Nancy Ke

Public Relations Campaign Strategies

Planning for Implementation

SECOND
EDITION

Robert Kendall
University of Florida
Gainesville

 LONGMAN

An imprint of Addison Wesley Longman, Inc.

New York • Reading, Massachusetts • Menlo Park, California • Harlow, England
Don Mills, Ontario • Sydney • Mexico City • Madrid • Amsterdam

Acquisitions Editor: Cynthia Biron/Deirdre Cavanaugh
Developmental Editor: Liz Hunzinger
Project Coordination and Text Design: Ruttle, Shaw & Wetherill, Inc.
Cover Designer: Kay Petronio
Electronic Production Manager: Christine Pearson
Manufacturing Manager: Helene G. Landers
Electronic Page Makeup: Ruttle, Shaw & Wetherill, Inc.
Printer and Binder: R. R. Donnelley & Sons Company
Cover Printer: The Lehigh Press, Inc.

Public Relations Campaign Strategies: Planning for Implementation, Second Edition

Library of Congress Cataloging-in-Publication Data

Kendall, Robert (Robert Leon)
    Public relations campaign strategies : planning for implementation
/ Robert Kendall. — [2nd ed.]
        p.   cm.
    Includes bibliographical references and index.
    ISBN 0-673-99692-1
    1. Public relations.   2. Public relations—United States.
I. Title
HM263.K395   1996   95-24103
659.2—dc20   CIP

04 05 06 - DOC - 12 11 10 9 8 7

Contents

Preface

This book is intended to help the public relations person plan public relations campaigns. What follows is intended both for the practicing public relations professional and for the student of public relations who has mastered the basics of writing; has a strong understanding of the media, layout and design, and research procedures; and has a basic understanding of the public relations function.

The book has been prepared for a junior, senior, or graduate course in public relations campaign strategies. Some of the material has been used as part of the *Accreditation Primer* (New York: Public Relations Society of America), a handbook designed for and available to practitioners preparing to sit for the $5\frac{1}{2}$-hour written examination offered by the Public Relations Society of America (PRSA).

The 1987 *Design for Undergraduate Public Relations Education*, produced by the Commission on Undergraduate Public Relations Education as the national standard for academic curricula in the field, suggests that a curriculum follow certain guidelines. Public relations education should be built on a 75 percent liberal arts foundation and constructed to reflect six categories within "public relations studies":

1. Principles, practices, and theory
2. Techniques: writing, message dissemination, and media networks
3. Public relations research for planning and evaluation
4. Public relations strategy and implementation
5. Supervised experience
6. Specialized advanced study

This book serves courses in categories 3 and 4.

Although academic programs determine their own prerequisites, most programs may be expected to follow the *Design* curriculum guidelines, which place the strategies course at the senior level after most other courses are completed. The book can, however, be adapted easily to courses without prerequisites.

Traditionally, the strategies course has been taught by persons who have (1) drawn from their professional experience; (2) used collected readings, often materials developed by professional counseling agencies; (3) required readings from case studies; and (4) assigned the planning and often the execution of a campaign as a class project. More recently, the literature has begun to reflect a growing body of theory and research on the process. Some teachers have begun to include this material, but it is difficult to include everything. This text attempts to combine the two approaches—incorporating the personal experience of those who write for trade publications in the field while relating the theory and research to the process—and provide them in one volume.

While the text is designed for the courses described above, it will adapt well to courses in business, marketing, political science, or other fields that undertake campaigns to shape public opinion or behavior. Case studies courses could analyze the cases in the book and use the chapters on planning as a basic for analysis. The book would also be appropriate for courses in applied research.

All those who are engaged in the cultivation of relationships among groups should find the approach to planning the campaign discussed in this book a useful tool. Those who see in public relations a strong social force for good—that is, a means of building a better world by improving relationships among the wide range of social entities—will find support in these pages.

Just as wholesome relationships among individuals bring benefits to both the individuals and society at large, so the wholesome relationship among groups of people will bring benefits to those groups and will benefit society by contributing to stability and understanding. Deception, deceit, and subterfuge can be just as destructive to relations among organizations as we all know they can be for relations among individuals. Just as the most wholesome relations among individuals result from truth, honesty, fair play, candor, and openness, so it is with organizations, whether they are corporations, nonprofits, government bureaus, or political parties.

This book offers a how-to approach to planning the public relations campaign—that is, the concerted effort on the part of an organization to build socially responsible relationships by achieving research-based goals through the application of communication strategies and the measurement of results. The approach assumes that a campaign must be planned prior to implementation, even if the plan must be altered during execution.

Based on a fundamental problem-solving model of research–adaptation–strategy–evaluation, the book is divided into six parts, an introduction, four parts dealing specifically with each of these four stages of the planning process, plus one part on presenting and implementing the plan. An overview chapter offers an orientation to public relations that serves as a review of the field to bring readers "up to speed" if they have not had an introductory course or had one some time ago. The overview chapter also sets forth the book's approach to public relations, which is designed to stimulate discussion and critical thinking on the nature of the field and the implications of a definition of public relations for the character of the practitioner's work.

To the second edition I have added short case studies to appropriate chapters as examples of how the aspect of the campaign being discussed at that point fits into an actual campaign. Most of these are summaries of 1994 Silver Anvil winning campaigns. Each case is presented in its entirety to show how the campaign element under discussion contributes to a successful total campaign. The reader is encouraged to note, for example, how research contributes to adaptation decisions such as goals, objectives, and target publics, and to strategies and tactics as well as to evaluation.

Acknowledgments

I would like to express my appreciation to the specialists who carefully reviewed and helped fine-tune the manuscript of the first edition: Glenn A. Butler, University of Florida; Robert Byler, Bowling Green State University; Pamela J. Creedon, Ohio State University; Elizabeth Dickey, University of South Carolina; James E. Grunig, University of Maryland; Jerry C. Hudson, Texas Tech University; Dean Kruckeberg, University of Northern Iowa; Jan P. Quarles, University of Georgia; Maria P. Russell, Syracuse University; and Elizabeth Toth, Southern Methodist University.

I would also like to express my gratitude to the following people for their help in reviewing and refining the manuscript for this edition: Lowell A. Briggs, York College of Pennsylvania; Robert A. Carroll, Ph.D., Northeast Louisiana University; Linda Hon, University of Maryland; Frank E. Parcells, Eastern Illinois University; and Nancy B. Wolfe, Elon College.

A special thanks goes to Cynthia Biron, my editor at HarperCollins; Liz Hunzinger, the developmental editor for this edition; and Marilyn Dwyer at Ruttle, Shaw & Wetherill, who guided the project through production.

For her patience during the many hours of preparation of this book, her indispensable proofreading, her reasoned judgment and feedback, I thank my wife Judith. For inspiration and support, I thank both Judith and my son Elliot.

Robert Kendall

PART
ONE

Introduction to Public Relations Campaign Strategies

An Overview

1

- The Public Relations Campaign
- Communications as Functions and as Tools
- Case Study: Levi Strauss & Co. "Responsible Sourcing"
- Defining Public Relations, the Key to Practice
- Case Study: Public Relations During the Des Moines Floods of 1993
- Ethical Practice at Different Organizational Levels
- The Campaign in the Cultural Life of the Organization

THE PUBLIC RELATIONS CAMPAIGN

The public relations campaign is a concerted effort of an organization to build socially responsible relationships by achieving research-based goals through the application of communicative strategies and the measurement of outcomes.

The term *campaign* in its general usage means a "connected series of operations designed to bring about a particular result."[1] That description fits the public relations campaign.

COMMUNICATIONS AS FUNCTIONS AND AS TOOLS

Public Relations and Related Functions

Within the communication field there is an interaction of various functions and tools. For example, marketing may serve as a tool of public relations, and public relations may serve as a tool of marketing depending on which function is being served. If the end result of an activity is to match goods or services to consumer needs (a marketing function), advertising, public relations, promotion, publicity, and the like become tools for that marketing function. If on the other hand the end is to advance the entire organization (a public relations function), marketing, advertising, publicity, promotion, and the like become public relations tools. In one sense, marketing is public relations for a product or service; public relations is marketing for the entire organization.

Public relations can create an advertorial and purchase space to publish it, and that is advertising; but because it is used to achieve a public relations end it is a public relations technique. The same can be said of product or service marketing techniques, of personnel training strategies, of voter preference tracking, or of other techniques that seem to be identified with various professional fields. The technique serves the function.

Other functions may also use public relations techniques: marketing, advertising, sales promotion, fund raising, political office seeking, and other fields use news releases, but releases are tools of those disciplines insofar as they are applied to achieving the goals of those disciplines. Public relations is frequently mentioned as an essential part of the "marketing mix." In that application, such as "gaining product exposure; announcing company, corporate and personnel changes; disclosing news related to company finances and well-being; and publicizing state-of-the-art engineering developments,"[2] public relations serves the goals of marketing.

There may even be techniques that are primarily public relations tools that may be used in other functions: news releases, publicity kits, news conferences, annual reports, and special events. These tools are public relations techniques to the degree that they are most commonly used to achieve public relations goals; they are equally legitimate tools of marketing when used to achieve marketing ends, or of fund raising when they achieve those ends.

Figure 1.1 illustrates the relationship between various functions and tools in the communication fields as they relate to public relations campaigns. To identify how any of the four functions across the top are served by tools listed down the left margin, read down the function column. The descriptions are necessarily brief simplifications; you are encouraged to make further elaboration of the way various tools serve these and other communication functions.

Notice the fine line that, at times, distinguishes both the functions and the tools. The practitioner, whether in public relations, marketing, or another job, will often engage in activities that involve a combination of the functions and tools. This analysis is offered not to split hairs but to help avoid territorial disputes and disagreements between people holding various job titles and responsibilities. Each of the communications functions is enhanced when they all work in concert, whether they are performed by a single person or represented in different job titles. The coordination of the full range of communication functions is often called "integrated communication."

FUNCTIONS (read across)

	Public relations	Marketing	Advertising	Sales promotion
	Public relations builds mutually beneficial associations with publics	**Marketing** matches product and/or service to consumer need	**Advertising** creates and places paid media messages	**Sales promotion** performs activity to win publicity in support of sales

TOOLS (read down)

	Public relations	Marketing	Advertising	Sales promotion
Advertising as a tool of:	**Public relations** creates media messages to publicize entire organization	**Marketing** creates media messages to publicize product or service		**Sales promotion** creates media messages coordinated with publicity-winning activities
Marketing as a tool of:	**Public relations** builds sound relations with consumers by serving their service/product needs		**Advertising** reinforces advertised messages with product/service well matched to consumer need	**Sales promotion** reinforces the activities that win publicity for sales of product
Public relations as a tool of:		**Marketing** creates well-perceived corp. as support for effective match of product/service to consumer needs	**Advertising** reinforces advertised messages by building a well-perceived organization	**Sales promotion** builds a well-perceived organization to support sales promotion goals
Promotion as a tool of:	**Public relations** uses events and activities to build beneficial associations with organization publics	**Marketing** uses events and activities to call attention to the match of goods to user needs	**Advertising** uses activities and events to call attention to advertised product or service	
Publicity as a tool of:	**Public relations** provides stories and information to media to tell about relation-building activities, etc.	**Marketing** provides information about benefits of product and/or services	**Advertising** provides information by buying space/time to tell benefits of product and/or services	**Sales promotion** provides information specific to product or service as aid to sales
Special events as a tool of:	**Public relations** stages events to win publicity for relation-building goals	**Marketing** stages events to publicize benefits of product or service	**Advertising** stages events to win publicity in support of advertised product/service	**Sales promotion** stages events to publicize product or service to support sales

Figure 1.1 Functions and tools in communication.

Goal of the Public Relations Function

The public relations campaign differs from other campaigns in its goals. Public relations seeks to build mutually beneficial relationships with constituent publics. When activities attempt to improve relations with employees, stockholders, customers, members, government, or any of the many publics on which an organization's well-being depends, the effort is public relations. When a collection of those activities is structured into an organized effort, it becomes a campaign.

Research and Evaluation

Research of the situation is necessary to ensure that the campaign solves the problem or achieves the goal it sets out to attain. Measurement of the outcome of the effort is also implied in the term *campaign* as it is used here. Thus, *evaluation* is the other side of the research coin: research identifies the conditions prior to the campaign; evaluation identifies changes in the conditions as a result of the effort.

Research may also be employed in each of the other stages of the campaign in addition to those labeled "research" and "evaluation." The adaptation plan may need to include continuing research of the dynamic changes in public opinion or in public behavior to make sure the campaign adjusts to day-to-day shifts. The strategy stage may need to test strategies prior to implementation, but also to plan for research of the effectiveness of different messages or of different media during implementation. Other research requirements during implementation may include those needed to deal with crises, such as the legal status of possible actions or the likely reaction of critical publics.

Public Relations and Public Communication Campaigns

One of the campaign types most closely related to the public relations campaign is the *public communication campaign.* The types are alike except in two respects: (1) The public communication campaign tends to focus on an immediate objective, such as stopping smoking, controlling wildfires, or reducing crime, and it relies primarily on mass communication. In contrast, the public relations campaign, as the term is used here, seeks such objectives as a means of building relationships with constituencies that may be involved, and while it may use mass communication, it relies on the complete spectrum of communication media. The difference is in orientation. (2) The public communication campaign has an affinity with the advertising campaign, in which the immediate objective has a minimal connection with the organizational mission; the public relations campaign fulfills a goal that contributes directly to the organization's purpose.

Paisley describes the public communication campaign in terms similar to those applied to the advertising or political campaign. "A public communication campaign seems to represent *someone's intention to influence someone else's beliefs or behavior, using communicated appeals.* Commercial advertising and political electioneering also fit this description, but as a rule they are not classified as public communication campaigns."[3] Paisley's effort to define the term focuses on the social purpose or "intention" and on an alternative approach he calls "process" as a "genre of *journalism* that might be called noncommercial advertising," which he characterizes as operating on the level of "technique."

> The definition of a public communication campaign can be approached either via *intention* or via *process*. Should campaigns be defined via intention? Are they strategies of *social control* insofar as one group intends to affect the beliefs or behavior of another group? Or should campaigns be defined via process? . . .
>
> When education is the only strategy that can be pursued or is worth pursuing, attention shifts to the level of technique—that is, to the *process* of communicating. Modern campaigns draw upon the techniques of journalists, media producers, educators, group counselors, and others. The campaign planner synthesizes these techniques into a matrix of possible approaches to target audiences. Combinations of approaches are pilot tested, and the campaign evaluator—newest member of the team—feeds back information on which approaches are working well, which approaches might work well after revision, and which approaches are not working well at all.[4]

Paisley traces the development of the campaign throughout American history. Traditionally, campaigns pursued the social intention of controlling society, as, for example, various campaigns in the women's rights, abolition, and temperance movements. Later campaigns concentrated on the process. "The earliest campaigns relied on personal persuasion backed by printed materials to disseminate the message; electronic media have augmented but not upset this winning combination."[5]

> Important changes have occurred in the entire *sequence* of activities that campaigns now consist of. *Preimplementation* activities typically include planning, coordination with other campaign sponsors, baseline research on audiences, preparation of materials and field arrangements, preliminary implementation, pilot testing, and revision of materials and arrangements. *Implementation* activities include, in addition to implementation of the campaign, a process evaluation of the conduct of the campaign and an outcome evaluation of the campaign's effects on its target audience(s). When the campaign terminates or pauses between implementation periods, *postimplementation* activities include analyzing the processes and outcomes of the campaign to determine how it may be replicated more cost-effectively.[6]

Paisley traces another trend in the development of the campaign. Whereas most early campaigns were reactive, in the sense that they were reactions to social problems that needed to be corrected, later campaigns tended to be proactive, in the sense of taking steps to avert problems before they developed. "In this period of transition from reactive to proactive campaigns, we see big stakeholders—federal agencies, private associations and corporations—learning the techniques of proactive campaigning first. Their new reasonableness ('come let us reason together') is evident in current campaigns focusing on health care, environmental protection, energy conservation, and so on."[7]

Campaigns continue to use both reactive and proactive modes, depending on the circumstances.

Design of the Public Relations Campaign

The design of today's campaign follows certain fundamental steps. The campaign begins with research, proceeds with goal setting, planning, and strategy decisions, and concludes with evaluation. Paisley identified five "principles" on which public communication campaigns are based:

1. assessment of the needs, goals, and capabilities of target audiences;
2. systematic campaign planning and production;
3. continuous evaluation;
4. complementary roles of mass media and interpersonal communication;
5. selection of appropriate media for target audiences.

The elements of the public relations campaign conform generally to the formula used for many years in planning programs for public relations. The RACE formula devised by John Marston and published in his *The Nature of Public Relations* [8] established research, action-communication, and evaluation as the basic ingredients of programing. Cutlip and Center added planning after research, but the procedure is still essentially the same. The "action" and "communication" parts of the RACE formula have often caused confusion. Action that must be planned within the campaign is often confused with action as implementation. Moreover, "action" may sometimes be inadequate to describe the full range of possible strategies. "Action" implies that something must be "done." At times the best response to a public relations problem is to do nothing at all; the campaign planning formula should allow for that option.

For example, a railroad management has chosen to make no response to requests for charitable use of railroad equipment. To respond to such a request, especially if the request is part of a well-publicized activity, puts the railroad in a defensive no-win position, losing control of outcome if the request is granted and seeming to be a "Scrooge" if it gives a negative response. In such cases calling public relations activities "actions" leaves no room for taking no action. Strategy is a better term. It implies the choice or nonchoice of a specific, planned, and measurable activity to solve a problem.

The alternative formula RAISE—Research, Adaptation, Implementation Strategy, and Evaluation—clearly involves planning at each stage. Although the research stage alone should be carried out, at least in part, in order to complete the other stages in the planning process, each of the remaining stages also needs to be planned prior to implementation.

For two notable reasons, the RAISE formula has helped students grasp the principles involved more quickly than other formula: (1) When the entire process is seen as a planning process, students tend to give equal weight, value, and importance to each of the stages, including research and evaluation, and not shortchange one or both. (2) When "action" and "communication" are planned as parts of the adaptation as well as the strategy process, and

▶ CASE STUDY: LEVI STRAUSS & CO. "RESPONSIBLE SOURCING"

Media stories of "worker exploitation in overseas 'sweatshops'" producing clothing and footwear for American consumers led Levi Strauss & Co. to institute guidelines for "responsible sourcing," as the practice of offshore production contracting is called.

RESEARCH

A company task force of staff from around the world identified issues relating to sourcing, researched existing standards, and studied the company's existing practices. The task force balanced company merchandising and production needs with corporate social responsibility and studied ways of dealing with international values. The group also identified and obtained regular feedback from 25 key internal and external stakeholder groups. In-depth interviews identified contractor practices on issues such as wages and benefits, working conditions, health and safety, use of child labor, prison labor and political/social stability, and human rights in various countries.

More than 50 countries where Levi Strauss & Co. contracts production services were assessed for human rights and political/social stability. A data base was created for ongoing monitoring of issues assembled from the U.S. State Department, the UN, Amnesty International and Freedom House, local legislation, and news media. High-ranking elected officials in several countries were interviewed including those at U.S. embassies, unions, business organizations, churches, and public interest groups.

ADAPTATION

Goal

Objectives: (1) Ensure that LS&Co.'s products were being made under conditions consistent with the company's long-standing commitment to corporate social responsibility; (2) distinguish LS&Co. from other companies that produce goods outside the United States; and (3) enhance and protect LS&Co.'s corporate reputation and brands.

Strategies: (1) Develop and implement comprehensive sourcing guidelines; (2) develop a communication and training program to educate internal audiences; and (3) use media and direct communications to carry messages to external audiences.

Target Publics: LS&Co. contractors, suppliers, retailers, employees, unions, manufacturers, human rights groups, consumers, and the media.

Budget: For internal and external communications and for manager training materials (excluding development and implementation of the guidelines): $200,000.

IMPLEMENTATION STRATEGY

Based on LS&Co.'s corporate values the task force developed the document "Sourcing Guidelines" outlining the "Terms of Engagement" for contractors and country selection criteria for countries contracting with LS&Co. A brochure explaining the use of the document was produced and translated into ten languages. Managers in various countries were selected to enforce the Terms of Engagement that set forth contractor standards. About 100 managers were sent to training sessions that covered guidelines, case studies, and exercises in decision making to prepare them for dealing with contractors, conducting audits, and making necessary improvements.

Continuous monitoring ensured compliance with the Global Sourcing Guidelines. Copies of the Sourcing Guidelines were distrib-

(*continues*)

uted to the American Apparel Manufacturers Association, which agreed to distribute them to its membership as well as to business leaders and partners. Other interested companies also received copies of the Guidelines to adapt to their own needs. Union support was cultivated by face-to-face meetings with Amalgamated Clothing and Textile Workers Union (ACTWU). Employees were educated about the Guidelines through meetings, memos, videos, and internal publications. Influential business and consumer media were targeted to position LS&Co. as a leader in worldwide business practices among otherwise negative sourcing organizations. A speakers bureau of senior company executives made 20 presentations to key international audiences including business schools, Business for Social Responsibility groups, and European trade unions.

EVALUATION

Objective 1. All of the company's seven hundred contractors worldwide have been au-

dited, 70 percent met the standards and about 5 percent have been dropped for lack of compliance. The company withdrew from Burma and China due to pervasive human rights violations and suspended sourcing from Peru due to employee safety concerns.

Objective 2. Guidelines have been cited as "the model of aggressive enforcement" of corporate social responsibility; the *Economist, Business Week, The Wall Street Journal, The New York Times,* and *U.S. News and World Report* cited the company for its efforts. *Business Ethics* awarded the company its 1993 Award for Excellence in Ethics. The company's brand image and reputation continue to benefit from the company's efforts as evidenced by praise from the author of "100 Best Companies to Work for in America."

Source: 1994 Silver Anvil Winners: Index and Summaries, Public Relations Society of America (PRSA), 1994.

are divided into the preliminary "adaptation" thought processes and the decision-making "strategy" choices, team members grasp the full range of the process and more easily see planning as distinct from implementing.

The two important alterations to the traditional formula in our approach are adaptation and implementation strategy. Adaptation seems more appropriate to what happens at this point in the process than does planning, because the primary task, after research, is matching the needs of the publics with the resources of the organization conducting the campaign—*adapting* resources to needs. The adaptation stage involves planning, but no more planning than is required for other stages, since they are all aspects of a planning process.

The Public Relations Program Versus the Public Relations Campaign

Although the distinction between "program" and "campaign" may not be universally recognized, there are advantages in differentiating the continuous "program" from the time-limited "campaign." The campaign planned for a month, six months, a year, or even two years is much more subject to measurement of effect and tends to involve greater precision in planning and execution than a continuing program that has no clear beginning and end. Plans for activities that have no deadlines tend to get pushed back in the scheduling of priorities.

Of course, for most organizations that undertake a campaign, there will also be continuing activities that have a public relations impact: the organization will continue to announce decisions to the press, publish the employee newsletter, and carry on other regular assignments; it will circulate memos, post notices on bulletin boards, and respond to media inquiries. In these respects the organization has a public relations program whether it realizes it or not. In contrast, the campaign is an organized and integrated effort to manage certain well-focused public relations activities, together with their supporting communications, to achieve a more controlled result.

Depending on the nature of the campaign, regular activities can be continued together with the concentrated effort of the campaign, but coordinating the ongoing activities with the activities of the campaign can give greater impact to both. For example, when the campaign theme and activities are incorporated into the newsletter, the bulletin board, and other communications, the additional notice will multiply the effect. Coordinating regular and campaign activities also enables the practitioner to measure the effectiveness of specific activities as well as to measure total effect, because it is easier to justify an effectiveness measurement for a total campaign than for a single memo or bulletin board notice. The campaign will also attract renewed interest in familiar communications and offer a chance to improve and to redesign them.

The campaign need not be a one-shot effort; a cycle of campaigns—each building on and profiting from previous ones—has much to recommend it over the indeterminate continuing program. The basic elements that make up a public relations campaign can simply be repeated with revisions, additions, and different directions for a more effective long-range program.

The cyclic continuing series of campaigns (see Figure 1.2) also has the advantage that the evaluation of one campaign can be incorporated in the research phase of the next. *Research* leads to *adaptation* of the organization's resources to the campaign situation, which leads to the public relations *implementation strategy* to solve the problem situation, which leads to an *evaluation* of the campaign.

The checklist for planning public relations campaigns is not a step-by-step process; a campaign may or may not require all of the steps. The steps are not necessarily to be taken in the order given, nor should they necessarily be completed in order. For example, groundwork on objectives may be necessary before publics can be selected; then objectives may need to be adjusted according to targeted publics. Many elements of the checklist need to be carried forward together. There is good reason to approach campaign planning on a broad front—completing parts of three or four steps, going on to other steps, then returning to continue working on the first steps.

The checklist for the campaign stages shown in Box 1.1 will serve as the structure for planning the campaign. The same outline will be used throughout the rest of the book.

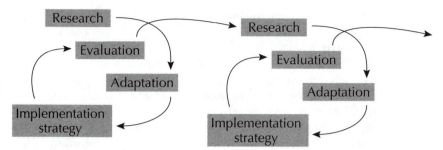

Figure 1.2 The campaign cycle begins with *research* of the problem. *Adaptation* considers the factors of problem statement/goal; target publics; strategy options; limitations of time, money and personnel; and maintenance of management support. *Implementation strategy* plans, tests, and calendars the elements in the strategy, including communication and budget, as well as "sells" the plan to management. *Evaluation* plans how the effectiveness of the plan will be measured during and following implementation.

Communication Plus Interpersonal Support

Research on why campaigns succeed or fail has tended to concentrate on the recipient of the campaign communication. From these studies a clear pattern emerged. Communication alone has little effect,[9] but when mass communication is tied closely to the personal involvement of the audience in one way or another the result can be quite successful. This pattern has emerged in a number of public communication campaigns, including the stop-smoking, forest fire prevention, and crime control efforts. McAlister notes of the stop-smoking campaign that beyond the three functions that have been achieved through the mass media—informing, persuading, and training—there is another critical element.

> A . . . notion to be emphasized . . . is the importance of *interpersonal support for mediated communications.* Mass communication media may effectively inform, persuade, and train their audiences but lasting change will not be achieved in the absence of a supportive social environment. . . . researchers now realize that campaign effectiveness may depend upon the creation of opportunities for interpersonal communication, participation, and social reinforcement. This has led to attempts to efficiently integrate mediated and interpersonal communication and thus further progress toward the identification of potentially effective strategies.[10]

The principle of media communication supported by interpersonal interaction was critical in the "Take a Bite out of Crime" campaign. O'Keefe reports what several researchers "have demonstrated empirically, people are more likely to act on information acquired from mass media sources when appropriate social and environmental supports are present."[11] As an auxiliary to the national public service announcements (PSAs) of the Advertising Council, local communities undertook a variety of neighborhood efforts. Those exposed to the PSAs "exhibited significant increases over those not exposed in how much they thought they knew about crime prevention" and that expo-

BOX 1.1   **A Checklist for Planning Public Relations Campaigns: Research–Adaptation–Implementation Strategy–Evaluation**

State the "situation" that prompts the campaign.

Research of the Situation and the Sponsoring Organization

1. Discover the facts to confirm or alter the situation.
2. Ensure dependable findings by using valid methodology.
3. Interpret data accurately and adequately.
4. Identify the problem(s) in statement form.

Adaptation of the Organization's Resources to the Situation

1. Subdivide the problem(s) into measurable goal statements.
2. Segment target publics in order of priority.
3. Research and brainstorm for possible solutions.
4. Make a "shopping list" of workable solutions to problem.
5. List resources and limitations: money, time, people, etc.
6. Develop a system for liaison with management.

Implementation Strategy for Solving the Problem/Reaching Goal

1. Select a strategy from "shopping list" above.
   a. Be sure targeted publics are addressed.
   b. Goal should dictate both strategy and targeting and be based on research findings.
2. Design the communication plan to support the strategy.
3. Calendar the entire strategy and communication plan.
4. Budget each action or event in per-action dollars/people.
5. Justify or "sell" the strategy/communication plan to a skeptical client or employer.

Evaluation of the Total Campaign Effort

1. Provide for establishing proof of success.
2. Measure degree of goal achievement, results, etc.
3. Consider three aspects of evaluation: in-process, internal, and external.
4. Collect pluses, minuses, and make projections.

sure was "significantly related to" increases in preventive activities. "Particularly noteworthy were campaign-related increases in neighborhood cooperative crime prevention efforts."[12] The effect of the campaign in Atlanta revealed the types of community activities that made the campaign a success. These activities included a Ten Most Wanted program, with circulation of pictures; a Citizen's Alert program to notify police of suspicious activities; an interface of police and private security; a Safer Atlanta for Everyone (SAFE) program; a Police Recruitment program; a Business Watch program; a Business Block Parents program; and an Atlanta Cares project.[13]

Research on Campaign Audience Response

Research has also focused on what happens within the audience during a campaign. Grunig and others have developed a model to explain different "situations" among audience members during a campaign. The reasoning behind the model goes like this: "The purpose of the communication campaign . . . is to increase the extent to which members of an audience perceive an issue as problematic and involving the hope that they will then seek more information, develop an organized idea, and do something about the issue." In other words, members of the audience targeted by a campaign have to see an issue, say crime, as a problem, see themselves involved as a potential victim of crime, seek information on the issue, formulate in their minds something that they could do about crime, and then actually do something about crime.

Grunig and Ipes describe their efforts in building the model: "The purpose of the research reported in this article was to develop a theoretical anatomy of a public information campaign—to describe the changes in the mind of a passive member of an audience who receives and uses messages from the campaign." The resulting model of campaign audience reaction or "situational theory" involves four steps: problem recognition, level of involvement, constraint recognition, and referent criterion.[14] In another study Grunig and Stamm identify these four steps by the questions asked of audiences to classify their status on each measure. "Problem recognition" asks, "do you stop to think about this problem often, sometimes, rarely, or never?" "Level of involvement" asks, "do you see a strong, moderate, or weak connection between yourself and this problem?" "Constraint recognition" asks, "could you do a great deal, something, very little, or nothing personally to affect the way these issues are handled?" "Referent criterion" asks, "do you have a great deal of knowledge or experience that would help you to make judgments about these issues, some experience, very little, or none?"[15]

The model has contributed to understanding the workings of a campaign by documenting the reactions of audience members in actual campaign situations. Grunig and Ipes explain the results of their study:

> The data suggest that a public communication campaign changes a passive public into a High Involvement Constrained Public or a High Involvement Problem-Facing Public. It seems likely, however, that many members of the problem facing

public were in that category before the campaign began, and that the major effect of the campaign was to produce the constrained public.

The members of a newly active public, then, develop simplistic cognitions, often remnants of solutions on the media agenda or simple notions such as the one that threatened punishment alone would solve the drunk driving problem. Members of the public do develop strong attitudes, but again, they seem to evaluate the simplest solutions most strongly. Seldom do they engage in behavior that requires much effort on their part. On this issue, however, increased recognition of the drunken driving problem may at least, make people aware of when they and others should not drive.[16]

The campaign audience "situation variables" describe what happens as a result of campaign communication efforts. The process begins, according to this model, with the "agenda setting" function of the media, which place the issue—crime, drunk driving, wildfire, or the like—on the public agenda. As people begin to deal with the issue now on their agenda (problem recognition), they experience several "cognition" states: whether they see themselves personally involved (level of involvement), whether they feel they can do anything about the issue (constraint recognition), and whether they have enough knowledge or experience to make a judgment on the issue (referent criterion).

The campaign may put a problem "on the public's agenda" and, by promoting various solutions, may succeed in "getting people to remember proposed solutions." If the issue is kept on "the media agenda for a long time" it creates an "active public" consisting of those who recognize the problem and "form cognitions, develop attitudes and engage in behavior related to the problem." The campaign planner, after placing information in the media, "hopes the information will cause the people who processed the information to recognize the issue as a problem and to perceive that drunken driving involves them." If the campaign is successful at this stage, "the people begin to seek information about drunken driving, develop solutions in their mind for the problem, and begin to change their own behavior or pressure legislators for changes in law."[17]

DEFINING PUBLIC RELATIONS, THE KEY TO PRACTICE

Definitions of public relations are not simply a common understanding to be decided upon so that a discussion of the field can proceed without confusion. A mature definition, more than anything else, determines the maturity of practice in the field.

Definitions reflect a range of sophistication in the duty the function owes to the society at large. This range of perceptions is evident today as well as through the history of the field. Ivy Lee saw public relations functioning as an honest broker of information and counseled the Rockefeller interests to change their behavior as a way to improve their publicity. Lee had pursued "his policy of advising Rockefeller to tell the truth and reshape his management to be acceptable to public opinion."[18] Sophisticated definitions focus on the deeper implications of the terms *public* and *relations* and concentrate on an understanding that reaches the full potential of relationships with publics in a free society.

This sophistication in a definition is not a late development. Some of the pioneers in the field learned by experience the value of such a conceptualization. L. L. L. ("Lou") Golden phrased such a concept of the field, "*Public consent does not stem from gimmicks or tricks. It exists because of performance in the public interest—plus an embedded policy of explaining to the public what an organization is doing and why.*[19] Note the phrase "performance in the public interest," which suggests a proactive effort on the part of the organization to do what is best for society whether society is petitioning for such behavior or even concerned about it. The positive effect on public attitudes and opinion (and credibility) toward the organization stemming from such an orientation can never be overemphasized.

Beyond the self-interest of the organization, which is best served by behavioral integrity, there is a social interest in every organization's behavior; organizations exist with the consent of society as long as they serve a useful public interest.[20] Corporations exist, for example, because society needs the jobs, the products, the well-being of all the people—suppliers, distributors, local merchants, schools, and churches—whose livelihood depends on the corporation. As long as the organization serves the public interest, it is free to operate relatively unencumbered. When the corporation takes that freedom for granted and abuses its responsibility to society, even to some segments of society alone, society imposes restrictions on its operations: regulations, higher taxes, impediments in the form of laws, ordinances, and the like in an effort to restore the balance of the public interest.

Harwood Childs confirmed the importance of the concept "the public interest" in a definition of public relations with his landmark book, *An Introduction to Public Opinion,* published in 1940. The book resulted from a series of lectures organized by the American Council on Public Relations, which was to merge in 1948 with the National Association of Public Relations Counsel to form the Public Relations Society of America. Childs, a political science professor at Princeton, defined public relations as "those aspects of our corporate and personal behavior which affect the public, the community; that the basic problem of public relations is to adjust those aspects of our behavior which affect others in such a manner as to promote the public interest; and that the public interest is what public opinion says it is."[21]

This definition rests on a concept of the common good, what is best for society at large; it focuses on behavior both corporate and individual to the extent that that behavior influences the public; and it presumes that any behavior not in the public interest will be adjusted in order to comply. If ethical behavior is conformity to the social consensus of what is right and wrong, this definition presumes that public relations *is* by its very nature *ethical behavior.*

If public relations is by its essential nature "publicity," then ultimately it may become press-agentry. If the essential nature of public relations is to act as an honest broker of information, then ultimately management may define what is the truth or whether or not to divulge information critical to the public interest. If the essential nature of public relations is ethical behavior, then it ultimately builds sound relationships based on mutual benefits.[22]

The application of the various definitions of public relations found in many textbooks deals with the relationships between business organizations and their "significant publics": employees, customers, investors, suppliers, dealers-distributors, plant community, and the like. In these textbooks the application of public relations procedures to other sectors of society, such as government, nonprofit organizations, and trade associations, is frequently presented as if it were designed for business and simply adapted to other sectors of society. Although the application to business may have merit, it fails to paint a broad enough picture of public relations in its full social function.

A Working Definition of Public Relations

The following approach to defining public relations builds on the definitions advanced by Edward Bernays, Harwood Childs, Lou Golden, and others who emphasize the social responsibility of public relations, or, more specifically, its commitment to serving the public interest. The definition asserts that public relations performs an essential social function:

> *Public relations is a phenomenon within societies by which advocates of a social entity manage that organization's performance in the public interest in order to*
>
> - *nurture mutually beneficial associations with all groups interdependent with the organization, by means of*
> - *the responsible use of all the appropriate instruments of one- and two-way communication*

A **phenomenon within societies** implies that public relations is a natural development within societies, that it has existed in societies throughout history, and that this function is essential to social well-being. The function by which segments of society develop and maintain relationships with each other has not had any other name or been identified except by the term public relations, but the function has operated in all societies, especially and most fully in free societies.

Advocates of a social entity suggests that public relations activity involves the intentional advancement of a cause—a cause or "social entity" that may be as diverse as the political ideal by which Sam Adams promoted the American Revolution; or the cause of the women's rights movement, which won for women the rights to vote and own property; or the cause a corporation like AT&T pursued in its mission of "universal service." Advocacy of the interests of such an entity implies the recognition of such a function and the delegation of persons to the task of advancing those interests before the court of public opinion, as a result of which society will best choose how to relate to that entity.

Manage that organization's performance proposes that the advocates are managers of the entity's relationships, including input into its philosophy and mission, its strategic policies, its goals and objectives in fulfilling its social role. Whether that social role is to produce a product or service, perform a political function, or provide higher education, public relations manages the relationships necessary to the organization's purpose.

In the public interest means that such an entity's performance should conform to what is in the best interest of the entire society. Much has been written about the part that public relations plays in social responsibility and about public interest. Some people suggest that social responsibility is *reactive* and that performance in the public interest is *proactive*. Although there may be times when public relations may be either reactive in responding to a disaster or proactive in taking a stand on an important public issue, a mature approach will be predominantly proactive. Proactive public relations means simply that the public relations function takes the lead in promoting the issues in ways that are in the best interests of both the public and the organization.

Taking the lead in dealing with public issues is a management function. Management in this context means the ultimate responsibility for directing what an organization does and how it does it. According to this definition, the management of performance in the public interest directs all an organization's functions from management of production and distribution to employee and consumer communication so that they are compatible with the public interest. Thus, management of an organization's performance requires taking responsibility for a social entity's character—the character which people perceive and on the basis of which they make judgments about an organization. The outcome is, in short, the organization's public relationships or the status of its reputation.

The meaning of this management role of public relations is illustrated in an anecdote related by one of the most respected practitioners in the field after a career in public relations for some of the largest corporations in the country. After working for a number of years as the senior public relations officer for a major New York financial institution, he said that he had never been invited to a meeting of the corporate board of directors, but he never missed a single one. He knew that his responsibility was to counsel management on the impact of their decisions on the public interest and that that advice was not always sought or even welcome. It was to his credit and honor as a practitioner as well as to the corporation's benefit that he provided that counsel.

The term *image* has often been used to describe the perception the public has of an organization. A related term, *identity*, describes efforts by corporations to establish how the public will perceive them. Downey argues that "corporate culture—which has been described as a company's shared values, beliefs and behavior—in fact flows from and is the consequence of corporate identity."[23] The "corporate identity" involves the corporate logo, with careful control of the precise colors involved, the signage used to identify the company, its letterhead, direction signs, vehicles, employee uniforms, and the like. James G. Gray Jr. describes the management of corporate image as the essential public relations activity for a corporation:

> Corporate managers are beginning to realize the importance of corporate image. A strong, positive image can see a corporation through a crisis as in the case of the Tylenol crisis at Johnson & Johnson or through a period of red ink as in the case of Chrysler. . . . Just as a corporation appears to be a living, breathing being, just as it develops a "personality," it must guard against allowing that personality to become misinterpreted or misunderstood. It must gain and hold public goodwill in order to succeed economically and even physically. Corporate leaders have begun to realize that they can not allow public goodwill to evaporate and then become replaced by hostility. . . . Managing the corporate image is the key to securing and maintaining public trust. . . . Business leaders who guide and shape the corporate reality safeguard the image by openly and honestly communicating with these publics.[24]

Performance in the public interest, for any organization, means having mutually beneficial relationships with all of its constituencies. Two parties to a relationship, whether individuals or groups, enter into an associations in which each contributes and each receives to a degree that satisfies the needs of each. The balance between giving and receiving may change over time but must be agreeable to both parties. Specific application of performance in the public interest means "to nurture mutually beneficial associations with all groups interdependent with the organization."

Characteristics of relationships as mutually beneficial associations are based on the emerging theory of "social exchange." The concept of social exchange was developed by analogy with economic exchange theory, which explains the process by which people exchange values such as money in return for needs such as food, clothing, and shelter. The idea of the marketplace determining the value for various products and services required by humans served as a model for explaining the system by which people exchange social, as opposed to economic, values that are required in wholesome relationships. One explanation of social exchange theory describes it as a way "to account for the emergence, persistence, and demise of sustained social relationships."[25] Friedman further explained, "Any model of individual action [the theory] relies upon must therefore have a component that permits consideration of the interests of the other (that is, the exchange partner). The relationship itself is the unit of interest; as such, some notion of the best outcome for the unit is required." Exchange theory thus attempts to account for stable relationships by identifying the noneconomic values exchanged as the basis for their establishment and maintenance.

The macro aspect of social exchange theory, involving the interaction between groups, is particularly useful in understanding the nature of relationships in public relations. Yet the micro patterns of interpersonal relations remains the model for understanding relations between publics. "An important issue in constructing macrosociological theory is the linkage with microsocio-logical theory. One approach is to start with microsociological principles and use these as the foundation for building macrosociological theory."[26]

The study of interpersonal relations has contributed a framework for understanding the nature of relationships. Cupach and Metts identified three "clusters" in the "relationship category" which threaten relationships:

1. problems associated with role expectations, performance, and violation;
2. problems associated with relational compatibility, cohesion, and intimacy; and
3. problems associated with the regulation of interaction.

An "external category" also included "(1) problems associated with a third party's intentional or unintentional involvement; and (2) problems associated with an unspecified, generally inanimate outside occurrence or circumstance."[27]

Interpersonal communication is fundamental to the relations between persons in all aspects of public relations. A wide range of literature is available on the nature of interpersonal communication and its adaptation to business and other professional settings.[28] It offers a model of relations between publics according to social exchange theory.

Characteristics of relationships between individuals parallel those of relationships between publics. A study using factor analysis identified three basic elements important to relationships: trust, involvement, and rules. Characteristics that correlated strongly with the trust element were honesty, confiding, trust, and fairness. One element correlated strongly with the rules factor: rewards. For the involvement factor, closeness, companionship, and emotional involvement were highly correlated. Two factors appear to have the most obvious application to public relationships: trust and rules. Values that were found to be associated with these factors suggest characteristics that might effectively define relations between publics: honesty, confiding, trust, fairness, and rules.[29] Rules, in this context, refer to procedures that are negotiated to govern the relationship in the future after the relationship has been threatened.

Ideal and real relationships may be two different things in interpersonal as well as interpublic relationships. Yet if we understand the characteristics that are important to mutually beneficial *personal* associations and apply them to the building of *public* relationships, there is hope for success. Public relations must be based on an informed understanding of the term that makes up half its name.

In discussing the meaning of public relations, it may be useful to think in terms of an ideal. While the ideal meaning of the term may be performance in the public interest so as to nurture mutually beneficial associations with all groups interdependent with the organization, and while achieving that goal may produce ideally profitable relationships, it is nevertheless true that organizations, like individuals, may fail to live up to the ideal. That fact should not deter the effort. Like individuals, organizations tend to achieve what is expected of them but seldom more. The historic experience of corporations,

> ## CASE STUDY: PUBLIC RELATIONS DURING THE DES MOINES FLOODS OF 1993

Julia Carey, APR, employee communications manager at Meredith Corporation, transformed a guest room in her home into a mini-office when the company's three downtown buildings closed. With the aid of her own PC and laser printer, a new phone line, and a fax machine and an extra computer brought home from the office, her three-person staff dispatched daily "flood updates" to employees. With phone lines jammed, faxes were zipped out after 10 P.M. A special phone hotline rang to the tune of 300 calls a day, thousands over the two-week period. A common question asked was, "Do we get paid?" The answer was yes.

During the crisis, Carey referred often to her "flood book," a three-inch binder containing the company's crisis communications plan. "I didn't go anywhere without my red book," she said.

Meanwhile, employee communications editor, Kathi Woods, who joined Meredith only three months ago, survived a crash course in communicating in a crisis. While churning out a special edition of *Insider Ex-tra*, a company newsletter, she got a taste of deadline journalism. In driving rain, she snapped pictures of the flood's devastation, interviewed stressed employees and concerned executives, and in less than a week, churned out an eight-page newsletter on a makeshift desktop publishing system set up at Carey's home.

Just to show good faith, when the buildings reopened, each of the more than 700 Meredith employees found a "Welcome Back" flier that wisely included tips on how to deal with emotional stress. Employees were also greeted with a water bottle bedecked with the Meredith logo on their desks, alongside one liter of much needed purified water. "We wanted to let them know we appreciated their sacrifices," said Craig Maltby, APR, manager of corporate and magazine group relations.

Adapted from: Shell, Adam, ed. "Briefings: The Flood of '93—Keeping Business Afloat During a Disaster." *Public Relations Journal* (September, 1993): 6.

such as AT&T and NCR, that have put mutually beneficial relationships with all constituencies ahead of profits provides evidence that an organization that comes even close to the ideal will be more profitable over time for all concerned than will an entity content with a one-sided short-term gain.[30]

Public relations also describes the *state of affairs* in all of an organization's varied relationships. Some of these relationships may be good, some "shaky," and others downright bad. Taking responsibility for those relationships means taking the necessary steps to improve them by moving in the direction of an ideal mutually beneficial association.

Public Relations as a Social Phenomenon

The approach taken in this book is based on the assumption that public relations is a social phenomenon and that society needs facilitators of relationships for groups as well as for individuals. It is further assumed that every group—every social entity of greater or lesser value to society—fulfills some mission for society, a "cause," which it must advocate, and that the advancement of that cause, within a necessary balance of public interests, is of benefit to society. Finally, it is assumed that every party to every conflict between one social entity and another should be equally well represented by an advocate for each point of view, with the confidence that society will best make up its mind in the ensuing debate.

This approach applies emphatically to business, but it applies to all other organized segments of society as well. It does not dispute the profit-making function of business, but suggests that the relations between business and society will be stronger and more beneficial if profit is placed in perspective. Profit serves an important and legitimate function within society, producing the capital necessary to bring the energies of hundreds of people to bear on solving a social need, but profit should be presented to society as the benefit it is: the return on investment that is essential to ensure that the money will be available to risk such developments as the Xerox machine, the Polaroid camera, the airplane, or the automobile. Every cause is better served by demonstrating the organization's contribution to society than by defining its right to take from society. The business organization should advocate its mission within society—providing goods and services in exchange for a return on investment—in such a way that the publics with a stake in the operation can understand and agree.

Public Relations as Advocacy of a Cause

The advocacy of a "cause" by every social entity involves the articulation of the organization's mission to society. The term "cause" implies a need to achieve understanding and acceptance of what the organization has to offer to society, often by overcoming formidable obstacles on the way to social approval and cooperation. A nonprofit group or a higher educational institution is easily recognized as advocating its cause, often with altruistic implications that what it is doing is good for society. Activist groups on either side of controversial issues plead their causes by emphasizing the benefit they offer to society.

Every group believes it offers some social benefit, however widely or narrowly conceived that benefit may be. For example, even a group that advocates a position not supported by law *offers* a benefit by proposing to convince society of the value of the position and the wisdom of making it lawful. The legalization of beverage alcohol in the 1930s followed a vigorous debate in which advocates for each side brought their case before the court of public opinion.

Regulation and deregulation of business are similar issues that focus the advocacy efforts of each side. Supporters of leveraged buy outs (LBOs) claim that such economic pressure increases the price of stock to realistic levels; opponents claim that LBOs force companies into unacceptable levels of debt, reduce social responsibility activities, and result in loss of jobs. The public relations function seeks to win public understanding and approval of the contribution that the entity makes to society against the arguments of competitors and detractors.

The fact that no one in a local environmentalist organization or a nuclear freeze group holds the title "director of public relations" doesn't mean the function is absent. Whether or not it is labeled as such, the advocacy of a cause is a socially important function that we call public relations. It is also important to realize that although organizations on one or the other side of these issues may have high-priced public relations counsel and huge financial resources, the public decides the issues on the basis of the force of truth advanced in the debate. The environmental protection group Greenpeace has successfully challenged the international whaling industry and foreign governments as formidable as the former Soviet Union.

Buying into the Cause   Clearly, the ethical public relations practitioner must believe in the cause he or she supports; the public relations advocate must "buy into" the philosophy and mission of the organization. Failure to do so, or loss of faith in the organization after once being committed, means the practitioner will not be able to bring full conviction to the task and will not perform at 100 percent. The practitioner who cannot buy into the cause is well advised to resign to protect both his or her professional reputation and the interests of the employing organization.

The Basis for Public Relations Ethics

The foregoing discussion has made a case for performance in the public interest as the cardinal value on which a definition of public relations is built. Such a cardinal value is implicit in two major codes of ethics in the field, the Public Relations Society of America's (PRSA) Code of Professional Standards for the Practice of Public Relations and the Code of Athens of the International Public Relations Association. Yet both codes specify a more rudimentary value as the basis of ethical practice: human rights. The PRSA code bases its professional principles on "the fundamental value and dignity of the individual, holding that the free exercise of human rights, especially freedom of speech, freedom of assembly and freedom of the press is essential to the practice of public relations."

The Code of Athens also specifies human rights as the core value of public relations practice: "all member countries of the United Nations Organization have agreed to abide by its Charter which reaffirms 'its faith in fundamental human rights, in the dignity and worth of the human person'."

How is this human rights foundation compatible with our emphasis on performance in the public interest? The meaning of "public interest" must have to do with the "general welfare," "life, liberty, and the pursuit of happiness," and other such intentions of the founders of the United States. It appears that the public interest is itself based on the more fundamental value of human rights. Organizational performance that is devoted to fundamental human rights will operate in the public interest.

The foregoing discussion of the meaning of public relations will provide a common ground for planning public relations campaigns. An ethically based understanding of public relations in the public interest will build relationships that are stable and enduring. An understanding of public relations as self-interested manipulation of publics through clever use of publicity and communication will result in relationships that are seldom mutually beneficial and that are unstable or even largely negative. An understanding of public relations as propaganda that makes use of press-agentry, deception, and half-truths may produce short-term gains but not long-term or mutually beneficial relationships. Propaganda may sway opinion or behavior, but because it does not produce stable relationships it does not fit our definition of public relations.

ETHICAL PRACTICE AT DIFFERENT ORGANIZATIONAL LEVELS

Even within an ethical definition of public relations, variations are evident in its practice at different levels in an organization. The entry-level person will focus on communications activities, while the senior public relations officer will concentrate on counseling management on serving the public interest. Nevertheless, each level of practice fits an ethical definition if it is oriented toward serving the public interest. Usually a senior practitioner manages the functions at each level to direct this ethical orientation. A brief description of how the public relations function fits into the usual organization at various levels will help with maintaining the liaison necessary for a successful campaign.

The public relations pyramids shown in Figures 1.3 and 1.4 illustrate how public relations functions at four levels within an organization. The four levels represent four types of public relations responsibilities required in carrying out the organization's mission. The levels also generally reflect the path of advancement for a person as promotions are given for higher levels of responsibility: from entry-level communications assignments, to responsibility for activities and events, to responsibility for the ongoing program of public relations, and finally to responsibility for the organization's performance in the public interest as counsel to top management.

These responsibilities will be combined in some organizations; in some organizations one person will be responsible for all levels. The model may be read from bottom to top to trace the practitioner's advancement through an organization, or from top to bottom to trace the functions of upper levels to lower levels of practice.

THE CAMPAIGN IN THE CULTURAL LIFE OF THE ORGANIZATION

Public relations is directly responsible for an organization's culture. If public relations is the management of relationships—mutually beneficial associations—between an organization and its significant publics, as these pages have argued that it is, those relationships are most acutely at stake in the currently popular concept of corporate or organizational culture. The public relations function in its reactive stance, of solving unexpected problems, but especially in its proactive stance, of solving anticipated problems and shaping the organization's identity, is responsible for the organization's culture. Stephen Downey contends that *corporate culture* is an overused buzzword and that the *corporate identity* for which public relations holds responsibility is a more fundamental term for what is involved.

> Corporate identity . . . I submit, is to culture what cause is to effect—unsurprising because identity is still too often thought of as "image" instead of being recognized for what it truly is: the very heart and soul of an organization. . . .
>
> I . . . argue that corporate culture—which has been described as a company's shared values, beliefs and behavior—in fact flows from and is the consequence of corporate identity. Specifically, I refer here to identity in its most basic sense; that is the fundamental style, quality, character and personality of an organization, those forces which define, motivate and embody it.
>
> This sense of identity should not be confused with corporate image, which is merely the way an organization is perceived by its various publics. Neither should it be confused with corporate identification or graphic presentation, which at their best are the verbal and visual expressions of well-planned, well-executed corporate identity programs. . . .
>
> In this sense, then, fundamental corporate identity is the sum of all the factors that define and project what an organization is, and where it is going—its unique history, business mix, management style, communication policies and practices, nomenclature, competences, and market and competitive distinction. Basic corporate identity is not only the source of the company's culture, but also the focus for the corporation's later identification; that is, its verbal and visual presentation, including the application of planned marketplace positioning and competitive differentiation at corporate, business unit, product and service levels alike.[31]

Public relations campaigns are an organization's "actions that speak louder than words" and, as such, celebrate the corporate culture by playing out its character in words and deeds. These actions may be reactive in reacting to crises or responding to emerging issues, but more often they may be proactive in exhibiting its character. A company may exhibit its character in a campaign to promote employee relations by establishing an employee day-care center, by improving and beautifying city parks, and by offering "flextime" employee work schedules. Such a campaign in deeds will do more to establish that the company is committed to its employees than will a well-worded company policy statement affirming responsibility to employees.

Public Relations as Guardian of Organizational Culture

Organizational culture is a fact of life throughout the entire range of organization types. Every company, university, nonprofit organization, government agency, and hospital has its own peculiar personality. The need to give careful

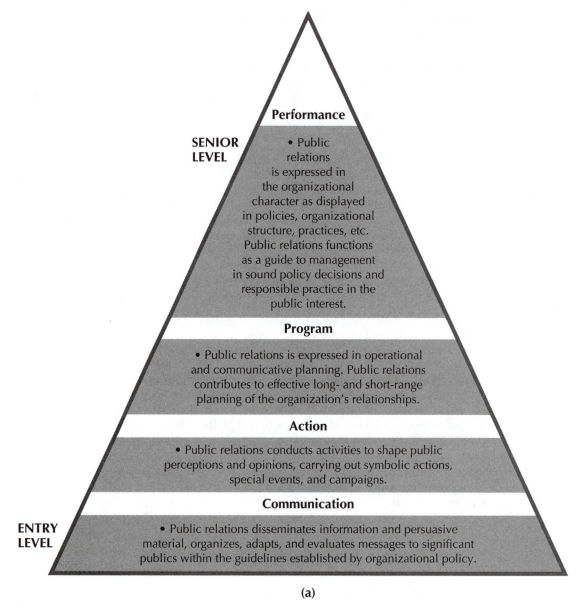

SENIOR
LEVEL

Performance

• Public
relations
is expressed in
the organizational
character as displayed
in policies, organizational
structure, practices, etc.
Public relations functions
as a guide to management
in sound policy decisions and
responsible practice in the
public interest.

Program

• Public relations is expressed in operational
and communicative planning. Public relations
contributes to effective long- and short-range
planning of the organization's relationships.

Action

• Public relations conducts activities to shape public
perceptions and opinions, carrying out symbolic actions,
special events, and campaigns.

Communication

ENTRY
LEVEL

• Public relations disseminates information and persuasive
material, organizes, adapts, and evaluates messages to significant
publics within the guidelines established by organizational policy.

(a)

Figure 1.3(a) The public relations pyramid model illustrates how public relations functions at different levels within the typical organization.

attention to organizational culture is well illustrated in the example of two hospital's cultural differences:

Memorial Hospital's culture cherishes self-reliance and efficiency. Memorial inhabits a stable niche of the health-care industry, as a "high-quality community institution that provides excellent basic health care but immediately refers out cases that are esoteric, complex, or that require sophisticated medical machinery."

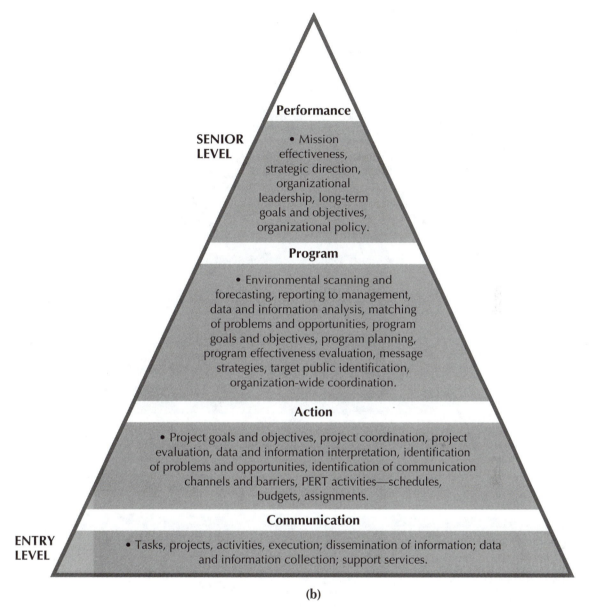

Figure 1.3(b) The pyramid model also illustrates the typical tasks public relations people perform at different levels in most organizations.

The administrator devotes about 90 percent of his attention to internal operations, and he actively discourages other personnel from joining hospital or professional associations, attending conferences, or forging external linkages. Subunits communicate infrequently because few fundamental problems remain to be solved. According to the administrator, "about 60 percent of the 'work' they do in other hospitals is nonessential." He singles out memos, meetings and conferences as "frivolous activities" that Memorial minimizes.

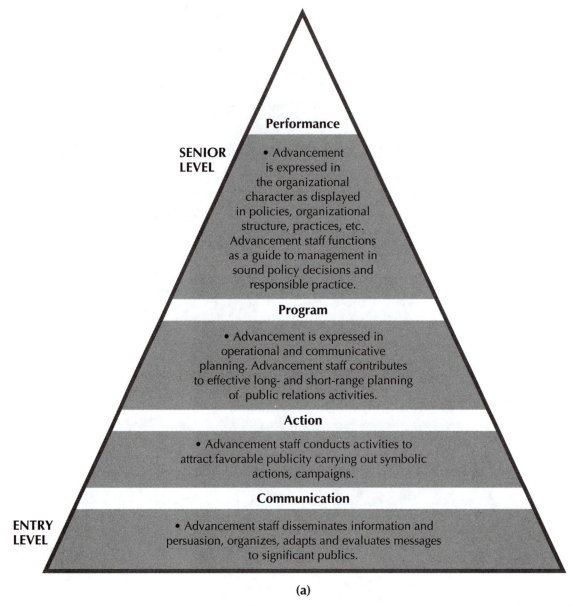

Performance

SENIOR LEVEL

• Advancement is expressed in the organizational character as displayed in policies, organizational structure, practices, etc. Advancement staff functions as a guide to management in sound policy decisions and responsible practice.

Program

• Advancement is expressed in operational and communicative planning. Advancement staff contributes to effective long- and short-range planning of public relations activities.

Action

• Advancement staff conducts activities to attract favorable publicity carrying out symbolic actions, campaigns.

Communication

ENTRY LEVEL

• Advancement staff disseminates information and persuasion, organizes, adapts and evaluates messages to significant publics.

(a)

Figure 1.4(a) The public relations pyramid model adapted to ''institutional advancement'' shows how public relations functions at different levels of the typical nonprofit organization.

The controller proudly characterizes the hospital as a "lean and hungry organization." This metaphor is substantiated by an uncommonly low ratio of employees to patients . . . everybody here does some benchwork . . . no administrator or department head has an assistant or a private secretary, the controller prepares and types his own financial statements.

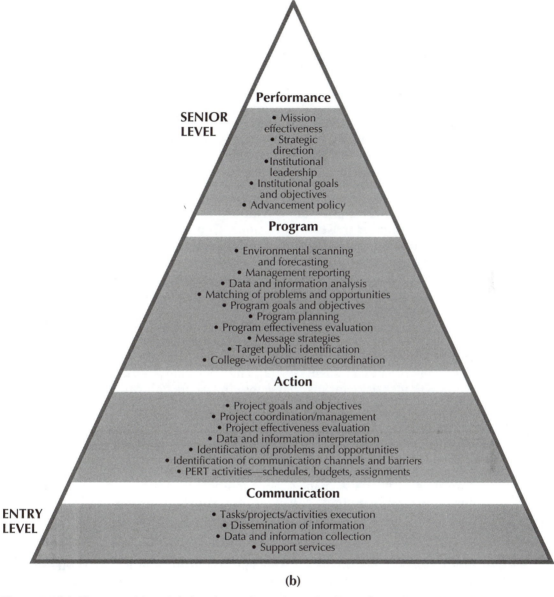

Performance
- Mission effectiveness
- Strategic direction
- Institutional leadership
- Institutional goals and objectives
- Advancement policy

SENIOR LEVEL

Program
- Environmental scanning and forecasting
- Management reporting
- Data and information analysis
- Matching of problems and opportunities
- Program goals and objectives
- Program planning
- Program effectiveness evaluation
- Message strategies
- Target public identification
- College-wide/committee coordination

Action
- Project goals and objectives
- Project coordination/management
- Project effectiveness evaluation
- Data and information interpretation
- Identification of problems and opportunities
- Identification of communication channels and barriers
- PERT activities—schedules, budgets, assignments

Communication
- Tasks/projects/activities execution
- Dissemination of information
- Data and information collection
- Support services

ENTRY LEVEL

(b)

Figure 1.4(b) The pyramid model also shows the tasks ordinarily performed by public relations staff at different levels of the nonprofit organization.

Picture now the second hospital as it is also described by people who work there:

> Community [Hospital] resembles a nearly decomposable system: a loose federation of heterogeneous components, many of which coalesce around distinct types of patients. This allows components to be grafted onto the organization or severed

with minimal disruption. The administrator devotes about 70 percent of his time to managing external relationships, and many sub-units link independently to patients, community organizations, and planning agencies. The bonds between Community [Hospital] and its environments grow . . . administrative and professional employees abound, and the hospital's entrepreneurial ideology and loosely coupled workforce encourage them to look outward. . . . One doctor commented that apart from reviewing physicians' recordkeeping practices, the hospital exerts minimal control over the quality of care. "This is a chaotic place," said one physician. "In fact, sometimes it reminds me of a mob." However, Community [Hospital] is an ideologically charged mob that values innovation, pluralism, and professional autonomy.[32]

Reflect for a moment which of these you would prefer to work for, especially if you were practicing public relations. Imagine what you would face if you were to undertake a public relations campaign to change the corporate culture of either of these organizations. Consider what approach you would take if you were charged with the task of capturing the corporate identity of either of these hospitals to preserve and maintain the current corporate culture. The challenge you would face in maintaining and promoting that corporate personality is what is involved when public relations is guardian and advocate of the organization's culture.

For two reasons, the public relations planner should consider the campaign as a way to build and or maintain the organizational culture: (1) Organizations, especially business organizations, have discovered that corporate culture holds the key to success.[33] (2) The responsibility of public relations for "corporate identity" means that public relations helps to shape and preserve organizational culture.

Corporate Culture Holds the Key to Business Success

A reading of business management journals on the topic will reveal statements such as: "Corporate culture is increasingly recognized as a *sine qua non* for the long-term success of a corporation," and "As many recent efforts argue that organizational culture is the key to organizational excellence, it is critical to define this concept." Both of these quotations from different issues of MIT's *Sloan Management Review*, one by a business professor at MIT and the other by an executive of AT&T, reflect a common assumption that corporate culture holds the key to organizational success.

What does corporate or organizational culture mean for the public relations campaign planner? The AT&T executive, W. Brooke Tunstall, says, "Clearly, the culture must be shaped, adapted, and reoriented to bring the value systems and expectations of AT&T people into congruence with the corporation's new mission and to prepare them for the competitive . . . battles looming ahead. Yet no AT&T manager is charged specifically with the management of corporate culture." He, of course, is concerned with creating a new AT&T in the wake of divestiture.[34]

Most broadly, Tunstall defines the culture-building process as having to do with "a general constellation of beliefs, mores, customs, values system, behavioral norms, and ways of doing business that are unique to each corporation." These are the very things that are often at the core of communications efforts, from annual reports, to company publications, to position papers, and other facets of the public relations effort.

Edgar Schein, the MIT professor, describes the process this way: "Organizational culture is the pattern of basic assumptions that a given group has invented, discovered, or developed in learning to cope with its problems of external adaptation and internal integration, and that have worked well enough to be considered valid, and therefore to be taught to new members as the correct way to perceive, think, and feel in relation to those problems."[35] These are the elements critical to the public relations objectives concerning new employees, dealers, distributors, and other publics essential to a business organization's success.

The popular concern about the way different cultural practices contribute to business success propelled William Ouchi's book *Theory Z: How American Business Can Meet the Japanese Challenge* to the best-seller list. In it he describes the cultural characteristics of the Japanese business manager's commitment to participative management and quality circles. His effort has led to reexamination of other cultures' business management styles, from European traditions to the Orient.

Perhaps the best reason for the growing belief that corporate culture holds the key to business success is the book by Deal and Kennedy, *Corporate Cultures: The Rites and Rituals of Corporate Life*. The authors studied some 80 corporations and found that the more successful were the ones with the strongest cultures. They believe the answer to "America's industrial malaise" is "to relearn old lessons about how culture ties people together and gives meaning and purpose to their day-to-day lives."[36]

They found that early business leaders did build strong cultures within the companies they founded. "The lessons of these early leaders have been passed down in their own companies from generation to generation of managers; the cultures they were so careful to build and nourish have sustained their organizations through both fat and lean times. Today these corporations still have strong cultures and still are leaders in the marketplace."[37] They name NCR, GE, IBM, P&G, 3M, and others as companies with exemplary cultures.

Now, let's have a look at how the elements of corporate culture mesh with the corporate identity responsibilities of the public relations officer.

Corporate Culture Matches the Public Relations Job

Deal and Kennedy name four basic elements that make up corporate culture. These four provide at least one way to compare corporate culture with the responsibilities of the public relations practitioner. They are "values," "heroes," "rites and rituals," and "communication networks." These include interpersonal communication networks as well as mediated communication networks. It takes no stretch of the imagination to compare these elements with what public relations people do. Because of the external relationships charged to the public relations officer, he or she often becomes the corporate *conscience*, the one to remind other executives of corporate social responsibilities. The public relations officer often is charged with drawing up or at least maintaining the corporate code of ethics and almost invariably with disseminating the code of ethics within the organization.

A packet describing responsibilities of the public relations officer of Ashland Oil showed that one of the booklets for which he was responsible included the company's code of ethics. It covered such topics as employee loyalty, how to avoid even the appearance of conflict of interest, a prohibition against serving on the boards of competing companies, and otherwise not working for competing companies. The booklet also explained how to comply with Securities and Exchange Commission rules against profiting from insider information in stock purchases. Overall, the booklet provided an example of how the public relations officer is the guardian of the corporate conscience.

The public relations officer is also responsible for corporate values as the collector, interpreter, and disseminator of what the organization believes and considers important. Values and ethics, as the responsibility of the public relations officer, place him or her at the very heart of the corporate culture.

But the public relations person is also intimately involved in the next cultural element Deal and Kennedy mention: heroes. One of the first tasks often assigned to new public relations employees is to compile or rewrite and update the corporate history. The public relations person thus becomes the company storyteller, the maker or chronicler of the corporate heroes.

The public relations person is also critical to another of Deal and Kennedy's elements of organizational culture: rites and rituals. "Many rituals or ceremonies seem like just a lot of hoopla," they write, "yet the underlying purpose is very serious, as in the case of one large company we know: the company recognizes many successful efforts by . . . the presentation of a plaque called the 'attaboy'." They further describe other ceremonies: "Whether they are cultural extravaganzas or simple events when employees pass particular milestones, ceremonies help the company celebrate heroes, myths, and sacred symbols. . . . Ceremonies place the culture on display and provide experiences that are remembered by employees. . . . Properly done, ceremonies keep values, beliefs, and heroes uppermost in employees minds and hearts."[38] The authors are talking about the responsibilities that fall to public relations: special events.

The fourth and final of Deal and Kennedy's elements of corporate culture—communications networks—should be the most obvious responsibility of the public relations person. Whereas formal communication is an important way people in an organization get information—through public relations newsletters, brochures, bulletin boards, and the like—Deal and Kennedy stress informal communication. Gossip, storytellers, whisperers, spies, and priests are terms they use. What they mean is that word gets around in any organization, and sometimes the informal is as important as the formal. The storytellers and priests, as Deal and Kennedy explain them, are those who have been with the company longer than most others—even than the chief executive—and know the anecdotes, the stories of overcoming great odds, and the stories of how something was accomplished.

Public relations cannot succeed without being plugged into this informal network, but a successful company also must have effective formal communication. Here is where public relations exercises its basic function as the communications center of the organization. As the coordinator of formal and informal communication, the public relations person directs the communication network and manages the organization's campaigns.

SUMMARY

The **public relations campaign** is a connected series of operations.

Communications as functions and as tools: Goals of the public relations function differ from those of other campaigns. How public relations campaigns compare with public communication campaigns suggest different applications. Different approaches to designing campaigns involve fundamental steps. The advantages of the time-limited "campaign" over the continuing "program" focus on its time frame. The checklist for a public relations campaign outlines the elements involved in the process. The key to successful campaigns is a combination of mass communication and interpersonal support mechanisms. Research on campaign audience response reveals the cognitive process involved.

Defining public relations, the key to practice: Factors in a definition include concepts such as a public, management, the nature of relationships, and communication. This book defines public relations as a societal phenomenon in which an advocate of a social entity manages the organization's associations in the public interest.

Ethical practice at different organizational levels: The public interest is the basis for public relations ethics. The public relations pyramid illustrates the role of public relations at various levels in an organization.

The campaign in the cultural life of the organization: Public relations serves as the guardian of the organizational culture. Corporate culture holds the key to business success. Elements that make up the corporate culture correspond to the public relations responsibility for corporate identity.

FOR FURTHER READING

Definitions of Public Relations

Harlow, Rex. "Building a Public Relations Definition," *Public Relations Review* 2 (Winter 1976): 34–42.

Harlow, Rex. "PR Definitions through the Years," *Public Relations Review* 3 (1977): 49–63.

Hill and Knowlton Executives. *Critical Issues in Public Relations.* Englewood Cliffs, NJ: Prentice Hall, 1975.

Olasky, Marvin. "Roots of Modern Public Relations: The Bernays Doctrine," *Public Relations Quarterly* 30 (March 1985): 25–27.

Professionalism

Barber, Bernard. "Control and Responsibility in the Powerful Professions," *Political Science Quarterly* 93 (Winter 1978): 599–615.

Brody, E. W., et al. "The Credentials of Public Relations: Licensing? Certification? Accreditation?" *Public Relations Quarterly* 29 (Summer 1984): symposium issue.

Grunig, James E. "Toward a Multipurpose Theory of Public Relations," *Public Relations Journal* 31 (January 1975): 12–14.

Kendall, Robert. "The Body of Knowledge in the Public Relations Profession," *International Public Relations Association Review* 8 (May 1984): 8–10, 14.

Marston, John. "The Hallmarks of a Profession," *Public Relations Journal* 24 (July 1968): 8–10.

Ethics

Andrews, D. K. "Difficulties in Assessing Ethical Policy," *California Management Review* (Summer 1984): 133.

Delattre, Edwin L. "Ethics in the Information Age," *Public Relations Journal* 29 (June 1984): 12.

McCammond, Donald B. "A Matter of Ethics," *Public Relations Journal* 39 (November 1983): 46.

Pastin, M. "Ethics as an Integrating Force in Management," *Journal of Business Ethics* 3 (November 1984): 293.

PRSA CODE, formal title: *Declaration of Principles, Code of Professional Standards for the Practice of Public Relations with Interpretations.* New York: Public Relations Society of America (1983).

Public Relations Journal: Register Issue, published annually, includes a copy of the PRSA CODE with interpretations, PRSA Bylaws with procedures of the Board of Ethics and Professional Regulation (formerly the Grievance Board), and procedures for the Judicial Panels.

Schaefer, T. E. "Professionalism: Foundation for Business Ethics," *Journal of Business Ethics* 3 (November 1984): 269.

PART
TWO

Building the
Campaign Plan:
The Research Stage

Introduction to Research for Campaign Planning

THE PURPOSES OF RESEARCH

Otto Lerbinger has observed that "public relations research is beginning to refer to the uses to which research is put rather than the methodologies employed."[1] In a study of 28 corporations and nonprofit organizations, he identified four main purposes for which public relations research is used: environmental monitoring, public relations audits, communications audits, and social audits. He has also arranged these in a grid to indicate the "universes" that are studied, whether the external environment, the organization, publics, messages, media, or effects. These universes include publics that would involve the organization itself and other organizations that have an interest in the same issues, but would also involve messages, media, and effects that are not precisely "publics" or people (see Figures 2.1 and 2.2).

I. External Environment	II. Organization	III. Publics	IV. Message	V. Media	VI. Effects
Environmental monitoring					
	PR audit A. Audience identity B. Corporate image				
	Communication audit				
		1. Readership survey 2. Content analysis 3. Readability survey			
					Behavior analysis
Social audits					

Figure 2.1 Lerbinger's model of research uses. The arrangement of research categories under the headings at the top of the table indicates the type of information that is studied in a given research project.

The functions of public relations research Lerbinger defines in a summary of the findings of his study. "Political strength estimates," noted in item II, refers to the general meaning of "organizational politics" in the sense of contriving to influence policy rather than the sense of activities to influence government or public policy.

I. Environmental monitoring—keeping track of what changes are taking place "out there" is the fastest growing area of public relations research.

II. The public relations audit is receiving renewed attention as organizations seek to identify more groups and organizations that might affect their welfare. More dimensions are being added to the audit, particularly a political strength estimate that examines the resources of a group and the tactics used.

III. Public opinion polls and other data-gathering services are increasingly being used by public relations practitioners.

Along with accountants and social scientists, public relations people are contributing to social audit research which attempts to catalogue, systematize and measure a corporation's social performance.[2]

BROAD CATEGORIES OF RESEARCH

Of the many ways to classify research, public relations has traditionally used research methodology, or how the research is conducted. Methods have been

Figure 2.2 Researchers use different methodologies to discover facts needed to plan successful campaigns, but most studies require collection and analysis of data. Here a researcher examines a computer printout of data analysis in preparation for writing a report of findings.

categorized by the three broad procedures of (1) examining the historical record (the historical method), (2) examining the status quo, or what exists (the descriptive method), or (3) testing formal research questions phrased as hypotheses by using sophisticated techniques such as the "double blind" (the experimental method). Some of these broad methods have been divided into more specific approaches. The historical method includes library research, communication logs, and results of past polls. The descriptive method includes surveys or polls, interviews, focus groups, content analysis, and the Delphi technique, among others. The experimental method includes such procedures as the controlled field experiment, laboratory product testing, and tests of communication effect.

QUALITATIVE VERSUS QUANTITATIVE RESEARCH

Qualitative research seeks to identify characteristics within publics that may be important to the campaign, such as discovering preferences for video over print information. Finding a corporate culture tradition of teamwork may suggest strategies that take advantage of such factors by setting up employee task forces. Once qualitative research identifies characteristic values in a population it is possible to use quantitative research to measure the actual numbers or the proportion or percentages of such values and the degree of commitment to them. By comparing percentages of people who hold these values with demographic characteristics such as age, sex, job title, and education it is possible to find out which demographic categories are most supportive of certain values and which are least supportive. If, for example, you find that preference for teamwork is more common among middle-age women with high school educations, the finding would suggest forming task forces from these people.

Qualitative research investigates the *value* of programs or activities, using such techniques as focus group interviews. Quantitative research *counts, measures*, and analyzes in numeric terms by either formal or informal methods, using such techniques as the random sample survey. Research by its very nature has tended to be empirical, that is, based on the five senses and the assumption that human knowledge should be derived from observations that can be duplicated by others. The ability to duplicate observations verifies that the observations were true. However, researchers in several fields are beginning to question the adequacy of empirical methods of research alone. Qualitative research is gaining respect as a means of deciding what facts are more valuable than others. The qualitative approach is especially useful in campaign planning.[3]

Indeed, the weaknesses of empirical research methods led to widespread interest in qualitative research, sometimes—especially in evaluation circles—called naturalistic research. "The case study, as the exemplar of the naturalistic perspective on inquiry and the use of qualitative methods, has been accepted into the ranks of viable evaluation alternatives by most of the evaluation community."[4] Qualitative research methods generally use variations on the carefully trained observer technique as it has been developed in the field of anthropology and applied to ethnographic studies. Moorhead suggests using an "ethnographic approach," because it offers a "potentially powerful methodology" for the technical communication researcher, a methodology that provides a useful balance to the strengths and weaknesses of experiments and surveys.[5] He suggests that the approach is particularly useful for research conducted on the job in business, industry, and government.

The major difference between quantitative and qualitative research is not in empirical observation alone, but in the use of representative samples and the measurement of probability in calculating generalizability. Emmert and Barker characterize the difference in the degree of precision:

> Indeed, the differences between *qualitative* and *quantitative* research modes are overblown. Both modes can and should be based on empirical observation. Quantitative research is more precise but narrower in focus than qualitative research. Qualitative research is less restrictive but also less precise than quantitative research. Both are indirect interpretations of reality. Recently, the intelligent position that the two methods can complement one another has been advocated by significant scholars.[6]

THE SCIENTIFIC METHOD

Scientific research is based on a concept that emerged during the Enlightenment—the rationalist movement that began in the 1700s in reaction against the social, religious, and political conditions of the time. The ensuing rational approach to understanding the natural world was focused in what the British

Royal Society called "the scientific method." One of the ironies of this now long tradition of rational thought is that so much disciplined scientific thinking has failed to produce an agreed-upon definition—or even a statement—of what the scientific method is.

James K. Feibleman has attempted to resolve the matter—with questionable success—in his book, *Scientific Method*. He explains: "It has been claimed that the greatest discovery in science was the method of discovery, yet there is no general agreement as to just what this method is." He approaches the task of identifying the scientific method by observing what scientists do. The resulting practical definition of the scientific method is not actually a definition but reduces the character of the scientific method to the typical activities of scientists. It may be as important to note why scientists do what they do as it is to note what they do. Scientists ultimately attempt to establish a true understanding of the natural world, including human nature, by relying on empirical evidence, that is, evidence that can be perceived by the five senses. Such evidence is usually sufficient proof to the scientist and others that the observations and conclusions, if they pass the critical examination of other scientists, are a true account of the aspect of nature being investigated. Feibleman addresses both the what and some of the why:

> The scientist makes observations, designs instruments, conducts experiments, collects data, takes measurements, makes calculations, draws conclusions. But if we would like to include in the account the process whereby he discovers the hypotheses we are hardly ready with an accurate and precise description, for such inductions are difficult to explain.
>
> Observations are made in order to uncover "provocative facts." This stage is one of purely descriptive knowledge. Inductions from the provocative facts are made next in order to discover hypotheses worthy of investigation. This is the stage of brilliant originative insight. The hypotheses are set up for testing in this fashion, then they are tested in three ways. The first way is the one peculiar to science; it involves testing the hypotheses by means of experiments. In the second way the hypotheses are tested against existing theories by means of mathematical calculations. This is the stage in which the quantitative laws are shown to be the necessary logical consequences of a few axioms or assumptions. Finally, the third way is to make predictions from the hypotheses and to use them as instruments to exercise control over practice. Those hypotheses which pass all three tests successfully are considered to be established, however tentatively, as laws.[7]

Feibleman also notes that working scientists do not engage in all elements of the scientific method at any one time or even in any one lifetime. It is a process involving scientists geographically dispersed, often even separated in time, who individually or in small groups add to the process a few steps at a time. An experiment is repeated again and again in a self-corrective process of starts and stops. Feibleman notes how the collective process involves both logic and intuition, "The formalized multi-stage process of the scientific method of investigation is a logical structure. But like all logical structures it needs to engage the intuition and constitutes an aid to it, not a substitute for it." Indeed, he says, intuition operates throughout the process, "We do not have the method complete unless we understand the role of intuition at every stage." Intuition is at work in deciding what to observe, in discovering hypotheses from the observations, in designing tests for the hypotheses, even the selection of mathematical calculations and demonstrating that the findings are consequences of certain axioms or assumptions, and most certainly in making predictions from the hypotheses. Intuition, of course, is that seemingly unscientific understanding that comes without conscious reasoning—the leap of cognition that springs to mind without apparent effort.

A Definition for the Mass Media Fields   Those who use the scientific method often resort to "operational definitions" adequate to that particular field of scientific inquiry, but which might not apply to all fields. Kerlinger says the scientific method is "a systematic, controlled, empirical, and critical investigation of hypothetical propositions about the presumed relations among observed phenomena."[8]

Wimmer and Dominick offer five "characteristics of the scientific method" and warn that research that does not follow these tenets cannot be considered a scientific approach:

1. **Scientific research is public**. . . . Researchers . . . must take care in published reports to include information on their use of sampling methods, measurements, and data-gathering procedures. Such information allows other researchers to independently verify a given study and support or refute the initial research findings.
2. **Science is objective**. . . . Objectivity . . . requires that scientific research deal with facts rather than interpretations of facts. Science rejects its own authorities if their statements conflict with direct observation.
3. **Science is empirical.** Researchers are concerned with a world that is knowable and potentially measurable. . . . they recognize that concepts must be strictly defined to allow for observation and measurement. Scientists must link abstract concepts to the empirical world through observations, which may be made either directly or indirectly via various measurement instruments.
4. **Science is systematic and cumulative**. . . . researchers always use previous studies as building blocks for their own work. . . . In its ideal form, scientists' research begins with a single, carefully observed event and progresses ultimately to the formulation of theories and laws. . . . researchers develop theories by searching for patterns of uniformity to explain the data that have been collected. When relationships among variables are invariant (always the same) under given conditions researchers may formulate a law.
5. **Science is predictive.** Science is concerned with relating the present to the future. . . . if a theory generates predictions that are supported by the data, that theory can be used to make predictions in other situations.[9]

Such a characterization of the scientific method is usually adequate for research in fields related to public relations. It should also be clear that archival and descriptive research are essential to the scientific method. Archival research is the means for placing any intended research within the context of any previous related efforts of the scientific community. Descriptive research consists of various ways to conduct observations or to *describe what exists.* The public relations practitioner should be at home with the creative intuition needed in the scientific method since it is the same creative intuition that practitioners use in solving other problems requiring creativity.

The creative intuition in experimental research requires the creation of new ideas, new approaches, and new techniques to problem solving as well as the precision of formal logic for which science is well known. Let us consider an example of how experimental research uses the scientific method to answer a question that might confront a practitioner of public relations.

An Example of the Scientific Method   Let us begin with an observation. The spokesperson for our organization seems more effective when appearing on television at certain times than at others. We use creative intuition to observe that in some videotapes the spokesperson seems to be looking up at the viewer and at other times seems to be looking down. We wonder if the position of the spokesperson relative to the viewer may have something to do with message effectiveness. A check of the literature reveals that other researches have found that a person standing over a seated person is perceived to be more of an authority than the seated person.

Observations   These observations and conclusions from previous archival research lead us to speculate—formulate a hypothesis—that our spokesperson is more believable when appearing to be looking down at the viewers. We then decide to test the hypothesis by setting up an experiment where we can measure the effects of these two factors—looking up and looking down at viewers—when they happen in a television interview.

The Test   We apply our creativity and intuition again in designing a test which will allow us to measure the difference between a television spokesperson looking down at the camera—perceived by the viewer to be looking down at the audience—and the spokesperson looking up at the camera. We need to rule out all other influences beyond those we want to measure, so we select a single spokesperson to make a speech and record it on two different tapes. In one, the speech is recorded by a camera below and looking up at the speaker; in the other, the camera is placed above looking down at the speaker. However, to make sure that there is not some element about the two camera angles we didn't anticipate that may still influence how the speaker is perceived, we position a camera at eye level for a third taping of the speech. This third camera position, which we judge to be a neutral position, will be used as a "control" condition against which to compare the other two. We now have the three videotapes of the same person giving the same presentation but recorded from three different camera angles.

The Sample   Next we need to arrange three different audiences to view the three tapes. Because our intuition tells us that the entire population is likely to respond uniformly to the experiment, the sample need only be drawn to represent the general population. If we suspect that segments of the population will respond differently—the educated different from the uneducated—samples would need to be drawn to accurately represent these segments.

For the general viewing population the audiences need to be as alike as possible, and we hope, as much as possible like the audiences our organization spokesperson will need to reach. We find representatives of these audiences and arrange for them to be divided into three equal groups. We know that random selection gives each participant an equal chance to be chosen in any of the groups. We arrange for the three groups to view the tapes at the same time—to preclude that time of day has any influence, and in viewing rooms as nearly alike as possible—to avoid the chance that something about the rooms might make a difference in the way the message is perceived.

The Instrument   Then we need some way of measuring how the audiences perceive the message as presented in the three conditions. We decide on a questionnaire that will give each participant a chance to respond without discussing the matter with any other participant—a questionnaire that will detect the degree the message is understood, the degree of credibility the speaker is perceived to have, and perhaps the degree of willingness to act on the speaker's message. Note that the first two topics are critical to confirm our hypothesis, that camera angle affects spokesperson believability, which other researchers have shown may involve both the viewer's *understanding* of the message and *credibility* of the speaker. The third questionnaire topic, behavior, is not important to confirming the hypothesis, but may be critical in applying the findings to improving our organization's presentations. Finding out how to make use of the findings of research may be as important to the practitioner as the basic research question itself.

The Experiment   We then carry out the experiment, record the responses in a data set, and proceed to analyze the data. We need to compare the total ratings from each group on a scale that allows easy comparison on each of the qualities being measured, especially understanding and credibility. Comparing findings on these two topics against indications of behavioral intent will help to identify whether understanding or credibility has the greater influence on the likely behavior of presentation audiences. By comparing scores of each of the three groups on each of the three scores for the characteristics of both understanding and credibility, as well as behavioral inclination, we can determine whether camera angle makes a difference in the overall believability of the spokesperson. We can also determine which aspect of believability has the greatest influence, and whether either or both aspects of believability might influence audience behavior. We would expect the scores on understanding to be nearly the same for all three groups, the scores on credibility to be higher for the group that "looked up" to the speaker, and the neutral viewing group to be between the other two groups' scores. We might expect scores on behavior to be the same as credibility, if somewhat less extreme.

The Hypotheses   This activity of "guessing" what we will find is the intuitive process of speculating on the results. It is the way hypotheses are determined. In this example the hypotheses could be stated as research questions: Will understanding of message content be the same for all three viewing conditions? Will credibility be higher for the spokesperson-looking-down condition and lower for the spokesperson-looking-up condition than the neutral-spokesperson condition? Will behavioral intent be higher for the spokesperson-looking-down condition and lower for the spokesperson-looking-up condition than the neutral-spokesperson condition? Many scientists prefer the null hypothesis form which states the hypothesis as a negative statement.

The Null Hypothesis   Karl R. Popper, scientist and philosopher, is well known for asserting that "scientific theories can never be proved through experimental tests but only disproved, or 'falsified'."[10] What he is saying is the basis for the null hypothesis. By stating hypotheses in negative or "null" form, any significant finding disproves the null hypothesis and thus provides positive evidence in support of the question being investigated. Asked if his theory of "falsifiability" is falsifiable, Popper responded that "it's a silly question" because the falsifiability question is "pseudoscientific" in the way that "Marxism or astrology or even psychoanalysis" are "metascience." Pseudoscientific theories are distinguishable from scientific theories or questions because the latter "offer predictions specific enough to be experimentally tested—and hence falsified." Such specific predictions rely on the scientists' intuition. "A theory is an invention, an act of creation, based more on a scientist's intuition than on preexisting empirical data."[11] Popper asserts that scientific theories as well as hypotheses can never be proven, only disproven or falsified.

Applied to our example, the first research question stated as a null hypothesis would be: There will be no difference in understanding of message content by the subjects in the three viewing conditions. The second null hypothesis would be: Viewers of the spokesperson-looking-down condition and the spokesperson-looking-up condition will not differ in messenger credibility from the neutral-spokesperson condition. The third null hypothesis would be: Viewers of the spokesperson-looking-down condition and the spokesperson-looking-up condition will not differ in behavioral intent from the neutral-spokesperson condition. If the experiment finds that any of these null hypotheses is false by revealing a significant difference in the viewing angle, the finding provides evidence to support the idea that viewing angle may indeed influence message credibility. The experimental findings that reject the null have falsified the negative hypothesis thus giving credence to the positive hypothesis. But, as Popper asserts, the process can only falsify the negative (null) hypothesis and cannot conclusively prove the positive hypothesis. The reason is there may be other influences at work that the experiment cannot control.

Furthermore, one robin doesn't make a spring, as they say. One indication that camera angle influences speaker credibility doesn't mean that this cause and effect relationship will always be true. Thus, scientists also calculate the probability that what has been observed is the result of the proposed cause rather than a result of chance alone. A small difference may seem to reject the null; but the null is rejected only if there is a significant difference. Whether the difference is significant involves statistical testing.

Testing Significance   In the communication field the most common tests of significance use statistical probability theory to compare experimental or survey results with what would happen by chance alone. If the difference observed in the experiment were within the range of what probability theory tells us would happen simply by chance, the difference is not significant. In fact, tests of significance are only tests of statistical probability; you can test the chances that four aces will be a winning hand in poker, but you can't test whether your opponent has a better hand at any given deal. That is, probability calculations cannot tell you whether a specific finding is accurate; only the chances—the probability—that it will be accurate.

Fink and Kosecoff suggest some basic guidelines for analysis of research data[12] that may be applied to a wide range of research conducted in the communication and behavioral sciences. They list commonly used survey data analysis techniques for four different types of analysis:

1. Descriptive Statistics (mean, mode, median, numbers, percentage, range, standard deviation)
2. Correlations (Spearman rank-order, Pearson product-moment)
3. Comparisons (Mann-Whitney U, chi-square, t-test, analysis of variance)
4. Trends (repeated measures analysis of variance, McNemar test)

In other words, the researcher must consider whether to simply describe the data according to basic statistical descriptions, in which case descriptive statistics would be used. If the need is to see how one set of variables such as reading habits correlate with demographics such as age, education, and the like, correlations would be used. If comparisons need to be made, specific statistical tests would be used such as Mann-Whitney U, chi-square, t-test, or analysis of variance, often called ANOVA, or, for a number of comparisons, Multiple Analysis of Variance (MANOVA). If the need is to track patterns over time or other patterns, trend analyses would be used such as McNemar, or repeated ANOVA, or MANOVA.

Analysis of data requires an understanding of the nature of the data, whether it is parametric or nonparametric, that is whether the measures are made according to equal appearing intervals or not. These categories are determined by the type of measurement used to collect the data. These four "levels of measurement" are:

1. **Nominal**—sorting responses into unordered categories, such as male–female, blue eyes-brown eyes;
2. **Ordinal**—placing responses into ordered categories along a single dimension, such as "not important" up to "very important";
3. **Interval**—classifying responses by a standard equal-appearing-interval scale, such as inches, Fahrenheit temperature, or picas;
4. **Ratio**—classifying responses where the ratio between values are meaningful as well as the intervals between them, such as income in dollars, weight, or time.

To measure eye color, for example, the first of these, nominal, may be either parametric, if measurement is in pigmentation level—or nonparametric—if the measurement is by self-identification. The second, ordinal, is a nonparametric measure, because the distance between the points on the scale may vary for different respondents. The last two are parametric measures, because the measurements are according to universally recognized standards of measurement. Most of the statistical analysis procedures assume the data is parametric, such as t-test, Pearson correlation, and analysis of variance. However, these analysis procedures have also been applied to nonparametric measurements at times. The danger is that the distance between one person's "agree" and "strongly agree" may not be the same as another person's. The assumption is false that this Likert type scale of agree-to-disagree is the same type of measure as are inches and feet. However, many scholars believe it is fair to use some statistical analyses of data that are based on measurements made without using equal appearing interval scales, such as Likert type scales.

The scientific method thus involves a combination of both careful logic and creative intuition. Perhaps the most important consideration in using the scientific method is in lending credibility to reports of research findings. The use of clear thinking in posing insightful research issues, phrasing those issues in carefully worded hypotheses, measuring those hypotheses by logically designed experiments or surveys, testing those designs, applying the most appropriate statistical procedures, and reporting these steps in clear language is the ideal way to give credibility to research studies.

RESEARCH TERMINOLOGY

Knowing research terminology can assist the practitioner in planning a research program that best fits the needs and resources of the organization and working with others without confusion.

Research broadly defined is studious inquiry designed to discover and interpret facts. *Distinct (but overlapping) categories* include:

1. **Empirical research**—relies on experience or observation using the five senses often without attempting to fit results into a system or theory.
2. **Basic or pure research**—investigation seeking factual understanding of phenomena often through the building and testing of theories, but with no intent to apply results to solving everyday problems.
3. **Applied research**—efforts to solve problems by applying results of investigation in phenomena associated with the problem.
4. **Social research**—basic or applied investigation of phenomena associated with the social sciences, including such fields as psychology, social psychology, anthropology, communication, and mass communication, but excluding the physical or hard sciences such as physics, biology, zoology, chemistry, and mathematics (most public relations research falls in the social research category).

5. **Evaluation research**—investigation of the effectiveness of programs to be applied to the improvement of those programs.

Research may be described in other ways:

1. *Classified by source,* that is, by the type of approach or procedure for gathering information:
    a. **Historical research**—collecting information that exists "on the record" including historic documents, personal papers, journals, and official records.
    b. **Descriptive research**—collecting information that describes existing conditions, the status quo, of individuals, or group opinions, attitude, or behavior.
    c. **Experimental research**—collecting data by using an experiment, usually designed to test a theory or hypothesis.
2. *Classified by the technique,* procedure, or method used:
    a. **Formal, scientific, or quantitative research**—rigorous use of the principles of scientific investigation such as the rules of empirical observation, random sampling in surveys, comparison of results against statistical standards, and provision for replication of results.
    b. **Informal, or nonscientific, research**—investigation without use of the scientific method, usually undertaken as exploratory and/or preliminary to more rigorous methods.
    c. **Qualitative research**—investigation into the value of programs, or probing other value judgment questions using informal or formal methods.
3. *Classified by immediacy of the information source:*
    a. **Primary research**—investigation of phenomena by gathering data personally or collecting information firsthand.
    b. **Secondary research**—investigation of phenomena by use of research findings of others, or collecting information secondhand.
4. *Classified by function:*
    a. **Formative research**—information gathered to use in making adjustments in the campaign plan during implementation.
    b. **Summative research**—information gathered in monitoring a campaign in order to document the effectiveness of the whole campaign or its parts.

Research Types and Techniques

The literature commonly uses the term *method* or *methodology* to describe both the information source and the procedure for collecting the information from that source. This book uses the term *type* of research to emphasize the source of information, usually in reference to the historical, descriptive, and experimental types. When a research method is used to describe a procedure

▶ CASE STUDY: CRAYOLA USES RESEARCH, CAPITALIZES ON ELEMENTARY RECOGNITION

Continuous research insights are phoned to Crayola headquarters via an 800 phone number. The device "gives us a direct pipeline into consumer reaction and thinking. From that we're able to glean the interesting relationship Crayola has with kids and adults. It's almost universally positive. That information is a helpful tool for us in developing our programs," Brad Drexler, manager of corporate communications at Binney & Smith in Easton, Pennsylvania, told a staffer at *pr reporter*.

In 1990, Crayola introduced eight colors, the first new ones in 18 years, and retired eight old ones. Focus groups with children ages 4 to 10 around the country sought consumer opinions—how they would improve or change Crayola products. This was "consistent with a new company philosophy to become more attuned to the needs of the end users."

Retired colors were enshrined in the Crayola Hall of Fame, built at headquarters. "It became a real attraction. People want to come and visit and see and touch. It drives a lot of traffic through our tour program."

At the time, a ground swell protested the colors' retirement. After being screened by phone, protesters' names and phone numbers were given to the media. "We felt the intent of individuals protesting our crayon color change was so tongue in cheek and benign, and the benefit derived in the form of increased awareness for the new colors so great, that the opportunity far outweighed the slight risk sales could be negatively impacted." Picketers were even invited to protest the Hall of Fame ceremony.

In 1993, the company celebrated its 90th birthday. A consumer contest named 16 new colors being introduced. Winners got (1) a trip to Hollywood for birthday party, (2) had their names printed (for a limited time) on the crayon each named, and (3) were inducted into Crayola Hall of Fame as the first nonemployees ever to name crayon colors. Over two million name suggestions were sent in—more from adults than from children. The contest was introduced in January, winners announced in November. Yearlong events brought much media attention.

To stay relevant, Crayola offers a line of multicultural products that began with crayons representing eight skin tones "to greater sensitize kids to cultural diversity." Products have since expanded to markers, paints, color pencils, and clay.

Adapted from an account in *pr reporter* 37 (September 12, 1994): 1, 2.

such as a survey or an audit, this book uses the term *technique* or *approach* to emphasize how the information is collected.

Where the terms *formal* and *informal* methods are ordinarily used, this book uses formal and informal without adding the word method. Two terms that are commonly used without association with the term *method* are primary and secondary research. These terms are used to indicate whether the information is gathered firsthand, that is, "primary" research, or secondhand, which is to say "secondary" research.

RESEARCH DESIGN

The research design is the plan for conducting the research project. Whether the research project is a library search, a poll, a content analysis, or an experiment, it must be planned; most researchers call this plan the research design. Suchman describes it this way: "The design is *the plan of study* and, as such, is present in all studies, uncontrolled as well as controlled and subjective as well as objective."[13] The design will differ from project to project.

Glen Broom and David Dozier suggest examples of reasons for selecting different designs. For planning purposes a "snapshot" or "freeze frame" analysis of conditions at one specific time, "called *cross-sectional* designs," may be appropriate. For evaluation purposes a *longitudinal* design, one that "gathers data at several points in time," may be needed.[14] Whereas execution of research projects demand precision and exactitude, developing the research design tests the scientist's creativity. Suchman notes, "There is no such thing as a single, 'correct' design." Nor is a research design "a highly specific plan to be followed without deviation"; instead it is "a series of guideposts to keep one headed in the right direction." In addition, "A research design must be *practical.*" A design must have flexibility: "any research design developed in the office will inevitably have to be changed in the face of field considerations."[15]

Research design often involves two levels. The first is the broader scope of research design, which includes (1) the statement of the problem, (2) a statement of research questions or hypotheses, (3) identification of the phenomenon to be observed, (4) tests or other measurements to be applied, and (5) the form in which the findings will be reported. The second, narrower scope of research design involves the specific procedure to be employed in the project: (1) *phenomenon* specifies the phenomenon to be observed and how the observation will be managed—by use of archival records, survey population and sampling procedure, or experimental subjects; (2) *measurement* specifies how the measurement will be conducted—the standard(s) to be used in collecting historical evidence, the survey questionnaire, or the experimental treatment (see Box 2.1).[16]

CHOOSING RESEARCH PROJECTS FOR THE CAMPAIGN

The choices to be made when selecting research projects for the campaign include when to do research, which specific research projects to do, whether to do a project in-house or hire it out, which research type or technique to use, and how to make use of the research results (see Figure 2.3). In the broad sense, the public relations practitioner should be involved in continuing research. He or she must be well informed in the news media, perhaps with a system of tracking issues that may affect the organization. The practitioner must maintain a continuous study of the organization to anticipate trends among employees, customers, dealers, suppliers, investors—indeed, all publics significant to the organization. These research "antennae" are but an

BOX 2.1   Research Design—An Aid to Preparing a Research Plan

Research requires a plan of action—that research plan has been called the research design. The research design involves five decisions:

1. **Where is the needed information to be found?** If the information is available in library holdings, or published records, the research effort will be a *library or literature research* project; if the information consists of people's opinions, attitudes, or behavior patterns, the project will involve a series of *interviews or a survey* in which you ask the people who hold those opinions; if the information consists, for example, of whether a print message is more credible than a video, the project will require *an experiment.*

2. **How will the information be selected?** *Library research* will select either all the information available—if there is not much—or narrow the topic down to what is most pertinent, or even sample what is available. *Survey research* will draw a random sample from the population in order to get representative results. *Experimental research* will select responses using a test instrument, for example, a device to test credibility.

3. **How will the selected information be measured?** The *library researcher* will employ criteria of how well the articles, books, or other information supports or contributes to the argument the researcher seeks to prove; the *survey researcher* will measure whether respondents agreed or disagreed with questions asked; the *experimenter* will use an instrument, often scaled responses such as agree-disagree, to measure credibility.

4. **How will the information be analyzed?** The *library researcher* will use a narrative in which the authorities identified will be quoted or cited and the collected information will be generalized to support the proposition the researcher set out to prove—or prove a new proposition that fits the evidence discovered. The *survey researcher* will calculate mean scores or averages, percentages of those who agree or disagree, and perhaps more sophisticated statistical procedures that answer the research question. The *experimenter* will use statistical calculations to determine whether the measurements recorded differ from what would happen by chance alone, and thus, for example, "prove" whether print messages are more credible than video.

5. **How will the findings be reported?** All research reports use narrative of one sort or another. *Library researchers* provide documentation in the form of credible information or quotations from writers, including survey and experimental research findings to substantiate a claim or to "prove" a proposition. The *survey researcher* reports the percentages

(*continues*)

of the sample that agree or disagree with the items asked in the interviews, and which thus represent the opinions of the population from which the sample was drawn in order to answer the research question. The *experimenter* reports the statistical probability that the findings are valid, their reliability, and the probability that such results would happen by chance alone, and, thus, "proves" that one medium is more credible than the other.

early warning system that may prompt further research to confirm an observation and perhaps suggest public relations action.

The question of when to do research is perhaps best answered by asking further questions: How significant is the threat or trend? How much money or goodwill is at stake? How precise do the answers to the questions have to be? In general, the more precise the answers and the greater the stake in dollars or other measures, the more necessary research will be. In terms of chronological time, the research must be done in time to take the necessary action.

The question of what project or projects to undertake involves deciding what information is needed and where the information is to be found. For example, a campaign to generate support and funding for a downtown development effort might include the following research projects: collect from other cities details of how they went about similar programs, interview area merchants both downtown and in outlying malls for opinions for and against, survey the public and shoppers to determine why they do or do not shop downtown, review state laws and local ordinances to identify regulations that make downtown less attractive, and do a financial analysis to identify financial inhibitions to a more attractive downtown. These are but some examples of research that would be appropriate for a specific campaign. Notice that each research project listed here identifies where the information is to be found (the research type) and how to collect it (the research technique).

Some research projects may be carried out by the practitioner; indeed, the practitioner would be the logical person to study the organization itself and perhaps to do the necessary library and legal research. Survey research will often be hired, and experimental testing of products or ingredients should usually be conducted by an independent research organization to give the findings credibility. The services of an independent research firm are strongly indicated when the results will be widely disseminated and the self-interest of the sponsoring organization is clearly evident. Employing an independent research firm will prove to be cost-effective when calculating the effect and credibility of the findings.

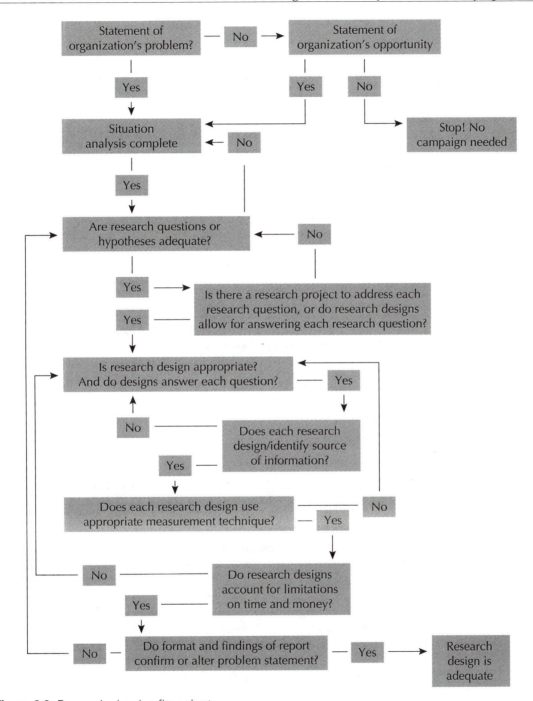

Figure 2.3 Research planning flow chart.

Example of the Challenge of Choosing Research Projects

A research challenge on "homelessness" confronting the federal and state governments illustrates what a campaign planner faces in selecting research projects for a campaign. Because the task involves the current status of the homeless, this is an example of a descriptive research type. Many estimates have been made of the number of homeless in this country, but such estimates traditionally have been obtained through "sample surveys . . . based on the reasonable assumption that everybody has an address." There are obvious problems in measuring homelessness by surveying people at home. The challenge is finding a method or technique for collecting the needed information.

Two projects attempted new approaches to counting the homeless, one in Chicago and one in Baltimore. In Chicago, Dr. Peter H. Rossi employed a "photographic negative" approach "based on the assumption that an address was precisely what everyone in the target population lacked."[17]

> In a two-week period in September and October 1985, and again in February and March 1986, professional interviewers from the National Opinion Research Center at the University of Chicago, accompanied by off-duty police officers, swept a representative sample of blocks around the city. Between midnight and 6 A.M. they checked every space to which the public had access—bus stations, building doorways and lobbies, even parked vehicles. They talked to every person they encountered to determine if he or she were homeless, and then conducted further interviews with those who were.
>
> In the same two-week periods, other interviewers talked to the homeless people in Chicago's emergency shelters. A total of 722 people were interviewed. From the data collected, Mr. Rossi and his colleagues at the University of Massachusetts' Social and Demographic Research Institute projected that, on an average night in Chicago, about 2,700 people were "undomiciled" for some period of time over the course of a year.[18]

The findings were immediately controversial because the standard figure for Chicago's homeless was a sharply higher 25,000. "Advocacy groups accused him of trivializing the problem and damaging their cause."[19] Advocacy groups on either side of this issue would need to choose research projects to support a campaign that would convince those holding the pro and con positions as well as those who were undecided. Quite apart from which side of the controversy one might take, the focus in this case was on the credibility of the evidence. At issue are precisely the two elements involved in selecting a research project for a campaign: the source of the information, or what is to be studied, and the technique, that is, how to go about collecting the information.

In Baltimore another technique was employed, but it was agreed that the best source of information was the homeless themselves. Dr. John Breakey challenged Rossi's method, claiming that the street survey "may have made many homeless people reluctant to identify themselves as such, thus artificially lowering Mr. Rossi's estimates."[20]

> [Breakey] and his colleagues conducted a study of homelessness in Baltimore in 1985 and 1986 using a technique known as the "capture-recapture method," origi-

nally developed for counting wildlife, which involves taking successive samples of a target population within a defined area.[21]

Beyond the question of how to take a sample of the target population, other technique questions are at stake in this research case. A definition of the homeless has not been settled. "So many people slip into and out of brief periods of homelessness that it can be difficult to tell who is without a home at a given moment."[22] Should the definition include only those who "literally have no place to stay" or also include the marginally housed, "families in welfare hotels, elderly pensioners in 'single-room occupancy' buildings, and others who survive purely by the good graces of relatives who are willing to put them up for a while"?[23] The problems of information source "type" and "technique" illustrated in this research case are similar to the research problems that confront the typical public relations campaign planner.

The public relations practitioner needs to do two things at the outset of a campaign: (1) prepare a situation analysis in order to gain a clear understanding of the nature of the problem requiring a public relations solution and (2) conduct research in order to confirm the initial understanding of the problem and determine the dimensions of the facts that must be addressed. Being able to choose the most appropriate research types and techniques will enable the practitioner to zero in on the information needed. Public relations research is directed at clarifying the situation that has prompted the public relations effort.

THE RESEARCH FUNCTION IN CAMPAIGN PLANNING

Often a public relations effort will be undertaken as a result of an executive's request. The chief executive officer (CEO), a vice president, or others may bring a request to the public relations department to "do something about the company image in the community." Or a nonprofit client of a public relations counseling firm may want to improve the organization's standing in the community as a base for more effective fund raising. In every case in which public relations activities are requested, the situation analysis must be confirmed. Research is needed to make an accurate appraisal of the situation.

It is possible that the CEO will request a public relations effort based on his or her perceptions of the situation—many cases of public relations actions are based on no more than that—but both the public relations officer and the CEO will be better off confirming that the perceptions are correct. Nager notes that the purpose of public relations research is "strategy," that is, the "policy . . . that derives from the knowledge which research provides." Indeed, "research can breathe life into public relations programs—finding direction for the campaign itself, providing substance for [printed] materials, steering counselors toward proper audiences, media and messages and, finally, evaluating the program's effectiveness."[24]

If the researcher discovers that the initial perceptions were not accurate, it is certainly better to know what the true situation is before undertaking a public relations campaign. In either case, research is insurance that time and effort, as well as money, will not be spent in vain.

The research procedures listed in the following pages are intended to guide the public relations practitioner in making an accurate appraisal of the problem that the public relations effort is expected to solve. Before this research on the public relations problem gets under way, it is essential to have a good understanding of the organization itself. The longtime employee may have a full appreciation of the personality of the organization; the counselor just beginning to work for a client will need to study the client organization carefully. For the new public relations employee, researching the organization will pay long-term dividends. Knowing the organizational culture will help the practitioner to avoid working at cross-purposes with the organization.

Know the Organizational Culture   The first step in the process of research for a public relations campaign is to study the sponsoring organization. Whether the practitioner is a new employee, a long-term employee, or a counselor employed by the organization, an effective campaign rests on a thorough understanding of the employing organization. Chapter 6 offers six aspects of an organization's "personality" to study in order to gain the necessary understanding of the organization.

These six aspects provide a framework for studying the organization's culture—the characteristics that distinguish it from all other organizations. Organizational culture has been described as "the way we do things around here." It is these characteristics of organizational culture that the uninitiated often find perplexing. Clearly, the public relations practitioner cannot be effective unless and until he or she knows "how we do things around here." The six aspects are: cultural history and mythology, competitive and environmental posture, philosophy and mission, operational policies, organizational structure, and trends analysis.

Know the Organization's Track Record   Beyond a knowledge of the organizational culture, and distinct from it, the practitioner should know what the organization has been doing, especially anything that relates to the proposed campaign. Thus, it is necessary to examine the organization's records—the archives—to determine whether the information needed already exists and what the collective memory of the organization offers about the organization's publics, its products or services, its communications, and the perceptions the various publics have of the organization.

Know the Situation That Prompts the Campaign   After examining the record, the researcher may need to explore certain questions in greater detail to be fully prepared to undertake the campaign. If the record reveals that the media have portrayed the organization in an unflattering way, it may be necessary to conduct descriptive research on the media and the general public to discover the true status of opinion and whether or not media coverage has had a lasting effect. This survey research requires the descriptive technique as outlined in Chapter 3. Such questions may be answered in many ways—through observation, interviews, polls, an opinion panel, contracted research, etc. The list and guidelines in Chapter 3 are intended to help the practitioner select the appropriate research procedures to find the needed answers.

The most common descriptive research procedure the practitioner is likely to use is the public opinion survey or poll. A detailed step-by-step guide for conducting an opinion poll is provided in Chapter 4. The outlined procedure is intended to be used by the practitioner as a checklist to make sure he or she has at least considered all the possible steps in conducting a poll. It should be especially helpful to practitioners who do not regularly conduct polls or who may need such a guide to deal effectively with a professional polling organization.

Consider an Experiment   The researcher may need to test the effectiveness of a public relations program or test the results of a communication effort. In such a case, an application of the experimental method may be necessary. At times, the services of an independent laboratory or research firm may be necessary to establish the credibility of facts beyond anything the organization's best efforts could establish. A research report from an independent research firm may be critical when the results of in-house research are questioned or when unimpeachable findings are required to achieve the needed level of credibility.

Examples of Fitting Research to the Problem

Suppose you are planning to market a new product that looks and tastes like eggs but has much less cholesterol than the real thing. You might test the product in typical cities by letting shoppers taste the product from an electric skillet set up in supermarkets and asking for their responses on a short questionnaire. After compiling and examining the responses from these sample "customers," you could tell what percentage liked the product, what percentage disliked it, what percentage would be willing to purchase it and at what price. You could also identify the obstacles the new product is likely to encounter by listening to the reactions of the sample customers. In this case, one rather simple research project could tell you all the facts you need to know to promote the product to its potential market, assuming supermarket shoppers are a representative cross section of the potential market.

Another example shows how complicated a research project can be. Suppose you have just been given the assignment of planning a public relations campaign for the public relations profession. You assume that there is a problem, or there wouldn't be a need for such a campaign, but you don't know specifically what the problem is. To begin, you would have to research the organization employing you to find out what prompted the campaign.

You discover that the society of public relations practitioners who hired you has a collection of press clippings, all of which in one way or another discredit public relations. You notice that the clippings tend to be byline news and opinion columns, which leads you to suspect that newspeople may have derogatory attitudes toward public relations. But you suspect that the general public may share those attitudes.

CASE STUDY: ST. LOUIS METROLINK

With the completion of its $351 million sleek light-rail transit system the Bi-State Development agency, Greater St. Louis's government-funded transit agency lacked the money to launch the new service in a community that was increasingly skeptical and critical of the system. Fleishman-Hillard Public Relations and the agency embarked on a six-month public relations campaign that successfully raised private funds to pay for the launch, reversed the tides of negative media coverage, and built significant community enthusiasm for MetroLink.

RESEARCH

History of the project revealed rapidly escalating costs, and a questionable base of support which led most politicians to regard the system as a boondoggle. Media were relentless in their negative coverage. Bus ridership was in decline and those remaining bus riders threatened to boycott the new system because it would scrap their bus routes, and because the minority bus riders—the MetroLink's chief potential customers—were offended that the new system would have to move 2,500 bodies from a largely neglected African-American cemetery.

Review of other light rail systems, including those in Portland and Los Angeles, indicated valuable information on how to explain MetroLink's payment system to passengers and how to avoid pitfalls in grand opening activities.

Community meetings helped to build rapport with the African-American community and heard the concerns of potential riders, particularly the bus route elimination issue.

A market research project was undertaken by Citizens for Modern Transit (CMT), a nonprofit mass transit advocacy group, and revealed public concerns that included crime, cost of fares, timeliness of train schedules, and location of train stations. Based on this research, the key messages emphasized that MetroLink was safe, useful, and cost

effective with stops close to St. Louis's top attractions.

Projections of ridership were derived from a St. Louis Systems Analysis document that provided the basis for the goals of the campaign.

The Problem

Six months before it was scheduled to open the MetroLink was in danger of becoming a colossal flop.

ADAPTATION

Goal

Raise private funds to redirect opposition and to achieve a successful launch of MetroLink.

Objectives

Achieve widespread community acceptance, as demonstrated by sustained daily ridership.

Overcome the opposition of the minority community.

Turn skepticism of the media into support and enlist them as allies.

IMPLEMENTATION STRATEGIES

Use the fund raising campaign to generate a sense of ownership and excitement about the system.

Reposition MetroLink as a useful, cost-effective, and accessible transportation system.

Build consensus and two-way communication with the minority community.

Work with the local Urban League chapter to facilitate relocation of African-American cemetery.

Arrange series of preintroductory system rides with key officials and opinion leaders to build enthusiasm and showcase the system's attributes.

Communicate MetroLink as a clean, safe, and accessible form of transportation with convenient schedules and stations.

Tactics

The fundraising campaign developed a highly visible plan to raise private funds and build ownership feelings; one element, the "Wall of Fame," rewarded donors with a wall plaque emblazoned with their names in an underground station. A "Rent the System/Station" offer allowed businesses to host preopening parties in MetroLink stations. A "Name the Car" program offered businesses the opportunity to name cars in exchange for donations.

A News Bureau was established within weeks of the fund raising effort to counter fears identified in the research; a series of story angles based on messages identified in the research were provided to the media; and key media were invited to participate in preopening for a first-hand look at the system.

Community involvement activities placed speakers bureau participants in over 50 community meetings for presentations to counter prejudices about MetroLink and build support for the system. A compromise was reached on bus schedules to allow bus routes to coexist with the MetroLink for a limited time.

Advertising/Promotions established the theme "Think MetroLink" to encourage sustained ridership.

Special events to generate excitement during opening day included: radio station sponsorship of parties at MetroLink stations, bands, a carnival-like atmosphere, and free rides. More than 7,500 St. Louisians were on hand to watch officials "flip the switch" to declare MetroLink open, and 67,000 rode the first day.

EVALUATION

Ten percent of the area population rode the system in its first three days, more than 200,000.

MetroLink served its one-millionth passenger after just five weeks.

Daily ridership exceeded projections by 76 percent during the first five months.

Daily ridership continues at 23,500, achieving the objective of sustained ridership.

MetroLink popularity increased bus ridership, reversing the expected decline.

African Americans embraced the system—instead of boycotting—making the East St. Louis station the busiest in the system. The East St. Louis park and ride lot had to be enlarged immediately after opening.

The East St. Louis station with minority business sponsors hosted the best attended station party.

With Urban League partnership a plan to notify families of cemetery relocation and to facilitate the process dissipated the opposition.

Extensive news coverage appeared throughout the state in spite of coinciding with the worst flood in 100 years.

The *Post-Dispatch* gave MetroLink its editorial support in the weeks leading up to the opening, with another supportive editorial two weeks after the system opened.

Almost $800,000 was raised in cash and in-kind donations to finance the campaign.

Young professionals—nontraditional users of public transit in St. Louis—crowded MetroLink at noon, riding to downtown lunch spots.

MetroLink is providing an economic boost to two downtown shopping centers on the rail line, where sales are up 20 percent and customer traffic 22 percent at one Union Station restaurant. MetroLink has contributed to a 20 percent increase in foot traffic at St. Louis Centre, and sales are up 8 to 9 percent.

The train itself has become a tourist attraction with families riding every weekend.

Neighboring St. Clair County residents so want the system extended to their community that they approved by two to one a tax to pay for extension.

St. Charles County residents, too, are clamoring for a MetroLink extension. These results document that a firm foundation has been built for MetroLink to continue into the twenty-first century.

Source: 1994 Silver Anvil Winners: Index and Summaries, Public Relations Society of America, 1994.

You are also shown a 1913 law that prohibits the federal government from funding "publicity experts"[25] and you are told that many in government hold public relations in low esteem. All of this leads you to conclude that the problem is very complex, involving many different publics with many shades of attitudes. You also realize that the concept of public relations is not easy to explain or to understand.

Obviously, no one research method or procedure will provide all the facts you need. The research of the organization's files will be only the first step. For example, the planner will need to examine the culture of the sponsoring organization, research government policy, survey public opinion among the general public and among newspeople, monitor published accounts of public relations practice, and perhaps survey practitioners themselves to discover the nature of their complaints and their understanding of the problem. The research problems of this assignment are multifaceted and complex.

The outline of research types and techniques in Chapter 3 will serve as a checklist from which to select projects to use in order to find needed answers. These research techniques are explained in detail in that chapter to help the student practitioner select an approach or approaches to fact-finding that fit a particular situation or a specific problem. The procedures listed may be used in formal or informal designs, depending on whether the scientific method is required. Other research procedures not using scientific rigor, and therefore not projectable to a larger population, may be quite useful and appropriate, depending on the circumstances.

The research procedures checklist should be used in just that way, as a checklist. Not all methods or procedures should be attempted in any given situation; methods should be chosen carefully to fit specific circumstances, budgets, time constraints, persons available to do the work, and the like. The list may be consulted after initial approaches have been tentatively selected to see if other methods might be more appropriate or cheaper.

SUMMARY

Like other parts of the public relations campaign, research requires a plan. This chapter has offered an orientation to research for the student building a research plan.

The purposes of research considers Lerbinger's categories of publics or universes that need to be studied and the approach to each.

Broad categories of research include historical, descriptive, and experimental research.

Quantitative versus qualitative research describes two research traditions: counting and measuring with probability sampling and statistical tests of significance, and the value-oriented "ethnographic" approach of the carefully trained observer.

The Scientific Method describes the procedure scientists use, defined here as it applies to mass communication fields with examples including hypotheses and techniques used to test for statistical significance.

Research terminology looks at formal and informal; primary and secondary; research methods including historical, descriptive, and experimental; and examples of fitting research to the problem.

Research design considers the plan of study to be used in conducting each research project.

Choosing research projects for the campaign involves knowing the range of types and techniques available and matching the information needed to the campaign to be carried out.

The research function in campaign planning covers knowing the organizational culture, knowing the organization's track record, knowing what prompts the campaign, and knowing whether to use an experiment.

FOR FURTHER READING

Brody, E. W., and Gerald C. Stone. *Public Relations Research.* New York: Praeger, 1989.

Emmert, Philip, and L. L. Barker. *Measurement of Communication.* New York: Longman, 1989.

Goodfield, June. "Humanity in Science: A Perspective and a Plea," *Science* 198 (November 11, 1977): 582.

Grunig, James E. "Special Section: The Two Worlds of PR Research," *Public Relations Review* 5 (Spring 1979): 13.

Lindenmann, Walter K. "The Missing Link in Public Relations Research," *Public Relations Review* 5 (Spring 1979): 33.

Moorhead, A. E. "Designing Ethnographic Research in Technical Communication: Case Study into Application," *Journal of Technical Writing and Communication* 17 (1987): 325–43.

Nager, Norman R. *Strategic Public Relations Counseling: Models from the Counselors Academy.* New York: Longman, 1988.

Pavilk, John. *Public Relations: What Research Tells Us.* Beverly Hills: Sage, 1987.

Thompson, R. W., and R. E. Roper. "Methods in Social Anthropology: New Directions and Old Problems," *American Behavioral Scientist* 23 (July/August 1980): 905–24.

Tirone, James F. "Education, Theory, and Research in Public Relations," *Public Relations Review* 5 (Spring 1979): 15.

An Outline of Research Procedures

3

- Research Types
- Archival Research
- Descriptive Research
- Case Study: Liberty Financial Young Investor Program
- Case Study: San Jose's "Recycle Plus"

RESEARCH TYPES

The summaries of research "techniques" in this chapter are offered as a guide to devising the research plan on which to build the campaign. The research plan is a series of research projects that the campaign planner chooses to collect the necessary facts and information needed to plan the campaign. Ordinarily, the campaign planner will need to carry out a range of research projects chosen from the catalog of approaches provided in this chapter. The research plan should identify the precise nature of the problem or opportunity and thus motivate the public relations campaign.

The material is organized into two general types of research most often used in the field: archival approaches, which examine what is on the historical record, and descriptive approaches, which examine the present status of the situation. A third approach, the experimental, tests research hypotheses to establish proof of hypothetical facts by applying the scientific method. Because space limitations prohibited an adequate explanation of that technique in this book, the reader is encouraged to refer to Broom and Dozier's excellent treatment of experimental research.[1]

ARCHIVAL RESEARCH

This type of research examines information that is "on the record" in order to answer questions about the organization, its internal publics, its external publics, its products, its communications, and other document-type information. The organization's records provide an account of past activities: reports, projects, plans, policy statements, minutes of meetings, reprints, back issues of publications, handbooks, memos, letters, and other such documents.

Whether the practitioner is a regular employee or a counselor working for several clients, the information needed to make an effective contribution in public relations is essentially the same. The practitioner needs to know the organization's personnel, history, current activities, problems, challenges, and the like.

Access to basic information about your client or employer organization is essential to effective public relations. The organization's files are as important to the practitioner as the newspaper's morgue is to the reporter. Nothing can substitute for the facts when they are needed.

Archives thus provide a repository of basic detailed facts about the organization that are more precise than people's memory; archives also provide the resources for background research, which is the essential first step in most other research techniques. Organizations have different archival systems, ranging from simple to complex.

A more elemental system might be a set of files containing records and minutes of meetings, letters and other correspondence, newspaper clippings, feature stories, biographies, brochures, annual reports, back issues of company publications, and the like. A more elaborate system may include a library complete with an archivist to manage the holdings. Unfortunately, archives often rate a low priority for time and funds. More often, collecting and maintaining the archives falls to the public relations person, either officially or as a necessary step in performing the public relations function.

In archival research (also called historical research), the information is to be found in recorded documents. It differs from survey research, where the information is collected from the minds of respondents, and from experimental research, where the information is found by comparing responses to the experiences of different groups of people. The technique used for gathering and reporting research also differs. Archival research is generally reported in the form of summary of facts, generalization, and "proof" in the form of quotations or other documentation.

The specific technique employed in archival research usually involves a set of research questions. The archival record is then examined in order to collect evidence in the form of quotations, numbers, dates, names, and places, with careful documentation of sources, all as a way to answer the research questions. An archival research report is ordinarily in the form of the familiar "term paper" in which the researcher summarizes the results of the investigation in a theme statement, an outline of the facts with quotations, and other evidence to support or "prove" the theme.

The Historical Record

The record of the past is as valuable as the organization's management chooses to make it. George Santayana's aphorism applies to the public relations staff: "Those who cannot remember the past are condemned to repeat it."[2] Every organization has a past, however long or short it may be. That past includes mistakes, successes, policies, and practices that represent different people's efforts to achieve certain goals. That past experience can be of great benefit in guiding the organization toward achieving today's goals. The type of material most useful will ordinarily include categories such as the following.

Important papers: charters, articles of incorporation, policy statements, earnings statements, annual reports, lists of employees, organizational charts, building blueprints, lists of committee and board members, sales reports, letters, memos, position papers, files of past and retired employees, list of constituents, inventory lists, minutes of meetings, conference programs and reports, summary reports of decision meetings, research reports, and published materials.

Newspaper back issues can provide a profile of the ebb and flow of community issues over time, a catalog of names and leaders, and can reveal networks of people who are involved in various community organizations or causes. Unfortunately, such collections can quickly become out of date and too cumbersome to be useful if not regularly maintained and updated. Local newspapers cannot be counted on to provide access to such back issues even if such a file is kept. A state university library may be the repository of state newspapers, usually on microfilm.

Clipping files, consisting of only pertinent items, are usually a preferred alternative to collections of newspapers. Some organizations employ clipping services to collect all references to the organization from a range of local and regional newspapers. Broadcast monitoring services can also be used to record and forward taped mentions occurring on radio or television.

Miscellaneous published materials include company newsletters and magazines, brochures, press clippings of releases, reprints, audio and video recordings, pictures, slides, speeches, monographs, books, trade publications of significance to the organization, and the like.

Communication Logs

A record of incoming communications can provide a useful diary when it includes telephone, mail, and other communications to and about the organization. The more common forms are telephone, mail, and conversation logs. There may be several variations on each of these; telephone logs, for example, may be used to tabulate complaints, record questions being asked, and note information requested, or to appraise the efficiency of employees who answer the telephone, including calls that must be referred.

The telephone log, as a system for tabulating incoming communication, may take several forms. The basic form usually will note the date, name and address of caller, nature of message, person to whom the message is directed for reply, and, if appropriate, the caller's telephone number and when and if a return call is required. In one example, the daily telephone log was sent around the office so that persons concerned with the subject or the reply could double-check that the call received full and complete disposition. Also, as daily log sheets accumulate, they can be examined for patterns, recurring issues, public concerns, and trends.

Past Research Reports

Past research should be examined critically; whether you did the work yourself or someone else did it, there is always room for improvement. Being removed from the deadline pressures lets you examine the process in perspective to see the weaknesses and problems more clearly. Specific uses of previous research depend on the current research needs, but the checklist in Box 3.1 may suggest some possibilities for using prior research.

A look at old surveys or other research reports offers insight into how the previously conducted research might be applied to current projects, in terms of how the findings might guide further inquiry and suggest suitable methodology. Past research, especially opinion polls, may provide answers to many questions the immediate research task has brought to mind. The organization may have conducted or contracted research several years earlier, and the resulting report may be available. Whether or not the project has any information to contribute to the current project, an examination of the prior effort can identify issues to reexplore as a basis for comparison with the prior findings. Failing that, the past research can help by revealing pitfalls to be avoided.

Some benefits that such an examination can offer include the following: (1) The study may suggest possible answers to specific questions needed in the current effort; these may need to be updated if the information is several years old. If you had planned to ask a specific question that was asked before, you can use the same phrasing again and see if there has been any change over time. (2) The previous study helps to identify follow-up questions, with the answers to the previous question serving as a base for the next question. (3) Questions from the previous study can be helpful in designing the new questionnaire. (4) A careful look at the research design of the earlier study can identify and avoid possible problems; the study may help in correctly identifying the population, for example. The sampling techniques can offer clues to

---

BOX 3.1   A Checklist for Using Prior Research

1. **Determine Characteristics of the Population** Look at both demographics and life-style, as well as whether the population does indeed have the information you need. Consider other findings that may apply to current research needs.
2. **Identify Media Use Patterns** Look for ways to reach the audience you need to reach in your public relations efforts, such as common organization memberships, common workplace, readership of one or two publications, concentrated TV viewing or radio listening, and the like.
3. **Consider Reanalysis of the Data** Applying analytic techniques to the data other than those used originally can provide new findings and save time and money, especially if the information is still current.
4. **Check for Reusable Questions** Look for items that can be repeated for the same or a different population. It may be important to determine whether there has been a shift in opinion since the earlier study. Repeating questions for comparison can yield information on changes over time.
5. **Note Useful Techniques for Conducting the Research** Every research project has unique aspects, some of which may be highly adaptable. Look for clever ways to identify the population or draw the sample, conduct the interviews, tabulate the data, compare subgroups, etc.

---

improvement; look carefully at each subgroup to see if large enough numbers were generated to produce a statistically valid representation.

Data Bases

Computerized records allow on-line access to the vast library of information now available on a wide range of topics in data banks, or data bases. Locating and retrieving information stored by computer has vastly expanded the capability of local libraries by providing worldwide access to billions of documents. Many local and university libraries provide access to the collections of information called data bases, most of which contain either numeric or bibliographic data.

Most data bases are reference lists of books and articles to be used in searching for relevant items on specific topics; a few contain the full text of articles. Certain categories of nonbibliographic information are available in data base systems, including lists of chemicals, trade opportunities, U.S. exports, U.S. public schools, the Foundation Directory, and so forth.

Data base accessing is analogous to library research; anyone familiar with card file indexes and the "stacks" that store thousands of library books can imagine the data storage system in which such resources are listed in a computer. The difference is that the computerized holdings are immensely greater than those in most libraries, and access to the information is much easier and faster. Although operating the computer terminal and "conversing" with the data base system in the computer's language can be frustrating initially, it is still more efficient than locating materials in the average library, not to mention trying to find information located in a library miles away.

Most data bases offer abstracts or reviews of articles; some include entire articles. The public relations Body of Knowledge (BOK) data base is available from the Public Relations Society of America (PRSA) in print or on disk for use in personal computers. The BOK data base includes reviews of articles and books selected by a panel of scholars as essential to public relations practice. Entire BOK articles are available from PRSA on loan. Box 3.2 shows an example of a review from the Body of Knowledge data base.

The five major data base services—Knight-Ridder Information, Inc., ORBIT-Questel, CDP Online, MEDLINE (the data bases of the National Library of Medicine), and the LEXIS-NEXIS systems—are universal libraries that are updated continually and available almost 24 hours a day worldwide. The reader may be familiar with the previous names by which these services were known before they were acquired by different companies or otherwise renamed—Knight-Ridder Information, Inc. was previously known as DIALOG; ORBIT-Questel, formerly known as Orbit, was bought by Questel; CDP Online was referred to as BRS (Bibliographic Retrieval Service, Inc.) before it was bought by CDP Technologies; MEDLINE used to be known as MEDLARS; and the LEXIS-NEXIS systems was owned by Mead Data Central before it was bought by Read Elsevier. The NEXIS system is of particular interest to the public relations practitioner because it lists newspaper and magazine abstracts. The New York Times data base in NEXIS, for example, includes entire articles. The LEXIS system is a collection of legal data bases.

Use of any of the systems requires a minimum amount of preparation and resources:

1. A dial access computer terminal.
2. The telephone number of the data base on-line service.
3. An account number and password, or cooperation of a subscriber who has both.
4. A clear idea of what information is needed, preferably with a list of key words to locate the information.
5. Some training in the language and the commands used by the data base; there are variations in language and commands between systems.
6. The necessary funds to pay for the search, approximately $15 minimum to about $125 maximum per hour of connect time.

BOX 3.2   Example of Book Review from the PRSA Body of Knowledge

KEY WORDS

MANAGEMENT, POLICY, IDEOLOGIES, GOALS, EFFICIENCY, MISSION, UNIONS, LIFE-CYCLE, CONTROL.

The third book in a series conceived as a review of the "systematic knowledge" on the "theory of management policy," this volume examines the nature of the influence that is brought to bear on organizations. Mintzberg approached the subject as a business management professor in order to aid business leaders, but the result also provides a social criticism in its analysis of the ways society controls its organizations.

Sections cover such topics as "how 'outsiders' try to control the behavior of organizations," how "ideologies develop in" and may "capture" organizations, how politics develop, "how organizations reconcile conflicting goals," why efficiency and other "systems" terms are "dirty" words that have displaced "mission" as a goal, why unions arise in dysfunctional organizations and make them even more dysfunctional, how destructive forces give rise to "life cycles" in organizations, as well as who wants to control organizations and why.

Mintzberg, Henry, *Power in and Around Organizations.* Englewood Cliffs, NJ: Prentice Hall, 1983.

Because each of the data base services uses a different system of languages and commands, a skilled operator is usually recommended. Many libraries have such operators and offer this service to the public. Such library services are variously labeled "Online Database Searching," "Information Retrieval," "Computer Assisted Research," and the like.

A copy service will make copies of uncopyrighted material as well as that protected by copyright and will pay the copyright fee and mail copies to you. The copy service charges for employee time and photocopying and assesses a royalty fee for rights to copy protected materials, which it forwards to the Copyright Clearance Center in Washington, D.C., for distribution to copyright owners. These charges, together with mailing charges, make this the most expensive method of getting copies of data base materials. Costs of a single magazine article can be more than the cost of the original magazine issue. Of course, if the material is unavailable elsewhere, the charges may be worthwhile.

For more specific information on data base accessing, the Information Services Series of books published by John Wiley & Sons is a good resource.

Standard Library Resources

Basic library research involves various reference books, book indexes, and special public relations resources. The basic library holdings, available in most public or university libraries, are indispensable for public relations research. Library research should be approached with an orientation to the nature of the materials available. Each of the collected publications has usually been designed for specific readers, a fact that may not be clearly evident on first examination. Standard and Poor's publications are designed, for example, for investors needing information to guide their investment decisions. These publications digest materials about corporations to show comparative strengths and weaknesses. Coincidentally, the same information can be very useful to the public relations person for quite different reasons: tracking the competition, plotting trends, and detecting the emphasis various companies are taking in a given industry.

Psychological Abstracts, on the other hand, is a collection of summaries of articles in current scholarly journals in psychology and is designed to help scholars locate information on topics within the discipline of psychology or related fields. To the public relations practitioner, *Psychological Abstracts* may be extremely useful in finding, for example, research reports on the effects of various methods of persuasion, how learning theory can be applied to communication with employees, or what visual perception research can offer in making graphic illustrations more effective.

Standard library references aid public relations researchers. The **Directories in Print** or **Directory of Directories** list of reference materials is arranged conveniently for the public relations researcher for doing library research, literature search, or background research. These directories are suggested as a starting point for exploring the background on a topic or issue to see what has been published in magazines or journals. Background research is standard procedure for any type of research. Any article in a scholarly journal begins with the background, in which it offers a review of the pertinent literature. A look at a typical journal article will reveal how such background research is done.

Case studies: By studying published "cases," one can discover how to find and use the ideas, techniques, and procedures spelled out in previous public relations efforts, which, with a little innovation, can be applied to other situations. Cases available in specialized library volumes are the records of public relations efforts, and offer an excellent resource for creative ideas. By putting together different ideas from various cases, or combining ideas from the cases with other ideas in new ways, the public relations planner can devise truly creative responses to problems. As a research resource, case studies serve primarily as a repository of public relations ideas, techniques, and approaches that may be adapted to different public relations situations. The body of literature in public relations has begun to accumulate a sizable collection of cases. Like library resources in general, the cases are published in books and in a few periodicals.

Cases may be divided into two categories: (1) case studies or case histories and (2) case problems. The case studies, or histories, are accounts of public relations activities, usually successful, covering the broad range of programs, campaigns of a political or promotional nature, print publicity, broadcast publicity, special events, direct mail, multimedia, or any combination of these.

The case problems are actual or simulated public relations problem situations used to challenge the creative abilities of planners to devise the most effective solution by drawing on a knowledge of past cases or other experience. Case problems test the reader's mastery of principles that would apply to the situation and that may be identifiable from the case studies.

DESCRIPTIVE RESEARCH

Descriptive research is a way of assessing the status quo of situations, such as public opinion, behavioral inclinations, communication effects, demographics, life-style, and media use patterns. It measures, counts, makes profiles, tabulates, and otherwise describes the conditions that exist at present within an organization, its communications, or the status of its public relations in the segments of society important to the organization.

The purpose of descriptive research is to *establish norms,* or an index of existing attitudes, opinions, facts, practices, and the like, as a benchmark against which to measure progress toward achieving improvements. The norm may be, for example, an index point of 5 (neutral) on a 10-point scale from 1 = unfavorable to 10 = favorable opinion. The index point helps determine a campaign *goal* by showing where the organization rates on the scale in relation to where it may wish to be. For instance, it may wish to improve employee attitudes and opinions from a neutral 5 on the scale to a more favorable 8. The status of other conditions as discovered in descriptive research may determine secondary objectives or directions to guide efforts or to assist in policy making. Descriptive research may help to *develop methods* by revealing the nature of a problem and suggesting how to advance from "where we are" to "where we want to be."

For example, a professional association may discover that it lacks proof of the effectiveness of its present public relations program with members. Descriptive research might *establish standards* of what members expect, determine a *rating* of membership services currently provided, *measure opinion* concerning programs offered to members, make an *evaluation of communications* used, and *collect facts* regarding other aspects of service to members. Each of these measures becomes a mark against which efforts to improve can be compared. A descriptive research project may undertake any of these tasks or may combine several of them into a single project.

Descriptive research may help to *establish campaign goals* by identifying discrepancies between what an organization thinks it is doing and what the facts show it is really doing. By revealing weaknesses, descriptive research indicates directions in which the organization needs to concentrate its efforts. Goals grow out of measurable reckonings of the status of the organization's activities, and the best goals are those toward which progress or achievement can be measured. By stating a goal in terms of a percentage of satisfaction, or approval, or sales, achievement can be measured. Descriptive research makes this kind of goal setting possible.

Descriptive research can also help to *determine audience segmentation* by finding out which people are concerned about an issue, have an interest in

➤ CASE STUDY: LIBERTY FINANCIAL YOUNG INVESTOR PROGRAM

The president of Liberty Financial Companies (LFC) and former president of the American Stock Exchange, Kenneth Leibler, visited his daughter's eighth-grade class for a presentation. His experience convinced him that students were poorly informed about, but were capable of grasping, relatively complex investment and economic concepts. A task force studied the situation and concluded that a program to educate young people about important economic and investment principles would succeed if (1) it responded to real needs of students, parents, and educators; (2) commercial footprints were nonintrusive, and (3) it could be built and sustained over several years. Additional corporate sponsors to share the costs would also be feasible.

RESEARCH

Two surveys were conducted. The first, a nationwide survey of 1400 secondary school students, under commission with Louis Harris/Scholastic Research, found a majority learned all they knew about money matters from their parents, but that parents rarely talked about family finances. Misconceptions included 29 percent who believed that unemployment was higher than 21 percent, and 60 percent who thought it was much higher than it actually is. Boys had better knowledge of financial issues than girls; boys were more prone to make riskier investments, and were less regular in saving. Most students wanted more formal instruction in personal finance. A second survey of 102 educators attending a national convention, conducted by Ruder-Finn, Boston, revealed that teachers were in desperate need of materials to help teach economics and personal finance and would welcome a program by any responsible corporation.

ADAPTATION

Goals

Generate broad public awareness of LFC and its commitment to families and children; strengthen LFC's ties to its employees, achieve a quantifiable impact on LFC's core mutual funds business, provide opportunities for customer banks, respond to budgetary limitations, and benefit current customers.

Objectives for Targeted Publics

Build awareness, provoke response in parents of young children; strengthen LFC associations with client banks throughout the United States; generate leads and memorable promotion items for field sales force; build awareness and provoke inquiries about educational materials among educators; create sense of corporate involvement and demonstrate leadership among employees; demonstrate LFC leadership to parent company, Liberty Mutual; position LFC as a leader and innovator in the industry and build awareness within financial news media; position LFC as a supporter of education and children and build awareness within educational/family media.

Strategy

Leverage release of The Young Investor Survey as well as the specially designed publication *Liberty Financial Young Investor Parents' Guide* to generate coverage of the introduction of Young Investor Program; leverage information in the release to generate "seasonal" spot news and features, and where possible, to tie in to information about children and education being released by other organizations; base effectiveness of program on responses from parents, educators,

(continues)

customer banks, and field sales force as well as track calls, leads, and shareholder conversion ratios.

Time Frame

Program would be sustained and grown over several years.

Budget

For 1993, $198,500.

IMPLEMENTATION STRATEGY

The two surveys noted earlier were conducted for publicity value as well as research. An attractive logo was designed for the program and incorporated into the *Young Investor Parents' Guide.* A toll-free hot line was set up for users of the *Parents' Guide* seeking more information, and a customer service setup captured personal data of all callers. Embargoed releases to key financial and educational columnists were sent out and, as a follow-up, media kits with releases, photos, and survey results were mailed a week later, including a "Saving for College" release corresponding to the College Board report of college costs. A pre-Christmas "investment gift giving" feature was placed in the November–December issue and a New Year's resolution feature in December–January was teamed with ongoing follow-up calls. Special events included a "Young Investor Day" for employees and their children (September) and an employee family holiday party in December at the Boston Children's Museum. LFC sponsored Junior Achievement and made a grant to the Children's Museum; Young Investor features were printed in employee and customer newsletters; the industry's first newsletter for young shareholders was launched; and coalitions were formed with Interactive Software, Junior Achievement, Lotus Development, and Tom Snyder Educational Software.

EVALUATION

Media coverage produced 1,061 reports in virtually all markets of the United States; 118 million impressions were generated at $1.26 per thousand; 31,800 leads were generated at $3.90 per lead—compared to the $25 industry average; custodial accounts (for children) grew significantly faster than normal, and a system to track lead-to-shareholder conversions was initiated; LFC won praise from parent company, which sought inclusion in program; LFC launched a new product—an industry first—a fund for young investors; employees increased investment in funds especially custodial accounts; 70 customer banks sought inclusion in Young Investor Program; 50,000 copies of *Guide* were sold out and a 100,000 copy second printing was ordered; budget for second year of program was doubled and expanded to include educational materials, newsletters, computer software, and scholarships; future plans included youth conferences, scholarships, an international component, and a celebrity honorary advisory board.

Source: 1994 Silver Anvil Winners: Index and Summaries, Public Relations Society of America, 1994.

---

the topic of the campaign, or are members of organizations with an interest in related subjects. If you were planning a campaign for an environmental protection group, for example, you could survey the general population by asking such questions as: How concerned are you about protecting the environment? What actions have you taken in the past month to protect the environment? Are you a member of any of the following (listed) organizations devoted to environmental concerns? By identifying persons who have expressed an interest, have indicated compatible behavior, or are allied with groups committed to the cause on which the campaign is focused, you can carefully define and more effectively target the audience the campaign needs to reach.

Descriptive research may also contribute to *establishing message strategy* for achieving goals. One technique for deciding on effective public relations message strategy is to include questions in research projects to determine how people get their information, what shaped a decision, what influences the opinion you are measuring, or what arguments would be most effective. This kind of information can, of course, be collected in other ways, but if you can document the influences at work on the public you need to reach, you can more easily figure out what messages will work best in reaching them. Descriptive research can identify how people make up their minds, what influenced their actions, or what factors brought about the conditions that the campaign addresses.

Descriptive research can combine these functions of establishing norms, setting goals, and deciding on messages as segments of a single study. Through careful design of the research project, each function can be addressed as an aspect of the overall study and addressed with greater efficiency than by approaching each separately. The research report should be in the form of a term paper or a survey research report (see Chapter 4). The report should offer careful documentation of facts by citing any relevant documents or specific research projects. In referring to projects you should cite, in addition to the relevant facts, the basics of the procedure: who conducted the study, when, what source of information was used, the number of subjects or interviews, and appropriate interpretation.

The descriptive research techniques that follow in this chapter may be employed either formally or informally. That is, the "formal research" findings of any of the techniques may be representative of the population being studied, whereas the "informal research" findings cannot be said to represent the total population.

Observation

This procedure collects information by noting what people actually do, as that behavior affects the organization. Observations are made of media use, traffic patterns, or equipment use for various groups and for various times of the day, week, or month. The deductive process as applied to observation produced the theories used to explain the physical world, theories that could be tested by experiment; the inductive method was developed to confirm that the observations were true.

The process of observation is the same for scientists who study the hard sciences and those who study the social sciences. Observation requires careful systematic monitoring, detailed record keeping, analysis of the record to detect patterns, and formulation of theories to explain the observed phenomenon. For the scientist, the observation technique ends with the formulation of the theory or hypothesis. Next comes the experimental testing of the hypothesis. If the hypothesis is proved by repeated and independent testing, it becomes a widely accepted explanation of the natural world, a law of nature.

Observation is perhaps the most fundamental technique in descriptive research, or even in research generally. By observing pedestrian traffic patterns, auto traffic flow, public reaction to an exhibit, employee lunchroom seating, bulletin board use, and the like, the researcher can collect descriptive facts that are nearly incontrovertible. If the method of collecting observations is adequately systematic, so that results are truly representative, the results are likely to be even more accurate than the responses people give if you ask them in a poll what they do in the same circumstances.

In planning an observation research project, keep several basic elements in mind: identify the purpose of the project, determine a suitable research design, and plan how you will codify and analyze the results. Observation research may be used in conjunction with other research techniques with several advantages; it can give a broad understanding of the nature of the reality being investigated and can identify factors for further study.

Guidelines for Research by Observation   The following simple procedure ensures that the observations will be systematic. The observer should be careful to record *all* observations, not just those that support the position he or she hopes to prove. Although a research question or a point of view that you hope to prove may have prompted the investigation, that bias should not prejudice the findings. By approaching the process of making observations with an open mind, the following guidelines can help to reach dependable conclusions.

1. Define the Phenomenon to Be Observed   An effective definition of the phenomenon to be observed should be reduced to a statement that is specific enough to avoid ambiguity about what is being observed and precise enough that the observations will be significant to the organization. By expressing the objective of the observations in a statement, the researcher establishes a norm or standard against which the observations can be counted as either meeting or failing to meet. For example, employee behavior under new work schedules might be observed in terms of a statement such as: "Employees are more productive than under the previous schedule when compared with: products finished vs. work hours clocked; work absences under old and new schedules; worker grievances under old and new; and assembly line management reports."

2. Establish Limits as to What Will Be Observed   To avoid biting off more than you can chew, set limits on the time for which the observations will be made, on the group or groups among which they will be made, and on the area or geographic location of the observations.

Such limitations further define the phenomenon to be observed. Limitations also provide measurements by which comparisons can be made. For example, day and night shifts can be compared when monitoring response to memos, break time can be designated as the time to monitor bulletin boards, and various media can be compared for treatment of a news release, all as ways of establishing such limitations.

3. Devise a System or Method for Observations   A system for making observations is needed to ensure that all examples of the phenomenon will be observed and that the observations will be made according to the same standard. There may, for example, be a tendency to pay more attention to observations that confirm the observer's expectations or what the observer wants to prove. Only a system that treats all observations impartially will contribute an accurate reading of the situation. For example, a student intern or new employee might be assigned to make the observations after being given careful training.

At the outset, the system should include plans for how many observations will be enough to ensure that all variations in the phenomenon are included, a time frame, a site selection procedure, and a way to classify each observation in an appropriate category. A certain number of categories may be determined in advance, but allowance must be made for some that may not be anticipated.

4. Record All Observations   Recording all observations means providing a system to account for the full range of possible responses, not just those hoped for. This may mean having a way to check responses to a news release that would record full use, partial use, incorporation in other stories, headline treatment, and no use at all; but responses such as telephone inquiry, original stories based on the release, follow-up stories, and related features may be observed and certainly should be recorded.

In direct observation of behavior, nonverbal cues may also be significant. A keen sense about nonverbal cues and even keener powers of observation may be needed to pick up some of these. In observing bulletin board use, for example, a list of award winners may be expected to elicit certain gestures of elation; a posting of restrictive regulations may elicit quite different gestures.

In cases in which the participant-observer procedure is appropriate, some method may be needed for making a record, especially if the participant-observer is too involved in interaction to be able to do so. An audio or video recording may be made, or an assistant may be used in these cases.

5. Analyze Recorded Observations   After all observations have been made, the entries in each category should be classified and counted. Classification of entries into predetermined categories requires determining how variations in what was observed fit the categories, such as whether comments in a specific category were favorable or unfavorable, positive or negative, or whether other evaluative judgments should be made. Comments may also provide a range of potentially useful information or suggestions. At this analysis stage, finer degrees of discrimination of meaning and application are appropriate.

Counting observations involves simply tallying recorded instances that fall into each of the categories. To make further sense of the numbers, averages may need to be calculated. For example, classifying the total responses or comments that are favorable, unfavorable, or neutral as a percentage of the total observations is an easy way to interpret what the pattern of responses means. Calculating the percentage in each category and arranging the categories in rank order from highest to lowest will reveal which are more significant and which may need to be addressed in a public relations effort.

6. Interpret the Patterns   Observations, whether tallied by predetermined categories or not, take on meaning when they are compared with a larger whole. The number of observations should always be compared with the potential number. If 35 people were observed using the bulletin board and there are 60 people in the organization, a majority have been accounted for. If 20 observations are made out of a potential of 800 bulletin board users, a different meaning should be given to the findings. Yet the greatest benefit of the observation technique is to provide an exhaustive list of the range of behavior being studied, whether or not the representativeness of the behavior is calculated.

Observation is essentially an intuitive exercise. By looking at the order of categories ranked by the number of observations and by integrating these with the overall impressions gathered from the observation experience, an intuitive meaning can be attributed to the observed phenomenon. Of course, intuition can never be more than a guess, an educated guess if a systematic method is used to gather observations. But the collected observations can be used to design an instrument that will be dependably comprehensive in measuring the true proportions in the population.

7. Apply the Findings   The results of the observation technique may be applied immediately to solving problems in many cases. If little investment is at stake in implementing the findings, the observation technique may be adequate. If, however, a great deal of investment in time or money is involved, it may be wise to confirm the observed findings with a more accurately representative research technique.

Interviews

A fundamental research technique is gathering information by asking people—employees, consumers, management, media, opinion leaders, and other constituents—for their opinions, their reasons for acting as they do, and their thinking on topics of interest to the organization or to the campaign. Interviewing is a fundamental element of descriptive research. The term *interviewing* is used here to mean planned, purposeful conversation. With this definition, interviewing fulfills a broad range of research applications, from gathering facts by talking to two or three people, to in-depth discussion with an elite group, to the questionnaire-guided collection of data from a random sample. Specific applications of interviewing to the polling technique will be covered in the chapter on the public opinion survey.

Interviewing may be appropriate at several stages of a research project. It is certainly critical to the initial stage for guidance in structuring the research design and in selecting topics to be covered and groups to be polled. Interviewing is important in the planning stages of research projects as a device for identifying the range of responses that the public being studied may be able to articulate on a particular question. In the later stages of research, interviewing is important as a way to identify and count the percentages of opinion on the various topics being explored and to elicit personal thoughts and observations on the topic.

In formal opinion research, interviewing is the only way to collect data so that the results are quantifiable, that is, expressible in numeric quantities. Interviewing as a method of formal research data collection can be used with small elite groups, such as corporate boards of directors, with small representatively chosen groups for in-depth interviews, and with large numbers of people where a few well-chosen topics are explored.

Interviews have been characterized as falling into either of two categories: (1) standardized or structured interviews, which collect the same data or the same categories of data from each interviewee, and (2) nonstandard interviews, which include a range of types that do not conform to the requirements of standardized interviewing.[3]

Standardized interviews generally require more preparation to ensure that each topic is well defined and the areas to be explored under each topic are well drawn. Nonstandardized interviews may be required for exploratory investigations that attempt to define topics or plot the extent of feelings or the range of options on an emerging issue. Standardized interviews require extensive "homework" to identify the issues and the range of attitudes or opinions that exist. Nonstandard interviews are one way of doing that type of homework.

Of the many groups that may be studied by interviewing, the groups characterized as elites require the most careful preparation and the most sensitive techniques. Louis Dexter has written a perceptive book in this area. Although the major emphasis for Dexter is interviewing high-ranking political personages, the information is appropriate for other luminaries as well.[4] Elite groups involve "people in important or exposed positions [who] may require VIP treatment on the topics which relate to their importance or exposure." Other terms for this genre of interviewing are "nonstandard," "exploratory," and "journalistic." The conditions in interviewing elites require letting the interviewee "define the situation," encouraging "the interviewee to structure the account of the situation," and letting the interviewee introduce "notions of what he regards as relevant instead of relying on the investigator's notions."[5]

The general checklist for interviewing shown in Box 3.3 may be helpful in planning for the use of interviews in research. The list is designed to be comprehensive, but some elements of the process may not apply to every type of interview situation. Consequently, the checklist should be used to make sure you have not overlooked something important; don't assume all the elements mentioned apply to any one interview situation.

BOX 3.3   General Checklist for Interviewing

1. **Determine That Interviewing Is Appropriate**   Establish that (a) the information is not available elsewhere; (b) the information needed is significant enough to justify interviewee participation; (c) the information can be obtained by interviews with representatives of particular publics; (d) you have adequately defined the problem requiring the interviews; (e) you have determined what is to be accomplished in the interviews, whether for "discovery" or for "measurement."

2. **Do Your Homework**   Discover essential information about (a) the issue or topic to be covered; (b) the interviewee's background, orientation toward the issue. biases, and the like; and (c) conflicts, controversies, and personalities surrounding the issue. In addition, (d) be prepared to document your credibility as an interviewer on the topic.

3. **Structure the Interviewee Selection Procedure**   Plan to (a) identify respondents by groups, key informants, or as individuals; (b) determine the number of interviews; (c) decide whether to "sample" or not; (d) establish a time frame; (e) choose the type of contact, whether scheduled with appointments or nonscheduled. Some types of publics to consider interviewing in doing research for a public relations campaign are current employees; current officers; retired employees or officers; board members, past and present; community leaders from such sectors as government, schools, media, business, civic organizations, community activist groups, consumer groups, churches, hospitals, social service agencies, associations, and neighborhood organizations.

4. **Outline the Topic(s) to Be Covered for Each Interview or Series of Interviews**   The outline can range from a series of topical items with subpoints to an open-ended questionnaire. Consider such guidelines as: (a) Begin with easy, nonthreatening questions. (b) Place crucial questions in the middle of the outline. (c) Build rapport before asking for sensitive information. (d) Structure the outline to facilitate dealing with the topics out of order, knowing the respondents may not follow your outline. (e) Have the subpoints progress from fact, to opinion, to motives. (f) Allow progression from topic to topic to be guided by your rapport with the interviewee.

5. **Complete Personal Preparation for Interviewing**   Allow time to familiarize yourself with the outline points and to become psychologically prepared immediately before the interview. Know and rehearse successful interview techniques: (a) Know your own personality and how to adapt to other personality types. (b) Practice useful techniques such as empathizing, listening, observing, separating fact from fancy, knowing the respondent's point of view and the opposing point of view. (c) Consider the "role" you assume in interviewing: avoid an "authority figure" role and consider adopting a role appropriate to the situation (courier, journalist, confidant, counselor). (d) Be straightforward in demeanor and avoid cleverness. (e) Rehearse your introductory remarks.

6. **Be Alert to Nonverbal Cues**   Consider the physical setting as well as

being aware of interpersonal cues. Make an effort to: (a) Control the site of the interview in order to promote free exchange of information; suggest "someplace where we can talk without being distracted." (b) Use care in seating arrangements to facilitate observing nonverbal cues. (c) Watch for significant cues: posture, physical bearing, personal grooming, gestures, facial expression, total body inclination, voice quality, rate, volume and inflections, and significant changes in any of these. (d) Probe for clarification of nonverbal impressions: "you seem to feel strongly about. . . . " (e) Note physical surroundings of interviewee's home or office for significant cues; ask for interpretation of notable observations when appropriate to interview topic.

7. **Manage the Interview Process** Assume responsibility for the interview situation: (a) Preface procedure by establishing an appropriate mood (pleasant, confident) to set the interviewee at ease. (b) Explain the purpose of the interview and method of selecting the respondent. (c) Deal with resistance to being interviewed; assure the respondent that "there is no one else who can provide the information, point of view, experience, etc." and that there are no right or wrong answers to this type of inquiry. (d) Assure the privacy and anonymity of the information and the source, unless it is "on the record." (e) Keep the interview "on track," but at the same time (f) allow for pertinent digressions. (g) Employ structured listening; take notes in *outline form* during the interview or when listening to tape recordings of the interview. (h) Allow for unhurried replies; distinguish awkward silence from thoughtful pause. (i) Ask only one question at a time. (j) Phrase questions carefully for maximum clarity and understanding. (k) Avoid leading questions that suggest answers. (l) Avoid impertinence; inappropriate lightheartedness may destroy the businesslike mood or damage your credibility. (m) Probe replies for correct understanding. (n) Allow for qualifications. (o) Build rapport before asking sensitive questions.

8. **Carry Through and Follow Up** Make the necessary arrangements to set up the interview: (a) Call back if interviewee is not available at first attempt. (b) Make appointments or other arrangements when necessary to assure input of key participants. (c) Arrange a series of interviews with the same people if required by the topic. (d) Use a time-delayed series of interviews to examine developments over time. (e) Call back as needed for clarification of critical points.

9. **Weigh What to Record and What to Report** Sort out the wheat from the chaff after the information is harvested: (a) The written record should be made as soon after the interview as possible, even if made from a tape recording, to ensure proper recall of details not recorded and to be able to recall words on the tape that are not clear. (b) A written record should be made from the outline prepared in advance, especially if data from different respondents are to be compared. (c) Tape-recording interviews requires the permission of participant; re-

(continues)

member that listening to the tape requires as much time as or longer than recording it. (d) In making the written record from tape, select information for its appropriateness to the purpose of the research, even when tempted to do otherwise. (e) For exceptionally long recordings, summarize information for the written record. (f) The written report of the interview should be structured and indexed using the outline as a guide for ease in locating specific points later.

10. **Validation of Data May Be Accomplished by Comparison with Other Sources** Remember that: (a) The option of validation will depend on how critical the information is to the sponsor of the research project. (b) Validation provides a check on the dependability of the information. (c) The level of validation depends on the nature of the information and the degree of dependability needed. (d) Internal validation can be accomplished by comparing replies to the same questions strategically placed in the interview.

Content Analysis

This research technique when used in public relations is applied primarily to evaluate communications by examining what may be observed in or during the communication, including the verbal, musical, and gestural elements. It may involve systematic analysis of any of several aspects of what a communication contains, from key words or concept references, such as company name or product; to topics, such as issues confronting the organization; to reading ease, of company publications; or to all elements of a company video production.

One of the more widely cited definitions of the technique describes it as "the application of scientific methods to documentary evidence."[6] Another states that "in general, content analysis applies empirical and statistical methods to textual material. Content analysis particularly consists of a division of the text into units of meaning and a quantification of these units according to certain rules."[7]

Using content analysis in public relations most often involves questions about the communicated message. There may be a problem with a message or series of messages, or there may be a situation in which the message is so critical that a potential message failure cannot be tolerated. These are the conditions that indicate the use of content analysis. In this case, the communication process must be examined to make sure that the failure is with the message and not with other aspects of communication, such as misplaced intention of the communicator, inappropriateness of the channel or medium being used, unreceptiveness of the intended audience, or weakness of the total communication within its context. Content analysis may be used to examine the encoding and decoding of communications to identify patterns in successful and unsuccessful messages.

Content Analysis of Problem Messages   Content analysis is most commonly applied when a message has failed. Once the source, channel, and receiver have been eliminated in appraising a message failure, content analysis can be used to pinpoint the elements that caused the failure. The encoding and decoding of communication is among the greatest challenges the public relations person faces. Selecting the right written language form—whether English, standard dialect, idiom, phrasing, connotation, or other semantic element—is demanding enough, but the challenge to be an unambiguous communicator in purpose and in message intention further complicates the process. Messages disseminated by committees are notorious for failings of ambiguity because the committees cannot decide on the purpose and intention.

If the message is sent through an audio channel, the many nuances of pronunciation should also be considered—rate, volume, pitch, and quality variation taken alone or in combination—as well as the possibility of music and sound effects adding to or distracting from the emotional impact of the message. If a video or cinema channel is chosen, the many subtle variations in visual communication should be added to the list of concerns: facial expression, gestures, head inclinations, body movement, framing and focus of the camera, background scenery, camera angle, and juxtaposition with other elements in the frame. These are only illustrations of the many variables that may cause a message to fail. Content analysis is the research technique best suited to identifying the elements that may have contributed to message failure.

Content Analysis of Critical Messages   Like messages that have failed, messages that must not fail can be examined by using content analysis to ensure success. The elements that should be considered are the same as those for failed messages. A failed message may strongly indicate the reason for the failure; a message not yet sent should be examined in all its aspects.

The procedure for content analysis is outlined in Box 3.4.

Advisory Panels

This research technique uses semipermanent representative samples of significant publics for periodic polls and in-depth interviews as predictors of attitudes, trends, or public reaction to a policy or product. The advisory panel is a practical variation on the survey approach to descriptive research. The panel, carefully chosen to represent the public of interest, becomes the "sample" for repeated polls on a variety of questions or issues that come up over the course of an organization's ongoing public relations program.

The key to successful advisory groups is the selection of panel members for their ability to represent larger populations. To the degree that the public relations practitioner may be able to recruit a representative group from among customers, constituents, employees, or other significant publics, the advisory panel may be among the most effective tools available for measuring critical perceptions on which to base important planning decisions.

The advisory panel may serve as both a research tool and a public relations action. While the research benefits of the advisory panel may be obvious, the benefits of the technique for achieving public relations goals may not be. As a device for achieving recognition, disseminating information, focusing persuasive influence, fund-raising, and even carrying out special projects, the advisory panel is well suited. Academic programs have long employed the tech-

BOX 3.4   **Content Analysis Procedure**

In his book *Mass Communication Theories and Research* (Columbus, OH: Brid, 1981, 51–53), Alexis S. Tan describes six factors in content analysis procedure. The six are necessary for the technique to work.*

1. **The hypothesis** is a statement of what the researcher expects to find as a result of the study. The hypothesis may take several forms: the research question is often the form that the objective of a research project takes at the beginning. It may be refined into a statement form or "research hypothesis" and further refined into a "null" hypothesis. Each provides projection of what the researcher hopes to prove.

    The research question simply phrases a question which the project seeks to answer. For example, "What is the difference between messages that achieve high reader response from a mailing and those that do not?" The same research objective may be reached more efficiently by refining the question into a research hypothesis in statement form such as, "Messages that have a high verb to noun ratio and frequent use of second person pronoun will generate more reader response to a mailing than messages that do not." Refinements offer more specific criteria to measure message success. One further refinement allows the researcher a more precise measure of the objective by proposing that there will be no difference between messages with high and low incidence of verb-noun ratio and second person pronoun; this becomes the *null hypothesis:* Messages with high incidence of verb-noun ratio and second person pronoun will achieve no greater reader response than low incidence messages.

    The hypothesis, whether it is a null or a research hypothesis, also helps to avoid what scientists call a Type I error, which is concluding that the hypothesis is true (or false) when the reverse is actually the case. The results can be tested for significance which calculates the probability of making a Type I, or *"alpha error."* Most tests of significance set an arbitrary acceptable level of probability at plus or minus .05 or 5 percent.

2. **The unit of analysis** should be determined. That is, the portion or portions of the text to be analyzed should be selected. The entire document may be subjected to analysis, but if it is too long to be manageable, a sample may be drawn.

3. **Sampling,** as with all scientific measures, produces more representative findings when it is randomly selected than if a nonrandom selection is made. A book, for example, may be sampled by choosing n page numbers between 1 and the end. These may be analyzed in total or, if a large number of pages is selected, paragraphs may be picked at random. The unit of analysis should seldom be smaller than a paragraph. The unit for analysis from other documents may be selected similarly.

4. **Categories of analysis,** or what will be counted and further analyzed, should be chosen very carefully. Verb-noun ratio, references to corporate name, industry mentions, issues discussed, and news versus feature treatment are examples of possible categories of analysis.

5. **Three independent coders,** or more, who count the incidence of the categories of analysis, each duplicating the other's work, should be employed to guarantee consistency in classification of whatever is being counted. With three or more coders the researcher can check on the objectivity of the ratings of the coders. Most researchers require 80 percent agreement or higher. Any incidences that do not achieve 80 percent agreement are eliminated from the analysis.

6. **Analysis** of findings ordinarily consist of average or mean scores of the incidence (with 80 percent + agreement) of each category of analysis as well as the percent of each in the total. Cross-tabulation of two related categories may also be calculated, which indicates when two incidents or variables occur together. The use of active verbs by two different writers may be compared by cross-tabulation, for example.

*See also Krippendorff, Klaus. *Content Analysis: An Introduction to Its Methodology* (Beverly Hills: Sage, 1980).

nique to form influential opinion leaders into working groups to recruit students, raise funds, evaluate academic programs, and generate favorable media and word-of-mouth attention for the school. These benefits are quite beyond the obvious research data collection capability of the procedure.

Representativeness of the panel may be achieved several ways. A panel representing employees may be selected from a list of current employees. The "Hawthorne effect," a bias resulting from the perception of being treated with special consideration, may be reduced by more frequent rotation of employees than would be required for panels representing other groups. A quota system may be more appropriate than a random selection procedure for choosing members, especially if the list of employees is rather small—under 3000 for example. Selection by quota with proportions chosen according to size from various departments, work sites, or type of work involved may do more to ensure representativeness of all opinions than random selection, particularly in small populations.

Panels representing consumers, association members, university students, voting citizens, or such populations can be selected randomly from available lists. Consumers can be selected by compiling a list of purchasers identified by coupon response, using coupons enclosed in products or distributed at the point of purchase. A prize can be offered as an incentive for completing the coupon, and the list can be used later to contact potential panel members. In the case of commercial enterprises, compensation for participation is generally expected.

Panel members representing any of the publics noted above may also be chosen for their special ability to represent their peers, their reputation for peer leadership, or their qualities of opinion leadership such as gregariousness, being well informed, and often being consulted for their opinions. In some cases, panel members may be elected by their coworkers or peers. The method of selection will depend on the type of information needed from the panel. Opinion leaders may be more important for panels in which focus group techniques or in-depth discussions will be used than for panels that will be consulted via questionnaires or other written methods of data collection.

The recruitment process may well take advantage of the perceived recognition or "honor" such selection implies. People are usually pleased at being called upon for some special assignment, especially employees. Other groups may be offered token recognition for their efforts, such as certificates or sample products, if they are likely to feel the organization is taking advantage of them. The researcher should be cautious of the Hawthorne effect in planning the recruitment of panel members.

Selected segments of the panel may be consulted on occasion. By selecting only female members of the panel, researchers can focus on products or issues that apply to women. Other demographic segments can be consulted selectively as the need arises. The panel also may be consulted either formally or informally, depending on the nature of the question. At times, relatively minor questions can be asked—how people would be likely to respond to a proposed communication theme or what the potential appeal of a message strategy might be. Such questions may be posed by a series of phone calls or even by mailing a questionnaire.

Panel members will need to be replaced periodically. Several reasons make this advisable: time demands can become a burden; with some, the ego satisfaction or the perceived power of the position may distort the ability to offer representative information; the different perspective that newer employees or constituents have to offer may require retirement of older members to allow for input from more recent members. A regularly scheduled replacement system will allay the appearance of being "dismissed" from the honored assignment.

Some system is needed to ensure that a sufficient number of panel members will be available for specific assignments to compensate for panel members who may not be available. Backup panelists or a list of panel members long enough for a sufficient number to be drawn at any one time will ensure that an adequate number is able to participate in specific assignments. With a long list, different panels can be chosen for different tasks by rotating through the list.

Focus Group Interviews

This technique employs skilled discussion leaders to lead group discussions in order to discover such factors as biases, opinions, motives, behavior patterns, or preferences. The technique works well for discovering the more detailed information for which polls are not practical.

To researchers, the focus group allows more depth and insight into the needs of consumers or other constituents. It is a "chance to 'experience' a 'flesh and blood' consumer . . . to go into her life and relive with her all of her satisfactions, dissatisfactions, rewards and frustrations she experiences when she takes the product into her home."[8] The advantages of such intimate insight into how a product fits into a consumer's life go far beyond anything a questionnaire could discern.

However, qualitative focus group research is no longer limited to studying consumer products, as it was when it was developed. "Now politicians, government agencies, and even social change groups are coming around to treating concepts as if they're soft drinks," says Marian Rivman, founder of Quality Respondents, Inc., a New York–based company that recruits focus group participants.[9] Public relations practitioners find the technique quite helpful in identifying attitudes and motivations of important publics.

Information obtained through focus group interviews is qualitative rather than quantitative, because it represents but doesn't measure feelings, attitudes, and ideas. It is an informal research procedure and does not produce hard data. Results should not be treated as percentages of people that can be projected onto an entire population. Like other direct observation methods, it is most useful in identifying the range of attitudes and opinions in the minds of participants. These opinions and attitudes can be tested later by quantitative methods to determine proportions in the population.

The focus group is not a substitute for quantitative research. Using it as such is the most common misuse of focus group results, especially as companies try to cut costs by eliminating expensive quantitative research and substitute comparatively cheaper qualitative research. Nevertheless, focus group results do have many important uses. "Qualitative information has been a closet kind of thing in the profession. It's often used only as a stepping-stone, but it can be much more useful than that," according to Bobby Calder,[10] a frequent focus group moderator and professor of behavioral science in management at Northwestern University.

Focus groups can be used in developing hypotheses that can be tested quantitatively to determine what questions to incorporate in a consumer questionnaire. In addition, they can aid in interpreting quantitative results. They can also provide information about general consumer feelings and changing attitudes toward a product category so that companies will not be surprised by any changes in consumer attitudes. Focus groups are useful for getting consumer reactions to new products when little other information is available. They can generate new creative ideas, new product ideas, and new uses for old products. "Focus groups are most important for the ideas that get killed," says Melvin Prince, market researcher at Burson Marsteller.

Here is an example of focus group results being put to good use:

When General Electric Co. tied for fourth place in microwave oven sales back in the late 1970's, the people in product development set up a number of focus groups—in-depth interviews led by moderators trained in group dynamics—in an effort to explore consumer attitudes toward their products and boost GE's weak market share. Of all the opinions that emerged, one gripe held the key: people hated the fact that the 20 inch-deep appliances cluttered up their counter tops.

GE's industrial designers had been toying with the idea of over-the-range microwaves, and focus group reaction confirmed that a desirable microwave should not be on the counter. The company thus introduced a new, over-the-range microwave in 1979 and called it the "Spacemaker," as though users would somehow be gaining space by adding an appliance to their crowded kitchens. Within one year, Spacemaker helped GE capture the Number One spot, with 16% of the market.[11]

The two main elements of the focus group interview are the participants and the moderator. Most researchers agree that the ideal group size is eight to ten people. "Fewer than 8 is likely to burden each individual, while more than 12 tends to reduce each member's participation."[12] Researchers disagree about the composition of the individual focus group. Within each consumer group are subgroups; for example, there are heavy-, medium-, and light-user categories. There are even more specific categories; for example, women using skin care products can be subdivided by age, with each age group having different needs and concerns. Some researchers believe that each focus group should consist entirely of one subgroup, whereas others feel that each focus group should be a heterogeneous mixture of subgroups.

There are problems with focus groups. One is that the focus group usually gives conservative evaluations, so it will often screen out new innovative products that either do not fall within the participants' range of experience or require a change of values for the product or idea to be accepted (e.g., miniskirts). The focus group "works against radical, but maybe profitable, changes."[13]

Some other problems are that earlier responses could bias later responses. Also, intimate personal topics are often difficult to discuss in a focus group setting. Despite the problems with focus groups, when they are used correctly they have many advantages. Besides being fast, they are flexible enough to pursue new concepts and product uses. Although focus groups are relatively expensive they bring the client closer to consumers, giving the client valuable information in understandable form. Instead of having to pore over confusing and often boring graphs and charts, the client has access to the ideas, feelings, and attitudes of people expressed in their own words.

Delphi Studies

This approach uses a multistep "discussion-by-mail" procedure to predict trends, identify issues, articulate concerns, and test possible actions. Delphi research may be called "discussion by mail" because the procedure records the responses of participants to an original mailed instrument and their subsequent collective reactions to follow-up mailings. Several cycles of questionnaires are mailed to participants, each incorporating responses from the previous cycle into a new and more refined questionnaire until respondents reach a consensus on the initial broad research question.

The Delphi procedure has the advantage that respondents can remain anonymous to each other; it thus overcomes the distortions that group dynamics impose on decision making. The technique may also broaden the base

➤ CASE STUDY: SAN JOSE'S "RECYCLE PLUS"

Between February and September 1993 the city of San Jose, California, began a new waste collection and recycling program. The public relations challenge included motivating the 261,000 city households to adopt new wheeled dumpsters for automated garbage trucks; to sort waste into three plastic bins of mixed paper, newspapers, and glass for recycling, to put used motor oil in special plastic jugs; and to place yard waste near the curb. A new waste collection tiered fee system rewarded recyclers and replaced a flat rate system.

RESEARCH

Procedures reviewed surveys previously conducted by mail and telephone and looked at focus group studies;

Surveyed 186,000 households for preferred cart size using a trilingual questionnaire.

A telephone sample survey of 400 measured attitudes toward recycling and determined messages that would be effective in customer acceptance and participation.

Focus groups in English and Spanish supplemented the telephone survey and pretested a "how-to-recycle" poster.

A shopping mall intercept survey pretested a modified poster.

Focus groups in Spanish and Vietnamese pretested direct mail and advertising materials.

The Problem

State requirements and an overtaxed landfill required generating public support for implementing a new waste handling and recycling program.

ADAPTATION

Goal

Generate public support for and participation in a new waste disposal and recycling program.

Objectives

Double the volume of recycling; substitute a tiered fee system to reward recyclers for flat waste disposal fees; reduce materials going into landfills by 50 percent by the year 2000; introduce recycling to 75,000 multifamily living units.

Strategy

Implement a multimedia campaign in coalition with numerous organizations and agencies.

Target Publics

English-, Spanish-, and Vietnamese-speaking households and 75,000 apartment dwellers among the city's 822,000 citizens.

Time frame

Efforts were concentrated into the months of February to September 1993.

Management Liaison

City Community Relations Division office chain of command reported to the city council.

Budget

A budget of $1.2 million was approved. Allocation was $60,000 for survey research, $735,000 for collateral materials, $100,000 for minority outreach, and $300,000 for advertising design and placement.

IMPLEMENTATION STRATEGY

Collateral materials were delivered to 186,000 homes with new garbage carts.

Newsletter inserts in waste disposal bills and later delivered as stand-alone pieces were distributed as direct mail. Materials were prepared in English, Spanish, and Vietnamese for ethnic communities. Print and broadcast media were involved in reaching targeted publics

(continues)

through news and advertising. A "Block Leader" speakers bureau and special events used volunteers to go door-to-door to discuss recycling. Western Waste, one of two contract waste collection companies, conducted a school education program. The other contract company, "Green Team," conducted a special outreach program to multifamily units. New city council members were oriented to the program. Purchasing staff were trained to select high-quality print materials. Staff were recruited and trained for the trilingual outreach effort. Response to negative publicity was provided when unexpected volumes of recycling caused problems at start up.

EVALUATION

After six months, residential recycling almost tripled at 2.7 times higher than previous and above the goal; yard waste recycling was up 30 percent; waste diverted from the landfill in-

creased from 29 percent to 45 percent and 56 percent from single family households; these results represent 50 percent of the year 2000 goal; and surveys of customers report "overwhelming" high satisfaction with the program. Editorial coverage continues to be supportive.

A follow-up customer satisfaction telephone survey of 500 measured opinion toward the recycling program and media preferences used in the campaign.

A computer tracking system coded and tabulated up to 4,000 daily customer requests for information or complaints. Calls declined from 4,000 a day to 1,100 a day by the end of December with fewer than 5 percent expressing dissatisfaction. Staff participating in the campaign experienced growth and fulfillment in the environmental protection effort.

Source: 1994 Silver Anvil Winners: Index and Summaries, Public Relations Society of America, 1994.

for decision making by selecting experts who are most often called upon as leaders in a field. By enlisting these leaders to participate, it ensures that the resulting findings and any resulting decisions will be reasonably representative of developments in the field. The Delphi technique can produce high-quality information, and it is well adapted to collecting information from relatively inaccessible corporate leaders.

Designed to reach consensus in groups for whom face-to-face meetings are difficult, the Delphi procedure calls for questionnaires to be distributed in cycles of about 45 days to a panel of experts or to a representative sample. The answers of participants are summarized, often with statistical analysis, and returned for participants to reconsider their earlier responses in light of the group summary. This procedure, of course, is applied to the *opinions* of experts, often about perceived future trends, and is not used to try to sway perceptions of fact. The feedback cycles continue until shifts of opinion seem to have stabilized, regardless of whether opinion is polarized. The resulting consensus serves as a base for making decisions, particularly about what should be done in light of the resulting projections for the future.

Application of the Delphi technique to public relations research should begin with the choice of using the procedure in preference to other research approaches. What the Delphi does best is to focus the opinions of a group of high-level individuals without interrupting busy schedules. Delphi has been used to focus scientific advances months or years before the information is available in the research journals. Indeed, Delphi grew out of a 1948 U.S. Air Force–funded Analytical Methodology Research program at the Rand Corporation. Delphi had a pioneering trial application in 1962 when Rand staffers Olaf Helmer and Norman C. Dalkey conducted and published "An Experimental Application of the Delphi Method to the Use of Experts."[14]

In addition to being used to pick the brains of a few select experts for factual information, the Delphi technique has also been used to measure opinion in policy making,[15] in land use and transportation planning,[16] in quality of life assessment,[17] in analysis of police corruption,[18] and in an assessment of priority research questions in public relations in the 1980s.[19]

The Delphi procedure includes the following basic steps, although more detailed steps are employed by some:

1. Assemble a design and monitoring team.
2. Select a panel or group of participants.
3. Design and mail questionnaires to participants.
4. Allow about 45 days for participants to complete and return questionnaires.
5. Mail a new questionnaire with a summary and analysis of the preceding one to participants.
6. Give participants one or more opportunities to reevaluate their initial positions on the questions being examined.
7. Prepare a report of final results with percentages for each position expressed and the majority consensus, and send a copy of the report to participants.
8. Incorporate findings into organization policy or planning.

A successful Delphi research project will depend on careful formulation of the initial broad question that identifies the focus of the study. Without precise phrasing of the topic for the study, participants cannot respond uniformly. The design and monitoring team should interview those who commissioned the research to clarify and confirm the precise information needed and to understand how the information will be used. The final formulation may differ significantly from the initial problem statement or research question.

The first questionnaire will usually consist of the one carefully phrased general question with a series of subordinate questions that examine the various aspects of the larger question. These first-cycle subquestions will usually be in open-ended form with ample allowance for respondents to offer other considerations. In the second-cycle mailing, each subquestion or segment of the general question should be ranked or otherwise rated to allow respondents in the second cycle to compare answers.

The second-cycle questionnaire will incorporate all the subordinate considerations, add new ones mentioned by respondents in the first cycle, and possibly drop some that rated very low. This second-cycle questionnaire can be closed ended and can use ranking or rating scales. The first- and second-cycle responses can be tabulated and analyzed with basic statistics: mean scores for scaled responses, ranking or rating, mode, and standard deviation. These statistics are provided to respondents with such other summary observations as necessary for them to respond in the subsequent cycle.[20]

Subscription Research Services

Syndicated research services offer the results of regular research studies that are generalizable to a range of users. Researchers such as Gallup Polls, Cambridge Reports, Response Analysis, Min-Research Alert, Roper Reports, and Simmons Market Research Bureau are examples. Subscription research services provide summaries or reviews of research conducted by the organization providing the subscription service. A syndicated research service is defined here as a research service offered by a firm or group of research firms conducting and/or collecting research findings on a broad range for general interest topics to be sold to newspapers, publications, corporations, and individuals.

Some research organizations offer free subscriptions to summaries of recent work; for example, "The Sampler" from RESPONSEanalysis is provided as a promotion for their services. Some organizations, like Min-Research Alert, collect research reports from other research organizations. Most of these research summaries give only minimum information about the results and may not offer detailed accounts of the research methodology, which would be needed for precise analysis and application.

Other research summaries available by subscription give more detail and will be more useful in making public relations decisions. These detailed research summaries are more costly, of course, and can be ordered only for studies required for a specific campaign. They are much more dependable in such applications as monitoring public demand for certain classes of products, tracking attitudes toward controversial issues, and anticipating public policy trends.

The **range of services** depends on the size of the research firm. One giant in the mass communication and marketing field is Simmons Market Research Bureau (SMRB), Inc. The company does an annual syndicated survey of 15,000 adults to measure media audiences, demographics, and extensive product purchase patterns; the service is described elsewhere in this book. Aside from syndicated surveys, SMRB also conducts custom audience research for newspapers, magazines, broadcast, cable, and other media as well as a biannual syndicated teen survey.

Syndicated research is also relatively cost effective; instead of incurring the rather large costs of conducting an opinion survey or of hiring one done, you can obtain the results of general surveys by subscription. For a fixed amount, the research firm supplies the results of studies the firm or others have conducted. In this way the public relations researcher can track major issues in public opinion such as trends in personal savings, support for presidential candidates, public use of tax preparation services, and women's use of perfumes.

What syndicated research cannot do is answer specific questions about your community or your corporation's employees. Syndicated research may offer a "benchmark" of employee satisfaction in ten major corporations, which may be used to undertake an in-house job satisfaction survey for comparison.

The primary function of syndicated research is in issues tracking, to compare the changes in issues over time as they might affect the organization. One broad-issue publication that includes brief reports of the range of polling organization findings is *The Polling Report*.[21] It covers a range of topics and cites the findings of many polling organizations.

An example of a popular syndicated research group is Louis Harris and Associates, Inc. The Harris group conducts research throughout the world on social, financial, industrial, and commercial topics. The survey covers all areas of current events and is syndicated to 200 newspapers twice a week. One of the larger research groups is Yankelovich Skelly & White/Clancy Shulman. In addition to syndicated research services, the firm offers market laboratory tests, custom research, and management consulting services. The firm covers the areas of marketing, social issues, public opinion, human resources, and industrial and policy research for corporations, associations, and the media.

Syndicated research is done not only by specialized research organizations. Some larger public relations firms, such as Hill and Knowlton, also offer these services through their research subsidiary, Group Attitudes Corporation, which specializes in image/issue survey research for planning, monitoring and evaluation of public relations, public affairs, communications, and marketing and advertising programs. Full-service, custom research, selected subscription research services including opinion-leader studies, financial or employee studies, and focus groups are some of the services the company offers, according to a Hill and Knowlton descriptive brochure. Other smaller research organizations offer a wide range of services, as they describe themselves in the membership directory of American Association of Public Opinion Research.

Omnibus, Piggyback, or Shared Research

This variation on the common polling technique lets two or more participants contribute questions to a common questionnaire and share costs. This cooperative survey research—also called omnibus, piggyback, Caravan (trademark of National Opinion Research Corporation, NORC), amalgam, and shared research—may be defined as a survey in which two or more clients participate by buying space in the interview instrument or in segments of the questionnaire as administered in a single survey.

The procedure is attractive to public relations people on tight budgets because the expenses of a national poll can be cut to a third or even a tenth of the usual amount, depending on the number cooperating. There are trade-offs, of course; the researcher is limited to a small number of questions and the population must be the same, usually the general public, for all those cooperating in the project. Furthermore, not all polling organizations offer the service.

Piggyback and shared projects are frequently put together as client interest can be identified, which poses the problem of finding suitable participants. The problem of having to recruit participants has led some organizations, including NORC, to abandon the practice.

For the pollster, the participant recruitment problem might be turned to an advantage by using the opportunity to solicit business that might not otherwise consider hiring a research service. The invitation to join in a survey may be extended to organizations that have never used contracted research, as a way of cultivating future business. For the research user, knowing that certain research organizations conduct cooperative projects, the prospective client may simply indicate such an interest to selected polling firms and wait for the opportunity to develop. Consult the American Association for Public Opinion Research (AAPOR) directory.

Participating in shared research is not difficult if the services offered are understood. Crossley Surveys, Inc., located in New York City, conducts a regular "Crossley Empire State Poll" as a shared-cost telephone poll of adults in New York State. Commercially oriented firms, as opposed to academic ones, are more successful with omnibus surveys because they have a larger number of clients and quicker turnaround in completing the polls. As an example of how to go about participating in an omnibus poll, a Crossley brochure explains:

> Each quarter Crossley surveys 1,500 New Yorkers asking questions for several survey participants. Participants can include in the Poll any questions they choose. Each participant has exclusive rights to the data generated by his questions. The CROSSLEY EMPIRE STATE POLL is the only shared-cost poll in New York State.

Crossley offers four advantages: sophisticated telephone interviewing, custom questions and tabulations, flexible geographic coverage, and minimum expense through shared cost. Adaptations to special needs are possible, such as expanding into neighboring states, and "when the number of questions is too large for a single interview, two samples of respondents will be surveyed." This means that the additional questions would be asked in a subsequent sampling. The Crossley brochure further states:

> The poll can provide measures of the effectiveness of advertising or promotion campaigns by using identical questions before and after the campaign. Repeating standard questions periodically can provide tracking measures on a wide variety of topics and issues. Attitudes toward brand names, politicians, the economy, organization images, capital punishment, and pollution control are examples of phenomena which might be usefully tracked.

The firm suggests that the shared-cost poll may be used for such things as evaluating programs, needs assessment, measuring public participation, tracking policy decisions, determining issue salience, and candidate evaluation. Product or service applications include awareness and usage, brand preference, local product availability, new product potential, inhibitors to adoption, and corporate image.

Contracted or Commissioned Research

The technique of hiring polling is often referred to as "farming out" research to professional research organizations; bids may be invited by distributing "requests for proposals." For all the emphasis on research in public relations, the literature offers little help in how to buy research.

There are three ways in which the client and researcher make contact, apart from whether they decide to work together. Researcher and client may find each other through (1) *personal contact,* a chance meeting where the parties discover their mutual interest or a meeting with someone who knows about a prospective researcher or client; (2) *published information,* a directory, an advertisement, an article by or about the researcher, or other reference the client may use to identify a researcher to contact; or (3) a *request for proposal (RFP),* an invitation to bid on the project, distributed to known researchers or published as an advertisement in appropriate periodicals. Of course, various combinations of the above may be used.

Whether the client and researcher initially meet each other or not, personal contact is often a part of selecting the researcher. The client will often want to confirm the competence of the researcher by talking with a previous client. The professional researcher is happy to supply a list of clients as references. A particularly effective way for researchers to make themselves and their work known is through publication in the literature read by potential clients. Research purchasers, for the same reasons, will find the literature in the field a good source for mentions of research and researchers as well as advertisements appropriate to research needs. The more popular trade publications are usually a good source of such information, but the scholarly journals will help to identify researchers, particularly those associated with a university.

Directories are also a source of leads in finding a researcher who fits the client's needs. The yellow or business pages in the telephone directory should offer some options for locating potential researchers, at least in the larger metropolitan areas. The Manhattan directory in New York City lists about one page of "public opinion" researchers. The AAPOR lists over 100 member firms together with the range of services offered; the American Marketing Association (AMA) directory lists about 300 researchers.

A third way to find a researcher or firm is through the widespread practice of inviting bids on the research project. The usual procedure is to send out a request for proposal (RFP) to researchers. The RFP can be sent to selected addresses published in a directory or to a list of local-area firms compiled from various directories and perhaps including universities that conduct research of the type needed.

The RFP can vary according to the needs of the user of the research. An organization contracting with an independent research organization must specify only an outline of needs, in some cases no more elaborate than a list of topics to be covered or subjects to be explored. In larger organizations, especially those regulated by the federal government, a series of forms will have to be completed as part of the proposal in order to comply with regulations, such as equal opportunity employment, patent rights, and insurance regulations. Various state regulations may also be involved. RFPs also include agreements on topics such as standards of work to be performed; costs and terms of payment; nonreimbursable costs, such as bad debts, fines, and plant conversion costs; independent research and development costs; travel; changes in the work plan; stop-work-order provisions; termination notices; deliverable documents (such as reports of work progress, legal notices, insurance certification, contractor's release, and assignments); data and records to be retained by contractor; publicity releases; property; subcontracting; and conflict of interest.

Once the contract between researcher and client has been made, an agreement satisfactory to both parties must be worked out. The contract provisions are usually spelled out by the research user in the RFP. Any deviations from these specifications must be worked out and included in the "proposal," which is the researcher's response to the RFP as the plan for conducting the research project. The proposal, with any revisions worked out by the two parties, becomes the contract under which the research will be performed.

One device for guiding the initial contact between research user and provider is a "research needs assessment form." The example of such a form shown in Box 3.5 indicates the questions that need to be addressed. The form will be helpful when the contract is less formal than proposals required by the federal government. The typical nongovernment RFP would need to incorporate many of the concerns covered in the assessment form. When there is no formal RFP or formal proposal, both parties to the agreement should work out a form that specifies the expectations of both to avoid misunderstanding.

Research service organizations vary widely in the range of capabilities and specialized services provided. Each firm has developed abilities based on its own research experience and interests. Directories list the self-descriptions of research organizations to help the purchaser of services match needs with the strengths of the service provider.

U.S. Census Data Analysis

Analysis of information collected by the Census Bureau and available from the census data base is an often overlooked research technique. The raw data are available from Bureau of Census repositories, especially the Public Use Documentation data base. The U.S. census data have the unequaled advantage of representing the entire U.S. population in the basic demographic informa-

---

BOX 3.5   **Research Needs Assessment Form (for Public Relations Polls)**

This guide is intended to help research user and provider to articulate a mutually satisfactory agreement when contracting or commissioning research.

Name of organization sponsoring the research:

1. What motivates this research project?
2. What problem(s) do you expect this research to help solve?
3. What specific questions do you expect the research to answer?
4. Are the questions answerable by asking for (check all that apply): opinions—preferences____, detecting attitudes____determining beliefs____, identifying values____, measuring behavior____, desires____, needs____, others____? (Explain):
5. Who has the answers to the questions to be asked? What public or segments should be polled? How should the population be defined?
6. Do you expect to find important differences between responses of different segments of this population? (Plans must be made to ensure that these segments are large enough to be an accurate measure of the phenomenon.)
7. How accurate do the results need to be? (How certain do you need to be that results represent the population?)
8. How should interviews be conducted? (How detailed do the questions or other material shown the respondent need to be?)
9. What specific question topics should be covered? (Need to supply a list of the "objectives.")
10. Are the qualities measured subject to change over a short time? (How much time can be allowed for interviews?)

---

tion asked in the most recent census. Because the census asks standard questions of all U.S. residents, the answers are available in percentages and in actual numbers, and a wide range of statistical analysis is possible. Moreover, answers to the researcher's questions can be provided for virtually any geographic area: counties, incorporated villages, towns and cities, county subdivisions, census tracts, enumeration districts, and city blocks.

The Census Bureau counts all residents of the United States, whether citizens or not. Residents of Puerto Rico, the Virgin Islands, Guam, American Samoa, and the trust territories of the Pacific Islands are also included in the count. Information can thus be obtained about any of these geographic areas or any tract within them. Answers to any one question or combination of questions may also be obtained, such as cross-tabulations, correlations, multivariate analysis, and the like.

BOX 3.6   U.S. Census Repositories of Computerized Data

U.S. Census Bureau microdata sets are held in repositories at the following locations:

City	Regional director	User service phone
Atlanta, GA	(404) 730-3832	(404) 730-3833
Boston, MA	(617) 424-0501	(617) 424-0510
Charlotte, NC	(704) 344-6142	(704) 344-6144
Chicago, IL	(708) 562-1350	(708) 562-1740
Dallas, TX	(214) 767-7500	(214) 767-7105
Denver, CO	(303) 969-6750	(303) 969-7750
Detroit, MI	(313) 259-0056	(313) 259-1875
Kansas City, KS	(913) 551-6728	(913) 551-6711
Los Angeles, CA	(818) 904-6393	(818) 903-6359
New York, NY	(212) 264-3860	(212) 264-4730
Philadelphia, PA	(215) 597-4920	(215) 597-8313
Seattle, WA	(206) 728-5390	(206) 728-5314

Data Available   The data are usually described as demographic, that is, descriptions of the characteristics of people as they are distributed geographically, or according to vital statistics. The major categories of information collected by the 1990 census are as follows, by census form question number: (1) name of person (this is recorded for follow-up but is not available); (2) household relationships; (3) sex; (4) race; (5) age; (6) marital status; (7) Spanish origin; (8–10) education; (11) state or country of origin; (12) citizenship; (13) language used; (H13) housing, with 32 descriptive categories; (14) ancestry; (15) housing tenure; (16–33) personal history, including work, college, military service, physical and mental health, children born, marriages, how get to work, job activity, type industry employed, occupation, employer, how much time employed, and income. See the U.S. census questionnaire for details.

All data from questions 2 through 32 are available in statistical form; that is, tabulations, percentages, and other analyses are available for public use. Income information is not available. The Census Bureau provides a staff that assists and educates the public on how to use the census data.

Accessing Census Data   Beginning with the 1980 census, the data are stored in a computer data base. Previous data were printed and copies distributed to regional repositories, where they are available free to the public (see Box 3.6). Portions of previous census data were even more widely distributed to libraries around the country. The 1980 and 1990 census data are accessible only by computer. However, portions of the 1980 and 1990 census, the microdata sets, are accessible at each state's designated repository, often a state university library or state computer system.

The director of the regional census repository office will explain how the data may be accessed. The service is no longer free, but access charges are not prohibitive. The cost of accessing the data files will reflect the cost of the computer and communication system, rather than fees for use of the data itself, and thus will depend on the complexity of the task, amount of computer time needed, and print charges.

The census data may be accessed by any number of computer software packages. Statistical Packages for the Social Sciences (SPSS), Statistical Analysis System (SAS), and Census Software Package (CENSPAC) are some in general use. CENSPAC, which may be used on any compatible computer, is published by, and is available from the Census Bureau.

Audits in Public Relations Campaigns

These popular research procedures actually combine several research techniques and methods to analyze the status of public relations, communication, and/or social responsibility of an organization. In recent years the audit has become a major qualitative research tool in public relations. As its name implies, an audit examines, describes, and evaluates the current status of an organization's programs in a specific area such as communications, public relations, or social responsibility programs and uses this information to generate suggestions for new programs to improve conditions.

An individual audit is designed specifically for the needs of the audited organization, but there are general methods that are used in most audits:

1. Identification of the public or audiences important to the audited organization.
2. Extensive interviews such as focus group or face-to-face interviews with internal publics (managers and employees) and external publics (shareholders, media contacts, and the like).
3. Opinion surveys of both internal and external publics using questionnaires.
4. Analysis of how publics or audiences view the organization.
5. Analysis of current programs, personnel, and materials.
6. Identification and analysis of trends and issues affecting the organization.
7. Recommendations to the organization concerning areas on which it must concentrate to achieve desired ends and to plan future programs.

An internal audit is conducted within an organization or department by the department or organization itself. An external audit is conducted by an outside firm that is independent of the organization it is auditing. However, the external audit usually consists of auditing both within and outside the organization.

A short description of the three types of audits, whose areas of responsibility overlap, follows.

The Public Relations Audit   This audit focuses on the public relations position of the company with respect to its publics, its current policies, and its promotion and communication programs.

The Communication Audit   This audit is concerned solely with the organization's communication and analyzes the organization's advertising, annual reports and other publications, audiovisual materials, news releases, memoranda, and other communication. It evaluates these for content and adaptation to the chosen audience. Tools used include surveys, interviews, readership (market) analysis, content analysis, and readability studies.

The Social Responsibility Audit   This examines an organization's positions and activities related to public affairs, relevant public policy issues, emerging social issues, and other aspects of its corporate citizenship. Overall, this type of audit is concerned with the organization's efforts to identify, examine, plan for, and deal with social trends and issues that are or will be affecting the organization. The SR audit is usually internal because it deals with the organization's civic responsibility toward society at large, and it may be a part of the organization's corporate planning or performance analysis. The auditing process consists of four broad steps:

1. Identifying issues that have social or civic implications.
2. Ranking of these issues based on
    a. proximity in time—when the issue will affect the organization
    b. effect on the organization, whether direct or indirect
    c. relative overall significance to the organization
3. Correlating issues with the organization—fitting them to appropriate departments.
4. Developing possible responses.

By its nature, the audit seeks and collects information but does not take steps to solve any problems that are discovered. The process is one of discovery and analysis, not strategic response.

Corporate social responsibility is a relative endeavor depending on economic, social, and, to a lesser degree, government conditions. The general public looks to the corporation as a guardian of the quality of life as a condition of its franchise to conduct business. Examples of social performance activities of corporations are shown in Box 3.7.

Who Conducts the Audit?   The question of credibility of findings dictates that audits be conducted by outside, autonomous organizations. The independence of the outside firm and its concentration on this line of specialization make the choice obvious. Public relations counsel with expertise in research offers these advantages:

1. Experience and expertise.
2. The counsel's exclusive time and attention to the client company.
3. Comparison of findings with those of other clients.
4. Objectivity and credibility of an independent firm.

BOX 3.7   **Corporate Social Performance Activities**

Examples of how corporations may discharge their civic duties through such activities as:

1. Promoting minority group employment and advancement.
2. Increasing overall productivity.
3. Improving business management.
4. Improving career opportunities.
5. Installing state-of-the-art pollution controls.
6. Ensuring equal opportunities for minorities and women.
7. Supporting private and government policies for economic growth.
8. Supplying direct financial aid to schools and colleges through scholarships, grants, and corporate funds.
9. Installing in new facilities equipment that lessens negative environmental effects, that is, that saves energy and produces less pollution.
10. Recruiting the handicapped and especially the impoverished as employees.
11. Encouraging adoption of open housing laws in the community.
12. Supporting the preservation of animal life and the ecology of the land.
13. Supporting local and state arts programs.
14. Building and supporting local hospitals, clinics, and community health care institutions.
15. Replenishing natural resources such as trees.
16. Building plants, offices, and outlets in ghetto areas.
17. Supporting day-care centers for the children of employees.
18. Restoring the beauty of used areas, such as strip mines and landfill dumps.
19. Supporting current schools and helping to establish new ones.

The public relations, communication, or social responsibility audit would have no more credence than a financial audit if the auditing firm were not independent and objective. Users of audits in the public relations field are buying the credibility of results as surely as financial audits do in selecting the auditing firm.

When Should an Organization Be Audited?   Consultants differ on how regularly an organization should be audited, with suggested time intervals between audits ranging from one to seven years. It is generally agreed that there are certain events or time periods affecting an organization to which an audit should be an almost automatic response. Various changes or conditions in an organization may indicate the need to reinforce credibility while at the same time making significant and overt policy changes. Conditions calling for an audit may include such examples as:

1. Installation of a new public relations director.
2. Engaging of a new public relations counsel.
3. Management perception that the organization should alter its current programs.
4. Significant change in the organization's structure because of merger, acquisition, or a new chief executive officer.
5. Continued labor or management unrest.
6. Periods of poor performance or declining earnings.
7. Organization review of its advertising program.
8. Public relations program needing more support from management.
9. A corporate crisis.
10. Profound changes in other companies in the industry which the corporation can exploit.

Audits in the public relations field share the same basic motivations as audits in the financial field: how does the condition of our firm measure up, compared with standard practices, against others in the industry, and how can we use the findings to bring our corporation more into line with confidence-inspiring practice? Whereas financial institutions are under strong, often legal, obligation to undergo an audit, the public relations function has only a moral obligation to undergo an audit; but that moral obligation is no trivial matter because the entire purpose of public relations is to achieve the moral approval of its constituencies.

SUMMARY

Archival research techniques examine what is "on the record," including the historical record, communication logs, past research reports, data bases, and standard library resources.

Descriptive research techniques describe what "exists" by using such approaches as observation, interviews, content analysis, advisory panels, focus group interviews, Delphi studies, subscription research services, omnibus or shared research, contracted or commissioned research, U.S. census data analysis, and audits in public relations campaigns.

FOR FURTHER READING

Auditing

Abt, Clark C. *The Social Audit for Management.* New York: AMACOM, 1977.
Goodman, Steven E. "Why Few Corporations Monitor Social Issues," *Public Relations Journal* (April 1983): 20.

Kopec, Joseph A. "The Communication Audit," *Public Relations Journal* (May 1982): 24–27.

Simon, Raymond. *Public Relations: Concepts and Practices.* New York: Macmillan, 1980.

Strenski, James B. "The Communications Audit: Basic to Business Development," *Public Relations Quarterly* (Spring 1984): 14–20.

Interviewing

Balinsky, Benjamin. *The Executive Interview.* New York: Harper, 1979.

Bingham, Walter Vandyke, and Bruce V. Moore. *How to Interview,* 4th ed. New York: Harper, 1959.

Dexter, Louis A. *Elite and Specialized Interviewing.* Evanston, IL: Northwestern University Press, 1979.

Downs, Cal W., G. Paul Smeyak, and Ernest Martin. *The Professional Interview.* New York: Harper, 1977.

Gorden, Raymond L. *Interviewing: Strategy, Techniques and Tactics.* Homewood, IL: Dorsey Press, 1969.

Kahn, Robert Lewis, and C. F. Cannell. *The Dynamics of Interviewing: Theory Techniques and Cases.* New York: Wiley, 1957.

Matarazzo, Joseph D. *The Interview; Research on Its Anatomy and Structure.* Chicago: Aldine Atherton, 1972.

Metzler, Ken. *Creative Interviewing.* Englewood Cliffs, NJ: Prentice Hall, 1977.

Richardson, Stephen A., B. S. Dohrenwend, and D. Klein. *Interviewing: Its Form and Functions.* New York: Basic Books, 1965.

Sherwood, Hugh C. *The Journalistic Interview.* New York: Harper, 1972.

CHAPTER 4

Steps in Survey Research

- Setting Objectives
- Defining the Population
- Drawing the Sample
- Developing the Questionnaire
- Determining Method for Administering the Questionnaire
- Questionnaire Wording
- Structuring the Questionnaire
- Questionnaire Pretesting
- Questionnaire Coding

- Training Interviewers
- Preparing Interviewer Packets
- Conducting the Interviews
- Debriefing Interviewers
- Verification
- Writing and Debugging a Computer Program
- Interpreting the Data
- Writing the Report of Findings

Survey research is one of the most common descriptive research methods. It measures public opinion, attitudes, or behavior by interviewing representative samples of appropriate publics. Random selection of appropriate numbers for the sample ensures that the results will represent the characteristics of the entire population from which the sample is drawn. The following steps are an outline of the process.

SETTING OBJECTIVES

By setting objectives for the survey the researcher can determine specific questions that need to be answered about the public being polled. Phrasing the objectives—that is, what you want to know—in a form to fit the answers you expect helps ensure that the results will be usable without reinterpretation. The public relations problem should dictate the type of answers needed to solve the problem; the form these answers will take guides the statement of objectives. The objectives point to the problem you need to solve; failure to follow objectives can mean that the findings will not match the problem you want to solve.

Objectives must be developed with the intended application clearly in mind. A list of question "topics" is helpful for generating questions. If the campaign or program is for a client, the objectives should be drafted by the client or developed in close cooperation with the client. If the campaign is to be conducted for a specific division of the organization, the management people who will make decisions based on the results should be intimately involved in listing the objectives. Realistic research objectives come from long-term involvement in the organization and its problems.

For example, a police department, in preparation for a public relations campaign, may begin with a number of questions or problems: How effective are current department public relations efforts? Which enforcement efforts by the department have the greatest public support? How much does the public know or understand about what the department does? Do people think there are enough officers? Is there support for a new headquarters building? Would the public be willing to make minor damage or loss reports over the telephone in order to allow officers to concentrate on more serious offenses? Do different segments of the public—youth, older people, males, females—differ on any of these questions?

These objectives must be studied carefully not only to determine specific items to be included on the questionnaire but also to decide what specific segment of the public or population to ask and how to conduct the interviews. Stated objectives will also help determine the size of the sample. Be revealing whether any of the information needed applies to only portions of the public, the objectives will indicate whether you need to *stratify* the selection. Stratification draws portions of the sample from the categories of the population whose answers may differ from those of others. Stratification ensures that the unique opinions of these subsegments will be represented in the findings. For example, if you want to find out whether people who have been involved in an accident in the last year differ from the rest of the population in their opinions about accident-reporting procedures, you would have to include in the sample people who fit that category to guarantee having representative opinions from this stratum of the population.

Objectives help determine:

1. Size of the sample.
2. Allowing for adequate subsamples.
3. What population—or public—to focus on.
4. Items to be included in the questionnaire.
5. Areas that need to be emphasized or compared.
6. How to conduct the interviews—face to face, by phone, by mail.

Objectives for a survey are of critical importance to many aspects of the process and must be compiled with care and knowledgeable input. The objectives should be listed either as problem areas or as general questions. The list should be discussed in some detail with the organization's management representative to clarify the stated problems and set priorities. Management should also guide decisions on which population will be surveyed, how the interviews will be conducted, the size of the sample, and the size of any subsamples. Possible survey objectives are shown in Box 4.1.

BOX 4.1   Example of Objectives for a Public Opinion Survey from a Municipally Owned Electric Utility

OBJECTIVES FOR PUBLIC OPINION SURVEY

Since Regional Utilities is owned by its customers, we have an obligation to provide them with reliable information ranging from national energy postures to the daily activities of our local system. For us to accomplish this, we require information concerning the following:

1. Public attitudes about the provision of services.
2. Types of information desired.
3. Most effective methods of providing the above information.

Some Sample Ideas for Questions

1. Do you as a citizen know exactly who owns and operates the utility system?
2. How do you feel about the service you receive from the telephone center? (Availability of lines, promptness.)
3. How do you feel about the services supplied by the utility?
4. Do you know what services are available?
5. Do you feel the utility should supply convenient payment locations such as "drop boxes"?
6. How do you feel about customer policies?
7. Do you know that the utility has a citizen's advisory committee?
8. What type of information do you feel the utility should supply to its customers?
9. Do you think the news coverage on utility issues is adequate?
10. Would you attend workshops to help you understand your electric bill? Would you watch special television presentations?
11. Do you like the billing statement form?
12. Do you read the "Bulletin" on your billing statement?

13. Do you think it is worth the additional expense to bury all transmission and distribution lines?
14. Do you think the utilities should provide loans for energy conservation measures? Supply energy conservation measures at a competitive cost?
15. How would you like to see fuel adjustment handled? (In the base rate or as it is now, a separate item.)
16. Do you think there is any energy problem?
17. What types of information need to be routinely supplied to promote "total customer awareness"?
18. Do you know what types of fuel are used to generate electricity?
19. Do you recall receiving the latest bill insert?
20. Have you seen or heard any information from Regional Utilities advising you how to conserve in your use of electricity, or not?
21. Where do you get most of your information about Regional Utilities?

DEFINING THE POPULATION

Precise identification of the population involves deciding who has the answers to the questions you need to ask or who are the most appropriate people to ask. In taking a survey for the police department, for example, the researcher has to decide when a person is a citizen. That may seem easy enough, just say at voting age. But many people who have important opinions about the police department are not yet of voting age. What about driver age? What about people in school to whom the "officer friendly" program is directed who are not yet of driver age? What about the resident of the neighboring county who drives to work in the city every day? What is the "community"—are those outside the city limits included? What if only city residents pay taxes to support the police department but suburbanites enjoy the benefits of city police protection; do we want to ask them if they want more services? Obviously, there are many questions to consider in defining a survey population.

If you need to know how various segments of the population differ in their opinions, you must be prepared to increase the size of the sample to ensure that subsamples are large enough to be representative, or take steps, such as stratified sampling, to ensure that these subsamples are adequately represented.

In practice, the population may be defined by the way the sample is selected. One way to draw a sample is to start with a list of the population; a city directory, a list of electric utility customers, or a list of employees is commonly used. With a list of everyone in the population it is easy to select a simple random or systematic random sample. In this case the list defines the population. If the list does not exclude any segment important to your purposes, the sample should be acceptable.

A population list must be inclusive. For a comprehensive list of the general population of a city, the list of subscribers to the electric utility is ordinarily suitable. Virtually everyone in the city uses electricity; more people use electricity than subscribe to telephone service. However, the service area of utilities may not correspond to the city boundaries. If more than one utility serves the population you wish to measure, you need to have both utility lists.

A population list is more appropriate for small populations than for huge multicounty or state populations. For those the multistage method with its variations is more suitable. Of course, a list of members of a national association, although it is national, would still be relatively small.

Methods of interviewing or methods of drawing the sample may have a major influence on how the population is defined. When you decide to do telephone interviews, the population must be defined as telephone subscribers. The results may then not be applicable to the total general population. If, for example, the poll asks for information about poverty conditions, it would probably not adequately represent those too poor to afford telephones. When you decide to interview shoppers at a certain mall, you are defining the population as _____ Mall shoppers. When you insert a questionnaire in an employee publication, you are defining the population as readers of that publication.

DRAWING THE SAMPLE

Sampling involves selecting a *portion* of a larger population in order to estimate characteristics of the whole. The challenge in any sampling procedure is to ensure representativeness. The scientific reliability of a survey, by the way, depends almost exclusively on sample selection, no matter how sophisticated other aspects of the project may be. The scientific technique that assures reliable findings is random probability sampling.

> *Probability theory, as far as sampling is concerned, is based on two principles: randomness and the law of large numbers.*

Put together, these two principles mean that if every individual in the larger whole has an equal chance of being selected in the sample (randomness) and if you select a large enough quantity in the sample, you can make very accurate predictions of how representative the sample will be of the whole population. The quantity selected—that is, the size of the sample—is much easier to control than the randomness of the selection process, which means that randomness needs critical attention at every step in the same selection process. More about randomness later.

The law of large numbers, described by various statistical theorists, is a basic physical law that applies to the way quantities of anything being measured accumulate. Imagine a railroad car of beans that are well mixed, that is, are homogeneous; if measured amounts are spilled out on a flat floor, the result is the law of large numbers of action. The first ten pounds will scatter over a large area with more in the center of the pile than at the perimeter. If another ten pounds are spilled and another, a pattern will take form. When enough have been added to the pile of beans the shape is very predictable.

If you could cut from top to bottom across and through the pile, the shape at the cut would be the familiar bell curve traced by the top of the pile (see Figure 4.1). The law of large numbers established that the accumulation of anything in quantity will produce this bell-shaped configuration. Down each side of the bell curve is a break point where the shape changes from convex to concave. If one draws a line from that point to the base of the curve on each side, the area inside the lines will contain 68.26% of the total. By dividing the bell curve into segments, using these first two vertical lines as the first segment, the curve can be divided into units called standard deviations. The second segment, or second standard deviation, is defined by a line drawn down through each side of the pile where the curve again changes. This second unit, or second standard deviation, contains an additional 27.18% of the total pile, combining both ends of the curve, for a total of 95.44% in the first two standard deviations. The third standard deviation accounts for an additional 4.30%. These standard deviations will always contain the same proportions when the distribution is normal, that is, when the accumulation takes place by chance alone.

By comparing the bell curve produced by any given collection of events, beans, people, or opinion with a normal distribution, many statistical procedures are possible. These procedures make estimations based on the difference between the *standard* distribution and what is observed in a specific distribution.

Based on this natural phenomenon, a statistical formula can predict the probability that the sample represents the whole, or show how close the sample would come to representing the whole if the sample were selected in the

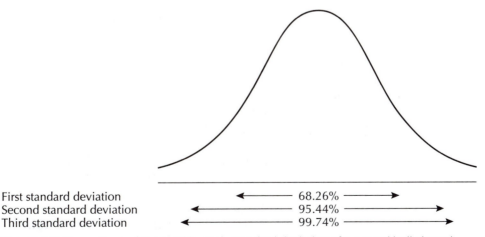

First standard deviation   ←———— 68.26% ————→
Second standard deviation   ←————— 95.44% —————→
Third standard deviation   ←————— 99.74% —————→

Figure 4.1 Proportions of the total in each standard deviation of a normal bell-shaped curve.

BOX 4.2   **Formula for Computing the Chance Sampling Error**

One common way to write this formula is

$$\sigma\% = \sqrt{\frac{p \cdot q}{n}}$$

where p = % of attributes to be measured which are assumed to exist
                  in the population, also called "homogeneity"
          $\sigma\%$ = chance sampling error
          q = difference between p and 100%
          n = size of sample

        This formula will apply to populations of up to 100,000. For larger populations, the formula adds an element:

$$\sigma\% = \sqrt{\frac{p \cdot q}{n} \cdot \frac{N-n}{N-1}}$$

where N = population size

---

same way an infinite number of times. The formula yields the *chance sampling error*, which is also called the *error of the estimate*, the *bound on error*, the *standard error of the sample*, the *sampling error*, and various other terms. The chance sampling error indicates by a percentage the possibility of how close the sample will come to representing the whole or, more precisely, by how much the sample would fail to represent the whole if it were drawn an infinite number of times in the same way. The chance sampling error formula is shown in Box 4.2.

It is important to understand the value of p in the chance sampling error formula. The p represents the uniformity or homogeneity of the population—that is, how uniform the opinions or attitudes are likely to be in the population. Expressed in another way, p is an estimate of the likelihood, given as a percentage, that the characteristic you want to measure will be present in the population—for example, that 50% of the population will have an opinion on the issue being measured. One might also think of p as the proportion of the population who would find that the least relevant question in the questionnaire makes sense or is relevant.

The factor p must be estimated from what can be surmised about the population being measured. Common estimates of p range from 50% to 95% or even higher. If you estimate that, say, 15% of the population would not have any awareness of the issue being measured, the value of p would be .85, which is to say that 85% of the population at least are aware of the issue being measured.

To represent an issue for which the chances are a toss-up that any respondent will have an opinion, the most conservative estimate should be used, the 50–50 chance or 50%, which means that p is .50. You assume there is a 50–50 chance that any respondent will have an opinion. The chance sampling error thus chosen will predict the representativeness of the sample on the least relevant issues but will be even more representative on other issues.

Working out the formula for populations under 100,000 is quite easy with a pocket calculator that has a square root key. There are four steps in working out the formula, as shown in Box 4.3. With a higher homeogeneity estimate in the population, the formula will yield even more desirable results, that is, a smaller chance sampling error. Assuming that 85% of the population has an opinion on the issue, the same sample of 200 would yield a sampling error of 0.02, or 2%.

The advantage of applying this formula to the sampling procedure is that you know how accurate your sample will be in representing the whole population. The formula can be worked out for different sample sizes. In general, samples of under 30 are not considered large enough for the law of large numbers to operate dependably and thus do not yield accurate estimates of the total population. For small populations, a 50% response rate is usually necessary to produce reliable results. For populations smaller than 60, a total count, or census, is recommended to ensure representativeness, assuming that a response rate of 50% or higher is achieved.

For larger populations of 100,000 or more, a sample of 1,500 is commonly used. But even for large populations, samples of 2,000 or 3,000 do not improve

---

BOX 4.3   Steps in Working Out the Chance Sampling Error Formula

$$\sigma\% = \sqrt{\frac{p \cdot q}{n}} = \frac{0.50 \times 0.50}{n} = \frac{0.25}{n}$$

$$= \sqrt{\frac{\overset{0.035}{\overline{0.00125}}}{200}} = 0.03$$

This calculation uses the most conservative estimate of homeogeneity, .50, and uses a sample size of 200. The calculation is for populations of under 100,000.

the sampling error very much beyond what would result from a sample of 1,500. To improve the chance sampling error beyond that produced by the 1,500 requires so many more respondents in the sample that the chance of mechanical and human errors outweighs the possibility of improving the sampling error to any significant degree.

Many professional pollers have observed that percentages of responses—of yes's versus no's or of approves versus disapproves—will usually not change significantly after the first 20% of a population are reported. This suggests that a trend may be determined after measuring 20% of a population, but the trend still leaves unanswered the question of how representative the results may be. Therefore, even when percentages of opinion in a population are determined, the chance sampling error must be calculated in order to indicate the degree of sampling accuracy.

Size of the sample may be determined by several considerations. How much can you afford to spend for interviews? How much can you spend on long-distance charges if a large geographic area is involved? How accurate must the results be, since size of the sample determines the chance sampling error? How much time can you allow for completing the survey, since a large number of interviews take longer than a small number?

Usually, most of these factors influence the decision about sample size. The chosen sample size is always a *projected* sample size because the number of completed interviews will never exactly match the number planned. The number of interviews that are uncompleted for all causes will vary greatly depending on the motivation for the respondent to participate. Some respondents will not be at home, some will refuse to participate, some will have moved, and some data will be incorrectly recorded and require either recoding the responses or repeating interviews.

To compensate for uncompleted interviews, the sample can be drawn larger than needed. Depending on the estimate of participation and interview completion, an extra 20 to 30% can be added to the interviews needed to offset the anticipated losses, with actual respondents selected from this list randomly. It is always better to have more interviews than necessary than to have too few. Any subsamples you may need to look at will require at least 30 respondents to be statistically representative at a nine-times-out-of-ten chance, so any numbers added to the total from extra interviews will be a plus, especially for subsamples.

Some Types of Random Sampling Procedures

There are many ways to draw a sample for measuring public opinion. All random samples are designed to represent the populations from which they are drawn. The key to representativeness is random selection, that is, selection so that every individual in the population has an equal chance of being chosen in the sample.[1]

Simple random sampling is both the simplest and the most sophisticated technique. It requires a list of the population that is, or can be, numbered.

Many populations cannot be numbered or even listed—residents of cities or statewide political constituents, for example. The difficulty of finding lists of populations is why this simple random technique is seldom used. However, with the advent of wide use of computer records, this limitation may be less a problem in the future. Because the simple random technique offers excellent randomization accuracy, it is recommended whenever a list is available. Public relations practitioners may find it is well suited to surveys of small populations within corporations or nonprofit organizations.

Individuals are drawn for the simple random sample by matching numbers on the list against numbers chosen from a table of random numbers. The matching can be done easily by using a computer, or it can be done by hand for very small samples. Because a table of random numbers is selected by a computer with every digit selected randomly, the numbers from such a table can be used in any order. Such tables may be found in statistics books or can be generated by a computer with a simple program. Numbers are usually listed four or five digits to a set and printed in rows and columns. Selection of numbers can be done by the pencil drop technique—using the number closest to the point of a pencil dropped on the sheet of random numbers—in this way single numbers or a combination or numbers in any configuration can be chosen randomly. Since each such choice is random, a list of numbers of almost any length can be built. Care must be taken to avoid combinations that are above the upper limit of the sample size; if selections are to be made between 1 and 300, 4 cannot be accepted for the first digit.

An example of how a sample was drawn using the simple random technique is shown in Box 4.4. The sample was used in a survey of alumni of a university to compare donors with nondonors. A larger than normal selection of business school graduates was drawn to provide a large enough subsample of business graduates to allow further analysis. When drawing such a sample, a decision must be made about what information to record about each name on the interviewee information sheet, such as phone number, zip code, and so on, to assist the interviewers to identify the correct respondents. Any changes in the information at the time of the actual interview can thus be written down by hand to confirm or update the computerized information.

Systematic random sampling is a technique recommended when the population is not numbered, or is difficult to number, but is represented on a list of names, preferably including addresses and phone numbers. City directories and phone directories are examples of such lists. The *first step* is to determine the size of the sample needed and add a percentage to compensate for projected losses. The *second step* is to divide the number of people on the list, or an estimate of the number, by the projected sample size: N/n, where N is the population and n is the sample size. This will divide the population into segments or blocks, each of which will supply one individual for the sample.

For the *third step*, select a number at random from the first segment or block. This "random start interval" number will provide randomization for selecting not only the respondent from the first block of names but also all subsequent blocks. This random number, selected by chance alone from digits

BOX 4.4   **Example: Simple Random Sampling Procedure**

A sample was drawn from an estimated population of 95,000, which included all living alumni of the University of Florida who had graduated since 1911 with good addresses and telephone numbers available in Alumni Affairs records. Alumni without a telephone number available were not included in the sample.

Out total projected sample of 600 was stratified to consist of 300 donors and 300 nondonors from all colleges and fund categories. To ensure a large enough subsample of business school graduates, a quota of 60 business college graduates was included in each category of 300. This ratio is greater than the actual ratio of business graduates, which is 36 per 300 or 12 percent.

The sample was chosen by simple random selection. Using the university's computer system, a program assigned numbers to all alumni for whom phone numbers and certain other information was available. The computer was then programmed to choose random numbers and select the alumni with the corresponding numbers. This random selection included graduates from all colleges and donors from all fund categories.

The simple random procedure followed these steps:

I. The alumni file was divided into four subfiles:
   A. business donors
   B. nonbusiness donors
   C. business nondonors
   D. nonbusiness nondonors
II. Individuals in these subfiles were each given a number and the random numbers generator program then selected:
   A. 60 business donors
   B. 60 business nondonors
   C. 240 nonbusiness donors
   D. 240 nonbusiness nondonors
III. This selection was then shuffled to make five donors and five nondonors per page with one page to be assigned per interviewer.
IV. The 60 pages were then shuffled in order to distribute pages to interviewers randomly.

The subsample of business graduates would yield a chance sampling error of .045. The chance sampling error for the total sample of 300 in each donor-nondonor category is .02. The actual sampling error varied in both cases depending on the total number of interviews actually completed.

between 1 and the last number in the block, is called the start interval because each succeeding name is selected by measuring the number of names in the block to find the right name in each subsequent block.

Selecting the random start interval can be a problem. If each segment contains 364 names, for example, three digits will have to be selected, but the first digit cannot be over 3. Moreover, the first name on the list cannot be ruled out, so zeros will have to be included to ensure that number 001 has the same chance of selection as number 364 and all numbers in between.

A table of random numbers, again, is an ideal tool for the actual selection process. Different techniques will work equally well for picking the digits because each digit is printed at random. The pencil drop technique is a useful method: let a sharpened pencil drop on a page of random numbers—without looking—and select the number nearest the point. Keep dropping the pencil until a digit acceptable for each of the three digits in the required number has been chosen.

After the random start interval number is selected, the *fourth step* is to count to that number on the population list and select that name as the first one for the sample. The distance between the first and second names will be the same number of entries as the block size and may be measured on a paper tape. The measured tape may then be used to measure between subsequent names to select the sample. Care must be taken that the tape measures lines of typed names only, adjusting for any blank space at the top or bottom of columns or blank space near headings in columns.

In the systematic random method, the *fifth step* is to count the number of names between the names to be chosen; this is called the skip interval and is the same as the block size. Since counting all the names is unnecessarily tedious, the space occupied by the names in the first full block can be measured using a heavy paper tape, as described above. If the end of the tape falls just short of a name or just beyond a name, some systematic method should be used to determine the name to choose: the first complete name beyond the end of the tape, or the name closest to the end of the tape.

If the systematic random method is used to select telephone numbers or prefixes, the same general technique may be used. However, not all numbers listed may qualify for selection—long-distance and 800 numbers, for example. In such cases a method of choosing alternate numbers before and after the unqualifying one may be used.

An example of systematic random sampling is shown in Box 4.5. Obviously, some variations in this procedure may be necessary or desirable in order to provide a sample of people more likely to have opinions on the topic of the interviews, or to balance representation between large and small units. The survey director will need to exercise judgment in designing the sample selection process that will be most suitable to the particular research situation.

Multistage random sampling is the preferred technique for very large populations. Polls of national voting-age populations generally use some variation of this procedure. The multistage random approach is well suited to populations for which there is no list or for which such a list would be too cumbersome to be practical.

BOX 4.5   Example of Systematic Random Sample Drawing Technique

OBJECTIVES

Provide a systematic random sample of population listed by name, address, and phone number on three-by-five cards in groups of ten phone numbers, or other required packet criteria.

PROCEDURE

Read entire instructions before beginning.

1. **Determine Sample Size.** Assume an acceptable sampling error of .05 percent or less. Using a pocket calculator with a square root key, work out the following formula (three people work independently and compare results; accept only results agreed on by at least two people):

$$\sigma\% = \sqrt{\frac{p \cdot q}{n}}$$

where p = .50 (or other percent of attributes assumed in population)
$q = p - 1$ (.50%)
n = projected sample size.

Accept a sample size that produces a chance sampling error of .05 or better, based on the projected sample size; if the chance sampling error is acceptable, the sample size is acceptable.
2. **Estimate Size of Population.** Using printout or other list of the population, count three or four pages to determine an average number of entries per page; then multiply the number on the average page by the total number of pages.
3. **Choose the Skip Interval.** Divide the population size estimate—— by the projected sample size.
4. **Select the Random Start Interval.** Use a table of random numbers; select digits between 1 and——(that is, the skip interval number). The pencil drop method may be used to select digits from a table of random numbers.
5. **Select the First Individual in Sample.** Count down the list to the entry number corresponding to the random start interval. Enter the required number of names, phone numbers, or other needed information on a different three-by-five card for each interviewer.

6. **Apply Skip Interval to Select Remainder of Sample.** Use paper tape or other method to measure distance between first name selected and each subsequent name; this distance is the skip interval.

MATERIALS NEEDED

- Packet of three-by-five-inch cards
- One to three pocket calculators
- List of population
- Pens and/or typewriter
- Patience

Note: Teams may assign these tasks to different people to speed the process; the most demanding task will be measuring to select names. One person may measure with two or three different persons taking turns recording names and phone numbers on three-by-five cards.

* Assuming 10 interviews per 45 students in class, or 450. (This will vary with different situations.)

In a national sample of consumer preference, for example, three or four regions of the country would be randomly selected; from these regions, states or cities would be randomly selected; from these, cities and rural areas would be randomly selected; from these, voter precincts are selected at random; from these, randomly selected city blocks or other units are chosen; from these, individual housing units are chosen, again at random; from these, individual respondents are selected, again at random. The random selections are done by the survey director, except for the last two stages—housing units and individual respondents—which are selected by the interviewer using random selection techniques provided by the survey director.

The multistage proportionate sample, also called the stratified proportionate random sample, is the same as the multistage random sample except that the units are selected in proportion to their size. Thus, if 25% of cities are under 25,000 population, 30% are 25,000 to 100,000, 35% are 100,000 to 500,000, and 15% are over 500,000 proportions of each of the categories selected in the sample are the same as the percentages of the population they represent. The same procedure would be followed where disproportionate size of units exists; that is, some units are extremely large or small. Sampling units are selected so that the percentage of subunits selected from the unit is proportionate to the size of the unit.

One variation of this technique, called stratified proportionate multistage sampling, selects a random sampling unit from each stage except the final stage, since proportionate selection is unimportant at the stage of individual respondent selection. This final stage selection is thus not proportionate. Another variation is to select sampling units at one or more stages—voter precincts, for example—because they have proved to be highly representative in the past or because they have qualities that make them desirable at representative "test markets."

Random cluster sampling selects units by random at all stages and interviews all people in the last stage. For example, to obtain a cluster sample of a public school system you might select junior and senior high schools at random, classrooms at those schools at random, and class meeting times again at random, and then interview all the students in the chosen classrooms at the randomly chosen times.

Stratified cluster sampling is a variation on the cluster sampling technique but without the stages. It selects clusters at random from available sampleable units. For example, a university might sample student opinion by using buildings as sampling units and select classrooms randomly as clusters, interviewing everyone in each selected classroom.

For the stratified random sample, "the population is first divided into two or more strata" or categories. In this method the population is classified by predetermined characteristics, the proportions of people representing the characteristics needed in the sample are then randomly selected from each category, and "the subsamples are then joined to form the total sample."[2] Randomization may be achieved by either simple random, systematic random, or random digit dialing. This method differs from the quota sampling method in that randomization is applied to selection of individuals in each category.

Random digit dialing (RDD) is a modern telephone technique that has much to recommend it if telephone interviews are acceptable and if there would be no problem in excluding those who are not telephone subscribers. RDD has the advantage of combining the final sample selection with the interviewing, which greatly simplifies the design of the survey. It also gets high marks for accuracy in representativeness of the intended population.[3] Box 4.6 shows an example of the technique.

A comparison of door-to-door interviews with RDD interviews in one experiment found that the telephone sample had "more missing data on family income, more acquiescence, evasiveness and extremeness of response bias and more and somewhat contradictory answers to checklist question." However, a different study found that telephone surveys were more accurate than face-to-face methods.[4] One explanation is that some people are willing to be more candid in telephone interviews than in face-to-face situations. The subject of the survey and the phrasing of questions may have much to do with variations in response to the technique.

I have found that a telephone interview log helps in checking on the work of interviewers as well as providing feedback on the number selection and interviewing process. The log can provide a record of numbers attempted, numbers completed, times of the calls, number of callbacks, and a brief note on the results of attempted and completed calls. The information can be helpful in

BOX 4.6 **Example of Random Digit Dialing (RDD) Sampling Technique**

Steps in the RDD Technique

1. Decide the size of sample needed from the identified population. However the population may be determined, it must be redefined as "telephone subscribers" because only telephone subscribers will be contacted.

2. Draw a proportionate number of the telephone exchanges that serve the population. This can be done most easily by drawing a systematic random sample of prefixes from the telephone directory. A systematic sample of the first five digits ensures that people in large and small exchanges have an equal chance of being chosen. By drawing the first two of the last four digits, a fit with actual numbers used in small exchanges is ensured.

   Another method is to use a city directory listing of phone numbers by exchange. Count the subscribers in each exchange to find the proportion of individuals to be chosen from each exchange. The same method can be used for multicity samples by using directories from the several cities; for larger populations the method can be combined with the multistage method (see corresponding heading in the text).

3. Assign one exchange prefix number per interview to each interviewer; that is, provide each interviewer with a proportionate selection of prefixes each of which will provide one interview. Provide each interviewer with a copy of a table of random numbers. Assign different blocks of random numbers to each interviewer as a way of reducing the chance of repeat calls to the same randomly chosen number.

4. Direct each interviewer to complete one interview for each prefix number assigned, which should be done by dialing the three-digit prefix plus two numbers, to which a two-digit random number is added (chosen from the block of numbers assigned). If the call and interview are not completed, go on to the next two random numbers, using the same prefix, until an interview is completed.

spotting weaknesses in the research design, such as exchanges with limited numbers of subscribers, and thus can help identify problems while they can still be solved.[5]

Random digit dialing, one should note, produces many calls to numbers that are out of service, disconnected, or otherwise unuseable. However, the technique also provides a highly accurate sample of telephone users, including unlisted numbers and recent hookups not yet listed.

DEVELOPING THE QUESTIONNAIRE

Preparing the questionnaire may be the most challenging part of survey research. Full-time polling professionals freely admit that questionnaires designed and approved by experts will often be found faulty after the interviews are completed. Questionnaire construction is an art; there is no foolproof set of directions to rule out mistakes. A wealth of pollster experience is available to anyone intent on doing the best job possible.[6] Some of that experience is described here.

The first task is to determine what information you want and in what form you want it. That is, you should imagine that you have finished the survey and are ready to use the results. Then, from that perspective, determine what information you need and in what form. By working backward you can avoid the unpleasant mistake of asking the wrong questions or asking them in the wrong way.

For example, you may be ready to ask, "Are you satisfied with your job at COBO Corporation? ( ) yes ( ) no." You plan to use the resulting information in an employee relations campaign. As you reflect on how you will use the results in your campaign, you discover that you need more precise information; you need to know what *factors* influence job satisfaction so that you can do something about improving it. So you rephrase the item: "How important are each of the following in the satisfaction you get out of your job at COBO Corporation? (Please mark 1 to 5, 1 for not important up to 5 for very important.)

( ) Your workstation   ( ) Wage or salary
( ) Coworkers   ( ) Lunchroom facilities
( ) Working hours   ( ) On-the-job health care
( ) Fringe benefits package   ( ) Your supervision
( ) Work load   ( ) Vacation policy
( ) Leave policy   ( ) Honors and recognitions
( ) Others that should be mentioned _____

The information the second question will produce is much more likely to be complete, to be more comparable, and to provide a more precise measure of the situation. The results from this item will also be much more useful in designing a public relations effort to improve working conditions. Designing the questionnaire involves this kind of thought for each of the items of information you need for the campaign as well as the demographic information you will need. The next step in conducting a survey is deciding how the interviews will be conducted.

DETERMINING METHOD FOR ADMINISTERING THE QUESTIONNAIRE

The decision of whether the interviews will be conducted face to face, by telephone, or by mail will usually be made in conjunction with other decisions: how much to budget for the survey, how to draw the sample, and what population to measure.

Factors in the decision about how to administer the questionnaire include cost, time, how accurate and how representative the findings must be, and the type of information needed. The time and cost are determined largely by the amount of information and the way it is collected. Accuracy, representativeness, and type of information needed are determined by the objectives, the size of the sample, and the rigorousness of methodology and procedure.

Time and Cost

The planning chart for selecting polling interview methods shown in Box 4.7 may help in making the decision of what polling method to use. By selecting the factors that are important to the particular survey and tallying the advantage rating of the methods, the one most appropriate to the case at hand can be selected.

Accuracy and Representiveness

Two factors that also play a role in deciding how to administer the questionnaire are (1) accuracy—how precise the data must be or how tolerant you can afford to be of human error, and (2) representativeness—acceptable chances

---

BOX 4.7   Planning Checklist for Selecting Polling Interview Method

Factors	Advantage rating[a]		
	Phone	Face to face	Mail
1. Time—start to finish	3	1	0
2. Cost—within local community	3	1	1
3. Cost—within state	2	0	2
4. Cost—within nation	1	0	3
5. Presentation of visual details	0	3	2
6. Security of interviewers	3	0	3
7. Easy-to-use respondent incentives	1	3	3
8. Can use semantic differential	0	3	2
9. Can use Likert scale	1	3	3
10. Likely rate of response	2	2	1
11. Wide geographic distribution	2	0	3
12. Ease of administering	3	1	2
13. Reliability of responses	2	2	1
14. Can use lengthy questionnaire	0	2	1
15. Items likely to avoid ambiguity	1	3	0

[a]Advantage rating: 0 = none, 1 = some, 2 = good, 3 = excellent.

that the findings will represent the population being measured, or the statistical error. Three types of error in survey research should be taken into account when designing the study, particulary when deciding how to administer the questions: methodological error, procedural error, and statistical error.

Methodological Error   A prime factor in *validity* of the survey, methodological error refers to whether the survey measures what it intends to measure. Errors of this type are a result of weaknesses in the survey design, including such things as asking the wrong questions, asking the right questions but of the wrong people, asking ambiguous questions that seem to ask one thing but are interpreted differently by some people, allowing some interviewers to vary the way the questions are asked, or interpreting the questions differently at different times. All of these possible problems result in findings that are not valid or are not true measurements. Methodological errors come into play quite apart from the two other types of error; it is possible to have a very desirable (low) statistical error in a survey that still fails to represent the sampled population because of methodological errors.

Procedural Error   This type of error, together with methodological error, determines the *reliability* of the survey. Procedural error has to do with human errors in the process of conducting the survey, such as recording a response in the wrong blank, writing numbers that are later misread, pressing the wrong key when entering data, or departing from the designed method for any aspect of the process. Procedural errors are quite difficult to detect; to check for such errors requires repeating the research using the same method to see if the results are the same; this is called *replicating* the survey.

   If the results are the same after replication, procedural errors can be largely ruled out. Checks can be made of the interviewers' work by repeating certain questions and comparing the results, but it may not be possible to test for other procedural errors. One critical step is to check the data very carefully to be sure they are error free. A standard system for checking is to enter the data twice, duplicating each line as it is entered. If the two lines are identical, they can be accepted as accurate. If there are any differences, the error can easily be detected and corrected. By including ampersands periodically throughout the data, numbers that have been added or left out by human error can be more easily spotted and corrected.

Statistical Error   The statistical error, or chance sampling error, describes the odds that the findings will fail to represent the population on the issues being measured, or the degree by which the sample is likely, according to probabilities, to fall short of accurately reflecting the characteristics of the population. Statistical error will always be present when a sample is taken. This error is not present if the entire population is measured in a "census"; it is strictly a function of sampling. Other terms frequently used to describe this error include standard error, standard error of the estimate, chance sampling error, sampling error, tolerated error, and bound on error, and there is no uniformity in the use of these terms. I prefer the term *chance sampling error* as the most descriptive.

The statistical error is frequently stated in two steps: (1) The chance sampling error describes the estimated percentage by which the sample falls short or representing the population sampled; .03 or 3% and .02 or 2% are often used. (2) The confidence level describes the degree of certainty that the estimated sampling error is accurate. This is sometimes called the confidence interval; confidence level is commonly stated in the same range of percentages as the chance sampling error but with the symbol < for "less than" or the symbol ± (also in percent) to indicate the range of confidence above and below the percentage of error. A typical report of these statistical errors would be a chance sampling error of .03, $p < .05$, which means you can trust that the 3% chance sampling error is wrong less than 95 times out of 100.

Newspaper reports of polls often state this statistical error as follows: "In theory, it can be said that in 95 cases out of 100, the results based on the entire sample differ by no more than 3 percentage points above or below what would have been obtained by interviewing all persons in the population."

This statistical error is based on probability theory and can be neither avoided nor eliminated. A sample will never be 100 % representative. There will always be a sampling error, however small it may be with increasingly larger samples.

Information Needs

A critical factor in deciding how to administer the questions is the nature of the information needed. To make sure of getting the information needed, it is important to start with a list of objectives when designing the questionnaire. The set of objectives will help to cover all the points necessary to get the needed information.

Once the list of objectives has been worked out, it can be used to design the questions. By using the objectives and combining or dividing them, a workable set of questions can be designed, consisting of "items" for the "instrument." The term *instrument* is frequently used interchangeably with *questionnaire*; some prefer instrument because the questionnaire may contain items that are not questions but rather statements with which respondents will agree or disagree. Rating or ranking procedures are also often phrased in statement form.

The questionnaire may be structured by outlining the topics, subjects, or other facets of the research problem in the order in which they should be addressed. The objectives list may mention two or three ideas that are related and should be presented as part of the same item or perhaps grouped together as related items. The topics covered in the instrument must be arranged in logical order so that the respondents will be able to follow the line of thought from one item to another. You should prepare the respondent for any abrupt shift of topics in the questionnaire with a transition that explains that you are moving from one topic to another.

Determine at this time what weighting is needed for the various topics, subtopics, or specific questions. Weighting can serve several purposes. It may be used to count certain cases more than once to compensate for not having enough persons representing a subgroup in the population to analyze opinions of that subgroup, or to give greater emphasis to certain topics in the questionnaire by using more items on that topic than on others.

Among other ways to weight in a survey questionnaire is to give certain answers more consideration than others. Responses to a single item may be given numerical values higher or lower than the simple numeric order of the item responses, and these values would have to be validated independently.[7] Another form of weighting involves selecting respondents by some quality important to your purposes and giving greater emphasis to the responses of the selected persons. A related method is to give a preference to certain types of respondents in the sample selection process in order to weight the responses of those types. SPSS and other analysis packages have weighting capabilities. SPSS selects cases at random to add to or delete from the sample to achieve desired proportions—for example, so that proportions of males and females in the sample can be made to match the population.

The researcher may need to get certain information from males 18 to 25 years of age about auto insurance. The experience of other surveyors indicates that males in this age group are difficult to find at home for interviewing. To make sure enough of these males are in the sample so that attitudes from this subgroup can be analyzed, the sample can be weighted to select a quota of young males. One technique for doing this is to ask for the youngest male age 18 or over.

QUESTIONNAIRE WORDING

Putting questions in just the right words is a continuing challenge to pollsters. The problem of wording is that the range of everyday life patterns supplies so wide a variety of meanings to words and phrases that what is understood may shift from one respondent to the next. The variation in semantic interpretation is greatest in surveys of the general public and somewhat less among smaller, more homogeneous publics. A checklist, based on Parten's list, can help avoid "wording" problems.[8] Such a checklist for wording questions is shown in Box 4.8.

Various writers in the field suggest other techniques for designing an effective questionnaire. One expert recommends that each item be followed by an open-ended or free-expression question to check whether the respondent understood the question, had an adequate frame of reference to answer it, and had sufficient knowledge to answer meaningfully.[9] The device can add precision to the process, but it does add costs to the survey and would be more important to some surveys than to others.

Above all, questions or items should be phrased in the natural conversational style of the respondent but should never use a patronizing manner, poor grammar, or any peculiar idiom of the respondents. The final test of a questionnaire's wording or phrasing is the pretest, in which typical respondents

BOX 4.8   A Checklist for Wording Questionnaires

Use simple familiar words, addressed as in conversation, to the respondent. Wording and phrasing may be of different levels of sophistication depending on the public polled. Surveys of children, or of public transportation users, for example, would require more care in wording and phrasing than would be required of college students or the peers of the questionnaire designer. Questions should be worded as if talking to a member of the population sampled.

Make items as short as possible, without sacrificing the conversational quality that gives the context for understanding the language used. Too much brevity can give the respondent too much latitude for interpreting the question; too many words in an item can get the respondent confused.

Structure each item to yield a single topic of information; each item should be designed to elicit the one precise bit of needed information. No item can do the double duty of asking more than one question. The use of conjunctions (and, but, or) in questions should be a warning of such flawed items. Items with "and" or "but" will mean that some respondents are answering what comes before the "and" and others answering what comes after. The result is that the data are useless.

Avoid multiple-meaning words. Some common words have a range of meaning that depends on the context in which they are used. "Strike" means different things in different contexts, whether the person is talking about baseball, bowling, labor relations, child abuse, theater scenery, or warfare. If you cannot avoid using multimeaning words, be sure to supply the correct context.

Avoid "tandem" items, which turn out to be two or more questions connected by a conjunction: and, but, or, etc. The presence of an "and" or "but" means you have two questions; decide which of the two to use, or whether to use both in separate items.

Avoid ambiguous words or phrases, that is, words or phrases that point in two or more directions. It is even possible to let ambiguity slip into phrasing without using an ambiguous word. Slang phrases should be especially suspect: "go down," "top it off," and "turn off" are three examples of the many ambiguous slang phrases.

Edit out leading questions that suggest a response or otherwise bias an answer. Examples of such items are: "Are you in favor of reducing crime?" "Do you favor gun control laws that would mean only criminals would have guns?" "How strongly do you support corporal punishment as a teacher's right?

(continues)

Prestigious names or words tend to bias responses. It is best to avoid incorporating associations with celebrities or status positions in questions: "Do you enjoy the president's favorite sport of horseback riding?" Such items would likely elicit biased responses from those who would identify either positively or negatively with the president and avoid entirely the intent of the item, to measure attitudes toward horseback riding.

Be careful with indirect questions. The question "How much should a person in a position such as yours give to charity?" may get around the problem of sensitivity to personal giving, but it would yield inaccurate and very subjective data about the patterns of individual contributions because it calls for a speculative answer. I used this item compared with actual giving patterns; people overestimate their United Way giving by about 15 percent.

Eliminate "pitfall" words that call for subjective judgment by the respondent, including words such as "reasonable," "medium," and "kinds," which are like using an elastic ruler because people differ so greatly in how they perceive the meaning of these terms. Similar to these terms are stereotype words, "green freshmen," "backwoods," "Madison Avenue." People respond to the subjective perceptions of these words rather than to the content of the question.

Avoid phrasing that "talks down" to the respondent. Questions that belittle the interviewee will bias answers. Examples of phrasing to avoid might include "simple factory worker," "soap opera fun," "underprivileged," and "nonworking mother."

Consider carefully before using the personal pronoun "you." Personalized items with "you" may lead respondents not to answer because they personally would not consider themselves included in the category posed by the question.

Allow for all possible answers. Closed-end questions, multiple choice items, should always have an "other" category to accommodate any answers that don't fit the list. Make sure the multiple choice list has all the possible responses by pretesting with members of the population, but also include an "other" category in case any options are missed.

Keep multiple choice options realistic. Don't use answer lists or check-off alternatives that leave the "right" answer obvious, or even suggest an answer.

Keep writing requirements to a minimum. Whether the questionnaire is to be completed by the respondent or the interviewer, written responses should be kept brief. Don't ask for information except what can be written with a few key words. Key words are easier to tabulate but may be difficult to interpret within the semantic meaning of the respondent.

Recognize limitations of type of interviews. Complicated questions require personal interviews; less complex ones can be mailed; the simplest ones can be used on the telephone.

Plan whether to include veracity checks. Confirmation of respondents' truthfulness can be built into the questions used. For example, after asking for whom the respondent voted in the last election, ask where the polling place is located. If the respondent doesn't know the location of the polling place, his or her answer may be discarded.

Don't ask about socially unacceptable behavior. Information collected about illegal activities can make the pollster legally liable. Unless a great deal of effort has gone into building rapport and trust, questions about immoral or unethical activities will not yield trustworthy data. Questions such as "Would you be more inclined to rob a bank or defraud the government?" is an example.

Avoid apparently unreasonable items. People will usually participate if there are logical reasons for asking the questions, but will grow impatient and cease to cooperate if the questions don't make sense or seem patently self-serving.

Arrange like-topic items together. Keep questions on the same subject together in the questionnaire. Exceptions may be veracity-check questions that test consistency; these rephrase items asked earlier to see if the person gives the same answer.

Remember that context influences item response. The proximity of one question to another can influence response to the later question.

Use general items before specific. When two items on the same topic are used, place the more general one first. Introduce successive topics by using a general question and then specific ones.

Beginning questions should be easy to answer. First questions in a questionnaire should be "icebreaker" types—nonthreatening, easy to answer, and designed to provoke interest in continuing with the rest of the questions.

Place sensitive or embarrassing items at the end. Questions about income, charitable giving, and other matters that people may be reluctant to divulge should come at the end of the questionnaire, so that the earlier part of the survey information is collected even if the sensitive information prompts the respondent to end the interview.

are asked the questions and are encouraged to voice any confusion or problems about understanding the items. Further insights can be generated by probing the pretest interviewees for their impressions or suggestions for improving the questionnaire. Interviewer sensitivity to answers in a pretest can spot potential problems, even if they come up only once in the pretest.

STRUCTURING THE QUESTIONNAIRE

The survey instrument, or questionnaire, should be carefully structured to fit the various topical segments into a smooth-flowing and integrated whole. A smooth-flowing questionnaire leads the respondent from one topic to the next in a logical or psychological order or, if no such connection between segments is possible, provides a transition that helps the respondent shift his or her thinking to the new topic.

The introductory statement is perhaps the most critical part of the whole instrument. The introductory statement should accomplish six objectives: (1) identify the caller and sponsor; (2) establish credibility and legitimacy for the interview; (3) identify and gain access to the person required for the interview; (4) assure confidentiality; (5) win tacit cooperation without actually asking respondents to "answer our questions," which offers the chance to refuse; all in order to be able to (6) ask the first question.

Respondents who do not have the time to respond will let the interviewer know; a request for an appointment "when it would be convenient" should be made when a respondent refuses. Some people will, of course, refuse to be interviewed at all, but these refusals can be kept to a minimum with careful preparation and a sensitive approach to each respondent.

An ideal introduction will point out that the respondent was specially selected and will create an interest in the subject matter of the survey in order to motivate participation. All of these elements should be achieved by the introductory statement, which should be adapted to the type of interviewing and should be as brief as possible.

The questionnaire itself should adapt the type of information needed to the type of question or item category. Such categories include the *factual or qualifying item,* which qualifies the respondent to answer certain other items, such as "Does the respondent recognize the _____ product?" or "Does the respondent live in _____ neighborhood?" *Behavior items* measure what people have actually done or do regularly. The most common item category is the *opinion item,* which is defined as "expressed behavioral inclination," or what the respondent says he or she is likely to do. *Attitude items* measure attitude, defined narrowly as "behavioral inclination," which means determining what people are likely to do without making them aware that they are giving the information. *Unobtrusive items,* such as the semantic differential and the forced choice, are two ways of measuring attitude. *Demographic items* record information that characterizes the respondents by age, sex, education, occupation, income, and the like.

The format of questions ranges across three classes: (1) open ended, free story, and essay, all of which call for the respondent to answer in his or her own words; (2) closed ended, checklist, recognition, preference, and multiple choice formats, which offer the respondent options from which to choose; and (3) rating, ranking, and recognition, all variations of the checklist or multiple choice format, which call for a judgment on each option.

Open-ended items also may be formatted as closed-ended items if the responses are in respondent's own words and the nearest listed answer category is checked. Bipolar questions, such as the Likert and semantic differential, give a choice between two options with a scale offering degrees of intensity between them. The eight types of questions that follow may be altered or combined to suit the needs of the researcher.

Filter or Qualifying Questions

These filter out those not qualified to answer, attempt to fit respondents into behavior categories important to the survey, or seek facts that may be important to classify respondents. These are ordinarily nonthreatening, easy-to-answer questions and appropriate to use at the beginning. Examples are: How many years have you lived in _____ city? Do you happen to recognize the name _____ (of product or company)? A similar type of question, a screening question, can be used to select certain respondents by asking for special information. Many researchers make a distinction between these factual/qualifying or "information" items and demographic items: qualifying items are usually screening, strata classification, or categorization items, whereas demographic items classify respondents by population characteristics such as geographic distribution and vital statistics.

To avoid research bias—imposing the researcher's values, perceptions, or language on the respondent in the way the questions are constructed—Patricia Labaw suggest asking questions in the context of two factors. Filter items should determine whether the respondent is "conscious" of certain information, that is, able to respond to the topic, to "arrange events and ideas together into new orders *within his head,*" whether such ordering has occurred in reality or not. This can be done by "filtering questions" that idetifying whether the issue or question is salient for the respondent's "structure," that is, "the operating environment of the individual, those factors which impinge on his ability to move or function in specific ways within this world."[10]

The factors that determine the operating environment include age, sex, health, race, reading level, mental skills, knowledge level, and physical, economic, climatic, and social boundaries. Labaw suggests doing more than collecting detailed demographic information. She suggests using this "conscious" and "structural" information to interpret each topic, or even each question, by incorporating appropriate filter questions with each topic. These filter questions establish whether the respondent is able to think consciously about the topic and has adequate knowledge to make informed responses.

Opinion Items

These are often not questions but statements with which the respondent indicates agreement or disagreement. Opinion items identify preferences, tendencies, and inclinations expressed by the respondent. That is, the respondent can state a preference, assuming he or she has the qualification—the knowledge or experience to support an opinion. Opinion items usually attempt to measure *intensity* of the inclination by using the Likert-type scale, offering a choice ranging from strongly agree to strongly disagree, approve or disapprove, or any similar bipolar concept on a three, five, seven, or nine point scale.

Neutral may indicate that the respondent is either undecided between the options or doesn't know. It is usually difficult to make a distinction between undecided and don't know consistently because neither respondents nor interviewers may be able to do so. To be sure you are distinguishing "neutral" and the categories of "don't know," "doesn't apply," and "no response" is not an easy task, but using a neutral point in the middle of the scale and another choice at one end of the scale for the other categories is probably the best technique.

Opinion items can also be asked as open-ended questions, but the answers are more difficult to tabulate. Actually, some authorities recommend two or more stages of questionnaire design in which a first-stage free response item identifies the full range of possible answers and a second stage uses the identified categories as options in a closed-ended item. The initial stage, using a small sample, establishes the categories, and the second stage, using a large sample, tabulates the numbers in each category. This can be done by using multiple choice items with an "other" category during the pretest and examining the "other" responses to expand the list of options. Of course, the final questionnaire still needs to have an "other" category in case the pretest failed to identify a category. If there are too many responses in the "other" category in the final survey, the questionnaire designer obviously failed to offer the full range of options.

Attitude Items

These are often similar to opinion items in format. They also may use scaled intensity measures—measures of preference, tendency, and inclination—but attempt to measure unconscious, subconscious, or unexpressed inclinations. Consequently, most true attitude items are indirect measurements. If the person *expresses* an inclination, the expression is an opinion; the attitude behind it is usually more complex. Some writers on the subject make little distinction between attitude and opinion, but careful students or human behavior see an important difference. Attitudes are probably more enduring than opinions and often are not consistent with other attitudes or opinions or even with behavior. Attitudes are, therefore, measured by indirect means, because they are much more difficult to discern and require questions more difficult to design.

One form of attitude question commonly used in national surveys on economic conditions is phrased: "Is this a good or bad time for people to purchase major household items?" Fabian Linden examined responses to this question and others over time and provided a validity check by comparing responses with real changes in the economy. The results indicate that an opinion question such as this one can indeed measure the underlying attitude about the condition of the economy.[11]

Another way to get at attitudes is the forced choice question, which offers two alternate answers equally higher and lower than the true answer. For example, if the rate of inflation for the preceding month was 8% the attitude of respondents toward whether inflation is getting better or worse can be determined by asking: "Can you tell me the rate of inflation for the past month? Was it (a) 7% or (b) 9%?" The question must be carefully structured based on a factual circumstance related to the attitude being measured. In planning the price of a new product, respondents could be asked whether the price was fair by asking alternate respondents to evaluate a price above and a price below the projected price.

A standard attitude question is the semantic differential, which measures attitude toward a single concept by responses on a seven-point scale usually to ten paired semantic terms. The procedure is described by Charles Osgood, George Suci, and Percy Tannenbaum.[12] Subjects respond to a "concept" by marking each bipolar scale on a seven-point continuum. The revealed attitudes have three primary dimensions, "factors" that are described as "evaluative, potency, and activity." The procedure can be used only in face-to-face or mail surveys with respondent-completed forms; telephone interviews cannot effectively use the semantic differential.

The factors discerned in attitudes toward a given concept, as determined by a statistical procedure called factor analysis, are described by the authors as follows: "A pervasive *evaluative factor* in human judgment regularly appears first and accounts for approximately half to three-quarters of the extractable variance . . . based . . . on the bedrock of rewards and punishments both achieved and anticipated." One might ask about a concept, "Is it good or is it bad?" "The second dimension of semantic space to appear is usually the *potency factor*, and this typically accounts for approximately half as much variance as the first factor—this is concerned with power and the things associated with it, size, weight, toughness, and the like. The third dimension, usually about equal to or a little smaller in magnitude than the second, is the *activity factor* which is concerned with quickness, excitement, warmth, agitation and the like."[13]

Scales, each with ten paired semantic terms, used in the semantic differential must be constructed for each concept being tested. The procedure is described in the book by Osgood et al, *The Measurement of Meaning*, along with the technique for validating the semantic terms used. Semantic paired-word scales used by the authors in a study of communication effects were, for the evaluative factor, "good-bad, valuable-worthless, fair-unfair, and pleasant-unpleasant; for the potency factor: weak-strong, heavy-light, and large-small; for the activity factor: active-passive, fast-slow, and calm-agitated."[14] The authors recommend reversing polarity of the terms alternately throughout the list of paired words. A semantic differential instrument on communication effects "concepts" would look like the example in Box. 4.9.

BOX 4.9   Example of Semantic Differential Form

Concept _____

Good	☐	☐	☐	☐	☐	☐	☐	Bad
Worthless	☐	☐	☐	☐	☐	☐	☐	Valuable
Fair	☐	☐	☐	☐	☐	☐	☐	Unfair
Unpleasant	☐	☐	☐	☐	☐	☐	☐	Pleasant
Strong	☐	☐	☐	☐	☐	☐	☐	Weak
Light	☐	☐	☐	☐	☐	☐	☐	Heavy
Large	☐	☐	☐	☐	☐	☐	☐	Small
Passive	☐	☐	☐	☐	☐	☐	☐	Active
Fast	☐	☐	☐	☐	☐	☐	☐	Slow
Calm	☐	☐	☐	☐	☐	☐	☐	Agitated

This example of the semantic differential form is administered in face-to-face interviews to test attitudes toward a concept such as a product, issue, or organization. Subjects place an X in one of the boxes between each semantic pair of terms. Scores may be calculated by assigning numbers 1–7 from the low end to the high end of each set of terms, or simply by drawing a line from top to bottom connecting the marks. Note the polarity of terms is reversed periodically.

Evaluation of the semantic differential is basically a comparison of distance between the "profile" of responses from one concept to another or from one respondent to another, or between groups of people. The profile can be determined by drawing a line from response to response down the scale list; the authors describe a statistical formula for doing the same thing based on plane geometry.

Behavior Questions

Behavior questions may also be used to infer attitudes by identifying actual behavior. For example, attitudes toward new innovative products can be in-

Figure 4.2 Survey and polling research both gather information on opinions and likely behavior by asking individuals selected to represent target publics. To assure consistent data is collected from all responded the questionnaire must be carefully designed and uniformly administered.

ferred from reports of comparable new products purchased by respondents. Other behavior patterns can also be identified: reasons for buying, where one prefers to buy, price, color, package size preference, and so forth. Further behavior information can be collected from present or past behavior. Life-style profiles of the buying public have been developed by the Newspaper Advertising Bureau, based on factual behavior-type questions. When research is used for public relations planning, an important behavior characteristic includes the media use patterns or other sources of information of the public being measured.

Self-Perception Questions

These questions are akin to other attitude items. One might want to know, for example, the potential for leadership among members in a trade association. Potential leaders might be asked a question such as the following:

Are you the type of person who (indicate a number between 1 for "goes the extra mile" up to 5 for "never lets people push you around"):

Goes the extra mile   1   2   3   4   5   Never lets people push you around

The paired concepts must be designed to avoid an obvious positive-negative polarity. Concepts should offer pairs of equally positive values.

Answers to self-perception items can help to distinguish people who would fit the desired personality type for a particular leadership role. The self-perception question can also be used for some other purposes: to identify market segments, to establish characteristics of a public, or to match publics with potential public relations activities.

Open-Ended Questions

Open-ended questions are of three types; one poses a very general question and records the two or three points each respondent makes. By using a predetermined checklist of answers, and without reciting the list, an open-ended item may be used as a closed-ended item, with the interviewer checking off the answers mentioned in the free response. Another valuable open-ended type of item is a follow-up to another attitude or opinion item that asks "Why do you say that?" Such responses identify the range of motivation or perceptions that underlay the preceding question and can also confirm whether the respondent was qualified to answer.

Closed-Ended Questions

Closed-ended questions simply offer the respondent a list of multiple choice options from which one or more may be chosen as they are read. A useful modification is inclusion of the "other" category to accommodate any choices not anticipated when designing the question. The closed-ended question may also be modified to make a ranking or rating question. Ranking items ask the respondent to place the response categories in order of preference, importance, frequency, or the like. Rating items differ by offering three or five rating numbers to be used in responding to each alternative; rating items are preferable to ranking items when the list of characteristics calling for response is so long that people may have difficulty sorting out the order.

When a closed-ended question offers more than one possible answer, the item becomes a series of yes-no items. As with yes-no items generally, it is desirable to collect more than either the yes or no by adding categories for "doesn't apply" or "don't know." The rating system, of course, solves the problem by collecting a range of responses on each option from very unimportant to very important, see the questionnaire example in Box 4.10.

Demographic Questions

These concern age, sex, income level, race, religion, education, occupation, housing tenure, marital status, memberships, and other population characteristics. They are useful for later comparison with other items to see if attitudes or opinions are peculiar to certain segments of an audience, if males and females differ on an opinion, or if education would account for differences in attitudes on an issue.

By comparing demographic variables associated with certain opinion or attitude responses, the research can determine the descriptive characteristics of people who hold the range of opinions. Other measures of association can also

BOX 4.10   Example of Questionnaire Survey of Infirmary Users

INTERVIEWER NAME _____   CASE # __ __ __ &
                                                            1   2   3   4

CALL BACKS 0 1 2 3 4 __   TELEPHONE NUMBER __ __ __ - __ __ __ __   &
                      5   6 7 8   9 10 11 12   13
                                 (for verification use only)

INTERVIEWER INSTRUCTIONS
• Boxed statements are interviewer instructions; do not read aloud.
• If there is no response or if the response given does not apply, then leave code space blank.
• Do not rephrase questions or comment on respondent's answer.

INTRODUCTION:
A. "Hello, I'm _____ , and I'm a student at the University of Florida College of Journalism and Communications We're conducting an opinion survey of UF students in Gainesville about health services."
B. "May I speak with a person at this number who is a student at the University of Florida?"

• If there is no person associated with UF—thank that person for the time and terminate interview.
• If target person is not at home or says that he will cooperate but not at this time. . . Find out when to call back. **TIME** _____.
• Repeat A if other than target person answered, continue with C and D. If not, skip to D.

C. "I understand you are a student at the University of Florida."
D. "Your phone number was drawn at random and your answers cannot be connected with you in any way and will be kept completely confidential. CAN YOU HELP?"
  1. Are you associated in any way with UF Student Health Services? If yes, discontinue interview and select another respondent.
  2. What is your present class status?

Do not read list; Enter code number from list of majors
EXAMPLES: 4 J M = 4 2 3; 3 L S = 3 2 7

__ __ __
14 15 16

---

3. When you are not attending the university, do you live. . .

• Read list

---

1. On campus   4. In Florida
2. In Gainesville   5. Out of state
3. In Alachua County   6. Out of Country   __
                                                            17

4. How many credits are you taking?

• Do not read list

---

1. 5 or under   4. 10–13
2. 6–9   5. 14 or more   __   &
                                                        18   19

5. Please rate the following in how you would choose ANY MEDICAL FACILITY. Tell me 1 for not important and 5 for very important.

• Code the rating number given (1 to 5)

___ 20 Convenient   ___ 25 Close to home
___ 21 Pharmacy facilities   ___ 26 Attractive facilities
___ 22 Waiting time for service ___ 27 Recommendation of friends
___ 23 Competence of staff   ___ 28 Privacy
___ 24 Congeniality of staff   ___ 29 Other (explain) _____   &
                                                                               30

6. What, if any, service providers have you sought out for medical care in the last year?

• Read list. Code 0=No, 1=Yes, 2=Not applicable

___ 31 Immediate/urgent care center   ___ 36 Private clinic
___ 32 Personal physician   ___ 37 Women's health clinic
___ 33 Public health service   ___ 38 UF infirmary
___ 34 Hospital   ___ 39 Other (explain) _____   &
___ 35 Emergency service   40

(continues)

7. How have you formed your opinion of Student Health Services? (i.e., the UF Infirmary)

> • Read list. Code 0=No, 1=Yes

___ 41 Personal experience   ___ 45 Information calendar
___ 42 Friend or associate   ___ 46 Other (explain) _____
___ 43 Alligator (student newspaper)   ___ 47 No opinion
___ 44 Brochures

8. How many times did you visit the Student Health Services facility on campus last year?

> • Do not read list. Circle one

0   1   2   3   4   5   6   7   8 or more   ___   &
                                                                  48   49

9. How far from the infirmary do you live? Please give your answer in minutes, either walking, driving, or by bus.

> • Do not read list.

1. 5 minute walk   5. 5+ minute drive
2. 5+ minute walk   6. 10+ minute drive
3. 10+ minute walk   7. 15+ minute drive
4. 15+ minute walk   8. By bus   ___
                                                                  50

10. I am going to read you a list of things related to Student Health Services. Based on your own experiences, please rate the quality of each item. Tell me 1 for poor to 5 for excellent, or tell me if it doesn't apply.

> • Read list. Code 0 for don't know or doesn't apply. Circle one

	POOR				EX	DK	
Infirmary building	1	2	3	4	5	0	___ 51
Easy to get to	1	2	3	4	5	0	___ 52
Appointment process	1	2	3	4	5	0	___ 53
Brochure information	1	2	3	4	5	0	___ 54
Check-in procedures	1	2	3	4	5	0	___ 55
Appointment procedures	1	2	3	4	5	0	___ 56
Billing	1	2	3	4	5	0	___ 57
Privacy	1	2	3	4	5	0	___ 58

&
59

11. I am going to read you a list of SERVICES that the Student Health Service provides. Please rate them using the same scale. Or tell me if you have never used the service. Rate 1 for poor to 5 for excellent.

> • Read list. Code 1 to 5 or 0=Don't know; doesn't apply

	POOR				EX	DK	
Physician appointments	1	2	3	4	5	0	___ 60
Trauma clinic	1	2	3	4	5	0	___ 61
Wart clinic	1	2	3	4	5	0	___ 62
Cold self-care clinic	1	2	3	4	5	0	___ 63
Blood pressure clinic	1	2	3	4	5	0	___ 64
Allergy injection clinic	1	2	3	4	5	0	___ 65
Cast clinic (i.e., for broken bones)	1	2	3	4	5	0	___ 66
Dermatology clinic	1	2	3	4	5	0	___ 67
Orthopedic clinic	1	2	3	4	5	0	___ 68
Women's clinic	1	2	3	4	5	0	___ 69
Urinary tract infection clinic	1	2	3	4	5	0	___ 70
Diagnostic (i.e., examination)	1	2	3	4	5	0	___ 71
Immunization clinic	1	2	3	4	5	0	___ 72
Mental health clinic	1	2	3	4	5	0	___ 73
Health education	1	2	3	4	5	0	___ 74
Sexual assault recovery service	1	2	3	4	5	0	___ 75
Observation unit	1	2	3	4	5	0	___ 76

&   &   &   &
77 78 79 80

CARD #2   CASE NUMBER ___ ___ ___ &
                        1   2   3   4

12. Student Health Services provides services besides medical treatment. I'm going to read a list of other services. Please rate the services with the same scale 1 for poor to 5 for excellent. If you have never used a service, please tell me it doesn't apply.

> • Read list. Code 1 to 5 or 0=Don't know; doesn't apply

	POOR			EX	DK	
Information service	1 2 3 4 5	0	___ 5
Medical records (of immunizations)	1 2 3 4 5	0	___ 6
Lab	1 2 3 4 5	0	___ 7
Pharmacy	1 2 3 4 5	0	___ 8
X-ray	1 2 3 4 5	0	___ 9
Business office	1 2 3 4 5	0	___ 10
Insurance office	1 2 3 4 5	0	___ 11

&
—
12

I am going to read some statements regarding Student Health Services. Please tell me whether you AGREE, DISAGREE, or have NO OPINION. Or tell me whether you feel STRONGLY either way.

> • Don't know=0

13. I think the Student Health Services facility is an attractive place.

> • Circle one

SA A N D SD DK
5   4 3 2 1   0 ___ 13

14. The waiting room is comfortable.

> • Circle one

SA A N D SD DK
5   4 3 2 1   0 ___ 14

15. The Student Health Service compares well with other professional health care facilities.

> • Circle one

SA A N D SD DK
5   4 3 2 1   0 ___ 15

16. The Student Health Service presents a professional atmosphere.

> • Circle one

SA A N D SD DK
5   4 3 2 1   0 ___ 16

17. The check-in desk is well managed.

> • Circle one

SA A N D SD DK
5   4 3 2 1   0 ___ 17

18. The medical staff at the infirmary is well qualified.

> • Circle one

SA A N D SD DK
5   4 3 2 1   0 ___ 18

19. I trust decisions made by all medical practitioners at the infirmary.

> • Circle one

SA A N D SD DK
5   4 3 2 1   0 ___ 19

20. The people at the check-in desk are always courteous.

> • Circle one

SA A N D SD DK
5   4 3 2 1   0 ___ 20

21. On the whole, the medical personnel have a cordial and professional manner.

> • Circle one

SA A N D SD DK
5   4 3 2 1   0 ___ 21

22. The records at the infirmary are always confidential.

> • Circle one

SA A N D SD DK
5   4 3 2 1   0 ___ 22

23. Weekdays 8 to 4:30 and Saturdays 8 to noon are convenient infirmary hours.

> • Circle one

SA A N D SD DK
5   4 3 2 1   0 ___ 23

24. I know—or could easily find out—how to get Student Health Services care after hours.

> • Circle one

SA A N D SD DK
5   4 3 2 1   0 ___ 24

25. I would be willing to tell a friend that I visited the mental health clinic.

> • Circle one

SA A N D SD DK
5   4 3 2 1   0 ___ 25

26. On your last visit were you seen by:

> • Check first; enter name later; 0=No; 1=Yes

CHECK   NAME
( ) Physician   _____ ___ 26
( ) Physician assistant   _____ ___ 27
( ) Nurse practitioner   _____ ___ 28
( ) Registered nurse   _____ ___ 29
( ) Resident physician   _____ ___ 30
( ) Other   _____ ___ 31

&
—
32

(*continues*)

27. How would you rate that person's competence, using the same scale as before, 1 for poor to 5 for excellent. Can you tell me the person's name? (Enter name above)

‾‾
33

28. For what reasons would you NOT go to the infirmary for health care?

> • Do not read list. 0=No; 1=Yes

There are no reasons to keep you away   ___ 34
It's hard to get to   ___ 35
Poor opinion of medical personnel   ___ 36
Long lines/waiting time   ___ 37
Better services are provided elsewhere   ___ 38
Poor experience with Student Health Services   ___ 39
Unsanitary   ___ 40
Uncomfortable waiting room   ___ 41
Not when I need specialist   ___ 42
Not for life/death situation   ___ 43
Have a personal physician elsewhere   ___ 44
Other (explain) _____   ___ 45

&
46

29. Could you explain to me how Student Health Services are funded?

> • Do not read list

1. Fee for Service—pay for service as it is used
2. Health Care Fee—calculated into tuition cost
3. Both Health Care Fee and Fee for Service
4. Other method given
5. Can't say (doesn't know)

‾‾
47

30. The current health fee for students is $3.33 per credit hour or around $40 for the average student with a 15-hour credit load. What would be the MAXIMUM fee increase per credit hour you would TOLERATE in order to build a new facility?

> • Do not read

1. No increase   4. Up to $1.50
2. Up to $0.50   5. Other _____
3. Up to $1.00

‾‾
48

31. What is the average time in minutes you feel walk-in patients would be willing to wait for service?

> • Do not read list

1. None, service immediately   5. 21–45 minutes
2. 1–5 minutes   6. Over 45 minutes
3. 6–10 minutes   7. Don't know
4. 11–20 minutes

‾‾
49

32. I am going to read a list of statements concerning possible changes in student health services. Please tell me if you oppose or support, are neutral, or if you feel strongly either way.

> • Read list. 0=Don't know

	OPP	N	SUP		
a. Longer daytime hours	1 2	3	4 5	0	___ 51
b. Eliminate after-hours treatment	1 2	3	4 5	0	___ 52
c. Expanded building/facility	1 2	3	4 5	0	___ 53
d. Fee increase for better facility	1 2	3	4 5	0	___ 54
e. Contract with Shands for after-hours treatment	1 2	3	4 5	0	___ 55
f. Refurbishing existing facility	1 2	3	4 5	0	___ 56
g. Credit hours for participating in the peer counseling groups	1 2	3	4 5	0	___ 57

&
50

33. Now, for statistical purposes, are you male or female?

> • Male=1; Female=2

‾‾
58

34. What is your age?

> • Enter age in years

‾‾ ‾‾
59 60

35. What is your race?

White   Black   Asian   Hispanic   or other
‾‾   ‾‾   ‾‾   ‾‾   ‾‾
1   2   3   4   5

‾‾
61

36. While you are attending the University of Florida, who pays for more than half of all your expenses? (includes tuition, board...)

> • Read list

1. Self
2. Parent or guardian

3. Financial aid (scholarship, loans, etc.)
4. Other (explain) ────────────────

‾‾‾
62

37. How much of your current expenses are covered by financial aid?

> • Read list

None　　Up to 25%　　Up to 50%　　Up to 75%　　Up to 100%

‾‾　　‾‾　　‾‾　　‾‾　　‾‾
1　　　　2　　　　3　　　　4　　　　5

‾‾
63

38. What kind of health insurance do you have?

> • Read list

1. Parent's policy
2. Student insurance
3. Own policy

4. No policy
5. Other (explain) ────────────────
6. Don't know

‾‾
64

39. Of the following categories, please estimate your yearly family income from all sources?

> • Read list

1. Under $5,000
2. $5,000 – $7,000
3. $7,000 – $10,000
4. $10,000 – $15,000

5. $15,000 – $25,000
6. $25,000 – $50,000
7. $50,000+
8. Don't know

‾‾
65

40. We're conducting this survey for Student Health Services. Do you have any suggestions or comments to improve the service?

> • Write answer on colored sheet.
> • Thank the respondent for his or her time and cooperation.

be used for a wide array of statistical analyses, such as correlation, multiple regression, canonical correlation, factor analysis, and loglinear analysis, all of which can be adapted to analyze survey data. These methods of analysis can identify significant details that might otherwise be overlooked.

Cross-tabulation is the most common method of survey data analysis and usually uses demographics. This technique, which can be executed by a computer, compares the answers to two questions, usually a demographic variable and a significant behavior, opinion, or attitude question. For example, if a large number of the sample expressed dissatisfaction with the employee newsletter, a cross-tabulation analysis would tell you the proportions who were male or female, which age category, what type of employee, and the like.

A technique related to demographic analysis is the measurement of "psychographic" and "life-style" characteristics. Psychographics describes people as they characterize themselves; life-style analysis describes how people actually live. The technique uses many of the previously mentioned question types to identify psychological types within a population or to categorize a population by preferred behavior patterns. Results may be helpful in segmenting publics as well as in offering guidance in selecting persuasive techniques. Advertising and marketing have long used the technique. The *Journal of Marketing* and the *Journal of Advertising Research,* among others, publish descriptions and applications of the method.

QUESTIONNAIRE PRETESTING

After the questionnaire has been drafted, it must be tested by asking individuals of the same type as and from the same population as those who will be polled to respond to the questions. These test respondents should be selected so that they will not be in the actual poll.

Questionnaire testing involves administering copies of the drafted version to several test respondents in order to identify problems in the individual items or questions and to see how the whole instrument "flows." If several interviewers do the pretest, the suggestions each one identifies must be incorporated in the final draft version. When the pretest of the questionnaire is completed it should be as nearly free of ambiguities, confused phrasing, abrupt shifts of topics, and other problems as possible.

QUESTIONNAIRE CODING

The coding system translates each response into a number. Each response is represented by a range of numbered options, each standing for an alternative response to a question—for example, 1 = strongly disagree, 2 = disagree, 3 = neutral, 4 = agree, 5 = strongly agree—so that each response can be identified and tabulated. Because IBM cards originally contained 80 columns and computer terminal screens now accommodate 80 columns, it is convenient to number the coding to 80 and then start over with "card 2" if more than 80 columns are needed. Each card must be identified with the case number, usually the first three digits, which identifies the interview, perhaps the interviewer, and the card number. This is necessary because the cards can get mixed up even on the terminal. The case numbers are also important in the verification process so that problem cases can be identified.

Every possible answer to each question must be assigned a number. Some responses that may occur in more than one item—no response, don't know, doesn't apply—can be assigned arbitrary numbers to be used throughout the questionnaire. This simplifies the computer programming task and provides a degree of consistency that helps in reading and understanding the resulting printout.

If more than ten possible answers can be selected for any item, two columns should be provided for answers to that item. Some items (e.g., zip code) will require three or more digits for a response, and the coding system must provide a column for each digit required for an answer. However, SPSS can accommodate only three digits per variable; if the entire zip code is needed it must be broken into two or more variables. For simple yes-no items, the preferable form is 0 = no, 1 = yes, 2 = don't know. This form avoids confusion for both the respondent and the interviewer; it also simplifies computer tabulation when the "no" answers don't have to be recoded to zero later.

TRAINING INTERVIEWERS

Both the skills needed for interviewing and the specific demands of the questionnaire being used require that interviewers be trained. Interviewers will vary in their interpersonal skills and their ability to conduct successful interviews.

Interviewers may be recruited in a variety of ways. In college classes studying survey research, each student may be assigned a quota of interviews. No better way exists for learning interviewing skills than to conduct a number of interviews under the direction of an instructor and later discuss with classmates the various problems encountered and the possible ways of dealing with them. Those who may in the future teach others the skills of interviewing need to experience the process firsthand.

Many companies or other organizations may offer incentives to regular employees to interview, either on company time or by other arrangements. Temporary help may be hired and trained for specific interviews. Most polling organizations employ part-time interviewers because the interviewing is done only sporadically, as various research projects are ready to conduct interviews at different times. College classes studying research methods also may provide trained interviewers, who may be recruited by pollsters needing temporary help.

Ideally, interviewers should be as nearly like the interviewees as possible: young interviewing young, black interviewing black, senior citizen interviewing senior citizen. This match of interviewer and interviewee is seldom practical, however. As a compromise, most pollsters employ middle-aged women, who are less threatening to most interviewees than male interviewers or those of other age groups.

General interviewing skills should be reviewed with people recruited to interview whether they are experienced interviewers or not. Role playing is specifically beneficial to cover the basics of the steps and fix them in the trainee's mind. An outline of the basics of interviewing techniques can be used during training sessions, and the interviewer can keep it for later reference when doing the actual interviews.

Participants in the interviewer training sessions should be provided with a packet of materials including (1) a copy of the questionnaire to be used in each interview, (2) guidelines for interviewers, (3) checklist for interviewers, (4) respondent identification and selection procedure, (5) special instruments for conducting the specific series of interviews, and (6) interviewer identification (for door-to-door work) and any other procedures being used in the specific interviews.

PREPARING INTERVIEWER PACKETS

Packets should be prepared for each interviewer, including everything needed to conduct interviews and to prepare the interviewer to "field the survey." A checklist of packet materials will help avoid overlooking necessary items. Packets will vary, but the following interviewer packet checklist can be adapted for a wide range of survey projects.

Packet envelope with interviewer identification (name and identification number). Envelopes must be large enough, 10×14 inches, to accommodate all materials and to prevent loss of items in the frequent handling they will get. Each interviewer must be identified by a number that can be used on the data cards to keep track of his or her work. A master list of names and identification numbers becomes the index for identifying interviewers in case errors must be corrected or other problems arise.

Copies of the questionnaire, either the correct number of instruments for completing the assigned interviews or a single copy of the questionnaire with a packet of response sheets. Costs can be kept down by using a single copy of the questionnaire together with a response form designed for the specific questionnaire. The response form must provide a space, either a blank or a set of parentheses, to record the number for the answer to each question. Note that each question must be briefly identified by a number corresponding to the question number and by column (coding) number. The form should be structured to reduce the chance of data-recording errors. Both questionnaire and response form should provide room for marginal notations and comments; interviewers should be encouraged to be faithful in writing marginal comments.

Interviewee selection procedure gives interviewers directions for selecting individual respondents and will vary with each survey project. With random digit dialing sampling, a table of random numbers must also be included in the packet with instructions for selecting the final digits from the table. When respondents are selected from a list, as in the simple random method, a segment of the list will need to be provided in the packet. Such a list can be made from a directory by photocopying segments of the list and marking individual assignments with a felt pen. The list should provide the information the interviewer will need to locate the proper respondent. The phone number, address, and name will be necessary, depending on the system being used.

When door-to-door interviews are being conducted, detailed instructions for locating the address will be necessary. A large map of the area can be used to locate addresses in relatively compact geographic sectors. Interviewers can then be assigned addresses in localized sectors. Photocopied segments of each sector of the map can be especially helpful to interviewers.

For other methods, a set of instructions that can be followed without much concentration is essential; interviewers will have to cope with a range of distractions while trying to locate respondents. When the multistage random sampling method is used, instructions for selection at the final stage must be provided. One such method is shown in Box 4.11.

BOX 4.11   Random Respondent Selection Procedure: For Final Stage of Multistage Random Sampling

Select respondent by first letter of respondent's first name, beginning with first interview and advancing to second block for the second, third, etc. Proceed through successive blocks at each interview until you locate a person whose name begins with a letter given.

Begin by asking: "I need to talk to the person whose first name begins with the letter A, B, C, D, or E;" if more than one person's name fits the same block, select by alphabetic method for the second letter of the name, etc. If a selection is not yet made, read five letters in succeeding blocks until a person is located whose name fits, and select that person, if otherwise qualified to respond.

Blocks:

1. A   B   C   D   E
2. F   G   H   I   J
3. K   L   M   N   O
4. P   Q   R   S   T
5. U   V   W   X   Y   Z

The purpose is to select respondents by chance alone.

Open-ended response sheets may be devised to collect "comments" or "suggestions" separately from the other items on the questionnaires in order to separate them easily and thus speed the process of typing and analysis of open-ended responses. These comment sheets can be of a different color than the questionnaire and other materials in the packet so that they can easily be separated out when the packets are returned.

Interview log form—a device for tracking each interviewer—keeps a record of "what happened" during each interview and serves several purposes. A log or record of interviews can help spot problems in the survey design that may emerge only during the interviewing; for example, when a long list of phone numbers from a certain exchange is not completed, one may suspect that the exchange is a small one with a limited range of numbers. This would call for a shift in the survey design, probably while the survey is under way. Interviewers should be instructed to call the survey director in case of such problems.

Data entry instructions, directions for putting results into the computer for late analysis. Interviewers or other employee(s) will need to transfer the coded numbers from the questionnaires into a computerized storage system, such as a personal computer disk, for later analysis. Instructions should include basic operating procedure for the computer system to be used.

Interviewer instructions: A summary of how to conduct interviews should be included for easy reference for interviewers. A list of "do's and don'ts" for interviewers may be based on general guidelines, such as those outlined in Backstrom and Hursh's *Survey Research*,[15] but may need to be adapted to particular situations.

Other inclusions: The specific needs of each survey design mean that the packet checklist will differ. Other items might include respondent cards, for use with detailed questions in face-to-face interviews, or special telephone instructions concerning time zones and area codes for multistate calls.

CONDUCTING THE INTERVIEWS

Directions for conducting the interviews should include dates and the times of day when interviewees will most likely be available. Dates should be limited to make sure that social or physical conditions in the general environment experienced by respondents will not have changed in such a way as to influence responses. Major news events, even those not apparently related to the survey, extreme weather conditions, and the like may influence responses and should be carefully monitored; a limited time frame for conducting the interviews is an important guard against the chance of such influences being present.

Time of day during which interviews are conducted is important, particularly if certain demographic categories are important to the sample. Working men and women are less often at home during daytime hours than during evenings. School-age children are at home in late afternoon and evenings. With some people it will be necessary to make an appointment for interviews.

DEBRIEFING INTERVIEWERS

When interviews are completed, a debriefing session can pinpoint unanticipated problems with the survey design or with the execution procedures that may bias the results. In the sessions, the survey director should find out whether the designated respondents were contacted and try to identify any deviations from the intended procedure. It is important to be nonjudgmental in debriefings in order to encourage candid accounts of interviewer experiences and to avoid attempts to distort the facts. By identifying mistakes or problems encountered in carrying out the interviews, it may be possible to make adjustments when processing or analyzing the data to compensate for errors.

For example, I conducted a survey in which the design called for a larger than normal proportion of young males to be selected, because their opinion was important to the survey and because young males are a demographic segment often not at home for interviewing. Debriefing interviewers revealed that the system may have been too successful and that we had interviewed too many males. The forewarning enabled us to compensate by reweighting that demographic segment.

The debriefing sessions may also be used to collect interviewer packets and check that all procedures were followed. Any mistakes in interpreting or recording answers to items or other clerical errors are much easier to correct while the interviewer has the materials in hand and while memory is still fresh. The debriefer can check for proper coding of the questionnaire, and if interviewers are assigned to do their own data entry, that can be checked. The data entry can be checked by asking interviewers to confirm certain columns: some should contain numbers that are easy to identify; yes-no items will have either 1 or 0. The final columns in the printout should all be even.

A practical device for reducing data coding errors is to include in the coding system, on the questionnaire, certain columns to be entered as ampersands (&). These ampersands should be typed or printed above the column number or otherwise associated column number, as in the example in Box 4.10, so that as the columns are punched in order, the ampersand will also be entered. If ampersands are coded near where errors are likely to occur, where a long series of ones and zeros may make it easy to skip a column inadvertently, the accuracy of cards can easily be examined by noting whether the ampersands line up when the data are printed out. The check can be made more easily by marking a line with a straightedge down the appropriate column of a printout of the data set. If an ampersand is in the wrong column, it will be immediately clear that some data in a preceding column are out of place. The questionnaire can then be checked for the correct data, using the case number, and the corrections can be made.

VERIFICATION

Confirmation of the accuracy of both the entered data and the interviews is important as a way of ruling out unintentional errors. Verification of data entry is designed to identify errors in either coding or data entry. Verification of the interviews is designed to certify that the interviews actually took place as reported. Fraudulent reporting of data is, of course, a serious form of cheating and should not be tolerated by either academic or professional pollsters.

Data verification people should check again for ampersands in the proper place. In surveys requiring two cards per interview, ampersands will appear on every other line of data. Both lines need to be checked. The computer will read lines 1 and 2 in that order even if by error you have placed them in 2 and 1 order. Only one missing card (line of data) is needed to throw off the entire data set. This type of problem may be inferred if the computer printout delivers bizarre results. A data base check of the complete set of interview response data to search for capital O and lowercase L will identify any of these two characters that may have been entered in place of "0" or "1," which are common mistakes.

Confirming that the interviews were genuine may be done by calling randomly selected respondents to ask a few well-chosen questions that will reveal whether the interview actually took place. The procedure outlined in the

"Verification Team Assignment" (in the Instructor's Manual accompanying this text) is designed to verify that interviews were actually conducted by noting the general behavior of respondents. Respondent demeanor is a better indication of the genuineness of the interview than a straightforward question, "Were you the subject of an interview on the subject of . . . ?" The person may have forgotten the incident and need to be assisted in recalling.

The verification team assignment procedure allows for the questionnaires to be out of numerical sequence and uses a randomization technique that allows verification to proceed without calling back several times to reach a certain phone number or a certain person. Verifiers can usually sense when something is amiss; the report will indicate questionable cases. Most respondents are pleased that their opinions are the subject of such careful attention and are quite helpful with the verification.

WRITING AND DEBUGGING A COMPUTER PROGRAM

A number of computer software packages are available for data management and analysis. The Statistical Packages for the Social Sciences (SPSS) is one such packaged program. The procedure requires writing a program of only a few control cards (lines in a computer program) that direct the SPSS software package to read and process the data placed in the data file. An SPSS computer program I used in analyzing the infirmary poll data from the questionnaire in Box 4.10 is shown in Figure 4.3. The SPSS software package, which can be obtained from SPSS in Chicago, is available for use on personal computers. A copy of the SPSS Manual is recommended as a resource for persons wishing to develop their skills in data analysis.

In addition to the mainframe version, SPSS also offers SPSS PC and SPSS for Windows that may be used on personal computers. The procedures and commands are quite similar except that the PC version uses periods in some places where the mainframe version uses slashes. SPSS PC for DOS and SPSS for Windows are both available in many campus bookstores in a student version for about $50. This "studentware" will run small numbers of variables and limited numbers of cases, but the graphic capability makes them quite attractive at the price. The Windows version operates much the way Microsoft Excel does.

Tabulation of survey research can also be done by hand; a copy of the questionnaire can be used to tally the number of responses for each item. For very short questionnaires used for only a few interviews that system may be desirable, especially if the alternative is using the computer for the first time. For two- or three-page questionnaires with 50 or more interviews, it will usually take less time to program the computer than to do the tabulation by hand.

The essential tasks are preparation of the control cards, variable label cards (short versions of the questions), and value label cards (short versions of the options). The control cards instruct the computer in how to proceed. The "cards" may be entered into a computer as lines on a terminal screen. Either a personal computer with a storage disk, from which the data can be uploaded later to a system that has access to the SPSS package, or an interactive terminal capable of storing the program in a mainframe may be used. Whether the computer reads the cards from actual cards or from a tape or a disk makes no difference; the computer regards the lines as 80-column IBM cards in any case.

Debugging the Computer Program

The process of eliminating errors from the computer program should be planned, no matter how careful the user may be in preparing the program. Several types of error can occur: faulty data, inconsistent matching of variables with data columns to be read, control cards out of the proper sequence, control cards improperly written, and others. Fortunately, most computer software packages will print out the results of attempts to run the program with error messages, which help identify the problem. The program must be run, errors corrected, and the program run again until all errors have been corrected. The end result of the computer program and debugging is an error-free printout of the analysis of the survey data.

INTERPRETING THE DATA

Determining what the findings mean is the final task in conducting a survey. Interpretation requires some system for relating each tabulation number and/or percentage on the printout to all the rest of the findings, sorting the important from the less important results. Such a system enables the reader of the research report to understand easily what it all means. To begin with, it is especially important for the researcher to make sense of the printout.

The best way to start is to plug the significant numbers and percentages from the printout into a copy of the questionnaire. This step does two things: it collects the answers in percentages or mean scores on a copy of the questionnaire, and in the process it acquaints the researcher with the results. Generally, the frequency tabulations in percentages together with the number of cases (valid cases) should be entered in the questionnaire. Where there is a series of similar items, Likert type, or rating scales, for some items the mean (average) score may be entered in the questionnaire. After this process the researcher discovers the surprises—which variables scored the highest and lowest responses—and otherwise sees what the results are. The completed questionnaire serves as a handy reference of results when writing the final report. A copy of this filled-in questionnaire should be included as an appendix to the report to the client.

After filling in the questionnaire, the researcher must place in order from highest to lowest the various answers to the questions on the questionnaire. This system makes it easy to see the order of importance of the responses. Generally they need to be reported this way, in graphs or charts, in the report to the client. Without such a system of ordering from highest to lowest, the results would have to be studied much more carefully. This step of ordering also

```
//INFRMPOL JOB (2007,0000,5,5),  KENDALL ; CLASS=A
/*PASSWORD
/*ROUTE PRINT LOCAL
//   EXEC SPSSX
RUN NAME     87 INFIRMARY POLL
DATA LIST  FILE=INLINE RECORDS=2
         /V1 14-16 V2 TO V3 17-18 V4 TO V13 20-29 V14 TO V22 31-39
         V23 TO V29 41-47 V30 48 V31 TO V39 50-58 V40 TO V56 60-76
         /V57 TO V63 5-11 V64 TO V76 13-25 V77 TO V82 26-31
         V83 TO V95 33-45 V96 TO V98 47-49 V99 TO V106 51-58 V107 59-60
         V108 TO V112 61-65
VARIABLE LABELS
            V1    CLASS STATUS
            V2    WHEN NOT ATTENDING UF LIVE
            V3    CREDITS
            V4    RATE MED FAC CONVENIENT
            V5    RATE MED FAC PHARM
            V6    RATE MED FAC WAITTNING TIME
            V7    RATE MED FAC COMPET STAFF
            V8    RATE MED FAC CONGENIAL STAFF
            V9    RATE MED FAC CLOSE TO HOME
            V10   RATE MED FAC ATTRACTIVE
            V11   RATE MED FAC RECOMMEND
            V12   RATE MED FAC PRIVACY
            V13   RATE MED FAC OTHER
            V14   SOUGHT IMMED URG CARE
            V15   SOUGHT PERSONAL PHYS
            V16   SOUGHT PUB HEALTH SVC
            V17   SOUGHT HOSPITAL
            V18   SOUGHT EMERG SVC
            V19   SOUGHT PRIV CLIN
            V20   SOUGHT WOMEN HEALTH CLIN
            V21   SOUGHT UF INFIRM
            V22   SOUGHT OTHER
            V23   OPIN SHS PERS EXPER
            V24   OPIN SHS FRIEND - ASSOC
            V25   OPIN SHS ALLIG
            V26   OPIN SHS BROCH
            V27   OPIN SHS INFO CAL
            V28   OPIN SHS OTHER
            V29   OPIN SHS NO OPIN
            V30   TIMES VISITED LAST YEAR
            V31   HOW FAR FROM INFIRM
            V32   RATE INFIRM BUILDING
            V33   RATE EASY GET TO
            V34   RATE APPT PROCESS
            V35   RATE BROCH INFO
            V36   RATE CHECK IN
            V37   RATE APPR PROCED
            V38   RATE BILLING

            V39   RATE PRIVACY
            V40   RATE SVC - PHYS APPT
            V41   RATE TRAUMA CLIN
            V42   RATE WART CLIN
            V43   RATE COLD SELF-CARE CLIN
            V44   RATE BLOOD PRESS CLIN
            V45   RATE ALLERGY CLIN
            V46   RATE AST CLIN
            V47   RATE DERMAT CLIN
            V48   RATE ORTHOPEDIC CLIN
            V49   RATE WOMENS CLIN
            V50   RATE URINARY TRACT CLIN
            V51   RATE DIAG
            V52   RATE IMMUN CLIN
            V53   RATE MENTAL HEALTH CLIN
            V54   RATE HEALTH EDUC CLIN
            V55   RATE SEX ASSAULT REC CLIN
            V56   RATE OBSERV UNIT
            V57   RATE INFO SERV
            V58   RATE MED RECORDS
            V59   RATE LAB
            V60   RATE PHARM
            V61   RATE X-RAY
            V62   RATE BUSINESS OFF
            V63   RATE INSUR OFF
            V64   THINK SHS ATTRAC PLA
            V65   WAITING RM COMFORT
            V66   SHS COMPARES WELL WITH OTHERS
            V67   SHS PRESENTS PRO ATMOSPHERE
            V68   CHECK-IN DESK WELL-MANAGED
            V69   MED STAFF AT INFIRM QUALIF
            V70   TRUST DECISIONS MADE INFIRM
            V71   PEOPLE CHECK-IN DESK COUR
            V72   MED PERS CORD AND PRO MANN
            V73   RECORDS CONFIDENTIAL
            V74   CONVEN INFIRM HOURS
            V75   KNOW HOW SHS CARE AFTER HOURS
            V76   WILL TELL FRIEND VIS MEN HEALTH
            V77   SEEN BY PHYS
            V78   SEEN BY PHYS ASSIS
            V79   SEEN BY NURS PRAC
            V80   SEEN BY REG NURS
            V81   SEEN BY RES PHYS
            V82   SEEN BY OTHER
            V83   RATE PERSON COMPETENCE
            V84   REASON NOT GO INFIRM - NONE
            V85   HARD TO GET
            V86   POOR OPIN MED PERS
            V87   LONG LINES
            V88   BETTER ELSEWH
```

Figure 4.3 Example of a computer program.

```
                V89   POOR EXP SHS
                V90   UNSANIT
                V91   UNCOMF WAITING RM
                V92   WHEN NEED SPEC
                V93   NOT RO LIFE-DEATH
                V94   HAVE PHYS ELSEWH
                V95   OTHER
                V96   CAN EXPL SHS FUNDED
                V97   CURREN HEALTH FEE IS
                V98   AVG WAIT
                V99   ABOUT CHANGES LONG DAY HRS
                V100  ABOUT ELIM AFTER-HRS
                V101  ABOUT EXPAND BLDG
                V102  ABOUT FEE INCR BETTER FAC
                V103  ABOUT CONTRACT SHANDS AFTER-HRS
                V104  ABOUT REFURB FAC
                V105  ABOUT CREDIT PART PEER COUNSEL
                V106  SEX
                V107  AGE
                V108  RACE
                V109  PAYS HALF+ EXPENSES
                V110  EXPENSES COVERED BY FIN AID
                V111  KIND HEALTH INS
                V112  FAMILY INCOME
VALUE LABELS    V1    01  ACCOUNTING  02  ADVERTISING  03  AEROSPACE ENG
        04      AGRICULTURE  05  AGRONOMY  06  ALLIED HEALTH  07  AMERICAN STUD
        08      ANIMAL SCI  09  ANTHROPOL  10  ARCHITEC  11  ART
        12      ASIAN STUDIES  13  ASTRONOMY  14  BOTONY  15  TELECOM
        16      BUILDING CONS  17  CHEMICAL ENG  18  CHEMISTRY
        19      CIVIL ENGINEERING  20  CLASSICAL STUDIES  21  CLIN DIATETICS
        22      COMPUTER INFO. SCI  23  CRIMINAL JUST  24  DAIRY SCI
        25      ECONOMICS  26  ELECTR ENG  27  ELEMEN ED  28  ENG SCI
        29      ENGLISH  30  ENTOMOL NEMOTOL  31  ENV ENG  32  FINANCE
        33      FOOD RES ECON  34  FOOD SCI NUT  35  FOREIGN LAN ED
        36      FORESTRY  37  FRENCH  38  FRUIT CROPS  39  GEOGRAPHY
        40      GEOLOGY  41  GERMAN  42  GRAPHIC ARTS  43  HEALTH ED
        44      HISTORY  45  HISTORY OF ART  46  INDUST & SYSTEMS ENG.
        47      INSURANCE  48  INTERDISP BIO MED SCI  49  INTERDISP. ENG
        50      INTERIOR DES  51  JOURNALISM  52  LAND SURVEY
        53      LANDSC ENG  54  MANAGEMENT  55  MARKETING  56  MATERL ENG
        57      MATH-MATH ED  58  MECH ENG  59  MECH ENGR  60  MECH AG
        61      MICROBIO  62  MUSIC  63  MUSIC ED  64  NEWS-ED
        65      NUC ENG  66  NURSING  67  OCCUP THER  68  ORN HORT
        69      PHARM CHEM  70  PHARMACY  71  PHILOSOPHY  72  PHYSICAL ED
        73      PHYSICAL THER  74  PHYSNS ASST  75  PHYSICS  76  PLANT PATH
        77      PLANT SCIENCE  78  POLITICAL SCI  79  POULTRY SCI
        80      PSYCHOLOGY  81  PUBLIC REL  82  LAW  83  REAL ESTATE
        84      RECREATION  85  RELIGION  86  RESO CONV  87  RUSSIAN
        88      SOCIOLOGY  89  SOIL SCIENCE  90  SPANISH  91  SPECIAL ED
        92      SPEECH  93  STAT  94  TECH COM  95  THEATRE  96  UNDECIDED
```

```
        '''''''97  VEG CROP  98  WILDL ECO  99  ZOOLOGY  00  OTHER /
        V2   1    ON CAMPUS   2   IN GAINSVILLE     3   IN ALACHUA COUNTY
            ''4   IN FLORIDA  5   OUT-OF-STATE      6   OUT-OF-COUNTRY /
        V3   1    5 OR UNDER  2   6-9   3   10-13   4   14 OR MORE /
        V4 TO V13    1 NOT IMPORTANT    5 VERY IMPORTANT /
        V14 TO V22   0  NO   1  YES   2  NOT APPLICABLE /
        V23 TO V29   0  NO   1  YES /
        V30  VISITS /
            '''V31 1   5 MIN. WALK   2  5+ MIN. WALK   3  10+ MIN. WALK
            '''4  15+ MIN. WALK   5  5+ MIN. DRIVE   6  10+ MIN. DRIVE
            ''''7  15+ MIN. DRIVE  8  BY BUS /
        V32 TO V63  1  POOR  5  EXCELLENT  0  DONT KNO /
        V64 TO V76  1  STRNGLY DISAGREE  5  STRNGLY AGREE  0  DONT KNO /
        V77 TO V82  0  NO   1  YES /
        V83  1  POOR   5  EXCELLENT /
        V84 TO V95  0  NO   1  YES /
        V96  1    FEE FOR SERVICE    2    HEALTH CARE FEE
             3    BOTH HEALTH CARE AND FEE FOR SERVICE   4  OTHER METHOD
             5    CANT SAY--DOESNT KNOW /
        V97  1    NO INCREASE   2    UP TO .50   3  UP TO $1.00
             4    UP TO 1.50    5    OTHER /
        V98  1    NONE    2   1-5 MIN. 3   6-10 MIN.   4   11-20 MIN.
             5    20+-45 MIN.    6   DOESNT KNOW /
        V99 TO V105   1  STRONGLY OPPOSE   5  STRONGLY SUPPORT /
        V106  1   MALE        2  FEMALE /
        V107  1   YEARS OF AGE /
        V108  1   WHITE   2   BLACK   3  ASIAN   4  HISPANIC   5  OTHER /
        V109  1   SELF
              2   PARENT OR GUARDIAN
              3   FINANCIAL AID
              4   OTHER /
        V110  1   NONE
              2   UP TO 25%
              3   UP TO 50%
              4   UP TO 75%
              5   UP TO 100% /
        V111 1  PARENTS POLICY   2   STUDENT INSURANCE   3  OWN POLICY
             4   NO POLICY  5   OTHER   6  DONT KNO /
        V112  1   UNDER $5,000  2   $5,000-$7,000  3   $7,000-$10,000
              4   $10,000-$15,000  5   $15,000-$25,000  6   $25,000-$50,000
              7   $50,000+   8  DONT KNOW /
MISSING VALUES V1 TO V112 (0)
FREQUENCIES VARIABLES = V1 TO V112
        STATISTICS = ALL/
        BARCHART/
BEGIN DATA
/*INCLUDE DATA1
/*INCLUDE DATA2
/*INCLUDE DATA3
END DATA
FINISH
/*EOJ
```

Figure 4.3 (Continued).

helps the researcher to understand the findings before attempting to explain them to the client or other reader.

With the findings in mind and a copy of the filled-in questionnaire in hand, the researcher is ready to write the project report. Of the several methods of interpreting data, no one system can be the best for any specific survey report. Each survey-report writer should select the method most appropriate for the research being reported; the design of the survey and the findings determine which will work best. The journalistic method is most readable and is growing in popularity. This system selects the findings in order of importance, summarizes them, and then, in later paragraphs, expands on the items reported in the summary.

The journalistic research report arranges the questions or items reported according to the priority in which the reader would want to know the information. That is, the items on the questionnaire should be rearranged in order of what is important to the reader or client. The items may be arranged in order of the impact they will have on the organization. Items may be significant for their positive findings (indications that opinion toward the organization is better than expected) or for their negative findings (opinion worse than expected). The fact that an organizational policy draws a high approval rating may be very significant, but a low rating may be even more significant.

The writer may combine findings from several items or especially significant items to arrive at a major observation, but any conclusions based on findings that are the opinion of the researcher should be confined to the conclusion section of the report. Less significant findings may be combined in a single list or summarized in one or two paragraphs and reported in the findings section.

The report writer should also remember that the reader may not understand the intricacies of the survey process and probably doesn't need to know. The difference between the SPSS table headings "frequency" and "valid percent" should be translated into plain English or at least interpreted for the reader who doesn't know these terms. Bar graphs, line graphs, and pie charts are especially helpful in understanding the findings. The *significant* results need to be sorted out from the *less significant*, at least for the narrative part of the report. The complete accounting of the results may be included in the filled-in copy of the questionnaire attached to the report as an appendix, for the reader who wants more details.

Because the results of a survey can easily be lost in lists of numbers and because the terms used in survey research reporting are prone to ambiguity, the first rule of report writing is *clarity*. The writer should be careful that the language used does not obscure the facts. Short sentences, simple comparisons, and consistent ordering of facts reported for each item will help to achieve clarity. Tables and charts showing relationships of items also aid understanding.

Percentage figures are usually the best way to report findings. Because in probability samples the sample represents the population, those percentages are the best indication of what exists in the population that will be important to the research project. In other words, the percentage of the sample agreeing with a particular statement reflects the percentage in the population that feels the same way. Listing *mean scores* for a series of Likert-type items is another way of representing results. In this instance, the mean score stands for the point on the scale of 1 to 5 where the average response fell. That average is a handy way to describe the feeling or inclination of the total population. Mean scores are also easier to understand when they are reported from highest to lowest for a series of scaled items.

Associated with reporting mean scores is the standard deviation; the larger the standard deviation number, the more the responses are spread out. A large spread of response means that the sample reflected a wide range of opinion on the topic; a small standard deviation means a narrow variation on the topic, or that people tend to be closer together in their opinion on the topic.

For items on which a respondent may choose more than one response (which total more than 100 %), only percentages for individual variables will be significant. These percentages are of those in the population who have that opinion and are not the percentages of those who answered the combined questions, because the percentages of answer-all-that-apply questions do not add up to 100 %.

Reports are most easily understood when the highest-to-lowest pattern is followed consistently in reporting the entire results, in reporting a series of items, and in structuring paragraphs as well as phrasing sentences.

WRITING THE REPORT OF FINDINGS

The objective of a research report should be the same as the goal of a news story using a summary lead: summarize the story in the first paragraph and then elaborate each major finding in the same order of importance in succeeding paragraphs in the body of the story. The report should be written in a style appropriate to the client. An "executive summary" that provides a one-page digest of the report is critical to the well-written report. Not all readers in the client organization will read the entire report; they need essential facts that are easy to find and equally easy to understand.

Guidelines for Research Report Writing

1. Executive summary   Should summarize the most important findings in two or three paragraphs, preferably on one page. The summary should be written after completing the other parts of the report; it will be easier to summarize after putting the entire report into words.

The summary may include a few of the significant conclusions and may even include interpretations or the writer's opinion of what the facts mean. Concluding interpretations should be saved for the final section of the report. Leave for the final concluding interpretations section any expression of what the results mean, your own opinions as to what should be done about the findings, and then label them clearly as concluding interpretations (the writer's opinions).

2. *Methodology*   The second section, should describe in detail how the survey was conducted, the steps taken from start to finish to carry out the survey as assigned to teams or otherwise completed. The minimum information to be included is given by the criteria for reporting survey research of the American Association for Public Opinion Research (AAPOR): (1) sponsor of the survey and who conducted it; (2) population sampled; (3) size of the sample; (4) exact wording of the questions; (5) the sampling error; (6) results based on part of the sample; (7) type of interviewing; (8) time frame of interviews. Additional details of methodology may be reported based on the main outline of elements of this chapter, being careful to select only the elements of the method that are significant to understanding the survey results.

3. *Findings*   The third section, should present the results in either narrative form or through graphs and tables, preferably a mix of both. The most valuable will be the most easily understandable explanation of the results. Tables, charts, graphs, etc., are usually helpful in presenting divergent details in a form easy to grasp. By beginning with items of greatest consensus and working to those of lowest consensus or greatest *dis*agreement throughout the entire questionnaire, the reporter gives the reader the most important information first.

Based on personal judgment, the research reporter may also give information on items with the least response, which offers a comparison that may put surprisingly low responses in perspective. A series of charts or tables, accompanied by sufficient narrative for the reader to understand what the tables represent and how to read them, will probably be the best approach.

4. *Concluding interpretations*   The final section, should present conclusions and interpretations of the findings. This is the place for explanations that cannot be based on the facts alone as discovered, the place for the writer's opinions about what the facts mean, and the place for warnings about drawing unsupportable conclusions from the facts reported. It is also the place to report mistakes in the research design or execution or other errors that may have influenced the findings. Too much emphasis on unimportant errors that do not affect the findings significantly calls into question the credibility of the entire research effort and serves no useful end.

Types of information that might be included in this section are widely divergent response patterns, items of outstanding significance on which agreement or disagreement was nearly total, and items in which the "other" category drew high response, indicating that the options did not cover the range of choices in people's minds. Results of debriefing interviewers may indicate how mistakes were corrected or other compensations were made for errors.

Flaws should be treated realistically as regrettable errors in a process that cannot anticipate all the possible pitfalls; they should not be described so as to discredit the entire survey.

Judgments may be offered on what the findings mean that may not be obvious, what comparisons of certain items mean, what new questions are suggested by the findings, and what further research is suggested by the findings. Interpretations generally should give the meaning of the facts by explaining the significance, which may be done by comparing the findings with what was expected, or by explaining what the percentages mean. Interpretations may also include the researcher's opinion, but be careful to avoid opinions that are not supported by facts. Suggested applications may fit here also, but it is the client who must decide what to do about applying the findings ultimately as a part of the public relations campaign you suggest.

SUMMARY

The 17 steps in survey research in this chapter serve as a guide for planning and conducting polls and surveys as well as a guide for those dealing with outside survey research organizations. **Setting objectives** helps ensure that the results answer the right questions. **Defining the population** accurately ensures that the people who have the answers to your questions are indeed the ones surveyed. **Drawing the sample** ensures that the relatively small number polled accurately represents the larger population; methods of randomsampling include the simple random, systematic random, multistage random, random cluster, stratified random, and random digit dialing methods.

Developing the questionnaire combines the researcher's skills with clarity of wording, conversational language, the continuity and flow of items; by starting with the form in which you want the information to appear, you can work backward to develop questions that produce what is needed. **Determining method for administering the questionnaire,** whether face to face, by telephone, or by mail, helps formulate the questions properly for how they will be asked.

Questionnaire wording requires following rules to use simple words and language, avoid ambiguities, weed out "red flag" words, allow for all possible answers, and use "icebreaker" items at the beginning and sensitive items at the end. **Structuring the questionnaire** requires a carefully constructed introduction to gain cooperation and a smooth-flowing set of questions, including information items, filter items, and opinion, attitude, behavior, and self-perception items, all formatted in open-ended or closed-ended form. **Questionnaire pretesting** submits the instrument to people from the population being studied for their feedback on the meaning and flow of the items and to identify other problems. **Questionnaire coding** requires a system for converting answers into numbers that can be identified with answers to questions for later analysis.

Training interviewers acquaints those contacting respondents with how to proceed, how to handle objections, and how to deal with people over the phone or in person, by following a list of do's and don'ts. **Interviewer packets** should contain all the materials needed to complete the interviews assigned, including any procedures that are unique to the survey. **Conducting the interviews** involves carrying out the procedure as planned. **Debriefing interviewers** collects experiences and impressions while they are fresh in the mind of interviewers so that variations on procedure can be taken into account or problems corrected.

Verification involves checking data to eliminate coding errors and calling respondents at random to authenticate interviews. **Writing and debugging a computer program** is necessary to analyze data produced by interviews; the SPSS computer package used as an example illustrates what is involved. **Interpreting the data** involves making sense of findings by separating the important from the less important. **Writing the report** puts the interpreted findings into readable and meaningful written form.

FOR FURTHER READING

American Association for Public Opinion Research: Agencies and Organizations. Princeton, NJ: AAPOR, annual directory.

Babbie, Earl. *Survey Research Methods,* 2nd ed. Belmont, CA: Wadsworth, 1990.

Bradburn, Norman M., and Seymour Sudman. *Polls and Surveys: Understanding What They Tell Us.* San Francisco, CA: Jossey-Bass, 1988.

Broom, Glenn M., and David M. Dozier. *Using Research in Public Relations.* Englewood Cliffs, NJ: Prentice Hall, 1990.

Cantril, Albert H. *Polling on the Issues.* Washington, DC: Seven Locks Press, 1980.

Frey, James H. *Survey Research by Telephone.* Beverly Hills, CA: Sage, 1980.

Kraemer, Helena C., and Sue Thiemann. *How Many Subjects: Statistical Power Analysis in Research.* Newbury Park, CA: Sage, 1987.

Payne, Stanley. *The Art of Asking Questions.* Princeton, NJ: Princeton University Press, 1980.

Rubenstein, Sondra Miller. *Surveying Public Opinion.* Belmont, CA: Wadsworth, 1995.

Singer, Eleanor, and Stanley Presser. *Survey Research Methods: A Reader.* Chicago: University of Chicago Press, 1987.

Weisberg, Herbert F., J. A. Krosnick, and B. D. Bowen. *An Introduction to Survey Research and Data Analysis,* 2nd ed. Glenview, IL: Scott, Foresman, 1989.

Wright, Sonia R. *Quantitative Methods and Statistics: A Guide to Social Research.* Beverly Hills, CA: Sage, 1979.

CHAPTER 5

Research Cases and Problems

- The Research Plan
- Case Study: Macomb Community College Bond Issue

THE RESEARCH PLAN

In order to carry out the research needed for a successful campaign, you must have a research plan that will focus the effort on essential research projects. The campaign ordinarily needs to collect a wide assortment of facts from a variety of publics by using a range of different research techniques. For example, the planner might begin by considering whether to carry out projects of the following types: (1) It may be necessary to measure public opinion on the central issue of the campaign. (2) It may be necessary to find out how other organizations solved the same or a similar problem. (3) It may be necessary to interview management concerning the range of their perceptions of the problem. (4) It may be necessary to discover what pertinent information on the issue exists in the organization's files. These are the more common research projects, but the entire checklist of possible projects given in Chapter 3 may be considered when drawing up the research plan.

The following outline is an effort to identify the thought processes involved in devising a research plan to address the needs of a campaign. The examples, drawn from cases described in this chapter, should serve as a guide to thinking out the best research plan for the campaign challenges facing you.

Problem: Outline a Research Plan

You are encouraged to test your facility with the research concept in the public relations campaign by planning such a research project. Use the client chosen for your class assignment or select a different client or department campaign needs. To construct such a research plan, you will need to outline each of the following numbered points in complete sentences:

1. State the research problem for each aspect of the client situation you will attempt to solve.

    The Macomb Community College case summary lists a range of research projects typical of well-designed campaigns. Seven research projects are listed under the heading "Research." The careful reader will also note that two research projects are described as part of the implementation strategy: "a major study explaining our community's pressing and immediate need . . . " and "A content analysis of the press coverage revealed . . . " The case also shows how research findings lead to specific strategies.

2. Identify the research projects that will have to be carried out from the range of possibilities determined in the situation analysis. Chapter 3 lists examples of such research project approaches.

3. Describe the research approach for each project. The procedure you will use to conduct the research should include, especially, (1) how you will define the group or population you intend to measure; (2) whether a census, a sample, or other measurement of the information source will be appropriate; (3) the technique or procedure to be used for executing the project; (4) any limitations imposed by circumstances, such as time or money; and (5) a proposed calendar for the project.

4. Describe how you will compile, tally, and/or otherwise report the findings of the research projects, that is, the form in which the results of each research effort will be reported.

Note: For polls or surveys, you should plan to include in your final research report to the client—in the plan book—at least these standard elements: population definition, sample drawing procedure, sample size, chance sampling error, interview method (face to face, phone, etc.), time frame for the project, and a copy of questionnaire with responses filled in. Other projects may be reported in such forms as summaries of interviews, lists of publics, descriptions of marketing channels, synopses of regulatory and legal factors, and organization factors.

Before deciding on the research plan, however, the *situation* that necessitates the campaign must be clearly understood. The *situation analysis* must be carried out in order to answer certain basic questions about the campaign even before beginning the research. The research plan should be designed to confirm or modify the situation analysis. The situation analysis may look something like the following.

Situation Analysis

The public relations campaign begins with a clear understanding of the situation that prompts the campaign. Most campaigns begin with a problem that the management of the sponsoring organization wishes to solve by undertaking a public relations campaign; or, the situation may be an opportunity that management seeks to exploit. The initial challenge in working with management is the perception and statement of the precise nature of the situation as a problem or opportunity. The situation analysis is the foundation on which the research plan is built.

Outline the situation. Your analysis of the situation that prompts the campaign should include:

1. A statement of management's perception of the situation stated as a problem or an opportunity.
2. The structure of the organization decision-making process, or specifying who makes the ultimate decision.
3. Explanation of how liaison will be worked out and maintained with the organization's management throughout the planning and implementation of the campaign.
4. An outline of the categories or types of facts needed to confirm or redefine the problem as it is initially perceived.

This research plan outline should be comprehensive enough to list all the preliminary research needs of the campaign planning process and, if the campaign is a team effort, should be easily divided among team members to execute. Each team member may select one of the research projects to plan and manage the project's execution. It may be necessary for each team member to help with the execution of other team member's projects in addition to having responsibility for one project.

The case history examples throughout this book are mostly drawn from campaigns that won the 1994 PRSA Silver Anvil Award and illustrate the variety of situations a campaign may address. Several cases are presented in considerable detail. In the Macomb Community College case that follows, the "facts needed to confirm the situation" are listed under the heading "Findings." However, the specific problem statement as phrased in the "Background" paragraph is: "by the mid 1970s, declining state support and inflation had badly eroded the once solid funding base and created a need to ask taxpayers for additional support."

You may find it useful to test your skill in selecting research projects by making a list of research approaches after studying case problems. For a number of reasons, possible research projects may not be necessary or appropriate in any given case. The proposed projects listed here are those likely to confirm the nature of the problem evident in the case situation.

➤ CASE STUDY: MACOMB COMMUNITY COLLEGE BOND ISSUE

The following extensive case study offers unique insights into the specific elements of the public relations campaign. Most case studies are brief summaries of a campaign. This case study draws from a complete copy of the case that won a PRSA Silver Anvil in 1989. The MCC case is a particularly valuable example for classroom study: (1) It focuses on the issue of education funding at a time when many institutions face similar challenges. (2) It offers an example of the full range of elements that make up a comprehensive campaign. (3) It provides specific examples of many aspects of a campaign seldom included in published cases, such as research results, detailed plans, memos, publicity clips, and evaluation research findings. (4) It shows the interrelationship between research, planning, implementation, and evaluation in easy to follow form; and it shows how to arrange for the participation of prominent people such as the president of the United States.

Each of the elements of the campaign may be the subject of further detailed analysis in this case: What constitutes adequate research in a specific campaign? How does the planning and strategy grow out of research findings? How does the planner fit the strategy chosen to research findings? How much communication is necessary? How often does the message have to be repeated? At what point does evaluation prove the campaign was a success? Does evaluation have to prove more than the success of the campaign?

As with all case studies, the greatest benefit is through intimate involvement in a case that offers a rich model for adaptation to other situations. The direct linkage is between research findings and strategy options, and the well-focused strategy statement with its specific implementation tactics. The case also affords an instructive comparison between goals and evaluation.

The following summary of the case study may be used to examine the interconnection between research and the resulting strategy, the connection between the research-based statement of the problem and the goal statement, as well as the link between the research and the tactics—listed here as headings under "Execution." The reader might also note that a content analysis research project constituted a part of the "execution" of the Speaker's Connection.

Situation Analysis—Background

Founded in 1954 to serve the blue-collar, ethnic community of Macomb County, MI, Macomb Community College grew over 35 years to its present size of 32,000 students. Residents enthusiastically voted the original one mill* to support college operations, but, by the mid–1970s, declining state support and inflation had badly eroded the once solid funding base and created

*One mill is a tenth of a cent.

a need to ask taxpayers for additional support. Macomb County, however, had become the hotbed of the antitax movement in Michigan. Between 1976 and 1986, the college mounted—and lost—five attempts to increase its millage base. In addition, the 1986 millage effort resulted in a widely publicized lawsuit (ultimately dismissed) alleging misuse of public funds to advocate a "yes" vote. By 1988, the college struggled to maintain operations on the lowest voted millage of all Michigan's 29 community colleges and faced the certainty of declining quality, downsized enrollment, and low employee morale.

Research

Existing data and original research were used to develop major campaign strategies:

Research	Findings	Resulting Strategies
Telephone survey of 500 county residents	Citizens support MCC, but are anti-tax	Publicize projects, not millage
Telephone survey of 300 community leaders	High support for bachelor's degree and upgrade of facilities	Mount two separate ballot proposals
Field reports, focus groups	Proposals confusing to citizens	Use simple titles and descriptive language
Previous election analysis	Larger voter turnouts are better for MCC	Propose issues during presidential election
Legal review	Advocacy not allowed	Use public information effort only
Census data	Diversity of citizenry; low education levels	Segment audiences and messages
Communication theories	Persuasion requires personal contact	use endorsements, speeches, events

Planning

Goals
  1. To increase the perceived value of higher education;
  2. To successfully pass two ballot proposals.

Strategies
  1. Conduct a highly visible public information program clearly demonstrating MCC's commitment to the community and promoting the value of higher education. Leverage ongoing communication programming to carry messages. Note: State law does not allow public institutions to advocate a "yes" vote on tax issues.

2. Effectively use national and community leadership endorsements. Concept: No one ever wants higher taxes, but they may be convinced of the value of the projects of higher education, Macomb Community College, or its two ballot proposals are endorsed (directly or subliminally) by leaders they respect.

Target Audiences   Those who make the decision (taxpayers), those who have a direct stake in the success of the institution (employees, students, alumni, vendors, donors, county decision makers, and business owners), and those who influence discussion on ballot proposals in the county (senior citizens' groups, ethnic groups, and the news media).

Messages Theme   "This College is the Community . . . our people, our problems, our families, and our future." Community relations message: There is value in higher education. Ballot proposal message: MCC has placed two projects on the ballot.

Budget   Most expenses were covered by incorporating messages into the college's ongoing communications and activities. Volunteer efforts also increased available human resources. An additional budget of $90,000 was set aside for the special public information effort, including $15,000 for research and planning, $65,000 for implementation, and $10,000 for evaluation.

Execution

Bush/Dukakis/Reagan Visits   MCC was the only college in the country to host visits by George Bush, Michael Dukakis, and Ronald Reagan. More than 15,000 voters came on campus during the visits. Students actively worked the crowds to distribute millage literature. Local and national media attention was focused on MCC.

Endorsements   Endorsements from 26 community, business, media, labor, education, and professional groups promoted third-party credibility. Their names were printed on brochures and used in speeches. An advertising campaign used photos and quotes from community leaders. Rep. Claude Pepper (education and senior citizen advocate) was a featured speaker at the college. A citizen's group formed to endorse and advocate proposals.

Voter Registration   A voter registration drive on campus resulted in 940 new registrations of students and also focused attention on the upcoming election date.

Macomb 2000: Toward a Brighter Future   A half-day seminar was conducted for 70 key business, community, government, and media leaders. The college president unveiled a major study explaining our community's pressing and immediate need for a shift from a skilled work force to an educated work force, and the impact of low educational attainment rates on a community. It was followed by 25 additional speeches and interviews on this topic.

National Higher Education Week   Held four weeks before the election, this week of special events celebrated the value of higher education. Activities included media and legislative delegation briefing breakfasts, a faculty dinner, student activities day, and a financial aid seminar for high school parents. Five full-page ads announced the week and quoted national and state leaders' views on the value of education.

Speaker's Connection   Utilizing a combination of news releases, interviews, on-campus events, and other media activities, the college was able to shift the focus of media coverage from the tax increase issue to the potential benefits to be accrued through passage of the ballot proposals. A content analysis of the press coverage revealed that more than 90 percent of the articles on the ballot proposals and related issues were positive. Editorial board meetings resulted in endorsements for the proposals by two major Detroit newspapers, the daily newspaper in Macomb County, and the major weekly in the county's largest city.

Advertising and Print Collateral   Letters were mailed to targeted audiences announcing the ballot proposals; buttons, posters, and fliers were distributed at special events; extensive coverage was placed in the alumni magazine and legislative newsletters; reprints were made of key newspaper coverage; and a voter's guide was direct mailed to 270,000 households two weeks prior to the election. In addition, all regular college publications carried information concerning the ballot proposals and 156,000 fact sheets were stuffed into outgoing mail and correspondence. Four full-page image ads carried the campaign theme.

Internal Communications   A steady flow of ballot proposal information ran in 15 biweekly issues of the internal newsletter, mailed to 1,800 full- and part-time employees. Campaign buttons were distributed twice with fact sheets to all employees. The president personally solicited support from faculty, managers, union leaders, and other staff.

On Campus   Student Activities and Organization Day increased student involvement. Posters were put up in every classroom (356) with the actual ballot language and a reminder to vote. "Rapsheets" were mailed to all students that answered the proposal questionnaire. Two mobile displays were moved to 13 locations during the campaign. Students organized a "chalk blitz" and covered all campus sidewalks with vote messages the week before the election. The student newspaper carried feature stories supporting the proposals.

Essay Context: "Why I Want a College Education"   An essay contest announced during National Higher Education Week gave junior and senior high school students an opportunity to win a $100 U.S. Savings Bond by writing a 500 word essay about the value of a college education. More than two hundred students from 40 county high schools entered the contest. Cosponsored by the county's daily newspaper, the contest winners were announced the day before the election in a major article. Photos of the winners and quotes from their essays ran in a double-truck advertisement.

Evaluation

The campaign successfully achieved both goals:

1. The perceived value of education increased among 14% of the residents. In a county-wide survey in January 1988, 79% reported a college education was important. After the campaign, 93% reported it was important.
2. The Bachelor's Degree Partnership Program passed 55% to 45%, and the Equipment Updating and Facilities Renovation Bonding Proposal passed 56% to 44%.

In a telephone survey three months after the campaign, 19% of the residents recalled the campaign theme, and 61% agreed with it. Half remembered receiving campaign literature in the mail, and 50% recalled seeing the newspaper advertisements. Among those who attended the Bush/Dukakis/Reagan visits, 97% reported that they voted "yes" for at least one of the proposals, and 92% of those who heard a speech supported them. A follow-up survey of employees found that a majority thought the communications for the ballot proposals were very good to excellent (eight, nine, or ten on a ten-point scale). The $90,000 investment in this community relations program netted $32 million in new resources for the college.

THE COMPLETE CASE STUDY: MACOMB COMMUNITY COLLEGE*

The Table of Contents of the complete campaign includes the following headings. Students may wish to examine specific elements of the campaign by requesting from the instructor copies of the elements listed below. Selected elements of the campaign are included as examples in the following pages.

Research

1. Telephone Survey of 500 Macomb County Residents
2. Telephone Survey of 300 Community Leaders
3. Focus Groups Survey to Test Wording

---

*Campaign to promote value of higher education and to increase tax millage base is available to instructors in the Instructor's Manual.

4. Previous Election Analysis
5. Legal Review
6. Census Data on Macomb County
7. Communication Theories

Planning
1. Public Information Program
2. Media, Advertising, and Publications
3. Presidential Candidate Visits
4. National Higher Education Week
5. Program Organization and Timelines

Execution

1. Bush/Dukakis/Reagan Visits
2. Endorsements
3. Voter Registration
4. Macomb 2000
5. National Higher Education Week
6. Speaker's Connection
7. Media Relations
8. Print Collateral
9. Internal Communications
10. On Campus Activities
11. Essay Contest

Evaluation

1. Survey of County Residents
2. Certificate of Determination of Election Results
3. Precinct Election Results
4. Summary of Employee Survey
5. Sample Reading Level Analysis of Communications
6. Implementation Costs

Research Project (example of one project)

Legal Review   First page of attorney general response clarifying use of public funds in connection with ballot proposals.

STATE OF MICHIGAN

Frank J. Kelley, Attorney General

COLLEGES AND UNIVERSITIES: Expenditure by community college district of funds to provide facts on ballot proposals.

ELECTIONS: Filing of reports by voluntary associations advocating for or against ballot proposal.

SCHOOLS AND SCHOOL DISTRICTS: Expenditure of funds to provide facts on ballot proposals.

School districts or community college districts may expend public funds to inform their electors in a fair and objective manner of the facts surrounding an upcoming ballot proposal or proposals to be voted upon by the school district or the community college district electors.

A voluntary unincorporated association receiving contributions and making expenditure therefrom to advocate for or against a ballot proposal is subject to the filing requirements of the campaign financing and practices act and may be subject to imposition of fines for violating the act.

Opinion No. 6531

Honorable Art Miller, Jr.

State Senator

The Capitol

Lansing, Michigan 40913

You have requested my opinion on several questions concerning the extent to which institutions of public education and voluntary unincorporated associations may expend funds in connection with an upcoming ballot proposal. It is my understanding that the term "institution of public education" refers only to school districts and community college. . . .

Legal Guidelines for Communicating Information   MCC ability to spend public funds on ballot proposal:

I. Macomb Community College CANNOT:
   a. Spend public monies to influence favorable vote;

    b. Spend public monies to advocate one side only without affording dissenters the opportunity by means of the same financed medium to present their side;

    c. Spend public funds on behalf of one side only (b. and c. are cited by the same authority);

    d. Spend public monies to "URGE" the public to support one side;

    e. Use public funds to tell the public that Macomb Community College's view "is the only logical one."

II. Macomb Community College CAN:

    a. Make reasonable expenditures to give voters relevant facts in aid to reaching an informed judgment when voting on a proposal;

    b. Spend public monies to inform the public in an objective manner;

    c. Use Macomb Community College supplies and materials to inform the publics as to the views of the individual members of the board of trustees;

    d. Present arguments to the public as to how the proposal would benefit/affect MCC/ the community;

    e. Assist the public at arriving at a proper understanding of the situation but without "urging."

Adaptation (Planning)

The adaptation stage, called "planning" in this case, adapts the findings of the research projects to identify goals and objectives, and from this conceptual framework selects specific activities to fulfill those objectives and reach the stated goals.

Objectives of the Planning Stage:

To clearly define goals and strategies for all who work on the program.

To provide for smooth, practical, and timely implementation.

To identify all targeted audiences and messages appropriate to them.

To ensure the best possible timing of activities, individually and as a package.

The following activities or implementation strategy and tactics identified by Roman numerals were selected as the best package of actions to reach the campaign goal.

I. Public Information Program

Theme: "This College Is the Community"

A base of well-planned, routine activities allowed for flexibility in adapting to the unpredictable opportunities of the presidential candidacies. Messages and objectives were developed for 12 different audiences. The program reached a peak of activity one month prior to the election and maintained momentum through election day.

II. Media, Advertising, and Publications

Definition of the Problem   Macomb Community College is funded through three primary sources: state aid, student tuitions and fees, and local community. Local community support over the years has failed to maintain its equal share of funding. In the November 8, 1988, general election MCC will place two proposals on the ballot which, if passed, will increase local community support. It is the responsibility of College Relations to lead an information-based effort to inform the community of the need for these proposals in order to maintain and enhance the quality of higher education in Macomb County.

Situation Analysis: External Factors

1. There are widespread negative attitudes throughout the county concerning millage issues. These attitudes relate to all millage issues, not just those of the college.
2. Recent studies (Macomb Opinion Surveys) have shown that taxes are again becoming a major concern of county residents.
3. Most recent millage proposals on the K–12 level have failed.
4. Voters have rejected MCC's last five millage attempts, including two in 1986, which offered similar types of bachelor's degree partnership proposals.
5. MCC enjoys a generally positive image among the general public as an institution of higher education.
6. Support for college millage issues has been low in areas with high concentrations of senior citizens.
7. In 1986, the media was broadly supportive of the millage proposals.
8. The media has consistently displayed an interest in covering college-related issues.

Situation Analysis: Internal Factors

1. MCC has approximately 1,800 full- and part-time employees. In the 1986 election, active support from employees was minimal.
2. In the past 12 months more than 37,000 people have taken courses at MCC.
3. Despite only a one percent increase in state aid in the upcoming year, and a budget deficit in the past fiscal year, there generally is not a feeling among employees or students of a need for increased revenues.
4. In the past year College Relations and the college's administration has not enjoyed a good relationship with the *MCC Journal*.

Goal of the College Media Relations and Advertising Activities   The goal of College Relations' media efforts in the upcoming campaign is to lead an information-based program to increase awareness of the need for bachelor's degree programs and renovation repairs among those segments of the population most likely to support it. Efforts to interest the media in communicating these needs, as well as advertising and publications, will be used to help increase this awareness. Notice that this media relations goal is consistent with the first goal of the campaign and contributes significantly to reaching that goal.

Media Program Strategies   A central part of the media strategy detailed some 20 different media releases distributed about three per month over a six-month period from June to the November election day.

Target Media	Date
A. News Releases	June–Nov.
"MCC Board of Trustees Place Proposals on November 7 Ballot"	June 22
"LaRosa Outlines MCC Board of Trusteee November Ballot Proposals"	July 7
"McCafferty Outlines MCC Board of Trustees November Ballot Proposals"	July 25
"LaRosa Speaks to Mount Clemens Rotary Club" (Photo and Cutline Only)	Aug. 4
"MCC Board Approves Ballot Language for November Ballot Proposals"	Aug. 17
"Concordia College to Offer Bachelor's Degree Program in Human Resource Administration at MCC"	Aug. 30
"(Speaker) Urges Voter Registration"	Sept. 14
"Citizens Advisory Group Formed to Boost MCC Ballot Proposals"	Sept. 15
"Classes Fill for MCC's Pilot Program Bachelor's Degree Partnership Offerings"	Sept. 19
"Making Your Mark on the Future" (Voter Registration/Civic Responsibilities Article)	Sept. 20
"MCC to Host Student Voter Registration Rally at South and Center Campuses"	Sept. 22
"MCC Rededicates Technical Education Center"	Sept. 29
"MCC Participates in National Higher Education Week"	Sept. 30
"Students Register to Vote at MCC Rally"	Oct. 3
"MCC Ballot Proposals Endorsed by County Chambers of Commerce"	Oct. 5
"(Activity) at MCC as Part of National Higher Education Week"	Oct. 10
"(Activity) at MCC as Part of National Higher Education Week"	Oct. 12
"(Activity) at MCC as Part of National Higher Education Week"	Oct. 14
"Citizens Advisory Group for MCC Ballot Proposals Grows"	Oct. 20
"MCC Students Show Support for College's Ballot Proposals"	Oct. 28

Additional news releases were also planned for issue on endorsements, highlights of Speaker's Connection activities, and other specific election-related developments as they emerge. Planners made arrangements for interviews, media briefings, and advertorial materials to appear in the *MCC Journal*, an in-house publication. Briefing breakfasts with reporters from some twenty local and area publications prepared media people to report upcoming events effectively by providing them with the story of the College's effort to address the funding issue that had become so critical to the future of the community. Separate briefings brought editors up to date on the same story.

B. Work with *Journal Adviser* in conjunction with LaRosa Interview   July

C. Media briefing with editorial staff and faculty adviser for *MCC Journal*   Aug.–Sept.

D. Advertorial materials for *MCC Journal*   Sept. 22
        Oct. 6
        Oct. 11
        Oct. 20
        Nov. 11

E. Reporters' Briefing Breakfast—
    Armada Times
    East Side News
    Tech Center News
    Journal (formerly the *Advertiser Journal*) *Adviser*
    Anchor Bay Beacon
    Bay Voice
    C & G Publishing (*Warren Weekly* and *St. Clair Shores Sentinel*)
    Italian Tribune
    Port Huron Times-Herald
    St. Clair Shores Herald
    Richmond Review
    Romeo Observer
    The Source
    The Reporter
    WBRB
    MCC Journal
    Macomb Daily
    Detroit News
    Detroit Free Press
    Crain's Detroit Business

F. Editorial Board Briefings: Oct.
    Macomb Daily
    Detroit News

Detroit Free Press
Warren Weekly

Advertising in local media included image advertising and recruitment advertising in 15 area newspapers to appear over ten days in August seeking supporters and volunteers. The ads also told the story of the college's effort in the course of advertising for support and volunteers. Education Week provided the opportunity for the college to place advertising that would establish its image as a community institution committed to advancing the interests of the community and its citizens.

A. Image Ads:

Macomb Daily	July 4 & 5

B. Recruitment Ads:

Macomb Daily	Aug. 2, 4, & 9
Detroit Free Press	Aug. 8
Detroit News	Aug. 7
The Source	Aug. 10
The Advisor	Aug. 10
Romeo Observer	Aug. 10
Richmond Review	Aug. 10
Warren Weekly	Aug. 10
St. Clair Shores Sentinel	Aug. 10
Journal Adviser (formerly the *Advertiser Journal*)	Aug. 10
Tech Center News	Aug. 8
Armada Times	Aug. 10
Italian Tribune	Aug. 5
Anchor Bay Beacon	Aug. 10
Bay Voice	Aug. 10

C. Higher Education Week Image Ads

Macomb Daily	Oct. 10–14

Thirty different story placements in area media emphasized topics with a local connection, but also advanced the objectives of the campaign. Examples include:

A. Points for Emphasis	June–Nov.
"Board of Trustees Place MCC Proposals on November Ballot"	June 24
"College Volunteers Needed for Public Information Effort"	
"Volunteer Group Meets to Discuss Election"	July 22
"Ballot Proposal Volunteers Begin Strategies for November Election"	Aug. 5
"Speakers Connection Increases Efforts for Ballot Proposals"	

"Board of Trustees Approves Ballot Language for Election Proposal"	Aug. 19
"Ballot Proposal 'Hotline' Established"	
"Macomb Daily's Ken Kish Comments in Support of Ballot Proposals"	
"Concordia College to Offer Classes at Center Campus This Winter"	
"Bachelor's Degree Classes Offered at Macomb During Fall Semester"	Sept. 2
"Speakers Connection Intensifies Efforts for Ballot Proposals"	
"Ballot Information Supplied to Continuing Education Faculty/Staff"	
"College Volunteer Activities Increase Community Awareness of Ballot Proposals"	Sept. 10
"Faculty Urged to Register to Vote at Sept. 22 On-Campus Rally"	
Higher Education Week Special Issue	Sept. 30
"On-Campus Voter Registration Rally Registers Voters"	
"Oct. 10 Deadline Nears for Those Still Not Registered to Vote in Nov. General Election"	
"List of Endorsements Grows for College's Ballot Proposals"	Oct. 14
"Reminder to Vote by Absentee Ballot"	
"MCC Joins Columbus Day Parade"	
Ballot Proposal Special Issue	Oct. 28
"Community Awareness Stressed as Election Day Nears"	
"Speakers Address Community Groups on Ballot Proposals"	
"Volunteers Intensify Activity in Final Week Before Election"	
"Membership Increases in Citizens Advisory Group"	
"Ballot Proposals Receive Strong Support from County Chambers of Commerce"	
"Speakers Connection Increases Efforts for Ballot Proposals"	
"MCC Employees Encouraged to Vote in Next Week's Election"	
"(Speaker) Says Whole County Impacted by Higher Education Issue"	

A news release offering the college's interpretation of election results was planned well in advance of the election date for release on November 11. Plans called for additional releases added or deleted as events would dictate. Two separate direct mail pieces were planned for distribution to "occupant" in the fall with a copy of the "Image advertisement" on the cover to make double use of the advertising copy.

Personal letters from the college president were planned for distribution to staff, students, and decision makers. Letters from other college officials, including the director of public relations, were planned for distribution to donors explaining the college's effort. Communications including fact sheets and proposed articles were planned to reach other media on and off campus.

Summary of Election Results	Nov. 11

Articles will be added, deleted, or revised as events emerge.

B. Fall '88 Occupant Mailer Image Ad on Cover	June 20
C. Letter of Explanation to Decision Makers —person responsible: Lorenzo	June 22
Letter of Explanation to MCC Staff —person responsible: Lorenzo	June 22
Letter of Explanation to Students —person responsible: Lorenzo	June 22
D. PACE Catalog	July
E. Letter of Explanation to MCC Donors —person responsible: Ahles	Sept.
Letter of Explanation to MCPA Donors —person responsible: Teal	Sept.
F. Fact Sheet	Aug.–Nov.
G. Adviser Newspaper Articles	Aug.–Nov.
H. Macomb Alumni Magazine Proposals Article	Sept. 19
I. Update Letter to MCC Donors —person responsible: Ahles	Oct.
Update Letter to MCPA Donors —person responsible: Teal	Oct.
J. Spring '89 Occupant Mailer Description of Proposals	Oct. 26

III. Bush/Dukakis/Reagan Visits

Letter of invitation to Vice President George Bush
Letter of invitation to James Baker III
Poster announcing the visit of Vice President George Bush
Invitation/ticket to the Bush rally
Ad announcing Bush visit
News release announcing Bush visit, September 29, 1988

The plan also included the following (not shown here)

Photos of Bush visit
Poster announcing the visit of Massachusetts Governor Michael Dukakis
Photos of Dukakis visit
Invitation/ticket to the Reagan rally
Photos of Reagan visit

Objectives stated for this event kept the purpose of the visits focused on the campaign goal:

To support the college's Ballot Proposal Public Information program and the overall public affairs goals of the college.

To bring people on campus and draw attention to the value of a college degree regarding earning power and family security.

To enhance the visibility and credibility of the college through local and national media attention.

To give residents a chance to learn the candidates' plans and policies for higher education.

Some preliminary results:

The college's fieldhouse (capacity 5,000) hosted visits before overflow crowds on the following dates:

- September 29, 1988 — Vice President George Bush
- October 28, 1988 — Massachusetts Governor Michael Dukakis
- November 5, 1988 — President Ronald Reagan

More than 15,000 voters came on campus during the three visits.

An organized group of 75 actively worked the crowds to distribute more than 10,000 pieces of millage literature.

The college benefited from candidates' declared support for the future of higher education in America.

Among those who attended the Bush/Dukakis/Reagan visits, 97 percent reported that they voted for at least one of the proposals.

The visits generated a significant level of awareness of Macomb Community College through local, state, and national print and electronic media outlets.

Specific arrangements for the participation of such prominent personages as the three national political figures reveal the technique for achieving such news generating events and managing the endorsements of these major political personages in behalf of the college's campaign.

A letter of invitation similar to the following was sent to the Dukakis campaign.

ON COLLEGE LETTERHEAD

August 22, 1988

The Vice President of the United States

Old Executive Office Building

Room 274

17th and Pennsylvania Ave., N.W.

Washington, D.C. 20501

Dear Mr. Vice President:

The issue of education—especially, the relationship of education to jobs for the American worker—is of vital importance to our nation and its ability to compete.

The Vice President of the United States

August 22, 1988, page two

In Michigan, Macomb County is a community where education is critical to the security and future of its 700,000 citizens (representing 8 percent of the state's registered voters), most of whom are no-nonsense, blue-collar working Americans.

During your acceptance speech for the Republican presidential nomination, you set a goal of creating 30 million jobs over the next eight years and made a commitment to visit every corner of the country containing people who want to work toward a better America.

We are such people. Because of this, I would like to invite you to visit the Campus of Macomb Community College during National Higher Education Week October 9–15 to outline your future plans, programs, and policies concerning higher education and jobs for American people.

Macomb Community College is an important part of our community, serving over 32,000 students at three campuses north of Detroit. As Michigan's largest community college, our leadership is sought within the state (indeed, nationally) when the topic turns to creating visions of the twenty-first century.

Macomb County is a living example of a work force desperately in need of access to higher education. Macomb County residents have the lowest educational attainment rate of the four-county Greater Detroit area. About one-third of the adults over 25 have not yet completed high school, and only 10.7 percent of the adults have attained a bachelor's degree. With 45 percent of the employment base in manufacturing (twice the state average and four times the national average), our residents long for a more secure future for their children and grandchildren.

Politically, Macomb is a swing county. Some 25 percent of the residents profess to be Republican, 22 percent Democratic, and 33 percent are independent. County voters are notorious for voting solidly Democratic in local elections but have voted staunchly Republican in the last two presidential elections.

The college has its own issue on the November 8 ballot. We have mounted a ballot proposal to establish a Bachelor's Degree Partnership Program, which would allow local four-year colleges and universities facilities on our premises to offer the second two years of a bachelor's degree program.

We are comfortable in our ability to accommodate the extensive preparations necessary for a presidential campaign visit, including the complicated security and communications arrangements. We successfully hosted a visit by President Reagan in October 1984 and received accolades from both the Reagan-Bush Advance Team and the White House Advance Team for our efforts. Virtually to a person, the team of college staff involved in that event is with us today. Macomb Community College Chief of Police Gary Evans can be reached at (313) 445-7135 for further details of his arrangements with the Secret Service and FBI during that visit.

Because we are very interested in hearing the future plans, programs, and policies of both presidential candidates as they relate to jobs and education, we have extended a similar invitation to Governor Michael Dukakis. We are hoping to hear from your staff in the near future so we can secure the date of your choice for your visit. If your campaign staff have any questions about our invitation, they may contact our vice president for college relations, Catherine B. Ahles, at (313) 445-7244, or my office directly.

Respectfully,

Dr. Albert L. Lorenzo

President

cc: James Baker III

      Frank J. Fahrenkopf

      Spencer Abraham

      Bob Parker

      William Broomfield

A letter soliciting support was sent to five national and state Republican officials and nine national and state Democratic officials.

ON COLLEGE LETTERHEAD

August 26, 1988

Mr. James Baker III, Campaign Manager

George Bush for President Committee

Treasury /Office of the Secretary

15th and Pennsylvania Avenue, N.W.

Washington, D.C. 20220

Dear Mr. Baker:

The issue of education and its relationship to jobs for the American worker has become a pivotal point in this fall's presidential campaign. Macomb County, Michigan, has been frequently cited by both Democratic and Republican leadership as a bellwether of national public opinion for working America.

Because of this, Macomb Community College has invited Vice President Bush to visit our campus during National Higher Education Week, October 9–15, to outline his future plans, programs, and policies concerning higher education and jobs for the American people (see attachment copy of letter).

I am hoping you will carefully consider this invitation and lend your support to our efforts to bring Vice President Bush to our campus in October. If you would like to discuss the ramifications of this invitation, please don't hesitate to contact our vice president for college relations, Catherine B. Ahles, at (313) 445-7244, or my office directly.

Sincerely,

Albert L. Lorenzo

President

CBA/es

Attachment

Personal visits to Capitol Hill enrolled national support of the college strategy to invite presidential candidates on campus during the campaign. The following letter was sent from the office of William S. Broomfield, congressman from the eighteenth district of Michigan.

September 8, 1988

Hon. James A. Baker III, Chairman

Bush/Quayle Campaign Committee

733 15th Street, N.W., Suite 800

Washington, D.C. 20005

Dear Mr. Baker;

I want to encourage you to consider an invitation extended by Dr. Albert L. Lorenzo, president of Macomb County Community College. I believe very strongly that a visit to southeastern Michigan will greatly help communicate the Republican vision of America. As you can see, this area is a classic example of a community in need of the Bush/Quayle message of education, jobs, and economic prosperity. The college has an annual enrollment of over 32,000 students. An appearance by George Bush or Dan Quayle could have an important impact on the large number of blue-collar Reagan Democrats who live in Macomb County.

As Dr. Lorenzo has also indicated, the college facilities are more than adequate for the special needs of the vice president and his staff, security, and press entourage.

I heartily recommend that you give Dr. Lorenzo every consideration. I am enclosing a copy of the original letter to the Vice President for your reference. If there is any way I can be of assistance in this matter please don't hesitate to let me know.

Sincerely,

William S. Bloomfield

Member of Congress

WSB/pr

Enclosure

An advertisement appeared in the September 28, 1988, edition of the *Macomb Daily* (circulation 55,082) announcing the Bush visit. Over 500 posters announcing Vice President Bush's visit were posted on the South Center and Fraser campuses. Both advertisement and poster contained the same copy:

MACOMB COMMUNITY COLLEGE

Presents its Kickoff to

National Higher Education Week with

Vice President of the United States

George W. Bush

September 29, 1988

2:00 p.m.

CENTER CAMPUS COMMONS

CLINTON TOWNSHIP

The issues of education and jobs for the American worker are of vital importance to our nation and its ability to compete in the future. As part of Macomb Community College's public service programming during this important election year, please join us in listening to Vice President George Bush outline his plans, programs, and policies for the future of higher education in the United States and, more important, the security of jobs for the people of Macomb County. This presentation is the first in a series of programs Macomb Community College will present during National Higher Education Week, October 9–15. In its efforts to celebrate the value of a college education, the college is committed to sharing the future of education in America with Macomb County residents.

News Release

Catherine B. Ahles,
Vice President for College Relations
14500 Twelve Mile Road
Warren, Michigan 48093-3896
(313) 445-7244

**Macomb
Community
College**

FOR PR NEWSWIRE

September 27, 1988
Contact: Catherine B. Ahles
445-7244

VICE PRESIDENT BUSH TO VISIT MACOMB COMMUNITY COLLEGE

WARREN, MI, Sept. 27, 1988 - -

Republican presidential candidate George W. Bush will visit Macomb Community College's Center Campus in Clinton Township this Thursday, September 29.

At an outdoor rally, scheduled to begin at 2:00, the vice president will discuss his plans, programs, and policies for the future of higher education in the United States.

"The issues of education and jobs for the American worker are of vital importance to our nation," said college President Albert L. Lorenzo. "In my view, the public policy effected by the next president of the United States will have a drastic impact on our country's ability to compete in the year 2000." he added. "To quote a recent study by the Roper organization and published in The Public Pulse; 'There is no doubt about it: A college degree is the ticket to material success in America today. It is, in fact, a necessity—virtually the only path to success and affluence in our modern economy,'" said Lorenzo.

Roper statistics indicate that in 1986, the average household income for college graduates and those with post graduate work was $49,610—50 percent higher than people who had only one to three years of college experience ($33,090); almost twice the level of high school graduates ($27,700); and nearly three times the income of people who did not complete high school ($17,900).

Macomb County currently has the lowest rate of bachelor's degree holders in the four-county greater Detroit area. About one-third of the adults over 25 have not com-

-more-

-2-

pleted high school. Macomb County is the only one of the top 100 counties in the nation which does not house a bachelor's degree granting college or university within its borders.

A proposal placed by the college on the November 8 general election ballot would provide for the establishment of a Bachelor's Degree Partnership Program between Macomb Community College and other senior colleges in Michigan. The proposal requires voter approval of a one-third mill funding plan for four years.

Macomb County, home of 8 percent of Michigan's registered voters, is considered a key area frequently targeted by both political parties during elections. Some 22 percent are identified as Democratic, 25 percent are Republican, and 33 percent are independent.

The remainder do not declare partisanship. Solidly Democratic in local elections, Macomb voters have voted Republican in the last two presidential races. Macomb Community College's Center Campus is located at 44575 Garfield, near Hall Road (M59).

The visit by Vice President Bush will be the first of several events at the college to celebrate National Higher Education Week, October 9–15. Macomb Community College enrolls 32,000 students at three campuses in Macomb County, a northern suburb of Detroit with a population of nearly 700,000. Its employment base is 45 percent manufacturing with the automotive industry dominating, and is the home of General Motors Tech Center, an 18,000 employee engineering and design center.

# # #

Plan of Action   Campus Visit of Vice President George Bush [Similar plans were developed for Bush/Dukakis/Reagan visits.]
Message strategies for candidate visits:

- Establish the current educational attainment level and dependence on manufacturing industries of the people of Macomb County.
- Describe the needs of employers for an educated (as opposed to skilled) work force in the year 2000.

- Raise the education issues of access, opportunity, and choice; relationship to economic development; cost; and quality.
- Describe Macomb County as a living example of a work force in need of access to education.

Communication Strategies:

- Focus on turning out employees, students, and homeowners through:
  Distribution of fliers
  Media publicity
  Advertisements
  Direct involvement of student clubs, athletes
  Invitations to all high schools
  Working with *Macomb Daily* for full front-page advance coverage
- Utilize protocol opportunities to tell MCC's story by:
  Selection of students with success stories as dias guests
  Selection of airport greeters
- Encourage all news media to tell MCC's story about the value of a college degree and portray MCC as one of the premier community colleges in the United States through:
  News advisories and releases describing why MCC sought the event
  Special briefings of local press
  Press kit distribution day of event
  One page fact sheet—value of college degree
    Al Lorenzo bio
    MCC fact sheet (one page)
  MCC president introducing the event
  Press conference or briefing
  College Relations presence in pressroom
  Special briefing of all staff involved, especially Macomb Center staff, to develop spokespersons
- Maximize coverage gained by:
  Using quotes from stories during remainder of ballot proposal campaign, especially during National Higher Education Week
  Audio- and video-taping remarks for future use
  Heavy candid photography for photo layouts
- Facilitate employee morale by:
  Seeking generous photo opportunities
  Create lasting impression of MCC and facilitate visibility among media, visiting dignitaries through:
  Student produces gift for Vice President Bush
  VIP mementos
  Inspirational performance by Macombers
- Support voter registration/public service objectives by:
  Beefing up K-building voter registration table to handle crowd
  Placing banners, signs reminding attendees to register
  Making reference during introductions or speech to voter registration importance/location

- Support ballot proposal public information program objectives by:
  Having literature available on the proposals
  Staging static display in visible but appropriate spot
- Create excitement and have fun by:
  Photo opportunity: Giving Bush baseball jacket
  Distribution of buttons and bumper stickers
  Distribution of T-shirts to students

IV. National Higher Education Week Scheduled Programming

National Higher Education Week, at Macomb Community College October 9–15, 1988 sponsored by the Council for Advancement and Support of Education, is an annual celebration designed to promote the role colleges, universities, and their graduates play in shaping our society. Each fall, since the program began in 1981, members of higher education communities across the United States and Canada organize state and local activities to focus public and media attention on the mission of higher education and to demonstrate the need for increased public and private support for all education.

For Macomb Community College to develop activities during Higher Education Week of October 9–15, 1988, is extremely fortunate. With two proposals on the November 8 ballot, Higher Education Week programming can be used to support the college's ongoing public information efforts—reaching all of Macomb's publics in the process. It is hoped that Higher Education Week will be a cornerstone in the college's ballot proposal master strategy.

What follows is a brief description of several on-campus activities currently being developed for Macomb Community College's celebration of National Higher Education Week.

Scheduled Events for Higher Education Week

1. Presidential Visit
   George Bush/J. Danforth Quayle   Michael Dukakis/Lloyd Bentsen
   Key Date: Whenever they are ready
   Audiences: Macomb County voters, media
   Responsibility: Ahles, Hohl, Delmotte, Smydra, Ross
   Role in Higher Education Week: An on-campus presidential candidate visit would not only bring national exposure to Macomb Community College, but could give the college's ballot proposal efforts a tremendous boost approaching the November 8 election. Invitations to the two candidates spoke to the importance of higher education in today's society and is a strong campaign issue this fall.
   Status: Initial inquiries from both campaigns have been made to the college. Dukakis campaign in Macomb County has called to determine the capacity of our fieldhouse. Bush campaign in Washington has made contact with Broomfield, Michigan congressman.

2. Working Title: CASE Conference on Higher Education
   Key date: Monday, October 10   @ Center Campus/7–9 P.M.
   Audiences: High school and junior high school parents and students
   Responsibility: Hohl, Ross, Savage, Healy, Donna Orem
   Role in Higher Education Week: The Legislative Briefing is an annual event sponsored by the college—although it is usually held in Lansing. This event will give our elected decision makers an up-close look at the college ballot proposals and give them the opportunity to ask any questions in the process. This is also our opportunity to stress the importance of higher education with our elected officials.
   Status: Invitation list is being compiled, as well as letter of invitation . . . it would be expected that members of the board of trustees be in attendance, as well as administration officials, including Lorenzo.

3. Legislative Briefing
   Key Date: Friday, October 14   @ South Campus/8–9:30 P.M.
   Audiences: Elected representatives for Macomb County in Lansing and Washington, D.C., and/or their administrative assistants.
   Responsibility: Rini, Ross
   Role in Higher Education Week: The Legislative Briefing is an annual event sponsored by the college—although it is usually held in Lansing. This event will give our elected decision makers an up-close look at the college ballot proposals and give them the opportunity to ask any questions in the process. This is also our opportunity to stress the importance of higher education with our elected officials.
   Status: Invitation list is being compiled, as well as letter of invitation . . . it would be expected that members of the board of trustees be in attendance, as well as administration officials, including Lorenzo.

Program Organization and Timeline   Over 95 volunteers served on 19 program committees. Over 200 additional volunteers assisted in the public information effort.

1986–1988
KEY CAMPAIGN DIFFERENCES

1986	1988
Complex Message	Simple Message
Abstract Title	Concrete Titles
Mass Media Approach	Group, Individual Contact
Promotion Approach	Fact-Based Approach
Small Implementation Team	Large Implementation Team
Mass Advocacy	Selected Advocacy

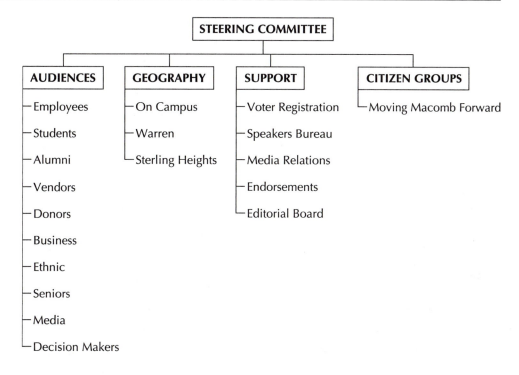

V. National Higher Education Week

Evaluation included two clippings form the *Macomb Daily* headlined "Getting to Know You . . . Worldwide Media Focus on Macomb's Voters" and "International Media Focus on Macomb County Voters:"

Endorsements

Contents:

> List of endorsements
> Brochure with principal endorsement listed on back
> Photo of Rep. Claude Pepper and Rep. David Bonior
> Sample letters of endorsement
> Editorial endorsements from major newspapers

Objectives of National Higher Education Week:

> To gain general support for the college's proposals through third-party credibility and/or by association.
> To leverage key endorsements such as major newspaper editorial boards, chambers of commerce, and civic groups to influence larger audiences.

Preliminary Results:

> Twenty-six key daily newspapers and a major weekly:
> • The *Detroit News*

"THIS COLLEGE *IS* THE COMMUNITY"

	JAN	FEB	MAR	APR	MAY	JUN	JUL	AUG	SEP	OCT	NOV	DEC

RESEARCH

PLANNING

EXECUTION

Employee annual meeting

Annual report to community

Speakers bureau

Image advertising

Macomb 2000 seminar

Press-public announcements

Continuous media relations

Continuous internal communication

Targeted letters/fact sheets

Endorsement activity

Legislative newsletters/briefings

Voter registration drive

Campus display

Alumni magazine

Presidential leadership visits

National Higher Ed Week

Ads, poster, media briefings

Forum, luncheon, alumni appeals

Student clubs

Mass mailed voters guide

Essay contest

EVALUATION

Implementation

Impact   until 2-89

- The *Detroit Free Press*
- The *Macomb Daily*
- The *Warren Weekly*

and major business and civic groups including:

- The Greater Detroit Chamber of Commerce
- Central Macomb County Chamber of Commerce
- Civic Searchlight

Endorsements:

> Key endorsements were identified, solicited, and tracked
> Letters requested and submitted

Twenty-six key endorsements were published on the second printing of the Guide of Macomb Community College Ballot proposals and distributed at the Reagan visit:

- AFSCME 1917 MCC
- Metro East Chamber of Commerce
- AFCME 2172
- Sterling Heights Area Chamber
- Macomb School Boards Association Civic Searchlight
- Romeo Community Schools of Commerce
- City of Center Line
- Lakeshore Public Schools
- Warren Consolidated School
- Macomb Community College
- Macomb Daily Faculty Organization
- *Detroit News*
- Macomb College Association of Administration Personnel
- Metro AFL-CIO
- Michigan Multiple Listing Service, Inc.
- Central Macomb County Chamber of Commerce
- Macomb Fire Institute Advisory Committee
- Warren Schools Credit Union
- Sterling Heights Police Command Officers Association
- Warren, Center Line, Sterling Heights Chamber of Commerce
- Greater Detroit Chamber of Commerce
- Macomb/St. Clair Private Industry Council
- Macomb County Chamber of Commerce Coalition
- Macomb County Community Growth Council

An endorsement of higher education made by U.S. Representative Claude Pepper appeared in a national Higher Education Week advertisement after he appeared on campus in September.

The following memo was circulated by the Greater Detroit Chamber of Commerce to its board of directors.

DATE: October 14, 1988

To: Board of Directors

FROM: Urban Affairs Committee

SUBJECT: Macomb Community College Millage Proposal

FOR CONSIDERATION/ACTION AT: October 26, 1988, Board of Directors Meeting

ACTION PROPOSED

The Urban Affairs Committee, with the agreement of the Taxation Committee, recommends the following: The Greater Detroit Chamber of Commerce supports the 1/3 mill increase proposal appearing on the November 8th general election ballot in Macomb County for the purpose of developing bachelor's degree programs at Macomb Community College through partnership with four-year colleges and universities.

BACKGROUND

Macomb Community College is asking voters to approve a 1/3 mill increase over the next four years raising $13 million in increased revenues. The purpose of the proposal is to generate funds to establish bachelor's degree programs to be offered on the MCC campus in partnership with senior colleges and universities. The partnership program will facilitate access to higher education for Macomb residents and create a more competitive work force for the county.

MCC currently has a successful experimental program which offers courses in health services, nursing, computers, statistics, accounting, business communications, economics, finance, and taxation. These experimental programs are being offered in partnership with the University of Detroit, Walsh College, and Wayne State University. Based on this experience, MCC feels the need exists to formalize and expand the partnership program. If the millage proposal is approved by voters, bachelor's degrees offered will be determined based upon student demand, community needs, and partnership agreements with four-year colleges and universities. In addition to the institutions mentioned above, consideration is also being given to Michigan State University and Eastern University as partners in the program. MCC itself will not become a four-year college.

Therefore, the Urban Affairs Committee recommends the Greater Detroit Chamber of Commerce support the millage proposal appearing on the November 8th general election ballot in Macomb County. The proposal would help assure a quality work force for the future and enhance overall higher education opportunities in the area.

(The current millage proposal is similar to a 1986 proposal supported by the Chamber which asked voters for a 2/3 millage increase in Macomb County for four-year educational programs at MCC. The 1986 proposal was rejected by voters. A copy of that action item is attached along with other supporting documentation.)

(attachments)

Implementation Strategy and Tactics*

Bush Scheduled to Talk Education at Macomb Rally
GOP Candidate to Meet Offspring of Middle Class
By Patricia Montemurri
Free Press Staff Writer

Republican presidential candidate George Bush, who promises to be "the education president," comes to Macomb Community College today to speak to the sons and daughters of Macomb County's blue-collar workers. But it is many of those students from middle-income families who have seen their college loans and grants dry up under the Reagan administration.

Macomb President Albert Lorenzo invited both Bush and Democratic rival Michael Dukakis to explain their ABC's for education and jobs at the college, the state's largest community college with 32,000 students on three campuses.

Macomb is home to many "Reagan Democrats," the ethnic, blue-collar voters who were raised as Democrats and support the party in local and state elections, but voted for Republican Reagan in 1980 and 1984.

Bush will speak at the school's Center for the Performing Arts auditorium at its Center campus in Clinton Township at 2:30 P.M., and then fly to Grand Rapids for a 5:15 rally and speech. School officials say they hope to bring Dukakis to campus.

The Macomb Daily
October 29–30, 1988
Page 1 A

Dukakis Boosted by MCC Audience
By Chad Selweski, staff writer

WARREN—Battling against the perception that he's headed for defeat in 10 days, Democratic presidential candidate Michael Dukakis told a massive crowd here Friday the race is "tightening up" and predicted he will pull off a surprise victory unlike anything seen in American politics since Harry Truman's win in 1948.

"There, too, they said Truman didn't have a chance. They said the other fella was way ahead and sitting on his lead," said Dukakis. " . . . My friends, it's not the

*Labeled "Execution" in the case study Examples of coverage of presidential visit.

pollsters that vote on election day, it's the people. And I think the American people are getting a little tired of being told how they're going to vote." The Massachusetts governor was buoyed by an enthusiastic audience of nearly 6,000 people packed into the Macomb Community College fieldhouse on the South campus.

A mixed crowd of senior citizens, union members and students waved Dukakis-Bentsen placards in a festive atmosphere capped by red, white, and blue balloons cascading from the ceiling at the close of the speech. The crowd appeared to be larger than the turnout for a highly successful campaign visit to the MCC fieldhouse almost exactly four years ago by President Reagan

Media Endorsements

The Detroit News
October 27, 1988
page 18-a

Yes to Macomb Millage, Part I

A little more than two years ago, this newspaper supported Macomb Community College's proposal for a two-thirds of a mill increase in county property taxes for 20 years. The tax would have financed a new program to allow Macomb residents to earn bachelor's degrees from existing four-year institutions without leaving the county. The voters, however, soundly defeated that proposal.

Now Macomb Community College is back asking for a scaled-down millage of one-third of a mill for four years in another effort to establish the same program. The college is also asking for a $19.2-million bond issue to make physical and structural improvements at the college. We support both proposals.

MCC's budget is more than $50 million a year. The college estimates that the millage proposal, if enacted, would provide a total of $12 million over its four-year life. That will permit the construction of a new $10.8-million, 60,000-square-foot building to house the four-year-degree program. Professors and instructors would be imported from schools such as Wayne State, Oakland University and the University of Detroit to teach courses in health services, nursing and computers.

How much would it all cost homeowners in the county? The college figures approximately $10 to $15 per household per year. And if residents take advantage of all property tax credits and federal deductions that are available to homeowners, the cost could be as little as $2.00. MCC President Frank Lorenzo is careful to point out that none of this means MCC is on its way to becoming a full four-year college.

The program is simply designed to make a full-course college education available to Macomb County residents without their having to relocate to East Lansing or Ann Arbor. Ultimately, college officials believe it will save many families in the county money, because they won't have to pay for the cost of room and board incurred when sending children away to college.

It is useful to remember, however, that both the University of Michigan at Dearborn and Oakland University also sprang from the same sort of modest beginnings as MCC, and spending programs designed to "save" money often don't in the end. We are also somewhat skeptical of the $19-billion bond to improve infrastructure. Where have the maintenance people been these last 20 years when the buildings began falling down? Some tighter management in this area seems appropriate.

Despite these reservations, we think there is a case to be made for additional four-year college capacity in the Detroit area. Michigan State is turning away qualified students for lack of space, and Oakland University is bursting at the seams. Macomb also has the lowest percentage of college graduates in the Detroit area and one of the highest unemployment rates. Since college graduates most always find jobs, education is clearly a way to help the county diversify its economy.

The money involved is not lavish and we are impressed with President Lorenzo's stewardship. The administration will have to come back to the people in four years if it wants the millage renewed, and the voters will then have another opportunity to judge whether promises have been kept or not.

The Detroit Free Press
October 29, 1988
page 8a

Macomb: Ballot Proposals to Aid the Community College Deserve Voter Support

The success or failure of two proposals on next month's Macomb County ballot will greatly affect both the quality of higher education available to county students and the economic strength of the county. One proposal would authorize . . .

A Side Bar to Read:
A proposal to borrow money to repair buildings and update equipment at Macomb Community College; and a proposal to levy a one-third mill tax for the next four years to allow the college to offer bachelor degree programs. VOTE YES ON BOTH.

The Macomb Daily
October 24, 1988
page 5a
    In Our Opinion

We Urge Approval of College Proposals

"Our progress as a nation can be no swifter than our progress in education."

Those words were spoken by John F. Kennedy, a man who used his education, experiences and abilities to become president of the United States.

We find a distinct similarity between President Kennedy's insight into educational benefits to our country and the values espoused by those who say an improved education foundation here in Macomb County will mean a better tomorrow.

Macomb's media strategy included using the Reagan visit to focus additional attention on its proposals.

The Detroit News
November 5, 1988
page 6B

Reagan Visit May Aid Bond Issue for MCC

By Tom Greenwood
News Staff Writer
    Like George Bush, Macomb County Community College is looking for votes out of today's visit by President Reagan to its Warren campus. But instead of presidential votes, the college wants support for its $19.2 million bond issue and a one-third mill increase proposal that will appear on Tuesday's ballot.

The bond money would be used to make major campus renovations and upgrade teaching facilities. The millage would establish a bachelor's degree program with four-year universities. "The visit may not sway any voters, but it will help draw their attention to the education issue facing Americans today," said Kathy Ahles, vice-president for college relations.

Reagan will speak at the college late this morning in one of his last election appearances on behalf of Vice-President Bush. He is expected to draw a standing room only crowd of 5,000. "Naturally, we're quite excited by the president's visit," Ahles said. "This marks the second time President Reagan has visited the college. He also came here in 1984."

Bush also came to the campus during the current campaign, as did his rival, Democrat Michael Dukakis. "As best we can determine, we are the only college, university, club or organization that has hosted both presidential candidates this year, as well as the president," Ahles said. "I think that says a lot about the school." "In their visits, both Vice President Bush and Gov. Dukakis stressed that education was the key to America's future and its economic development." The president will speak inside the field house on the MCC south campus, near the Martin-Hayes intersection. The doors open at 9:00 A.M.

Coverage of the Ballot Proposals   More than 15 stories, side bars, and editorials resulted from ballot proposal activities.

Briefing Sheet

Macomb Community College
- Has two proposals on November ballot:
  Bachelor Degree Partnership Proposal (1/3 mill)
  Equipment Replacement and Facilities Renovation (bonds)
- Only college to host three Campaign 88 visits.
- Largest of Michigan's 29 community colleges: 32,300 students.
- Third largest of all colleges and universities in the state, behind University of Michigan and Michigan State University.
- Fourth in the nation in number of associate degrees awarded.
- The only institution of higher education in Macomb County.
- 126 degree programs in arts and sciences, preprofessional, and occupational areas.
- Accreditation from eleven national professional associations, including a ten years renewal by the North Central Association of Colleges and Schools—the highest it awards.
- Three campuses:
  South Campus (Warren: largest, houses technology programs)
  Center Campus (Clinton Twp.: houses health, music, art)
  Fraser Campus (Professional Adult Continuing Education)
- Strong reputation; highly respected in the county and nationally
- Student Demographics:
  56%—under 25 years old, 52% female
  28%—25 to 34 years old, 48% male
  11%—35 to 44 years old, 19% full-time
   5%—45 years old or older, 81% part-time

- Courses taken by students:
  54% Arts & Sciences
  25% Business and Information Management
  14% Design, Mechanical, & Applied Technology
  5% Health & Human Services; Public Service
- Funding: 23% from local property taxes
  42% from state aid
  26% from student tuition

Macomb County
- Population: 700,000
- Education is critical to the future economic well-being of this manufacturing community and its metal-bending craftsmen.
- Employment base: 45% of the work force is employed in manufacturing, twice the state average and four times the national average.
- Lowest educational attainment rate of the four-county Greater Detroit area (about one-third of the adults over 25 have not completed high school and only 10.7 percent have attained a bachelor's degree).
- Typically blue-collar workers, many second or third generation of Italian, Polish, or Ukranian descent.
- Home of the GM Tech Center, largest manufacturing design center.
- Automotive plants for each of the Big Three manufacturers.
- Boating Capital of the World (more boats per capita).
- Recreation: boating, bowling, and softball.
- Main concerns: crime, job security, taxes, education.
- Values: family, hard work, straight language.
- 22% Democratic, 25% republican, 33% independent, 20% undeclared.

The county, known for its "ticket-splitting" voting patterns, has solidly voted Democratic in local elections, but has voted Republican in the last two presidential elections.

Messages   Macomb Community College has been using the slogan, "This College is the Community . . . our people, our problems, our families, and our future."

In American government today, the office of the president is the embodiment of America . . . its people, its problems, its families, and its future.

Macomb Community College's ballot proposals encourage taxpayers to continue to support the only institution of higher education in Macomb County. As technology begins to dominate the production processes of industry, the key to the future of this manufacturing county is the education and training of its highly skilled work force.

Quotes generated by campaign activities available for use in media communications.

> "If you have a college degree, you're virtually certain to have a job. That kind of success is not only true for individuals, but communities as well."
> —*Doug Ross, Michigan Department of Commerce*

"Every person must be trained for the future . . . it will be the only way to stay ahead in the global competition. Supporting education is not an expenditure, but an investment."
—The Honorable Claude Pepper, U.S. House of Representatives

"For too long, the community college system has been underappreciated. People don't realize that community colleges are a great asset. They fill a very special and important role in higher education."
—Donald L. Bemis, superintendent of public instruction, State of Michigan, and Macomb Community College, class of 1955

"In the future, we're going to have to ask workers to put their brains, not their backs, into their work."
—Roger Smith, General Motors Corporation

The coverage of campaign activities included the following: a photo of Vice President George Bush addressing a press conference; satellite coverage of the president's visit; ABC newsman Sam Donaldson working the crowd prior to Dukakis's speech; newsmen from around the world filing stories from MCC pressroom; network television interviews of local citizens; cable network during live coverage.

Evaluation

Evaluation Objectives
To determine if the community relations program accomplished its goals.
To measure the effectiveness of the communications used in the program.
To make program adjustments as found to be needed.
To provide a basis for future recommendations on millage election efforts.

Evaluation of Results
Impact evaluation shows that both stated goals of the program were achieved: the perceived value of education increased among 14% of the residents and the MCC ballot proposals passed with at least a 10% margin.

The communications used received high marks by county voters for recall of messages three months later (19%), and for agreement with the message (61%).

Employees rated the adequacy of information about the proposals at very good to excellent, with an average of 7.3 on a 10-point scale.

Preparation and implementation evaluation occurred throughout the program. Examples are:
• Changes in the content of the fact sheet and the "Guide to Ballot Proposals" based upon market testing.
• An Editorial Board reviewed and evaluated all print collateral prior to printing.

- An evaluation form was distributed to all Macomb 2000 attendees.
- Documentation of evaluation is available for future use.

Assessment of MCC Public Information Campaign

A. *Introduction*   This research report is one of the final steps of Macomb Community College's Public Information Program "This College is the Community," which was put into action early in 1988. The goal of the program is to increase the level of support for Macomb Community College among its constituents as measured by:

Passage of MCC ballot proposals
Increases in the perceived value of higher education among the county's residents

MCC commissioned Market Opinion Research to conduct this postelection survey of Macomb County voters to assess the impact of the public information campaign measuring campaign awareness and recognition; assessing increases in the perceived value of higher education; and assessing MCC's image as an institution of higher education.

The survey is based on interviews with a representative sample of 418 voters who actually voted on one or both MCC proposals on the ballot November 8, 1988. They were interviewed January 17–23, 1989.

B. *Campaign Effectiveness*   Overall, the campaign was successful. Both the equipment updating and facilities renovation bonding and the four-year partnership millage proposal were passed November 8, 1988, by margin of 56.44% and 55.45%, respectively. Campaign themes and messages were mentioned by many voters as reasons why they supported the proposals.

One quarter (27%) of supporters of the equipment updating and renovation bonding proposal gave reasons for proposal support such as: "need it to improve education," "investment in future college students," and "it's important to a community college for the people."

More than a quarter (26%) of the four-year partnership supporters gave similar mentions: "education is the most important thing," "would be good for the community," and "money spent for education is well spent."

C. *Campaign Awareness*   Most voters were aware of the campaign to promote the ballot proposals. This is indicated in recognition and recall of specific campaign activities.

One-fifth (19%) recall hearing or seeing the campaign theme, "This College is the Community." Six-tenths (61%) agree with it.
Half of voters (50 %) recall receiving literature in the mail on the ballot issues.
Half (50%) report seeing newspaper ads referring to proposals.

Of the 5% of voters who report attending speeches or presentations on MCC, virtually all were proposal supporters (96%).

D. Making MCC a Speaker Platform in the County   Almost one-tenth of voters (8%) visited MCC in 1988 to hear one of the presidential candidates, George Bush and Michael Dukakis, or President Ronald Reagan speak. A large majority (83%) of residents feel that MCC should continue to invite national and international figures to speak at the college.

E. Increase in Perceived Value of Higher Education   Macomb County voters present an overall positive attitude towards education. Nine-tenths (88%) agree that a strong community college is important for the strength of Macomb County. A strong majority, 86% agree that supporting education should not be seen as an expenditure but as an investment. Virtually all voters (93%) agree that a college education is more important today than it was ten years ago.

In comparing current findings to a Macomb Intermediate School District County assessment conducted in January 1988, 79% agreed that a college education is more important today than it was ten years ago. The increase to the 93% level in this survey, even given the slight question wording change and the narrower sample base of this survey of only those who voted, suggest that at least some increase in the perceived value of higher education has occurred since January 1988.

F. Image and Reputation of MCC   MCC has a very positive image among county voters. The college should have little trouble positioning itself as a prestigious institution among county residents, who hold this perception:

Two-thirds (65%) of voters regard MCC as a prestigious institution and 75% of ballot supporters, but only 41% of opposers, hold this view.

Half (51%) of voters feel MCC is regarded by county residents as being their first choice for higher education. Again, those who supported the MCC proposals are more positive (57%) than are proposal opponents (30%).

Nine-tenths (88%) would recommend MCC to someone else.

The majority of voters (59%) feel that MCC spends the monies it receives well, while 29% of ballot proposal opponents disagree and feel the college spends its monies poorly. Nearly all, 21 out of 22 people who heard speeches or presentations about the college voted yes on one or both MCC ballot proposals.

G. Election Results by Precinct   Photocopies of county election records identifying results by each precinct are kept on permanent file:

CERTIFICATE OF DETERMINATION

STATE OF MICHIGAN

> County Clerk's official notice of the
>
> successful passing of the proposal.

County of Macomb

The Board of County Canvassers of Macomb County having ascertained and canvassed the votes of the several cities and townships of the county, of the General Election, Special Election for the Macomb Community College Proposition, held on Tuesday, the Eighth day of November, A.D., 1988.

On the Proposition Proposal Equipment Replacement and Facilities Renovation Bonding Proposal I of the Community College District of the County of Macomb, that YES received the largest number of votes and it is declared that said proposition DID carry in this county.

IN WITNESS WHEREOF, we have hereunto

set our hands and affixed the seal of

the Circuit Court for the County of

Macomb on November 22, 1988.

BOARD OF CANVASSERS

ATTEST:

CLERK of BOARD of COUNTY CANVASSERS

CHAIRPERSON of BOARD COUNTY CANVASSER;

We hereby certify, that the foregoing is a correct statement of the Board of County Canvassers of the votes given in such county for the proposition at the General Election, held on November 8, 1988, to the votes cast for said proposition, as appears in the transcript of the County of Macomb in said statement, so far as it relates from the original statement on file in the office of the County Clerk.

IN WITNESS WHEREOF, we have hereunto set our hands and caused to be affixed the seal of the Circuit Court for the County of Macomb

November 22, 1988.

COUNTY CLERK

Summary of Media Coverage   Accounting balance (direct costs only). Throughout the campaign there was a concerted effort to utilize existing programming, including dual-duty for activities and events and piggybacking on regular publications and mailings. These expenditures would have been made whether or not this program had been undertaken. An additional $90,000 was set aside and dedicated to this public information program.

A total of $252,615 of financial resources and hundreds of hours of volunteer staff time were accessed and utilized, including the $90,072 of dedicated monies spent on this community relations program.

BOX 5.1   **Classification of Research Project Types Identified in 1994 PRSA Winning Silver Anvil Campaigns**

I.   Research of organizational culture
    30   Investigations into organization
    14   Research of legal/regulatory status of situation
II.   Archival Research
    22   Library research/Historic research
    18   Reviews of past research
    15   Research of organization's records
    13   Accessing of data base information
    4   Examination of case studies
    3   Studies of published polls
    2   Communication logs
III.   Descriptive research
    52   Poll/survey/marketing studies
    27   Content analysis projects
    20   Interview projects
    15   Focus group projects
    9   Audits
    7   Contracted research projects
    5   Observation projects
    3   Advisory council/panel
    1   Use of research subscription services
    1   Omnibus research
    0   Delphi studies
    0   Census data use
IV.   Experimental Research
    11   Message testing
    7   Program/strategy testing
    3   Use of independent laboratory/firm
    2   Product test projects

IMPLEMENTATION COSTS COMPARED TO BUDGET

Expenditure	Annual Budget	Expend-itures	Information Budget	Expend-itures
Research	$15,000	$15,000	$8,000	$8,000
Consultation			7,000	7,000
Printing	38,000	38,000	25,000	26,220
Postage	64,000	64,449	23,000	23,156
Advertising	22,000	21,257	9,000	9,429
Promotional Items	1,600	1,597	5,000	4,743
Special Events (incl. food)	2,500	2,245	3,000	2,509
Bush/Dukakis/ Reagan visits				18,995*
Evaluation		2,000	10,000	9,000
	$143,100	$140,540	$90,000	$90,002

*Not included in sum; paid by the Presidential Candidate Campaign funds.

SUMMARY

This chapter provides **an extended case study** of a classic campaign, the Macomb Community College effort to raise funding by successfully passing a bond issue in a "no new taxes" atmosphere. The summary lists the range of research projects undertaken for the campaign, with the details of that research provided for study in the pages that follow. Also the beginning summary of the campaign reveals how research led to specific strategies.

The case also reveals how specific **adaptation decisions were based on the research** findings, and how particular actions or tactics were designed to address the problems discovered in the research stage. Two examples of **research carried out as a part of the implementation strategy stage** are reported in the case.

The evaluation stage of the case shows how **evaluation research** documented achievement of the goals as well as other accomplishments of the campaign. The case provides an opportunity to study how the many elements of a campaign came together to overcome the seemingly impossible task of winning voter approval of increased taxes when state law prohibited the college advocating such a vote.

PART THREE

Building the Campaign Plan: The Adaptation Stage

Adapting the Campaign to the Organizational Culture

- Adapting to Organizational History and Mythology
- Adapting to Organizational Philosophy and Mission
- Adapting to Organizational Structure
- Adapting to Organizational Environment
- Adapting to Organizational Operational Policies
- Adapting to Organizational Trends

To be effective, the campaign should fit the organizational culture. Research on organizational culture is somewhat different from the research approaches described in other parts of this book, but it is research nevertheless. The research needed involves close and careful observation. The observation may involve the study of documents as well as people and behavior, but it seeks to construct a useful description of the organization's personality and character. The campaign then needs to be adapted to that personality or character.

ADAPTING TO ORGANIZATIONAL HISTORY AND MYTHOLOGY

Organizational history research projects explore the artifacts of the organization's personality, investigate why it does things the way it does, and set the stage for managing the public relations function for the organization, including campaigns. This type of research is background for other types of research.

Cultural History and Mythology

Research on the history and corporate mythology involves looking at organizational origins and why the entity was established, the founder's vision, and mileposts in the life of the organization. Research on the organization's culture—the collective "schema"—should logically begin with how the organization perceives itself and its place in the world and where the organization came from, that is, its roots or its cultural history. Cultural history differs from other types of history by its concentration on the events that have shaped the organization's personality, as opposed to its financial history or its history of leadership. Cultural history traces the impact of the leaders, events, rituals, and stories for the meanings they have had in shaping the character of the organization, together with other factors that have left their mark on the way the organization does things.

Reports about the Walt Disney organization have described the decision-making process since the death of Walt Disney as often inhibited by the deceased founder's still imagined presence. "That's not the way Walt would do it," they say. Habits of deferring to the wishes of a leader of an organization are hard to break, but these habits are the substance of an organization's culture. Cultural history traces these influences to their source and constructs a mosaic that can help its members know the organization in a way that would be impossible for most people without such aid. Mythic aspects of a culture may have a more profound effect on the way employees behave than the more "objective" facts of history.

A body of literature attests to the popularity of the histories of corporations. *The Dream Maker*, Bernard Weisberger's story of Will Durant, the founder of General Motors, is one example; Robert Sobel's book (1981) on Tom Watson Sr., the founder of IBM, is another. These corporate biographies and others like them recount the founding events that are inextricably bound up with the contributions of the visionary leaders. The mythic elements that make these stories such powerful representations of the respective organizations, and can inspire people both inside and outside the companies, consist of the *interpretations* given to contributions of these leaders and the events. Myth or schema, after all, is what an organization *makes* of the facts, and after the process is under way it is difficult to separate the facts from the interpretations.

Understanding the organization's mythological history is important because it is the interpretation of the facts more than the facts themselves that motivates and inspires people. It is this inspired motivation more than anything else that provides the solid foundation for an effective public relations campaign (see Figure 6.1). If a campaign violates unwritten values, or contradicts the mission of the organization, or opposes policies based on its founder's orientation, the plan faces severe obstacles.

I will suggest in the following pages an approach to discovering an organization's mythology, the interpretations the organization's members give to

Figure 6.1 Corporate culture is represented in this photo from an Annual Report of American President Companies. Like this company, every organization has a distinctive "way of doing things" including the clothes its people wear, the display of the corporate logo, the attitude of its people toward the public, and the many other cues that distinguish organizational culture. This company provides distribution and transportation services for containerized freight within and between Asia and North America. (Courtesy of American President Companies, Ltd.)

the shared experiences. This process of interpreting the facts of history gives an organization a vital self-consciousness; interpretation is the myth-making act. The richest organizational cultures, those most able to inspire and motivate employees, are those with the strongest mythologies.

As a guide to research on corporate mythic history, this book makes two assumptions: (1) Corporate culture is more a product of mythic interpretations than of "objective" or "factual" history. (2) An organization's mythology develops in six stages. These six stages may occur consecutively, or at least some of them may develop simultaneously. However, the tendency is to develop in the order listed.

Myth, as defined here, is a process of organizational self-identification. That is, mythic meaning is what people attribute to an organization that fulfills their need as individuals for self-identification and that they achieve by their association with the organization. In other words, people bring to the myth-building process their own need for self-identification and fulfill that need by attributing to the organization with which they are affiliated the characteristics that give the organization the qualities they cherish. The mythic process infuses the organization with the attributes people wish to believe about themselves collectively, shaping how people think and feel about themselves as part of the group.

The mythic process of social self-identification is the self-conscious personality of a group, whether a tribe, a nation, or a corporation. It is akin to the self-awareness so important to the individual that is expressed in self-confidence and an ability to live a full and productive life. A corporation is able to live a full and productive life in direct proportion to its ability to offer mythic social self-identification. A campaign plan that contributes to this performs an important function in the organization's life and brings to the campaign an important criterion for success.

Myth, as social self-identification, consists of six stages. These six stages are listed below:

> Founding events
> Existential interpretation of the events
> Institutionalization of the events
> Social and ethical values that emerge from the events
> Belief system developed on the basis of the events
> Doctrine and rituals evolved to explain and celebrate the events

Not all of the stages are apparent in all organization's myths; at least not all stages may be observable in any particular organization's mythic history. These six characteristics may be observed in varying degrees or inferred from corporate behavior; they are the building blocks of corporate culture.[1] A campaign may create new rituals, celebrate old ones, restate cherished values, retell old stories, or otherwise renew the organizational myth.

ADAPTING TO ORGANIZATIONAL PHILOSOPHY AND MISSION

Philosophy and mission describe the overall purpose of an organization, but within this larger purpose is a range of intentions. The guidelines by which an organization operates range along a continuum from specific to general aims. The most specific is the organizational *objective* to be achieved in the next month, six months, year, or other time frame and usually involves a specific project. Behind the immediate objective(s) lie the more general, more long-term purposes or *goals* that describe the aim of a series of projects, a campaign, or something the company as a whole seeks to achieve over a period of one, two, or five years or more. In contrast, *mission* usually describes an indeterminate or permanent aim or intention that changes only if conditions change to the degree that the overall purpose of the organization must change. On the other hand, *philosophy* is not an aim or intention but an attitude that shapes the range of purposes.

In his study "The President and Corporate Planning," Myles Mace found, "The more common president is one who is rarely satisfied with nominal growth rates, who stretches the forecasts of divisional or functional managers, and who establishes new and challenging standards of performance for the organization to achieve." The chief executive officer (CEO) formulates performance guidelines in some form or document, he says, and "the composite documents constitute the corporate plan for the stated period of years ahead. Sometimes these 'working papers' are regarded as 'company goals or plans.' In other cases, the significant elements of them are formalized into 'corporate goals,' . . . the corporate plans for achievement are spelled out in great detail. The mission and the plan for achievement are thus clearly defined."[2]

Organizational mission is a term used to describe the long-range organizational guidelines. A mission statement need not be lengthy, however. "A statement of purpose can become the contemporary replacement for the traditional strategic plan. It is not a bound volume, but only one or two pieces of paper. It is a summary statement of outputs, clients, values, and strategy that have been made specific by long-range objectives in the key performance areas that will determine business success."[3] The mission statement, nevertheless, is carefully drafted to reflect, in summary, the organization's most incisive purpose. In his extensive study of corporate philosophy and mission statements, Thomas Falsey concludes, "The words of a mission statement make for good public relations."[4]

According to Stonich, the mission statement for a business should involve three major elements: (1) a customer description, (2) a description of customer needs, and (3) how the organization's product or service fulfills the need. "The business definition includes definitions of market, function, and technology. *Market* reflects the customer group being served; *function* refers to the customer needs being satisfied; and *technology* describes how the company's products or services satisfy customer needs."[5] As simple as these elements seem, the business world is filled with examples of enterprises that failed because one or more of these elements are misunderstood. The same elements apply to nonbusiness organizations as well. See Figure 6.2 for examples of corporate mission statements.

The organizational mission does not change rapidly but reflects the long-

Our Commitments

We, in Squibb, are committed to these values:

To increasing shareholders' value. We seek to maximize total return on investment for our shareholders in terms of capital appreciation and current income by gradually increasing both ⋯n the business and dividends.

⋯*e in science and innovation.* Squibb science must be, and be perceived to be, ⋯ss stature in each of our areas of specialization in terms of basic biomedical ⋯duct formulations and clinical research. All of our operations must excel in terms ⋯ctive technologies and in terms of product innovation. Squibb will not enter, or ⋯field in which it cannot technologically excel.

⋯*xcellence.* All of our products must be of top quality, deliver the benefits they ⋯be cost effective. The "Priceless Ingredient" is as priceless as ever.

⋯*service.* We must excel in meeting the needs of our customers for prompt and ⋯ice. A squibb customer must be a satisfied customer.

⊛ The Westinghouse Purpose

The basic purpose of Westinghouse, in all its decisions and actions, is:

1) To attain a continuous high level of profit which places it in the top ranks of industry in its rate of return on investment capital, recognizing that Westinghouse can serve society only if it is financially viable.

2) To operate all elements of the Corporation throughout the world in a manner which contributes to the improvement of society and which is sensitive to the natural and human environ⋯

3) To achieve steady growth in profits, sales⋯ productive investment at rates exceeding th⋯ economy as a whole.

4) To be responsive at all times to the need⋯ people by providing quality products and se⋯ continuously and by creating new products⋯ increase user satisfaction.

5) To distribute equitably among owners, e⋯ fruits of improved productivity and efficient⋯ and capital.

6) To maintain a dynamic business structur⋯ investment form areas which have lost their⋯ business fields where potential for growth i⋯

7) To create a environment in which, witho⋯ employes are enabled, encouraged and stim⋯ highest potential of output and creativity an⋯ possible level of job satisfaction in the spirit⋯ Creed.

8) To conduct all affairs of the Corporation⋯ highest ethical and legal standards.

These eight points are indivisible. Together,⋯ basic purpose and fundamental manageme⋯ Westinghouse Electric Corporation.

⋯ipatory management ⋯the decision-making ⋯naking at the lowest ⋯ion systems; and the ⋯organization.

⋯uipment, our human ⋯bing the skills of our ⋯career planning and

⋯l mutual self-respect ⋯ grow professionally ⋯vironment contribut- ⋯and reward superior

⋯we contribute to the ⋯lo business, and are

⋯ity of its maker"

MISSION STATEMENT

RHW Hotel Management Company, Inc.

We hereby dedicate ourselves and our resources to the provision of TOTAL GUEST SATISFACTION of profit, by selecting and developing individuals within each job classification, whereby each can best utilize his talents for self-fulfillment and for the benefits of our guests... in the form of superior guest service, an always friendly and helpful environment, and the cleanest, most comfortable accommodations in our industry.

Figure 6.2 Examples of mission statements.

range view of the organization's strengths and its role in society. Tourangeau describes this "charter of objectives" as a "statement of the needs of society to which the organization intends to address itself . . . taking into consideration its own unique capabilities and resources."[6] The needs of society which the organization "intends to address" are simply alternate approaches to what Stonich called the customer and his need, together with the organization's technology to fulfill that need.

Organizational philosophy is an orientation that lies behind the mission statement. Philosophy means, as the American Heritage dictionary defines it, "a system of motivating concepts and principles, a viewpoint." In these terms, philosophy is the pattern of beliefs, attitudes, opinions, and values that under-lies decisions. An organizational philosophy lies behind the organization's stated mission and may contradict its apparent purpose. Research for a campaign that fails to detect a contradiction between philosophy and mission risks a failed campaign.

A *Harvard Business Review* article cites an extreme example of companies illustrating such a contradiction. They came to decisions based on very personal and, one would feel, irrational motives.

> I know of a company, very closely held, the executives of which (after a great deal of probing action) finally admitted they were primarily interested in maintaining the prestige of other members of the family. The top executive was not going to jeopardize his income or that of four or five members of his family. His could have been a growing and healthy company if it had brought in and held executives, but he could not keep people for very long. It took five years [for most executives] to realize what the real objectives of this company were.
>
> In another company, the president made a review of a five-year forecast of sales and profits based on the continuation of status quo operations. It seemed possible with existing products, he reasoned, to maintain the same flat curve of sales and profits . . . He concluded . . . that the company's plan would be to maintain this level of performance and not try to grow. . . ."If I grow and take on more people, I am not too sure I could do it. And even if I could, I am not willing to pay the price of the extra effort required."[7]

If these two examples are representative of even a small percentage of organizations, the public relations campaign planner may expect to discover or infer such motives in many organizations being studied. The research findings detailing the organizational philosophy will help the public relations person make effective decisions, whether they are to leave the organization or to adapt to this kind of organizational philosophy and plan public relations efforts accordingly.

ADAPTING TO ORGANIZATIONAL STRUCTURE

The way an organization is plotted in the organizational chart identifies how the organization's functions are related to each other. The effectiveness of the public relations executive depends on a thorough understanding of the structure of the employing organization. Traditionally, the organizational chart has been understood as a map of this structure. But like the map of a growing city, which easily becomes outdated as new buildings are erected, new streets are built, and even concentrations of business or professional activities shift, the organizational chart is a tentative representation of an organization's structure.

The formal structure depicted on the organizational chart, the *organigram*, may be the formal structure, but an informal power structure may be an even more important indication of how decisions are made. Shifts in organizational structure represent the normal evolution of a growing organization as new and more efficient ways of doing things are discovered and implemented. Informal structures are more common in certain types of organizations than in others.

Organizational structure is an *important diagnostic tool* for the public relations officer. It can be used to discern the true nature of the functioning of the organization for which public relations efforts are being undertaken.

> Organizational structure is much more than the boxes and lines that appear on a chart. It involves . . . how individuals, groups, and units function. At the most basic level, organizations are segmented into units and patterns of [relatively stable] relationship among units. [The "function of units" includes] how people are hired and placed in jobs, how they get rewarded, how jobs are grouped in units, what reporting relationships exist, how information moves, what reward systems are employed, how the career development system functions, how the organization determines if it is doing well or poorly, etc.[8]

Organizational structure, if it is called to the attention of people throughout the organization, affects behavior by controlling "people's *expectancies* of the consequences of their behavior," the "*effort*" that people bring to their tasks, and other determining factors in their "*performance.*" The expectancies fostered by the structure influence "*motivation*"; the way the structure operates either "*constrains or facilitates*" effective behavior.[9] For example, Walter Chrysler left General Motors to found his own company because the structure that evolved under Will Durant allowed little delegation of decision making and made it impossible to confer with the CEO or to get approval on critical decisions.[10]

In addition to the operational patterns of an organization, such as personnel recruitment and development, rewards and sanctions, and design of tasks, specific structural aspects define the organizational configuration: *aggregation*, the grouping of roles or positions into units; *intraunit relationships*, either informal or formalized structuring within work groups; and *interunit relationships*, the coordination and control between work groups.

Communication is often the key to the effective working of the organizational structure. Because different tasks vary in "uncertainty," the need for communication varies: that is, the more carefully defined the task, the less important the communication. Understanding the organizational structure is also important in determining the organization's personality, the corporate culture. Researchers in business management have produced evidence that structure is often the determinant of corporate personality, not the other way around.

> Underlying most efforts at organizational design is the basic assumption that how individuals and work units are grouped and linked together makes a difference in how an organization performs. Both the managerial experience and organizational research indicate that, to a large degree, this assumption is true. Organizations operating in the same environments with the same types of resources may be more or less effective depending on the appropriateness of their structures.[11]

The conclusion that structure determines organizational character grows out of the evolution of the theory of organizational structure. The military chain of command or formal "scalar structure," together with the scientific management forms of the 1920s, produced the machinelike organization with its highly standardized tasks and low worker morale. In reaction, the "human relations" school of thought sought to demonstrate that "reliance on the formal structure specifically on the mechanisms of direct supervision and standardization, was at best misguided, at worse dangerous to the psychological health of the workers."[12]

Mintzberg, on the basis of "over 200 books and articles" in the field of organizational structure, has described five types of structure into which all organizations seem to fit. The five types of structure (described below) are based on nine "design parameters" that describe a range of elements that determine structure. The design parameters are the "formal and semiformal means" that "organizations use to divide and coordinate their work in order to establish stable patterns of behavior."[13]

Mintzberg's nine design parameters are (1) **job specialization,** the number of tasks required of the worker and how broadly or narrowly each task is defined; (2) **behavior formalization,** the way the organization standardizes its work processes: (3) **training and indoctrination,** how the organization teaches job skills and knowledge (training) and how it inculcates norms of behavior; (4) **unit grouping,** how positions should be grouped; (5) **unit size,** how large groups should be; (6) **planning and control systems** that standardize vertical and lateral linkages for "mutual adjustment," including (7) **liaison devices,** formally established permanent or temporary positions to communicate directly, bypassing vertical channels; (8) **vertical decentralization,** the "dispersal of formal power" for decision making down the chain of command; and (9) **horizontal decentralization,** the extent to which nonmanagers control the decision process.[14] Mintzberg argues that organizational structure is determined by how an organization works out each of these nine elements in organizational life; it is not a decision imposed by management alone.

Management idealization of organizational structure should give the public relations person important clues to how best to carry out the public relations function. Mintzberg's five types of organizational structures will guide

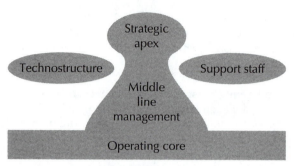

Figure 6.3 Mintzberg's model of the five basic parts of a typical organization, showing the relative relationship of position and function.

the researcher in identifying the dominant influences in the organization being served. These five "structural configurations" are the "Simple Structure, the Machine Bureaucracy, the Professional Bureaucracy, the Divisional Form, and the Adhocracy." To help in understanding Mintzberg's approach to organizational structures analysis, Figure 6.3 shows his model of the organizational structure, with an explanation of the psychological pull each element exerts to enhance its special prerogatives.

The strategic apex includes senior management—the CEO, president, and board of directors—and exerts a pull for centralization of authority at the apex of the organizational structure. The **technostructure** includes strategic planning, comptroller, personnel training, production scheduling, and the like and exerts a pressure toward design of standards for and regimentation of all employees. The **support staff** includes legal staff, public relations, industrial relations, research and development, payroll, and so forth and exerts pressure to form "work constellations," to decentralize power into ad hoc groups governed by mutual adjustment. **Middle line managers** include vice presidents, supervisors, and managers of the organization's operations and exert pressure to "balkanize" or to fragment the organization so as to concentrate top management and worker decisions in the hands of middle management. **Operating core** includes the workers who produce, sell, and distribute the product, and this core exerts pressure to professionalize its member's functions, give them more decision-making power, and enhance their skills. Mintzberg gives an example of the way these influences work:

> Consider, for example, the case of a film company. The presence of a great director will favor the pull to centralize and encourage the use of the Simple structure. Should there be a number of great directors, each pulling for their own autonomy, the structure will likely be Balkanized into the Divisionalized Form. Should the company instead employ highly skilled actors and cameramen, producing complex but standard industrial films, it will have a strong incentive to decentralize further and use the Professional Bureaucracy structure. In contrast, should the company

employ relatively unskilled personnel, perhaps to mass produce spaghetti westerns, it will experience a strong pull to standardize and to structure itself as a Machine Bureaucracy. But if, instead, it wishes to innovate, resulting in the strongest pull to collaborate the efforts of director, designer, actor, and cameraman, it would have a strong incentive to use the Adhocracy configuration.[15]

The minimum outcome of this research on organizational structure should be an organizational chart, an organigram, if one is appropriate to the organization. The research may attempt to fit, or at least compare, the organization to one of the five types of structure presented here, and to explain what pressures are exerted on the various functions within the organization. An analysis should be made of where and how public relations fits into the organization and how best to relate as the public relations officer to the organization.

➤ CASE STUDY: BRISTOL-MYERS SQUIBB, SYRACUSE "LIFTING THE VEIL"

For decades chain link fences circling the Bristol-Myers Squibb 70 acre site in its Syracuse, New York, division conveyed the message to the community, "Stay off the property and out of our business." It was no surprise that by the early 1990s most of the media and community focus was on Bristol's environmental troubles. In particular, the community's daily newspaper committed most of its Bristol Syracuse division coverage to environmental bashing. The negative focus caught the attention of corporate leadership in New York City to such a degree that it jeopardized future investment in the Syracuse division. The message was clear: without significant improvements in community relations, the future of the site and its more than one thousand jobs were in serious jeopardy.

RESEARCH

Despite being one of the community's largest employers and one of its last remaining major manufacturers, neighbors, community leaders, media, and elected officials were in the dark about Bristol's remarkable achievements. They knew little of the Syracuse operation's historic role in pioneering the world's first wonder drug—penicillin—at the peak of World War II. Few people were aware of the company's modern-day breakthroughs in biotechnology and anticancer research.

The Bristol-Myers Squibb/Eric Mower and Associates team turned to community opinion research completed in late 1991. The statistics confirmed that the sustained attention to negative environmental news combined with the "no comment/no access" mentality had badly damaged perceptions of the company.

More than half of the community residents, 51% responding to a telephone survey, held a negative opinion of the site.

Only 26% has a positive opinion.

Fully 91% of those reporting a negative opinion cited environmental concerns as their reason for the rating.

Readers of the daily newspapers were twice as likely as nonreaders to give negative overall opinions of the company.

(continues)

Among all the negative findings, the research found one strategic positive:

Neighbors and the community were overwhelmingly supportive of the site's scientific research effort.

It was agreed at the start that a postcampaign opinion survey would be conducted in early 1994 to measure results of the community relations initiatives and lay the foundation for future strategies.

Problem

A corporate culture at the site that had prompted the original "stay out" attitude needed to shift to one of community involvement, and an effort was necessary to communicate a new cultural attitude to the community and to media.

ADAPTATION

Goal

Demonstrate measurable improvement in community relations to Bristol-Myers Squibb decision makers.

Publics and Objectives

Improve community perceptions among neighbors, elected officials, and community leaders as measured by the 1994 community opinion survey.

Introduce a "balance" to media coverage beyond environmental issues as measured by a content analysis of news clippings.

Stimulate employee and retiree involvement in outreach activities as measured by actual employee/retiree participation.

Strategies

Translate support for scientific research into demonstrable community pride in the site.

Establish "linkages" with community partners to gain third-party support for the site.

Invert "no comment/no access" mentality into "open/accessible" mentality.

IMPLEMENTATION STRATEGY AND TACTICS

The Bristol-Myers Squibb/Eric Mower and Associates team executed a year-long community relations campaign to capitalize on the operation's fiftieth anniversary in Syracuse.

Theme and Logo

A theme and logo consistent with the scientific message were developed for use with all outreach activities. "Project 2043: Science at Work" projected a forward-thinking message about the site's important work in the next 50 years.

Community Outreach

Brochure. A four-color, 16-page site brochure presented the rich history and promising scientific future of the operation in a distribution to more than 5,000 neighbors, employees, retirees, elected officials, media, and community leaders.

Science Horizons. The Summer Science Adventure. In a linkage with Syracuse University and the State University of New York College of Environmental Science and Forestry, the company launched an innovative, week-long science camp for 50 seventh- and eighth-grade students from all public and private middle schools in the county. An entire day was devoted to a visit inside the Bristol site. Student, parents, and educators gave high marks to Science Horizons, and the program generated a steady flow of print and broadcast media coverage.

Community Open House. For the first time ever, the company broke down traditional barriers and opened the site to hundreds of neighbors, elected officials, media, and community leaders. Guided by employee volunteers, visitors went inside laboratories and manufacturing areas that were previously "off limits."

Bristol Omnitheater. Bristol provided the community with a long-lasting symbol of its scientific leadership: a $700,000 naming grant to the local Museum of Science and Technology to build a high-tech omnitheater. More than 400 community leaders attended the announcement ceremony at the future site of the giant dome-screened theater. The contribution drew live TV coverage and front-page coverage, including a newspaper editorial that called the gift "corporate citizenry at its best."

Media Relations

Media Briefing/Editorial Board. To lay a solid foundation for future media coverage, site management held a "no holds barred" luncheon briefing at the site and a private editorial board meeting with the two daily newspapers. Bristol's corporate vice president for policy and planning attended both sessions. More than 20 news directors, editors, and reporters participated in the meetings representing every major news organization in the region.

"Post Standard" Feature Series. Syracuse's morning newspaper was granted unprecedented access to the site's world-class research and development laboratories. The paper ran a three-day, front-page series entitled "Bristol Lifts the Veil" detailing the site's global scientific leadership.

Ongoing Media Outreach. An intense print and broadcast publicity campaign capitalized on each outreach initiative and emphasized science-related messages.

Employee Involvement

Employee Kickoff. Recognizing the importance of employee participation, employee meetings were held to introduce the year-long slate of activities. All employees received a commemorative coffee mug bearing the "Project 2043" theme and logo.

Volunteer Committees. All major events and programs were directed by committees made up of employee volunteers.

Project 2043 Report. Bristol's corporate management and all site employees received a monthly update on the community relations efforts.

Anniversary Luncheon. A thank-you luncheon for 1,200 employees, retirees, elected officials, and community leaders captured the attention of the community—and the corporation. The event featured presentations by the site's senior corporate officer and by the two legendary retirees who were instrumental to the clinical and business development of the company. Twelve corporate officers who flew to Syracuse for the event were greeted by political, community, and business leaders.

Budget

The budget of nearly $390,000 was set for the community relations program. Costs included all communications materials, site brochure, Science Horizons, open house, Anniversary Luncheon, and announcement of Bristol Omnitheater. Total costs at the end of the year were approximately $350,000.

EVALUATION

In clear, quantifiable terms the fiftieth anniversary community relations program met and exceeded all objectives.

Community Perceptions. A comprehensive community opinion survey was conducted in February 1994 using the same methodology as in 1991. In addition, interviews were conducted with media, commu-

(continues)

nity leaders, and elected officials. According to the research:

Negative perceptions of the company were nearly cut in half to 29% from 51% in 1991.

Positive perceptions increased by 50%.

Readers of the two daily newspapers were less likely to hold a negative opinion of the company than nonreaders—a direct turnaround from the 1991 study.

Fully 85% of media, political, and business leaders interviewed had a positive perception of the company.

Other measures of community success were:

The Metropolitan Development Association, Syracuse's most influential business organization, presented the company with a Community Appreciation Award recognizing five decades of achievement.

Science Horizons received an international "Creative and Innovative" Special Merit Award from the North American Association of Summer Session Administrators.

In concert with corporate decision makers, the local site has committed to sponsor Science Horizons for a second year. The hands-on program is also being considered a prototype for all Bristol domestic operations.

Media Coverage. Media coverage and relationships dramatically improved from 1991 to 1993.

The 60% of coverage received in 1993 was unrelated to environmental issues, and negative environmental coverage decreased by 65%.

Coverage on Bristol's community relations activities increased by 86%.

All—100%—of reporters surveyed gave unaided accurate descriptions of the company's products and business.

Contrary to previous environmental reporting,

an agreement with the state's top environmental agency received accurate and fair coverage. A *Syracuse Herald Journal* editorial called the agreement "the kind of public/private cooperation that will help Central New York prosper into the next century."

Employee Involvement. Hundreds of employees played an active role in the community relations program.

100 percent participated in at least one initiative.

Over 700 employees participated in the kickoff meetings at the start of the program.

Nearly 20 volunteer employee committees and subcommittees were formed.

840 employees and 230 retirees attended the Anniversary Luncheon.

Corporate Commitment. Corporate investment in and commitment to the Syracuse site have been solidified.

In 1994, work will be completed on $110 million in new site construction.

Another $10 million worth of projects will begin in 1994.

SUMMARY

Taken together, these concrete measurements verify Bristol's dramatically strengthened position within the community and among its media and political leadership. Among employees, the most important testimony to the increased stability of the Syracuse site comes from Kenneth E. Weg, the Bristol-Myers Squibb corporate president who oversees the facility. In praising the Syracuse site's diversity and vitality, Weg told employees, "Syracuse has grown into a critical link in the Bristol-Myers Squibb structure."

Source: 1994 Silver Anvil Winners: Index and Summaries, Public Relations Society of America, 1994.

ADAPTING TO ORGANIZATIONAL ENVIRONMENT

A study of the competition and environmental conditions will discern where the organization fits within its natural and social surroundings and its standing among its competitors. To fully appreciate all the publics that can influence a campaign, this discussion looks at the two aspects of the environment within which any organization exists: the geographic-social and the competitive.

Geographic-Social Environment

The geographic-social environment encompasses where the publics are located and the status of the relationships. Publics may be local, statewide, regional, national, or international, or they may be concentrated in one geographic place with one or two elsewhere. United Way, an organization that functions primarily at the local level, is still concerned with coordinating its efforts with the national annual fund drive. A university may be a state institution, but its alumni and often its student recruitment efforts are distributed nationally. The organization's relationship with each of these publics may be different and may require different strategies for each.

By knowing the geographic scope and the status of the organization's relations with its social fabric, the practitioner can better select media, better identify the channels that best match the geographic distribution, and better select groups for cooperation or for coalition building. Of course, any planning should take into consideration the priority of each public and concentrate efforts on those at the top of the list.

An organization with international scope will require more complicated media planning, particularly if several different languages are involved. Translation of messages containing cultural nuances should usually be done by employing foreign nationals. Failures in this area can be disastrous. On a visit to India, John F. Kennedy planned to distribute as favors autographed photos framed in the best Texas cowhide. Fortunately, he discovered in time that attitudes in India toward the sacred cow would have made the gesture a severe insult.

Competitive Environment

Of special importance to a campaign's success is a thorough understanding of the competition, and every organization, even those classified as nonprofit or governmental, has competition. A campaign's success will depend on what the competition is doing, has done, or is likely to do, especially during the campaign. Most competitive situations are so specific that each should be considered by itself. However, the following describe some elements to consider when analyzing the competition.

Competitive Situation   When thoroughly examined, the competitive posture of an organization will reveal the pressures or potential pressures on the organization that will continue to make an impact; all of them will be significant for the public relations campaign effort. Analysis of the competitive environment should strongly influence the campaign strategy, particularly the goal.

Especially for product-oriented companies, strategy is the response to the competition. Frank F. Gilmore, writing in the *Harvard Business Review*, notes that "the relationship between the company and its competitive environment is expressed by the strategy of the enterprise." Competitors affect an organization at its most critical level: if a competitor can offer a better product at a lower price—other factors being equal—the organization will have to meet the competition or go out of business.

To meet this competition requires research to discover the strategies the competition is using and to build strategy accordingly. Paul Stonich explains how to fashion a strategy to meet the competition: "In strategy formation, the strengths and behaviors of competitors are examined to determine the competitive position they hold in the marketplace and which ways they are likely to move given various trends and events."[16] Analysis of the competition is the first step in developing the basic elements of a strategic plan for any organization. The public relations plan should fit into the overall corporate strategy. Both plans should incorporate an understanding of the competition and focus on a strategy to meet the competition.

Competitive Analysis in Regulated Industries   One segment of the business world that will not precisely fit the foregoing profile of competitive business is regulated industries—electric and gas utilities, telephone companies that are regulated by the states, and cable TV companies that operate under city franchise agreements. In such cases, competition takes on an entirely different guise.

For regulated industries, competition takes the form of industry regulators. In the case of the former Bell System companies, for example, "In the absence of external competition, Bell management necessarily focused high-level attention on the industry's regulators, working assiduously to create a favorable 'regulatory climate' in Bell territories."[17] Such regulated monopolies face *indirect* competition. Only when the quality of service is so poor that regulators cancel the utility's franchise do competing organizations vie for the right to provide service under a new franchise.

The threat of losing a franchise—almost the equivalent of bankruptcy—keeps utilities ever vigilant to provide quality service. Employees are well trained, and management is carefully groomed to be sensitive to customer complaints, which are the equivalent of pressure from competitors in other businesses.

Another group of organizations, the nonprofits, differ from both regulated monopolies and the business community. Nevertheless, nonprofit organizations face their own type of competition. These organizations, such as the American Heart Association, the American Cancer Society, many hospitals, boys clubs, Scouts, service organizations, trade associations, and professional societies, compete in four major areas.

Competitive Analysis in Nonprofits Competition for support among nonprofit organizations involves four main ares: funds, members, media attention, and influence. Competition for nonprofit support usually means vying for funding sources. Whatever the nonprofit organization's mission, in practice the primary objective is fund-raising. Of course, membership recruitment—often a major source of fund-raising—becomes a close second in priority. Because favorable media coverage of the organization and its activities is critical to recruiting and retaining members, media relations also becomes a major concern.

Competition for funding pits every nonprofit against other nonprofits, especially those that appeal to the same people, represent similar social values, or attempt to solve the same social problem. The American Heart Association and the American Lung Association both appeal to those concerned about the danger of smoking; March of Dimes and Planned Parenthood both address the problem of birth defects. The agencies in each community that appeal to the same citizens for funds are in direct competition, but they dare not appear mean-spirited by discrediting competitors, which would endanger the nonprofit organization's image as a benevolent institution.

Nonprofit organizations that participate in United Way or other similar cooperative funding efforts work together in an annual fund drive, but they compete every year when budget requests are made (see Figure 6.4). Budget requests are seldom fully funded, but the system does reduce the efforts of organizations to raise funds on their own. Since the cooperation agreement limits the fund-raising activities of participating organizations—usually prohibiting individual group solicitations—the nonprofit must look elsewhere for any additional financial support.

Alternative fund-raising, in addition to unified solicitation, is thus largely limited to seeking grant money and holding special fund-raising events. Competition for grant funds is such that experience in grant writing and knowledge of grant providers' policies and priorities are almost necessary for success. Several foundation directories list grant-giving institutions, together with contact persons and funding criteria. These directories are available in larger libraries.

Fund-raising events remain the most promising supplement to cooperative solicitation and grantsmanship. Such events are limited largely by the creativity of the leadership and the nature of the constituency from which donations are sought. Participants in fund-raising events are, of course, the source of the funds to be raised; one cannot expect to raise a million dollars

Figure 6.4 United Way of America represents the successful effort to manage competition between nonprofit organizations. To avoid continuous and repeated solicitiation for funds by every nonprofit organization in a community, United Way combines into one annual fund drive the fund-raising activities of participating agencies. (Courtesy of United Way of America.)

unless the potential participants in the event can afford collectively to part with a million dollars.

Here, again, competition enters the picture. No group of people, particularly those who can afford to make large donations, will be ignored by other fund-raising organizations. What this means in practice is that nonprofit constituencies should be segmented into subgroups with just as much rigor and sophistication as the best business marketing plan. Research on the competition in the nonprofit sector can use some of the same devices marketers use in identifying what the competition is up to.

In nonprofit segmentation, one should look not only at the *dollar potential* of a constituency but also at *how often* donors may be approached. The motivations that are most effective with contributors often differ; some people may be more motivated to give by the festive appeal of an event than by the purpose of the nonprofit cause itself.

Fund-raising events—the successful ones, that is—generally combine several of these "appeal" factors. A golf tournament, for example, may be sponsored by the nonprofit or jointly sponsored with another organization that can appeal to a peripheral constituency. The event may motivate participants to contribute a large entry fee if it is to benefit the organization, especially if the potential entrants are favorably disposed toward the nonprofit organization and have the resources to make substantial contributions. Loyal members of the organization may be willing to give both by participating in festivities and by making outright donations, as well as contributing annual membership dues.

The motivation of individuals for donating to nonprofits is an esoteric consideration. One body of research suggests that the motivation which produces the largest proportion of charitable contributions is, in a very broad sense, guilt. Guilt includes the feeling of many wealthy people that they don't deserve the wealth they have, whether inherited or accumulated. The feeling that one must atone for misdeeds and/or the feeling that one must reciprocate for favors received account for the well-established success of the free fund-raising dinner. In this familiar device, carefully selected people are given an elaborate meal at no charge, after which contributions are solicited.

Competition for members and volunteers between nonprofit organizations comes down to the fact that every nonprofit needs both dues-paying members and volunteer workers. While fund-raising, especially through dues, is closely tied to membership, the day-to-day functioning of many nonprofits depends heavily on the free labor of volunteers. From the large art museums to the local scout troop, the pattern is the same: members are the ones who volunteer and do most of the work.

In most nonprofit organizations, membership and volunteer work involve the same people. In others, auxiliary organizations of volunteers may supplement the work of members or even undertake specific tasks, such as those performed by "candy stripers," the teenage girls who volunteer to help with patients in hospitals. Students or interns who seek experience in a field as preparation for professional entry are other sources of volunteers. A group's members are often people who are most committed to the organization's cause and who make major contributions of both time and money.

The personal gratification that volunteers seek takes many forms. Some volunteers may need to feel useful and important and may achieve this by being associated with a famous, large, or renowned institution. Others may wish to gain or expand their experience in a career field. College interns and professionals who serve in association offices or undertake committee assignments provide valuable volunteer services to advance their careers. Still others may wish to find personal satisfaction or fulfillment.

Such individuals are easily recruited away from an organization if they do not receive expected support and recognition for their efforts. Effective management of volunteer members is a fine art that requires skill in interpersonal counseling and practical insights into human psychology. The perceptive nonprofit leader will look carefully at the competition for dollars as well as for members and volunteers. A careful analysis should produce ideas for improved efforts for both money and people. Allied with both of these is the competition for media attention.

Competition for media attention is both vital and volatile for nonprofits. A nonprofit that is not well known—that is, is *unfavorably* known in the community—works at a disadvantage to achieve both adequate contributions and dedicated volunteers.

The nonprofit campaign planner must be aware of what other nonprofit organizations are doing and the media attention the activity is generating. Media attention enhances the prestige of the organization as an "institution," which both motivates popular support and reinforces the commitment of those who have contributed time and money.

Nonprofit organizations generally find that the media respond to the traditional how-to of media relations. The media are usually cooperative in using releases on or even covering local-angle events that involve local names in newsworthy activities. A skilled observer will be able to identify elements of media relations that work well for other nonprofit organizations and can emulate them.

A basic work on media relations, such as Wilcox and Notle's *Effective Publicity* (HarperCollins) or Newsom, Scott, and Turk's chapter "Working with the Media" in *This Is PR*, or a basic public relations textbook, of which there are many, will provide guidance in the technique to use.

Competition for influence engages all nonprofit organizations in a variety of activities to advance the cause they espouse. The three major aspects of influence for which nonprofits compete are (1) *political favor* at all levels of government, from city and county to state and nation; (2) the result of *effective services* provided to constituents, whatever segment of society is being served; and (3) *public reputation*, which is the cumulative effect of the organization's public relations efforts.

Competition for political influence will often find nonprofit organizations vying for licenses, government grants, favorable ordinances or laws, and favorable review by regulatory agencies. This type of activity is no different from the lobbying that plays so important a role in corporate, especially regulated utility, life.

The effective nonprofit leader will gain much from observing the lobbying efforts of other nonprofits and adapting techniques that prove productive. Much effective lobbying involves a shrewd combination of personal contacts with power brokers and skilled orchestration of grass-roots support. It involves knowing who in government needs to be convinced and directing a letter-writing campaign to persuade that person.

Providing services to constituents is equivalent to satisfying customers in a business enterprise. If a service-providing agency does not provide service that is appropriate, timely, and professional, other service providers may expand to fill the void, or government licensing or regulating agencies may slip in to correct the situation. Although the competition to provide service is not as immediate as that of business, the competitive threat is there.

On the other hand, a record of providing superior service not only will forestall competition from other service providers but also will develop a broad field of supportive constituents who can be counted on to endorse or testify to the work of the organization.

A happy constituency of those who have received services as the most fundamental level on which all organizations compete—the basis of the public relations the organization has achieved. Competition for public reputation is the total of an organization's performance in the public interest. An analysis of the public relations effectiveness of other competing nonprofit organizations can reveal both strengths that can be emulated and weaknesses that can be exploited.

By carefully analyzing competing nonprofit organizations, the campaign planner can discover how each achieves its influence within government and within its own constituency as well as how each achieves its public reputation. Simply by studying the competition, the nonprofit campaign planner can discover how best to direct his or her own organization to achieve the most effective public relationships.

Competitive Analysis in Government Organizations The nature of competition in government is quite distinct from that of business organizations. In democratic societies, government operates with the consent of the people, that is, by the consensus of the voting public. Short of impeachment, government officials are insulated from competitive pressures by the term of their office. In addition, many civil service positions are virtually lifetime appointments in which competitive pressures can be exerted only by a supervising elected official, if at all.

A *Harvard Business Review* article analyzed the difference between business organizations and government organizations with a view to improving understanding between the two and developing a better working relationship.

➤ CASE STUDY: NASA: THE CASE FOR SPACE

The "Case for Space" campaign was designed to gain broad congressional and administration support for the U.S. space program.

RESEARCH

- Regular monitoring of Congress by Washington, D.C., senior Rockwell officials' discussions with NASA, and news reports found congressional approval of the NASA budget and the Space Station was in serious doubt.
- Awareness, based on Yankelovich national surveys taken for more than a decade and commissioned by Rockwell, found that Americans strongly support the space program.
- Research on past space support efforts indicated the best methods of gaining continued backing from target audiences.

Promotional items highlighting space benefits well-received by similar target audiences.

Space related educational programs for students and teachers showed increased understanding of math and science.

ADAPTATION

Objectives

- Gain active support for the space program by building audience enthusiasm and demonstrating benefits to individuals primarily through emotional appeal.
- Channel support for the space program into quantitative messages sent to budget decision makers in order to achieve congressional approval of NASA budget and Space Station for fiscal year 1994.

Target Publics

Groups having the ability to get involved in the project and impact Congress's decision to approve NASA budget, including the Space Station; focus on cities and states with the largest space interests and activity:

- Rockwell employees totaling 15,000 at the corporate level and businesses directly related to space activities.
- Legislators and government officials, about 1,000, including members of Congress, mayors, and governors in key states.
- Vendors, about 2,500, including outside businesses supporting Rockwell space projects.
- General public, about 20 million Americans, able to voice support of space to legislators and other target groups.
- Space organizations, some 200 key officials of space organizations, including NASA.
- Educators, some 150 K–12 science and general teachers and their students.

Strategy

Create variety of opportunities in which to educate target publics and fulfill objectives:

- Media targeted based on areas where Rockwell and other aerospace companies have the largest presence, including Southern California, Florida, Texas, and Washington, D.C.
- Decision makers such as legislators and government officials were also targeted.
- Due to the depth of the issue a variety of media and presentation methods were selected, including print, broadcast, television, speeches, interviews, special events, and opinion pieces.

Creative Strategy

- Thought-provoking theme lines developed to appeal to a wide range of publics:
- "We Need Our Space," "I Need My Space," "Space. Our Presence Is Our Future."
- Theme lines were to be incorporated into a variety of promotional items and events. Items distributed to target publics to build enthusiasm and spread messages included: some 70,000 "I Need My Space" buttons, attached to cards carrying space support information; some 50,000 postcards with space theme and information were used for sending messages to Congress and to government officials; the postcards were also highly recognizable when delivered.
- Contemporary "break the mold" graphics were incorporated in all materials.

Budget

Costs were split between corporate and two main aerospace businesses totaling about $120,000, including the Yankelovich national opinion survey research.

IMPLEMENTATION STRATEGY AND TACTICS

- Informative and inspirational events were designed for specific target publics and timed to key congressional votes to maximize impact of positive responses.
- Luncheons/forums were conducted with congressional representatives illustrating the value of space exploration by relating to constituent needs such as health care improvement through space research.
- Presentation of promotional items to politicians, and celebrities with media coverage.
- Employee "I Need My Space" events with participation by senior management, politicians, and celebrities.

- Results of national survey of Americans' views on space.
- Programs set to aid educators in their teaching of science and technology.
- Media outreach included background information, articles, and opinion pieces distributed to target areas.

Aware of the failure of programs with similar goals to get off the ground in the past, the campaign focused on ensuring that this effort was well-developed, creative, contemporary, and attractive enough to be approved and funded. One of the measurement tools for responding to the anticipated large numbers of queries, Space Hotline, was not implemented due to lack of staffing support.

EVALUATION

Measurement

- Congressional approval of space funding.
- Number, prominence of people actively supporting the program's objectives.
- Broad, targeted media coverage.
- Thousands of letters written to key members of Congress.
- Other companies or organizations requesting to be a part of the campaign.

Results

- Ultimate sign of success was the approval of funding for the space program, especially the Space Station. In addition, Rockwell received a portion of the Space Station contract.
- The effort netted more than 75 million media impressions.
- Participation and support from target audiences: government officials included President Bill Clinton, California Governor Pete Wilson, Los Angeles Mayor Richard Riordan, California State Senators Dianne Feinstein and Barbara Boxer,

(continues)

cabinet members, and 250 members of the press.

- More than 20,000 space postcards were sent to members of Congress by employees, vendors, schools, and the general public.
- One vendor's employees sent 3,800 postcards to Congress; in addition, the company posted billboards with the message to President Clinton, which were seen by 300,000 people a day.

Media Coverage

- Continuing coverage in print media of the space support events included the *Los Angeles Times, The New York Times, Florida Today, Los Angeles Daily News,* Associated Press, and UPI; CNN; and other national radio and television outlets also covered the events. Many of these features were syndicated nationally.
- *Los Angeles Times* business column lauded the Space Station as a good idea, "Local and Global Reasons to Fund a Space Station." The story demonstrated

dramatic change in newspaper's approach to Space Station coverage. One year earlier one headline read, "Space Station . . . Big Science . . . Big Mess."

- A special three-page section in *Florida Today* detailed dozens of medical, scientific, and technological improvements resulting from space exploration; the feature was written by the business staff.
- Interviews and a major opinion piece appeared in *USA Today,* and the *Houston Post,* bylined by two U.S. senators—written by Rockwell staff—appeared after the space/health event.
- Articles and editorials by Rockwell executives appeared in *USA Today, The New York Times, Los Angeles Times,* etc.
- National space survey results were carried throughout the United States, including by Reuters, UPI, *Florida Today,* and other wire services.
- The materials generated reached more than 75 million readers.

Source: 1994 Silver Anvil Winners: Index and Summaries, Public Relations Society of America, 1994.

The author characterizes the difference between the two sectors as based on two different values. Most *business* systems rest on "the principle that managers should make the most efficient and effective use possible of the resources at their disposal." In contrast, most *government* systems rest on "the principle that managers should try to ensure that the system treats fairly most of the people it affects."[18]

A **competitive analysis of government organizations** will necessarily focus ultimately on the political opposition. Officeholders at any level are extremely sensitive to public approval and disapproval. Thus, the political opposition constitutes the competition for government organizations. If an elected official fails to satisfy major segments of the public, he or she risks being turned out of office.

Rather than concentrating on the efficient production of goods or services, "political managers see issues in the context" of an array of issues of interest to a wide range of constituents. "When attention does turn to a specific issue—altering a piece of tax legislation, keeping a plant open, or getting an increased appropriation for an agency's regional office—politicians instinctively measure how any given stance will be viewed by political allies and opponents and equally important, how it will play in the media."[19] Competitive pressure in government organizations takes the form of constituency and opposition interest in whatever is at issue.

Competition expresses itself—for government—as issues around which organized groups and individuals coalesce to exert pressure for or against a possible decision on a legislative bill. For the public relations campaign planner who serves a government organization, the investigation in preparation for planning a campaign will have to concentrate on the ebb and flow of public issues. A relatively new tool of the public relations profession, "issue tracking," may also be quite serviceable for government public relations officers.

In making a competitive analysis, all organizations—whether business, nonprofit, or government—do essentially the same things. The entity should assess its position in relation to other organizations that do or may do the same thing; analyze the extent of the public served, whether local, regional, national, or international; determine how it is distinct from all competition; and plan how it can marshal its resources to serve its constituency effectively.

From the viewpoint of business, a competitive analysis would include "the firm's relative competitive position, market share, regional and national market standing, distinct advantage, and market resource capabilities."[20] The competitive analysis is an important tool for planning how the organization will go about its mission and specifically how it will design its public relations campaigns.

ADAPTING TO ORGANIZATIONAL OPERATIONAL POLICIES

Policies constitute an immediately practical day-to-day set of rules for conducting business, in contrast to the longer scope of the philosophy, mission, goals, objectives continuum. Policies are guidelines for the conduct of daily operations. Most writers on the topic stress that the effective top manager should spend his or her time concerned with the longer-term philosophy and mission and should delegate most policy decisions to midlevel management.

One CEO, Thomas H. Melohn, president of North American Tool & Die, Inc., attributed a 600 percent corporate earnings increase to a participative management system that, among other things, gave the CEO the task of setting long-term goals and beyond that "let managers manage." The writer noted, "My job as CEO is to outline the company's objectives and the strategies to attain those goals. To achieve them, we place heavy emphasis on true delegation of responsibility. . . . we let our managers alone. . . . Each foreman is responsible for on-time production with no rejects and at maximum efficiency. How he does it is totally up to him."[21] If middle managers need to establish policies, they should be free to do so within the framework of organizational goals and objectives. Policies frequently evolve in response to practical problems. Seldom does an organization operate "by the book," or at least by the book alone.

In the absence of any general corporate guidelines to the contrary, policies may reflect our unspoken organizational philosophy or individual philosophies or even personal style. Joseph L. Bower describes two organizational philosophies that are so widely assumed in organizations that they are seldom articulated.

The efficiency orientation, is followed in most business organizations and "rests on the principle that managers should make the most efficient and effective use possible of the resources at their disposal." This orientation is geared to the "achievement of efficiency and effectiveness in the production and distribution of goods and services."

The equity orientation, followed commonly in government organizations, "rests on the principle that managers should try to ensure that the organizational system treats fairly most of the people it affects." This orientation is "geared to the equitable, or at least legitimate, distribution of costs and benefits to which there are common or overlapping claims."[22] Though neither of these orientations is confined to business or government, organizations in either the business or government community are likely to reflect one or the other orientation but without a clearly articulated statement of such. The orientation—or philosophy—will often have to be determined from a careful examination of the organizational philosophy.

Accordingly, individual philosophies or personal styles may also play a part in organizational policies. Managers, like other people, were found to approach their work according to eight different personal styles. J. Marshall and R. Stewart, in a study of managers' perceptions of their own jobs,[23] found that managers' work strategies fell into eight distinct approaches (Box 6.1).

These work strategies are likely to prompt policies. Work strategies, for the authors, consisted of "how the individual tackled the job." These strategies fell along a continuum from "reactive" to "proactive." Reactive strategies are essentially passive responses; proactive strategies generally involve "actions . . . within usually externally defined guidelines."[24]

In researching an organization, the public relations person will need to discover policies from a wide range of sources. Some policies will be written; the more formal will likely be printed and distributed among employees in a handbook, for example, and the less formal may be announced in memos or posted on bulletin boards. Other policies may be applied to so small a group of employees that they will be circulated only among those few people. The

BOX 6.1   Eight Working Strategies

The eight strategies which suggest personal styles or philosophies that in turn shape policies are as follows, in order of their most common appearance in the research sample:

1. **The project approach** (29 percent) found that managers approaching "their jobs in terms of phases or sequences of tasks and activities over time . . . working toward . . . medium-term objectives were the typifying characteristics." One might expect the policies set by this type of manager to take on characteristics of the formalized solution to a recurring problem.

2. **The shapers** (22 percent) were more "opportunistic" managers "who believe they shape their own jobs. Many are in peripheral, service, or new roles which make this more possible." Policies under this type of manager may seem idiosyncratic, but at the same time may be amenable to change.

3. **Planning** (12 percent) managers were list makers who were concerned with "organizing their time at work to make a regular . . . listing of work to be done and periodically assessing their direction in the job." Because these managers are intent on their control over efficiency, one may expect their policies to attempt to shape the work into systems or structures that would seem to promise efficiency.

4. **Yielding** (10 percent) managers "let situations develop rather than deliberately steer them. Their reactions [to problems] are then directed at reestablishing the *status quo*." One might expect policies under this type of manager to be sporadic, inconsistent, or even absent.

5. **Controlling** (8 percent) managers see themselves as "riding a tiger" and so they set "lots of commitments and deadlines to make the thing manageable." They see the job "as progressively eliminating all possible choices and variations until the job can be done simply and routinely. . . . [O]ne of the main motives for their subsequent behavior" is the feeling of being "overloaded at work." Policies under this type of manager one might expect to be the most complex and restrictive of the various types of manager.

6. **Hustle and bustle** (8 percent) managers see their jobs as offering "no time to think, no need to decide what to do, things just come at you." Policies under this type of manager, one might expect, would be transient if present at all and with lax enforcement.

7. **Instinct** (8 percent) managers "see their jobs as large and diverse, but do not worry about that or take containing or controlling action. [They

(continues)

feel] no need to set boundaries or arrive at definitions of duties. . . . They take the job as it comes." They have a "high tolerance, even liking, for uncertainty." Policies under such managers are most likely to be absent or in the form of "understandings" which are not formally written or widely understood.

8. **Bypassing the system** (6 percent) managers "work to the same objectives as the official system, or their own particular interpretations of them; they feel these objectives can be achieved more effectively by alternative means." These managers "fully understand the official procedures first" but pay due attention to them in "modifications." Policies under such managers would likely be "understandings" rather than formally stated. Such understandings, of course, risk not being understood at all or misunderstood, and can lead to serious disruptions of work.

eight manager styles listed in Box 6.1 may help the researcher determine what type of policies to expect in a given department or division.

Policies may be established at various levels throughout the organization from top to bottom. Policies set by a supervisor will apply only to his or her department and employees. Policies set by top management will usually be applied throughout the organization or within a particular division. Policies, especially at the corporate level, may be called other things: strategies, rules, regulations, or codes of conduct.

Codes of conduct provide a broad outline of organizational policies as the individual employee is affected. Such codes are usually guidelines on ethical questions. One study of corporate policy statements on codes of conduct found that ten specific elements appeared in 60 percent of such codes. One may expect these ten elements to be reflected in most organizational policies: a position on (1) a general statement on ethics and philosophy; (2) the acceptance of gifts; (3) general conflicts of interest; (4) compliance with laws, and specifically, regulating contributions to government officials and political parties; (5) stock trading on insider information; (6) conflict of interests concerning relatives, associates, suppliers, customers; (7) undisclosed or unreported funds or assets; (8) false records or book entries; (9) misuse of organizational assets; and (10) use of confidential information.[25]

Recently, codes have begun to incorporate rules governing love relations between executives in the corporate hierarchy. Most articles on the topic conclude that love affairs between management staffers sow dissension and suspicion among other staff persons and that the woman is usually the one to suffer dismissal.[26] Two issues that have recently found their way into organizational policy statements and codes of conduct are drug testing of employees and decisions involving employees who have acquired immunodeficiency syndrome (AIDS). These issues involve wider social and ethical questions that society is in the process of debating.

In researching an organization's operational policies, it is important to remember that the terms used in this discussion—general to specific guidelines, as well as philosophy, mission, strategy, goals, objectives, and policies—are not used uniformly in the literature of the field. The terms do describe organizational guidelines, but the point where the terms fall on a general-to-specific scale should be determined from usage in the specific organization. Some writers in the field use the terms interchangeably. The important information to distill from study of an organization is what the term *means*, whichever term is used.

ADAPTING TO ORGANIZATIONAL TRENDS

Knowing a company means knowing how it approaches the future, including issues identification and tracking, plans for dealing with emerging issues, and contingency planning. Anticipation of what the future holds for an organization involves identifying and understanding the full range of influences that impinge on the organization or that may impinge. The researcher will need to consider how the organization approaches the question of what the future may bring. In case the organization has no such program, the researcher may need to plot such a program.

The challenge of the future and what to do about it is really much more complicated than analyzing trends. Since the mid–1970s, public relations practitioners have become responsible for the whole spectrum of dealing with the future. The term most frequently applied to this new public relations responsibility is *issues management*. The January 1980 *Public Relations Journal* observes, "The emerging issues of the 80's and their impact on the practice of public relations is a principal concern of practitioners at all levels and in all areas of the profession. Identifying, analyzing, and planning for emerging issues are now listed among the practitioner's major responsibilities."[27]

Issues management generally includes responsibility for these four often overlapping elements of the process: (1) futurology or forecasting, in its broadest sense of predicting what will happen in the future; (2) identifying and tracking emerging issues or plotting the genesis and probable prognosis of topics of public concern; (3) anticipating the impact of issues or predicting how matters of public concern will affect an organization and with what magnitude; and (4) managing the organization's response to the emerging issues or planning, executing, and evaluating contingencies for the various public concerns that threaten to impinge on the organization.

The significance of issues management has increased noticeably in the fields of public relations and public affairs. Some research efforts reported in *Public Relations Review* and elsewhere, as well as mentioned in trade publications, confirm the regard that issues management has achieved among leaders in these fields.

The nature of issues management has not always been clear, especially in the more popular literature. The concepts involved, the techniques employed, opinions about the process, and especially the importance of this new specialization to the field of public relations have remained somewhat clouded. A national survey of 130 members of the Public Relations Society of America (PRSA) and 34 members of the Issues Management Association (IMA) has brought some clarification of these questions.[28]

How important is issues management? Survey participants who were familiar with the term regarded issues management (IM) with a high degree of understanding and as important to the practice of public relations and public affairs. A significant 94% of those who recognized the term think it is very important or important for the profession today, and 90% believe IM will continue to be an important factor in the future.

An equally significant finding was that 33% of PRSA members were "not familiar with the term or concept of issues management." Of those familiar with the term, most agreed that IM is "an efficient instrument (64%), a reliable procedure (63%), and an important new field (62%)." Slightly over half of the sample (55%) perceive issues management as public relations' "new frontier."

What does issues management seek to accomplish? Of the ten basic goals or objectives for IM identified in the literature, survey participants selected the following three as the most important: (1) create and maintain awareness of important issues among senior management (96%); (2) identify, analyze, and interpret emerging issues (95%); and (3) develop and manage policies or strategies in response to specific issues (87%). The two least favored IM goals were "influencing the outcome of an issue" and "striving to control the issue." These results reflect the often expressed opinion of experts that issues cannot readily be controlled or managed.

What is involved in IM? The survey revealed that the least complicated techniques are used most frequently in the practice of IM: monitoring (91%), scanning (85%), and trend impact analysis (71%). Techniques like trend extrapolation, scenario writing, technological assessment, and cross-impact analysis are seldom used; and Delphi, nominal group techniques, and computer simulation are hardly ever applied.

As far as issue forecasting is concerned, less than half of the combined PRSA-IMA sample (41%) employ this procedure, and those who do use it primarily for short-range forecasting—under one year. Only "issue identification," the first step in the issues management process, is used "always" by a solid majority of participants in the study (77%).

The other five stages of the process of IM are "always" applied by less than half of the sample. Determination of response strategy was always used by 46%, implementation of action program by 40%, issue analysis and ranking by 39%, evaluation of results by 38%, and issue forecasting by 33%. These findings lend credence to the opinion that a majority of issues management programs are still in the initial stages of development.

Defining issues management: A composite definition of issues management was constructed from respondents' comments on a proposed definition that was derived from definitions in the literature. Asked to express agreement or disagreement with the proposed definition by indicating inadequate words or phrases, a high (95.6%) proportion of the sample gave their consent to the proposed definition. A number of modifications were suggested, some of which were incorporated into a final definition, which reads as follows:

> *Issues management is the systematic process of identifying, analyzing, ranking, and monitoring emerging and current trends and developments, internal or external, to an organization; forecasting their likely direction and magnitude of impact; developing, implementing, and evaluating timely policies and/or strategies that minimize their threats and maximize their opportunities, in a coordinated effort to manage the organization's response to change.*

What specializations use issues management? Issues management is seen as "most useful" in large companies or corporations (93.8%), in political parties (87.3%), in associations (82.4%), in banking and financial institutions (81.4%), and in small companies or corporations (80.2%). Surprisingly, IM is rated less useful for multinational organizations; nonprofit organizations; federal, state, and local governments; and media. Multinational organizations and higher education tied for lowest in indicating the usefulness of issues management.

SUMMARY

This chapter explores how to adapt the campaign plan to six aspects of organizational culture: history and mythology, philosophy and mission, organizational structure, competitive and environmental posture, policies, and trends.

Adapting to organizational history and mythology. Adapting to an organization's history and mythology means relating to the personality of the organization as shaped by the founder, stories, rituals, and other significant aspects of organizational life.

Adapting to organizational philosophy and mission. Fitting the campaign to the organization's philosophy and mission means coordinating it with the unique reason for the organization's existence and its long-range purpose.

Adapting to organizational structure. The campaign must relate to the organization's structure from the top executive level to the operational or line worker level.

Adapting to organizational environment. Adapting the campaign to the environment means ensuring that it suits the competitive position of the organization as well as how the entity fits into its environment, including relations with other organizations, as well as the natural and social world.

Adapting to organizational operational policies. The campaign must also be adapted to the operational policies of the organization; in other words, it must be compatible with the day-to-day flow of decision making and practices.

Adapting to organizational trends. The campaign also must be compatible with the trends that are or will be affecting the organization.

FOR FURTHER READING

Bozeman, Barry. *All Organizations Are Public.* San Francisco, CA: Jossey-Bass, 1987. The book makes the point that organizations are no longer affected by economic or political factors alone but must be responsive to the public interest.

Deal, Clarence E., and Allen A. Kennedy. *Corporate Cultures: Rites and Rituals of Corporate Life.* Reading, MA: Addison-Wesley, 1982. This analysis of corporate cultures is rich with examples of companies familiar to most readers.

Falsey, Thomas A. *Corporate Philosophies and Mission Statements: A Survey and Guide for Corporate Communicators and Management.* New York: Quorum Books, 1989. Prompted by the observation that the mission statement of Johnson and Johnson guided the company through the Tylenol crisis, the author went on to study the role of mission statemens in other companies.

Golden, L. L. L. *Only by Public Consent.* New York: Hawthorn, 1966. Accounts of how major corporate leaders (e.g., General Motors, AT&T, DuPont, U.S. Steel, etc.) came to revere social responsibility and sound public relations practices.

Golner, Andrew B. *Social Change and Corporate Strategy.* Stamford, CT: Issue Action Publications, 1983. This book argues that organizations must harness the forces in interdependence through sound public affairs programs.

Harvard Business Review: On Managment. New York: Harper & Row, 1975. A collection of articles that appeared in HBR, all on various aspects of management.

Hickman, Craig R., and Michael A. Silva. *Creating Excellence: Managing Corporate Culture, Strategy and Change in the New Age.* New York: New American Library, 1984. The authors argue that neither corporate culture nor strategy alone can cure corporate ills, but in combination they can.

Peters, Thomas J., and Robert H. Waterman, Jr. *In Search of Excellence.* New York: Warner Books, 1984. This popular examination of corporate cultures focuses on factors that contribute to outstanding performance.

Sobel, Robert. *IBM: Colossus in Transition.* New York: Times Books, 1981. The story of the Thomas Watsons and the founding and growth of IBM.

Weisberger, Bernard. *The Dream Maker.* Boston: Little Brown & Co., 1979. The story of Will Durant and the founding of General Motors.

CHAPTER 7

Adaptation in the Campaign Plan

- Situation Analysis
- Problem/Opportunity Statement
- Setting the Goals
- Segmenting and Targeting Publics
- Listing Strategy Options

- Case Study: Aerosol Industry Battles CFC Misinformation
- Enumerate Resources Available
- Develop a System for Management Support

The adaptation stage of the campaign fits (or matches) the research findings articulated in the problem(s) statement to the resources of the organization and to the publics involved, in order to select a strategy that will solve the problem by achieving a carefully devised goal. The process focuses on what is widely discussed in the literature as public relations or communication "planning."

This book deals with what is traditionally called planning in two stages: adaptation and strategy. The term *adaptation* refers to the stage that fits together the preliminary parts of the planning process (or adapts them to each other). The object of the adaptation stage in public relations campaign planning is to achieve the optimum fit in putting together all the preliminary planning elements in the public relations campaign. These adaptation plan elements are:

1. **Situation analysis.** The situation analysis examines the campaign motivation, or the situation that prompted the effort; a careful definition of the situation helps to identify the questions that need to be answered during the research stage.

2. **Problem statement.** The stated problem or opportunity that results from research projects and confirms or modifies the situation analysis.
3. **Goal statement.** The goal statement that transforms the problem/opportunity statement into a form that can be achieved and measured.
4. **Target publics.** Segmentation of the public into prioritized "target publics."
5. **Tentative strategies.** A "shopping list" of tentative strategies from which the ultimate strategies will be chosen.
6. **Statement of limitations.** A statement describing the limitations of time, money, and personnel.
7. **Management liaison.** A plan for maintaining rapport or liaison with management, to ensure that plans are compatible with policies of decision makers.

SITUATION ANALYSIS

Every public relations campaign begins with a reason, or some form of motivation or perceived situation for which a public relations effort seems appropriate. Motives may vary greatly. The organization may have experienced *problems:* a slowdown in requests for service or a downturn in sales. Membership may be declining or growing more slowly than that of a competitor. A product may have decreasing sales. A government agency may not have enough public support to justify adequate funding from the legislature. Employee turnover may be too costly. Public opinion may have turned against the organization, its product, or its service. A campaign undertaken to solve such a problem will be a *reactive* public relations effort.

There may be an *opportunity* to expand the organization or to establish a new enterprise; a decision may be made to address an emerging issue before it becomes a threat; the organization's executives may wish to do something for the community or the arts; the organization may be approaching its twenty-fifth or fiftieth anniversary; the organization may have enjoyed excellent relations with all its publics over the years and want to celebrate those good relations. Whatever the circumstances, the public relations campaign begins with some incentive for conducting a public relations campaign. A campaign of this type is called a *proactive* public relations effort. The program management, PM, approach to campaign planning, which parallels the approach used in this book, describes this need for the campaign as a "mandate."[1]

Whether the campaign is a reactive or proactive effort, the initial situation as it is perceived must be fully researched. All aspects of the situation must be thoroughly studied to discover what attitudes, opinions, or behaviors should be changed, among which public or publics, and what communication will be necessary to accomplish these ends. That investigation is part of the research task. Research should go beyond the initial investigation of the situation analysis by carrying out appropriate research projects, such as the possible projects listed in chapter 3. Whatever is done must be complete enough to as-

Figure 7.1 The adaptation stage of campaign planning usually requires getting a number of people together to make crucial decisions. Whether the decision makers are company executives, a campaign planning team, or government officials, the decisions are often the same: What is the nature of the problem we face? What should our goal be? What publics have a stake in the decision? What strategies are most likely to succeed? What limitations do we face? Here, George Bush and advisers make a decision during his tenure as UN ambassador. (AP/Wide World.)

certain what the problem is, with regard to which publics, and what strategy will be necessary to solve the problem. Decision makers often work in teams to solve problems as Figure 7.1 illustrates.

B. F. Goodrich Co. faced an unusual public relations situation in 1988 when it concluded the sale of its tire manufacturing operations to Uniroyal Inc. Goodrich was no longer in the tire business. After its long-term name confusion with Goodyear Tire and Rubber Company and its corporate-identity blimps, Goodrich had a different identity crisis; nobody knows that it doesn't make tires. Now solely in the business of producing specialty chemicals, plastics, and aerospace products, the company needed to counter years of advertising that people still remember. "The primary problem has been the company's advertising campaigns from the past, especially the 'We're the Other Guys' campaign aimed at distinguishing Goodrich from Goodyear—and its ubiquitous promotional blimps. 'That (ad) hasn't been run for 13 to 15 years,' says Mr. [Foster] Smith, Goodrich [spokesman], 'But people remember it as if it was yesterday'."[2] The situation called for research to find out whether people, especially business leaders on whom the company would depend for its future success, knew of its changed circumstances.

PROBLEM/OPPORTUNITY STATEMENT

The object of public relations campaign research is a well-documented statement of the problem. A problem and an opportunity both require investigating what constitutes the circumstances surrounding the campaign. Problem research may involve any of the research techniques.

The end product of research for a campaign, of whatever type, is the statement of the problem or opportunity in such a way that the problem can be solved or the opportunity successfully exploited. The 18-to-25-word statement should be phrased simply in a straightforward subject-verb-object construction to reflect the writer's clarity of thought.

This is the reason the problem statement is critically important—not because of the inherent value of a written statement, but because of the resulting clarity of thought and the precise direction it gives to the campaign. The time spent in phrasing and polishing, rewriting, rephrasing, and editing the statement is time well spent because it is the indication of rigorousness of thought.

In the B. F. Goodrich case, the problem statement would depend on research findings into the true nature of the situation. Foster Smith, the company spokesman, says, "We haven't met anyone who knows we're out of the tire business and that we don't fly blimps."[3] Results of a focus group research project revealed that 100 percent of business leaders questioned were surprised to learn that Goodrich no longer makes tires and never flew blimps. The research probed the perceptions of a select group of New York portfolio managers and Fortune 1000 executives. The documented problem statement that Goodrich no longer makes tires and never flew blimps was converted into a goal statement incorporated in its first-ever corporate advertising campaign headline: No Blimp, No Tires. The tag line of this ad, which appeared in several major financial and trade publications, reads, "Chemicals and Aerospace, Not Tires."

Stating the Problem

Dividing the problem into its parts—into specific achievable and measurable elements—may be necessary as a first step in developing the problem statement. If the problem involves more than one public or several segments of a primary public, it may be necessary to break the statement down by publics. That is, the problem may not be quite the same for different segments of the public you are dealing with. Suppose you were doing research for an employee relations campaign and the research revealed that of the 85% who felt they lacked information, 95% were assembly line workers and 35% were clerical workers. A further breakdown of "team feelings" revealed that 52% of line workers and 48% of clerical workers feel they are not part of the team.

Segmenting the employee public in which the problem has been identified would go something like this: (1) Almost all (95%) of assembly line workers want better information about decisions that affect them. (2) About a third (35%) of clerical workers want better information. (3) About half of all workers feel they are not part of the team. The difference between 52% and 48% is very small and probably not statistically significant; that is, it is probably an artifact of the statistical measure and not a real difference. Therefore, team feelings are a problem equally among about 50% of both line and clerical personnel.

The target public involved in this example is employees. The public was broken down into segments or, more specifically, targeted groups within the overall public. Target public, as the term is used here, means the public the campaign seeks to reach with its message; segmentation refers to the identification of specific groups within larger publics who, because of their specific activities, memberships, media orientations, or the like, make themselves easier to reach as a group.

Moving from problem statement to strategy options requires knowledge of a range of theories and how they apply to the campaign at hand. The campaign planning grid shown in Figure 7.2 offers some theoretical factors that must be considered in devising a strategy to solve a problem. The campaign planner should begin with a statement of the problem and filter it through the columns of factors to determine how each factor's main points and subpoints might influence the selection of a strategy to solve the problem.

To move from the statement of the problem to the selection of most appropriate strategy requires considering the points under each column of factors as a possible influence on the strategy selected. The columns are brief summaries of theories that affect the decisions that must be made in choosing a strategy to solve a problem. All the listed factors are discussed in other parts of this book, with the exception of the communication factors; the reader will find a discussion of these factors in William McGuire's chapter 2 in *Public Communication Campaigns*. The factors in organizational culture are discussed in chapter 6 of this book; audience factors are based on Grunig's "situation theory" discussed in chapter one of this book. The list of strategy options is presented in more detail later in this chapter.

After stating the problem, the first step in developing a strategy is refinement of the problem into a goal statement. Other steps leading from problem to strategy include targeting publics; listing limitations of time, money, and people; and brainstorming for possible ideas. The process should end with a shopping list of possible strategy ideas.

SETTING THE GOALS

The goal statement is a converted problem statement. The goal of the public relations campaign is the other side of the problem "coin." Time spent on the problem statement will contribute directly to the effectiveness of the goal or goals statement. If the problem is clearly stated, the goal is much easier to see.

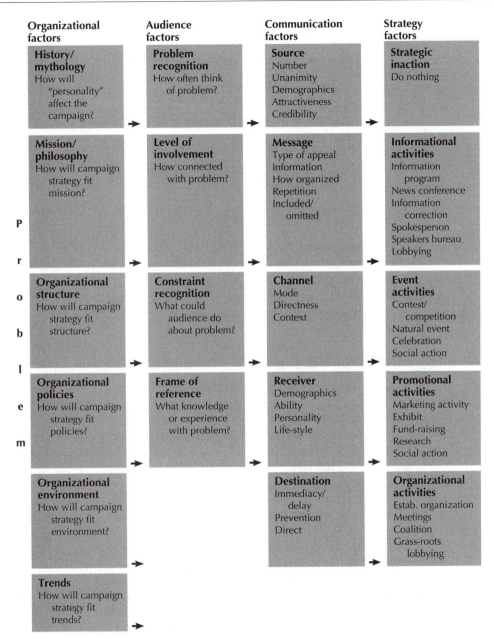

Figure 7.2 Campaign planning grid. The grid is an aid to thinking. It helps the campaign planner to think through the interconnected factors involved in planning strategies. To use the planning grid, state the problem the campaign seeks to solve, then filter the problem through the considerations represented in the columns. In other words, when determining solutions to the problem, each possible solution should be subjected to the listed factors involved in organizational structure, in audience, and in communication. The resulting choice of possible strategies should thus fit the peculiar circumstances of the campaign situation.

The obstacle to problem statements, as well as the obstacle to goal setting, is narrowing the problem to manageable proportions. If the problem can be narrowed to a single purpose or a reasonable set of challenges, the goal becomes the achievement of that end or the meeting of those challenges. The public relations problem can often be subdivided into more specific and thus more manageable portions.

The subdivided problems can be expressed as campaign goals. For best results, goals should be stated in measurable form; this keeps the goals specific and makes evaluation possible. The percentages stated in the goals become a mark against which improvement can be measured. For example, the stated goal might be to improve employee relations by increasing team feelings by 20% and information by 50%. The way problem statements lead to a goal statement can be illustrated as follows:

- Problem statements:
  Almost all (95%) of assembly line workers need better information about decisions that affect them.
  About a third (35%) of clerical workers need better information.
  About half of all workers feel they are not part of the team.
- Goal statement:
  The campaign will improve employee relations by increasing team feelings by 20% and increasing information by 50%.

It is important to remember that measurable goals begin with quantified research, that is, research findings that can be expressed in numbers. Measurable research produces measurable goals, which result in measurable achievements. Goals from our research example and problem statement might be expressed in a single statement: The campaign will seek to increase by 20% the team feelings of employees, increasing by 50% the level of information perceived by all employees. The goal might be better stated in terms of each problem segment, that is, employee department or subdivision. That aspect of segmentation will be considered in the discussion of segmenting publics in the next point below.

Specific objectives may need to be established for the goal or for several goals. Objectives are usually more specific than goals, with each objective contributing to goal achievement. Objectives may involve independent actions, each designed to contribute toward reaching the goal, or they may be related to each other so as to constitute a "package," either a consecutive series of activities or activities chosen to correlate with and enhance each other. As with goals, objectives are best stated in measurable terms.

Achieving the goal (or carrying out the strategy) in our example might include such objectives (or tactics) as:

1. Management approval for the release of information that affects employees.
2. Initiation (or redesign) of the organization newsletter to appeal to assembly line workers, with a regular column on executive policy decisions.

Figure 7.3 Campaign planning requires a careful mix of factors determined by the nature of the sponsoring organization, by the nature of the target publics, and by factors known to govern successful communication all brought to bear on selecting the most promising strategy.

3. "Bulletins" on important policies distributed in the employee lunchroom.
4. Creation of an employee advisory council to provide feedback to management and to serve as a channel for disseminating accurate word-of-mouth information.
5. Establishment of a monthly "suggestion award" for the employee who contributes most to organizational teamwork feelings.
6. Setting up a system of employee reporters to provide news from various sections of the organization to be used in the newsletter.

Compare research findings with organizational mission. This means that you look carefully at the discrepancies between what the organization attempts to do, its mission, and what it actually is doing according to research findings.

If the organization's mission is to "promote the practice of psychology," for example, and research reveals that only 30% of the public knows what psychologists do, then you can identify a problem in the discrepancy between the mission and the fact that less than a third of the population understands what is involved in the practice of psychology. That difference points to the problem which the psychological organization faces: Many people in need of psychological services don't know how to take advantage of those services because so small a portion of the public understands the nature of psychological services.

You may further define the problem by comparing the mission against other research findings. Suppose you discover that only people with incomes of $20,000+ and some college education make use of psychological services. The problem could be further defined as: Psychological services have a market limited to middle to upper socioeconomic levels. This leaves you with further questions: Should services be expanded to accommodate lower socioeconomic levels, or do lower socioeconomic levels need to be educated about the value of psychological services? The problem needs to be examined until you fully define all of its dimensions.

Structure the problem by identifying all its aspects. By arranging the problem according to all the elements that can be corrected, you can better see how to solve it, or at least see which aspect to solve first. It may be necessary to state the problem in hypothetical form. If research is incomplete or a research project cannot be finished in time to contribute to goal setting and strategy planning, you may have to project what you think the findings will be and proceed with the planning stage based on a hypothetical problem statement. After the planning and research are complete, the actual percentages can be plugged into the goal statement. Unless you have guessed very wrong, the strategy will still be appropriate and should require only minor changes in emphasis.

It is especially important to state the problem with all its dimensions, including such facts as misunderstanding and false information on the part of a significant public. The problem statement may require several individual statements, each addressing one aspect of the problem.

Convert the problem statement to a goal statement. For example, the problem statement:

> *People needing psychological services cannot receive them because only 30 percent of the public understand those services.*

becomes the goal statement:

> *. . . to increase effective delivery of psychological services by increasing public understanding of such services from 30 percent to 70 percent.*

There are various ways to state both problems (or opportunities) and goal statements. These are only examples.

Note that problems and opportunities as well as goals may be simple or complex. The goal statements are restatements of the problem statement in a form that can be dealt with or solved more easily. Where there are multiple problem statements and multiple goal statements, one problem statement does not necessarily match a comparable goal statement, but all together the goals are translations of the problem statements.

While working on the statement of problem/opportunity and its resulting goal, the planner must also give attention to the publics that must be addressed for the goal to be reached and the problem solved. This calls for identifying the most important public and segmenting it into the subgroups that are most concerned with the problem/opportunity.

SEGMENTING AND TARGETING PUBLICS

In general, targeting and segmenting refer to aspects of the same process. Targeting refers to selecting the audience or public to be reached in the campaign. Segmenting refers to breaking the public or audience down into smaller and more manageable parts. The campaign planner may start with a particular public in mind, segment that public into parts, and target the most important of those to be reached.

Segmenting and selecting publics in order of priority of their importance to the campaign means identifying groups that have some stake in the problem or some characteristic in common that is important to the goal of the campaign. The actual segmentation[4] is best accomplished by identifying— from research findings or by other means—groups of people who share attitudes or opinions and the ability to act for or against the goal of the campaign.[5] These publics or segments of a public may also share characteristics that facilitate communication, such as all being employed by the same division of a company or all being members of the same service organization. With such commonality, these segments can be reached by posters, memoranda, speeches, articles in the organization newsletter, or, by using the organization's mailing list, direct mail.

In our example, the segment most important to the goal would be assembly line workers because their opinions and attitudes, by percentage, are farthest from those set as the goal. This segment thus provides the greatest challenge in its need for communication as well as the greatest chance of improvement. The reader may note that assembly line workers' perceptions may be quite accurate—that they are not given sufficient information about management decisions that affect their lives and they respond by expressing dissatisfaction and quitting. If our observation of line employee dissatisfaction is correct, solving the problem requires identifying the public that feels the distress, monitoring that public as steps are taken to correct the problem, and finally determining whether the perceived problem was solved.

Since assembly line workers need information more than any other group of employees, changing the situation for them holds the greatest promise of achieving the goal of the campaign. Consequently, these assembly line workers should be the public of first priority. Assembly line workers also share a common characteristic. They all work at one place, the assembly line. A public concentrated in one place is easy to reach with communication: posters, pay envelope memos, and public address announcements.

A segment that differs in attitude or opinion from other segments, as our assembly line workers differ from clerical workers, leads one to suspect that past communication practices may have been uneven or biased against the segment. If assembly line workers feel they lack needed information, research may reveal that the information went only to supervisory personnel, who felt possessive about the inside information and failed to pass it on to line workers—even if management expected them to do so. Or it may be discovered that the information was distributed to line workers, but it was in the form of multipage bulletin board notices and written in language unappealing to line workers, so they did not get the message.

Another important segment in our example is management, but since the management team is not as large a group as either line or clerical workers and yet may have a more profound influence on the situation, the analysis of this segment may take a different form. Personal interviews with executives in the communication chain may reveal a number of things. The interviews may reveal that (1) management attempts to communicate the information but does so ineffectively, (2) management thinks employees are not interested in such information, (3) top management dispenses the information but it is quashed by junior executives, or (4) management provides the information but in a form that employees don't understand or can't decipher. Whatever the problem turns out to be, the difference between management perceptions and what research determines to be the facts will establish the nature of the problem.

If management policy or practice is part of the problem, it may be solved much more simply than problems in larger groups. It may be sufficient to show one executive the problem as identified by your research findings to bring about a policy change that immediately solves the problem. The problem also may be solved by more careful directions from management to the persons responsible for the problem. The point is that although management is an important segment in a campaign, the management team need not be included in the publics to which communication is directed throughout the campaign, except as recipients of the material as information items.

The object of segmentation is to identify the groups important to the campaign's success. Prioritizing means simply that the most important public segment receives primary attention and perhaps the primary allocation of time and money. If resources are limited, it is important to accomplish the most critical part of the plan before time and money run out.

Identification of publics focuses campaign planning. Dividing the public you are dealing with into smaller, more manageable, and more homogeneous groups greatly increases the efficiency of the campaign and makes it easier to accomplish. Messages can be adapted more effectively to smaller like-minded groups than to large masses. Usually, members of smaller groups will already belong to one or more other organizations that share values, orientations, and mind-set.

Segmenting by Identifying Like-Minded Groups

By identifying the organizations to which the people you want to reach belong, you have not only targeted the group but also uncovered ready-made channels for reaching them. Most organizations have membership lists and even newsletters that regularly reach the group. Segmenting publics can target the people you want to reach and make the communication job much more efficient.

Segmentation should be planned in the research stage of the planning process. The discovery of the problem or opportunity usually also identifies the concerned public. Identifying segments of the public may be a matter of reflecting on what logical interests would bring those people together. Often it will become clear that those you want to reach on a given issue are already concerned about that issue and have organized to do something about it. Moreover, they will usually welcome an ally, especially if cooperation will contribute to their goal as well as to yours.

Segmenting by Research Questions

Demographic information derived from research may be used to segment publics in another way. When a survey or poll is taken of the public of concern, demographic, psychographic, and life-style questions can identify the segments you need to target. Demographic items in a questionnaire ordinarily ask age, occupation, education, and the like; that information is important, but you can also ask about group membership and media use patterns that will facilitate communicating with the target public.

The questions shown in Box 7.1 are typical of those used by the major research organizations in this field, such as Simmons Market Research Bureau. For further information about its procedures or extensive syndicated research reports, see the information in Chapter 3 on subscription or syndicated research services.

A media-use-pattern item would be phrased something like this:

How do you get information about important issues in your life? Tell me how important each of these sources of information is for you; tell me 0 for not important to 4 for very important:

_____ Radio; which station? _____

_____ TV; which station? _____

_____ Newspaper; which? _____

_____ Friends or family _____

_____ Magazines; which? _____

_____ Other _____

Explain _____

_____

Segmenting by Media

One important segmentation technique is to use the media audiences. Media audiences have segmented themselves by their selection of favorite media. In radio and magazine audiences, the listenership or readership is very highly segmented because of the specialized nature of each medium. Radio was the first to segment its listenership and did so largely in response to competition. The result is a selection of radio "sounds" to match the listener's preference. Top 40, easy listening, classical, rock, country and western, blues, news, etc., may attract the very segment you want to reach. In that case, you can simply use that radio segmentation medium to reach your audience.

The same is true of magazines to an even greater extent. Magazines are produced for every conceivable special interest, from recreational vehicle

---

BOX 7.1   **Psychographic and Life-Style Questions
Identify Audience Characteristics**

Psychographic items ask for the respondent's "self-perception," such as:

On a 1 (low) to 5 (high) scale check a number for each:
I consider myself—broadminded, open-minded, tolerant, liberal.
  1   2   3   4   5

I consider myself—affectionate, passionate, loving, romantic.
  1   2   3   4   5

I consider myself—stubborn, hardheaded, headstrong, obstinate.

Life-style items, on the other hand, ask about actual behavior patterns, such as (using the same scale):

I always look for the name of the manufacturer on the package.
  1   2   3   4   5 (brand loyalty)

I prefer to buy things my friends and neighbors would approve of.
  1   2   3   4   5 (conformists)

When in the story, I often buy an item on the spur of the moment.
  1   2   3   4   5 (impulsive)

---

fanciers *(Motor Home)*, to Appaloosa horse breeders *(Appaloosa Journal)*, to runners *(Runner's World)*, to wind surfers *(Windsurfing)*. These specialty publications are listed in *Standard Rate and Data Service* (SRDS) in the *Business Publications* volume, where you will also find publications addressed to building contractors, insurance adjusters, police officers, nurses, physical therapists, archivists, antique collectors, and a host of other industrial and professional special interests.

If the audience segment you need to reach is the general public, but concentrated in one geographic area, you can make use of the geographic segmentation of newspapers and other media. Several directories list daily and weekly newspapers, some by geographic circulation area.

Standard Rate and Data Service (SRDS) offers seven volumes, one each for daily newspapers, weekly newspapers, spot radio, spot TV, popular magazines, business publications, and outdoor advertising. As an example of segmentation, the *Spot Radio* volume offers a comprehensive list of stations by programming format. A list of the format types included in the volume provides the range of "sounds" as new ones emerge from time to time that appeal to the various segments of the listening audience.

Bacon's Publicity Checker lists magazines and newspapers in three volumes. The magazine volume lists business, trade, professional, industrial, farm, and consumer magazines as well as over 300 special-interest newsletters. These are all indexed by market classification, contact data, circulation figures, required format, photo use, and types of releases accepted. The newspaper volume lists both dailies and weeklies by state and city with contact data, frequency, circulation, and editors' names for 25 news departments. The magazine volume is cross-referenced for easy targeting of over 160 markets, and the newspaper volume includes special sections to target specific groups. *Bacon's* is designed specifically for public relations use, unlike *SRDS* and most other directories.

Editor and Publisher International Yearbook (E&P Yearbook) lists daily newspaper section editors and international newspaper contacts in the United States. By selecting editors of specific sections—business, gardening, or food— you can zero in on a well-segmented readership. It is seldom effective to send material to a newspaper without addressing a specific editor; if you do, the material will be sent from desk to desk until it is too old to use before it gets to the right person, if it ever does.

IMS/Ayer's Directory indexes popular magazines and newspapers, including publications in such fields as agriculture; colleges; foreign languages; religious, fraternal, and ethnic groups; and trade and technical fields. Required mechanical specifications for submitting material are included, along with circulation maps and phone numbers of persons to contact. Marketing data includes facts about populations, agriculture, and industry of key cities and towns, with advertising rates. It is designed for advertisers, publicity people, media buyers, writers and agents, nonprofit organizations, and so on. State-by-state breakdowns are offered in a cross-referenced section. It can help the public relations person target geographic, special-interest, or industry markets.

Working Press of the Nation (WPN) publishes six volumes, one each for (1) newspapers, (2) magazines, (3) TV and radio, (4) feature writers, (5) photographer, and (6) internal publications, formerly *Gebbie's House Organ Directory*. WPN, like *Bacon's*, is designed for public relations people rather than for advertisers.

PR Newswire is a wire service, like Associated Press or Reuters, except that the service is paid for by the distributor rather than the subscriber. The cost is about $50 per 400 words of copy plus an annual fee of $60. It sends to 150 major media; to an investors network; Nexis, a computerized data base of news stories, including *The New York Times* content; and special media lists that can be customized to distributor needs. The service may be of little value for one-time segmentation but may be useful for reaching previously targeted publics, such as financial or business editors.

Newslink, a satellite distribution service similar to PR Newswire, beams television clips to 300 local TV newsrooms. The clips must be produced by the customer, and the charge is about $1,000 per minute of transmit time. When compared with the cost of mailing videotapes to even a small number of stations, the price is reasonable.

Derus Media Service, Burrelle's, and others distribute print material in camera-ready "slicks" or photo mechanical transfers (PMTs) for use by offset news operations. The material is usually feature material or photos, seldom if ever hard news, and is directed to the "busy newspaper editor," usually on a small weekly, who needs something to fill a news hole and may be desperate for anything that fits.

Segmenting by Syndicated Research Services

Services such as Simmons Market Research Bureau conduct random-sample interviews of adults to gather media use patterns for newspapers, magazines, and radio and TV stations, including programs watched as well as other information about product use. Psychographic and demographic data are also provided. The data are extremely valuable for segmenting in very careful detail, but the service is expensive. The set of more than 50 volumes is continually updated with results of drop-off questionnaires followed by in-home interviews conducted around the country. The service is usually purchased by advertising agencies or large public relations firms who use it regularly.

Segmenting by Mailing Lists

Mailing list companies offer lists of names and addresses segmented by a range of special interests, professions, geographic area, and industries, as well as by magazine subscribers, contributors to specific charities, association memberships, political cause contributors, and the like. Lists are regularly updated and may be manipulated to select such specifics as contributor, reader, membership, or zip code characteristics. A rule of thumb for mailing list response is 2 percent. That is, you can expect a response rate of about 2 percent no matter how often you use the mailing list or what type application you are making of it. That rate can, of course, vary depending on how much self-interest appeal the mailing has for the recipient.

Segmented mailing lists are available in the indexed categories of your choice at costs ranging from $25 to $50 per thousand names. Lists are available on computer tape to print out on your own computer, on gummed labels, or for use on Cheshire system, plain computer paper, with 4 addresses across and 11 down per page, which the machine will cut and glue on each piece. You can ask for a catalog from any of the major mailing list houses—Dow Jones, Ruth Roman, Zeller, Dunn Hill, or others—to select categories. A complete list of mailing list houses is available from the Direct Mail Marketing Association or from advertising reference books. The services available are described in the catalogs.

Mailing houses, not to be confused with mailing *list* houses, will take your direct mail pieces in bulk, together with a computer printout of mailing labels *arranged by zip code* and run them through the Cheshire machine, sort by zip code, and deliver to the post office for about $20 to $50 per thousand pieces. The post office will not accept bulk mail if it is not presorted by zip code. It is usually less expensive to have the printout of the mailing list mailed to you for delivery to a local mailing house than to mail the much more bulky direct mail pieces to the mailing list house for mailing. Consult your local telephone directory for mailing houses; most cities of 50,000 and larger will list one or more.

LISTING STRATEGY OPTIONS

This is the step in campaign planning where creativity comes into play. The planner should make a list of possible activities or strategies; from this list the most appropriate strategy can be chosen, but creativity is required to come up with such a list. Box 7.2 clarifies terms that are closely related to strategy with examples of the terms as defined by the PRSA Accreditation Board. Creativity is the ability to relate or put together two or more old ideas and come up with a new idea. The obvious major resource for creativity is a wealth of ideas, activities, or procedures for solving problems that have been used in the past. These ideas can be gleaned from case studies, from reports of activities appearing in the newspapers, from approaches to problem solving appearing in specialty publications, from explanations of formal procedures for official actions, and from a person's own experience, judgment, and common sense.

In planning campaign strategy, one rule is basic: Any strategy will succeed, other things being equal, if the strategy appeals to the self-interest of all participants. This means, of course, that the activity, special event, etc., serves the special interest of every participant organization and individual and that self-interest is made apparent in recruiting participants. In anticipating the self-interest of possible participants, consider whether the activity will increase the profit, public recognition, favorable attention, or ego satisfaction of potential participants.

Sources for Creating Strategies

Of all the listings of ideas, the one indispensable resource for strategic planning is in the planner's own mind: experience, judgment, and common sense. The planner must know a lot about people: their motivations, their self-interests, the limits on their attention, their talents, their time. A knowledge of the culture and what activities appeal to people, an understanding of history and the possible appeals of nostalgia, a familiarity with the annual calendar[6] of events—all these and more will be helpful for the campaign strategy planner, and they all need to be in the planner's own mind. Chase's annual events directory lists events throughout each calender year.

Background readings in public relations case studies also prove quite useful. Ideas from cases read over the years serve as models and as inspiration for ideas appropriate for specific campaign plans.[7] After extensive reading in the field, which the practitioner should do regularly as a matter of professional preparation, the practitioner can draw upon the store of ideas. You might be able to adapt an approach taken by an organization quite different from yours and under quite different circumstances or you might be able to blend together ideas from several cases in a new way to accomplish your goal. Don't

BOX 7.2   **A PRSA Standard for Definitions of Campaign Planning Terms**

The following has been adapted from the "Conventions for Program Terminology Use" developed by the Accreditation Board of the Public Relatoins Society of America (PRSA) as a standard to encourage uniform use of terms in preparation for and writing accreditation examinations.

Mission. Goal. Objective. Strategy. Tactic/tools.

Perhaps no other set of related words has so many definitions in public relations practice. Is a goal supposed to be measurable? Does "position the company as a leader" express an objective or a strategy—or does it express imprecise thinking? Is a strategy an action or a way of thinking? Do tactics/tools achieve objectives or express strategies or both?

The Accreditation Board that manages the accreditation testing process recognizes that the debate about terminology probably will never be resolved in day-to-day public relations practice. However, that fact is of little use to candidates preparing themselves for the accreditation examination.

For the purpose of the accreditation examination, the following *operational definitions* should guide candidates' responses to questions in the examinations that use these terms.

MISSION OR PURPOSE

Operational Definition

The overarching reason that the organization came into existence; sufficiently large in scope that it can guide the organization's planning for many years.

Example 1: To bring affordable transportation to the common person.
Example 2: To end world hunger.

GOAL

Operational Definition

Usually a more specific expression of a mission or purpose. Often related to one specific aspect of the mission or purpose, and commonly described as the desired outcome of a plan of action designed to solve a specific problem over the life of a campaign. Note that the four elements of an objective are either stated or implied in a goal, but are more general and long term. Goals are conversions of problem statements.

Problem: Roadway use is above planned capacity but mass transit use is only 60 percent of capacity.

Example 1 (a behavioral goal): To increase public use of mass transit to at least 75 percent of capacity.

Problem: Only 60 to 80 percent of world population has an adequate food supply.

Example 2 (a communication goal): To introduce multi-yield agricultural practices to farmers in developing countries.

Comment: Only when a goal statement includes a quantitative target can it be measured and thus assure that evaluation can document the degree of success. To that end, the above goals might be restated:

Measurable example: To increase by 10 percent the public use of mass transit by the end of the campaign.

Measurable example: To introduce multi-yield agricultural practices to 20 percent of farmers in selected developing countries within five years.

OBJECTIVE

Operational Definition

An objective usually addresses a specific aspect of the problem with each of several objectives contributing toward achieving the goal. Objectives must: (1) address a specific desired communication or **behavioral effect,** (2) **designate the public** or publics among whom the effect is to be achieved, (3) designate the expected **level of attainment** or accomplishment, and, (4) designate the **time frame** in which those attainments or accomplishments are to occur.

Example: To increase by 8 percent [level] the ridership of public transportation in the Los Angeles Metropolitan Area [behavioral effect] by workers earning less than $25,000 per year [public] within the first six months [time frame] of the communication program.

Example: To recruit at least 15 percent [level] of freeway drivers [public] into a park and ride [behavioral effect] within the first two years [time frame] of the program.

Other objectives that might contribute toward the goal might target: (a) downtown workers in the second six months, (b) drive time motorists frustrated with traffic jams, and (c) during the peak smog season those concerned with protecting the environment. Objectives may also be designed to evaluate the effectiveness of the public relations effort, as in the following example.

(continues)

Example: To have at least 10 percent [level] of a randomly selected sample of riders of public transportation in the Los Angeles Metropolitan Area [public] identify as their reason for riding public transportation one of the communication tactics employed in your public relations campaign [behavioral effect] by the end of the second year of that campaign [time frame].

Example for second goal: To have 50 percent [level] of the farmers of one Asian, one African, and one South American developing country [public(s)] be reported by field agents as applying multi-yield agricultural practices [behavioral effect] by 1999 [time frame].

STRATEGY

Operational Definition

Strategies indicate the conceptual approach in selecting specific actions to be taken to achieve objectives and reach the goal. A strategy expresses the thoughtful plan to maximize resources and/or address the unique characteristics of the situation. It is an overall approach to selecting the activities ultimately undertaken that, in the aggregate, will solve the underlying problem. A strategy may address a problem that involves a single target public, but more often will be a series of strategies, each one addressing an aspect of the problem involving a different target public.

Example 1: Establish public transportation as the style choice of the 1990s.

Example 2: Identify indigenous leaders to serve as role models for agricultural innovation in their communities. Establish a coalition with other groups such as Agency for International Development and Oxfam to share technology and communication networks. Design information packages showcasing program successes to appeal to local media.

TACTICS/TOOLS

Operational Definition

Tactics/tools are the activities conducted to carry out specific objectives and thus to implement the overall strategies of a public relations program. The full range of the tactics/tools needed for each objective all depend on specific personnel, costs, and other resources. While tactics generally include activities that involve the participation of target publics, tools, in general, seek to achieve a desired response from a public.

FIRST GOAL

Example Tool: Design, produce, and distribute radio, television, and print public service announcements featuring celebrities endorsing mass transit.

Example Tool: Initiate Mass Transit Logo: "A Transit Fare Means Cleaner Air."

Example Tactic: Launch a "Why I'd rather be riding than driving" essay contest.

Example Tactic: Introduce a lottery prize drawn from mass transit pass numbers.

SECOND GOAL

Example Tool: Design, produce, and distribute video training materials for use in demonstrating the benefits of multi-yield agricultural techniques.

Example Tactic: Launch farmer cooperative demonstration projects to provide role models of successful multi-yield techniques.

Example Tactic: Sponsor a World Hunger Conference with participation of coalition partners with special invitation to local and world media.

limit creativity to cases. The creative person can take parts and pieces from a wide range of sources and come up with a winning campaign idea.

A word about plagiarism. It is extremely unlikely that there are any "new ideas" in the world, only old ideas put together in new ways. In recognition of this fact, the copyright law (U.S. Code 17) specifies that ideas are not copyrightable—only *expressions* of ideas are. The law specifically protects only that which is "fixed in a tangible medium of expression"; in other words, it must be written or otherwise permanently "fixed." The same basic principle applies to patents; only the specific plans for an invention, as expressed in drawings, are patentable.

Although there may be little reason to be concerned about borrowing *ideas* from others in planning a campaign, written material and such things as slogans, themes, logos, cartoon characters, photos, artwork, and music are protected. To use copyrighted material requires the written permission of the copyright holder, who is usually the author or publisher.

In adapting an old idea to a new situation, the expression of the idea will necessarily be different. The same principle guided the Copyright Office in its decision not to make graphic elements copyrightable. There would be pure chaos if all the design and layout elements of brochure and print graphics were not available for everyone to use, simply because they have been used and borrowed since the invention of printing.

Many resources are available to stimulate the creative processes of the campaign planner, or the team responsible for designing the strategy. In the absence of wide-ranging experience, one can collect the experiences of others by reading reports of public relations efforts or related projects.

Newspaper and Magazine Reports   Reports of community or corporate activities, planned events, and individual exploits can be rich sources of ideas for a "strategy shopping list." Most newspapers include accounts of activities that could be used, with some variation, in public relations campaigns.

Examples of campaign strategy ideas may be found in most daily newspapers. It's just a matter of identifying the type of public relations activity in the report. The Aerosol case study and the Ford Tractor case study provide examples of campaign strategies.

▶ CASE STUDY: AEROSOL INDUSTRY BATTLES CFC MISINFORMATION

Following the Environmental Protection Agency ban of chlorofluorocarbons (CFC) and the resulting popular attacks on all aerosols as the cause of ozone depletion, the Consumer Aerosol Products Council (CAPCO) with Ketchum Public Relations launched a campaign to correct the misinformation.

RESEARCH

Aerosol sales leveled off and dropped in 1990, when environmental coverage in the news and entertainment industries was on the rise. A Roper Organization surveys in 1991 and 1992 found that 86 percent of American adults and, 77 percent of teens were unaware that aerosol products do not contribute to ozone depletion. Nearly half of educators surveyed at a National Science Teachers Association meeting were unaware that aerosols no longer use CFCs. More than 500 instances of misinformation appeared in the news media since 1990 and nearly 30 in entertainment media. Examples included a Johnny Carson joke that said "Candace Bergen's hairspray destroys the ozone layer" and comic strip character Ziggy who told readers to "avoid aerosol products."

ADAPTATION

Goal

Balance misinformation in the media with accurate information about aerosols and CFCs.

Target Publics

Adults and young people, the news media, and the entertainment industry.

Strategy

Develop a two-pronged effort to relay the "no CFCs" message, including: (1) an education unit for middle school students, and (2) a media relations program to reach consumers and the news and entertainment industries.

Time Frame

Initial campaign was scheduled for 1992–1993.

Budget

For 1992–1993, $700,000 divided into $425,000 for time and $275,000 for expenses of production and distribution of education unit.

IMPLEMENTATION STRATEGY

Education Program Strategy

Work with science teachers to develop an education unit for middle school students with accurate information to balance inaccuracies in the media and to reach adult consumers and influentials with a brochure on aerosols and the environment.

Educational unit reached students bombarded with inaccurate aerosol information as they were studying atmospheric science. A hands-on packet included two demonstrator aerosols, a 13-minute video, a classroom poster, a student worksheet, an informative teacher's guide, a teacher evaluation pre- and post-test, a "free loan" unit available at educational trade shows, direct mail to middle school science teachers, media outreach information, and advertisements in teacher/science trade magazines.

To reach consumers and influentials Ketchum created a colorful, reader-friendly brochure on aerosol products, "Aerosol Works For You," promoted by direct mail to supermarket consumer affairs representatives and professional home economists.

Media Relations Strategy

Pair research results with examples of inaccuracies in entertainment industry and generate in the media the "no CFCs" message. Appealing to their "watchdog" role, reporters were shown dozens of examples of misinformation to generate positive "no CFCs" message in media. Personalized media relations tailored research findings to reporters' needs. Industry response letters and contact with third-party spokespersons in National Science Teachers Association, U.S. Environmental Protection Agency, and Competitive Enterprise Institute to provided each reporter with a compelling story. The inaccurate cartoons and sitcoms themselves proved most supporting as evidence of misinformation; reporters contacted industry representatives asking them to explain their errors. A "Green TV" kit on aerosol misinformation was direct mailed to network and publishing representatives pointing out poorly researched scripts.

EVALUATION

The goal of balancing misinformation with accurate aerosol information is being realized as aerosol sales figures are showing a strong recovery two years into the campaign. Nearly 600,000 students and teachers have viewed "The Aerosol Adventure" in class and more than 75 percent of teachers rated it a four or five on a five-point scale. More than 100,000 "Aerosols Work for You" brochures were sent on request from top supermarkets Proctor & Gamble, Minyard Food Stores, and Spartan Grocery Stores. More than 100 million Americans have seen stories about entertainment industry misinformation in national media, including in the *Wall Street Journal*, *TV Guide*, *Newsweek*, *USA Today*, *Seventeen*, and *Omni*, and on *CNN*. A 1993 follow-up survey of national environmental reporters found nearly 100 percent knew the facts about aerosols and CFCs. *Bonus results included:* Producers of aerosol misinformation have removed inaccurate programs or products. Random House no longer prints the inaccurate "ABC's for a Better Planet." CBS no longer airs reruns of an inaccurate episode of "Northern Exposure." DIC Productions, makers of "GI Joe," will no longer distribute an incorrect episode called "The Nozone Conspiracy."

Source: 1994 Silver Anvil Winners: Index and Summaries, Public Relations Society of America, 1994.

Problem-Solving Techniques from Specialty Publications   Several newsletter-type publications directed toward public relations people offer summaries of recently noted solutions to public relations problems.

The *pr reporter* includes brief summaries of current strategies and other effective public relations efforts:

> In the wake of the Union Carbide disaster at Bhopal, India, which left hundreds dead and thousands injured after a deadly chemical leaked into the atmosphere, the Chemical Manufacturers Association developed programs to give the public greater access to information on hazardous chemicals as well as emergency and medical services. If the industry doesn't deliver, CMA's chairman Edwin Holmer predicts, "a nervous public and impatient government decision-makers will dictate the actions we must take."[8]
>
> After details of misuse of millions of dollars of monthly mortgage payments in a bankruptcy case became known, a U.S. bankruptcy judge in Detroit hired a public relations firm to help deal with calls from the media for information and from the public who expressed fears of losing their homes. The firm chose to do personality profiles of the judge and other court figures to help restore confidence in the court system. Bar Association guidelines against reporting on pending cases and against communications which have an "air of advertising" limited public relations activities from which they could choose.[9]

Identifying Useful Ideas from Case Studies   Most case studies tell the story of a public relations effort as reported by someone involved in it. Some are reported by outsiders who interview those directly involved. For these and other reasons, case study reports follow no predictable outline, and the standard elements that make up a public relations effort are thus not easy to identify. The structural outline in the Ford Tractor Operations case study will help you to organize and recognize the essential elements in public relations campaigns. Of course, not all public relations efforts are limited-time campaigns or even ongoing programs and so will not fit this structure very well. But identifying elements that can be adapted to a campaign being planned will be easier if you can spot the function of various case activities and match it with the corresponding function in your plan.

Careful analysis of case studies can provide ideas for such things as coalition building, communicating through related organizations, and taking advantage of existing government-sponsored research that can be applied to campaign planning.

Arrangements for Official Action   Strategies may include requests for official actions such as a proclamation issued by the mayor or the governor, a model legislative bill to be introduced in state or federal legislatures, a document read into the *Congressional Record*, or a proposal for a special-issue U.S. postage stamp. For each possible official action there is a procedure that should be followed. The rule of self-interest applies for all requests for official action: the action must promote the official's political career to an important segment of his or her constituency; if the action is in the public interest, the government official will be happy to sponsor the action; if the action is controversial, a sponsor should be sought among officials representing supporters of the action.

Official proclamations are probably the easiest official actions to arrange. A draft of the proclamation is the first step. It can be to establish "physical fitness day" or "visit a friend day" or "free enterprise day"—whatever would fit into the campaign being planned. A telephone call to the governor's or mayor's office explaining the requested proclamation and the cause for which it is being requested will often be sufficient to get approval or at least to discover the procedure.

Model legislation, like the official proclamation, will find ready cooperation from legislators if the bill is in the public interest, or if the bill is in the interest of some legislator's constituency in the case of controversial issues. The bill must be drafted, the legislator contacted, and a final draft approved. If there is any controversy on the issue, it is advisable to have an attorney familiar with that aspect of the law examine the bill to make sure it is in proper legal phraseology, to avoid a court challenge and possibly having the bill declared invalid.

Having a document read into the *Congressional Record* (CR) of the federal Congress is simply a matter of having it requested by a member of your state or district legislative delegation. The document should have some public interest, and it is valuable largely for the publicity value of reprints that may be distributed afterward.

Special-issue stamps to honor various contributions to American life may be proposed to the U.S. Postal Service. The possibilities for use in a campaign might include an inventor associated with your company or its products, a prominent figure in your nonprofit organization's history, an anniversary of a landmark court decision, and the like. A brief study of a stamp collector's handbook should offer some useful ideas. The Postal Service has a brochure available on the procedure for requesting a special-issue stamp; one requirement is that the person to be honored must be deceased.

Creative Research   Creative ideas may come to mind after consulting a list of resources available for public relations applications. Creative thinking puts previously staged events together with the needs of a campaign plan and comes up with a new idea. Such ideas may come from a list of directories.[10] Some suggestions for possible campaign applications are offered after each entry in note 10; these should be used as thought starters, not as the only way the resource can be used.

A Shopping List of Possible Strategies   A list of potential strategies allows the planner to focus attention on what might be used before a commitment is made to any set of strategies. The list should not exclude ideas that may cost too much, take too many people to implement, or otherwise seem unmanageable. Those problems may be solved later; first you need a list of possibilities from which you can refine and select. The list should be two to four times longer than the actual number of events or strategies needed. The longer the list, the more opportunity for creating the ideal approach. One way to develop

▶ CASE STUDY: FORD TRACTOR OPERATIONS

CASE STUDY ANALYSIS

For each outlined element below, identify that element in a case study you wish to analyze. Describe how each element was carried out. Make note of any special value or advantage in the way the element was implemented.

Criteria for Analysis of Public Relations Case Studies

Basic Elements:

1. **Research** What research was used, whether done by the organization, hired, compiled from other research, or otherwise?
    a. What facts were discovered, which were crucial to the case, and how were they stated?
    b. How was the problem or opportunity stated and how did they analyze the situation that motivated the effort and refine that analysis into a usable statement of what needed to be done?

2. **Adaptation** How did they fit together the critical parts of the planned effort, especially including the following?
    a. How did they state the goal? This is usually the result of the research stated as "the problem" but converted into a goal statement.
    b. Into what groupings did they target the public or how did they segment it into groups to promote efficiency?
    c. What budget advantages, economies of scale, or cost savings were evident?
    d. How did they maintain liaison with management to ensure support and approval at every stage of implementation?

3. **Implementation Strategy** What was the strategy or action they chose in order to reach the goal or to solve the problem?
    a. Identify each element of the strategy or package of activities that was chosen to achieve the goal, including any tie-ins, tradeouts, coalitions, or partnerships with like-minded organizations.
    b. Identify each element of the communications plan, message, and media used in the strategy or to enhance the strategy. Note especially the effectiveness of any communications used before, during, and after events or activities in the strategy.
    c. What timing or calendaring advantages are evident, in both the placement of advance publicity and the fitting of actions to the calendar of public awareness?
    d. Were there any special advantages in the assignment, deployment, or co-ordination of people needed to implement the effort?

4. **Evaluation** How were achievements measured or determined and what lessons were learned from the experience?
    a. How did they determine whether goals were reached and to what degree?
    b. How were positive or negative outcomes recorded? Were any results used to make future projections?

EXAMPLE OF CASE STUDY SUBJECTED TO ANALYSIS USING THE STRUCTURE ABOVE

Case study no. 2,018 published in PR News, volume XLI, no. 32 (August 19, 1985) tells the story of Ford Motor Company's Ford Tractor

Operations (FTO) effort to relate more effectively to women farmers.

1. **Research** At least two research projects were used, the application of recent findings from studies of the U.S. Department of Agriculture to the market for Ford tractor products, and results of a "test" of a strategy to determine its potential further use.

   a. Facts discovered: (They discovered these facts on which the campaign was built) 6 percent of farms are operated by women; 85 percent of male farmers have wives, of whom 55 percent are joint operators with their husbands; of the same 85 percent, 61 percent are responsible for budgeting and finances and 46 percent help make decisions about major equipment purchases. The test of the strategy proved it worthy of continuation; in addition, it provided "useful ideas" including the fact that "farm women play an important role in purchasing of parts and in demanding quality service."

   b. Problem statement: The stated problem or opportunity was, "it would be desirable to develop closer relationship with these influential people."

2. **Adaptation** They fit together these critical elements:

   a. Goal: The goal as stated was: to develop a closer relationship with women farmers and "in addition to making them more amenable to purchase of FTO equipment, they also could provide valuable information feedback."

   b. Segmentation: A particularly effective segmentation technique, for the public they wanted to reach, was accomplished by targeting ten major North American farm organizations through which they could reach women farmers.

   c. Budget: While budget details were not provided, the economy of scale by which they could reach all women farmers through existing farm organizations and at a fraction of the cost of reaching them otherwise, not to mention the added credibility of working through respected organizations, was ingenious.

   d. Management liaison: Management rapport was maintained in two notable respects: the responsibility for developing and implementing the program rested with the Assistant Public Affairs Manager, and top executives of FTO were always present and participated in the effort.

3. **Implementation Strategy** The strategy of establishing a council of women farmers and working through existing farm organizations was particularly effective.

   a. Strategy: Specific elements of the strategy included conducting educational seminars for farm women in conjunction, that is, as tie-ins, with national conventions of various farm women's organizations as well as at gatherings sponsored by educational institutions (University of Western Michigan, for example); establishing the National Agricultural Women's Council with representatives appointed by each of the ten farm organizations.

   b. Communication plan: Communication elements included approaching the ten farm organizations, asking them to select representatives; discussions at the meetings; initiation of advertising to women; reprints of ads featuring women as equals in farm operation distributed to women's organizations and to national print and electronic media; speakers drawn from FTO as well as from outside on current topics of interest to farm women; packets distributed to farm women attending sessions; media conferences conducted at council meetings, with press packets including photos and biographical sketches; synopses of speakers' remarks prepared to use in follow-up releases.

c. Calendaring: Timing of announcements and advance publicity as well as repeat scheduling of council meetings appeared to be effective, but calendaring the activities to fit the national conventions already meshed with the farm planting and harvest calendar was noteworthy.

d. Special advantages: The special advantage of working through the existing organizations was that the campaign was accomplished with apparently one staff person from FTO and presumably a minimum of expense, though the study does mention the FTO picked up the costs of participants in the council meetings.

4. **Evaluation**   Achievements were enthusiastically recorded, including media results as well as executive approval.

a. Goal achieved: Achievement of the goal was simply affirmed: "accolades demonstrate that FTO is establishing its desired relations with the woman farmer." Measurement of this achievement was based on extensive media clips, letters applauding the effort from women, from farm organizations, from top officers of USDA, and from FTO management, which termed it a "huge success."

b. Outcomes: Only positive evaluations were made, and its success strongly recommended continuation of the National Agricultural Women's Council.

a list of tentative strategies is to conduct a brainstorming session with a group of people who are equally intent on devising the best strategy and are up to speed on the campaign situation, its background, and its research findings.

Box 7.3 provides a checklist of categories of possible strategic approaches that may be considered in coming up with a shopping list. This checklist of strategy types does not represent the final form any strategy shopping list will take; it is intended to be used as a thought starter in conjunction with brainstorming or other creative techniques. The actual strategies must be specifically adapted to the client or employer situation.

Organize a Brainstorming Session   Brainstorming is an interpersonal communication technique for creating new ideas by sharing ideas, discussing possible improvements, combining ideas, and generally taking advantage of group creativity in a way that one person alone can never do.

Some ground rules for brainstorming:

1. Ideally five to ten people is the best number; all rank or position of authority must be suspended, and no ideas may be derided or ridiculed.

2. Everyone must be allowed to contribute, with no one person dominating the discussion; someone must be designated moderator and someone designated recorder.
3. The recorder must rapidly write down every idea presented, preferably on a large newsprint tablet that everyone can see, sheets from which can be taped to walls for reference; the moderator must keep the discussion on track and make sure recorded ideas accurately reflect the contributor's thought or with acceptable improvements.
4. The task must be clear to every participant, and a time limit is recommended, usually from 15 to 60 minutes.
5. First a list of ideas or possible solutions to the problem should be written on the tablet.
6. Next the group should discuss the ideas that seem best, combining various ideas or going on to consider other ideas until the possibilities are exhausted or until a solution is reached.

As applied to the task of planning strategies for a public relations campaign, the brainstorming session should produce a refined list of strategies or a package that offers reasonable hope of solving the campaign's problem or reaching the goal. The strategies may still be tentative, subject to change as further details of the campaign plan take shape, but the best possible strategies should be identified by the brainstorming session. If the campaign is being conducted for a nonprofit organization, at least one of the strategies or events should ordinarily be a fund-raising event.

The next step in planning for a public relations campaign involves an inventory of the organization's resources. Because the campaign will require considerable amounts of time and money and the contributions of various people, it is necessary to take stock of what you have to work with.

ENUMERATE RESOURCES AVAILABLE

The planner should take stock specifically of the money, time, and personnel available for the campaign. The situation analysis and research should have identified the major limitations, but if these are not known, they must be investigated at this time.

Timing: Careful attention must be given to how the campaign will fit into the annual calendar, as well as the chronology of what happens in the campaign. When a commitment is made to a tie-in with a calendar event, the die is cast. Everything must be back timed from that date. Estimates of time required for research, for planning, and for preparation of campaign print or broadcast materials, as well as allowances for the unexpected, must be made to permit implementation of each within the time available.

BOX 7.3   Types of Public Relations Strategies

STRATEGIC INACTION

1. **Do nothing**—the decision that under the circumstances the proper response is to take no action, as in a challenge from a disreputable source.

INFORMATION DISSEMINATION ACTIVITIES

2. **The public information program**—the dissemination of information emphasizing the point of view of the sponsoring organization, official endorsement, position statement, testimony.
3. **News conference**—an invitation to the simultaneous announcement to all media of significant, timely news from a knowledgeable spokesperson.
4. **Lobbying**—the legitimate function of providing accurate information to lawmakers and feedback to the organization, all to promote the organization's interests.
5. **Personality appearance, spokesperson tour**—the selection of a celebrity or expert to represent and disseminate information about the organization or product/service.
6. **Speakers bureau**—providing expert, trained employees, or others, for the programming needs of clubs, service organizations, and schools and valuable publicity for the sponsoring organization.
7. **Misinformation correction or false allegation response**—the effort to correct false information, usually from sincere but misguided sources. Often accomplished by action that refutes the falsehood without lending credence by direct denial.
8. **Information booths/exhibits/displays**—the dispensing of information important to a group of people gathered in one location; also traveling exhibit.

EVENT ACTIVITIES

9. **Natural events**—the reaction to a naturally occurring event, from mergers, profit statements, discoveries, and inventions, to acts of heroism, executive appointments, etc.
10. **Celebration events**—occasions marking special day(s), week(s), or month(s) to recognize laudatory acts or memorable times: anniversary, founders' day, national secretary day, etc.
11. **Staged/media events**—activities invented solely to attract media attention and/or generate publicity: dedications, groundbreakings, tree plantings, high-wire walking, pole sitting, etc.

12. **Contests, competitions**—the attempt to establish the best, fastest, largest, smallest, and to set a "world record," awarding of prize, or other mark of excellence.

PROMOTIONAL ACTIVITIES

13. **Marketing-related activities**—focusing efforts on matching of consumer products with the needs of the consumer: especially trade shows, product/services demonstrations, product tests, new product introduction, book release.
14. **Demonstration/dramatization**—demonstrating how a product or process works; dramatic portrayal or group concern, as in a strike; performance having emotional appeal, a vignette.
15. **Fund-raising**—efforts or events destined to raise money from foundations, the public, corporations, etc.; often used to supplement a limited campaign budget.
16. **Research findings**—contracting for independent documentation of facts on a controversial issue, or release of other research results; useful in answering misinformation and in achieving credible publicity.
17. **Social responsibility efforts**—activities in which an organization or its employees engage and which benefit the community and have publicity value.

ORGANIZATIONAL ACTIVITIES

18. **Establishing of an organization**—enlistment of supporters of an organization into an identifiable group for cooperative effort and cohesiveness.
19. **Coalition building**—construction of working alliances with groups that share goals/objectives in order to carry out mutually beneficial programs.
20. **Meetings, conventions, seminars**—capitalizing on the publicity value of information-exchanging assemblies to build recognition of the organization, disseminate information, etc.
21. **Indirect (grass-roots) lobbying**—effort to influence the legislative process by organizing voters to bring pressure to bear on the legislature.
22. **Negotiation or adjudication of conflict**—intervention of a disinterested authority figure to resolve differences between groups.

A tentative calendar of activities may help at this point to fit together the possibilities for the campaign. Refinements can be made throughout the planning process and incorporated into the final calendar, which becomes a part of the "strategy" stage of the campaign plan.

Personnel needs must also be estimated. The people needed to carry out strategies will have to be projected based on educated guesswork. If large numbers of people are going to be required to implement parts of the plan, it will be necessary to plan for cooperation of nonprofit groups for volunteers—the Scouts, for example, or the Jaycees. Certain extraordinary needs for people to help with campaign tasks can best be covered by hiring temporaries. The possibility of hiring interns from nearby colleges or universities should not be overlooked; public relations interns can usually be given responsibilities for major aspects of the campaign planning and execution.

As another example, if your plans call for a number of people to "host" an event, you need to know whether people in the other departments of the organization would be available on company time. If additional clerical staff may be needed during the campaign, you may have to find out how to secure the temporary transfer of people, look into hiring temporary help, or find another solution.

Money: Budget limitations must also be known at the outset of a campaign planning process. Usually funds are limited, never enough to do everything you would like to do. This limitation of budget should not, by itself, be a hindrance to planning the most effective effort. If the funds are not in the budget, an appeal can be made to allocate resources from contingency funds or, that failing, to include fund-raising events in the plan. For most nonprofit organizations it is often a foregone conclusion that fund-raising events will be part of the campaign.

If funding is severely limited and the campaign can't even get off the ground, it is possible to include fund-raising events in the campaign to pay for expenses. The fund-raising event can, with careful planning, provide income and at the same time make a substantial contribution to the campaign goal.

In addition to resources available, the organization's policies must be investigated. Particularly important is discovery of any policy, written or unwritten, that might have a bearing on the campaign. If, for example, you have suggested that a company picnic be held on company time, you need to know if there is a policy against releasing employees from assigned duties during working hours.

The campaign planner may wish to use the worksheet shown in Box 7.4 in making an inventory of limitations.

DEVELOP A SYSTEM FOR MANAGEMENT SUPPORT

There must be a plan for maintaining liaison with management. Because the campaign must ultimately be approved by management decision makers, it is usually desirable for management to approve the campaign plan at each stage

BOX 7.4   Resource Inventory for Public Relations

This form will help to identify resources available as public relations campaign planning gets under way. Specific information may be available, or estimates may have to be used. The more realistic the projections, the more valuable the resulting information will be.

TIME LIMITATIONS

1. Campaign implementation deadline: _____
    (Time campaign execution must begin.)
2. Campaign printed material delivery date: _____
    (Should allow for reprinting in case of errors.)
3. Advance publicity beginning date: _____
    (Needs to generate sufficient participation in campaign.)
4. Printed publicity material delivery date: _____
    (Available in time to include in mail-out packages.)
5. Planning completion date: _____
    (Should include all arrangements needed for campaign.)
6. Research completion date: _____
    (Indicate when final results are needed for plan book and if research is likely to run over into planning time; some facts may be needed sooner than final report deadline.)

The above should be back timed from implementation deadline. Other plans should be calendared from implementation. For example, implementation and evaluation both must be scheduled; implementation should be back timed from any critical impact date (when results are to be achieved), and evaluation should be scheduled at various times after the end of the campaign.

IMPLEMENTATION SCHEDULE

1. Integrated and coordinated event/activity dates: _____
    (Highlight critical dates for beginning and ending events that must fit together.)
2. Evaluation schedule dates: _____
    (Indicate beginning dates for various evaluations.)

BUDGET CONSTRAINTS

1. Total budget available: _____
    (Clarify flexibility of budget; if inflexible, plans for fund-raising activities need to be included in campaign.)

(continues)

2. Itemize budget for each campaign event/activity: _____
    (Costs for events/activities that can be implemented independently of other campaign elements need to be specified; costs of communication are the most basic.)
3. Reduce budget costs by specifying any tradeout considerations: _____
4. Final budget calculations: _____
    (Campaign costs, less initial budgeted amount, less any tradeout considerations; resulting balance to be raised by special fund-raising efforts.)

PERSONNEL NEEDS ESTIMATE

1. Estimate of person-hours needed to implement campaign: _____
2. Number of full-time people available for campaign: _____
    (Number of persons multiplied by 40 hours per week.)
3. Number of hours for which temporary help will be needed: _____
    (Most responsible positions will have to be filled by regular employees or temporaries under salary or wage contract.)
4. Number of hours available from volunteers: _____
    (Include loaned executives, interns, employee volunteers, service organization volunteers, etc.)
5. Deficit person-hours: _____
    (Indicate how additional hours will be filled from above categories.)

of development. In this way, adjustments can be made whenever potential problems arise that might otherwise eventually conflict with management policies. The term *management* here means the person or persons who are ultimately responsible for the organization, its total operation as well as its public relations efforts. Usually that is the chief executive officer (CEO), whether the organization is a corporation or a nonprofit and whether the campaign is planned as part of the activities in a corporate public relations department or by a counseling firm for a client.

Develop a procedure for maintaining management support. When planning is under way for an extensive campaign effort, rapport with management is critical to ensure that management will accept the final plan. It is often too late to win approval of the plan if it is in final form before it is submitted to management. Nothing is quite as discouraging as spending months on a plan, working out exhaustive details, only to be told, "we can't do it." The way to avoid this pitfall is to gain and keep management understanding and support for the project throughout the planning stages.

Interpersonal communication skills are particularly important in interacting with top management. Knowing how to interact with superiors requires mastery of interpersonal verbal as well as nonverbal skills. J. T. Wood has outlined a useful orientation to the process in her book *Human Communication.*[11] Of course, interacting with management is only one application of interpersonal skills for the campaign planner or manager.

Know the chain of command. One problem with management support is that the chain of command may not be easily discernible. The organization may not work quite the way the organization chart says it should. There may not even be an organizational chart. In any case, it is wise to draw up an organizational chart to reflect the current, actual lines of authority. With every change in personnel there is likely to be some shift in how things are done. The most important thing to find out is who will make the final decision to approve the campaign plan and decide to execute it. Several people may have to "sign off" on aspects related to their areas of responsibility.

The task of working with you on the plan may be assigned to a middle management executive who will present the final plan to the CEO for approval—that, by the way, is a treacherous arrangement. The junior executive may have reason to sabotage the undertaking or at best have little interest in the success of the project. Whatever the means of approval, the wise planner will design a careful strategy for presenting and winning approval of the plan in addition to giving careful attention to the plan itself.

Another possible obstacle to approval of the plan may be the gatekeepers who control access to the decision makers. Secretaries are valuable allies, and it never pays to alienate one. A good secretary can facilitate access to the chief executive by control of the agenda and can often insert an important item for decision into an already full agenda for the executive's day.

Get the Plan Approved. Once the decision-making process is identified, a system must be developed for gaining approval for the various parts of the developing plan and making sure critical go-ahead decisions are made promptly throughout the planning process. A prearranged schedule of meetings, or at least a time for phone calls with the decision maker, is critical to the planning process. The essential ingredient in the plan for liaison with top management is regular access. The system may consist of regularly scheduled meetings with management, regularly scheduled meetings with a contact person designated by top management, regular reports submitted to management, special project reports, progress reports on the campaign, or a combination of these. The liaison system should be worked out in a way that satisfies both the practitioner's need for liaison and the CEO's scheduling restrictions.

Things that should be communicated officially include recommendations for actions or programs, progress reports, research results, and—especially if the CEO is a client rather than an employer—costs and billings. Recommendations for actions should be communicated because the purpose of the liaison is to get management reactions to such things. Reports of progress on the campaign will give the CEO the opportunity to react to the details of the plan as well as the overall direction it is taking. Research results should be reported because there may be more far-ranging applications of the findings than just the campaign; in any case, management is always interested in results of any research involving the organization. Costs, especially if they show the good news that you are under budget, are valuable in building a sound relationship with management. Bad news about costs are important to report to management, in writing, so that they will not be blown out of proportion and so that they can be dealt with effectively. Billings for services, as long as they are within a realistic range, should simply be included in regularly scheduled reports.

SUMMARY

The adaptation plan—spelled out in detail in this chapter—covers seven steps.

The situation analysis describes the problem or opportunity that motivated the campaign.

Stating the problem. In the analysis of the situation the planner has identified the mandate for the campaign, including management's perceptions of the situation and expectations for dealing with it. Research has confirmed the true nature of the situation by defining the problem to be solved or the opportunity to be exploited. This research has employed all appropriate techniques to discover relevant facts to confirm or modify the situation as perceived. With these findings, the planner has subdivided the problem into manageable parts.

Setting the goals. With the problem carefully defined and subdivided according to how it is perceived by the various publics, the problem has been converted into a goal or goals. The goal(s) has translated the problem into a form that can be measured as a way to monitor its achievement. *Establish objectives.* With the goal(s) determined, various objectives have been identified that will contribute to reaching the goal(s).

Segmenting and targeting publics. Drawing on research findings, the various publics that have an interest in the situation have been identified and segmented into those of high and those of low priority. Target politics have also been analyzed to identify attitudes and opinions that have a bearing on the case. Appeals that will be most effective with these target publics have been identified. *Brainstorming for ideas.* With a wide range of case studies in mind, the planning team has been able to conduct successful and productive brainstorming sessions to construct a list of possible strategies.

Listing strategy options. As problems, goal, and target publics have been clarified, some thought has been given to possible solutions to the problem—potential strategies. These have been listed in a "shopping list" of strategies.

Consider limitations. The team has considered the time frame during which the campaign must be executed. Constraints of personnel to carry out the plan have been considered. The availability of funds to execute the campaign has been carefully considered and solved.

Develop a system for management support. Throughout the adaptation stage the attitudes, policies, and judgment of management decision makers have provided a constant check on ideas and decisions. An efficient system for management rapport has led to a plan that reflects management approval. With these decisions made, the team is ready to proceed to the strategy-building stage of campaign planning.

FOR FURTHER READING

On Planning

Cantor, Bill, ed. "Planning the Process." *Experts in Action.* New York: Longman, 1984.

Crow, Richard T., and Charles A. Odewahn. *Management for the Human Services.* Englewood Cliffs, NJ: Prentice-Hall, 1987. See especially pp. 118–128.

Govoni, Narman, Robert Eng, and Morton Galper. *Promotional Management.* Englewood Cliffs, NJ: Prentice-Hall, 1986.

McElreath, Mar, P. "Planning Programs for Exceptional Events." *Public Relations Review* 5 (Fall 1979): 35–40.

Middleton, John, ed. *Approaches to Communication Planning.* Paris: UNESCO, 1980.

Nagelschmidt, Joseph, ed. "Part Five: Grassroots," "Part Six: Communication," and "Part Seven: Education and Training" in *The Public Affairs Handbook.* New York: AMA-COM, 1982.

Nager, Norman R., and Richard H. Truitt. *Strategic Public Relations Counseling: Models from the Counselors Academy.* New York: Longman, 1987.

Peter, J. Paul, and James H. Donnelly Jr. *A Preface to Marketing Management*, 3rd ed. Plano, TX: Business Publications, Inc., 1985.

Rice, Ronald E., and C. K. Atkin, eds. *Public Communication Campaigns.* Newbury Park, CA: Sage, 1989.

Salmon, Charles T., ed. *Information Campaigns: Balancing Social Values and Social Change.* Newbury Park, CA: Sage, 1989.

Simmons, Robert. *Communications Campaign Management: A Systems Approach.* New York: Longman, 1990.

Stricharchuk, Gregory. "Just Read Our Lips: No Blimps, No Tires, No Blimps, No Tires." *Wall Street Journal* (Friday September 30, 1988) sec. 2, p. 29.

Swanston, David and Robert Kendall, *Accreditation Sourcebook.* New York: Public Relations Society of America, 1994.

On Events

Anderson, James A., and Timothy P. Meyer, Chapter 4, "The Social Action of Mediated Communication," in *Mediated Communication: A Social Action Perspective.* Newbury Park, CA: Sage, 1988. Offers a thoughtful perspective on the role of public relations activities in the wider social context.

Bernays, Edward. *Public Relations.* Norman, OK: University of Oklahoma Press, 1977. This autobiography includes, among others, the classic Ivory Soap carving contest story.

Chase's Annual Event Directory. New York: Contemporary books, annual. Lists events, special days, etc., in the annual calendar.

Edelman, Murray. *Constructing the Political Spectacle.* Chicago: University of Chicago Press, 1988. Analyzes actions, enemies, and strategies in political campaigns.

McFarlan, Donald, ed. *Guinness Book of World Records.* New York: Bantam Books, annual. Lists world records as a standard for planning to challenge the records.

No Secrets: Case Studies for the Goal Quill Awards Program. San Francisco, CA: International Association of Business Communicators, annual.

Case Studies

Center, Allen, and Patrick Jackson. *Public Relations Practices: Managerial Case Studies and Problems,* 4th ed. Englewood Cliffs, NJ: Prentice-Hall, 1990.

Hendricks, Jerry A., *Public Relations Cases,* 3rd ed., New York: Wadsworth, 1995.

pr reporter, includes summaries and highlights of cases. P.O. Box 600, Exeter, NH, 03833–0600

PRSA Silver Anvil Winners, 33 Irving Place, New York, NY, 10003, annual. Summarizes annual winners of PRSA public relations competition.

PRspectives. Muncie, IN: Ball State University, Department of Journalism, annual.

Public Relations News, 127 E. 80th St., New York, NY 10021. Includes a 1–2 page case study in each issue.

Simon, Raymond and Frank W. Wylie, *Cases in Public Relations Management,* Chicag: NTC Business Books, 1994.

Valverde, Fernando E., APR, *Relaciones Publicas en Accion: Casos de Programas.* San Juan: PR, Publicaciones Puertorrequenas, Inc., 1994.

The Adaptation Plan: Cases and Problems

- Case Study: Sporting Events Sponsorship—A Public Relations Campaign Strategy in the Spotlight
- Case Study: Student Team Campaign: University Police Department Community Relations and Recruitment

---

➤ CASE STUDY: SPORTING EVENTS SPONSORSHIP—A PUBLIC RELATIONS CAMPAIGN STRATEGY IN THE SPOTLIGHT
by Karen Livingston

What better way to appeal to a nation obsessed with sports than to give it what it wants. Many corporations are doing just that in the form of public relations campaigns built on sporting events. Companies such as Saturn cars, Motorola Communications, Timex watches, and Coors beer are sponsoring everything from mass participation fun runs to drag races to speed boat exhibitions all in the name of better relations with their customers.

Use of Sports Events as a Public Relations Campaign Strategy.   Public relations counselor Art Stevens, writing for the *Harvard Business Review*, describes special-events marketing as the process that "promotes products by linking them to events, issues, or ideas of inherent interest to consumers" (Harris, p. 193). He contrasted traditional product publicity, which focuses on the product's features and benefits, with event sponsorship, which he labeled "brandstanding." By engineering links that connect the product to an event of public interest, brandstanding establishes a rapport between consumers and a product.

According to International Events Group, publishers of "Special Events Report," more than 3,700 companies spend over $1.8 billion in fees alone to sponsor special events. Add to that the money spent on advertising, promotion, and public relations activities supporting these sponsorships, and the number exceeds $3 billion annually (Harris, p. 194). This field is growing at a rate of 30 to 40 percent annually.

As an offshoot of this trend, sports sponsorship by far is the special-events category most favored by corporate America. Success in such mega-events as the 1984 Los Angeles Olympics and the 1988 Festival of Lights Celebration in Calgary, Canada, which was held in conjunction with the winter Olympics there, has spawned a growing number of companies specializing in sports which include the "Big Three"—International Management Group (IMG), ProServ, Inc., and Advantage International, Inc. A number of public relations firms have established special-events departments. Burson-Marsteller says its credentials in sports- and entertainment-event marketing are "among the best in the world" (Harris, p. 195).

Barry Frank, senior corporate vice president of International Management Group, remarked on the role of public relations in sports marketing:

> When a company spends hundreds of thousands or even millions of dollars to sponsor an event, it seems rather foolish to me not to spend the additional relatively small amount required to tell people you're doing so. Public relations is the final ingredient required to ensure the success of the buy; to fail to use PR seems kind of like buying a car without the engine; it still looks pretty but it won't go very far (Harris, p. 200).

One example of a public relations/ sports marketing special event is Seagram's Coolers "Send the Families" program, which sent 550 family members, one for each athlete in 23 participating sports, to Seoul, Korea, for the 1988 Summer Games. The company described the program as "Seagram's Coolers' effort to reward the team behind the team—families of U.S. Olympic athletes." A key public relations component was a giant greeting card that traveled 9,000 miles across the country, collecting 50,000 signatures and 200 million media impressions (Harris, p. 207).

In its never-ending quest to find new and different ideas, a program entitled the "Canadian Mist Thumb Wrestling Tournament" was created by the Edelman public relations firm to build brand awareness through media attention, promote product trial, and strengthen the ties among manufacturer, distributor, and customer. The public relations firms set the rules for the 60-second match and added to the fun by creating the International Thumb Wrestling Federation, which sanctioned the Canadian Mist Thumb Wrestling Tournament as its first and only tournament. More than 1,000 bars and restaurants ran tournaments. Each received an instructional videotape, posters, T-shirts, buttons, and other publicity-oriented paraphernalia. The event attracted print coverage and was carried on "CBS Morning News." The tournament also provided an occasion for Canadian Mist tasting, a strategy that resulted in increased orders and hundreds of new accounts (Harris, p. 216).

Frigidaire Bike Race

Frigidaire long enjoyed an illustrious history, since Will Durant, the founder of General Motors (GM), purchased a mock-up of the first refrigerator invented and began producing Frigidaires as a division of GM. When in 1979 GM sold the Frigidaire division in order to concentrate on the automobile business, the appliance company began operations as part of White Consolidated Industries. Today Frigidaire Company is the North American appliance arm of the world's largest appliance maker with offices in Columbus, Ohio.

The new company conceived as its mission statement: "the design and manufacture of services that satisfy our customer's needs. We have a deep concern for safety, the economy, and our environment. Because leadership is not a static condition, we cannot rest with the quality we have achieved; we must continue to innovate and improve" (personal communication from P. Gostomsky, October 30, 1994). Frigidaire remained in the 1990s one of America's leading manufacturers of appliances. In keeping with the well-earned respect of a generation of homemakers, and with its mission statement, the company wanted to address certain research findings that posed a problem for its continued growth.

Research

Previous research had revealed that Frigidaire consumers consisted primarily of adults over age 45. Their main competition, Whirlpool and General Electric, held the largest market share of younger consumers, those in their "family building years" (personal communication from J. Baumeister, November 13, 1994). While adults over 45 are still a major market segment, they probably would not be interested in buying too many more appliances during their lifetimes. Frigidaire felt that it needed to attract younger consumers who would be interested in purchasing three or four refrigerators during their lifetimes. They specifically wanted to target young adults age 25 to 35.

"Surveys are still probably one of the most viable forms of communication research that you can use," according to David Clavier, executive director of Husk Jennings Overman Public Relations. Nevertheless face-to-face interviews can deal more effectively with complicated issues and can generally decrease the number of "don't know" answers. Interviewers can also make important observations aside from responses to questions.

Accordingly, Frigidaire's in-house marketing department used survey research as the first phase of its public relations campaign research. They used results from a nationwide, ongoing telephone survey of Frigidaire dealers. Whenever a dealer calls Frigidaire, sales representatives are instructed to gather statistics on consumers. They also get reports from their field representatives and make use of a direct mail–type survey when new consumers mail in their warranty cards.

Adaptation

In public relations campaigns, as in many other applications, the planning or adaptation process can mean the difference between success and failure. As Ginnie Duffy, a Florida communications manager, notes, "Think of planning as a blueprint for success" (FPRA Newsletter, p. 8.). Using findings from their survey research, Frigidaire came up with a series of questions which formulated a problem statement.

Problem   How do we attract a younger consumer to the Frigidaire brand? How can we assure the people of central Ohio that we are a company interested in their community? From these questions Frigidaire established two campaign goals.

Goals   To attract younger consumers to the Frigidaire brand and to establish themselves within the central Ohio area as an active community-minded corporation.

Frigidaire listed their specific objective.

Objective   Create a brand name association between Frigidaire Company and young, "family-building," central Ohioan consumers as well as between bicycle racing and Frigidaire. This would be measured in an on-site survey conducted by the members of the task force team. The objective was limited in this way because of the shortness of the public relations campaign. If all went well with this event, Frigidaire would expand to make this an annual event with more specific objectives.

Segmentation   They succeeded in segmenting and targeting their public of younger consumers and central Ohioans, and came up with a short list of strategy options.

Strategy Options   Tony Evans, the director of communications, said, "Frigidaire has been looking for the right kind of local event to promote." Because of the steady input from several enthusiasts both inside the company and in the Columbus-area community, a bicycle-oriented campaign was already chosen. The list of options for this campaign included: adding an event to an already established local race series, putting on a separate race, sponsoring a women's racing team, hosting a postrace dinner for top racers in the event, conducting week-long school visits about bike safety, or hosting a family ride throughout the city of Columbus.

Timing and Budget   Frigidaire wanted to implement the campaign as soon as possible. The budget was limited to $40,000.

Liaison   To maintain open lines of communication with company management, the outside public relations firm was to work with Frigidaire's communications director. Once the decision to sponsor the bicycle race was made, weekly meetings were held. A task force to direct the event was made up of ten people within the company, the public relations firm, and the company's director of communications.

Implementation Strategy

The decision to sponsor a bicycle race came after a big push from the local bicycle race promoter. The combination of internal enthusiasm for the idea—there were numerous bike enthusiasts within the company—the persistence of the local race promoter, and the survey and field research indicating the appeal of a local, healthy, "young" event sold Frigidaire's corporate decision makers (personal communication, J. J. Baumeister, October 28, 1994). The one-day race would be tied in to an already existing autumn race series which attracts an elite level of bicycle racer. According to Tony Evans, Frigidaire's director of communications, "We are continuing efforts to make Frigidaire Co. an active participant in the central Ohio community, and this is a wholesome event that interests people from all walks of life. A person does not have to be a sports enthusiast to enjoy watching one of the top bicycle races in the world" (*Dublin Villager*, p. 21).

Analysis of strategy revealed that it measured up on at least five criteria for successful events. One key element in successful event strategy is *an obvious relationship* between the activity and the sponsoring organization. A highlight race of the event was the "Women's Professional North American Championships" that linked the company to women as the primary decision maker in appliance buying. Frigidaire believed that a sporting event held in Grandview Heights in the Columbus, Ohio, area would link its name to central Ohio by sponsoring a community-minded, healthy event including two men's bicycle races as well as the one for women. *News value* was proven when local and national media came out in full force to cover the event. *The name of the event* also reinforced the link between the company and the three races they called "The Frigidaire North American Professional Criterium Championship." *Tie-ins* were made with an already established race series held in a neighboring town that was to continue through the weekend; participants were willing to pay the expense to fly into town. In addition the local community was already familiar with the classic race series that the area held in high esteem. Because this particular part of the series boasted such a large prize list it immediately became the event's "crown jewel" (*The Athens Messenger*, 1994). Tradeouts with local businesses contributed race support including a local Lincoln-Mercury dealer to provide pace cars and support vehicles for the race.

Testing the strategy was done by traveling to a similar bicycle race in Atlanta, and evaluating the demographic makeup of the crowd. This field research was then reported back to the company.

The communication plan was put primarily in the hands of the hired public relations firm, SBC. They would be in charge of press releases, advertisements, public service announcements, banners, posters, fliers, and invitations.

Figure 8.1 Frigidaire Bike Race poster announced the "Women's North American Pro Criterium" Championship Pro Am cycling event to the local community. (Graphic courtesy Frigidaire Company.)

The race promoter, who was hired from the bicycle community, was in charge of getting athletes in town a week early to talk to local schools about bicycle safety and to talk to the local media about the race.

The calendar was set with the date of the race falling on a Thursday night, September 22, 1994. All scheduling of communications worked backwards from that date.

The budget of $40,000 was divided into $20,000 for the race prize list and the other $20,000 for publicity. Other local sponsors kicked in an estimated $5,000 for additional press and prize lists. Also, local Frigidaire dealers contributed $5,000.

Evaluation

Sponsors evaluation of sporting events traditionally have depended on measurement of direct advertising during a major football or basketball game. Re-

Figure 8.2a Frigidaire cycling event contestants pass official booth in the "Women's North American Pro Criterium" Championship event in Grandview Heights, Ohio. (Photo courtesy of Frigidaire Company.)

cent research has shown, though, that editorial coverage of televised sports events can be just as effective as running the sponsor's commercials (Harris, p. 199). Frigidaire's evaluation methods took various forms including the accumulation and tabulation of press clippings, an on-site survey, staff feedback, observations of the extent of on-site media coverage, and a follow-up participant survey. According to Pat Gostomsky, sales representative and member of the bicycle race task force for Frigidaire, the race was officially declared a success within the Frigidaire company. Two days after the race was over, and the results were tabulated, plans for next year's event were beginning. Preliminary tabulations of a survey of 100 spectators during the race revealed a high recognition rate of Frigidaire as the primary sponsor of the event. The survey also found that demographically the spectator makeup included a high number of young families, which fit the targeted audience perfectly.

Staff feedback was used as a form of in-process evaluation. Biweekly task force meetings permitted the ongoing evaluation of the project. This method was also employed after the special event took place and was very valuable in "winning over" upper-level management. Because the communications director and members of the management team were skeptical about the use of a bike race as a public relations campaign strategy, a number of feedback meetings were held afterward with task force members, the communications director, the outside public relations agency, the race promoter, the mayor of the suburb of Grandview Heights—where the race was held—and a bicycle racer.

This immediate feedback was used to determine the first impressions after the race and whether plans should begin for a repeat performance the following year. It was determined from this group that most aspects of the event ran smoothly. A couple of changes were recommended, including holding the race during the day so that more families could make an entire day of it. The decision was also made to change the date from a Thursday night to a Sunday so that more people, participants and spectators, would be able to attend.

Media coverage was gauged by observation including assessing the number of press corps attendees. On the night of the race all three local television stations carried the race finish during their sports segments. The following day two Columbus papers as well as two papers in nearby communities printed the results and accompanying stories. Tabulation of coverage took the form of employing a press clipping service—Luce Press Clippings—which gathered and recorded 30 different news stories in 11 different publications including two business magazines and various local newspapers and journals.

A follow-up survey went out a few weeks after the event; members of the "race committee" called the participants to do short phone interviews to determine the level of quality that the racers felt needed to be attained in order to attract some international riders. In preparation for the following year's event it was determined at a task force meeting that the event needed to be placed on the "international calendar" to attract even more media attention. The phone survey was a follow-up to the race as well as preliminary research for the next event (personal communication from J. Baumeister, November 12, 1994).

Contingency plans help to avert potentially negative feedback. For example, a housing development located near the race course housed over 100 senior citizens. Initially they were very upset by the fact that they would not have immediate access to their cars or the bus because of changed traffic patterns on the night of the race. The race promoter solicited the help of a nearby country club by organizing a shuttle service in the form of golf carts for anyone who wanted to be transported to their cars or to the bus stop. This potentially negative situation turned out to be one of the most publicized aspects of the special event. Some of the area residents and the mayor of the community said they were very impressed with the community-minded spirit of the Frigidaire company (personal communication from J. Baumeister, November 19, 1994).

Frigidaire was pleased with the outcome the evaluation revealed. They are making plans for a bigger and better event next year with the hope of better relating to their target market by associating their name with a leisure, life-style activity like bicycling. The success of the initial effort led the company to ex-

Figure 8.2b Winners in Frigidaire's Championship cycling event celebrate victory. First place went to Karen Livingston, graduate student in public relations who later wrote this account of the event. (Photo courtesy Frigidaire Company.)

pand the objectives for future events. Frigidaire is just one of a growing number of companies using sports events in their public relations campaigns. It is the special-event category "most favored by corporate America—it continues to grow at 25 to 30 percent a year" (Harris, p. 198). With the Olympic Games just around the corner, more and more companies are expected to take advantage of sporting events to assure successful public relations campaigns.

▶ CASE STUDY: STUDENT TEAM CAMPAIGN: UNIVERSITY POLICE DEPARTMENT COMMUNITY RELATIONS AND RECRUITMENT

Situation Analysis Summary

1. *Statement of Perceived Problem.* A University Police Department (UPD) approached public relations faculty for help in recruiting officers for its

understaffed and overtaxed department. The UPD became the "client" for a team of students in a public relations campaign planning course.

2. *Identification of Ultimate Decision Maker.* A team of officers were appointed by the chief to spearhead the recruitment effort led by a lieutenant and the public relations officer. The university police chief, in consultation with the university administrative vice president, would make the ultimate decisions regarding the campaign.

3. *Explanation of Liaison Arrangements.* After an initial presentation of the situation to the class, one member of the six-person team was selected to meet weekly with the UPD public relations officer. The campaign plan proposal in both written and oral forms would be presented to the department at the end of the semester.

4. *Outline of the Facts Needed to Confirm the Nature of the Problem.* The reasons for vacancies and low applications for available officer positions would need to be explored, including measuring public perceptions of police work, perceptions of current officers, and comparison of department working conditions with other occupations and with other police departments. Facts about employment trends generally and trends in police work specifically, as well as facts about people making career shifts, would need to be examined.

Research Plan

The research plan involved the following steps, which covered the facts needed to confirm the nature of the situation as it was initially perceived.

1. State a research question for each aspect of the situation in a form that can be solved by conducting one or more research projects. In this case there were several research questions:
   - What conditions exist in the organizational culture and historical background that might affect staff vacancies and low applications?
   - What are public perceptions of police work and UPD that might be influencing applicants for officer positions?
   - Are there trends in other police departments that suggest this is a national rather than a local problem?
   - What patterns exist in employment statistics to indicate whether there may be reduced numbers in the job market? Are employment counselors aware of any bias against police work among people making career shifts?

2. Identify the research projects that will need to be carried out to answer these questions. The research projects to answer these questions included the following.
   - The team researched the organization, the University Police Department, in terms of its history, mythology, and personality.

The UPD has a history as old as the university itself. Beginning with an obscure subdepartment of the Physical Plant Division called Campus Security, the police had a staff of 30 for a student population of 13,000. Moved to a separate building in 1957, Campus Security changed its name to University Police Department as a separate division under the administrative vice president. In 1972 the state legislature amended existing laws so that university police officers became "law enforcement officers of the state." The change meant that UPD officers began carrying guns, were required to complete 600 hours of police training, and exercised the same powers as other sworn law enforcement officers.

The department's chief reported to the vice president of administrative affairs. Two assistant directors report to the chief of police and are responsible for three divisions each. A captain supervises each division including Patrol, Education, Training, Communications, Investigations, Personnel, and Crime Prevention. There is a separate Office of Public Information specialist, who handles all correspondence with the media and reports directly to the chief while working closely with the crime prevention division. The crime prevention division sets up all auxiliary programs sponsored by UPD, such as Student Nighttime Auxiliary Patrol, Nighttime Building Security, property engraving, and Traffic Safety Day. UPD also directly supervises 16 traffic and parking officers and 20 auxiliary and reserve officers.

Interviews with current police officers revealed many positive aspects of police work and the department's commitment to increasing citizen participation in local law enforcement. A system of three levels of entry into police work enables people to try it as part-time auxiliary officers while undergoing on-the-job training, to advance to the reserve officer level with a commitment to work 16 hours a week after meeting other application requirements, and finally, after completing police academy training, to serve as a full-time officer.

General requirements for recruits are that they must be 19 years of age, have a valid driver's license, and have a high school diploma. Additional requirements are a good driving record, passing a background investigation and polygraph test, and having a medical examination. Auxiliary officers, who wear a light blue uniform, must work with a regular officer for 225 hours. Reserve officers wear a regular uniform, but with different badges on the lapel, and must be eligible for the police academy.

- The team also conducted a survey of public opinion to determine the degree to which public perceptions might influence recruitment efforts.

The survey built on a previous survey conducted nine years earlier. This allowed certain questions to be repeated in order to measure any changes that might have occurred in public perceptions over the intervening years. The earlier study interviewed by telephone a randomly selected sample of 267 drawn from the university community of students, faculty, and staff. The second drew a random sample from the same population and also conducted telephone interviews. Major findings were as follows:

A similar proportion knew where UPD offices were located:

1979	73%
1988	86%

Regarding contact with the police unit, 35% had no contact, 18% one contact, 18% two or three contacts, 14% four or five contacts, and 10% six or more contacts.

Significant proportions of the sample revealed attitudes toward the police department which suggested that the university community would not encourage friends or acquaintances to enter police work. Most (41%) disagreed or strongly disagreed that "policemen try to be fair," with 30% neutral and 29% agreeing or strongly agreeing. Most (46%) disagreed or strongly disagreed that "UPD officers are courteous and helpful while on the job," while 32% agreed or strongly agreed and 22% were neutral. The sample also did not believe UPD "capable of handling serious crime on campus."

Although these results indicated that more of the sample held negative attitudes than positive attitudes toward UPD, larger proportions believed that "UPD can help me if I need them" (51% to 32%) and "would recommend the auxiliary/reserve program to someone" (39% to 28%). Significantly, 18% "would be interested in joining the auxiliary/reserve program."

As an aid to segmentation and media planning, most students were found to be members of political organizations (17%), professional organizations (16%), or social fraternities or sororities (15%); 25% were members of no organization. The campus daily newspaper was the most common source of information about UPD (35%), with friends (27%), the student union calendar (17%), and personal experience (13%) also rated as important sources.

- Trends in other police departments were investigated to determine whether conditions were similar elsewhere.

Personal telephone interviews with other similar departments revealed little difference between the local situation and that in other localities. However, a review of the literature, including journal articles, polls, and media coverage of public perceptions of the police, established a pattern of weak public confidence.

A 1950 study of New York police officers found a tendency toward authoritarianism and a hunger for power. These tendencies increased the longer an officer stayed on the force. Today these tendencies are less common, according to Peter Manning. He says that most recruits are very idealistic and want to help people. Some authorities have found that these idealistic attitudes frequently lead to burnout and job turnover when the idealism is not matched by public appreciation.[1]

Public opinion polls over the past 20 years have reflected public dissatisfaction with police officers in general. Based on findings from seven published studies and references from the local campus newspaper, one must conclude that the public has a low confidence in the training programs for police officers. This low confidence leads to overall displeasure with the way the police officers do their jobs. Moreover, positive public perceptions are imperative to police work. The more confidence people have in the police department, the more likely they are to report crime. Conversely, if people believe their police department is ineffective, they are less likely to participate in reporting crimes.

The team concluded from these findings that public perceptions of police work in general and local coverage of UPD, which reveals experiences with rude officers and unprofessional conduct, contribute to recruitment problems. These findings indicate that recruitment efforts should be supported by a strong general public relations effort to improve public perceptions of UPD.

- Employment statistics and consultation with employment counselors reveal that the low number of applications for positions with UPD are not due to low numbers of unemployed but rather to lack of information about the availability and requirements for police work in general and the openings at UPD specifically.

Problem Statement   Based on the above findings, research confirms the perceived staffing shortage, which forces officers to do more paperwork instead of patrol work and experience job burnout and turnover. A recruitment problem arose based on largely false perceptions of low pay, long hours, and job risk. The problem must be amended to reflect the larger problem of negative public perceptions of police work. The revised statement of the campaign problem is: UPD faces a recruitment shortfall and job turnover in part because of lack of information about the career opportunities at UPD, but also because of negative public perceptions of police work in general and of UPD specifically.

Adaptation Plan

The adaptation stage fits the research findings, as summarized in the problem statement, with the needs and resources of the organization (UPD) and the perceptions of the target publics. The question is how the recruitment problem can be solved, given the conditions at UPD and the perceptions of the public, which will influence potential recruits in their decision to apply and from which recruits will have to be drawn. The adaptation plan consists of the following seven elements:

1. Problem Statement (subdivided into specific achievable and measurable elements) (a) UPD faces a staffing shortage and recruitment shortfall, largely due to inadequate information about working conditions and benefits of police work at UPD. (See Figure 8.3.) (b) UPD, together with other

Figure 8.3 University Police Department (UPD) faced a staff shortage with attendant staff turnover; recruitment problems; false perceptions of low pay/high risk, and long hours; and a general negative public perception of police work. (Photographer/Investigator Nick Vellis/University Police Department, University of Florida, Gainesville FL.)

departments, suffers from negative public perceptions about police work, which leads to unfavorable attitudes toward recommending or applying for such work.

2. Goals Statement   (a) The proposed campaign will seek to increase participation in the auxiliary/reserve program of UPD by 10 percent. (b) To support this primary goal, the proposed campaign will promote a more positive public perception of UPD within the organization itself and within the university community. In order to achieve these goals, the proposed campaign will also seek to achieve two objectives: to provide full and factual information about the UPD auxiliary/reserve program to high school and college campuses, and to promote among university student leaders and faculty opportunities to serve as liaison to UPD.

3. Target Publics   Research findings, together with a growing preference at UPD for recruiting college graduates, suggest that university and community college students constitute the primary target public for the campaign. These findings identified organization membership as a significant factor among respondents; furthermore, 18 percent of respondents indicated a willingness to consider applying for auxiliary positions at UPD. Therefore, the target public will be segmented into campus organization members, such as student leaders, law-related students, and faculty as a secondary public capable of facilitating reaching and encouraging the primary target. Research also identified media as a major channel by which the target public get information about UPD; therefore the campus media will be a secondary public.

- Primary target publics: college and university students
- Segments: campus organization members
- Secondary publics: faculty, media

4. Organizational Assessment Many officers among the UPD staff of 65 have backgrounds as students or former students at the university. In addition, many officers have an active interest in athletics. These factors will be drawn upon to design a campaign strategy for addressing the problem. A wide range of auxiliary programs have established a track record for UPD's involvement with students, which will also be drawn upon in choosing strategy options.

5. A "Shopping List" of Possible Strategies Potential activities or strategies to reach the campaign goal included:

- A public information program
- Cycling for safety, an in-place distance attempt
- Safety Squares, a "Hollywood Squares" type game
- A crafts festival of UPD officers' hobbies
- Designated day for safe driver awards
- Barbecue/dunkathon carnival-type fund-raiser
- Campus display of UPD programs and safety tips
- Pedal to safety demonstration of alcohol effects
- Establishing a UPD Advisory Board
- Auxiliary/reserve officer workshop
- Officer Olympics of police skills
- UPD hoop-law basketball tournament
- Crimes on Campus seminar
- Enter a UPD marching band in homecoming parade
- UPD awards banquet
- Groundbreaking event for new building

6. Limitations No time limitations for completion of the campaign have been set, but there is an urgent need to solve the recruitment problem as soon as possible. This urgency may dictate that the campaign be undertaken prior to Law Enforcement Week in the fall. No *budget* has been established for implementing the proposed campaign; therefore, it will be necessary to include one or more fund-raising events in the total campaign to raise sufficient money to pay campaign expenses beyond what regular funding might cover. Since the Fair Labor Standards Act prohibits officers from volunteering their *time*, any involvement of regular officers will have to be during duty hours. Auxiliary officers can be asked to volunteer their time, and it is possible to recruit student volunteers.

7. Liaison   A system for regular contact between the student team and the UPD each Thursday was established. A similar arrangement might be decided upon during implementation of the campaign. During implementation, continuing contact between UPD and the campaign manager would be essential.

Strategy Plan

The strategy stage of the campaign planning process builds the most promising combination of strategy options into a coordinated package of activities. These strategy options are selected from the "shopping list" put together in the adaptation stage. The strategy stage supplies the details for the selected options and organizes them into an integrated whole. The details that must be provided in the strategy-building stage include the points outlined in the strategy plan for the UPD campaign.

The problem statement and goal statement are repeated here to ensure that the strategy fits the problem and goal precisely. If any minor adjustments in stating either the problem or the goal become necessary to accomplish this fit, it can be done at this time. These adjustments can also be incorporated into statements of the problem and goals made earlier in the campaign plan.

1. Problem Statement   (a) UPD faces a staffing shortage and recruitment shortfall, largely due to inadequate information about working conditions and benefits of police work at UPD. (b) UPD, together with other departments, suffers from negative public perceptions about police work, which leads to unfavorable attitudes toward recommending or applying for such work.

2. Goal Statement   (a) The proposed campaign will seek to increase participation in the auxiliary/reserve program of UPD by 10 percent. (b) To support this primary goal, the proposed campaign will promote a more positive public perception of UPD within the organization itself and within the university community. In order to achieve these goals, the proposed campaign will also seek to achieve two objectives: to provide full and factual information about the UPD auxiliary/reserve program to high school and college campuses, and to promote among university student leaders and faculty opportunities to serve as liaison to UPD.

3. Selection of Strategy Options   These are integrated into a campaign package to be called "UPD Awareness Month: They're On Your Side."

The proposed activities are designed to increase positive perceptions of UPD as a humane and dependable defender of public safety worthy of highest recommendation as a career field. These activities have been selected as the

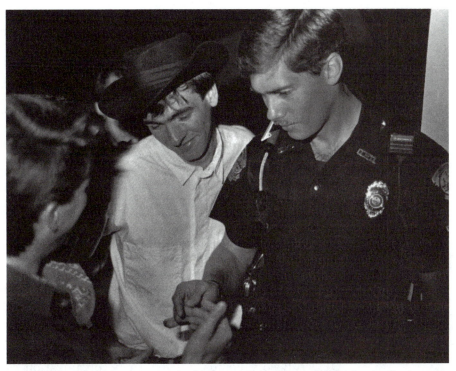

Figure 8.4 The campaign strategy for UPD sought to increase participation in the police auxiliary and reserve programs by 10%, and to promote a more positive perception of UPD police work by encouraging students and facility to accept opportunities to serve as liaisons with UPD. (Photographer/Investigator Nick Vellis/University Police Department, University of Florida, Gainesville FL.)

optimum way to reach the target public of college and university students as segmented into campus organizations, with support from secondary publics of faculty and media. (See Figure 8.4.) The selected activities and events also take optimum advantage of available coalitions, tie-ins, and special resources available within the target public community.

"UPD Awareness Month: They're On Your Side" will take place during the month of April, to be designated as UPD Awareness Month. The activity package will consist of the five activities or events summarized here and described in detail after the summary:

1. "Auxiliary/Reserve Officer's Workshop" will be held the first Saturday in April. The A/RO Workshop will offer special training in interpersonal interaction to prepare officers to act as role models and take advantage of interpersonal communication in their interaction with members of the target public during the UPD Awareness Month and afterward. The workshop will prepare officers to promote recruitment by covering such topics as communication skills improvement and leadership styles.

2. "Cycling for Safety" will be held outside the student union as part of the annual Campus Safety Awareness Day, during which UPD distributes information on cyclist and pedestrian safety on campus. The proposed event will add competitive interest and appeal by including a marathon cycling ride on a stationary bicycle seeking to set an endurance record, with participation by members of the campus cycling club, and a continuous video demonstration of safety tips.

3. "Safety Tickets" is an activity designed to reward motorists and cyclists for safety and to counter the negative associations of receiving traffic tickets. Officers will stop motorists and cyclists and reward them for safe operation with a ticket that can be redeemed for a beverage or ice cream at the student union. Positive interpersonal interaction offers benefits not available in mediated communication, a fundamental principle in campaign planning.

4. "Officer Olympics" is an event designed to increase positive perceptions among the target public of the abilities and competence of UPD officers by offering students the opportunity to compete in a contest of skills required of UPD officers. The Officer Olympics will include a foot race, target shooting, an obstacle course, and an automobile obstacle course. Contestants will rotate on schedule so that the events will be going on at the same time. Winners will be chosen by top score in each event.

5. "UPD Advisory Board" will be a new organization established to increase university student participation in and feedback about the operation of UPD. The board will be composed of about twenty students representing various segments of the campus community and will meet monthly to discuss perceptions of UPD and make policy recommendations. The department may ask the board to address special problems as they emerge during the year.

Two additional events are recommended as possible replacements for any of the above events, if they turn out not to be practicable, or additions to the above events if time and money allow. "Safety Squares" is a game show patterned after the "Hollywood Squares" TV show and will feature public safety questions. The event will involve Greek organization members and perhaps people from other organizations and have UPD officers as the "squares" "UPD Hoop-Law" is a basketball tournament between UPD officers and students designed to increase mutual contact and understanding. The event manager can give further consideration to any of the strategy options listed in the adaptation section.

Detailed Event Plans

"Auxiliary/Reserve Officer's Workshop"   The day will begin at 9:00 A.M. with an informal coffee and donuts breakfast for the participants and guest speakers. The breakfast will be held in the public activities section of the student union. The workshop will be held in the student union from 9:00 A.M. to 2:00 P.M. with a luncheon from 12:15 to 2:00 P.M.

Sessions. After breakfast, officers will attend the first session, "Communication Processes." This will be conducted by a university speech communication professor and will cover such basic topics as the following:

1. The benefits of the auxiliary/reserve program with emphasis on highlighting these benefits in interpersonal communication.
2. Integrating auxiliary/reserve, part-time service into an academic program.
3. Responding to questions from potential recruits.
4. Ways to recruit applications from different academic areas.

A "Leadership Styles" session will be conducted by an administrator from student services, perhaps the dean of student services. The session will be from 11:30 A.M. to 12:15 P.M. and will cover

1. Effective leadership styles.
2. Requirements of leadership styles for a UPD officer.
3. Displaying effective role model characteristics in recruiting for UPD.
4. Utilizing leadership qualities in recruiting students to UPD.

A luncheon session will feature a keynote speaker from the university administration addressing the topic of services provided to the university by auxiliary and reserve officers. An open forum will follow, during which participants at tables will discuss assigned topics and give summary reports at the end of the session. To conclude the luncheon session, the activities of the Awareness Month will be described, including how officers will be involved throughout.

Contingency Plan. To deal with unforeseen developments, backup speakers and session leaders will be identified when arrangements are made for speakers. Arrangements for the use of buildings and rooms will be made at the earliest opportunity after the event is approved.

Communication Plan. Communications will be prepared in three phases. Announcements and other publicity, such as invitations, department memos to officers, fliers, and a poster, will be prepared prior to the event. Communications to be prepared during the event include an information packet of programs and name tags. Introductory remarks and an outline of events to be announced at the close of the luncheon will also be prepared. Communication after the event will include thank-you letters, certificates of completion, and a summary of the decisions reached during the sessions.

Evaluation Plans. At the end of the workshop, the officer participants will be asked to complete questionnaires, which will be collected at the door. The questionnaire will (1) determine the officers' confidence in applying the skills covered in the sessions during interactions with students in the coming events and (2) obtain demographic information to compare effectiveness between auxiliary, reserve, and regular officers. The event manager will also maintain a diary of impressions, suggestions for follow-up, and observation concerning possible improvements.

Campaign models and forms used in the UPD campaign are shown in Box 8.1.

"Cycling for Safety" This event is a combination bike-a-thon, featuring the university cycling club in a stationary bicycle endurance effort, and videotape demonstration of bicycle safety in conjunction with the annual Campus Safety Day distribution of safety information.

Once the date has been established (the second Wednesday in April is preferred), arrangements must be made for use of the student union colonnade. The facility is available without charge to student and university groups. The contact person can be reached at 393–1645. Arrangements must be made as early as possible to avoid being preempted by other organizations wanting to use the facility. The student union will provide the necessary table, chairs, and videotape machine.

The university cycling club has agreed to participate for the publicity value for their club. The president of the club can be reached at 379–0032 and the faculty advisor can be reached at 393–8833. The cycling club will be responsible for providing the bicycle and the stationary stand for the marathon and riders who will participate. A blackboard will be used to post the distance achieved by riders at the end of each hour through the day. Students may deposit forms with their guesses of distances logged for each hour in a collection box at the site during the week prior to the event. The deposit box will also serve as an announcement of the event with a poster explaining the contest (Box 8.2). These forms will be included on brochures distributed before the event to generate interest in drop-by visitors during the day and to generate excitement. Event managers may post names of entrants who come closest to actual miles posted. The student who makes the closest estimate per hour and the total miles achieved will win a special prize of a bicycle with safety gear. A second prize of bicycle safety equipment will be awarded to the winner who comes closest to estimating the total miles and who deposits an entry before noon on the day of the marathon.

In addition, the cycling club will demonstrate tangible safety equipment. Previously printed brochures about bicycle safety will be provided by the UPD information office. On the day of the event the display must be set up by 8:00 A.M. and members of the cycling club will be responsible for it. UPD officers will be on hand at the display to answer questions and distribute materials. The display must be disassembled and removed by 5:00 P.M.

Contingency Plan. The most serious obstacle to the event's success would be failure of the cycling club to provide equipment and riders. Although the self-interest of the club would make that development unlikely, a backup source of bicycle and stand, such as a local bicycle shop, should be identified. In case club members do not show up, riders might be recruited from other student groups, which should be identified in advance. The availability of a backup videotape player should be determined in advance also.

Arrangements for dealing with emergencies, such as a fall from the stationary bicycle or any accident involving students or other participants, will

BOX 8.1   UPD Campaign Models of Forms and Communications

EVALUATION FORM

(Please answer the following questions in your own words)
1. How well do you think the sessions in the workshop prepared you to deal with students as prospective recruits for UPD?

2. How well did the workshop measure up to your expectations of how it would help you to interact with students?

3. How well did the "leadership styles" presentation help you develop skills in these interpersonal situations?

4. How well did the communication presentation help you to develop your communication skills?

5. In what other ways could the department help you to be a better role model in attracting quality recruits for UPD?

6. Do you have any other comments?

PARTICIPATION/RESERVATION

Auxiliary /Reserve Officer's Workshop

Officer name _____

Home phone _____

Are you planning to participate in the Auxiliary/Reserve Officer's Workshop?
     (   ) yes, I'll be there from 9 to 2
     (   ) no, I can't make it

If you can make it to only some sessions, which ones?
         (   ) Communication   9:00 to 11:30
         (   ) Leadership   11:30 to 12:15
         (   ) Luncheon   12:15 to 2:00

Please return to UPD Box _____

give the UPD officers present an opportunity to demonstrate their skills in dealing with such emergencies.

Communication Plan. Before the event, simple one-color $8\frac{1}{2}$-by-11-inch three-fold brochures will be distributed at literature display sites throughout the campus, to residence halls, and through student organizations. These brochures will announce the event and will include a form for estimating miles logged by marathon cyclists. A news release (Box 8.3) announcing the

DRAFT OF LETTER TO SPEAKERS

(On UPD Letterhead)

Date
Name of Speaker
address

Dear _____,

This is a follow-up on our telephone conversation about your participation in the University Police Department workshop as a part of an effort to improve recruitment of auxiliary and reserve officers. The purpose of the session you agreed to lead is to prepare officers to be effective role models for college and university students who will recommend or apply for a position as an officer with UPD.

Your skills in teaching interpersonal communication will be especially helpful to officers not in the program to take advantage of their experience in dealing with potential student recruits. As we mentioned in our phone conversation, the workshop is scheduled for Saturday April ___, 19 ___ from 9:00 a.m. to 2:00. Your session is scheduled for _____ in room ___ of the student union.

Thank you for agreeing to make this contribution to the continued strength of the University community. If you have any further questions about your participation do not hesitate to call me.

Sincerely,
Name Workshop Director
University Police Department

BUDGET

Item needed	Cost	Donated	Actual cost
50 Chairs (rental per doz.)	$ 5.00	yes	0.00
Flip chart	15.00	yes	0.00
Room rental	75.00	yes	0.00
Publicity			
100 fliers	10.00	yes	0.00
100 invitations	10.00	yes	0.00
Food and catering			
Coffee for 50	25.00	no	25.00
Donuts for 50 (4 doz.)	10.00	no	10.00
Luncheon for 50 ($2.85 each)	142.50	no	142.50
	$ 292.50		$ 177.50

BOX 8.2   **Copy for UPD "Cycling for Safety" Poster**

UPD'S CYCLING FOR SAFETY

Learn the valuable motorist/cyclist rules you need for survival on campus.

When? April ___, 19___
8:00 a.m. to 5:00 p.m.
Where? Student Union

See the University Cycle Club set an endurance record as they ride a stationary bicycle throughout the day. Win a first prize bicycle or a second prize of safety equipment by guessing the number of miles logged. Entry forms are available at residence halls, the student union, and other places throughout the campus.

event and competition will be sent to the campus and city daily newspapers and to radio stations serving the campus.

During the event the brochure will be distributed to visitors at the event for estimating total miles. In addition, a videotape demonstration of safety equipment and other tips will be shown continuously. Campus maps with designated bike routes and other safety information will be displayed for pickup.

After the event, follow-up releases will be sent to the campus daily and other media telling the number of miles ridden, details about the cycling club participants, and the two winners. The release will relate the event's purpose and include additional details about UPD and employment opportunities as auxiliary and reserve officers.

Evaluation Plan. Participation will be measured by a count of entries for the prizes prior to and during the event. The impact of the event on bicycle accidents on campus will be calculated by comparing accident statistics for the month after the event with statistics for the same month the previous year. If data seem marginal or further comparisons seem warranted, comparisons may be made for additional months.

Media coverage will be monitored and collected for content analysis of favorable mention of UPD. Yearly comparisons may also be made. Campus infirmary records of accidents involving bicycles will be analyzed and compared with previous years to determine if the degree of injury has changed after the event.

A follow-up survey to measure the impact of the entire campaign will include specific questions to track exposure to the event's publicity and to de-

BOX 8.3   Model News Release for UPD "Cycling for Safety"

On UPD Letterhead

Contact:
    Phone:

"Cycling for Safety" Shows Students Safe Cycling Rules

Gainesville, Florida, (date)—The University of Florida Police Department will sponsor "Cycling For Safety," a demonstration of bicycle safety at the student union ___date___, from 8:00 A.M. to 5:00 P.M. A competition to guess the number of miles logged by a stationary cyclist features a bicycle as first prize and safe cycling equipment as second prize.

Angie Tipton, UPD public information specialist, said, "This event gives UPD the opportunity to emphasize the importance of safe bicycle operation on campus, at a time when cycling accidents pose an increasing danger to preoccupied students. We hope a large number of students drop by the demonstration and try their hand at winning a bicycle."

Members of the University Cycling Club will demonstrate safe cycling practices while answering questions from visitors. Club members will also man the stationary marathon bicycle to establish a distance record.

By sponsoring the event UPD hopes to increase awareness of bicycle safety rules for all campus cyclists. UPD believes that an increase in safety awareness will lead to a lowered rate of cycle accidents on campus.

– 30 –

termine the extent of word-of-mouth reference to the event. These evaluations will be incorporated in planning future repetitions of the event.

The UPD "Cycling for Safety" budget is shown in Box 8.4.

"Safety Tickets"   This activity, to continue throughout UPD Awareness Month, seeks to offset the negative experience of getting a traffic ticket by awarding "safety tickets" for good driving practices. During the month, UPD officers will issue safety tickets redeemable for a free beverage or ice cream at the student union.

BOX 8.4   **UPD "Cycling for Safety" Budget**

	Budget	
Item	Estimated	Actual
Printing	$100.00	$100
Chairs and table (rental)	20.00	no cost
Videotape player (rental)	30.00	no cost
Video production	150.00	no cost
Totals	$300.00	$100.00

Officers will be supplied with a quota of safety tickets for the month, which they may issue any time they observe a safe operating practice on the part of a pedestrian, cyclist, or motorist. Officers should attempt to single out practices that are most prone to violations leading to accidents. The size of the quota will depend on the number of free treats that can be arranged.

Contingency Plan. If the union food service cannot underwrite the total expense of the treats as a tradeout promotion for the ice cream shop and the food service generally, another underwriter may be arranged. A local radio station may find the opportunity an attractive tradeout to demonstrate support for UPD and campus safety. The station may wish to interview safety ticket recipients as a further service to listeners.

Communication Plan. A news release and public service announcement (PSAs) on the activity will be distributed to prepare motorists and others and to reduce their alarm at being stopped. A poster (Box 8.5) will be distributed throughout campus. Other releases used during the UPD Awareness Month will mention the activity as well.

During the activity a safety brochure prepared for UPD Awareness Month will be given with the safety ticket. Possible radio and newspaper interviews with those receiving the tickets will be pursued. After the activity, follow-up releases will explain the results of the program and possible ties to lowered accident rates.

Evaluation Plan. To get a measure of the impact of the activity, the overall campaign evaluation will include questions about the students' impressions and about discussions they have participated in where safety tickets were mentioned. Individuals who received safety tickets will be randomly contacted and interviewed for their reactions and suggestions. Media coverage will be tracked and recorded for content analysis to discover the degree of favorable treatment of the activity and of UPD.

BOX 8.5   **Copy for "Safety Ticket" Poster and Ticket**

POSTER COPY

WE WANT YOU
TO GET A TICKET!

Get Stopped By UPD

During the month of April good driving practices may be rewarded with a "Safety Ticket" redeemable for a treat at the student union. So drive safely—and

Get Stopped By UPD.

SAFETY TICKET COPY

Record of safe driver / cyclist / pedestrian Name_____ Phone number_____ Campus address_____ **YOU HAVE BEEN STOPPED FOR BEING A** **SAFE DRIVER / CYCLIST / PEDESTRIAN**	detach here	Good for one free treat when presented at the Sugar Cone in the student union before May 10, 19___ Sponsored by UPD.

The budget for the "Safety Tickets" event is shown in Box 8.6.

"Officer Olympics"   In an effort to increase participation in the auxiliary/reserve officer program of UPD and to promote a more positive perception of UPD on campus, a competition between university students and UPD officers will demonstrate basic skills required of police. The "Olympics" will feature four events: a foot race, an obstacle course, target shooting, and an automobile obstacle course. All four events will be held simultaneously, with participants rotating through the four events. If participation is large, heats may need to be arranged with a manageable number competing at one time.

The event will be held during the third week in April as a part of UPD Awareness Month. The course will be laid out on an easily accessible parking lot near the center of campus. Bleachers will be set up to accommodate spectators. Registration to participate will be in advance, with possible late registration if advance registration is low. Name tags will be prepared for shirt fronts, and numbers will be attached to the shirt back of participants.

BOX 8.6   **Budget for "Safety Tickets" event**

	Budget	
Item	Estimated	Actual
Printing of safety tickets	$200.00	$200.00
Treats (10 per day for 30 days at $1 per treat)	300.00	no cost
Totals	$500.00	$200.00

Contingency Plan. In case of inclement weather the event will be rescheduled for one week later. Registrants will be given coupons good for "preferred seating" for the following week good for two admissions—as a way to encourage attendance.

"UPD Student Advisory Board"   To promote a more positive perception of UPD and to provide feedback from the primary target public, a group of about twenty students will be appointed to a newly established UPD Student Advisory Board. Members will be appointed to represent as nearly as possible students graduated from area high schools and junior colleges, as well as major constituencies of the university student body. Members will be selected on the basis of recommendations from faculty members and a commitment to community service as indicated on a formal application form.

Students selected will receive a formal notice of appointment with an announcement of the first meeting. The initial meeting will include an official induction ceremony and members will be organized into committees, such as traffic and parking, crime prevention, communication, education and training, and patrol. In each committee, board members will receive a briefing on the operation of these police services and the problems of relations with students most common to each. Board members in return will offer advice and suggestions for improving relations with students, staff, and faculty in each area. UPD administrators will be free to assign additional duties to the board or to certain members.

At the initial meeting, the members will receive a list of advisory board members, a statement of purpose prepared in consultation with the chief, and a list of committee assignments. The major agenda item of the first meeting will be orientation to UPD and the more significant problems in human relations and relations with the campus in general.

The media will be invited to the initial meeting and will be supplied with a list of board members and the board's statement of purpose. Interviews with members will be encouraged, in an effort to identify board members to the

BOX 8.7   **Overall UPD Campaign Budget**

| | Budget | |
Production Items	Estimated	Actual
Applications	$40.00	$40.00
Letters and postage	50.00	50.00
News releases	20.00	20.00
Certificates	30.00	30.00
Miscellaneous	50.00	50.00
Totals	$190.00	$190.00

campus community as contacts for feedback from students to UPD. The site of the first meeting will be UPD headquarters, which members will tour as a part of the orientation.

Contingency Plan. A list of backup members will be kept on file in case appointed members resign or fail to participate. Three unapproved absences from meetings will be cause for replacement. The UPD management will review the procedures of the board at the end of the first month, the first six months, and the first year and recommend adjustments.

Communication Plan. No less than a month before the first meeting of the Advisory Board, a letter describing the program and inviting applications will be prepared and mailed to deans of the various colleges and schools throughout the university. The letter, accompanied by application forms, will solicit their help in identifying students who would be interested in and qualified to serve on the UPD Student Advisory Board. Telephone contact with faculty designated by the deans may be necessary to follow up on the initial letter and encourage nomination of worthy students. The application form will be designed to include a statement of purpose and background criteria for selection. A news release will announce creation of the UPD Student Advisory Board and describe its purpose. A memo will be sent a week before the first meeting inviting media to attend.

During the first year, members will receive notices of meetings, notes of previous meetings, and other communications related to board activities. A newsletter may be used to disseminate appropriate developments to members periodically. After a term of service on the board, members will receive a certificate of service; extraordinary service should be appropriately rewarded.

Evaluation Plan. The overall impact of the UPD Student Advisory Board will be assessed by the survey used to measure the effectiveness of the entire campaign. In addition, members will be asked to complete a simple form in which they address problems and achievements of the board. Exit interviews will be used with members who complete their term on the board to assess strengths and weaknesses of its practices and procedures.

The overall UPD campaign budget is shown in Box 8.7.

SUMMARY

A **professional campaign** offers insights into adaptation. This chapter has illustrated some of the critical aspects of the adaptation stage of the public relations campaign. The reader may apply some of the insights gleaned from these actual cases in understanding and using the adaptation outline when planning other public relations campaigns.

Situation analysis is tied to the research plan. A careful review of the situation analysis gets the campaign planning process started right. In the Frigidaire bike race case, management wanted to build relationships with the new community of central Ohio as well as with younger "family builders," but additional research was needed to confirm the nature of the situation. The situation analysis described in the first paragraphs helped to focus on the research questions that needed to be answered.

The adaptation stage focused on the problem, goals, objective, segmentation, strategy options, timing/budget, and liaison arrangements. The Frigidaire bike race case reveals the interrelations between the critical factors in campaign planning: the research-defined statement of the problem is converted to a statement of goals, objective, and target publics on the one hand and the strategy options on the other.

The strategy options illustrate the thought process of deciding among a series of possible actions what is often involved in selecting the best strategy. The analysis of the strategy chosen also shows how the criteria for strategy selection is applied in a specific case. The case also reveals how research was used to test strategy.

The evaluation plan provides an example of the range of values that may need to be considered in an evaluation. Examples of staff feedback, media coverage, follow-up survey research, and a contingency plan in action show how a range of evaluation considerations come into play.

A **student-planned campaign** shows the adaptation process. A University Police Department's request for help led students to identify the basic problem. Students designed a **research plan** that identified public perceptions as a major influence on lagging recruitment; these research findings led to a quantifiable goal statement. The case also illustrates the close relationship between research findings and organizational research in determining target publics. The value of a broad range of strategy options is shown in a case offering 16 choices, from which the final selection of 5 was made. The case illustrates how limitations often pose *degrees* of restrictions on a campaign; time and money were more critical than personnel in an acceptable plan.

Strategy plans illustrate factors in selecting the best options. When the strategy options that best reach the goal are chosen, the problem is also most effectively addressed.

Evaluation plans *assess the entire campaign as well as events.* Effective evaluation must focus not only on the overall goal achievement but on the effectiveness of each of the events that make up the campaign.

This chapter helps the campaign planner to apply the lessons of case histories of effective campaigns. It illustrates the decision progress in planning campaigns. The two cases described here show how the principles covered in the chapter on adaptation work in practice.

FOR FURTHER READING

Case Studies

Center, Allen, and Patrick Jackson. *Public Relations Practices: Managerial Case Studies and Problems,* 4th ed. Englewood Cliffs, NJ: Prentice-Hall, 1990.

pr reporter, includes summaries and highlights of cases. P.O. Box 600, Exeter, NH, 03833–0600.

PRSA Silver Anvil Winners, 33 Irving Place, New York, NY, 10003, annual. Summarizes annual winners of PRSA public relations competition.

PRspectives. Muncie, IN: Ball State University, Department of Journalism, annual.

Public Relations News, 127 E. 80th St., New York, NY, 10021. Includes a 1–2 page case study in each issue.

Robinson, William. *Best Sales Promotions.* Chicago: Crain Books, annual.

Simon, Raymond. *Public Relations Management: Cases and Simulations.* New York: originally published by Grid, purchased by Macmillan, 1977.

Spezzano, Vince. *Promoting the Total Newspaper,* 2nd ed. Reston, VA: International Newspaper Promotion Assn., 1973.

Frigidaire Bike Race Case

"Frigidaire Sponsors Cycling Event," *Dublin Villager* (July 19, 1994):21.

Harris, T. L. *The Marketer's Guide to Public Relations.* New York: John Wiley & Sons, 1991.

"Pro Am Cycling Event Comes to Columbus," *The Columbus Dispatch* (September 1, 1994): C3.

"Sponsorship Is Cool," *The Athens Messenger* (August 29, 1994): D 13.

"10-Step Plan Could Save You From Non-Planners Anonymous," *Esprit* [Date ?]p. 2.

PART
FOUR

Building the Campaign Plan: The Implementation Strategy Stage

Graphics in the Public Relations Campaign

by Deborah M. Gross

- Research on the Use of Graphics in Campaigns
- Challenges of the New Technology in the Adaptation Stage of the Campaign
- Implications of New Technology on Preparing for Strategy Implementation
- Updating Evaluation with New Technology

Visual communication and the use of desktop publishing have become growing areas of study. Researchers' curiosity has led them to investigate the significance of visual communication and the impact that graphics technology may have on public relations professionals.

High-tech companies are growing, and the rapid changes are causing firms to reevaluate public relations needs. Distinguishing characteristics of new technology require that professionals balance traditional and modern public relations methods, gain new expertise and skills, and help convince high-tech companies that public relations is important. Firms that know how to communicate with the public using technological advances will succeed. Successful public relations practitioners will be those who plan and implement specific strategies to achieve objectives based on research findings.

RESEARCH ON THE USE OF GRAPHICS IN CAMPAIGNS

Some of the research on this topic is qualitative. The researchers make general statements about the nature, working, and effects of visual communication and technology, specifically relating to the public relations profession. This information is largely derived from informal research, without use of the scientific method.

Other research is more formal in nature. Weathersby (1988) used a focus group survey to determine public opinion and attitude. Similarly, Miga (1994) used focus groups and observation to identify key problems in an organization. This research was combined with a more scientific study, which analyzed responses to randomly distributed surveys.

Consider the Audience

To communicate effectively, public relations practitioners need to consider their audience. If their objective is to get their material published, they must consider the needs of the editors. One way to get material published is to include visual items (Lindeborg, 1993–94; Marken, 1993; Kornegay, 1993). A study done by the Internal Revenue Service and the University of South Carolina showed that informational graphics make news releases more appealing to editors (Lindeborg, 1993). Similar findings occurred with cartoons (Lindeborg, 1993) and with photographs (Marken, 1993).

Beyond the editorial decisions, publications must be attractive to the intended reader. Research shows that effective use of graphic design may be the foundation for a successful corporate identity package (Weathersby, 1988). Kornegay (1993) found that more stories were read when they incorporated graphics.

Ward (1992) conducted research on the effectiveness of sidebar graphics using a review of the literature and an experiment. By reading the literature on visual communication and graphics technology, public relations practitioners in the future would learn which techniques researchers have found to be successful. An experimental research method would be particularly useful for testing the effectiveness of a public relations program or the results of a communication effort using graphics technology.

Importance of Visuals

When focusing on visual communication, it is important to note that we are living in a very graphic world. Visual images are so pervasive that we may not be consciously aware of how often we encounter them. Increasingly, public relations professionals are realizing the impact visual items may have in printed material. This realization has been largely due to the expectation of clients, who are no longer looking solely for consulting advice. Potential clients want public relations professionals who are capable of putting publications together. There is a growing need to integrate a knowledge of printing, typography, and graphics (Conover 1990; Weathersby, 1988; Gordon, 1989).

Marken (1993) found that most public relations people have a talent for giving life to the spoken and written word but tend to disregard the value of visual images. To improve the quality of the written piece, Marken (1993) sug-

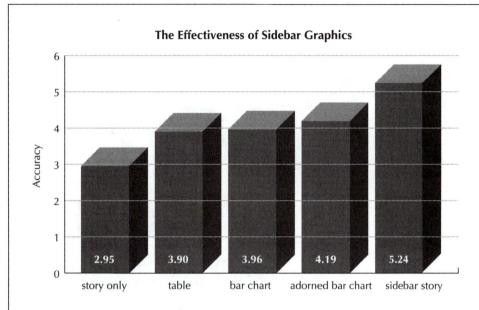

Figure 1.1 Douglas B. Ward (1992) attempted to show whether a bar chart that accompanied a news story aided reader comprehension. Two versions of a graphic and story were tested against a lone story, a story and table, and a story with sidebar. This bar chart reflects an accuracy score for 13 questions—right answers minus wrong answers. Subjects who read the story and sidebar had the highest comprehension scores. The results suggest that graphics need to be kept simple and that they need to contain more explanatory information.

gests thinking of visual effects along with thinking of copy. This process of thinking visually will help to promote more exuberant writing and will assist in stimulating visual images in the reader's mind. By practicing this technique, public relations practitioners can increase the impact of their message. The greatest advantage of this high-impact message is that visuals have both immediate and long-lasting effects.

Other researchers have found similar conclusions. Conover (1990), Lindeborg (1993), and Kornegay (1993) believe that graphics can simplify information, improve readability, and attract attention. Visual images also serve to set a tone or to entertain (Conover, 1990).

Desktop Publishing

The advent of desktop publishing has transformed the use of visual images and, in turn, has influenced the role of the public relations practitioner. Adding to the complexity is the term *desktop publishing* which is a misnomer (Gordon, 1989; Andrews, 1994). As Gordon (1989, p. 24) states, "'Desktop lay-

Desktop publishing is actually a misnomer, authorities claim. "Desktop layout" or "desktop page layout" would be more accurate terms because the process involves not publishing, but layout and design.

out' or 'desktop page layout' might be more accurate." The current term is misleading since it implies that anyone can publish material.

Despite implications of the term, many researchers and public relations practitioners view desktop publishing as an invaluable tool (Gordon, 1989; Horton and Shinbach, 1994; Spiegelman, 1993). The benefits that have been cited by most practitioners include: profitability, speed, timeliness, control, creative flexibility of presentations, and higher employee productivity. All of these factors may contribute to another important benefit, gaining new clients. High-quality work produced in a timely manner will contribute to improved business opportunities (Gordon, 1989; Conover, 1990).

Descriptive research would be a useful method for assessing the benefits of desktop publishing. As noted elsewhere in this book, "The purpose of descriptive research is to establish norms, or an index of existing attitudes, opinions, facts, practices, and the like, as a benchmark against which to measure progress toward achieving improvements." Descriptive research procedures include: observation; interviews; content analysis; advisory panels; focus group interviews; Delphi studies; subscription research services; omnibus, piggyback, or shared research; contracted or commissioned research; U.S. census data analysis; and audits.

Kotcher (1992) noted that desktop publishing will continue to affect our perceptions of visual communications. The ability of graphics to simplify complex information in an effective and powerful manner can be extremely beneficial during a crisis, especially when time and funds are limited.

With all of these benefits, researchers wonder if desktop publishing is cost efficient. In a study by Gordon (1989), frequent users said the answer is yes. Companies can save money by doing their own typesetting and layout. Other researchers believe that desktop publishing is an investment in the future of the organization and will greatly increase productivity in the long run (Gordon, 1989; Horton and Shinbach, 1994; Kornegay, 1993). These savings can be passed on to the clients or can be reinvested in the company.

Wes Thomas of Wes Thomas Public Relations in East Northport, New York, summarized his view of desktop publishing by saying, "It's too difficult to estimate how long our system took to justify itself. It's saved us a lot of time and aggravation. I don't know how to put a dollar value on that" (Gordon, 1989, p. 27). Other practitioners might use a computer-assisted statistical analysis such as the *Statistical Package for the Social Sciences,* commonly called the SPSS (Nager and Allen, 1984; Holzer, 1992).

Problems with Desktop Publishing

Similarly, a company needs to examine the effect desktop publishing may have on the corporate identity. According to Gordon (1989), Horton and Shinbach (1994), and Conover (1990), desktop publishing can actually be detrimental to the company image if it is placed in the wrong hands. One of the major problems with desktop publishing is design quality. A common error is the use of too many elements or type styles, which creates a confusing, fragmented design piece. Practitioners should research basic elements of design before producing materials for publications. Gaining design knowledge will enhance the capabilities of desktop publishing software and will enable practitioners to produce more effective communication publications (Gordon, 1989; Conover 1990).

As the use of graphics technology continues to grow, practitioners need to maintain quality as their top priority. As Gordon (1989) found, too often people sacrifice publication quality because of the limitations of the system. As communicators, we need to maintain high quality standards and use desktop publishing to enhance our materials.

Inherent in desktop publishing research are decisions regarding hardware and software. Choosing between Apple and IBM-compatible equipment is a decision that involves more than cost. According to Gordon (1989), users feel that the Macintosh allows greater graphic flexibility and may be more user friendly to new desktop publishers. However, some offices are already equipped with IBM hardware and it would be wise to invest in desktop programs designed for existing equipment.

Choosing Graphics Technology

The difficult decision regarding hardware choice may be eased by using one or more of the following services: dealers, consultants, customized services, news wires, publications, newsletters, directories, or training and education services (Information Access Company, 1994). Practitioners must keep in mind that the perfect computer depends on who you ask and how you look at the question. No computer is perfect for everyone (Miller, 1993).

Publications such as *PC Magazine* and *MacWorld* have done reviews of both hardware and software. Magazines, journals, and news wire services include reviews of current software that are specifically related to the public relations practitioner (Spiegelman, 1993; Horton and Shinbach, 1994). While these reviews may be helpful, practitioners need to be wary of biased reviews in publications that accept paid advertising.

The Information Highway

Closely related to news wire services is the topic of the information highway. Technology has had a significant impact on the public relations field and will continue to change the way public relations practitioners communicate. Companies who have invested in desktop publishing materials may also want to invest in on-line services. While there are great benefits to this technological revolution, research shows that many potential users are not comfortable with the rapidly growing technology. Their discomfort may stem from an unfamiliarity with the broad range of users of the services. Flanagan (1994) suggests that part of the problem is the media's inaccurate portrayal of users of electronic services as "kids" and "computer nerds." In addition, potential users may have a misconception that the services are too costly (Flanagan, 1994; Bovet, 1994b).

Since much of the attention regarding electronic communication focuses on sending E-mail, public relations practitioners need to be aware of the various benefits electronic technology can offer. Words, designs, and pages can be sent by modem over electronic networks. Technology allows newspapers to receive newsletters, brochures, press kits, and graphics electronically. Once the material is transmitted, the receivers have the option of editing specific items on their own computers (Lindeborg, 1993–94; Flanagan, 1994; Duffy and Palmer, 1994; Middleberg, 1994; Wiesendanger, 1994). Similarly, Lindeborg (1993–94) stated that commercially available broadcast fax technology allows practitioners to send press releases and graphics from an agency computer to any newspaper in the nation.

The relationship between the message sender and receiver is changing. Practitioners who have been frustrated with limitations on interpersonal communication will find that new technology greatly increases the likelihood of one-on-one and small-group communication. Technology also allows for instant feedback from our audiences (Nager and Allen, 1984).

With all of the discussion of various research techniques, how do practitioners decide which method to choose? Nager and Allen (1984, p. 227) suggest that professionals should not use any research method exclusively. "Public relations practice is too complex to be dominated by a single tool. Indeed, the most fertile research comes from a combined approach of various methods."

CHALLENGES OF THE NEW TECHNOLOGY
IN THE ADAPTATION STAGE OF THE CAMPAIGN

Technological growth is transforming the role of the public relations practitioner and is affecting the manner in which communications professionals view, perform, and evaluate their jobs. In a rapidly changing environment, strategic plans for public relations campaigns need to be flexible, adaptable, and proactive. As Charles Darwin observed about the evolution of species, "Adaptation is the route to survival and prosperity" (Grates, 1993). Organizations that undertake careful research will plan more effectively and make informed decisions for their long-term communication goals.

Implications of New Technology

The implications of new technology are far-reaching and pose important challenges for communications professionals. Research indicates that public relations practitioners need to be aware of the following issues: cutbacks in public relations and other communication expenditures, sharply higher levels of client expectations, increased competition, growing impact of special-interest groups, globalization, and corporate downsizing and industrial consolidation (Grates, 1993; Eilts, 1990; Bovet, 1994b; Warner, 1993; Graham, 1991; Hauss, 1993a).

In light of decreased communication budgets, the public relations professional must maximize campaign effectiveness and be able to justify any high costs involved (Grates, 1993; Eilts, 1990). Clients expect an agency to plan ahead, be adaptable, offer multiservice capabilities, be responsive to client needs, and show outstanding creativity (Grates, 1993).

Increasing competition has made high-quality products and service a top priority for public relations practitioners. Successful companies will be ones that establish a positive relationship with their customers and can anticipate consumer needs. Creating product awareness, timing, and positioning are especially crucial for the high-tech industry (Eilts, 1990; Skolnik, 1994; Grates, 1993).

To ensure a long-term positive relationship with consumers, communications professionals need to take creative approaches to employee relations, team building, and labor management programs. By using quality management techniques, the company is making a long-term investment in ensuring an ability to attract, develop, and keep talented employees.

To support an image of high-quality products, companies need to establish and maintain an effective corporate identity program (Gorman, 1994; Selame and Selame, 1988). "Most successful companies are based upon clear, powerful, visual and verbal manifestations of their strategies," commented Chris Gorman, president, Chris Gorman Associates, Inc., New York (Gorman, 1994, p. 41).

Most important, communications professionals need to dedicate the resources and efforts necessary to completely understand their clients' needs.

This includes an accurate perception of their corporate structures, organization, products, strategies, short-term and long-term goals and objectives, and the environment in which they operate (Grates, 1993; Gorman, 1994).

Transformations brought on by the technology expansion are causing companies to reevaluate public relations needs. Unique qualities in the electronics industry require that public relations professionals maintain a balance between traditional and nontraditional methods, gain new expertise and skills, and convince technology businesses that public relations is important. "Technology is moving much, much faster than people's ability to absorb or use it," stated Robbin Goodman, senior vice president, Makovsky & Company, New York (Eilts, 1990, p. 23).

Confronted not only with a growing demand for technology expertise, but also with the globalization of high-tech organizations, small public relations firms are consolidating and being acquired by worldwide agencies. Increasingly, clients are demanding international representation, a benefit that large public relations firms are more likely to offer (Eilts, 1990; Bovet, 1994a; Warner, 1993; Graham, 1991; Hauss, 1993a).

Strategic Planning Techniques

The literature suggests a variety of techniques for strategic planning. A basic framework, which seems common to most techniques, includes seven elements: situation analysis, problem statement, goal statement, target publics, tentative strategies, statement of limitations, and management liaison (Hainsworth and Wilson, 1992; Ehrenkranz and Kahn, 1983; Rice and Paisley, 1981; Cantor and Burger, 1984).

While the concepts may be similar, there are slight variations in the definitions of the planning elements. For example, this book defines situation analysis as "the campaign motivation, or the situation that prompted the effort; a careful definition of the situation helps to identify the questions that need to be answered during the research stage." Ehrenkranz and Kahn (1983, p. 178) identify situation analysis as "the industry, company background or personality profile, competition, and prospects for the future." Cantor and Burger (1984, p. 295) restate situation analysis as "the overview," which includes strengths and weaknesses, company objectives, results of research, assumptions, and problems.

While Rice and Paisley (1981, p. 16) follow a similar planning model, their definition of a plan is "proposed actions derived from agendas and policies." The difference in definition may stem from the type of campaign which is planned. Rice and Paisley focus on public communication campaigns, which tend to concentrate on an immediate objective and use mass communication. In contrast, the public relations campaign seeks an objective as a means to forming relationships with involved constituencies and relies on a broad spectrum of communication media.

Another difference is that the public communication campaign, as noted elsewhere in this book, "has an affinity with the advertising campaign, in which the immediate objective has a minimal connection with the organizational mission; the public relations campaign fulfills a goal that contributes directly to the organization's purpose".

Schultz (1990, p. 121) further illustrates a variation of a plan definition, from an advertising perspective. "The advertising plan is the background, history, and past records of the advertising programs that have been conducted for the brand." The elements of the advertising plan include: an executive summary, a situation analysis, marketing goals, a budget, advertising recommendations, media recommendations, other marketing communications programs, sales promotion recommendations, public relations, direct marketing, evaluation, and conclusion.

Schultz (1990) views public relations as a marketing communications technique. The advertising planning model proposes one similar to public relations being used as a planning approach, which includes objectives, strategies, and tactics.

Conversely, advertising can be considered a tool within a public relations campaign. For example, we propose that advertising could be one of the items on the "shopping list" of tentative strategies within the adaptation plan. A company planning to have a special event may want to advertise on television to attract a larger audience.

Additional planning techniques include: flow charts, the Program Evaluation Review Technique (PERT) chart, the Decision Event Logic Time Activity (DELTA) chart, and the C-R-E-A-T-E system. Each technique is designed for specific types of campaigns. For example, PERT is a flexible design which allows the public relations planner to examine the time schedule for completing a project. The DELTA chart is a decision-making tool which is commonly used in industry and government (Nager and Allen, 1984).

Strategic Planning Techniques—Communication Technology

Other research on campaign planning has focused specifically on communication technology and would be particularly useful for planning use of graphics technology in public relations (Middleton, 1980; Frankwick, Ward, Hutt, and Reingen, 1994; Cutlip, 1994). Companies involved in communication technology have needs which vary from the traditional planning models.

One of the most important requirements for communication technology planning is forecasting or scanning the future. Rapid technological innovation and development necessitate proactive planning, for short-term or long-term campaign goals. If a company wants to keep up with the pace of technological change, the public relations planner needs to anticipate and understand future possibilities. Valuable planning results can be achieved if there is a systematic process for examining the likely future based on specific trends and possible events (Middleton, 1980; Forbes, 1992).

Short-Term Planning

Middleton (1993) outlines four key phases of short-term campaign planning: technological assessment, data acquisition, forecasting, and decision making. Technological assessment includes an understanding of present conditions based on a literature search, technical interviews, and state-of-the-art analysis. Data acquisition is derived from a collection and analysis of existing records and dates. This phase may also include a market survey of existing and prospective users. Once the data is collected, planners need to validate the information and establish a data base (Middleton, 1980). This step would be particularly useful for graphics technology.

Forecasting, which was briefly discussed above, is a two-step process including a variety of factors. The first step includes calibration of analytic models, isolation of causal factors or statistical interrelationships, and model construction (judgmental, extrapolative, and dynamic). The second step includes growth and usage forecasts, saturation levels, and sensitivity analysis. Both of the steps are based on statistical research and are used to establish relationships for short-term forecasting.

The fourth phrase in the short-term model, decision making, includes investment analysis, policy assessment, and "early warning" planning. The results from this phase are based on operations research methods and are applied to project management and investment analysis. Strategic implication of forecasts are assessed and planning may be revised.

Long-Term Planning

Long-term communication planning examines possible scenarios to predict the future. According to Middleton (1980, p. 196), "A scenario is a clear statement about postulated future environments of significance, and usually embraces social, political, economic and/or technological possibilities." Traditional long-term strategy plans are of little use for rapidly changing technology, since a long-range plan may be obsolete before it is fully implemented.

In terms of graphics technology, contingency planning may be more effective. Due to the lack of certainty in predicting the future, trends identified in the forecasting process can be translated into three scenarios: an optimistic outcome, a pessimistic outcome, and an outcome somewhere in the middle. These scenarios would serve as the framework for contingency planning for each of the three possible outcomes (Forbes, 1992; Middleton, 1980; Yosri, 1993; Ceriello, 1992; Warner, 1993).

Middleton (1980) distinguishes contingency planning for technical prospects and nontechnical scenarios. When both themes have been examined, a forecast or common planning variable(s) from each set of possibilities is considered. Strategic implications are assessed and a systematic monitoring procedure is established to prove early-warning signals of significant new developments and trends.

Monitor the Campaign Progress

Inherent in the entire planning process is a need to constantly monitor the progress against the objectives, goals, and mission of the client (Forbes, 1992; Warner, 1993; Skolnik, 1994). Planners should maintain a liaison with management to ensure that all of the steps in the plan are compatible with company policies (Warner, 1993; Hainsworth and Wilson, 1992). Above all, public relations planners must realize that technology can be a tool for communicating information and keeping us in touch with our clients, coworkers, and the media. Communication technologies should complement, not replace, personal relationships.

IMPLICATIONS OF NEW TECHNOLOGY ON PREPARING FOR STRATEGY IMPLEMENTATION

In a rapidly changing environment, public relations campaign strategies need to be flexible, adaptable, and proactive. As Catherine M. Eilts, APR,* (1990) stated, "The public relations professional must anticipate, define and communicate the implications of these [high-tech] changes."

Strategy Selection

Campaign planners usually begin with a shopping list of tentative strategies. These strategies are a collection of ideas, drawn from various sources. Preparing such a list allows the public relations practitioner to select the most appropriate strategy.

* Accredited in Public Relations

One way to create a list of strategies is to conduct a brainstorming session. As noted elsewhere in this book, "Brainstorming is an interpersonal communication technique for creating new ideas by sharing ideas, discussing possible improvements, combining ideas, and generally taking advantage of group creativity in a way that one person alone can never do." And also, "the brainstorming session should produce a refined list of strategies or a package that offers reasonable hope of solving the campaign's problem."

Some public relations firms are using technology to aid the brainstorming process. Michael Finley (1993) discusses electronic meeting systems, a tool which allows the computer to record and mediate team members' ideas, insights, and strategic solutions. These systems permit a more anonymous brainstorming session, which appears to make people "more objective, more creative, more participative and less afraid of being shot down" (Finley, 1993 p. 40). Similarly, James L. Horton and Peter L. Shinbach (1994) suggest using Idea Fisher, a software program described as "a consultant in a box and an idea generator." This program provides the public relations practitioner with a systematic way to think through problems from many different angles.

Choosing the best implementation strategy requires careful thought, based on experience and the ability to match the current situation with an appropriate strategy. As stated elsewhere "Strategy is the heart of the public relations campaign." Campaign planners should base the implementation strategy on research findings, the organization's goals, and the target audience (Domeshek, 1993; Thompson, 1992–93; Hauss, 1993b).

Before implementation, the selected strategy should be tested to refine and improve its effectiveness. This step is especially important with new technology, since there may be a high investment of time and money in the campaign (Eilts, 1990). Hauss (1993b) further suggests that programs should be evaluated at each step in the campaign process. This activity will assist in maintaining liaison with the management and will ensure that the strategy stays closely tied to the organization's goals and objectives.

Communication Plan—With Examples from the New Technology Industry

Once the strategy has "passed" the pretest, the public relations practitioner must design the communication plan, which includes communication before, during, and after strategy implementation. One of the fundamental communication techniques is publicity, achieved by using the media of mass communication—print, cinema, radio, television, brochures, billboards, newsletters, multimedia presentations, news clips, etc. Other types of communication include: announcements; feedback; follow-up; incentives; informative, meeting management; PR department management, personal, and reminder.

Techniques such as extensive consumer research, product spokespeople, promotions, and speaker training can be effective for new technologies. To succeed in today's marketplace, companies need to build quality products positioned as offering a benefit to the target audience. Planners need to know the psychographics and demographics of the people who make and influence the purchase decision. This knowledge will allow the planner to target a strategy to the appropriate audience (Domeshek, 1993; Thompson, 1992–93; Eilts, 1990).

Graphics technology may be thought of as an "evolutionary product," a term that Boston marketing and communications firm Duval Woglom Brueckner & Partners, Inc., uses to describe groundbreaking products. These products are difficult to market because they are new and different—people may not use graphics technology they don't understand.

Domeshek (1993, p. 8) said, "when people think about new ideas, they tend to think about them in terms of things they already know." For example, when the automobile was first introduced, people called it a "horseless carriage" and some people put horse head imitations on the front of the automobiles to make them less frightening to horses (and people). After realizing the benefits of a car (an "evolutionary product"), people accepted the new concept and began to replace their horses with an automobile.

When promoting an evolutionary product, campaign planners need to communicate the product's full potential through communications channels. Evolutionary products, such as graphics technology, break new ground and may be solving a problem that people don't even know they have. The communication strategy needs to emphasize and illustrate the value of graphics technology and the benefits it has over the competitors. A company should approach this step with a "beginner's mind," since the benefits of the product may not be obvious to the target audience.

Furthermore, planners need to understand the target buyers' mind-set, their needs and their perceptions (Domeshek, 1993). Research suggests that public relations professionals are no longer restricted to media monitoring and distribution services. Today's practitioners are buying research tools, such as on-line data bases, equipment, and programs for use in desktop publishing, and many other communications services (Hauss, 1993b). In 1988, 2 percent of public relations firms bought their computers from desktop publishing and presentation graphics (Gordon, 1989). In 1993, the percentage of desktop publishing systems purchased by public relations firms increased to 40 percent (Hauss, 1993c).

Desktop Publishing

Gordon (1989) states that public relations professionals are using desktop publishing to prepare: business proposals, newsletters, posters, briefings, impact statements, employee communications, fliers, business cards, stationery, invitations, data sheets, name tags, certificates, press releases, and even some annual reports. Her research suggests that desktop publishing is used for

For the public relations practitioner, desktop technology has proven most useful for producing midlevel projects such as business proposals, newsletters, posters, fliers, invitations, data sheets, and news releases. In keeping with the strength of the new technology messages should be simple, clear, forceful and persuasive.

middle-level projects. When four-color art or graphic design skills are required, a more traditional approach is used.

Similarly, Kotcher (1992) believes that desktop publishing systems can be particularly useful during crises. Graphic images are a powerful and effective tool for simplifying complex information and presenting it when time and funds are limited. Improved resolution and color faxing will further improve the use of visual images to communicate (Kotcher, 1992; Kindeborg, 1993–94).

Media Strategy and Bandwagon Effect

With an evolutionary product, such as desktop publishing software, Domeshek (1993) suggests that campaign planners determine the best media strategy. Thoughtful public relations will lay the groundwork by educating target buyers and creating a positive perception of the new market category. All of the communications messages—press kits, news releases, pitch letters, and phone calls—should include the essence of the product position. Messages need to be simple, clear, forceful, and persuasive to reinforce the value of using graphics technology. This public relations strategy can be complemented by advertising or direct mail campaigns.

Elsewhere we suggest that two elements—saturation of the media with the message and mass participation—will be involved in achieving the bandwagon effect. The bandwagon effect is "a critical point in any publicity effort when the message becomes the subject of popular conversation. When the point the publicity has been trying to make becomes a topic 'everyone is talking about,' the publicity has achieved a bandwagon effect".

In terms of media, Eilts (1990) suggests that bylined articles, application stories, media tours, and press seminars continue to be important publicity techniques. She further states that the selection and timing of these tools need to be closely related to specific objectives. "Timing and positioning are particularly crucial for new high-tech entities" (Eilts, 1990, p. 23).

To ensure that news releases are published, public relations firms need to make materials more attractive to editors. Lindeborg (1993–94), Marken (1993), and Kornegay (1993) suggest that visual material is an effective way to catch editors' attention and will increase the chances of publication.

Corporate Identity Program—Logo Design

Developing an effective corporate identity program can be a powerful and effective communications tool. Research indicates that over 80 percent of what we learn is through visual stimuli. Thus, when intelligently applying good design, public relations practitioners can achieve a powerful subliminal effect. As Edward L. Bernays stated, "Nothing has changed, appearance still matters a great deal" (Selame and Selame, 1988, p. 8).

The first step in implementing a corporate identity program should be an examination of how the corporate logo is treated. This may be a refinement of an existing logo, or "explorations" of an entirely new logo design. Once the logo has been kept, redesigned, or created, other elements, such as typography, color, layout, and imagery, are considered.

The next step usually involves applying the logo to the company's stationery. This process is followed by developing a graphic standards manual. What characterizes a successful corporate symbol is its simplicity and ability to quickly communicate product information and corporate aura.

Corporate identity is a true reflection of corporate culture—successful programs should reflect clear, focused, sound business ideas. The implementation of the corporate identity program should communicate the strengths, competitive position, and market to the company's various audiences, both internal and external (Selame and Selame, 1988; Gorman, 1994; Weathersby, 1988).

Computer-Related Strategies

Similarly, Middleberg (1994) believes that "marketing to the computer literate is the opportunity of a lifetime." Middleberg (1994) suggests that the computer has been ignored as a marketing tool by public relations professionals because of "fear" and "status quo." Research indicates that there will be a growing demand for marketing through computer disks, on-line multimedia networks, and information superhighways (Middleberg, 1994; Flanagan, 1994).

Middleberg (1994) proposes that public relations planners use press kits on computer disk. He supports this strategy by stating the following advantages: a disk is small and compact for easier and cheaper mailing; disks provide easy access to information; editors can transfer original visual material directly from a disk to their computer; photography animation, color graphics, film and sound can make the material more memorable; disks are interactive, encouraging personal, rather than passive involvement; and disks cost less to update.

Middleberg (1994) also suggests that public relations practitioners put electronic brochures on computer disk, since paper brochures are usually unread and thrown away. Research indicates that when the words "diskette enclosed" are printed on the outside of an envelope, 90 percent of the people open the package and use it. The appeal of the electronic brochure is further demonstrated by the 12 percent response rate.

To promote a company, Middleberg (1994) suggests creating an animated greeting card, a sports trivia game, or holiday recipes complete with visual images—all on computer disks. These strategies can be implemented for a low cost, serve as an effective sales promotion, and enjoy a long shelf life.

Other effective strategies are on-line services and in-house bulletin boards. On-line services, such as Prodigy and CompuServe, can be used to include company news on the information libraries, which have millions of subscribers. These services can also be used for confidential E-mail and for bypassing overnight mail, overnight express deliveries, and messenger services.

When public relations professionals create a company bulletin board, customers and the media can tap into the company's information library. More exciting is the opportunity to interact with anyone who is on-line (Middleberg, 1994; Flanagan, 1994).

The Future—Multimedia and Interactive Technologies

Multimedia and interactive technologies have begun to influence company messages for select audiences (Duffy and Palmer, 1994; Capps, 1993). "The expansion of interactive television, especially cable or closed circuit, will allow public relations professionals to get greater visibility with the press, the public wholesalers, distributors and employees in a more congenial and direct fashion" (Capps, 1993). This may be an area to explore the use of graphics technology.

Duffy and Palmer (1994) define the term *multimedia* as any "computer-mediated communication that integrates any of these elements: text, audio,

Taking advantage of the future developments of technology will depend on adapting the new technology to the old principles: establish a product/service position, develop an effective message, and select the best method of communicating it to the public.

graphics, photo stills, animation, and video." Today's digital technologies include CD-ROM publication and digital links, both of which can be used on a desktop PC and Macintosh. Research predicts that by 1996, multimedia use will be more prevalent in the business sector and will account for $10 billion in revenue.

Duffy and Palmer (1994) suggest that multimedia can be used for annual reports, periodicals, press kits, and virtually any other class of publication. Performance graphs, still photos, infographics, illustrations, animations—all with voice-overs—are just a few of the content possibilities.

Additional predictions include implications for a more customized strategy, in terms of target audience. Multimedia products are "self-contained, custom data bases on disk created for traditional top-tier targets of influence, among them media decision makers, market researchers, institutional investors, and securities analysts" (Duffy and Palmer, 1994). Similar to Middleberg (1994) and Flanagan (1994), Duffy and Palmer (1994) suggest multimedia use in a data base and on the superhighway. As the transmission capacity of the Internet improves, multimedia periodicals are likely to arise under corporate sponsorship and may replace CD-ROMs as the mode of choice for reaching target audiences with multimedia packages.

The implications of new graphics technology are far-reaching and pose important challenges for communications professionals. The companies that are going to succeed are those that establish a product position, a message, and a method of communicating information to the public. Inherent in the strategy must be a strong benefit for the target audience. Graphics technology can be a valuable tool to public relations practitioners, consumers, and the media. The key is how to communicate the advantages effectively.

UPDATING EVALUATION WITH NEW TECHNOLOGY

In the 1980s, evaluation techniques focused on activity levels—such as quantity of clips, press releases, kits, and brochures—and avoided matters of substance. Technological advances have improved the measurement and evaluation of public relations campaigns. Research information is more accessible to public relations firms and "the days of mainly clipping articles for the decision maker to review are gone" (Hauss, 1993b, p. 16). A study conducted by Hauss (1993b, p. 18) suggested that "demand from top management for measurable, bottom-line results and accountability has caused a shift toward a more structured way of measuring results of public relations campaigns and programs."

After conducting research, planning, and implementing chosen strategies, public relations practitioners need to evaluate the campaign. Nager and Allen (1984) and Cantor and Burger (1984) discuss the previous misconception that public relations objectives could not be measured. Practitioners had a false notion that "what we do in PR is intangible and therefore unmeasurable" (Nager and Allen, 1984, p. 173). Donald K. Wright clarified this misconception in a *Public Relations Journal* report:

> Once it was possible to avoid public relations measurement on the ground that the field was nebulous and had a nature that prohibited measurement. Communications measurement became more essential in helping to determine how much public relations programs were contributing to the attainment of overall goals . . .

Evaluation and measurement never supply all the answers in public relations, but they often provide enough information in planning for the future to make them essential functions in leading organizations.

Research suggests that there is a rapid trend toward measurability and evaluation of public relations objectives. In a "growing climate of accountability," Hauss (1993b) believes that evaluation techniques are necessary for helping clients to determine whether they gained a return on their investment. A highly competitive business environment has caused clients to have higher expectations and to become more budget conscious. As this trend continues, campaign planners need to emphasize the importance of devoting time and money to research and evaluation (Thompson, 1992–93; Hauss, 1993b; Grates, 1993; Nager and Allen, 1984). James E. Grunig of the University of Maryland suggests that public relations agencies or departments make research, planning, and evaluation a specialized role within the department (Nager and Allen, 1984).

Emphasis on evaluation allows public relations practitioners to take positive steps toward increased professionalism and personal achievement. By demonstrating the results of their campaign efforts, practitioners add to the credibility of public relations (Nager and Allen, 1984; Brody, 1992–93).

Types of Evaluation

Advances in technology have vastly improved the measurement and evaluation of public relations campaigns. "In the old days, data was filed away in clip book files and data bases that weren't doing anyone any good," said Katherine D. Paine, president of The Delahaye Group, in Hampton Falls, NH (Hauss, 1993b). The age-old media clip book is being replaced by computer software packages, CD-ROM disks, and on-line interactive data bases from which clients can continually draw conclusions. High tech equipment, packed with nitty-gritty details, will eliminate the grunt work from the campaign evaluation process.

To achieve the most accurate appraisal of public relations efforts, the practitioner needs to apply appropriate evaluation methods. The diverse nature of public relations and the wide range of functions are difficult to measure and evaluate. Since there are various types of functions, Lesly (1990) believes that there are various levels of measurability: specific measurement, product publicity, financial news, personnel announcements, starting or pushing a trend, and coverage of an event.

Some researchers suggest that qualitative evaluation techniques are more valuable than quantitative methods. By limiting evaluation to quantitative measures, practitioners may emphasize superficial data and limit thinking and creativity (Wiesendanger, 1994; Lesly, 1990).

Similarly, Nager and Allen (1984) discuss the characteristics that distinguished Silver Anvil winners from nonwinners. Most winners included desired behavior of audience among their objectives and did not claim media coverage as their favorable result (Nager and Allen, 1984).

When Should Evaluation Take Place?

Many researchers suggest that evaluation should begin at the planning stage and continue after the campaign is over (Grunig, 1992; Hauss, 1993b; Nager and Allen, 1984; Hendrix, 1992; Hainsworth and Wilson, 1992; Lesly, 1990). Hauss (1993b), Grunig (1992), Forbes (1992), and Lesly (1990) discuss pre- and postprogram research as well as breaking down the problem into measurable goals and objectives. "Benchmarks" can be used to make program adjustments as necessary.

Some researchers separate evaluation purposes into formative and summative evaluation. M. Scriven (1967) stated that formative evaluations provide information for the development and implementation of a new program (Nager and Allen, 1984). "Summative evaluation is aimed at determining the essential effectiveness of a program and is particularly important in making decisions about the continuation or the termination of an experimental program or demonstration project" (Holzer, 1992).

Two perspectives for designing evaluations—process and impact—are closely related. Process evaluation focuses on the extent to which a particular policy or program is implemented according to its stated guidelines. For evaluation within this framework, the administrator is provided with information about activities, side effects and by-products, staffing and personnel, resources, and utilization and costs. Impact evaluation focuses on the extent to which a policy causes a change in the intended direction (Holzer, 1992; Rice and Paisley, 1981; Nager and Allen 1984).

Grunig (1992) discusses three levels of evaluation: preparation evaluation—quality of message presentations, appropriateness of message content and organization, and adequacy of background information; implementation evaluation—number who attend to messages, number who receive messages, number of messages placed in the media, and number of messages sent; and impact evaluation—social and cultural change, goal achieved and problem solved, number who repeat desired behavior, number who behave in desired fashion, number who change attitudes, number who change opinions, and number who learn message content. Each level reflects a different point in the public relations process.

Similarly, Nager and Allen (1984) suggest that it is useful to think of evaluation as occurring in several stages: a preliminary or planning stage (program design), a midcourse review stage (implementation), and an end results or assessment stage (program objectives). The CIPP Evaluation Model, developed at Ohio State University by Daniel J. Stufflebeam, offers an example of the ongoing process of evaluation. CIPP is an acronym representing four types of evaluation: **C**ontext, **I**nput, **P**rocess, and **P**roduct.

Rice and Paisley (1981) discuss six types of questions that evaluation intends to answer: audience, implementation, effectiveness, impact, cost, and causal process. The nature of the campaign objectives will determine which question type(s) will be emphasized.

Rice and Paisley (1981) further propose three major paradigms: advertising-type surveys, monitoring impact studies, and experimental studies. Advertising-type surveys are inexpensive and focus on the beginning of the causal chain where effects are of lower policy relevance. Monitoring impact studies are even less expensive, yet they concentrate on concepts at the end of a causal chain where policy relevance is highest, but so is the risk of false negative findings. Experimental studies are likely to be large-scale, comprehensive, and expensive, yet they are likely to produce more valid results and may have higher potential policy relevance in the longer term.

In terms of graphic technology, the third paradigm would be most appropriate, given enough time and money. According to Rice and Paisley (1981), large-scale experiments should only be used if the planner has some assurance that the message will have an effect if they reach the target audience. Typically, this assurance involves formative evaluation prior to beginning the campaign.

Examples of prior graphics research include studies on color, side bar graphics, and text and graphics. Color seems to convey particular messages

(Telford, 1994), side bar graphics aid reader comprehension (Ward, 1992), and background material in both graphic and text forms increases reader understanding (Griffin, 1992). Other research has shown that material is more likely to be published and gain attention if graphic material is included (Lindeborg, 1993–94; Marken, 1993; Kornegay, 1993).

The Effect of Technology on Evaluation

Nager and Allen (1984) discuss the effects of technology on public relations research. Computers allow practitioners to analyze data using complex, powerful statistical and mathematical techniques. In a more recent article, Bovet discusses informational data bases that can be tracked for electronic "clippings" of articles in business or consumer publications. A growing number of tools and techniques are available for disseminating, tracking, and evaluating the impact of messages. Fax-on-demand and electronic mail are two examples of services which provide inexpensive, fast, and effective communication.

Some researchers have focused on the use of data bases in public relations evaluation (Duffy and Palmer, 1994; Wiesendanger, 1994; Masterton, 1992; Hauss, 1993b). Masterton (1992) discusses the "virtually limitless" uses of data bases, citing the major benefit as allowing practitioners to gather timely information, which enables a firm and its client to respond quickly and effectively in any given situation. Desktop mapping software, press contact data base, news clipping trackers, and mailing labels are just a few of the possibilities available.

Flanagan (1994) further suggests that the information highway allows public relations practitioners to gain instant audience feedback through formatted information including newsletters and graphics. Business Wire in New York City provides a good example of this development. In 1993, they split high-tech news wires into three groups according to specialty: hardware news, software news (including graphics), and communication news (including data and telecommunication). Information can be transmitted via one, two, or all three.

Another example is Burrelle's "News Express," a same-day clipping service covering 48 newspapers. Pertinent clips are culled and faxed to clients by 9:00 A.M. on the day of publication. In addition to speed, the services' main selling point is graphic integrity—the clip appears as it did in print, complete with headline and photos.

Specific Evaluation Techniques for Graphics

Holzer (1992) discussed the Graphic Evaluation and Review Technique (GERT), a model which allows the manager to portray the various paths that a project might follow and determines the statistical completion time of the various activities, or stages of the process and the probabilities for each outcome. GERT also allows cost improvement, storage capacity, and other advanced, economic concepts of concern into the model. Data base capabilities and data management routines have been developed to support the analysis capabilities.

Similarly, Brody (1992–93) suggests the use of multicolored graphs, charts, and similar devices to impress clients and employers. One data service monitors "tone," article type, prominence of coverage, and audience as well as article content, and offers to track competitors' media coverage as well. Data are available in graphic and prose form. Statistically valid techniques can be applied to analyze consumer behaviors.

Other researchers suggest observational evaluation techniques. Kornegay (1993) suggests that public relations practitioners observe the pickup rate of their publications. Similarly, Lindeborg (1993–94), Marken (1993), and Kornegay (1993) emphasize the importance of graphics in getting material published. A close analysis of this occurrence could be a useful evaluation technique.

Weathersby (1988) conducted an employee focus group survey and found that employees wanted more timely, focused information in brief publications that told them more about how the corporation really operated, rather than listing notices of weddings and anniversaries. After replacing the monthly publication with a news-oriented quarterly and a biweekly newsletters, the company conducted an "after" survey to identify employee's attitudes.

Other techniques can involve calculation of changes in cost and time expenditure. Since a growing number of firms are using desktop publishing systems, time-saving and cost benefits are likely to occur. A careful observation of this occurrence may provide an encouraging evaluation of graphics technology (Shell, 1992; Holzer, 1992; Gordon, 1989).

Base Evaluation on Objectives

With all of the new technology available, practitioners need to remember that the point of analysis is to evaluate quality, not quantity. By focusing only on quantitative data, the practitioner will not comprehend the subtleties of the public relations program, something that only the human mind can integrate. Technology should serve as an aid, rather than a replacement, for human communication.

Most important, practitioners need to remember that evaluation should flow from research and should attempt to measure campaign objectives and goals (Nager and Allen, 1984; Forbes, 1992; Hainsworth and Wilson, 1992; Levins, 1993; Brody, 1992–93). According to Brody (1992–93, p. 48), "data of this nature is far more valuable to public relations practitioners than mere analyses of media exposure." By following through with measurable objectives, public relations practitioners have concrete evidence of what they accomplish (Nager and Allen, 1984).

SUMMARY

Research On the Use of Graphics in Campaigns considers how the new computer technology allows for more sophisticated audience analysis, incorporation of graphics in communication, desktop publishing, and the information superhighway.

Challenges of the New Technology in the Adaptation Stage looks at changes associated with computerization, adopting new technology to the planning process, using new communication technology, implications for short and long term planning, and monitoring the planning process.

Implications of New Technology on Preparing for Strategy Implementation considers selection of strategy, the communication plan, desktop publishing, media strategy, corporate identity, computer related strategies, and the future of multimedia and interactive technologies.

Updating Evaluation with New Technology offers a review of evaluation in light of new technology, the "when" to do evaluation, some effects of new technology on evaluation, the effect of new technology graphics on evaluation and the objectives of evaluation.

REFERENCES

Andrews, Paul. (1994), A New Page: Mr. Desktop Publishing Embarks on His Post-Computer Existence. [On-line]. *Pacific* 12. Available: NEXIS. Length 1238 words

Bovet, Susan Fry. (1994a), Building an International Team. *Public Relations Journal* 50 (7), 26–30.

Bovet, Susan Fry. (1994b), Technology Speeds Message Delivery and Monitoring. *Public Relations Journal* 50 (2), 2.

Brody, E. W. Ed. D., APR. (1992–93), Go Beyond Message Anlayses. *Public Relations Quarterly* 37 (4), 23,48.

Cantor, Bill & Burger, Chester. (1984), *Experts in Action*. New York, NY: Longman Inc.

Capps, Ian. (1993), What the "New Technology" Really Means for Communications Professionals. *Public Relations Quarterly* 38 (2), 24–25.

Ceriello, Vincent. (1992), How to Sabotage HRMS Planning. *Personnel Journal* 71 (10), 102–103.

Conover, Theodore E. (1990), *Graphic Communications Today*. St. Paul, MN: West Publishing Co.

Cutlip, Scott M. (1994), *The Unseen Power: Public Relations. A History*. Hillsdale, NJ: Lawrence Erlbaum Associates, Inc.

Domeshek, David (1993), How to Market Groundbreaking Products. *Public Relations Quarterly* 38(3), 8–11.

Duffy, Robert A. & Palmer, Michael. (1994), How Multimedia Technologies Will Influence PR Practice. *Public Relations Quarterly* 39 (1), 25–29.

Ehrenkranz, Lois B. & Kahn, Gilbert R. (1983), *Public Relations/Publicity: A Key Link in Communications*. New York, NY: Fairchild Publications.

Eilts, Catherine. (1990), High-Tech Public Relation: An Upstart Matures. *Public Relations Journal* 46 (2), 23–27.

Finley, Michael. (1993), Meeting Tools Organize Brainstorming Process. *Public Relations Journal* 49 (3), 39–40.

Flanagan, Patrick. Information Access Company. (1994), Demystifying the Information Highway. [On-line]. *Management Review* 83 (5), 34. Available: NEXIS. Length 3936 words. ISSN: 0025–1895.

Forbes, Paul S. (1992), Applying Strategic Management to Public Relations. *Public Relations Journal* 48 (3), 31–32.

Frankwick, Gary L., Ward, James C., Hutt, Michael D., and Reingen, Peter H. (1994), Evolving Patterns of Organizational Beliefs in the Formation of Strategy. *Journal of Marketing* 58 (2); 96–109.

Gordon, Judy A. (1989), Desktop Publishing: Separating Dreams From Reality. *Public Relations Journal* 18 (1), 9–15.

Gorman, Chris. (1994), Developing an Effective Corporate Identity Program. *Public Relations Journal* 50 (7), 40–42.

Graham, John. (1991), A 10-Point Plan to Manage for the Future. *Public Relations Journal* 47 (6), 39–40.

Grates, Gary F. (1993), Competing in the 90's. *Public Relations Quarterly* 38 (2), 20–23.

Griffin, Jeffrey L. (1992), Influence of Text & Graphics in Increasing Understanding of Foreign News Content. *Newspaper Research Journal* 13 (1&2), 84–97.

Grunig, James E. (1992), *Excellence in Public Relations and Communication Management.* Hillsdale, NJ: Lawrence Erlbaum Associates, Inc.

Hainsworth, Brad E. & Wilson, Laurie. (1992), Strategic Program Planning. *Public Relations Review* 18 (1), 9–15.

Hauss, Deborah. (1993a), Global Communications Come of Age. *Public Relations Journal* 49 (8), 22–26.

Hauss, Deborah. (1993b), Measuring the Impact of Public Relations. *Public Relations Journal* 49 (2), 14–21.

Hauss, Deborah. (1993c), The Purchasing Power of Public Relations Practitioners. *Public Relations Journal* 45 (11), 24–30.

Hendrix, Jerry A. (1992), *Solving Public Relations Problems.* Belmont, CA: Wadsworth Publishing Co.

Holzer, Marc. (1992), *Public Productivity Handbook.* New York, NY: Marcel Dekker, Inc.

Horton, James L., APR & Shinbach, Peter L., APR. (1994), Shrink-Wrapped Presentations From Your Desktop. *Public Relations Journal* 50 (4), 11–18.

Information Access Company. (1994). Other Services; For Financial Professionals; Buyers Guide. [On-line]. *Wall Street & Technology* 11 (8), 167. Available: NEXIS. Length: 8953 words. ISSN: 1060–989X.

Kornegay, Van. (1993), A Graphic Is Worth a Thousand Words. *Public Relations Journal,* 49 (5),6.

Kotcher, Raymond L. (1992), The Technological Revolution Has Transformed Crisis Communications. *Public Relations Quarterly* 37 (3), 19–21.

Lesly, Philip. (1990), *Lesly's Public Relations Handbook.* Chicago, IL: Probus Publishing.

Levins, Ilyssa. (1993), Can Public Relations Actually Move Product? *Public Relations Qurterly* 38 (1), 18–19.

Lindeborg, Richard A. (1993–94), New Ways to Break into Print Reliably and Often. *Public Relations Quarterly* 38 (4), 25–27.

Marken, G. A. (1993), Public Relations Photos . . . Beyond the Written Word. *Public Relations Quarterly,* 38 (2), 7–12.

Masterton, John. (1992), Discovering Databases: On-line Services Put Research at Practitioner's Fingertips. *Public Relations Journal* 48 (11), 12, 17, 19, 27.

Middleberg, Don. (1994), Marketing to the Computer Literate Is the Opportunity of a Lifetime. *Public Relations Journal* 50 (2), 14.

Middleton, John. (1980), *Approaches to Communication Planning.* Paris, France: UNESCO.

Miga, George P. (1994), Quality Presentations Boost Decision-Making Power, *Public Relations Journal* 50 (2), 24–30.

Miller, Michael J. (1994), The Changing Office. *PC Magazine* 13 (11), 113–122.

Miller, Michael J. (1992), How Reliable Is Your PC Vendor? *PC Magazine* 11 (10), 113–115.

Miller, Michael J. (1993), The Perfect PC. *PC Magazine* 12 (13), 106–107.

Nager, Norman R. Ph. D., APR & Allen, T. Harrell, Ph. D. (1984). *Public Relations Management by Objectives.* New York, NY: Longman Inc.

Patton, M. Q. (1980), *Qualitative Evaluation Methods,* Beverly Hills, CA: Sage.

Rice, Ronald E. & Paisley, William J. (1981), *Public Communication Campaigns.* Beverly Hills, CA: Sage Publications Inc.

Schultz, Don E. (1990), *Strategic Advertising Campaigns.* Chicago, IL: NTC Business Books.

Selame, Elinor & Selame, Joe. (1988), *The Company Image.* New York, NY: John Wiley & Sons, Inc.

Shell, Adam. (1992), Communicating in Tough Times. *Public Relations Journal* 48 (8), 22–24.

Skolnik, Rayna. (1994), Portraits of the "Most Admired" Companies: How Public Relations Helps Build Corporate Reputations. *Public Relations Journal* 50 (5), 14–18.

Speigelman, Lisa. (1993), Resolution: Get Organized. *Communication Arts* 34 (8), 140–141.

Strenski, James B. (1992), How to Survive Till '95. *Public Relations Quarterly* 37 (1), 39–40.

Telford, Anne. (1994), Color Predictions. *Communication Arts* 35 (8), 90–95.

Thompson, Gary W. (1992–93), Consumer PR Techniques in the High Tech Arena. *Public Relations Quarterly* 37 (4), 21–23.

Ward, Douglas B. (1992), The Effectiveness of Sidebar Graphics. *Journalism Quarterly* 69 (2), 318–328.

Warner, Harland W., APR. (1993), Working to Establish Public Relations as a Strategic Management Tool. *Public Relations Journal* 49 (4), 18–23.

Weathersby Jr., William. (1988), Family Ties: Are Corporate Publications Kith or Kin? *Public Relations Journal,* 44 (4), 20–24.

10 Developing the Campaign Implementation Strategy

- Building a Campaign Strategy
- Factors in Selecting a Strategy
- Testing the Strategy
- Designing the Communication Plan
- Understanding Campaign Publicity
- Calendaring the Total Strategy
- Budgeting Each Item of Strategy
- Justifying the Strategy Plan

Strategy is the heart of the public relations campaign. Choosing the best implementation strategy requires the wisdom of experience and the ability to sense the most suitable match between the situation and the strategy. The problem and the organization must be carefully paired with the publics and the activities chosen to address the situation. Choosing the strategy involves selecting special events or a package of activities most likely to achieve the goal(s) established for the organization and reach the most significant publics.

The term *strategy*, from a Greek word meaning generalship, has been adapted to fields other than warfare or statecraft as the art or science of affording maximum support to adopted policies. For our purposes, strategy is the plan of action chosen as the most promising means of achieving the campaign goal. This chapter will consider how to select the one best strategy and the details that go into shaping and preparing that strategy for implementation. Adaptation can zero in on the options for the types of action that can be taken, but finally the campaign planner must choose what to do in response to the problem, in light of the situation analysis. That is the strategy, the heart of the campaign.

The final choice will usually be selected from the "shopping list" of possible strategies for achieving the goal(s) put together in the adaptation stage. The selection will reflect careful consideration of all the elements in the research and adaptation stage, especially company policy and budget. The use of the term *strategy* includes the possibility that the best plan may be to take no action.

In his landmark book *Crystalizing Public Opinion* (1923), Edward Bernays first defined the role of the public relations counsel to include "devise a plan of action for the client to follow and determine the methods and the organs of distribution available for reaching his public."[1] He was describing what has come to be called public relations strategy. Bernays recognized that the ability to conceive and design a plan that would bridge the gap between the client's need and the perception and behavior of the public whose response is critical to solving the client's problem is "the chief contribution of the public relations counsel." Bernays described the strategy-designing capability of public relations counsel as follows:

> His ability to create those symbols to which the public is ready to respond; his ability to know and to analyze those reactions which the public is ready to give; his ability to find those stereotypes, individuals and community, which will bring favorable responses; his ability to speak in the language of his audience and to receive from it a favorable reception are his contributions.
>
> The appeal to the instincts and the universal desires is the basic method through which he produces his results.[2]

One of the historic functions of public relations in general, and the way it guides publicity in particular, is to shape popular ideology. Throughout history, and for periods ranging from a few years to a decade or more, social thought has focused on one particular "orientation" after another—the anti–Vietnam War movement, the environmental movement, civil rights, women's liberation, the new right. These popular ideologies are like fads in the sense that they capture the popular imagination and become "the topic to talk about," the "in thing," the "fashionable way" to behave or to think.

The range of strategic possibilities is restricted only by the resources and mission of the sponsoring organization, the accessibility of the significant publics, the goals of the campaign, and the types of activities that would be appropriate under the circumstances. Whether gleaned from readings, generated in brainstorming sessions earlier, or amended at the strategy stage, the actual ideas to be used as the implementation strategy will be those most appropriate to and most likely to achieve the campaign goal.

BUILDING A CAMPAIGN STRATEGY

The steps in the strategy-planning stage must be prepared as a single integrated plan, with careful attention to coordinating the strategy with the goal and with the targeted publics, as well as with communications and the calendar. The budgeting and justification aspects of this stage are no less important.

Strategy building as part of the campaign planning process involves at least the following elements:

1. **Select a Strategy.** Choose from the shopping list those actions that offer the best hope of reaching the goal or solving the problem.
2. **Research and Test the Strategy.** Subject the strategy to the scrutiny of comparison against standards, or test the approach against a representative sample of the target public.
3. **Design the Communication Plan.** Provide details of communications that will support the strategy before, during, and after each action or event, including the timing, the messages, and the media.
4. **Calendar the Total Strategy.** The calendar must show how all the elements are coordinated, which means entering on a calendar each part of the action/event package from the beginning of its implementation to the end of its evaluation.
5. **Budget Each Action or Event in the Strategy.** Provide the cost for every item that has a dollars and cents value, even tradeout and donated items, and list in dollar amounts the cost for each item in each event and the total cost of each activity.
6. **Justify the Plan to Management.** Trace the research-based decision-making process that the planning team used in putting the strategy plan together in order to convince management that it is the best plan possible.

The remainder of this chapter will give these elements in the campaign strategy more careful examination. The explanations presented are intended to give the campaign planner direction in adding the details necessary for the strategy to succeed.

FACTORS IN SELECTING A STRATEGY

The strategy or activity package consists of one or more activities chosen from the shopping list prepared in the adaptation stage. The strategy may be a single event or a series of related events or actions carefully coordinated to achieve the goal. See Box 10.1 for a list of award-winning strategies and tactics.

Special events and public relations actions are designed to win publicity, that is, to stimulate the reporting and dissemination of information needed to shape a social reality consistent with the employing organization and society's standards. Favorable public recognition and understanding can result from a range of activities: from the day-to-day practices and policies of the organization, to the way the organization deals with naturally occurring events, to the organization's own carefully orchestrated and symbolic actions, to its rituals and celebrations. But the same activities can just as easily result in negative public recognition and lack of understanding if their public relations management is neglected.

The key to creating social reality consistent with both the organization's purpose and the ethical standards of society is demonstrating a sound relation-

BOX 10.1   **Strategies and Tactics Used in 1994 Silver Anvil Winning Campaigns**

NUMBER OF USAGES	ACTIVITY/TACTIC USED IN STRATEGY
175	Public information program
94	Promotional materials
74	Staged or special events
61	News conferences or media activities
33	Meetings, conferences, seminars, etc.
23	Marketing-related activities
23	Coalitions, tie-ins, volunteer groups
19	Personality appearances, presentations
16	Demonstration, dramatization
13	Direct mail
11	Reaction to misinformation
10	Celebration event, festival, ceremony
9	Advertising
8	Contracted and/or sponsored research
7	Information booths, trade show exhibit
7	Speakers bureau, spokesperson
7	Survey research
6	Establishment of an organization
5	Contest, competition, award
5	Lobbying
4	Indirect lobbying
4	Social responsibility effort
3	Fund-raising
2	Natural event response
2	Grant making

ship between the organization and the society it serves. Just as an individual builds a reputation by behavior consistent with society's standards, so an institution achieves a reputation, and credibility, by its ethical behavior. But ethical behavior must be managed. Unlike individuals, who argue only with their conscience when faced with an ethical dilemma, institutions must resolve the differences of opinion within a management team holding a wide range of ethical convictions. It quite often falls to the public relations manager to be the social conscience and defender of the organization's reputation.

In building a reputation, actions speak louder than words, for both individual and institution. Institutional behavior wins both the interest of the media in disseminating accounts of the deeds and the interest of the public in perceiving the beneficial implications of the deeds, especially when the deeds are ethically sound in the sense of acting in society's best interests. The "Hay Train" case, described in the next chapter, is a good example of media interest in ethical corporate behavior. Another example appeared in *PR Week:*

> [National Cash Register (NCR)] is now generating newsroom copy because of the way in which it recently reorganized its public relations department.
> First, [Guiseppe] Bassani was named vice-president, stakeholder relations (he is believed to be the first ever to carry that title); then an annual report was dedicated to an academic interpretation of the stakeholder theory; then ads ran explaining the company's beliefs to the public; then a student essay competition was devised and advertised—the subject: "Creating Value for All Stakeholders in a Corporation."
> All of this activity generated publicity both positive and not so positive. *Industry Week* appeared favorably disposed towards the idea. . . .
> However, John Boland, writing in the *Wall Street Journal*, seemed concerned that shareholders might really be losing out. . . .
> Guiseppe Bassani, who prefers the name Pino, insists that there is no conflict, that in creating a "win win" situation with each of the company's constituencies, NCR also creates a "win win" situation for its shareholders. . . .
> ". . . it was my job to deal with all those people who had a stake in NCR—employees, customers, shareholders, suppliers, local communities—and create a win win situation with each of them.
> "I felt then that it was important to balance all of their interests if the company was to operate efficiently, and also that what was in the interest of one group was generally in the interest of all. . . ."
> Stakeholders are those groups on whom a company depends—the people who can help it achieve its goals or stop it dead in its tracks. This includes shareholders and members of the financial community, customers, employees, suppliers, government and other communities.
> Bassani says that NCR has been a stakeholder oriented company since its inception 103 years ago. For example it was one of the first U.S. Corporations to introduce a kindergarten for employees' children. It was one of the first to give distributors exclusive territories and salesmen large commissions. It was a leader in the area of women's rights.
> When Dayton [location of corporate headquarters in Ohio] was hit by a flood of the Miami River, founder John Henry Patterson mobilized the company to build boats for the community, explaining his action in two words: "It pays."[3]

Managing organizational behavior begins with the corporate social conscience, but the day-to-day practices and the planned activities require careful management too. Daily practices that are socially responsible and well-planned events can contribute more to a solid reputation than a never-ending supply of news releases that are inconsistent with an organization's performance in the public interest.

Strategy selection should be made within the context of all the adaptation decisions: (1) strategy should be chosen to reach the publics targeted for the campaign; (2) each element of the strategy plan should be coordinated with various segments of the targeted public and at this step reexamined for fit; (3) the goal should dictate both strategy and targeting, which means the strategic action package and the segmentation must be chosen because they offer the best chance of reaching the goal; (4) the strategy should be chosen for optimum consistency with limitations of time, personnel, and funds; and (5) the strategy chosen should be compatible with the inclinations of management.

In the final choice of campaign strategy, it is also wise to consider the effect the strategy will have on the wide range of entities inside and outside the organization. Pfeffer and Salancik note that "the organization, in responding to one set of pressures, may set in motion actions that will turn some previously satisfied group into a very unhappy one." Although a constituency that has been well served by the organization may not voice objections simply because it has not felt the full brunt of the new strategy, the potential damage should be fully considered. "It is, therefore, imperative for the organization to consider the implications of any given action or decision on *all* the groups and organizations with which it is interdependent."[4]

As a guide for creating a sound institutional reputation and at the same time a strategy for achieving the campaign goal, the following seven criteria can strengthen the public relations campaign. Consider carefully whether the tentatively chosen strategy measures up on these seven criteria for effective special events or actions. This process can help in selecting the best events for the strategy. Every event should meet most, if not all, of these criteria:

Criteria for Building Strategic Actions/Events

1. An obvious relationship is needed between the activity or event and the sponsoring organization. If the event reveals the organization's public-spiritedness without the organization having to point it out, the individual discovers this fact and registers the subtle insight, feeling like the insider in an inside joke. For example, when Midas Muffler conducted a noise pollution control program, they didn't have to say that everyone would enjoy more peace and quiet if more people used Midas mufflers.

If the event involves use of the company's product, the individual catches on that the product contributes to the better things of life. For example, when Kinney Shoes conducted a campaign to encourage walking, with its "walking tours" packets for touring historic homes and the like, it didn't have to say "our shoes help you enjoy life."

If the event invites others to share in celebrating the value of its most important commodity, participants understand that the organization cherishes the same thing they do. For example, when a savings and loan company decided to hold a ground breaking for a new building, it scattered $200 in coin in the loose sand of the building site and invited the children of depositors and neighbors to help them break ground by digging for the money. The event had tremendous media appeal—especially for TV and newspaper photographers—because even children could be counted on to celebrate the value of the money, which was the stock in trade for the S & L.

2. Inherent news value increases the impact of the activity or event. To assure that the event will attract media attention, it must have news value. Hard news happens to organizations. Crises, emergencies, and disasters are never chosen as a way to gain media attention, but the fair, evenhanded, sympathetic manner in which the organization deals with such events can do as much as or more for the public's perception of the organization than a long record of special events. Johnson & Johnson would not choose to undergo a Tylenol crisis, but its director of public relations commented to me that the result of their approach yielded positive benefits.[5]

Mergers, acquisitions, discoveries, and executive appointments are hard news also, and careful planning is needed to obtain the best possible media attention. Campaigns may be built on such natural events as an anniversary of the founding of the organization, the announcement of a new product, or a monumental discovery.

Soft news events, however, are the most common type used in campaigns. Achievements, competitions, and records of various sorts are examples of this category. Athletic events are often efforts to achieve individual or team records. These establish a "winner" and thus make news. A wide range of events that identify the "first," the "largest," the "tallest," the "oldest," or the "smallest" have news value because people are always interested in keeping track of their lives by making comparisons with the status of virtually anything.

For example, the United States achieved worldwide renown because of President Kennedy's decision to push toward being the first country to land a man on the moon. Quite apart from the built-in relationship of the event to the technical ability of the United States, the fact of the landing was monumental news, with both hard and soft news implications. Records of the Kennedy administration indicate that the decision was indeed motivated at least in part by its public relations value for the United States. Such a news event can have as much value internally as externally; it can do as much to bind the nation together as to promote the interests of the nation among other countries.

Various entities take pride—and a good deal of publicity—from the fact that they own the tallest building, have the largest ranch, are the oldest city, sell the most hamburgers, or produce the most wheat. Special events also have human interest—the struggle of the climber to scale the tallest mountain, the effort to cram the most students' bodies into a phone booth, and the training required to run the fastest marathon.

Special news value accrues to events that require runoffs at various levels. McDonald's restaurants win favorable publicity at the city, state, district, and national level every time they hold the Great American Band Contest. Publicity is obtained not only during the competition itself but also every time the huge band performs.

3. The activity or event needs an appropriate name. There is an art to selecting the right name for an event, as there is to selecting the right name for a story or an organization. Daniel Yankelovich has observed, from his long study of public opinion and public issues, that an issue doesn't achieve national prominence until it gets a name. The name is necessary for people to be able to talk about it and thus form an opinion. He notes that the rights of minorities did not become a public concern until someone gave them the name "civil rights."

Effective names must be descriptive and memorable, that is, short and novel. Names will be enhanced if they have characteristics of literary devices, such as alliteration, repetition of letter sounds; synecdoche, a part representing the whole; metaphor/simile, a stated or implied comparison; redundancy, repetition of the idea; irony, understated comparison; and the like. Advertisers are usually very adept at names, as are other skilled writers, and provide many examples that can be studied in order to emulate their style. An event requires a name before people can grasp its significance and before the media can talk or write about it.

For example, the March of Dimes as a fund-raising effort may not have had an obvious relationship to the disease (polio) for which it struggled to find a cure, but the name both described the effort and contributed a certain magic. The organization began by collecting coins in movie theatres; they "marched down the aisle" of countless cinemas after a filmed appeal from President Franklin D. Roosevelt. The magic was due to the fact that FDR was a victim of polio, and while he was never pictured struggling with his crutches—the result of an agreement among reporters—everyone knew. There was a strong emotional value in sharing that information. The name added overtones of irony and allusion: the victims of the disease could not march, but the dimes could march, to fight the disease.

Consider the implications that we read into events with names such as these, whether planned or unplanned:

- Miss America
- Liberty Weekend
- Rose Bowl
- Indianapolis 500
- Poster Child
- Exxon *Valdez*
- Golden Gate

All were events in the classical sense of public relations campaigns. Some were carefully chosen to promote an associated cause; one was bestowed by the media. All are key terms that enable the public to identify, think of, and talk about an event.

4. A bandwagon* effect means people are talking. A critical point in any publicity effort comes when the message becomes the subject of popular conversation. When the point the publicity has been trying to make becomes a topic "everyone is talking about," the publicity has achieved a bandwagon effect. No one knows for sure how to achieve that critical point or to estimate in advance how much publicity will be required to reach it. How much self-interest the audience has in the event or its purpose may determine how much publicity is required to reach the critical point. Obviously, a "low-involvement" product like toothpaste or soap, one with so small a price that purchasers need not investigate before risking a purchase, will require a great deal of publicity to achieve a bandwagon effect, if it is even possible with such products, though musical jingles have often succeeded.

Two elements seem to be involved in achieving the bandwagon effect: saturation of the media with the message and mass participation. *Media saturation* means repetition of the message over time and in a wide range of media so that it will be perceived repeatedly. Add to this the mass participation of people who will be motivated to talk about the matter, and the bandwagon effect is all but assured. To achieve a bandwagon effect requires a well-planned and well-coordinated effort.

Examples of media saturation almost always involve product marketing and advertising, because control of the full range of media placement is possible only with high-cost advertising. Advertising is required especially with low-involvement products. If the audience has considerable self-interest in the message, relatively less dependence on advertising is necessary.

To achieve a bandwagon effect using pubic relations and little or no advertising, you must concentrate on mass participation. Edward Bernays organized the well-known Ivory Soap carving contests for grammar school children in the 1930s. The children brought bars of Ivory Soap to school and carved "art" objects. Winners were chosen from each classroom, school, city, and state, with publicity generated at each round of competition.[6] When a national winner was announced, it was the culmination of a vast number of participants' efforts, interest, and attention. The more people who can be persuaded to participate in an event, the more likely is the person-to-person communication that stimulates the bandwagon effect. The Campbell Soup label-collecting campaign is another example of a mass participation event.

Political parties succeed in large part because of their ability to attract

---

*This term is used here in its common dictionary definition sense: "a party, faction or cause that attracts adherents or amasses power by its timeliness, showmanship or momentum." The term was also used by the Institute for Propaganda Analysis in 1937 to identify a propaganda device. Propaganda attempts to have a viewpoint accepted by thought distraction, appealing to some basis for acceptance other than the merits of the case, often using strong emotional appeals, one-sided arguments, and/or half-truths intent on short-term goals. No thought-distracting processes are intended or implied in the use of the term bandwagon here. There is no other word that conveys the meaning of socially stimulated interest intended here.

mass participation. Local school bond issue campaigns are effective when they can generate mass participation of the community in knocking on doors and performing other volunteer chores. The power of interpersonal communication is a potent element of any campaign action or event. The result of all this mass participation is word-of-mouth communication about the activity. No other form of communication is as effective as people talking to each other about something; that is how the bandwagon effect comes about.

5. Tie-ins multiply the effect of an activity/event. Relating the event to other events or to special calendar days takes advantage of the publicity about the correlated event or day. Every time a person hears about an event it registers in the memory, but the memory is short term and fleeting. If the memory is reinforced by another repetition of the publicity message, the impression is made a bit more indelible. That type of reinforcement is achieved not only by repeated exposure to planned publicity but also by exposure to tie-in publicity. A Fourth of July marathon to benefit crippled children derives publicity not only from announcements of the event itself but also from mentions of the Fourth of July, assuming, of course, that the publicity for the benefit marathon has succeeded in making impressions.

Tie-ins are possible with a wide array of events—political events, sporting events, anniversaries, and national celebrations such as the bicentennial of the U.S. Constitution. Many companies have taken advantage of the national fitness fad by making tie-ins with physical fitness: Post Cereal's Fitness Festival, Tone Soap's Measure-up Contest, Campbell Soup's "Souper" Weight Control program, Mr. Peanut's Guide to Physical Fitness. Motion picture producers increasingly develop tie-ins with businesses that produce novelty item replicas of things that appeared in the film, to the mutual benefit of both film and business.

A popcorn distributor in Kansas City tied in with the national presidential elections by packaging his product in both Democratic and Republican containers. By tabulating sales of each type of package, he predicted quite accurately the outcome of the election. The tie-in worked in a number of ways: the packaging associated the product with an important civic issue and duty, appealed to party loyalties, and took advantage of all the publicity associated with the election campaigns, and the associated voter preference tally took advantage of the speculation about who the winner would be.

6. Tradeouts are bartered joint ventures. Tradeouts take advantage of the shared interests of other organizations or individuals to barter goods or services in order to conduct an event in which both parties gain by reaching the same public. A simple tradeout agreement might involve a soft drink distributor contributing beverages for a United Way agency "fair" in exchange for advertising in the program for the event. A radio station might agree to provide "live remote" coverage of a tennis tournament in exchange for being the exclusive tourney advertising medium for a block of advertisers who are supporting the tournament. The advertisers in turn contribute trophies, shoes, balls, towels, etc., and receive discount advertising rates plus frequent mention during coverage of the event.

A fashion magazine might work out a more complicated tradeout in which a fashion house agrees to provide its latest fashions for a photo spread in the magazine; a modeling agency is recruited to provide models in exchange for mention in the article; a photographer is located to take the pictures in exchange for credits for the photos; and an airline is brought in to fly the whole group to a posh hotel in the Bahamas, where they will all stay in exchange for pictures of its facilities and mention in the magazine article—the airline gets the tail logo of its airplane as background for fashion shots.

The Coca-Cola company put together a similar tradeout package called the "Denimachine" Sweepstakes. Ten Ford Motor Company vans were "converted" by Van Goodies of Chicago, as designed by the editors of *Hot Rod* magazine, with Levi's denim upholstery. The vans were exhibited at racetracks and football games and were to be given away by Coca-Cola as first prizes in a drawing. The second prizes were 7,500 denim jackets and pants or women's skirts and T-shirts fashioned by Levi Strauss & Co. According to a news release on the event, "The 'Denimachine' Sweepstakes is designed to appeal to teenagers and young adults who drink more Coca-Cola, wear more jeans and drive more vans than any other age group." The sweepstakes was also featured in Coca-Cola's multimedia advertising campaign to run concurrently.

7. A series of related events multiply publicity effects. When a series of events take place under an umbrella theme, the publicity for each event becomes publicity for each of the other events, resulting in multiple publicity value. A theme, like the name for a single event, lets people and the media talk about the event package.

"Liberty Weekend," for example, was a theme that united a wide range of events—New York Philharmonic concert, "OpSail" parade of tall ships, fireworks, dedication of new Statue of Liberty, and others—to celebrate the 100th anniversary of the Statue of Liberty. Each event, by being related to the statue, shared in the publicity of the other events under the "Liberty Weekend" theme. Most publicity listed the events or described a single event, but the overall theme gave them all a special relationship. David Wolper's diary of "Liberty Weekend," reprinted in Box 10.2, offers rare insight into the working of an event manager when a wide range of events are scheduled under a single theme.

After you have chosen the best strategy and adjusted it so that if conforms as well as possible to the seven event criteria, consider whether it is the best possible way to reach each of the targeted publics. Check also whether the events in the strategy match the goal or goals. Some adjustment may be necessary if the events overlook an important public or do not cover all the goals.

Although a well-planned and well-managed activity or event will generate publicity, no event succeeds without its supporting communication. The principle is similar to the axiom that you have to invest money to make money. A certain amount of communication and publicity must be invested in an event before it will produce the desired return of media interest and thus achieve the desired public perception.

BOX 10.2   Wolper's Worries End in Weekend of Triumph

His diary offers peek backstage at celebration

Liberty Weekend Producer David Wolper—the mastermind of *Roots, The Thorn Birds,* the opening and closing ceremonies of the 1984 Summer Olympics—kept a diary for *USA Today* throughout the weekend, taking us behind the scenes.

JULY 3

Up at 7:45 A.M. Discuss preparations for New York Philharmonic Concert on the 5th. Suggest against New York Parks Department request to put in a VIP section. I say "No." Parks Department says "Yes." They win—it's their park.

Receive a call from Tommy Walker (producer of the fireworks show). He tells me the final fireworks are all set for tomorrow's July Fourth event.

Call Liberty Island to check that lighting system for statue is ready; also the backup system. Check with Pier 12, where VIPs are to arrive, to assure preparations are in order. Go backstage and visit with Elizabeth Taylor, Kenny Rogers, Neil Diamond.

Strong wind on island. Nervous, very nervous about VIP dinner tent where 2,000 people are to be fed.

Call National Weather Bureau to get final weather reports for Liberty Weekend. All looks good. A great relief. My biggest fear: Rain, the one thing I couldn't do anything about.

Go to my booth high above the stadium, where I'll be during the show, and speak to Roone Arledge at ABC; check if all preparations are ready for the evening.

It's 6 o'clock. I change my clothes for the evening's activities and freshen up. Decide that the wind is so strong we do not want to chance the VIP tent going down. So we decide to hold the dinner party in our open area. We'll be a little more crowded, but I don't want to risk anybody getting injured.

As the guests arrive, I see a lot of my friends, my family. Although it's very crowded they seem to be in good spirits.

Visit with Prince Albert of Monaco. Discuss last minute preparations with Lee Iacocca. Have a last minute talk with producer Gary Smith. Everything seems to be ready. A few glitches back stage but they will be fixed on time.

8:30 sharp: The show begins. I come down from my booth when I'm introduced to go on stage. After I give my speech and a few others speak,

(continues)

the president comes on stage and gives his talk, pushes the button to light the torch. I turn around and I, who've been talking about goosebumps, get them myself when the Statue of Liberty is lit as the orchestra and choir sing *America the Beautiful.*

I look over toward the president. His eyes are slightly watery. He catches my look and gives me a wink. I look to Lee and he gives me a thumbs up. It seems he's happy with the start.

I return up to my booth. The weather is very, very cold. Our medical services group brings all the emergency blankets they have to people and the guests, and especially give them to the older people in the audience.

The wind is very heavy. Some people leave because of the cold.

At the conclusion, I feel good the ceremony went off without a glitch. It didn't rain. It was a little cold.

After I get home, I sit with my wife until the late hours discussing the meaning of it all, the hard work.

JULY 4

Up early At 8:15. helicopter to Governors Island. Check everywhere to be sure the cleanup crew did their work and everything is ready for the new guests. Check to see that the food tent didn't blow down during the night. It is beautiful and ready with the food for the guests today.

Check over at Liberty Island to see that the stages and everything are being prepared for the July 5th's opening of the statue with Mrs. Reagan. They tell me the fireworks materials are being cleaned up, the island will be in tip-top shape.

Sit down next to Donald Regan. Much to my surprise he tells me we met years ago when I did a film on Wall Street and he was a member of a Wall Street firm. I confess to him that I didn't remember.

President arrives, and the opening ceremonies for OpSail go off without a hitch. A very beautiful ceremony directed by Tommy Walker, who is the best at a ceremonial event.

I have the feeling the lead ship, the Eagle, is going to get there before the president starts the parade. But fortunately they slowed the Eagle down just so it was timed perfectly.

About 2 P.M. I leave by helicopter for the Meadowlands. Watch final rehearsals of the tappers and the square dancers.

Speak to Tommy Walker and he tells me his firework barges are all under way. A lot of relief with the fireworks. We did not have our insurance until two days before the event, and for a few minutes along the way, I thought the fireworks show might never take place.

I helicopter back to my home about 5 to clean up and change for the evening. I had arranged a party (on board the yacht Maxim's des Mers) for the stars and people who contributed their time.

For the first time in four days I have a chance to see my children, who are on board. We take off and go to a wonderful spot to watch the fireworks and have a chance to relax away from the public's eye.

Get a call from Tommy Walker. He said three minutes to go and thumbs up. I wish Tommy the best of luck. I know he will do a terrific job. He's the best when it comes to fireworks in this country.

The fireworks are spectacular. You can hear the people cheering across the water.

Return home. Make a final call over to Liberty Island to see that everything is ready for opening ceremonies the next morning.

JULY 5

Leave by helicopter from 60th Street. Take a private boat to the opening ceremony on Liberty Island.

Walter Cronkite is on board. He and I chat about the meaning of the weekend, how things are going and how I am. When I take my boat trip to Maine, he is going to be on his boat at the same time and we will meet somewhere on a little island off Marine to talk just for fun.

Arrive on the island. Go over and meet the Christa McAuliffe family.

I want the opening ceremony for the Statue of Liberty to be a children's affair for two reasons: I want an event that's centered on children, and it would save me the headache of deciding what politicians are going to be the first to enter the Statue of Liberty.

It is a beautiful ceremony, very warm. I have a chance to speak to Lee Iacocca and we bring each other up to date on how the weekend is going.

Mrs. Reagan is gracious. She tells me how well she thought things were going for the weekend.

I rush by private boat and then by helicopter to the Meadowlands to watch rehearsals for both the sports show and the closing ceremony.

Finally after six months of work I am beginning to feel good. I have a feeling we are on the way.

Arrive at the Meadowlands at 12:15. Get report people already are at Central Park for classical concert with their blankets and having a good time.

Meet with the head of the Meadowlands complex and discuss security for the stars. He's worried.

Go over to the sports arena and chat with Peggy Fleming, Dorothy Hamill, Bart Conner, Peter Vidmar and some of the other participants in the show. Meet with director Don Ohlmeyer. He's having lots of technical problems and is going crazy.

Dorothy Hamill reminds me she hasn't performed live before so

(continues)

many people for a long time. The same with Peggy Fleming. They are a little nervous.

Receive a visit from the vice president's people and discuss with them how he will arrive, get to the stage, leave the stadium for closing ceremonies.

Meet with Boy Scouts who are little disgruntled they are not part of the closing ceremony. I remind them they were an important part of the Statue of Liberty earlier during the day. I give them some tickets.

I speak to producer David Griffiths at Central Park and wish him good luck. Dress rehearsals start at Giants Stadium. We have an audience of about 30,000 people, friends and relatives of people in the show as well as people who were invited from the racetrack.

The opening number of the dress rehearsal is so strong the audience is immediately swept into the show.

Receive a phone call from Roone Arledge at Central Park. The police estimate there are 700,000 people there, the largest group ever gathered for a classical performance. We draw more than Bruce Springsteen. I'm thrilled.

At the conclusion of the dress rehearsal I feel very good. I know it's going to be a smash show. There's plenty of glitz but that's the way I wanted it. I congratulate everybody, change a few things.

Fly home to my wife. She encourages me with the feeling that people are feeling great about the weekend.

JULY 6

Go to the Liberty Conference and give a short talk to the people there and thank them for being an important part of Liberty Weekend.

Plans for the rest of the day: sports salute, closing ceremonies, press conference, a party—then it's all over. Hope to be home by 1:30 A.M.

I can only hope that the weekend did what I wanted it to do—that people had a good time. I didn't expect to solve any problems of the world. I wanted people to have a good time, to feel good about themselves, to feel good about this country. I hope I accomplished it.

Source: "Wolper's Worries End in Weekend Triumph," *USA Today,* July 7, 1986.

TESTING THE STRATEGY

Once a strategy has been selected, at least tentatively, it may be tested to determine whether it will produce the desired results. Such strategy testing is not conducted in all cases, but the greater the investment of time or money in the campaign, the more a test of the strategy is appropriate. Tests of the strategy as a whole and of the "message strategy" are central to the process.

In the chapter "Shaping Persuasive Messages with Formative Research" in *Public Communication Campaigns,* Edward Palmer describes how formative research was used to test strategy at Children's Television Workshop (CTW) in preparing the Health Minutes Project series of public services messages to improve health practices. Formative research in this instance tested "specific elements of the presentation responsible for its intelligibility, appeal, memorability, capacity to elicit active learner participation, and so on."[7] For strategy building, pretesting the strategy involves investigating public response to the strategy in order to refine and improve its effectiveness. Palmer notes:

> In general, formative research can focus on providing any information that might contribute to the design of more effective communications. This can include information on any or a combination of learner or audience characteristics, both individual and social; characteristics of the medium (or media), with emphasis on how the medium is to be programmed; and characteristics of the situation in which the learning, the persuasion, or the application thereof are to occur. . . . It also includes perspectives on the features in media design which may importantly affect desired outcomes and rules of thumb concerning the incorporation of these features into the design of communications. These latter are especially important, for they constitute the "tricks of the trade" by which powerful theoretical effects involving perception, learning, cognition, motivation, memory, social interaction, and the like are translatable into applied situations through media. [As well as] valuable precedents . . . [that] can shape . . . objectives into media forms; guidelines for maintaining the quality of interpersonal relationships and achieving the interpersonal communication necessary for effective collaboration among diversely qualified experts; and caveats for helping to avoid expensive mistakes.[8]

Palmer describes how the strategy design and testing took place in producing the Health Minutes. Building on the research and experience that went into the production of the programs "Sesame Street," "The Electric Company," and "3–2–1 Contact," CTW divided the Health Minutes strategy design process into two parts. "The first was the preproduction phase," involving a literature review and a survey. "The second, the pilot testing phase, consisted of field tests on 10 experimental health minutes, produced expressly for this purpose in the form of animatics." The animatics or storyboard, "an artist's rendering of the visual elements to be contained in the segment," served both for screening the project for staff and adviser evaluation and for "formal field testing." The testing enabled the producers to "become generally sensitive to important dimensions of audience reaction" that could be applied to production of the additional 40 television and 25 radio segments. "Separate tests were carried out" on pilot versions of print materials that were to accompany the Health Minutes.[9]

The pilot testing part of the strategy design process involved tests of "six characteristics of the audience, the messages, or the recommended health practices. These included tests for comprehension, credibility, identification, relevance, doability, and intention." In addition to the contribution of the CTW experience to the campaign planner's understanding of the strategy-building process, the research that went into the project may have produced some findings that have broad potential application. They found it "important not to present anything that would create unreasonable feelings of frustration or guilt and not to admonish the audience about their existing unwise health practices." "Message salience" was carefully considered to make sure "key points were not overpowered by other elements in the presentation." "Memorability" and the "comparative effectiveness of integrating the health messages into drama versus inserting them" into factual narration were also important results of the research that went into building strategy for the Health Minutes.[10]

DESIGNING THE COMMUNICATION PLAN

The communication plan should include what will be necessary to communicate *before* the strategy is implemented, what is communicated *during* strategy implementation, and what is communicated *after* the strategy is carried out. This assumes that the strategy will be one or a series of activities or events. If the strategy involves only communication without the support of social interaction activities, it is still appropriate to use communication in advance of a distribution of news releases or publicity kits (see Figure 10.1). Some advance notice that communication materials will be arriving will improve receptivity for the material.

One of the fundamental means of shaping our collective interpretation of the reality around us is publicity. Publicity in its broadest sense is making something "known." What is known, however, is not necessarily correct information or true to the facts. Nevertheless, we make our collective judgments, we buy, we vote, we pass on our perceptions, and we shape our own perceptions. The result is the social reality within which we live.

It may be more accurate to define publicity as the public dissemination of information from which people construct their perceptions. It includes, of course, the mass media. But word-of-mouth conversations, advice seeking, offhand comments, snatches of overheard conversations, not quite complete glimpses of written messages, body language, symbolic actions, good deeds and bad all make up the texture of publicity.

Publicity plays an important role in society. An understanding of the role of publicity in society will help in constructing the campaign plan as well as in selecting the strategy. The strategy itself, with all its communication aspects, must be seen within the larger social frame of reference. Publicity is a social force. It focuses public attention; it sets the agenda of what people think about; it feeds the public debate on the issues of the day; and in these ways it helps shape public opinion. At a deeper level, using the same techniques for shaping the public consciousness, its fashions beliefs and values. The campaign may perform a monumental role by focusing public attention on relevant issues, stimulating public deliberation and decision, and thus guiding the progress of popular culture.

The impact of publicity is often in shaping a popular ideology or fostering

Figure 10.1 Communication materials during a campaign often include devices to get the message in the hands of targeted public members. The National Crime Prevention Council (NCPC) offers ''Trick or Treat Bags'' for use at a time when crime safety is a major concern. As an inducement to buy promotional materials, the NCPC offers a ''12-inch-tall McGruff the spokesdog.''

current fads in thinking or behavior. The faddish notions created by publicity are often transient ideas that have simply captured wide and repeated media attention. There is a bit of a pendulum swing to this, as adherents of one popular ideology readily become adherents of its opposite with the swing of fashion. Yet there are loyal adherents who, in sensing the swing away from their once popular outlook, remain loyal, and silent.[11] Thus there may be competing popular ideologies, but only one in ascendance. This publicity phenomenon may focus on a cause or an issue, but it is more often the orientation or outlook that serves as a rationale for championing a cause or an issue.

Mass media are the foundation of strategies. In order to reach a mass audience, publicity must make use of the mass media of communication. It is easy to overlook the fact that the terms *media* and *mass media* both really mean "mass media of communication." What is involved is communication through the media or channels appropriate to reach masses of people. Note also that the term *media* is the plural of "medium" and indicates more than one channel; there is no such term as *medias.* The careful student of the mass

---

BOX 10.3   The Publicity Media of Mass Communication

	Primary	**Secondary**
Print	Newspapers	Brochures/outdoor advertising
	Magazines	Posters/skywriting
	Books	Handbills/dodgers/fliers
		Newsletters/house publications
Cinema	Commercial films	News clips
	Public relations films	Film strips
	Documentaries	Short subjects
		Closed-loop presentation films
Radio	Commercial AM, FM	Low-power broadcast
	Public AM, FM	Carrier current
		Closed-circuit radio
TV	Commercial TV	Closed-circuit TV
	Local/network TV	CATV, cable
		Multimedia presentations

---

media will not make the embarrassing and revealing error of incorrect usage of these terms.

There are two approaches to understanding the relationships between the media: (1) in terms of the four major mass media, or primary media, in order of their historical development, and (2) in terms of the secondary media that may be used to supplement the primary media. Although these categories have been useful in the past for keeping the various functions distinct in the user's mind, historical distinctions have begun to fade as videotex, view data, satellite transmission of print galleys, graphic data bases, and the like have developed. The classification in Box 10.3 may still help keep the different possibilities in mind as communication planning gets under way.

In designing effective communication, the campaign planner can gain helpful insights into the process from some understanding of the well-known communication model outlined in Box 10.4. The Shannon and Weaver model helps to conceptualize the factors involved in communicating. The basic model was designed to aid in understanding how the telephone works and to help identify obstacles in the process. It proved to have valuable applications to understanding human communications as well as the mechanical process.

By looking at each step of the process the planner is involved in, and by reflecting, one can discover the trouble spots or potential trouble spots in communication. Consider number 3 in Box 10.4. Suppose the organization expresses its respect for employees in its actions toward them, but employees observe uneven treatment of some female employees and interpret this as discrimination against women. The model may help identify the organizational behavior that leads to the interpretation, or it may indicate that the interpretation is an inaccurate perception of organizational behavior. In either case, the model helps to locate the problem.

The model operates within a total communication environment, and the channels are subject to noise that might interfere with the process. For instance, everything else in the communication plan worked perfectly, but the

---

BOX 10.4   The Communication Environment

The model illustrates different communication processes. Each number illustrates a different possible example of the communication process:

1. Is the basic spoken-language process.
2. Represents the process as it might be used by a public relations practitioner.
3. Represents the process as it might be applied to an organization as a whole.
4. Shows how the process might apply to a news release item.
5. Shows that personal appearances combine sender, encoder, and channels in one person as an example of interpersonal communication, and decoding and receiving is combined in one response.
6. Shows how the public relations campaign might be applied.
7. Shows it applied to investor relations.

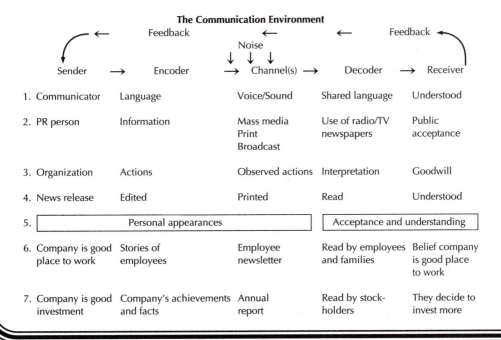

The Communication Environment

	Sender →	Encoder →	Channel(s) →	Decoder →	Receiver
1.	Communicator	Language	Voice/Sound	Shared language	Understood
2.	PR person	Information	Mass media Print Broadcast	Use of radio/TV newspapers	Public acceptance
3.	Organization	Actions	Observed actions	Interpretation	Goodwill
4.	News release	Edited	Printed	Read	Understood
5.	Personal appearances			Acceptance and understanding	
6.	Company is good place to work	Stories of employees	Employee newsletter	Read by employees and families	Belief company is good place to work
7.	Company is good investment	Company's achievements and facts	Annual report	Read by stock-holders	They decide to invest more

day your story was to be on television there was solar activity that interrupted the satellite signal, only a few people were able to decode the message, and thus most couldn't understand it. An example of noise in the newspaper channel would be smeared print or underinking. The model helps to identify problems that would otherwise not even be considered in communicating a message to an audience.

Designing a Communication Package

Few public relations activities take place without a broad range of communications associated with the activity: invitations, announcements, brochures, posters, memos, public service announcements (PSAs), news releases, feature stories, position papers, fact sheets, maps, rule books, programs, etc. The full range of communications must be planned—those needed before the event, those needed during the event, and those needed afterward for follow-up. Box 10.5 shows some communication types by categories.

This step of "designing the communications package" must be carried out in concert with planning for media or channels for the communication. Choice of communication vehicles often dictates the media channel that must be used. Frequently, communications planning reveals the need for various specific media or channels. Where specific channels are necessary, the media planning can be done to take advantage of the best possible "media mix." In deciding on the media mix, of course, you need to concentrate on the reach and frequency of message reception to take advantage of repetition of the message through several media.

In planning communication for a specific event, the before–during–after formula helps to coordinate communications that, under the press of deadlines, may lack cohesiveness. Communication cohesiveness can be achieved by employing a continuity of theme, paper stock, logo, or other identifying elements for all communication related to the campaign.

Before the event, invitations to speakers and special participants, memos, approval from management, calendar clearance, and other such preliminary arrangements require specific communications. During the event, such items as programs, maps, directions, and rule books are usually necessary. After the event, thank-you notes, follow-up releases, photo releases, fact sheets, and publicity kits can supplement earlier coverage or help reporters cover the event. Follow-up communication can even gain coverage from media not involved in previous coverage.

UNDERSTANDING CAMPAIGN PUBLICITY

The purpose of the public relations strategy is to shape public perceptions. For example, a special event generates news by creating a socially significant occasion that the media choose to report, resulting in publicity; the outcome may be a shift of public perception. There are many ways to generate public-

BOX 10.5   Some Communication Types by Categories

To assist the campaign planner, the following communication types are categorized by the most likely application. Some types will necessarily be repeated in more than one category. Some might be used in categories under which they are not listed. The list is provided to help make sure you have considered at least some range of possibilities. It is not an exhaustive list; other types of communication more specific to the event being planned should occur to the planner.

Announcement Communication (to make a coming event known)

Memoranda	News releases
Photo releases	Posters
Wire service release	Public service announcements (PSAs)
Teletype	Videotex, electronic mail, etc.
Satellite services	Audio, video cassette releases
Sandwich man	Skywriting/airplane trailers
Billboards	Door hangers/fliers/handbills
Personal invitations	Fax announcements

Announcement Events (events announcing other events)

Press conference	Speakers bureau
Dramatization	Spokesperson tour
Demonstration	Reenactment
Parade	Establishment of organization
Ritual/ceremony	Speech/debate/panel discussion
Sponsorship	Designation of special day/person
Scholarship to honor . . .	Endorsement by notable person

Feedback (communication received)

Clippings	Questionnaire
Letters	Media monitoring results
Notes	Personal contact
Memoranda	Interviews
Focus groups	Consumer/opinion panel
Observation of behavior	Debriefing sessions

(continues)

Follow-up (of other communications)

Reprints

Summary of proceedings

Proclamations

Resolutions

Photo releases

Memoranda

Publicity kits

Speech manuscripts

Announcements of decisions

Audio, video actualities

News/feature stories

Position papers

Incentive Communications (to motivate participants)

Certificates

Awards/prizes

Production graphs

Invitations

Matching offers

Diplomas

Wall progress reports

Sales/fund-raising graphs

Designation of special day/person

Honors/recognition letters

Informative Communications (to disseminate facts)

News releases

Posters

Memoranda

Brochures

Reprints

Comic books

Instruction manuals

Data bases

Fact sheets

Photo releases

Signs

Booklets/pamphlets/handbooks

Biographical/historic sketches

Exhibits/mobile exhibits

Position papers

Inserts in payroll, utility bills

Floppy disks with message

In-house magazine/newspaper

Media Communications (to provide information to the media)

News/feature releases

Press/media conference

PSAs

Speeches

Teletype

Paid advertising

Editorials

Position papers

Junkets

Tradeouts

Radio-TV scripts

Media tour/open house

Audio, video cassettes

Reports

Fillers, slicks, PMTs, clip sheets

Historic/bibliographic sketches

Letters to the editor

Photo opportunities/releases

Slides/audiovisuals

Fact sheets/tip sheets

Meeting Management Communications (for use with meetings)

Schedules of events	Agendas, programs, action items
Displays/exhibits	Presentation scripts
Flip charts	Slides/film strips
Badges/name tags	Directory of participants, etc.
Films	Training aids
Memoranda/letters	Reports

PR Department Management Communications (most with logo)

Letterhead stationery	Memo pads
Mailing labels	Forms (of all kinds)
Name badges	Postage meter
Parking decals/spaces	Uniform jackets
Pager/walkie-talkie	Bullhorn

Personal Communications (sent)

Personal contact	Phone contact
Letters	Memoranda
Telegrams	Electronic mail (E-mail)
Invitations	Reminder notes

Reminder Communications (to reinforce other messages)

Memoranda	Fliers/handbills/dodgers/door hangers
Picture mounts	Calendars (desk, wall, wallet)
Novelty items	Rolodex cards (with organization's name)

ity, in the broadest sense of "making something or someone known." Although media coverage may be the most obvious form of publicity, it is not the only one. The planner hopes that the event will create enough public interest to warrant media coverage, but the event can be enhanced to improve that coverage. When the circus came to town it never did so quietly; it put up posters, bought advertising, and staged a parade.

Campaign Communication as News

Multiple news interests can provide "insurance" against the failure of one news angle to achieve the desired coverage. News means two things here—what people "need to know" to cope with life, and what is "nice to know" to make life worthwhile. A. J. Liebling defined it this way: "the press should inform the people of the events and situations that have a real effect upon their lives and upon society as a whole . . . in a form that is clear, honest, accurate, fair, concise, meaningful, interesting, and, where appropriate, entertaining."[12] A local event of average news interest can be enhanced by including in the event a speaker with intrinsic news value. By adding elements that have their own news value, such as announcements of contest winners and setting of new records for the event, one can enhance its news value.

Wilbur Schramm adds a realistic perspective on the meaning of news: "As a small town daily newspaper reporter, the most important thing I learned is that news exists in the minds of men. It isn't an event, but something perceived after the event. . . . The news report of an event is put together from a gestalt of eyewitness accounts, second-hand reports, third-hand comments and explanations, and the reporter's mind set. It is then coded for transmission, usually by persons who have had no connection with the event. It is coded to meet mechanical requirements, anticipated needs and preferences of the audience, and what the editor thinks."[13]

Experienced public relations people are familiar with the charge that they create "media events" in order to manipulate the media into promoting their particular special interest. These "pseudo events" as Daniel Boorstin calls them,[14] discredit the field. Indeed, those who manipulate the media for their own private interest do indeed bring discredit on public relations because they fail to relate the event to the public interest. If an enterprise is operating in the public interest, as our definition of public relations asserts it should, its activities should be consistent with the public interest. To fail to make that fact clear is a disservice not only to the enterprise but also to the field of public relations itself.

In addition to the built-in newsworthiness of the event, the campaign planner can provide prepared materials for reporters. Providing such aids helps to focus the reporting task and should include the facts that serve the public interest, but should never distort the facts to the benefit of the planners' self-interest. To do so risks loss of credibility, without which public relations is impotent. Providing complete factual information helps to make coverage more accurate and creates goodwill with the media. Either collected in a publicity kit or distributed separately, prepared materials may include fact sheets, photos, brochures, position papers, and the like. In covering conferences, lists of participants, with the names spelled correctly, and copies of their speeches are especially valuable to reporters.

Word of Mouth

One of the most desirable forms of publicity is word-of-mouth dissemination of information, which includes the emotionalism that is possible only in interpersonal communication. Adler, Rosenfeld, and Towne offer a succinct outline for effective interpersonal communication.[15] When people talk to one another, enthusiasm, peer pressure, and interpersonal dynamics come into play in addition to the facts. Although interpersonal communication cannot be depended on to get the facts straight, there can be no substitute for the emotional reaction to the event that is possible in face-to-face contact. However, the reaction may be negative as well as positive, especially if the planner hides an ulterior motive or manipulative intent. To announce a "surprise celebrity" appearance and then start a rumor that it will be a much more popular personality than the one scheduled is an example of such a tactic that is almost guaranteed to backfire.

Positive word-of-mouth publicity is difficult to attain and more difficult to guarantee. To get people talking about an event requires careful planning. Beginning with an event with popular appeal, using repetitive publicity, and providing an early behavioral commitment opportunity, such as a chance for people to buy a ticket, are the bare-minimum criteria for stimulating word-of-mouth publicity. The element of competition to participate will also be helpful. The rock concert phenomenon is almost a classical example and is worthy of study as a guide to word-of-mouth publicity.

The choice of a campaign strategy with popular appeal requires knowledge of the community. There must be an awareness of the self-identification process within the society or culture, that is, how people identify themselves collectively as football fans, as patrons of the arts, as country and western music fans, or the like. Repetitive publicity must be carefully back timed so that the publicity builds to the critical moment just before the event: allow enough time for people to talk about the event but not so much time that people forget about it. A behavioral commitment opportunity is a chance for prospective participants to take action of some sort: buy tickets, call in reservations, buy and wear T-shirts. The various elements of the process of generating word-of-mouth publicity work together, so that publicity stimulates behavioral commitment and behavioral commitment stimulates further word-of-mouth publicity.

Perhaps the critical element in generating word-of-mouth publicity is creating a sense of social significance, a sense of history in the making. In this respect the planned event shares at the deepest level the character of a mythic event, an event that offers social self-identification. A conceptual understanding of this mythic process, which is elaborated in Chapter 6, can help the event planner fit the event into the cultural and ethical fabric of the community he or she seeks to reach.

Designating Media

Designating media or channels for communication is an important and related element in a communication package. It involves the selection of the means by which the communication will be disseminated most effectively to the segmented publics (see Box 10.6). Traditional mass media categories are losing their meaning in an age of communication technology innovation. Edwin Parker describes one innovation as an "information utility."

This new communication medium, which is coming to be called an information utility, will have one radical new property that previous mass media lack: what is transmitted over the communication channel can be controlled more directly by the receiver than by the sender of the message. It may look like a combination of a television set and a typewriter, function like a combination of a newspaper and a library, and permit a communication network that is something like a combination of a telephone and a telegraph system.[16]

The new technology holds a challenge for communication aspects of the campaign: reaching target publics may dictate ways completely foreign to traditional mass media thinking. Teletex can broadcast print information, video recording is perceived the same way as film, closed circuit TV is not broadcast through the air, video news releases are beamed by satellite to TV newsrooms nationwide, and direct mail may give way to electronic mail (E-mail) and fax. The viewer makes little distinction in the technology; campaign planners should concentrate on the end result. Channels should be chosen for the efficiency with which they will get the message to the targeted public.

The appropriateness of the channels needed for the communications chosen must be examined to discover whether the channels reach the desired segments of the public. Invitations, one might think, must be sent by direct mail, but a second look at the situation may suggest better channels: telephone, electronic mail, or, particularly if time is crucial, mailgram or telegram. Working through a third-party booking agent to reach a famous personality will be not only convenient but necessary. Experience with how the communications world works, together with a good portion of creativity, can help in selecting the best media channels for your message.

If research has shown that 60 percent or more of your public receives information about your organization from television, the plan would clearly call for television as the most important medium. Indeed, in this case, the channel would dictate that the communication be through television with clear limits for other media such as newspapers, radio, and billboards.

Channels of communication may be dictated by other considerations as well. If the public is geographically widespread and relatively small in number, a highly specialized approach may be called for. In one case, a small public of top executives, widely dispersed and perpetually busy, posed a special challenge. Providing each with an audio recorder complete with a taped message proved quite effective, and because the audience was small and critical to the success of the campaign, the plan was cost effective.

The process described so far in this strategy stage of the campaign plan requires considering a number of elements simultaneously or at least with a clear understanding of their interrelationship. Selecting strategy, segmenting, coordinating with objectives, tie-ins, communication, and channels all must be done in concert. One way to proceed is by calendaring or scheduling the elements for best results.

Once the strategy is selected and the channels determined, the planner must consider the list of communications that will be needed to ensure the success of the event. The planner will need to communicate before an event—

BOX 10.6　Guidelines for Some Typical Forms of Communication

THE BACKGROUNDER

Much like a term paper in format, the backgrounder provides information of the type found in a fact sheet but with more detail. The backgrounder gives the rationale or facts and opinion to back up the position taken by the organization on an issue of public concern. As with most communications, the backgrounder is enhanced by documenting the sources of facts and opinions in footnotes or endnotes.

Summary

Backgrounders frequently lead with a statement of the issue, continue with the documented facts in logical order, and conclude with a summary of the facts to support the position of the organization. Documentation should be in the form of footnotes or endnotes; documentation in the text is usually a third option.

Content

Material should be presented in nonjudgmental, objective, neutral language. Let the facts speak for themselves. Include historical details that clarify the issue by showing how it evolved. Be careful to include important names, dates, and other facts accurately and spelled correctly—as in facts sheets.

Structure

Present the documented facts in the order the reader is likely to want to consider them. Marshal the facts to lead to the conclusion the organization advocates. Follow an outline of the material and incorporate the outline in left margin and run-in headings. If you haven't made a habit of using headings—such as this document does—begin developing the habit now. Headings should be key words that identify for the reader the main topics developed in the document and the content of each section or paragraph.

Documentation Style

Documentation serves the same function as attribution in news stories—it gives credibility to the information by "borrowing the credibility" of the source, whether it is a quotation from a respected person or a summary of statistical facts from a credible source. The form for documentation should follow the standard stylebooks: Turabian, *A Manual For Writers . . .;* the *Modern Language Association* (MLA) *Stylesheet;* or the *American Psychological Association* (APA) *Publication Manual.* Each has a slightly different method of identifying the source of information used in a document. It is

(continues)

probably best to select one (Turabian or APA) and concentrate on learning that style. Note that documentation in footnotes differs from documentation of bibliographical references.

Documentation in the text is usually footnote information included in parentheses, but it does not duplicate information, such as the author's name, that is given in the text. *Check Modern Language Association Stylesheet* or Kate Turabian's *A Manual for Writers of Term Papers, Theses and Dissertations* for in-text notation procedure.

A Public Interest Orientation
Remember to approach the issue from a public interest point of view. Show that the organization's concern about the issue is consistent with the general public interest.

DIRECT MAIL PROMOTION PIECE
Direct mail has the advantages of face-to-face communication in that it is one-to-one and it can control the message, its style, what is emphasized, the appeals used, and the people who will receive it, but it still fits that category people call "junk mail." Direct mail ordinarily includes whatever the mailer selects to put in the packet or envelope, from a single "self-mailer" with address label attached, to a packet with response card, return envelope, multifold list of arguments, backgrounder, brochure, poster, or a wide range of other possible items. Research suggests that three items in a direct mail piece will be more effective than other configurations.

Background
The trade association Direct Marketing Association focuses on the interests of marketers who use direct mail, but that should not lead one to conclude that it applies only to marketing. Public relations practitioners use the technique across the spectrum of organization types from nonprofits to trade associations to government agencies.

Purpose
The direct mail piece usually seeks to achieve either of two classic purposes of communication, to inform or to persuade; the third classic purpose, to entertain, may be incorporated as a tool for either. The Tucker, Derelian and Rouner (TDR) text mentions calling attention to a "need, concern, or interest" together with a "desired behavior" as a response. Usually the piece offers detailed coaching as a guide for the desired behavior.

Target Audience
Because of the comparative cost of direct mail it is often used with opinion leaders or other carefully segmented publics, including from opinion

leaders to opinion leaders and opinion leaders to their constituencies. When direct mail is used with purchased mailing lists for sales or contributions pitches the response will usually be about 2 percent. The more the material appeals to the self-interest of respondents the higher the response rate.

GUEST EDITORIALS AND LETTERS TO THE EDITOR

The function of the editorial page is to draw a "pattern of meaning" out of what is in the news columns and to encourage understanding and coping with those realities. Knowing that, the public relations practitioner can bring to the public debate the opinions and solutions that represent his or her organization's point of view. The format (usually): (1) ties the editorial to a news development, (2) presents a point of view, (3) marshals persuasive arguments to convince the reader, (4) answers anticipated counterarguments, and (5) ends with a clear, firm summary. This pattern applies equally to both formats.

Tie to News

The piece should refer directly and specifically to a published item that prompted the editorial including date, page, and name of the newspaper where it appeared. The news item should be cited to identify the issue the editorial addresses. If the reference is so derogatory that it should not be repeated even to deny it, simply state the issue. If the issue is the correction of an inaccuracy, the identification of the issue should include, as a minimum, the name of the paper, date, page, incorrect information, correct information, and name of the letter writer.

Point of View

The public relations practitioner represents the organization in formulating and stating the point of view on the issue. If the practitioner is not fully aware of the organization's views it will be necessary to interview decision makers to determine how best to state the point of view, or at least to get reactions to a proposed statement. The statement should be brief, without qualifying phrases, and should be couched in terms of the public interest.

Convincing Arguments

To support the point of view, the writer should offer the most compelling arguments in the form of: quotations from authorities, statistics, comparisons/contrasts, logical reasons, precedents, relevant laws, and the like. Anticipate the arguments the opposition will use, or has used, and respond to them. A few strong arguments are better than many weak ones. If

(continues)

the issue is controversial, the strongest arguments stated first will be most effective.

In general, the arguments should be arranged for best effect, usually one argument per paragraph. Blatant emotional appeals as well as threats of litigation or other recriminations are usually counterproductive and should be avoided. State the case professionally and tactfully without accusation, name calling, or other derogatory comment. Remember to maintain good media relations; don't anger or alienate the reporters or editors with whom you must deal regularly.

Summary Conclusion

Reiterate the position you have presented using alternative phrasing, so that you say the same thing again in different words. Repeat the point of view and the arguments, especially the action or policy that you advocate.

THE POSITION PAPER (three to five pages)

The position paper takes a stand on an issue and provides the evidence to support it. In contrast, the backgrounder is written in a more quasi-formal, detached, reportorial style, with neutral and objective language. The position paper presumes that the statement will convince readers of the soundness of the stand and will persuade them to agree, or at least to soften their opposition.

Format

The structure of the position paper starts with an introduction that lays out the issue, then any background including historical development that may be needed, followed by discussion of the opposing side including a statement of the organization's position and a summary of arguments supporting it, and finally a suggested course of action.

Persuasive Devices

Among the effective persuasive techniques established in the persuasion literature that may be adapted to the position paper, are deductive and inductive reasoning, counterargumentation, source credibility, structural devices, appeals involving group dynamics, and personality factors. Consider each of these:

Deductive persuasion makes its case by stating a position and offering reasons or justifications. Arguments could include logic, statistical supports, credible opinion, and derived benefits.

Inductive persuasion starts with a variety of generalizations or evidence that carefully leads to the inescapable conclusion that the position must be supported.

Counterargument "inoculates" the audience against the opposing position by presenting that case in a weakened form with responses to known or anticipated arguments.

Source credibility "borrows" the credibility of sources in one way or another, listing names of supporters, quoting strong statements that favor your position, citing arguments of credible persons, or giving the expertise or strong social status of supporters.

Experience with structure suggests that the stronger arguments be used first when facing a hostile audience. When facing a friendly audience one should build up to the strongest arguments. Innoculation is effective with a neutral audience.

Group influence on persuasion has found that group dynamics, including identification with group norms, peer pressure, and compliance with group values, exert strong influence and are quite persuasive when one knows a group with which the audience wishes to identify.

Personality factors in persuasion include knowing that as low or lowered self-esteem increases response to persuasion, that people tend to continue their habitual behavior, and that people tend to resist change.

if no one knows about the event, it cannot succeed. The effort will have to include communication during the event. Many remember the shouted slogan of the vendor at the baseball game: "You can't tell the players without a program." It is true for more than baseball games. The event also needs communication afterward—to disseminate summaries, resolutions, and analyses and to thank the people who made it possible. Let's look at these three rules in more detail.

Communication Prior to the Event

Communication prior to the event must make potential participants aware of and motivated to join in the event. The type of communication also must be adapted to the audience segments. It is appropriate to send news releases to the media if you need to reach the general public; speakers require personal invitations, if not personal negotiation. Other prior-to-event communication types might include posters, radio and TV PSAs or spots, talk show appearances, fliers (handbills), and even other events to announce an event. In-house techniques can also be used, especially if the target public is concentrated in specific organizations; then announcements such as bulletins, memos, and bulletin board notices can be used as well as in-house newsletter stories.

Prior communication must be widespread, repetitive, and integrated to ensure the target public will be exposed to the message adequately to make a decision and to respond. As noted above, themes are valuable in focusing attention as well as in multiplying the effects of publicity. Diversity of advanced publicity, repeating the basic message in a variety of media, ensures that low media users will be exposed and provides the reinforcement that comes from repetition. It is usually better to have too much publicity rather than too little. Special events can also be used to announce other events, as, for example, the circus traditionally used a parade to announce its presence in town.

Communication During the Event

Communication during the event serves two basic purposes: It provides participants with needed information, such as programs, maps, schedules, and highlights. It may also take advantage of actions and publicity generated at the event by disseminating information favorable to the sponsoring organization, such as a resolution passed during a conference on an important public issue.

To ensure smooth functioning of the event, participants must know what is going to happen as well as where and when. Thus a schedule of some sort is necessary: a typed agenda for small meetings and a printed program for larger, more formal conferences and conventions. Other types of communication that may also be necessary include maps of the site, a guide to travel arrangements, parking instructions, registration information, name badges, signs directing participants to meeting sites, an information booth, special information about meals and/or room accommodations, an action agenda or copies of proposed resolutions, mementos, position papers, committee reports, biographical sketches of speakers, pamphlets, reprints, letter of welcome, note pad, pencil, directory of participants, and an evaluation questionnaire.

A basic function of events is to generate publicity, and this fact should not be forgotten in the press of planning, making arrangements, and managing execution. Publicity resulting from an event is usually in greater quantity and more depth than would be possible through news releases alone. As it progresses, the event continues to fulfill the overall publicity goals by generating coverage of several possible types. Reporters may cover the event, and if they are supplied with fact sheets, speech manuscripts, photos, and other facts, they will likely provide both accurate and valued media stories.

Pressrooms can enhance this process by collecting the necessary items in one place and supplying the reporters with phones, typewriters, paper, pens, coffee, and secluded places to conduct interviews, as well as help in arranging interviews. Pressroom items that may be especially useful include milestone achievements, numbers, and distances traveled; photos representing personalities or achievements of major interest and device demonstrations or videotape "actualities" of these; background information on personalities, devices, or the organization; and information kits with fact sheets, statistics, historical and/or biographical sketches, official statements, position papers, and the like. Coverage can be enhanced, or mollified in the event of disaster, by providing facilities such as these for media representatives.

Communication After the Event

Communication after the event should include such follow-up considerations as summaries of the event to be distributed to the media, packets of materials, and media kits including items noted above. When distributed afterwards, these materials can add to publicity produced during the event.

Praise should be distributed generously; a favorable lasting impression will accomplish a great deal in encouraging future participation in such events. Speakers, employees, and leaders should receive commendations even if they are paid for their service. Few better opportunities will come to the public relations person to win good feelings than passing out laurels and accolades after a successful event.

In planning the communications that will be most effective for the campaign, the checklist of events with typical supporting communication types shown in Box 10.7 will help ensure that the best possibilities have been considered.

BOX 10.7 Checklist of Events with Typical Supporting Communication

The following checklist will aid the campaign planner by showing how typical communications support various event types.

Naturally Occurring Event
News release
Position paper
Photos
TV actualities
Policy statement
Interview arrangements

Establishment of Organization
Membership IDs
Brochure (on benefits, purpose)
Maps/display/instructions
Constitution and bylaws
Achievement awards
Newsletter
Handbook

Meetings/Conventions/ Seminars, etc.
Schedules of activities
Direct mail (registration information)
Speaker arrangements
Lodging information
Badges/name tags
Exhibits/displays
Travel information

Press Conference/Press Luncheon
Invitations
Tip sheet/fact sheet
Badges/media kits
Handouts/facts/position statement

(continues)

**Personality Appearance/
Spokesperson Tour**
News releases/audio TV cassettes
Grass-roots participation
Traveling display/exhibit
Autograph party
Talk show appearance
Photo opportunity

**New Product Announcement/
Book Release**
Demonstration
Autograph party
News release/press kit
Photos/photo opportunity
Special publication/special issue
Specifications/endorsements

Carnivals/Pageants/Fairs
Costumes
Competitions
Dramatizations
Parades
Picnics/barbecues
Gifts/awards/souvenirs
Maps/guidebooks/rules

Information Booth(s)/Exhibits
Maps
Personal contact
Brochures/kits
Directory

Research Report Presentation
Summaries
Personal appearances
Policy statement

Speakers Bureau
Brochure
Biographical sketch
Information sheet
Model speech
Schedule

Contests/Competitions
Rules book/brochure
Posters/bus cards/Outdoor ads
News releases/kits
Endorsements
Advertising coupons
T-shirts, hats, etc.
Judge selections
Prizes/awards/certificates

Dedication/Ground Breaking
News release
Mementos
Parade/parade float
Speaker(s)
Invitation/open house
Printed programs
Supplementary events (tree
    planting)
Time capsule burial

CALENDARING THE TOTAL STRATEGY

Calendaring fulfills two purposes. It relates the action and events to the days
and months of the calendar year, and it reveals the timing of various events
and their supporting communications. Whatever type of calendar is chosen, it

should show the major elements of the strategy at a glance and preferably show enough of the communication plan details that the timing can be appraised and corrected if necessary.

Timing of the often complex interconnected parts of a communication plan is the second consideration in calendaring. Ordinarily the communication plan should be back timed from the launch day of the strategy events or action package. Major considerations in back timing involve mostly judgments learned from experience. For example, in planning a conference (working backward):

1. How close before conference day can the final registration number be delivered to food service? That will dictate registration cutoff.
2. How long before registration cutoff is it feasible to mail a follow-up announcement and registration information for the event?
3. How long after the first mailing is a second mailing appropriate? This requires estimating delivery time and allowing a reasonable delay in responding.
4. How long before the event is it necessary to send advance announcements to allow people to mark their calendars to avoid conflicts? Or should the registration information be sent early enough to serve this purpose?
5. How long in advance of the first mailing is a final mailing list needed?
6. What is a reasonable time for the printer to deliver mailing pieces? They should be delivered in time for affixing mailing labels to meet mailout deadline.
7. When must the copy be ready for the printer?
8. When do all these planning details have to be finished to get the process rolling?
9. When does planning have to start to get everything done to ensure a successful campaign? Often it is a matter of how late it can start.

This example could be applied to the planning for most strategies, with variations, of course. Back timing is not a hard-and-fast rule but it is usually a good idea. In the back timing analysis of the strategy the planner must be sure to include all the essential parts—especially those that require advance copy preparation and/or production. By looking carefully at the timing of the calendar to see if there is slack, the process can be delayed or speeded up if necessary. Anticipate or at least plan for delays and emergencies that will consume valuable time. Try to schedule the elements that will be most subject to delays at times where adjustments can be made. Be prepared to make difficult decisions if promises are not kept (See Figure 10.2).

The Calendar Chart The strategy should fit the calendar year in some reasonable, logical fashion. Picnics should be planned for the warmer months,

Figure 10.2 The communication tactics needed to support a campaign strategy often include a broad range of mass and interpersonal media often relying on newspapers. Whether the tactical messages is designed for newspapers or other media it must be carefully planned.

Christmas-related activities in early December, and holiday events on or just before the calendar holiday; family activities should avoid school days; events appealing to farmers should avoid planting and harvest seasons; and events should be planned to coincide with other known or regularly scheduled events. The risks of unfavorable weather, if not precluded by planned shelter, should be carefully calculated.

The calendar plan can be represented graphically in several ways. The simplest is a series of one-month calendar sheets marked with the dates in squares, to which the major elements can be added in one color and communication details can be added in another color. The entries can be made by hand, or they can be typed in and highlighted with different colors to help coordinate related activities.

The wall chart calendar displays the months in quarterly, semiannual, or full-year-at-a-glance form. The advantage of this method is that all elements and their interrelations can be seen at once as a constant reminder of what needs to be done next. One disadvantage is that the calendar is not easily folded for insertion into an $8\frac{1}{2} \times 11$ plan book for transportation outside the office. These wall calendars are available from office supply stores or mail order office equipment outlets. One is the "Re-Markable," available from Remarkable Products, Inc., 245 Pegasus Ave., Northvale, NJ 07647.

The Public Relations Society of America (PRSA) provides its members with a meeting checklist for coordinating activities with other PRSA activi-

---

BOX 10.8   Example of Gantt Chart

Gantt Chart for Public Opinion Survey

	Sept.	Oct.	Nov.	Dec.	Jan.	Feb.	Mar.	April	May	June	July	Aug.

Survey steps

Survey steps												
Background study	———											
Develop questionnaire		————										
Draw sample		——										
Phone interviews				————								
Computer program					——							
Frequencies printout					——							
Analysis of printout data						————						
Run subprograms and analyze						————						
Analysis of findings						———						
Final research report							———					

---

ties and other factors. Another technique is the Gantt chart, which lists activities down the left margin and indicates timing of activities by time lines under days, weeks, or months across the top of the page. Box 10.8 shows how a research project was calendared using a Gantt chart.

The task-timetable narrative is another type of calendar. The tasks to be completed are listed opposite a monthly, weekly, or daily timetable. Box 10.9 shows how the method would be used in a school bond issue election. One expert warns against building the community to a peak too soon or too late by failing to time the critical activities precisely. Bond issue elections seem to prove that the campaign launch day should be exactly three weeks prior to voting day. This type of campaign depends heavily on a front-porch personal contact information program. If adequate time is not allowed for this element, the campaign will not achieve its goal.

BUDGETING EACH ITEM OF STRATEGY

To ensure the most defensible budget, the cost of every part of the strategy must be listed at the end of each event or activity. The approach easiest to sell to management will identify each item of value—goods or services—and list the estimated cost in a column to the right of the items column. It may be

BOX 10.9   School Bond Issue Voter Approval Campaign

Time Before Election	Tasks to Be Performed

4 months	Citizen advisory committee/precampaign planning
	    Leadership organized
	    Survey of community attitudes
	    Past campaigns studied
	    Plan voter registration drive

3 months	Citizen committee elects chair
	    Necessary committees appointed
	    Committees collect background data
	    Set timetable
	    Adopt budget
	    Plan election strategy
	    Select theme
	    Begin work on presentation and brochure

8 weeks	Announcement to papers of board meeting to set details Board meets to set date and details of bond election News story of board action Details of board action explained to school staffs Information meeting for all school staffs Board has information meeting with cross section of community Citizen committee chair announces effort, invites all citizens to special committee meeting Workers organized at this meeting Campaign funds solicited
7 weeks	Basic presentation completed Outline of speech and audiovisuals for presentations completed Basic brochure copy completed Voter registration drive started

6 weeks	Citizen committee meets, assigns jobs
	    Review basic presentation
	    Set deadlines
	    Committees report on plans
	    Progress report on registration drive
	    Keep newspaper informed of progress

5 weeks	Brochures ready for delivery from printer
	Posters, fliers, etc., should be ready
	Speaker groups should be trained
4 weeks	Campaign kickoff
	Community dinner held for opinion leaders
	First presentation of campaign plan at dinner
	Media representatives invited to dinner
	Voter registration drive ends
	Factual story in school paper about campaign
3 weeks	Begin speeches and presentations to community groups
	Election feature story to newspaper
	Letter, brochure to new registered voters
	Coffee hours in private homes
	Story on groups' endorsement to news media
	Preelection survey conducted
2 weeks	Advertisement 1 to run in local papers
	Block captains drop brochure at each home
	Letters to community ministers, priests, rabbis
	Election feature story 2 to newspaper
	Editorial to newspaper
	Preelection survey 2 conducted
	Coffee hours in private homes
1 week	Localized fliers distributed in neighborhoods
	Story on endorsements to news media
	Advertisement 2 to run in newspapers
	Last preelection survey
	Endorsement advertisement in newspaper just before election day
	Coffee hours conducted in private houses
Election day	Telephone campaign starts; babysitter service for voters
	Transportation service to polls; poll watchers
	"Vote Yes" cards distributed near polls
2 days after election day	Thank-you letters to all workers
	Financial report to all contributors
	Thank-you advertisement in paper
	Postelection survey conducted
	Thank-you party held for all workers

Source: School Finance Campaign Handbook, Washington, D.C.: NEA, 1969.

necessary to call a local business for cost estimates; if cost estimates are based on local contacts, include the contact person's name, the name of the company, and the telephone number. This will give the person who carries out the plan somewhere to start. The documentation of cost estimates in a plan gives additional credibility to the plan and gives credibility to the planners for their attention to detail.

Items provided or donated should also be included in the budget, such as the site or building where the event is to be held, contributed supplies, production or transportation and tradeout items—any item provided without cost. List the estimated cost for the item in an expenses column and enter "donated" in an actual cost column. In this way, the dollar value of items you have arranged for will be impressive, and the cost of items that must be purchased will be more palatable to the client. If there are any fund-raising events in the strategy, those should also be listed as revenue sources in a column with a separate heading and deducted from the total cost of the campaign. In most cases a fund-raising event will generate more revenue than it will cost; that, of course, will impress the client.

An example of a budget planned for an open house (Box 10.10) illustrates the points made above and shows how one might list different categories for various types of items. The "amount" column specifies the number of the listed items needed.

In another example—also an open house—a budget was calculated by estimating the value of no-cost items in order to come up with a total cost. The figures are an impressive indication of the dollar values that can be arranged by negotiating with organizations that share the same goals and by tradeout agreements (Box 10.11).

JUSTIFYING THE STRATEGY PLAN

The justification, or selling, of the campaign plan should be treated as part of the strategy plan. What may seem to be a wonderful strategy idea to the planning team often seems unappealing to decision makers. Even if there has been a close liaison with management during the planning process, it is necessary to convince management of the appeal of the total campaign plan, whether management is an instructor or a client.

If the planning process has taken the necessary steps, the best justification is a recitation of the logical decisions the planning team made in arriving at the final plan. Focus on the research that proved to you your selected strategy was best—most clients will find this the most compelling evidence. Liaison with the client should have indicated what arguments will be most effective, but if that is not known, assume a skeptical client attitude.

Such a sales pitch ought to be included in the campaign plan book so that the person reading the plan will be convinced. These justifications should also be included and elaborated on in the presentation to help sell the plan. This process is treated in the chapter on presentation later in this book. (See "Planning the Presentation at Two Levels," in Chapter 14.)

BOX 10.10   **Budget Plan for Open House for a Small Nonprofit Organization**

Item	Amount	Cost	Donated	Actual Cost
Supplies				
Podium materials	1	n/c	13.00	3.00
Box for "drawing"	1	handmade	15.00	
Tables	7	n/c		
Chairs	200	n/c	70.00	
4 cases of napkins		10.00	in stock	
Paper plates	200	6.75		6.75
Plastic utensils sets	200	17.00		17.00
Name tags	300	1.25 each		37.50
Bullhorn	1	n/c	10.00	
Subtotal			108.00	64.25
Production cost (print)				
Brochures	500	.05 each		20.00
Fliers	500	.04 each		20.00
Tickets (for entry)	300	3.00		
Coupons	200	4.00 per pg.		8.00
Schedules	200	.04 each		8.00
Thank-you letters		1.50	1.50	
Film for photo releases		32.00		32.00
Design of advertising		9.25 per day		55.20
Postage		25.00		25.00
			144.50	280.20
Transportation				
Delivery of communications, use of volunteers' cars		20.00	x	
Delivery of food		15.00	x	
			Total cost	487.95
Value of donated items			less	$144.50
Total actual cost				$343.45

BOX 10.11   **Budget for Open House Sponsored by Child Abuse Care Agency**

Item	Cost	Actual Cost
Film	$100.00	$100.00
R/TV PSAs	0.00	0.00
Fliers	20.00	20.00
Booklets	550.00	0.00
(Paid by tradeout advertising)		
Play	1,500.00	0.00
(Live production, cost estimated for 200 people at $5.00 per admission, all donated)		
Total cost	$2,170.00 Actual cost	$120.00

SUMMARY

Building a campaign strategy involves choosing the best strategic option to reach the campaign goal and providing the necessary details for the strategy to be effectively implemented. Steps in designing the specific strategy include (1) selecting the strategy, (2) testing the strategy, (3) outlining the communication plan, (4) coordinating all elements of the strategy on a calendar, (5) budgeting each action or event in the strategy, and (6) justifying the strategy to management.

Seven criteria contribute to successful strategies: (1) relationship between activity and sponsoring organization, (2) news value, (3) a compelling name, (4) a socially stimulated interest—the "bandwagon effect," (5) tie-ins, (6) tradeouts, and (7) a series of related events.

Testing the strategy. Before deciding on a strategy, an effort should be made to test its ability to perform as expected with the target public.

Designing the communication plan. The plan, based on insights of the Shannon and Weaver model, should include what will be communicated before, what will be communicated during, and what will be communicated after the events or actions package. Designating media channels poses new challenges with the advent of emerging media technologies. Before-, during-, and after-the-event communications each have specific requirements. A checklist of events with supporting communication types helps the strategy planner match events and communications.

Calendaring the total strategy. Timing a campaign involves fitting campaign elements to the annual calendar as well as the chronological sequence of various elements. Methods include wall calendar, Gantt chart, and chronology.

Budgeting each item of the strategy. Include actual costs as well as donated contributions of value. By using a "zero-based" budget approach that assumes *everything* in the budget must be paid for, it is easier to convince management that the cost of the campaign is a bargain when only certain items require cash. This can be accomplished by listing at fair market value those items that will be donated as well as those that will ordinarily be covered by the organization's regular budget.

Justifying the strategy plan to management "sells" it to decision makers by emphasizing the strategy plan and the logic that guided formulation of the plan.

FOR FURTHER READING

Atkin, Charles K. "Mass Media Information Campaign Effectiveness." In *Public Communication Campaigns*, ed. Ronald Rice and Wm. Paisley. Beverly Hills: Sage, 1981, 265–79.

Chase, William D., and Helen M. Chase, eds. *Chase's Annual Events.* New York: Contemporary Books, published annually.

Corbett, William. "Special Events." In *Experts in Action: Inside Public Relations*, ed. Bill Cantor and Chester Berger. New York: Longman, 1984, 227, 238.

Finn, David. "The Elements of Sound Public Relations Planning." In *The Forum.* New York: Ruder and Finn, Summer 1984.

Grunig, James E., and Todd Hunt. "Defining and Choosing Goals and Objectives." *Managing Public Relations.* New York: Holt, Rinehart & Winston, 1984, 114–37.

Heitpas, Quintin. "Planning." In *Experts in Action: Inside Public Reactions.* New York: Longman, 1984, 291–309.

Hyman, Herbert H., and Paul B. Sheatsley. "Some Reasons Why Information Campaigns Fail," *Public Opinion Quarterly* 11 (Fall 1947): 412–23.

Koestler, Frances. *Planning and Setting Objectives: Guidelines for Non-Profit Organizations.* New York: Foundation for Public Relations Research and Education, 1977.

Lerbinger, Otto. *Design for Persuasive Communication.* Englewood Cliffs, NJ: Prentice-Hall, 1972.

Mendelshon, Herold. "Some Reasons Why Information Campaigns Can Succeed," *Public Relations Quarterly* 37 (1973): 50–61.

Nager, Norman R., and T. Harrell Allen. "Creating Goals and Objectives." In *Public Relations Management by Objectives.* New York: Longman, 1984.

Tucker, Kerry, Doris Derelian, and Donna Rouner. *Public Relations Writing,* 2nd ed. Englewood Cliffs, NJ: Prentice-Hall, 1994.

Tucker, Jack. "Budgeting," *Public Relations Journal* 37 (March 1981): 14–17.

VanLeuven, James K. "Theoretical Models in Public Relations Campaigns," presented at the Conference on Communication Theory in Public Relations, Illinois State University, Normal, May 1987.

Implementation Strategy Cases

- Case Study: The "Pastahhh" Campaign of the National Pasta Association
- Case Study: The CSX Hay Train: Strategy in Action

➤ CASE STUDY: THE "PASTAHHH" CAMPAIGN OF THE NATIONAL PASTA ASSOCIATION[1]

The Pastahhh Situation Analysis Summary

1. **Statement of Perceived Problem-Situation.** The National Pasta Association (NPA) decided it was time for a change in its public relations effort on behalf of pasta to create excitement where "ho-hum" perceptions had existed.
2. **Identification of Ultimate Decision Maker.** The directors of the NPA would select one proposal in an open competition; the board of directors or a subcommittee would make the decision on which proposal to adopt based solely on the plan presented.
3. **Explanation of Liaison Arrangements.** No liaison for feedback on ideas would be possible because each proposal would be submitted competitively.

4. **Outline of Facts Needed to Confirm Nature of the Problem.** The campaign planner might need to (1) establish public perceptions of the product, (2) discover findings of previous research involving the product, (3) interview media editors, (4) consult experts on the status of the product, (5) study the history of the product and the culture associated with its consumption, (6) search computerized data bases for information on the product, (7) consult library sources, and (8) study the organizational culture of the client organization. Figure 11.1 shows how the culture of pasta differs throughout the country.

Pastahhh Problem-Situation

The public relations effort of the pasta industry trade association had been carried out by the same public relations firm for 35 years. These efforts had attempted to position pasta as a health-benefit food that is not fattening. The NPA felt that the program had created the public perception that pasta is a good basic food but is unexciting. In an effort to change this perception, the NPA invited proposals for a campaign to turn perceptions of pasta around. The research conducted in preparing the winning proposal confirmed the suspicions of the NPA.

The reader is encouraged to identify how this public relations campaign differs from what would be involved in a marketing campaign. Check your perceptions against the analysis of the difference between public relations and marketing in Chapter 1.

The Pastahhh Research Plan

After the situation is carefully analyzed and the possible research approaches have been listed, it is time to consider the research plan itself. The research plan is an outline of the research approaches or projects that will have to be carried out in order to collect the facts essential to planning the campaign. The approaches outlined in Chapter 3 will serve as a checklist for selecting the most suitable approaches to collecting these facts.

Note the range of research projects incorporated in the Pastahhh campaign:

1. The Research Problem Possible research projects as listed in the situation analysis include: establish public perceptions of pasta, discover findings of previous research involving pasta, interview media food editors, consult nutritionists on status of pasta, study the history of pasta and the culture associated with its consumption, search computerized data bases for information on pasta, consult library sources, and study the organizational culture of NPA. Of the list, six projects were obviously carried out, two were not, and three additional projects were discerned that had been conducted as the need arose. The case study reveals these elements of the actual research plan:

Figure 11.1 The Pastahhh campaign provided graphic art for use in publications telling their story. Such photo mechanical transfers (PMTs) as these help editors tell a story when using printed material supplied in a public relations effort.

- **Public perceptions.** Two projects were mentioned in the case study designed specifically to determine public perceptions of pasta: focus group interviews and in-supermarket interviews. The case also mentions that restaurant reviewers were "balloted," but no other mention of this research project is included in the report.

- **Previous research.** Reference in the case study to "secondary research" indicates the importance of examining existing research findings.
- **Media food editors.** Survey of leading food editors noted in the "research" section of the case study confirms the significance of this type of research.
- **Nutritionists.** No indication of consultation with nutritionists is evident in the case study. However, the article "Pasta" in the October 1987 *Atlantic Monthly* reveals considerable research into the nutritional value of pasta. The research was evidently done but not mentioned in the case study.
- **History and culture of pasta.** Again, the case study did not mention research into the lore of the product. The *Atlantic Monthly* article is a rich store of information about the cultural tradition of pasta from its origins to the associations with the various cultural heritages related to it in this and other countries.
- **Search of data bases.** No evidence is apparent in the case study or elsewhere of the use of data base searches for information about pasta.
- **Library research.** Mention of "secondary research" in the case study, as well as ample evidence of such in the published stories, indicates that this type of research played an important part in the campaign. A mention of "per capita consumption" of pasta also reveals that detailed data on the product were collected, probably from library research.
- **Study of organizational culture (of NPA).** Published material from the campaign effort gives clear evidence that this type of research was done, but the technique is not mentioned in the case.
- **Lobbying support.** Research to support the need to influence legislation is not mentioned in the case, but it is evident that such a need existed and that research on that need was conducted.

2. Identification of Research Projects   The case summary gives no detailed information about how any of the projects were carried out. One may presume that the focus group interviews, balloting of editors, and in-supermarket interviews were conducted as specific research projects. Other projects were more in the nature of fact-gathering research of a less sophisticated nature.

3. Description of Research Design   No research design is mentioned for the more formal techniques of focus group interviews, balloting of editors, and in-supermarket interviews. One may presume that these and the fact-gathering techniques were organized with some formal structure.

4. Research Report Form   Research reports in general should be summaries of the findings of the project. The fact-gathering information summarized will be different from a survey and from library research, but the information will be in summary form in either case. For simple fact gathering the report need be only a list of findings with a summary of the list and an indication of how the information was collected. Some facts may simply be listed.

Each research project is an effort to find an answer to a research problem. The problem in the Pastahhh case was: What is the nature of the lack of excitement about pasta, and how do attitudes differ among the public? Such a problem cannot be solved until it is phrased in the form of a suitable research question. Several questions suggest themselves: Why are food purchasers and others unexcited about pasta? What feelings do they have about the product? How did they come to have such attitudes? How many people feel that way? Is the perceived lack of excitement true?

Not all of these questions are important to the public relations effort. Two major research questions need to be addressed in this case:

"What is the nature of the lack of excitement?" Which issues should guide construction of the message to correct misunderstandings or misconceptions?

"What are the dimensions of the lack of excitement?" How many people share the feeling, and to what degree? In what segments of the population are they concentrated?

By allowing for responses across the full range of attitudes or inclinations toward the situation, the research can identify the categories of information and misunderstanding that describe the true nature of the situation. This can be done by collecting demographic descriptions of those who supply answers to these questions, such as age, sex, eating habits, purchasing patterns, and media use, as well as life-style descriptions, such as frequency of eating out, preference for pasta, and the context of eating pasta. The answers to these questions help the researcher judge the nature and dimensions of the problem.

Once the problem has been refined into a research question that can be answered by the appropriate people, and to the degree that it identifies the nature of the public relations challenge to be met, the research plan is well focused. Next, the procedure for answering the research question, or research design, must be determined.

The research procedure, often called methodology, involves *how* you expect to find the answer to the research question. The research types and techniques described in Chapter 3, as well as the list used in Silver Anvil winning entries described later in this chapter, may help in deciding which procedures would work best. The two most commonly used research techniques mentioned in the Silver Anvil entries are polls and interviews. This fact suggests that these at least should be considered. Library research, observation, research of the organization's records as well as its culture, review of past research, and case studies are also popular approaches.

Specific aspects of the research procedure that should be decided are the types of research: (1) Where is the information to be found? It may be a certain group of people, it may be the library, or it may be in studies conducted by others. There are many possibilities. The research techniques also need to be decided: (2) How will the information be collected? Will a questionnaire be used, as used in focused interviews or as used in polling? Will you use a list of topics or questions, as used in individual interviews, library research, or in observation? (3) How confident do you have to be of the results? Will you need to use random sampling to ensure that results are representative? Will you need a system for collecting information to increase its representativeness, such as is often used in library research? (4) What is the time frame for conducting and completing the research project?

Based on research findings on the topics above, the following adaptation plan was devised.

Adaptation Plan

1. Problem Statement (repeated here for convenience)   Consumers think pasta is fattening; NPA is not recognized among food editors; consumers and food editors like the product, smiled when thinking of it, but generally had a "ho-hum" reaction; NPA members felt it was a good product but unexciting.

2. Goal (repeated here for convenience)   "The Pastahhh public relations effort was designed to add emotion to the product, to excite consumers, the media and members."

3. Target Publics   Two major and two minor publics were identified: consumers, divided into working women, singles, and families; the media, especially food editors; NPA members; and government, in order to "pave the way for good relations on Capitol Hill." Research helped to identify the target publics for the campaign; "Statistics tell us that the heaviest users of pasta are mothers, aged 35–44, in households with more than five persons. This consumer buys pasta because it is economical, nutritious, and convenient for her large family. (Interestingly, the black counterpart to this consumer uses much less pasta.)"

Further characterization of the target public resulted from careful study of Simmons market research data and the results of focus group interviews. "More recently, pasta is playing a more prominent role in other major lifestyle trends of the eighties and nineties. These trends mainly center around 'baby boomers.' This large consumer group is upscale, educated, interested in fitness, looking for convenience and economy but demanding a certain amount of 'chic' in much that they do."[2]

4. Organizational Assessment   The National Pasta Association for 35 years had carried on a program through the same public relations firm promoting the health benefits of pasta, emphasizing that it isn't really fattening. While not exactly "stodgy," NPA had the capacity to be much more exciting.

The proposal contains this analysis of "The Industry":

The U.S. Pasta Industry was once made of 250 small, regional companies with strong individual distribution ties. Since then, large food marketers have recognized the opportunities to be found in complex carbohydrate foods and caused a structural change of the industry by acquisition.

In the past two decades, six large food corporations have been responsible for the acquisition of 19 local-regional pasta producers. This has resulted in considerable consolidation and increased advertising of pasta based products with the long term goal of establishing a national brand.

Regional brand loyalty and regional distribution systems having remained strong have caused some of the big names to abandon the national brand. Mekessen, Pillsbury and Coca-Cola have all sold or agreed to sell their pasta interest because of the lack-luster response to the strategy of a national brand.

But this glitch has not impeded others trying to establish a national brand or the overall vigor of industry sales. The pasta industry is still growing three times faster than other dry groceries and new companies, such as General Foods, are entering the market. Marketers are also moving to new market strategies such as the establishment of value added products like frozen food pasta dishes, high protein pasta and "diet" or light pasta.

Competitive behavior of other marketers has been making inroads into the dry pasta industry. Fresh pasta products are found in most supermarkets today and imports have reached $55 million with its market growing 50% this year.

In addition, aggressive marketing efforts by competitive food products such as potatoes will continue to affect the pasta industry. The recent introduction of pasta fast food chains is one area where the impact on the pasta industry is yet to be determined.[3]

5. A "Shopping List" of Possible Actions or Objectives   The guidelines were to: create news, add fun, involve audiences, target different programs to different audiences, and focus on "big ideas" that would go "beyond recipe drops to big feature coverage." Specific objectives were identified: generate favorable "emotional" media coverage, increase visibility of NPA among media, pave the way for good relations on Capitol Hill, support industry goal of increased per capita pasta consumption, and excite NPA members about the campaign.

The proposal contains some 21 activities within the campaign. As an indication that a shopping list of ideas was used to come up with this list of 21, three additional activities are suggested in an appendix labeled "Other Ideas."

6. Limitations   Although no time limit was specified in the case summary, the campaign was based on the annual calendar. The possibility of changing aspects or emphasis of the campaign in ensuing years could thus be monitored and incorporated. Budget and personnel limits were specified as $275,000, which covered staff time plus direct expenses. As indicated elsewhere in the proposal, the firm offers the services of 55 full-time employees, and four persons will be assigned to the account team.

7. Liaison   Once the campaign proposal is accepted by the client management, a regular working arrangement must be determined that will be satisfactory to both parties. The proposal included a suggested assignment of staff to the new account:

Account Team
Staffing of an account within the agency is always a crucial decision. Providing the account with the proper experience, talents and staff support can make all the difference in the quality of the results. Finding the experience and skill for NPA's public relations campaign within HJK&A is not difficult; there are a number of account service professionals who have worked on accounts which incorporated similar challenges.

We offer NPA the following account management team:

Senior Management Supervisor for the account will be _____, CEO of HJK&A. He will be involved in the long range strategic planning of the account.

Account Supervisor for the account will be _____, who will be responsible for the management of the public relations program and will serve as chief coordinator of the various program elements.

An *Account Executive* will be assigned to assist _____ in the day-to-day operations of the account.

Creative Supervisor will be _____, who will be responsible for the creative development of collateral.[4]

A close and continuous liaison between Kaufman and the client NPA may be inferred, since the summary noted that NPA's president visited top food editors in the editors' own offices and reacted favorably to the *Pastahhh Newsletter* as "a guaranteed smile for pasta four times a year." Also, material from the campaign was incorporated into the NPA annual meeting.

Strategy Plan

1. Problem Statement (repeated here for convenience) Consumers think pasta is fattening; NPA is not recognized among food editors; consumers and food editors like the product, smiled when thinking of it, but generally had a "ho-hum" reaction; NPA members felt it was a good product but unexciting.

2. Goal (repeated here for convenience) "The Pastahhh public relations effort was designed to add emotion to the product, to excite consumers, the media, and members."

3. Strategy Options The campaign proposal listed a number of possibilities. One was a "Campaign Umbrella—Theme/Graphic" that would be used "to convey the primary message in a believable and memorable way." The rationale for the actual theme/graphic (Pastahhh) (see Figure 11.2), called a "themeline," was presented this way:

A theme unifies each element of the program so that the whole campaign works together to be more than the sum of its parts. At the end of the year, when you put all the campaign elements on one conference table it should look like a campaign—with color scheme, design and message—all unmistakably NPA and clearly from the same source. This kind of coordinated effort helps develop a positive, recognizable image for NPA's PR program among members, media, and, in time, consumers.

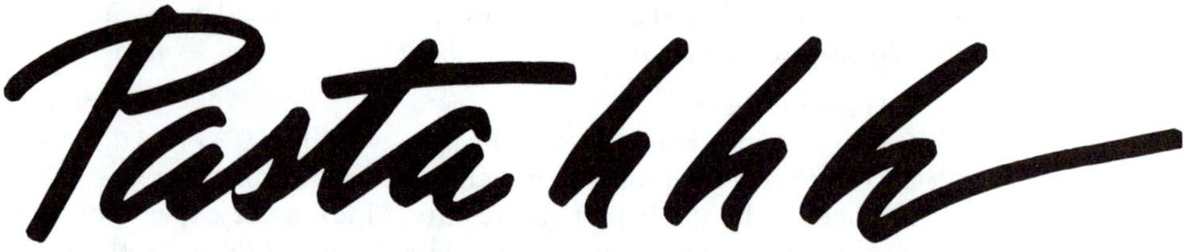

Figure 11.2 Pastahhh themeline.

Developing a theme at the start of a campaign also saves money. How? By avoiding the expense of "re-thinking" the design of every campaign element to be produced. Whether it's a press kit, news release, letterhead, a pamphlet, a newsletter, banner or a press invitation, the graphics would be consistent.

There are some very specific criteria we would use in developing a Pasta themeline. First, we feel the themeline must be broad enough to serve as the banner, or umbrella, for all of the product's benefits. Any themeline that only extols one or two virtues of Pasta would be limiting. Second, we feel that the themeline, like all good themelines should be short, "catchy," and memorable. Third, we don't want the themeline to be static. We want a themeline that emanates a positive, happy feeling—a feeling that reflects the smiles we want to come to people's faces when they talk about Pasta.[5]

Other possibilities for the strategy included both the suggestions incorporated in the proposed campaign and "other ideas." The specific campaign elements were:

Target Pamphlets—a series of pamphlets which personalize our message to specific target audiences, each with a section of basic pasta facts that communicate NPA's complete message (see Figure 11.3).

Project—Food Editor's Pasta Yearbook—a "keep-on-the-shelf" three-ring notebook to elevate the status of pasta in the minds of food editors, from noodles under the sauce to an awareness that pasta is a whole food category deserving regular and varied editorial coverage.

Pasta Yearbook Plus—print overruns of selected portions of the above yearbook to be mailed to targeted specialty publications: items of interest to senior citizens mailed to publications with heavy readership among seniors, for example.

Pasta Cooking Seminar for Food Editors—an annual event in which food editors would be invited to cook-along-with-the-chef; with invitations on aprons, reminders on pasta cooking utensils, print materials for distribution, and photos with the celebrity chef mailed with thank-you notes and diploma.

Feature Article Placement—articles tailored to specific targeted readership of magazines offering a target pamphlet; *Working Woman, Working Mother, Weight Watchers Magazine, Good Housekeeping, Parents, Bon Appetit*, for example.

Pasta Newsletter—a four-page quarterly to reach a wide range of media people and influentials with "short, breezy and interesting information about Pasta" (see Figure 11.4).

Figure 11.3 Pastahhh campaign brochures were designed for subgroups of the targeted public, each of which was found to have different needs as pasta consumers. Families were told "You want to keep within your food budget—but not at the expense of your family's nutritional needs." To working women, the brochure suggested in a headline: "Home at 6, dinner by 6:30." To singles, the brochure noted: "Reducing a recipe for six to a serving for one may take more time than you want to put into a meal. Let pasta do the work for you."

The Pasta Lover's Club—everyone's a pasta lover, but this makes it official; offers visible evidence of a growing interest that deserves editorial attention and news hooks for such events as annual cooking contest, annual awards, and honorary memberships for celebrities/athletes.

Spokesperson—carefully selected and approved by NPA to appear on radio, TV, and interviews for print, in bimonthly city tours, and as a participant at selected special events.

Suburban Newspapers—to target Middle America, "we recommend distributing targeting columns to 3,800" of these publications that are well read by the family-oriented who are also interested in home cooking.

Market Expansion Program—a specific budget proportion devoted to black and Hispanic "underutilizers of Pasta," with rice-alternative recipes; to minority newspapers, magazines, and radio stations; and to tie-ins with such as National Blood Pressure Education Program.

Pasta on Radio—three radio features each quarter highlighting a special event to form the basis for a radio news feature to be distributed by satellite, with narrative and actuality interview.

Figure 11.4 The Pastahhh newsletter, designed to reach a wide range of media people and influentials, includes such regular features as letters to the editor with answers, popular recipes, quotable quotes, and with an application for membership in the Pastahhh Lover's Club along with a note that Clint Eastwood, Garfield the cat, Johnny Carson, and Michael J. Fox are all honorary members.

Pasta Restaurants of the Year—survey of restaurant critics to select leading pasta restaurants in country's top-ten markets, with a map of these distributed to media for coverage; event has many offshoot possibilities.

Political Pasta—to emphasize industry's importance to the U.S. economy, politicians would be served a wide variety of pasta dishes, perhaps a favorite recipe from each state, with high potential media coverage.

TV News Features—a two- to five-minute video news feature about pasta using "Pastamania" theme, with a two-minute harder news piece for satellite release using NPA executive, spokesperson, footage from Political Pasta or Pasta Lover's Club; analysis of usage to be by telephone survey.

Meal Planning Competition—directed at institutional meal planners for eventual exposure to important trade audiences, with use of follow-up materials in promotions such as quotes used as "pastamonials," all targeted to such publics as students, nursing homes, hospitals, schools, food contractors, and others.

In addition to the specific campaign elements suggested in the proposal, three "other ideas" are offered:

Personality Pasta Gala—a special media event with a Hollywood host and invited celebrities and athletes designed for a late-night TV format such as "Entertainment Tonight."

Game Shows—arrange for a client's most important message to be the topic for a question on, for example, "Hollywood Squares."

Supermarket Pasta Meals—in a coalition with other generic food associations, feature a pasta recipe of the week with point-of-purchase flags for ingredients. After gaining one store's cooperation, use case histories to promote the program with others and place related features in magazines such as *Progressive Grocer*.

4. Strategy Fit to Target Publics   The elements of the strategy were selected to match the publics targeted for the campaign. Moreover, the strategy elements often double up to reach the critical publics in several complementary ways. The primary target publics were identified as blacks, Middle America, working women, singles, and entertainment personalities. In addition, several intermediary publics were identified through whom the primary publics can be reached by means of coalitions and tie-ins or tradeouts. These included the media in general—food editors, suburban newspapers, specialized publications editors, television producers, and radio programmers; politicians; show business and sports personalities; other generic food associations; food-serving institutions; restaurant critics; and professional associations with interest in food and nutrition.

Examples of matching strategy elements to targeted publics would include:

- Target pamphlets—to food editors and consumers with specialized interests in particular types of pasta
- Editor's yearbook—to food editors
- Yearbook plus—to specialized publication editors
- Cooking seminar—to food editors
- Feature article placement—to general-interest and food magazines
- Newsletter—to influentials and pasta enthusiasts
- Pasta club—to influentials and pasta enthusiasts as well as media editors who receive information about club activities
- Spokesperson—to event participants, media editors, and general public
- Suburban press editors—to reach families and home cooking specialists
- Market expansion—to reach minorities
- Radio features—to general public
- Restaurant of the year—to reach food editors

- Political pasta—to reach politicians and, through them, editors and the general public
- Meal planning competition—to reach institutional food organizations and those who eat there, as well as the media and the general public

5. Use of Special Resources, Coalitions, Tie-Ins, and Tradeouts   A number of creative strategic ideas are included in the campaign proposal, including coalitions with such organizations as institutional food servers, American Heart Association, American Dietetic Association, and National Food Service Association, who have a mutual interest in Health foods and appealing to institutional diners' palates. The Political Pasta event brought together NPA's interests with politicians' interests in the public benefits the pasta industry offers and the tie-in with favorite state recipes. The interests of NPA and the black community converged in the common concern about blood pressure.

The proposal specifically addresses the tie-in potential of the campaign as follows:

Tie-Ins

Through our public relations program, consumers will be persuaded to eat more pasta. While NPA members will reap the greatest benefit from the program, there will be a residual effect for the manufacturers of other pasta-related products, i.e. sauces, cookware, etc.

Therefore, it makes good marketing sense for other manufacturers to support NPA's efforts. With our tie-in program, we'll explore the possibilities of staging joint publicity events and special promotions in order to maximize NPA's budgets. One example of a tie-in effort might be to arrange for distribution of our Pasta pamphlets in every spaghetti pot which is sold. Another is coordination with sauce makers to include Pasta Club membership information on every label. There are a number of other possibilities and tie-ins with food associations, cooking utensils, wines, etc.[6]

6. Communication Before, During, and After   Each of the many strategy elements would require an announcement of some sort directed to the targeted public. Not all of these details are included in the case history or in the proposal to the NPA. Examples of these may be seen in the "Pasta Cooking Seminar for Food Editors." *Before* the event, "invitations would be sent on Pasta aprons" and "reminders would be sent on Pasta cooking utensils." *During* this event, attending editors would receive a copy of the Food Editor's Pasta Yearbook and a premiere issue of the Pasta Newsletter. Photographs would be taken of each of the editors with the celebrity chef. *After the event,* follow-up thank-you notes would include this photograph, framed, along with a diploma signifying successful completion of the cooking seminar.

Evaluation Plan

1. Problem Statement (repeated here for convenience)   Consumers think pasta is fattening; NPA is not recognized among food editors; consumers and food editors like the product, smiled when thinking of it, but generally had a "ho-hum" reaction; NPA members felt it was a good product but unexciting.

2. Goal (repeated here for convenience)   "The Pastahhh public relations effort was designed to add emotion to the product, to excite consumers, the media, and members."

This goal was expanded to five specific "objectives:" generate favorable, "emotional" media coverage; increase visibility of NPA among media; pave the way for good relations on Capitol Hill; support industry goal to increase per capita pasta consumption; and excite members about program. Each of these is directly addressed in achievements listed below.

Second year variation: "Fun; sell emotion, not product; use health/diet secondarily."

Third year variation: "Continue to use Pastahhh as an umbrella for various messages about pasta; continue to position pasta as a fun food that makes you feel good but de-emphasize pasta being fashionable now; use pasta's varied attributes to create new story angles as per needs of individual editors; support pasta's move to mainstream by associating pasta with established (not fad) health and nutrition recommendations."

3. Contingency Plans   The initial (first year) Pastahhh campaign contingency plan consisted primarily of additional activities that could be included in the plan at the discretion of the client and according to availability of funds. Three contingent activities were proposed: a Personality Pasta Gala, involving celebrities and athletes in a Hollywood Pasta Party; game shows, arranging for NPA topic as a question on such programs as "Hollywood Squares"; and Supermarket Pasta Meals, featuring a pasta recipe of the week with ingredients flagged at point of purchase.

Second year variation: "Part of this budget will be used for unforeseen opportunities that arise such as the many requests from editors and reporters for nutritional information, calorie counts, photographs, recipes, entertaining ideas, cooking tips, etc. Almost everyday something comes up that doesn't fit into our other programs."

In addition to this basic contingency plan, the second year proposal also included "Recommended Programs (if additional funds become available)." In priority order, these included the following: (1) A Meal Planning competition, inviting entrants from such categories as students, schools, nursing homes, hospitals, and food contractors to develop a one-month meal plan. Executives of the American Dietetic Association (ADA) and the National Food Service Association and editors of appropriate trade journals would be selected as judges; program would reach decision makers, future decision makers, and influentials in food service by providing useful source material for publicity and promotions. (2) A Political Pasta variation on successful first-year effort, would serve famous Democrats' and Republicans' favorite pasta dishes or invite political wives to cook. Media coverage would again be encouraged at local and national levels. (3) A Pasta Month Editor's Kit based on 1985 requests for editorial material would contain recipes for each day of Pasta Month, photos, press releases, camera-ready art, and backgrounders. (4) A Trade Press Program would develop press release, pamphlets, newsletter for in-store use, and a feature-length article all targeting food service and restaurant trade publications.

A subsequent variation: Two activities were proposed as "Optional Programs:" (1) A Radio Pasta Series of cooking "demonstrations" consisting of three prerecorded spots with our spokesperson or other authority to discuss trends and provide cooking tips to be mailed to stations throughout the country and (2) an NPA Recipe Collector, beginning with NPA members' favorite recipes with space for consumers and food editors to add their own favorites.

4. List of Ways to Collect and Codify Data   The first year proposal for Pastahhh included three approaches to be used to measure the effectiveness of the public relations campaign. The proposal gave these specific suggestions:

> It is important to measure the effectiveness of any communications campaign in terms of its effect in the marketplace. There are a number of possible ways to do this. A few of these methods are described below.
>
> - *Industry volume measures.* Any changes in the volume produced by the pasta industry can be attributed to the campaign, all other variables being equal. Reports prepared by Simmons provide this type of information on a total basis as well as by various demographic breakouts. A copy of the 1983 Simmons report is included in this proposal.
> - *Individual consumption measures.* Although the changes brought about by the pasta campaign may not be dramatic enough to significantly change the industry volume, they may change individual consumers habits. Consumption is typically measured through a diary panel (i.e. consumers who have agreed to monitor all their food/drink consumption over a period of time. The monitoring is done by completing a daily diary of consumption). A measure of consumption for all pasta can be made before the campaign to establish a benchmark and once again well into the campaign to determine any changes.
> - *Advertising/communications awareness research.* This type of research can measure the specific impact of the advertising in terms of whether consumers are aware of the campaign and what they think of it. Once again, this is done on a pre-cost basis. However, it should be pointed out that such techniques may not be sensitive enough to measure differences in this instance because of the nature of public relations campaigns.
>
> Industry volume measures are not typically measured through market research. The other two, however are. Diary panels such as NPD and NET are available and purchase of various categories of data can be made. Awareness is typically custom designed.[7]

5. List of Ways to Measure Degree of Goal Achievement   The case study report summary listed five measures of goal achievement: extensive media coverage, change in recognition of NPA, an improved lobbying environment, increased per capital consumption of pasta, and incorporation of Pastahhh materials in all of NPA activities.

Media coverage was described as "extensive" with exposures totaling over 600 million (see Figure 11.5). "What's more, publicity has been favorable, fun

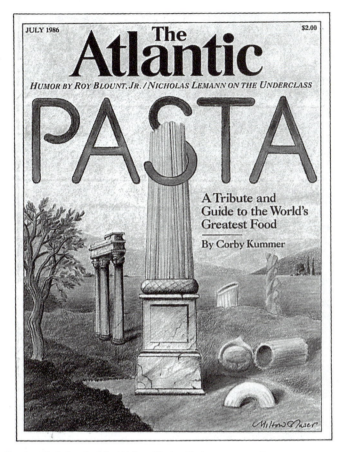

Figure 11.5 Cover of *Atlantic Monthly* with lead story on pasta.

and emotional. 'Pastahhh' is a frequent headline. Major features have appeared in *Good Housekeeping, McCalls, Parade, Food & Wine, Atlantic Monthly, Seventeen, Restaurant and Institutions, American Health, Shape, The Runner, Ladies Home Journal* and many more. Newspaper color food features regularly cover the news created by all our program from Pasta Month to the Spaghetti Search."

These measures are specific achievements of objective number two, which was to generate favorable "emotional" media coverage. While coverage was well documented, documentation of the "emotional" nature of the coverage rested on the emotional appeals of the coverage and the fact that editors "loved" the newsletter.

Recognition for NPA improved dramatically. "Virtually every food editor who was called in a follow-up survey was familiar with NPA, remembered getting the *Pastahhh Newsletter* and loved it." This achievement was a fulfillment of part of the goal, which was to increase visibility of NPA among media.

The lobbying environment on Capitol Hill improved largely through the newsletter, NPA staff–issued congressional product mailings, and Political

Pasta. The mailing of products to congresspeople appears to be the only activity not directly carried out as a part of the planned campaign. As a result of these activities, the case study report notes, "During a difficult year for many commodities NPA was singled out among dozens of trade associations to state its case to trade representative Clayton Yeutter during a formal hearing." This achievement fulfilled the objective of paving the way for good relations on Capitol Hill.

The proposal was careful to point out that "all other things being equal" changes in volume of consumption "can be attributed to the campaign." The evaluation thus took credit for an increase in per capita consumption, "up 1 lb, from 11 lbs to 12 lbs a year." This achievement fulfilled the objective of supporting industry goals of increasing pasta consumption.

The incorporation of the Pastahhh campaign into all NPA activities was achieved, as evidenced by campaign materials "appearing on everything from annual convention materials to gifts for influentials." The report of the campaign's evaluation noted, "Member awareness and satisfaction is high."

6. Record of Lessons for Future Applications   The campaign recorded results for incorporation into future plans in two ways; the summary of the campaign listed "a few specific examples," and each year a plan for the coming year used the results as a basis for a new round of activities.

The specific examples included the following:

- Together, the *Pastahhh Newsletter* and the Pasta Lover's Club have generated more than $20,000 for NPA.
- Over 900 entries were received for the Great American Spaghetti Sauce Search.
- *Good Housekeeping* had no plans for pasta feature in 1987. After our Press-Event-in-a-Basket visit, the I Love Pasta cookbook 23-page feature was scheduled.
- *Pastahhh Newsletter* topics and art are often picked up directly.
- Hundreds of editors requested Pastahhh media kits for Pasta Month 1986.
- The *Pastahhh Newsletter* has over 3,000 paid subscribers.
- The Pasta Restaurants program has resulted in local coverage and restaurant promotion. The *Chicago Tribune* has just launched a Pasta Restaurant Challenge fashioned after our concept.[8]

The results of the previous two years' effort were incorporated in the proposed plan for continuing the Pastahhh campaign for 1987–88. Incorporated into the introduction for the "National Pasta Association Public Relations Plan for 1987–88," the application of campaign results for the next year are detailed as follows:

Both the consumer marketplace and the National Pasta Association have changed dramatically since late 1984 when HJK&A first presented the product promotion program plan in New York.

   By all measures, it has been a dynamic period for NPA. The trade case on imported pasta has been a roller coaster of good news and bad news with, fortunately, a favorable resolution at last which may have tremendous positive impact as time goes on. Government monies to promote American pasta abroad have been made available to domestic manufacturers through NPA, opening the door to new opportunities and new markets. The pasta industry is shrinking, with large conglomerates buying up small and not so small pasta manufacturers. The industry has continued to move from family business to big business, changing the nature of the companies involved as well as the profile of the people in leadership roles.

The marketplace has changed too. Pasta is moving from trendy to maindstream. This is evidenced by an infusion of new pasta and pasta-related products from jarred pasta meals to an abundance of frozen prepared pasta dinners to the new product category of dry and liquid prepared pasta sauces and pre-mixed spice and cheese preparations. Our guess is that a consumer survey today would find an increase in the number of Americans who call pasta "pasta" as opposed to spaghetti, macaroni or noodle.

One thing statistics do show—both per capital consumption and gross sales of pasta are up:

EVALUATION BY COMPARING CONSUMPTION PATTERNS

Per capita pasta consumption

1984	11.6 lbs per person
1985	11.2 lbs per person
1986 (projected)	12.0 lbs per person

Gross pasta sales

1984	$1.34 billion
1985	1.37 billion (up 2.2%)
1986 (projected)	1.53 billion (up 11.7%)

Source: U.S. Department of Commerce.

What happened in 1985 to reverse the downward trend in per capita pasta consumption? What happened in 1985 to increase gross pasta sales more than ten percent? Is it coincidence that these increases directly paralleled the launch of the "Pastahhh" public relations effort? We find these "coincidences" often with generic marketing programs for associations.

Reviewing the results of the PR effort in terms of numbers of communications exposures sheds more light on impact:

COMMUNICATIONS EXPOSURES
1985–1986

Newspaper	1,399,074,225
Magazine	425,877,558
Broadcast	2,984,000
	1,827,935,783

Other measurements of success for the PR program include:

- 904 entries were submitted for NPA's Great American Spaghetti Sauce Search
- 3,700 members of Pasta Lover's Club ($18,500 income)
- 3,300 paid subscribers to *Pastahhh Newsletter* ($6,500 income)

Where do we go from here? The following recommendations for 1987–88 reflect our thinking in light of the changes in the marketplace. We want to keep the momentum going for media exposure in the billions and sales increases in the double digit percentages. That is what this plan is all about.[9]

➤ CASE STUDY: THE CSX HAY TRAIN: STRATEGY IN ACTION

I always believed if you stop and help somebody out, someday the good will come back to you.
  —*William Lappin, a North Liberty, Indiana dairy farmer, and one of the many volunteers who helped load the "Hoosier Hay Express"*

This statement reflects the proactive public relations strategy employed by the more successful corporations of our day. Businesses as well as individuals have found that a policy of being a good neighbor and helping out those who face hardships will bring a good return. Wise business leaders realize that the general public is informed, alert, well educated, and interested in the full range of business activities; they will therefore understand that public scrutiny of their enterprises has increased to the point where today's public opinion may become tomorrow's legislation for better or worse. Lou Golden quotes the chairman of General Motors:

The goals of General Motors are to serve society and in so doing to benefit its owners. This is accomplished first of all, by producing and merchandising products that are attractive, dependable and of high quality. A second requirement is that the company be alert to the development of new products and new processes. It must be a good place to work, a good neighbor in its plant communities, a good firm to do business with, and a good corporate citizen.[10]

Astute corporate leaders have long recognized, as Lou Golden observed, that "people won't be fooled by verbal smokescreens or moral pretensions behind which institutions can operate as they choose." Golden's insight, a result of serving an impressive number of major corporation executives, is that today's consumer is too savvy to believe undocumented claims of corporate social responsibility. Public relations will falter if it is carried out by the top management of the organization simply as an ornamental affection. No business decision may be considered without regard for its potential public impact.

Often, American business has taken the myopic view that business exists to create profits that will eventually trickle back into the society. The political environment of public opinion, however, has changed the acceptable norms of business practice. The public will no longer accept a narrow definition of corporate social responsibility. For anyone who doubts such claims, a look into the investment, consumer affairs, and employee rights litigation that pervades corporate life will reveal the degree to which business leaders are held accountable for their actions. The citizen's relationships with various business enterprises, reflecting the interests of society as a whole, are expressed through government legislation and regulation.

BOX 11.1   Strategies Used in 1994 Silver Anvil Winning Campaigns

Based on the checklist of responses to public relations problems listed elsewhere in this book, the approaches most often used are presented here as a guide to planning campaign strategy. Since most campaigns use more than one type of activity, the numbers in the list do not reflect the total number of 36 campaigns in the series of winners.

Number of Usages	Activity Type Used in Strategy
68	*Public Information Program*—the dissemination of information and publicity material emphasizing the point of view of the sponsoring organization: news releases, brochures, magazines, books, etc.
30	*Staged or Special Events*—activities invented to attract public and media attention and/or to generate publicity, such as dedications, ground breakings, tree plantings, seminars, and conferences.
22	*Personality Appearance, Spokesperson Media Tour*—selection of a celebrity or expert to represent and disseminate information about an organization or product.
13	*Promotional Materials*—use of novelty items, caps, T-shirts, buttons, pins, and the like as collateral material in promoting an organization or event.
11	*Meetings, Conventions, Seminars*—capitalizing on the publicity value of information-exchanging assemblies to build recognition of the organization and disseminate information.
10	*News Conference or Editors Conference*—invitation to the announcement of significant, timely news by a knowledgeable spokesperson to all news media.
10	*Contests, Competitions*—attempt to establish the best, fastest, largest, smallest—to set a record or other mark of excellence.
9	*Demonstration, Dramatization*—acting out or showing how something works or representation of popular sentiment on an issue.
8	*Contracted and/or Sponsored Research*—independent documentation of facts on a controversial issue, useful in answering misinformation and in achieving credible publicity.
6	*Marketing-Related Activities*—focusing efforts on matching consumer products with the needs of the consumer, especially trade shows, product demonstrations, product tests, and product publicity.

(*continues*)

5	*Information Booths, Exhibits, and/or Displays*—dispensing information important to a group of people gathered in one location.
5	*Celebration Event*—occasion marking special day, week, or month to recognize laudatory acts or memorable times, including anniversaries, founder's day, and national secretary's day.
3	*Speakers Bureau*—providing expert, trained speakers for programming needs of clubs, service organizations, and schools, as well as valuable publicity for the sponsor.
2	*Natural Events*—reaction to a naturally occurring event, from mergers, profit statements, discoveries, inventions, to acts of heroism and executive appointments.
2	*Establishment of an Organization*—enlistment of supporters of an organization into an identifiable group for cooperative effort and mutual benefit.
1	*Lobbying*—legitimate function of providing accurate information to lawmakers and feedback to the organization to promote the organization's interests.
0	*Indirect (Grass-Roots) Lobbying*—effort to influence the legislative process by organizing voters to bring pressure on legislators.
0	*Reaction to Misinformation or False Allegation*—effort to correct false information, usually from sincere but misguided sources; often accompanied by action that refutes the falsehood without lending it credence by direct denial.
0	*Fund-raising*—efforts or events designed to raise money from foundations, the public, or corporations; often used to supplement a limited campaign budget.
0	*Social Responsibility Efforts*—activities in which an organization or its employees engage as a benefit to the community or society at large and offer positive publicity.

The public relations professional has the opportunity to prove the broad social value of an enterprise by demonstrating how the corporation fulfills its good neighbor role. By employing such a strategy for the long-term goodwill of all its publics, a business can establish its enduring benefit to customer and community alike. As Golden reminds us, "On the day that management forgets that an institution cannot exist if the general public feels that it is not useful, or it is anti-social . . . the institution will begin to die."[11]

The CSX Hay Train Case

The Hay Train case examines a corporate good-neighbor policy as it was expressed in a natural event within the CSX service area. The corporation, in its current configuration, was conceived in an era of regulation and adapted its changing responsibilities to the bottom-line demands of business and the neighborly respect of its public constituency. The strategy not only promised benefits for the corporation for years to come but also won the corporation wide recognition for its immediate benefit to the people of the states it serves and the farm community in a much larger circle.

The corporation's general statement of purpose, or mission statement, is that it seeks to become the premier international transportation and resources company by serving its customers and fulfilling its role as a good citizen in the communities in which it is privileged to operate. The company's response to the drought crisis request reflected a long-standing policy of being a good neighbor and, according to Lindsay Leckie, was simply the "code we have lived by for years."

The case evolved out of a spontaneous natural event and a chance opportunity. By its strategic response to this "opportunity," CSX Transportation garnered more extensive and generous press than nearly all other organizations combined that were involved in the effort. Indeed, critical examination of the "Hay Train" reveals that all the strategic elements necessary for conducting a successful campaign are present: an obvious relationship between the event (a drought relief effort need for transportation) and the sponsoring organization (CSX Transportation), news value (the plight of farmers in the southeastern United States), a memorable name (Hay Train), tie-ins and trade-outs (with state governments, volunteer organizations, employees, etc.), and a series of related events (the series of drought relief transportation efforts).

The following account examines each of these elements, the role of CSX in the successful effort, the public relations decisions, and the outcome. (See Figure 11.6)

The CSX Organization was created in 1980, at the onset of federal deregulation. Since its inception, the corporation has taken several strategic actions in order to streamline its structure and better equip its ranks to anticipate, deal with, and respond quickly to fundamental economic and market shifts. One of its primary goals is to keep a competitive edge in the global transportation marketplace.

CSX Corporation is involved in four primary lines of business: transportation, energy, technology, and properties. Its transportation business was the primary one involved in the Hay Train effort. CSX Transportation, created in 1986 by consolidating departments of the former Chessie System and Seaboard System railroads, is divided into four units: CSX Distribution Services, CSX Equipment, CSX Rail Transportation, and American Commercial Lines.[12]

Situation background began with the culmination in 1986 of a five-year drought in the southeastern states. The drought, the worst in a century, was compounded by an intense heat wave through most of the summer. By mid-

Figure 11.6 CSX railroad made history by applying its company policy of being a "good neighbor" when it agreed to ship hay free of charge to southeastern farmers in the grip of a devastating drought. Hay donated by midwestern farmers saved threatened livestock and helped farmers in the drought-stricken states survive. (Courtesy of CSX Transportation.)

July, heat and drought had killed 52 people, caused 400 forest fires, and led to emergency restrictions on water use. Agriculture suffered most. Official estimates of crop and livestock damage were $2 billion or more, more than $400 million in South Carolina alone. The drought-stricken area reached from the Mason-Dixon line to northern Florida.[13]

Shortages of food and water forced many of the Southeast's farmers to feed their cattle the winter reserve hay, leaving nothing to tide them over the coming winter months. Without adequate feed supplies, many farmers were facing the grim choice of either selling their cattle, including breeding stock necessary to rebuild herds, to auction houses, or watching the animals starve to death. To compound the crisis, with such an influx of "beef going on the block at auction barns, the prices fluctuated wildly, leaving farmers to gamble even on the scale of their losses."[14]

The **strategic response to opportunity** began when one farmer, Tom Thrantham, was the subject of an ABC News telecast. Thrantham appeared on the network telling about his cattle approaching starvation. The story so moved Gayle McFarland, an Indiana farmer watching the telecast, that "he called agriculture officials and offered to donate hay if they could find a way to haul it south."

That one phone call led the governor's office in South Carolina to contact Ed Whitfield, CSX vice president of state relations, asking what CSX could do.

Immediately, both Whitfield and Ray Bullard, then vice president of CSX Transportation, thought shipping the hay was a worthy cause and a great idea.

Although there was no formal policy on the subject, there was a long-standing consensus among management people that the company would take every opportunity to act as a good neighbor. Within 12 hours after receiving that first phone call, top management representatives, who would become key players in the Hay Train, met to discuss goals and strategy. The executives drew on their combined experience, research into relevant cases, knowledge of the capabilities of CSX, and their professional judgment. Among those present were Ed Whitfield; Ray Bullard; R. Lindsay Leckie, CSX Transportation's manager of news and media relations; Jim Eaton, director of customer field service; and N. L. "Buck" Riggle, director of marketing-agricultural products.

Goals and Objectives   The planning team, according to a pledge by Whitfield and Bullard, agreed that CSX as a good neighbor would ship, free of charge, one trainload of hay of up to 100 boxcars and distribute the hay to each state in the CSX service area. In addition, CSX would then offer attractive discount rates for shipping hay until the drought situation eased. Two follow-up determinations were required as a result of this meeting: the company president would have to assess and approve the proposed action, and the equipment and coordination needed for the effort would have to be decided.

Steps to avoid two possible complications were considered at the initial meeting: to ensure that no profiteering would result from the effort and to take all possible safety precautions in shipping the flammable cargo. Apart from an unspoken consensus that the offer to ship the hay free of charge was the right and responsible thing to do, there was no discussion of the reason for the shipment.

Strategy   The primary goal of the hay shipment effort was to be a good neighbor by helping out the farmers in need. To accomplish this goal, further objectives were determined: (1) to ship the donated hay in a timely fashion, (2) to do so not seeking publicity but purely as a gesture of goodwill and friendship, and (3) to refrain from promoting the effort in any way as a media event. In practice, these objectives had the effect of giving authenticity and genuineness to the publicity that did result.

To further the aim of not seeking publicity, it was decided that all media communications and events were to be under the jurisdiction of the states involved. This decision also absolved CSX of any responsibility for managing the activity. CSX would not contact the media but would respond in a cordial and factual manner to any inquiries. Each respective state set up its own conferences and events. Some states worked out of the governor's office, while others worked out of the governor's press relations office. In addition, the departments of agriculture in the respective states provided relevant information. In most cases, a combination of all of these sources carried out the promotion and provided the necessary information.

In order to attain the goal of shipping the hay in a timely fashion, several strategies were employed. CSX would rely on the donating state governor's office and agriculture department to coordinate the donation, collection, and loading aspect of the operation. Included in the state's task would be selecting the proper drop-off point for donated hay and recruiting volunteers to transfer the hay to the train. The agriculture departments of states receiving the hay would be in charge of determining which farmers would receive the hay and assessing how much hay was needed in each case. Again, volunteers and coordination of information were critical. Farmers had to be informed about how they could receive the hay, and volunteers had to be recruited to move and transport the hay and feed the volunteers.

To streamline communications between all interested parties, CSX's R. L. Leckie became the chief liaison between the state agencies, the state information departments, and CSX officials who were in charge of marshaling and transporting the equipment. Having one person in charge of relaying critical information was essential to the continuity of decision making, efficiency, and timeliness of the effort.

Contagious goodwill led to a broad range of organizations to become involved. Upon hearing of the plans of their management, many members of the Brotherhood of Locomotive Engineers (BLE) and the United Transportation Union (UTU) followed suit by volunteering their labor to run the trains. Thus the "Hay-lo Specials" were born. In fact, the effort engendered pride among all employees. Some were so proud of their company that they worked extremely long hours in the volunteer effort, and one even took his vacation time to help with the relief effort.

The contagious spirit of CSX's generosity didn't end there. The 76-car "Hoosier Hay Express," estimated to cost $80,000, was the first train CSX delivered, and it captured the most significant public attention. More than 2,500 Hoosier (Indiana) volunteers loaded the 1,700 tons of donated hay from midwestern farmers. The hay, worth an estimated $145,000, came from 250 farms in 50 of Indiana's 92 counties. It took only $1\frac{1}{2}$ weeks to collect this amount. Midwestern farmers who had donated the hay also worked all night to bale it, and among those loading the hay the following three days were "Amish boys, prisoners, Mennonite and German Baptist faiths, National Guardsmen and hundreds of other uncompensated workers."[15]

Indianapolis restaurants, local industries, the Red Cross, the Salvation Army, and Indiana Bell donated food, transportation, communications, security, and other services as the first Hay-lo Special was being loaded. All counted, the train represented a contribution of more than $300,000, including the cost of the hay, $50,000 from Indiana truckers who transported it, $80,000 for the train, and the time volunteered by the railroad workers. The trainload was the largest single hay shipment into South Carolina during the summer's drought.[16]

After the loading was completed, the nearly mile-long train left Indianapolis on July 27, bound for Columbia, South Carolina. The train's departure time, speed, and stopping points were arranged so that it would arrive in daylight "for maximum publicity" for the train and to accommodate "the politicians who wanted to greet it."[17] Along the route, the hay train was assisted by volunteer BLE members and was cheered on by well-wishers. On the last leg of the journey, South Carolina's Mike Daniels and Indiana's John Mutz, both then lieutenant governors and both running for the top office in their respective states, boarded the lead locomotive.

The men unfurled their state flags and the train pulled up to its destination at the State Fair Grounds, to the strains of "Happy Days Are Here Again." There, farmers awaited the hay in a convoy of trucks. The fanfare and local, regional, and national media coverage were extensive. All together, about 1,000 people were present. The politicians took half an hour to make speeches from the bed of a "red truck driven by dairyman Sam McGregor, the first farmer in line to receive hay."

Governor Riley of South Carolina "proclaimed it 'Hoosier Day' in his state." Riley said, "Let me also thank the generous people of CSX Corporation for donating this first train and offering the service of additional freight trains at substantially reduced cost."[18] South Carolina's lieutenant governor, Mike Daniels, whose office was credited with proposing the train, said, "Twenty years from now, when the drought of 1986 is a harsh but distant memory, what we will remember is not the absence of rainfall, but the flood of human kindness."[19] Daniels specifically mentioned CSX: "This train, carrying nearly 2,000 tons of hay was made possible because a corporation like CSX believes that the free enterprise system is based on good corporate citizenship. This old-fashioned idea of citizenship is contagious. It spread to the railroad employees who were willing to donate their time, even when it meant working all night."[20]

In addition to the elected officials, CSX Rail Transport President John W. Snow praised the labor organizations. "A lot of people might look upon this situation as a chance to make a lot of money, but we look upon this as a chance to show what good neighbors are for. . . . We're delighted to be the pipeline between the farmers in Indiana and the farmers in South Carolina. We've been a part of the economy of South Carolina for 150 years. We've benefited from the good times, and we've suffered in the bad times. When Governor Riley called our office and laid out the problem we responded in the only way possible, and that was neighbor to neighbor and friend to friend."

Following the speeches, a small group of growers, cleared by the state agency, began unloading boxcars with the help of volunteer inmates from a minimum-security wing of the South Carolina Department of Corrections. In another state, additional volunteers came from a food distributor who donated a warehouse for storage. A local restauranteur opened up his business for CSX officials and others who were involved in the Hay Train operation.

Although Hoosier Hay Express received most of the national press coverage without any involvement of CSX officials in direct management of the operation, the coverage of this and additional hay trains was more than adequate by any public relations measurement standard. Accompanying the train all along its route were press conferences, special ceremonies, and news coverage.

Illinois The second Hay-lo Special, a 93-car train, was dispatched from Illinois on July 30 and arrived in Atlanta the next day. From there it went to the Georgia State Farmer's Market. This train's hay, loaded throughout Illinois, was only partially donated; a total of 48,260 pounds of hay was donated and 726,940 pounds was bought at $50 a ton. There were no intermediary expenses, and the Georgia Department of Agriculture collected the money from Georgia farmers and mailed it directly back to the farmers in Illinois.

Volunteer groups who assisted in loading the hay were public work crews from several Illinois correctional institutions, county farm bureaus, and the University of Illinois. As an extra gesture of camaraderie, before the train departed, CSX executives poured coffee for the crew.

Kentucky   The third train, the Kentucky Hay-lo Special, was the largest of the trains, with 105 boxcars of hay donated by farmers throughout the previous week. National Guard members loaded some 71,000 bales, including hay rolls. Special ceremonies were held when the train stopped in Lexington to add cars. Among the featured events were the ceremonial closing of a boxcar by Governor Martha Layne Collins and speeches by representatives of CSX and the railroad labor unions. As a special feature of the ceremony, a Norfolk-Southern Railroad employee, Richard McGibony of Rossville, Georgia, performed a song he had written about the relief effort, "Trainload of Hay." For the ceremony, McGibony added lyrics in the song to include CSX's name. When CSX officials had first heard of McGibony's song, they quickly sent him to a professional studio to record it. Although the song was never successfully marketed, McGibony had established that any profits from it would go to the relief effort.

Minnesota and Wisconsin   The fourth and last full trainload of hay consisted of 89 cars carrying 70,000 bales loaded from Soo Line points in Minnesota and Wisconsin. The train originated in Chicago and arrived in Birmingham, Alabama, for disbursement to several cities with appropriate ceremony. Messages from CSX Rail Transport President John Snow and the Soo Line President R. C. Gilmore were read to the Birmingham crowds. Engineer C. W. Crownover spoke, as did Lindsay Leckie, chief coordinator of the Hay Trains. In addition, farmers from Wisconsin were flown in for the ceremonies to be thanked personally.

After the last full trainload, CSX shipped approximately 100 carloads of hay in regular train service without charge. They would have transported more, but the hay donations had slacked off.

Evaluation   The standard criterion for evaluating a public relations activity involves measuring goal achievement. In this case, the goals set by the CSX Transportation executives were amply achieved: hay was provided to those in need in a timely fashion, CSX was perceived as a good neighbor, and the event was not perceived as a CSX media event. Furthermore, neither profiteering nor safety breaches occurred.

CSX set out to help the farmers in need. Although no one could meet all the needs of the drought-stricken farmers, CSX accomplished its goal with the amount of hay the company did ship. In the words of Lindsay Leckie, they "shipped enough to make a difference." The good-neighbor gesture made a lasting impression not only on the farmers but also on the media and government leaders.

By adhering to their goal of not promoting the Hay Trains as media events, CSX gained respect from all involved in the relief effort. In fact, by allowing the states to handle all the publicity, CSX avoided being caught up in several "attribution skirmishes" with politicians. The company was also spared in several articles that criticized the politicians and the states involved for trying to benefit "politically" at the expense of farmers.

As for being perceived as a good neighbor, in all the coverage CSX was portrayed in a respectful and dignified manner. Not being personally involved in the ceremonial events contributed to the perception of CSX as being above personal gain. The company was always depicted as a concerned corporate citizen. Adding to the glowing accounts in the media, the speeches made by CSX officials drove home and reinforced the primary goal of the company's involvement, to be a good neighbor and responsible citizen.

An example of the irony of how this "nonmedia event" worked well for CSX was the gratitude expressed to the corporation by journalists when CSX added a press car to the Hoosier Hay Express. By not seeking the press coverage, CSX reaped even more glowing coverage. The corporation also received letters from newspeople expressing personal thanks and commending CSX for its actions. Further evidence of the publicity value of not seeking publicity came with the estimates of those outside CSX speculating about the company's costs for the effort. CSX had not stopped to count their expenses, and the guesses appearing in the media generated even more favorable coverage.

The delivery of the hay shipments to farmers at the time of most critical need attested to the appropriateness of setting timeliness as a major goal. Achieving this goal depended to a great extent on the dedication of CSX's coordinator, Lindsay Leckie, who spent a grueling four weeks attending to details of the project and related matters. Two others who made significant contributions to the effort on a daily basis were Jim Bradley and Bill Eyler of the transportation department. The public-private partnership of CSX and the state agencies contributed to the project's success in avoiding profiteering.

Following the CSX lead, it did not take long for other railroads and their employees to "jump on the hay wagon." Among the railroads were Burlington Northern, Conrail, Illinois Central Gulf, Union Pacific, Chicago & North Western, Southern Pacific, Grand Trunk Western, Santa Fe, and some smaller ones. Moreover, businesses such as Adolph Coors Co. and SCE&G provided trucks and other contributions to the relief effort. Among all these contributors, CSX garnered the most press by far. Considering the amount of hay it shipped compared to that shipped by other railroads, CSX received the greater publicity dividends. CSX moved 370 carloads in four trains and was expecting to deliver up to 300 more carloads in regular service; other railroads exceeded that amount—Norfolk Southern alone shipped 1,300 carloads.

The comparative public relations success of CSX had more to do with initiating the idea and the symbolic value of trains loaded entirely with hay than with the amount of hay shipped. All other efforts received favorable treatment in the press, but often only as a sidebar to a story featuring CSX's effort. A contributing factor was the media preference for the symbolic 100 percent hay train. CSX's solid trainloads of hay met the criterion for special events that they can be given names that make them easier to talk and write about: "Hay Train," "Hoosier Hay Express," and "Hay-Lo Special." The coalition of CSX with the various participating groups, including state agricultural agencies, labor unions, and governors' offices, all based on mutual self-interest in the project, also contributed to the public relations success of the effort. The Hay Trains also met other criteria for successful special events: an obvious relationship between the event and the sponsoring organization, news value, and a series of related events.

Finally, through the Hay Train effort CSX provided a major segment of the American people with an event with overtones of our frontier heritage, where good neighbors were often valued above individual success. The Hay Train events offered an opportunity to participate in celebrating that revered heritage. A common theme in the remarks by farmers, officials, union members, and politicians was the "American spirit" prevalent in the event and that "it was about time to get back to the basic roots of helping one another." CSX, as the catalyst for this outpouring of good neighborliness, stands to collect dividends for a long time to come from its policy of social responsibility in managing its relations with its publics.

[AUTHOR'S NOTE: The Hay Train case study was written by Robin Wrinn, a graduate student at the University of Florida.]

SUMMARY

The **Pastahhh case study** shows how strategy and tactics are devised to address a specific situation analysis. One unusual aspect of the case is that the situation focused on the clients' perception that pasta lacked "excitement." Thus the strategy called for generating emotional response. The strategy and tactics outlined in the case illustrate how to stimulate emotional reaction to a product.

The **implementation strategy and tactics** put together in this case illustrate the range of activities available to the campaign planner. Not only does the case give examples of how to create emotional response in a target public, but how to package a series of interrelated activities and events to reach a full range of publics. The case also provides a good example of how campaign planners develop strategy options, not all of which may be implemented because of time or budget limitations. In the Pastahhh case optional strategies that couldn't be implemented the first year provided an attractive incentive to continue and expand the campaign in a subsequent year.

The **Hay Train case study** of strategy in action shows how corporate policy can be focused in a regional crisis to demonstrate corporate concern for a major constituency.

FOR FURTHER READING

Hay Train

Arthur, B. "Hay Express Winds Its Way to S.C.," *Charlotte Observer* (July 29, 1986).

Arthur, B. "Hay Train Unloads Boxcars of Good Will," *Charlotte Observer* (July 30, 1986).

Barnett, B. "Cargo of Hope Rolls into Town from Kentucky," *Charlotte Observer* (August 4, 1986).

Clark, C. "Hay Train Scheduled for Howell Yards Pit Stop Today," *Evansville (Ind.) Courier* (July 28, 1986).

"CSX Annual Report." Jacksonville, FL: CSX, 1986.

Cummings, W. "Haylift Is Good for the Spirit Too," *Atlanta Constitution* (August 13, 1986).

Fladung, T. "Indiana's Hay Arrives in States," *Columbia (S.C.) Record* (July 30, 1986).

"Hay, There's Hope," *BN News* (October 1986).

"Hay Train Leaves Kentucky for Carolina," *AP Monitor* (August 3, 1986).

"Hoosier Hay Express Brings Relief to Parched S.C. Farms," *AP Monitor* (July 29, 1986).

"It's a Rainy Day in Georgia as Prayers for Relief Go Out," *AP Monitor* (July 28, 1986).

Malone, F. "Railroads Pitch in to Help Drought-Stricken Southeastern Farmers," *Railway Age* (September 1986).

Patterson, R. "Trainload of Hay from Indiana on Way to Help Southeast Farmers," *Philadelphia Inquirer* (July 29, 1986).

Plipen, A. "'Americans Helping Americans' Is Motto of Hay-Bearing Train," *Cincinnati Enquirer* (August 3, 1986).

Powell, S. "A Yankee Hand for a Stricken South," *U.S. News & World Report* (August 18, 1986).

"Prayer Answered with Downpour, But Too Late," *AP Monitor* (August 4, 1986).

Rick, J. "Area Pitches in 24 Boxcars of Hay for Dried-Out South," *Commerical News* (Danville, IL) (July 29, 1986).

"South Carolina Greets 'Hoosier Hay Express'," *AP Monitor* (July 30, 1986).

"Sweet 'Hay-Lo Specials' Swing Through the Southland," *Locomotive Engineer* (August 29, 1986).

"12 Boxcars Ready to Carry Hay Equipment," *AP Monitor* (August 2, 1986).

Uehling, M. "Sweltering in Southland," *Newsweek* (July 28, 1986).

Building the Campaign Plan: The Evaluation Stage

CHAPTER 12 Evaluation Plan

- Evaluation Categories
- Nine Evaluation Purposes
- Choosing Evaluation Methods for the Campaign
- Three Essentials in Campaign Evaluation
- Case Study: Peanut, Pennsylvania, Celebrates Its Namesake
- Evaluation Based on Standards

The evaluation of a public relations campaign requires establishing convincing proof of the campaign's effectiveness. Dozier found that "three evaluation styles" are used among public relations practitioners: (1) scientific impact evaluation, (2) seat-of-the-pants evaluation, and (3) scientific dissemination evaluation.[1] *Scientific impact* evaluation uses primarily quantitative (counting effects) and social science methods of data collection in evaluating a program or campaign. "Samples of publics are drawn, surveys are taken, messages are tested, and public opinion poll data are monitored as part of scientific impact evaluation."[2] *Seat-of-the-pants* evaluation consists of "personalized, subjective evaluation in which anecdotal, casual observation or the judgment of the practitioner is used to estimate the effectiveness of a PR program."[3] This type of evaluation frequently uses peer recognition and the

403

winning of awards to document the effectiveness of a campaign. *Scientific dissemination evaluation,* as the name implies, focuses on distribution of the message and is often based on "numeric analysis of clip files, a log of column inches or air time, the reach of the media used, or a content analysis of those clips." Pavlik notes that "impact is inferred from that process . . . [assuming] the more widely a message is disseminated, the greater its (potential) impact."[4]

A growing body of literature is being produced by those employed in evaluation of government programs, social service agencies, nonprofit groups, schools and colleges, and corporate programs of various sorts. Many of those so engaged are members of the American Evaluation Association (AEA). The association publishes the journal *Evaluation Practice* and a series of monographs titled *New Directions for Program Evaluation.* The list of evaluation types in this chapter excerpted from Patton's *Practical Evaluation* reflects the range of evaluation activities of interest to the AEA membership that are relevant to public relations practice. It should be evident from a cursory reading of the list that much of what is being done in the field is of interest to public relations and many techniques may be applicable to our field.

EVALUATION CATEGORIES

Basic categories of evaluation that offer proof of success or effectiveness include: goal achievement, measurement of improvement, measurement of results, cost efficiency of the campaign, unexpected effects of the campaign, effects of the campaign on the organization itself, and perhaps unarticulated hopes that leaders of the organization may bring to the campaign. Let's consider what is involved in each of these categories.

Goal Achievement

Goal achievement implies that a goal was determined from a careful analysis of the situation, that research identified the true nature of the problem confronting the organization, and that the goal and the criterion for its achievement were based on these results. Achievement of a goal also implies that there are some quantitative element in the goal, a numeric scale, and that reaching some point on the scale was determined as "success."

Public relations campaigns often face the need to convince government regulators, legislators, and the general public, as in the case of an oil company seeking to build public trust in its research findings on energy problems. Samuel Bleeker recounts the campaign of one company that "felt it essential to pave the way for its multi-million dollar research effort with a long-range public information program." The company had "spent a sheik's ransom telling the public that conversion from oil heat to gas heat was, in most cases, uneconomical." The public reacted with skepticism: "of course few people be-lieved the oil industry claims . . . the public did believe a consumer group which said much the same things."[5]

The goal of the public information campaign sought both an effective technique for the public information campaign and building public trust.

> So the goal of a public information program was to explain the company's effort, to place it in the context of a larger national effort, and to minimize the public's ready distrust of corporate strategies and recommendations that naturally would issue from the studies.
>
>   In addition, the company was quick to realize that candor could accomplish several other essential corporate goals. It would:
>
> - reaffirm and enhance the company's stature and prestige in the international scientific community.
> - encourage wider recognition of the company's capacity to perform scientific research that is far-reaching in scope, outstanding in quality, and relevant beyond the company's immediate sphere of business interest.
> - help enhance the credibility of the company's discoveries bearing on the Green-house Effect. And
> - remind government leaders, social activists, labor and other critical observers that business can take the initiative in undertaking research that serves the highest public interest.[6]

Measuring goal achievement is the most prominent evaluation procedure. Evaluation should seldom be confined to one procedure, however. Included with other means of evaluation, goal achievement can demonstrate the effec-tiveness of the campaign most convincingly.

Measurement of Improvement

Measurement of improvement suggests that a benchmark of some sort was used to calculate the effects of the campaign. Such a benchmark may be a sur-vey taken before the campaign against which results of a postcampaign survey will be measured to determine "success." Benchmarks may also include such things as sales records, profits, or stock market value of company stocks, broadcast ratings, and rate of growth. Virtually any measurable aspect of an or-ganization's life that may be influenced by a public relations effort may be-come a benchmark for evaluation.

Among the skills future practitioners will use, according to Broom and Dozier, will be "evaluation research to monitor the program, to detect changes in the situation and to make program adjustments. Programs will be evaluated against outcome criteria spelled out in the objectives that guided program strategy."[7] Outcome criteria may be based on benchmark studies that determine a specific level of opinion, or attitude favorable to the organi-zation. Improvement is then measured from that beginning point. Improve-ment may also be measured from a standard established in prior efforts. Broom and Dozier suggest, "Goals and objectives are quantified using precise measures of impact obtained from an equally precise record of previous program accomplishments and/or failures."[8]

When measuring improvement or change as a means of evaluating a public relations campaign, it is critical to measure the public in which improvement or change was sought. Grunig claims that a "theory of publics" is crucial to the future of public relations practice, largely because "publics develop because of situations they face," and that change or improvement must be measured as it occurs in those publics. The situations that give rise to publics, or issues, provide the variable to be measured. Grunig has found that publics "differ in the extent to which they are active or passive." Passive publics are so transitory that little change can be expected, but active publics who seek out information and get involved in the issue are a much more promising category of public in which improvement or change can be measured.

Grunig suggests that his research on the nature of publics, especially active publics, provides a basis for public relations research and evaluation.

> Results of this research on publics have many implications for public relations policy, but they are especially important for formative and evaluative research in public relations. To plan a program or campaign, practitioners must know the kind of publics they are dealing with. To evaluate the program, they must know the likelihood of success for each objective. A realistic objective for an active public will be totally unrealistic for a passive public. I have found enough regularity in the kinds of publics I have found for many types of issues so that I do not believe every organization needs to research its publics from scratch. Most practitioners should be able to generalize from my research to identify their most likely publics.[9]

Measurement of improvement in public relations evaluation implies a starting point against which change is calculated. Change may be calculated for improvement in opinion, for behavior based on a benchmark established by a previous measure, or by comparison with results of a previous campaign or program. Change or improvement is calculated in the public targeted for the campaign.

Measurement of Results

Measurement of results is different from previously noted evaluation methods in that results do not necessarily imply goal achievement. Press clippings have long been used as a measure of public relations results, apart from whether they prove the campaign contributed to a solution to the organization's problem. Although measurement of effect by counting press clippings "is an intuitively attractive idea," as Pavlik notes, "an overwhelming amount of research shows that presentation of the message . . . does not equal reception of the message. Moreover, there is no way to tell the manner in which the message is received or distorted."[10] To reject media-monitoring tallies as ineffective evaluation may be premature.

If media use is tied to other measures of effect, such as shifts in public opinion or purchase patterns, it is possible to track those influences over time.

Krippendorff and Eleey offer a model for just such monitoring of an organization's environment: "the mass media are seen as providing the interface between the organization and a public that may not even coincide entirely with the public relevant to that organization." They illustrate the process in a graphic model with goods and services flowing from the company to the public and "revenues/support" and feedback flowing from the public back to the company. Information flowing to and from the organization includes "public relations effort, advertising activities, the mass media and public opinion processes," and the authors note, "Each of these is potentially subject to measurement."[11]

Measurement of results may involve more than press clippings. Such things as an improvement in sales, an increase in membership, and a certain number of people attending your open house are also "results." Results generally do not require a starting point, but often infer improvement over the existing status.

Formative evaluation, in which results of the planning or implementation of the campaign are applied to refinement of the plan, may fall into this measurement-of-results type of evaluation. The term "in-process evaluation" is used here and elsewhere, because it takes place while the campaign is in process. McClintock describes an approach to formative evaluation based on a "concept of organizational learning." It is most useful at the planning stage because it seeks to open up the full range of options in the approach of the campaign, but the end result is to offer more specific short-term effects and cost estimates. He suggests that the evaluator "work with program stakeholders to increase uncertainty about program structure," thus opening the process to a broader range of possibilities than might have been considered for "alternative strategies and organizational arrangements for defining problems and delivering services."

McClintock cites a method for "expanding the domain of thinking about concepts and their interrelationships" as a way of formative evaluation. The method calls for the evaluator to "1) play with ideas (for example, by using metaphors), 2) consider contexts (for example, by making comparisons with problems from other settings), 3) question assumptions (for example, by treating assumptions as both true and false under different conditions), and 4) systematize conceptual frameworks (for example, by specifying the relationships among concepts)."[12]

Measurement of results can include any of a range of evaluation approaches, from tabulating media coverage to formative or in-process evaluation that seeks to shape the campaign while it is still in the planning stage or while it is being implemented.

Cost Efficiency

Cost efficiency evaluation attempts to measure the success of a campaign by calculating the dollar value of results in relation to the effort and/or dollar value investment in the campaign. Campaign effects would thus be calculated in comparison with some given value, such as advertising costs for a comparable amount of media space or time. Person-hours, calculated in salary or wages; readership of company publication, calculated in terms of cost to produce and distribute it; and performance of volunteers, calculated in terms of costs of recruiting, training, and managing, are examples of how cost-effectiveness evaluation could be built into a campaign.

A variation on this method is cost-benefit analysis. This procedure compares the values gained against the resources sacrificed to achieve them. The result can help decision makers choose or reject a campaign plan. "Benefit-cost analysis compares the benefits and costs of alternatives when the outcomes can be accessed in monetary terms. It lends itself especially well to those alternatives or interventions in which the outcomes are market-oriented." The system requires that "both benefits and costs be assessed in monetary units" and compared.[13]

Regarding cost-benefit analysis, Levin makes the significant point that the method may be used to justify a program or campaign that produced a statistically small effect according to quantifying evaluation methods. When results of a campaign show that very small numbers of people have been influenced, it is easy to say the campaign was a failure, but "apparently small effects may be justified on cost-benefit criteria because the benefits exceed the costs for obtaining those effects." Attempts to modify behavior, such as campaigns to reduce obesity, alcohol or drug use, and smoking, may produce barely measurable results but may still be cost effective. "What is not considered is that even small effects may have relatively large benefits in relation to cost." Levin cites a stop-smoking campaign as an example:

> The conversion of the results into a cost-benefit analysis revealed that the benefits [or outcomes] in relation to costs were so high for the employer, that even if only one participant out of 20 quit smoking, the cost-benefit ratio could be favorable. Costs . . . amounted to about $30 per participant, and the lost wages of the participant during the program, which amounted to a value from about $46 to $117 depending on the gender and age of the participant. The total costs per participant varied from about $76 to $147 per participant.
>
> Benefits included the savings to the firm in reduced costs of fire, life, health, and workman's compensation insurance, as well as the savings from excess absenteeism and reduced productivity that are associated with smoking. . . . the benefits exceed costs by from $2,700 . . . to over $30,000.[14]

A cost-benefit analysis evaluation requires that costs and benefits be translated into comparable units of measure, such as dollars. When these units are entered in an accounting ledger system, the two totals can be compared. Indeed, Levin has described a computer spreadsheet software program that would accomplish the same thing with less effort.

> The cost analysis would be based on the techniques described[15]. . . . These can be developed in a simplified form by incorporating a standard type of financial spreadsheet analysis. The decision maker would be provided with guidance in developing the ingredients. A data base program would be used to store the costs of most of the standard inputs, such as the costs of different types of personnel, facilities, and equipment. The user could update this cost matrix on a periodic basis and could

add costs as they were needed. Assistance would be provided on determining the cost of each ingredient through a help menu. Calculation procedures for annualizing costs and carrying out other types of cost analysis would also be included.[16]

Cost-efficiency evaluation measures should especially be used in campaigns where costs are met by fund-raising events. In such campaigns a benefit would be very easy to demonstrate because the organization incurred virtually no expense in conducting the campaign.

Organizational Change

Organizational change involves evaluation *of the organization* as a result of the campaign. Such changes may be either positive or negative. A major public relations campaign targeted to the organization's most significant public will often have as great an impact on the organization conducting the campaign as on the target public. The Texas Eastern Corporation offers an example. In its effort to marshal public support for its plan to build a convention center arena in downtown Houston, the company had to mount an employee participation effort unmatched in its prior experience. The result was not only success in achieving the campaign goal but also an unexpected enhancement of employee morale and team spirit.

Well-managed public relations activities often have a significant influence on the sponsoring organization because of its involvement in programs to build relationships with constituencies. The rapport between evaluator and client that leads to a shared understanding of the organization's culture can help focus the impact of the campaign on the organization itself. Faase and Pujdak explain how their evaluation of a religious organization enabled the client organization to incorporate the evaluation outcome into its cultural life. "The client-evaluator relationship can be analyzed usefully to explain the importance of a shared understanding of organizational culture."[17] By planning to evaluate the organization's own response to the campaign, such as a renewed pride in the organization, a new appreciation of the corporate culture, or a new feeling of partnership between employees and customers, campaign planners can take advantage of this important campaign effect.

A related approach has been termed "internal" or "performance measurement" evaluation. Ciarlo and Windle describe an example of this concept as it was applied in a federal evaluation of community mental health centers. "At the local CMHC level, most internal evaluation activities, even though quantitative, were mainly descriptive and seldom challenged the CMHC's performance. Judgments of the success of such self-evaluation efforts were mixed."[18] By using internal performance evaluation, some evaluators found "greater local relevance" and the "opportunity for inserting evaluation findings into local decision making."

These performance measurement evaluations have been applied by social service agencies in evaluating the services they provide to their "clients," but the techniques may well be appropriate in evaluating public relations efforts to reach employees, association members, or other constituencies. For example, employees can be asked for their reaction; association members' response to efforts can be assessed. Efforts have also been made to measure "client outcome" of social service agencies. Ciarlo and Windle saw the "importance of client outcome data to the newly developing" demand for accountability in the "performance measurement system." The attempt to "evaluate changes in client functioning as a result of treatment"[19] in the mental health field might offer guidance in evaluating public relations efforts to change behavior in various constituency publics.

Campaigns may also change organization management's perceptions. Walt Lindenmann describes two top corporate managements whose minds were made up about how constituencies thought before the public relations effort was undertaken. Both were surprised by the outcome.

> A corporation once retained my organization to do an opinion-leader survey of two audience segments—those in the financial and business press and those in top positions in the federal government sector—congressmen, White House officials, and regulatory executives. The firm was heavily dependent on the U.S. government for its business and the public relations director told us at the start of the project, "We already know the views of Washington government opinion-leaders toward us and our industry. Our business depends on that. We want you to poll the government leaders just as a double check. We don't think you will tell us anything we don't already know. On the other hand, we really want to probe the media because we're not sure of their views."
>   . . . the findings from the poll of the media turned out not to surprise them in the least. But, the findings of the interviews with government respondents were totally unexpected. Government officials, it turned out, were telling corporate leaders one message in public, but conveying a completely different message in private.
>   . . . It can work the other way as well. A chairman of a manufacturing firm postponed for two years the conducting of an employee attitude survey because he was convinced his work force was highly critical of management and he was afraid to have the bad research findings—which he felt certain existed—confirmed by a poll. When he finally did give us the go-ahead to survey workers, to his surprise he discovered the staff was nowhere near as anti-management as he had suspected.[20]

Public relations efforts both at the research stage and at the strategy implementation stage can have a profound impact on the organization as well as the intended target public. Campaign evaluation plans that include what happens to the organization as a result of the campaign will have one more proof that the campaign made a difference.

Unplanned Results

Unplanned results of a campaign may be of interest in evaluation. Seldom should these be the only thing evaluated, but unanticipated desirable outcomes of a campaign may be convincing evidence that public relations in general and the campaign in particular are worthwhile endeavors. It is difficult to imagine the full range of unexpected effects, but employee morale, newly discovered values of teamwork, and a new appreciation of the public relations function are some and may suggest others.

The case of Texas Eastern Corporation's campaign to win voter approval to build an arena in downtown Houston cited a number of unexpected results in the evaluation. The campaign built a much stronger sense of employee cohesiveness and morale, and the values of public relations to the company became so evident that a full-time public relations position was created solely as a result of the campaign.

In working with multiple constituencies in a campaign, various segments of those involved may have different expectations. Scheirer refers to these different constituency-based expectations as "theories" and states that "a program evaluation design focused primarily on outcomes is likely to overlook the diversity of underlying program theories." She gives some examples of such unplanned outcomes.

> Federal agency staff may be primarily interested in satisfying political constituencies (client groups, legislators, or lobbyists). Their major criteria of success may be to demonstrate equity of resource allocation across the country or positive subjective response for local levels rather than valid empirical evidence of positive program outcomes. At the local level program theory specifying cause-and-effect relationships *may* provide a real point of guidance for designing and testing program components. Alternately, other local stakeholders may bring to the program a variety of other interests, from perceived client needs to staff members' career advancement.[21]

Because the campaign goals of various constituencies may differ, Scheirer suggests that the real goals of the campaign may need to be suspended pending a decision on what should be done as a result of the evaluations. "Evaluation of the program usually requires a suspension of judgment concerning the real objectives of the program."[22] The difference between planned and unplanned outcomes of a campaign is most likely to be of concern in cases of large multiconstituency organizations such as government. "This distinction between evaluating against a priori standards (an accounting approach) versus evaluating to address cause-and-effect relationships was well articulated in a recent article by the head of the program evaluation unit within the U.S. government's General Accounting Office (Chelimsky, 1985)."[23]

Taking into account the unplanned outcomes of campaigns in the evaluation stage can help to maintain relationships with all constituencies, but it also keeps the practitioner's perspective sufficiently broad. Campaign evaluation planners need to keep in mind that there may be constituencies other than those stated by management. There may even be unstated evaluation considerations important to management.

Unarticulated Hopes

Unarticulated hopes of management may be a problem for evaluation. If the campaign solves a problem that has been a major worry of management, it can be a strong advantage. But the advantage is lost if the achievement is not credited in the evaluation as a result of the effort. If the campaign fails to achieve something that management assumed would result but never mentioned, there may be a serious negative impact on the campaign, simply because the matter was not incorporated in the campaign for evaluation.

One example of unarticulated hopes is mentioned in a discussion of counselor-client relationships by Renee Miller. She quotes a fellow practitioner's experience: "Often, after a year or two, a client will simply stop paying his or her bills," said Nann Miller, president of Nann Miller Enterprises. "He or she might have wanted or expected bigger results—like the cover of *Newsweek*—and never communicated this."[24] Because unrealistic expectations pose a serious threat to campaigns when they remain hidden, every effort must be made to identify all expectations in discussions with management.

By identifying the possible unarticulated hopes of management for inclusion in the campaign evaluation, the planner can avoid the pitfall of a campaign that achieves its goals but nevertheless fails management's expectations. Even if all unarticulated hopes of management cannot be identified, the wise evaluator will not fail to credit the campaign with positive results that were not expected. Management may be pleased at renewed media attention to an issue of importance to the organization, quite apart from other results. Occasionally, management will respond enthusiastically to the ego boost that comes from publicity about the company or its leaders.

These examples, while not exhaustive of all the possible approaches to evaluation, do nevertheless suggest the wide range of evaluation types.[25]

NINE EVALUATION PURPOSES

Evaluation may be regarded from another point of view: what purposes does it serve? The National Academy of Sciences perceives nine different *purposes* of evaluation: (1) needs assessment, (2) basic research, (3) small-scale testing, (4) field evaluation, (5) policy analysis, (6) fiscal accountability, (7) coverage accountability, (8) impact assessment, and (9) economic analysis. Most public relations campaigns would, no doubt, use impact assessment most frequently. Others include needs assessment, to determine the feasibility of an anticipated new information program; small-scale testing, to find out what reactions might be to a proposed series of public service ads in the company publication; and field evaluation, to see how a new product promotion campaign is working.[26] A list of evaluation types is outlined in Box 12.1

CHOOSING EVALUATION METHODS FOR THE CAMPAIGN

Most evaluations, in public relations campaign planning, are measurements of goal achievements, results, or improvements of some kind or other. The before-and-after method, which establishes a benchmark against which achievement can be measured, is often the best way to demonstrate the success of the campaign.[27] The challenge in using various measures is in deter-

BOX 12.1   **Catalog of Evaluation Types**

A catalog of evaluation types is suggested in Michael Patton's book *Practical Evaluation.* The following list is based on Patton's "short list." Interpretations have been added to the category types. The types that seem most applicable to public relations evaluation are indicated with an asterisk (*) and marketing evaluations with a number sign (#).

     1. *Certification evaluation* asks whether the program meets minimum standards. It assumes the existence of certification standards and a mechanism for enforcing them.

* 2. *Appropriateness evaluation* investigates the nature and depth of information the publics should be receiving.

*3. *Awareness focus* determines who knows what about a program or issue and what they know about it.

#4. *Cost-benefit analysis* looks at the relation between costs and the dollar return on investment in the campaign.

#5. *Cost-effectiveness evaluation* looks at the relation between costs and nondollar investment.

* 6. *Criterion-referenced evaluation* is similar to goal achievement evaluation; criterion may be from sources other than problem identification research.

     7. *Decision-focused evaluation* asks what the campaign has produced to aid decision making.

*8. *Descriptive evaluation* is a nonjudgmental effort to find out what happens or happened in the campaign, apart from its goals.

*9. *Effectiveness evaluation* looks not just at goal achievement but also at the degree of goal achievement.

  10. *Efficiency evaluation* focuses on whether outcome can be increased without an increase in input for the campaign.

*11. *Effort evaluation* appraises personnel, staff, and time as an indication of investment in the campaign.

*12. *Extensiveness evaluation* asks to what degree the campaign solved the problems identified.

  13. *External evaluation* uses an outside evaluator to get an objective view of the campaign.

*14. *Formative evaluation* asks, either during or afterward, how the campaign can be improved.

  15. *Goal-attainment scaling evaluation* determines the achievement of the goal on a five-point scale.

*16. *Goal-based evaluation* simply measures the attainment of the goal.

  17. *Goal-free evaluation* measures the actual effects of the campaign apart from the goal.

(continues)

*18. *Impact evaluation* determines the direct as well as indirect effect of the campaign.

19. *Internal evaluation* means the staff conducts whatever evaluation method is used.

20. *Longitudinal evaluation* measures the campaign and participation in it over time.

21. *Meta evaluation* asks whether the *evaluation* was well done and was worth doing.

22. *Needs assessment evaluation* determines what the needs of the public or market may be and how they can be met.

23. *Norm-referenced evaluation* compares the campaign with a norm or a reference group.

24. *Outcomes evaluation* asks the degree of client desired outcomes and/or the campaign's effect on the client.

*25. *Performance evaluation* appraises the change in the behavior of the various target publics.

26. *Personnel evaluation* measures or rates the staff of the campaign.

27. *Process evaluation* looks at the strengths and weaknesses of the day-to-day operations.

28. *Product evaluation* measures the quality of the product being produced.

29. *Quality assurance evaluation* asks whether the standards for the campaign execution were met.

30. *Social indication evaluation* determines the overall impact of the campaign on society.

31. *Summative evaluation* determines whether the campaign should be continued or repeated at another time.

32. *Systems analysis evaluation* compares the outcome of the campaign with alternative options.

33. *Utilization-focused evaluation* measures effectiveness of the campaign by the degree to which the results were used.

Source: Patton, Michael Q. *Practical Evaluation* (Beverly Hills: Sage, 1982), 45–47.

mining appropriate results—how much improvement is realistic, significant, or acceptable, and whether the goal is an accurate reflection of what should be achieved. An evaluation method is selected by formulating questions and standards or criteria by which to evaluate. Whatever the approach, the evaluation planner or team must reach a consensus on the method to be used.

The before-and-after method is frequently called benchmark evaluation. In civil engineering, a benchmark is a reference point embedded in the ground for use in starting a land survey. In public relations campaigns, a benchmark is simply a point of comparison from which subsequent measures will be made. A word of caution is necessary here: Benchmark studies lack the careful controls of laboratory experiments but may imply that the results are equally rigorous. The danger is in attributing the results to the campaign when, in fact, some other factor may account for the effect. Frankly, most practitioners are less concerned about assigning credit than about justifying the investment of time and money in the campaign. The careful and conscientious practitioner must understand the logical basis for his or her evaluation efforts.

Evaluation is more than deciding whether to measure goal achievement, results, improvement, cost-benefit analysis, organizational changes, unplanned outcomes, or any of the other factors, alone or together, that can be measured. Methodology involves creating a *research design,* or the detailed procedure to be followed in making the measurements. The basic factors in a research design are the same whether it is for the initial fact finding for a campaign or for evaluation research of its results.

Those factors in basic research design include (1) careful identification of the *population to be measured;* (2) selection of the *portion to be measured,* whether a random sample, an informal nonrandom sample, or a census, as is often suitable for small populations; (3) the *degree of representativeness* needed, which involves the size of the sample or the precision required to yield the required accuracy; (4) the *measurement technique,* whether counting incidence from observation, a questionnaire administered by telephone, or comparing results of two or more activities as in an experiment; (5) how the *report of findings* will be carried out; (6) the *analysis procedure* to be used, whether a simple tally, cross-tabulation to compare segments, or more sophisticated statistical techniques; (7) *interpretation of findings;* and perhaps (8) *application of findings* to future campaigns, organizational policy, or other uses that may be indicated.

For specific guidelines in evaluation research design the reader is encouraged to refer to the research chapters in this book or to other volumes on research design. In a chapter titled "Thoughtful Methods Decisions" in his book *Practical Evaluation,* Patton discusses in considerable detail the comparative values of "qualitative" versus "quantitative" methods of evaluation research designs.

> Of course, the real options are much more complex than a simple choice between "qualitative" and "quantitative" paradigms. In any given study there are a host of methods choices.
>
> 1. *Measurement options:* What kinds of qualitative data should we collect? What kinds of quantitative measures should we use?
> 2. *Design options:* How much should we manipulate or control variance in the settings under study? (Options vary from controlled experiments to naturalistic field studies with a lot of variations in between.)
> 3. *Personal involvement options:* What kinds of interpersonal contacts, if any, should the researchers have with the subjects under study?
> 4. *Analysis options:* To what extent should the study be open to whatever emerges (inductive analysis) and to what extent should prior hypotheses be examined (deductive analysis)?[28]

Whatever the research plan—even if it is a package of several approaches each with its own design, which is probably most desirable—the campaign plan must include a well-thought-out procedure for conducting the evaluation. The following discussion focuses on the approaches to evaluation that are usually most appropriate for the typical public relations campaign.

THREE ESSENTIALS IN CAMPAIGN EVALUATION

The most important considerations in choosing a campaign evaluation plan are *in-process evaluation, internal evaluation,* and *external evaluation.* Ordinarily, the campaign planner should select from the wide range of evaluation methods at least one approach to apply to each of these three aspects of the campaign. The approaches chosen should be those that offer to provide the best proof of the campaign's success.

In-Process Evaluation

In-process evaluation monitors the campaign while it is being implemented. Just as an effective game plan can best direct an athletic team if it can be fine-tuned or even radically altered in response to the realities of the playing field or the strengths of the opposing team, the campaign plan will be most successful if it is evaluated during its execution with the option of altering the plan itself if circumstances warrant. This aspect of campaign evaluation has also been called "formative evaluation," but generally the term has been used in reference to evaluating federal social services programs rather than public relations campaigns.[29]

Methods for monitoring the campaign during implementation include keeping a campaign diary, holding staff meetings to report feedback and observations, making reports of on-schedule progress, and holding debriefing sessions to collect minute details that can reveal significant facts otherwise not discernible.

In-process evaluation includes the responsibility for setting in motion contingency plans or for altering the plan in response to developments. Emergency, crisis, and/or disaster plans are also the province of the campaign manager and are logically a function of in-process evaluation. The campaign implementation manager must also be responsible for the criteria used in deciding to alter the campaign plan. The campaign manager must have authority to decide when to implement contingency plans and must be responsible for deciding which contingency plan to choose if it becomes necessary.

Closely related to responsibility for the contingency plan is the "troubleshooter" function. The troubleshooter is the problem solver who constantly monitors the progress of the campaign and solves problems as they arise. The person designated as troubleshooter must have authority to make

➤ CASE STUDY: PEANUT, PENNSYLVANIA, CELEBRATES ITS NAMESAKE

RESEARCH

A national research study of attitudes and opinion about peanut butter found that Americans "overwhelmingly identify peanut butter as a food that is 'fun' to eat . . . and adjective that they don't transfer to competitive foods like cheese, hamburgers, bologna, etc." Ketcham Public Relations and their client the Peanut Advisory Board researched place names to find a suitable site for promoting peanut butter. The choice, Peanut, Pennsylvania, a small unincorporated town of 140, offered a perfect setting as host for the planned celebration. Research of the town, Peanut, found it was "a typical, middle-income rural community within an hour's drive of a regional media center—Pittsburgh." The town actually is named after a type of coal that used to be mined here.

Problem

To convince an entire town to stage a celebration in its honor.

ADAPTATION

Goal

Convince town to stage celebration event as a means of generating product publicity.

Strategy

Capitalize on consumers' perceptions of peanut butter as a "fun" food with a unique event that generates national publicity.

Objectives

1. Convince an entire town to help stage and support a celebration in honor of peanut butter.
2. Convince townspeople to attend such an event.
3. Publicize the event to reinforce the concept of peanut butter as a "fun" food.

Target Publics

Residents of the town; residents of surrounding towns; the town's civic and business organizations; local, regional and national media.

Budget

For all out-of-pocket expenses not including consumer research: $7,000.

IMPLEMENTATION STRATEGY

Designed as a charitable fund-raising event for a local library and food bank, the "Peanut Butter Lovers' Festival" featured the world's largest peanut butter and jelly sandwich. Created by residents of the town, the sandwich measured nearly 40 feet long and contained 100 pounds of peanut butter and 50 pounds of jelly. Road signs erected at the town limits read "Welcome to Peanut, Pennsylvania. We're nuts about you!" A peanut butter recipe contest was conducted for local residents, with prizes and publicity for the winners. Communication included media mailings, public service announcements, news advisories, and extensive phone contacts and generated newspaper, radio, and TV publicity in the Pittsburgh area the week prior to the event. Follow-up contact insured on-site coverage.

EVALUATION

Objective 1

Groups supporting the effort included: local organizations—chamber of commerce, Girl and Boy Scouts, high school, band boosters, moving van company, senior citizens club, school board, food bank, and the largest local employer, Pelikan, Inc., statewide—the governor of
(continues)

Pennsylvania and State Senator Porterfield; and nationally—national food companies donated products for sampling.

Objective 2

Attendance of 950 people from Peanut (population 140) and surrounding towns. The $2 admission fee raised $1,800 for the local library. A school food drive the week before the event generated $1,000 worth of peanut butter which was donated to the local food bank.

Objective 3

National publicity included the Associated Press, United Press International, Cable News Network, CNBC-TV, *The Wall Street Journal, The Washington Post,* and television network affiliates in New York, Boston, Philadelphia, Atlanta, Houston, Cleveland, Tampa, Miami, Minneapolis, Baltimore, St. Louis, Orlando, and Hartford among major cities. Local publicity included all Pittsburgh TV stations, KDKA Radio, and the *Pittsburgh Post Gazette.*

---

major alterations in the campaign plan as well as minor ones. Major problems might call for a shift in emphasis from one target public to another or redirection of publicity from one medium to another. Minor ones might require dropping ineffective public service announcements or offering rain checks to overflow crowds at a planned event. The troubleshooter will also be responsible for correcting mistakes made in planning that come to light in execution or for mistakes made in the implementation itself. This implies that the troubleshooter must be able to *identify* problems that cry for solution when others may not recognize that a problem exists.

Monitoring the campaign while it is in process also involves appraising unforeseen developments that may have an impact on the campaign. The campaign manager will have to evaluate and solve such problems. He or she must deal with challenges and should be prepared to take advantage of opportunities that emerge from the campaign or that develop apart from the campaign but may have implications for the campaign effort.

The campaign diary can be used to record facts, impressions, relationships, and other pertinent details of the progress of the campaign, and it offers a perspective that can be used to adjust the plan. The diary can also be used to preserve the details of the campaign for later use in evaluation. Reading a campaign diary some time after a campaign has ended can provide useful guidance for future campaigns by revealing the difference between the worries and anxieties during the campaign that proved to be of no consequence and the matters that proved to be genuine problems. Knowing the difference between these can be valuable in planning for future campaigns.

Internal Evaluation

Internal evaluation differs from in-process evaluation in that it measures the campaign after execution. Many of the methods are the same—feedback, observations, and reports of various kinds—but they are used after the fact rather than during the campaign. The campaign evaluation plan should include the procedure that will be followed to accomplish this function at the conclusion of the campaign, but the plan must be complete before the campaign begins.

Staff meetings following the campaign may be an excellent method of recording the full range of observations about the campaign. Problems will have to be noted, of course, but so will the insights of those close to the campaign regarding its timing, personality conflicts, and jealousies. A record may be made of people in the media who were particularly helpful or who posed obstacles. The staff may make personal evaluations of the coordination with tie-in or tradeout groups and have other perceptions gained by working in the campaign.

Individual performance of team members or project personnel may also be evaluated by the supervisor. Evaluations may be based on assigned duties, projects, achievements, performance, the quality of work produced, or a combination of these. Performance may be measured by the people themselves in the form of self-evaluations. People may also be evaluated in terms of their achievement of a set of objectives, such as their record in meeting or failing to meet deadlines, or the increase in sales resulting from various projects. Evaluations may be based on the people in charge of various tasks, or on the quality of the tasks performed by the team (e.g., editing, layout, artwork, or the end result). The team or project may be evaluated in terms of the effectiveness of the group's output or its total effort.

Project feedback offers another major method of evaluating in which the constituent parts of the campaign are examined. Having people within or outside the organization carry out a careful study of the campaign effort project by project or event by event makes it possible to compare the parts as well as the whole. This may be done by people in the organization or by trained evaluators from outside public relations. It may also be done by public relations staff who use carefully developed measurement instruments to reveal the relative effectiveness of the campaign in each of its many facets.

Evaluation by observation is akin to "management by walking around." Like the executive officer who learns more about the company by walking around the factory or office complex than by reading reports, the campaign manager may learn more about the nature of the campaign through personal contact with the people who are conducting it than by waiting for the reports to be submitted. Opportunities for observing problems as they happen, as well as the performance of the persons who solve them, give the manager a vivid appraisal of the campaign as well as of its staff.

External Evaluation

External evaluation looks at the effect of the campaign on factors outside the organization, such as the targeted publics, media coverage, cooperating organizations, and public behavior in general. Specific measurements would include changes in the various targeted publics, tabulations of measurable results, media monitoring, gatekeeper evaluation, audience media usage, and comparison of public (i.e., commercial) media with private, controlled media. By analyzing the campaign's effect on these external factors, the campaign manager-evaluator can get a very good understanding of its overall impact.

Follow-up measurements of public attitudes, opinion, and/or behavior can be compared with a previously established benchmark to reveal improvements that may be attributed to the campaign. This approach, of course, requires previous research to establish the benchmark or use of a benchmark established by some other research, such as census data, syndicated research, or sales of membership records. The measurements may be of attitudes and opinions, as mentioned above, or of such factors as information gain, product recognition, and source of information about the issue.

Tabulation of measurable results is one of the simplest evaluation methods but can be one of the most significant. An increase in sales, for example, is very simple to measure, but it may tell the whole story as far as effectiveness of a sales promotion campaign goes. Other factors that lend themselves to easy tabulation include membership increase, volunteers, donations, inquiries, and responses to a publicized offer. Tabulations can, of course, be both positive and negative; praise and complaints both tell important stories. Box 12.2 is a tabulation of Silver Anvil evaluation methods.

Media monitoring tallies clippings and broadcast usage, analyzes content, and otherwise evaluates the potential impact of the issue as it is carried by the media. The appearance of an issue or a point of view in the media is by itself no guarantee that the targeted public will receive the message. It is, however, a time-honored indication of the likelihood of message impact. With some subsequent research, such as measuring the readership or perception of an issue by use of a random representative sample, the results can be projected to the total readership of the media to give a quite respectable indication of the public's response to the issue or point of view. Content analysis can measure principally the media's position on or interest in an issue by such methods as counting key words in a sample of newspaper stories or tallying a range of words and phrases that indicate concern about a topic. Media monitoring, by whatever method, can also give a good indication of what media are most effective.

Gatekeeper evaluation keeps track of how well you are able to reach the people you need to make contact with in order to carry out the campaign. A record of the best methods for reaching critical people, reporters, management decision makers, and liaison persons with cooperating organizations could provide valuable insights for future dealings with gatekeepers. For example, learning the work habits of a critically important reporter could vastly improve future effectiveness, or knowing the best procedure for regular contact with a business executive who is important to the campaign could enhance future efficiency when dealing with executives. Many lessons may be learned for dealing with secretaries, who are often critical gatekeepers for access to executives; an alienated secretary may come back to haunt you when he or she conveys your message ineffectively or with a negative bias.

The media employed in the campaign may be evaluated by seeing which media usage patterns are most conductive to reception of your message. Study-

BOX 12.2   Evaluation Methods Used in 1994 Silver Anvil Winning Campaigns

Number of Usages	Method of Evaluation
48	Tabulation of publicity, placement
45	Tabulation of materials usage, requests, samples
39	Tabulation of participation, attendance, etc.
35	Cost savings, donations, sponsorships, sales, dollar value
32	Media participation/coverage of event
31	Measures of client improvement (traffic, tickets sales, business, etc.)
20	Post campaign poll or other comparison survey
20	Tabulation of column inches, air time, clippings, etc.
18	Tabulation of praise, recognition
17	Tabulation of "impressions"
13	Reaction of the competition/opposition
11	Tabulation of exhibit viewers, exhibitors, volunteers
8	Tabulation of coalition/cooperation
5	Comparison of stock position
5	Corporate social responsibility action
2	Talk show appearance, legislative testimony
2	Legal action
2	Interviews
1	Tabulation of contest or event entrants
1	Event performance count

ing the reach and frequency figures of the various media may show that the medium with the greatest circulation is not necessarily the one most used by your target audience. Some publications, for example, are read by three or four different people; this is more valuable information than circulation numbers. But when you know that each of those people picks up the publication an average of three different times, you know that reach is greater than circulation and that frequency added to it makes an impact figure of at least ten times the circulation figure. In this regard, public relations people have much to learn from advertisers, who developed the measures of reach and frequency.

Evaluation of public versus "controlled" media attempts to determine whether the public or commercial media are more effective in the long run than the private or controlled media. That is, is placement of material in newspapers, magazines, or television as effective as placement in an in-house publication, where you control exactly what is said and how it is distributed? Of course, the credibility of the public media is a factor if the audience is likely to question the credibility of the source of the information. On the other hand, if the audience is favorably disposed to the message, it might be more effective to use your own medium and distribution channels, since the credibility of the public media would not add anything to the process.

BOX 12.3   Minimum Criteria for a Good Entry Based on a Study of PRSA Silver Anvil Selection Process

1. Well-written two-page summary, supported by text; a clear, succinct statement of program goals and impact desired—87.8% (these two tied for first).
2. Whether research preceded planning and was linked to evaluation through results—73.5%.
3. Innovativeness, originality—67.4%.
4. Applicability to category and PRSA criteria—49%.
5. Correct grammar and spelling—44.9%.
6. Need for program—42.9%.
7. Applicability to audience; cost-effectiveness specified—36.7% (tied for seventh).
8. Broad focus and depth—30.6%.

Three Most Important Elements in a Good Entry
1. Proven effectiveness through results—71.4%.
2. Professional execution—67.2%.
3. Careful advance planning—32.7%.
4. Research to define goal and objective—22.5%.
5. Fit of program with other organization goals—12.2%.
6. Valuable to society—8.2%.
7. Congruence among program elements—3.7%.
8. Use of unique or new techniques; use of variety of media; succinct, crisp, exciting—2.0% (these three tied for eighth).

EVALUATION BASED ON STANDARDS

Standards for evaluation are suggested in a study by Hill, Moore, and Patterson in *P R Casebook.* The authors polled the Silver Anvil judging teams to find out the "minimum criteria" for a good entry and the "most important elements of a good public relations program." The criteria are presented here not as the ultimate standards for what makes a good campaign but as the standards used by peers who judge campaigns in this competition. The two lists in order of highest to lowest in percentage as given by respondents are shown in Box 12.3.

Box 12.4 shows a checklist of some appropriate evaluation methods as they might be applied to various public relations activities. The strategy list is the same one used earlier in the text. The list of evaluation techniques is not intended to be exhaustive, nor are the suggestions necessarily the most appropriate for a given situation; the intent is to provide suggestions and examples to aid the planner in selecting the best alternatives for the specific campaign being planned.

BOX 12.4   Evaluation Procedures with Strategy Types

Type of Public Relations Strategy	Some Typical Evaluation Techniques
1. Nothing	Impact assessment; media monitoring; tabulations
2. Public information program	Polls; pre/post tests; behavior modification measures
3. News conference	Media monitoring; clippings; gatekeeper evaluation
4. Coalition building	Direct and indirect effects measures; needs assessment; effects over time
5. Natural event response	Outcome evaluation; impact on society; public opinion poll
6. Commemoration events	Tally of participation; attitude survey; tabulation/rating of volunteers
7. Celebrations	Tally of attendees; media monitoring; staff brainstorming/debriefing; participant rating measures

(continues)

8.	Contests/competitions	Media monitoring; staff feedback; rating of event by judges; cost-effectiveness
9.	Personality/spokesperson	Staff reports; bookings evaluation; tally of contacts; opinion polls
10.	Establish organization	Comparison/tally of membership figures; volunteer feedback; member assessment of goal achievement; donations; polls
11.	Marketing activities	Consumer panels; sales tabulation/comparisons; focus groups; polls
12.	Meetings, conventions, etc.	Registrations tally; inquiry tally; program evaluation; participant feedback
13.	Information/exhibit booth	Materials pickup tally; tally of request forms filled out; business card collection "game"; visitor tally
14.	Fund-raising event	Donor tally; prospect list; opinion poll; feasibility study; pledges
15.	Contracted research	Behavior change study; media monitoring; audience-response test of results
16.	Social responsibility efforts	Focus interviews; opinion polls; opinion leader interviews; public relations audit
17.	Speakers bureau	Audience rating of speaker; issues rating questionnaire; booking tally
18.	Lobbying	Media analysis; legislation monitoring; interviews with legislators; polls
19.	Grass-roots lobbying	Polls, media monitoring; voting analysis; issue tracking
20.	Misinformation response polls	Content analysis; media monitoring; interviews; observation

Planning the evaluation procedure requires a familiarity with the options for evaluation, most of which have been listed and briefly described. The next step in the process of evaluation is to develop a set of usable ways to carry out each of the evaluation procedures chosen.

Evaluation methods, the techniques used for carrying out any of the evaluation types, ordinarily involve some mathematical procedure. The most common of these procedures are compiling, tallying, counting, averaging, sampling, comparing, and testing. Evaluation methodology and procedures, of course, imply a research design of some sort. Indeed, the evaluation methodology, with its research design, is identical to the methodology and design of the research stage of the campaign. Thus, the campaign planner should consult the research stage of the planning process for guidance on specific evaluation methodology and design. Broom and Dozier's book *Using Public Relations Research* will be especially useful for this task.

SUMMARY

Categories of evaluation include distinctive academic and practitioner orientations. *Six factors that can be measured* in public relations evaluation are goal achievement, improvement, results, cost efficiency, organizational change, and unplanned results. The National Academy of Sciences lists **nine purposes of evaluation.** Some thirty-three *examples of evaluation types* serve as a catalog from which to construct an evaluation plan.

Basic elements go into **research methodology and design** for evaluation practice. Some criteria help in selecting an evaluation method. There are **three common ways to evaluate a campaign:** in-process, internal, and external.

Effective **evaluation can be based on existing standards:** *Silver Anvil competition campaigns, especially a tabulation of evaluation methods used in 1994 campaign competition winners, as well as examples of evaluation approaches that might be appropriate for various strategies. A concluding note suggests procedures for planning the evaluation.*

FOR FURTHER READING

"Applied and Evaluation Research" chapter 16 in Kidder, Louise H., and Charles M. Judd, *Research Methods in Social Relations* 5th ed. New York: Holt, Rinehart and Winston, Inc., 1986.

Bickman, Leonard, ed. "Using Program Theory in Evaluation," *New Directions for Program Evaluation* 33 (Spring 1987).

Braverman, Marc T., ed. "Evaluating Health Promotion Programs," *New Directions for Program Evaluation* 43 (Fall 1989).

Cordray, David S., Howard S. Bloom, and Richard J. Light eds. "Evaluation Practice in Review," *New Directions for Program Evaluation* 34 (Summer 1987).

Dehar, Mary-Anne, Sally Casswell and Paul Duignan. "Formative and Process Evaluation of Health Promotion and Disease Prevention Programs," *Evaluation Review* 17 (April 1993): 204–20.

Hedrick, Terry E. "The Interaction of Politics and Evaluation," *Evaluation Practice* 9 (August 1988): 5–14.

House, Ernest R. *Evaluating with Validity.* Beverly Hills, CA: Sage, 1980.

Lam, Tony C. M. "Analysis of Performance Gaps in Program Evaluation: A Review of the Gap Reduction Design" *Evaluation Review* 16 (Dec. 1992): 618–33.

Mark, Melvin M. and Lance Shotland, eds. "Multiple Methods in Program Evaluation," *New Directions for Program Evaluation* 35 (Fall 1987).

Moffitt, Robert. "Program Evaluation with Nonexperimental Data," *Evaluation Review* 15 (June 1991): 291–314.

Nowakowski, Jeri, ed. "The Client Perspective on Evaluation," *New Directions for Program Evaluation* 36 (Winter 1987).

Patterson, Blossom H., et al. "Evaluation of a Supermarket Intervention: The NCI-Giant Food Eat for Health Study," *Evaluation Review* 16 (Oct. 1992): 464–90.

Patton, Michael Q. *Practical Evaluation.* Beverly Hills, CA: Sage, 1988.

Patton, Michael Q. *Qualitative Evaluation Methods.* Beverly Hills, CA: Sage, 1980.

Pavlik, John V. "Major Research Findings," chapter 3 in *Public Relations: What Research Tells Us.* Newbury Park, CA: Sage, 1987.

Seltzer, Michael H. "Studying Variation in Program Success: A Multilevel Modeling Approach," *Evaluation Review* 18 (June 1994): 342–61.

Wiener, Richard, Christine Pritchard, Shannon M. Frauenhoffer and Mabel Edmonds. "Evaluation of a Drug-Free Schools and Community Program: Integration of Qualitative and Quasi-Experimental Methods," *Evaluation Review* 17 (October 1993): 488–503.

Wimmer Roger, and Joseph Dominick. "Research in Advertising and Public Relations" chapter 15, and "Research in Media Effects" chapter 16 in *Mass Media Research: An Introduction,* 4th ed. Belmont, CA: Wadsworth, 1994.

Wye, Christopher G. and Harry P. Hatry, eds. "Timely, Low-Cost Evaluation in the Public Sector," *New Directions for Program Evaluation* 38 (Summer 1988).

CHAPTER

13

Evaluation Cases

- Case Study: Camp Crystal Lake: A Student-Planned Campaign
- Case Study: A Water Utility Launches Conservation Campaign—1989–93

An evaluation plan describes the methods by which the specific campaign will be evaluated. The most appropriate evaluation techniques should be chosen from the various approaches for evaluating public relations efforts. The basic question is, "How well did we do in solving the problem?" To answer this question requires comparing the status of the situation at the beginning of the campaign with the status after the campaign. Other factors may be evaluated, including the degree of improvement, various results, cost-effectiveness, unexpected results, and unspoken hopes.

Situation Analysis Restated   Before making choices for any evaluation plan, however, the *situation* that necessitated the campaign must be recalled. The *situation analysis* that was carried out at the beginning of the campaign should be restated with any changes dictated by planning for other stages of the campaign. Having in mind the precise situation as refined by research and other fine-tuning keeps the evaluation planning decisions focused. As an example of evaluation planning, we will examine the evaluation aspects of the student campaign plan that follows.

► CASE STUDY: CAMP CRYSTAL LAKE: A STUDENT-PLANNED CAMPAIGN

Organizational Research

Camp Crystal Lake is an outdoor environmental education center located on 140 acres of land next to Crystal Lake. Originally built as an air base in 1942, the Alachua County (Florida) School Board purchased the land from the federal government in 1948 to be used by schoolchildren for overnight camping throughout the year and as a summer camp during the summer months.

The camp is an outdoor/environmental education center for all ages, however priority use is given to fifth graders. During the school year, students spend from one to five days and nights at Camp Crystal Lake, studying the environment, enjoying recreational activities, and participating in programs to improve self-confidence and cooperation skills.

The program focus is learning about nature through a holistic approach. It is based on the concept that learning by doing in the outdoors is an effective method to develop awareness, knowledge, and skills for future effective environmental management. The sessions in the environmental education program are designed to maximize hands-on involvement. Observations, exploration, and interaction are the key to each activity.

The School Board

The School Board of Alachua County is one of only a few school systems in the nation to own a yearlong resident outdoor education center, such as Camp Crystal Lake. Combined with classroom knowledge, students learn about ecosystems, natural history, and geology at Camp Crystal, which gives them the opportunity to better understand natural concepts. The camp complies with all policies, rules, and regulations set forth by the school board, which are the same rules governing schools in Alachua County. The board makes all decisions concerning Camp Crystal Lake.

The camp is funded by grants created by the state education department to strengthen and enhance the public school program. Also, the School Board of Alachua County sponsors four camping sessions each summer. More than 100 children spend up to two weeks as recreational campers, while learning water skiing, archery, horseback riding, photography, and hiking.

Camp Staff

Camp Crystal Lake's staff consists of the camp director, three full-time counselors, a part-time secretary, and a part-time custodian. Teachers, parents, and other volunteers participate as program leaders.

Potential Risks

In the event of an emergency at Camp Crystal Lake, the School Board of Alachua County has developed guidelines in *Health and Emergency Procedures* for school officials to follow. In addition, the camp director at Crystal Lake follows emergency guidelines set forth by the American Camping Association.

Hazardous Waste   A confirmation study of Camp Crystal Lake (the former Keystone Army Air Field) by the U.S. Army Corps of Engineers identifies two landfill sites near the camp. The following conclusions are based on work performed for the confirmation study:

- No additional Department of Defense–related areas were identified.
- Nearly all inorganic and organic contaminants analyzed were below limits or detected at very low levels.
- Iron (in all wells), chromium (in three wells at Landfill One), mercury (in four wells at Landfill Two), and lead (in three wells at Landfill One) concentrations exceeded groundwater standards. Lead is a common metal found in shallow groundwater in Florida.

Hazardous Waste Crisis Response

The U.S. Army Corps of Engineers suggests further contamination assessment through a "consent order" between the responsible agencies and the Florida Department of Environmental Regulation. This assessment would determine the degree of environmental impact of degradation caused as a result of this dumping site.

Presently, the levels do not pose a threat to campers. The groundwater is periodically tested to determine if contaminants exceed recommended levels. However, if the chemicals threaten the safety of students, measures should be taken to ensure their safety.

Alachua County Demographics

- In northeast Florida.
- 901.47 square miles (land), 68.0 square miles (water).
- Population density: 199 persons/square mile.
- Population growth: year 1990   2000   2020
                       pop. 190,600* 218,700* 267,800*
                       *projected
- The greatest part of the population is located in Gainseville and surrounding area. Alachua, Newberry, and High Springs are the other major cities.
- Age segmentation (1987):   Age   % of pop.
                             0–7   7.1
                             10–19   16.7

20–29	27.1
30–39	15.5
40–more	33.5

- The average annual percent population growth (1980–88) in Alachua County was 2.6%, compared with a state rate of 3.4%.
- Race distribution (1987): 79% white and 21% nonwhite.
- Income rate (1986): $11,838 (34th highest in state).
- Educational level:
  a. 5.5% of the population has graduated from high school.
  b. 29.4% completed four or more years of college.
  c. The high school graduation level is 60.8%.
- Economy (1987): The labor force totaled 94,046 persons with the following distribution: government (38.1%), services (21.9%), trade (23%), and manufacturing (6.1%). The University of Florida is the major government employer in the county. Printing and publishing, transportation equipment, and fabricated metals products firms are the greatest employers in the manufacturing sector.
- Unemployment rate (1987): Alachua County is 3.4%, the United States is 6.1%.
- Farmland distribution (1987): Mainly located in the north are 465,590 acres with the following distribution, 41% forests, 39% crops, 20% pastures and rangeland.
- Natural resources:
  a. 42 natural ecological communities (including uplands, wetlands, and aquatic communities).
  b. 62 species of plants.
  c. 400 species of native vertebrate animals (36 are endangered or threatened, according to federal and state law, including the bald eagle).
- The final report of comprehensive inventory of natural ecological communities of Alachua County has recommended the following priority ranking for Alachua County upland ecosystem (considered critical to the county's environmental quality). The priorities are ranked according to five criteria: vulnerability, rarity, connectedness, manageability, and nature-oriented human use potential.

Rank of Priority

1. Prairie Creek
2. Santa Fe River
3. Loch Loosa Forest
4. Barr Hammock
5. Watermelon Pond
6. Hickory Sink

Lifestyle (Gainesville—1989)

- Education

Elementary school (0–8 years)—16.1%
High school (1–3 years)—13.3%
High school (4 years)—28.4%
College (1–3 years)—17.9%
College (4 or more years)—24.4%
- Sex/marital status
  Single male—25.7%
  Single female—26.2%
  Married—48.1%
- Children at home
  At least one—23.5%
  Children age 0–7—16.7%
  Children age 8–12—8.5%
  Children age 12–15—8.0%
- Stage in family life cycle
  Single 18–34, no children—25.8%
  Single 35–64, no children—13.4%
  Married 18–34, no children—6.5%
  Married 35–64, no children—15%
  Single, any child—5.3%
  Married, child under 13—11.2%
  Married, child 13–18—7%
- Good life activities
  Attend cultural arts events—21.2%
  Career-oriented activities—17.2%
  Community/civic activities—12.4%
- Outdoor activities
  Camping/hiking—22.9%
  Fishing—25.9%
  Wildlife/environmental activities—19.3%

Media Use Research Findings

This research project was to gather facts about the media use of environmental-oriented organizations in Alachua County. Because Camp Crystal Lake is a government-sponsored organization, the focus was other government or public works organizations. This was a qualitative study to determine the best course for Camp Crystal Lake to complement current environmental information programs and find the best way to be distinctive.

The list of organizations was obtained from the area phone book and a "snowball" effect from those interviewed. Each organization was called at least twice. The first call was the initial contact requesting an interview with the person responsible for the public relations, public affairs, public information, or related office. In many instances a callback was requested since the person was out.

Interviews were completed with:

Gainesville Public Works—Dan Jesse
BFI Waste Management—Public Information Officer
Alachua County Parks and Recreation—Steve Russell
Environmental Protection Agency—Chris Bard
Florida Defenders of the Environment—David Godfrey

These organizations answered questions regarding the purpose and services of their organizations, their audience segmentation, and their media use and response.

Results

All organizations interviewed used print, television, and radio media to relay their message. All employed active public relations and public information campaigns. All directed at least part of their public relations programs at the general public specifically. All said that their public information efforts were most successful when all three media were used in an organized campaign effort:

BFI and Alachua County Parks and Recreation officers commented on the great success of the "Big Blue" recycling program. A detailed plan including radio, newspaper, television, and magazine advertisements was designed by Bob White Productions. Also, a "Big Blue" character was created to act as a "goodwill character" to appear in schools and communities. "We essentially flooded the entire market with advertising," said the BFI public information officer. Before the plan started, about 35 percent of Gainesville and Alachua County residents were recycling. Now BFI estimates that 52 to 57 percent of those residents are recycling.

Alachua County Parks and Recreation sponsor an advertising campaign for their annual "Toxic Roundup." Utilizing mainly the public service announcements on local print, radio, and television, the campaign informs residents of when to bring their household toxic chemicals to a designated place for proper disposal. The campaign's effectiveness is currently under study by the county.

Some methods were thought to have had a greater impact than others in disseminating information:

Dan Jesse of the Gainesville Public Works spoke about the utility organization's efforts to promote conservation of water and electricity use. He stated that the use of a conservation newsletter listing conservation tips and economical information enclosed with monthly bills had gained a higher response than other media.

"When we promote a new program, such as the home energy audits, in the newsletter, we always get a high response." He went on to state that while they hadn't formally studied it, the newsletter coupled with other media gets the most responses for a program, although the newsletter alone is strong as well.

Since all organizations interviewed agreed that a well-planned multimedia campaign was the most successful in getting information about environmental issues to the public in addition to getting them involved (i.e., requesting home energy audits, participating in Big Blue), Camp Crystal Lake should utilize all media when planning its campaign.

Also, the spokespeople said that more personal forms of communication, such as sending an officer to speak with homeowners one-on-one about home efficiency or sending Big Blue to local schools, got people more involved in actual conservation efforts. Camp Crystal Lake should utilize strategies that offer services and chances at personal communication about environmental issues in addition to traditional media.

Public Opinion Research

Executive Summary

This research project serves as a benchmark study and is developed for periodic repetition in order to measure changes in environmental awareness and involvement, opinions about environmental issues and environmental education, as well as acquaintance with Camp Crystal Lake (CCL).

The most important findings of the initial telephone poll are:

- Only 35 percent of the respondents are aware of the fact that a Floridian generates more garbage than the average U.S. citizen.
- On the average, 54 percent of the respondents are practically involved in protecting the environment. However, only 11 of the 100 respondents are involved in environmental action groups.
- Nearly 75 percent of the respondents on this question showed their concerns regarding (hazardous) waste disposal.
- About half of the respondents had ever heard of CCL; however, only 29 percent could tell more about CCL than its name.
- Some parents state that they become more involved in environmental issues through their children, while others strongly disagree with this.
- The poll confirms the importance of multimedia use for distributing environmental-related issues.

Methodology

The poll was executed by the "general public" team by telephone. The questionnaire showing the exact wording of the questions follows the report. The population for the poll are the households of Alachua County, including Gainesville, Archer, Hawthorne, Micanopy, Newberry, Alachua, High Springs, and Waldo. The telephone book was used as the source to identify the households and because not every household has a telephone, it is better to redefine the population as "telephone subscribers." The telephone book contains about 72,500 private telephone subscribers in Alachua County.

Since less than 100,000 households have telephones, we can use a simple formula for computing the chance sampling error ($\sigma\% = \sqrt{p^\star q/n}$). We chose a sample size of 100, for which the sampling error is 0.05. However, because a telephone book sampling method is biased, by excluding households without telephones—probably low-income residents—the poll results will be less than

95% representative of the population. Besides, some questions are only based on a part of the sample—for example, most questions about environmental education are based on answers of households which include school-age children (35% of the sample). The result is a higher chance sampling error for those questions.

The sample was drawn using the Random Digit Dialing (RDD) Sampling Technique. A systematic random sample of the first five digits of telephone numbers was drawn from the telephone book, selecting each 725th number. Every team member received a list with 20 prefixes and a table of two-digit random numbers to add to the prefixes. An interviewee was contacted by adding random numbers to prefixes until a suitable respondent was found. Interviews were completed between November 4, 1991, and December 2, 1991, at various times of the day.

Research Findings

Knowledge/Awareness   Only 35% of the respondents are aware of the fact that a Floridian generates more garbage than the average U.S. citizen. Only 9% of the respondents realize that the average amount of garbage, per person, in Florida counts even more than two times the national average. A more detailed analysis of these data shows that respondents over 30 years of age are less aware than younger respondents.

Knowledge about organizations devoted to protecting the environment was quite limited for the residents of Alachua County. More than a quarter did not recall any name of such an organization, and only 15% could tell the names of at least three environmental organizations. The international organization Greenpeace is, by far, the most well-known. The respondents seemed to be less familiar with local/state organizations.

Behavior/Involvement   On the average, 54% of the respondents are involved in recycling, purchasing recycled products, conserving water, reducing gasoline use, purchasing products with reduced packaging, working with environmental action groups, and seeking information about the environment. The highest number of people is involved in recycling, namely 84 out of 100. However, only 11 of the 100 respondents are involved in environmental action groups.

Opinion/Importance of Involvement   Nearly 90% of the respondents recognize recycling as an (or very) important matter. Besides, also more than 80% of the respondents consider conserving water important (or very), especially those older than 30 years. Working with action groups scores much lower in the opinion of Alachua County residents; 13% even considered it not important at all.

Environmental Concerns   In answer to the question "What special environmental issues concern you as a resident of Alachua County," about 80% of the respondents stated one or more of the twenty-five received concerns. These twenty-five answers are reduced to categories related to:

1. (Hazardous) Waste disposal
2. Development (population growth)

3. Water and air pollution
4. Conserving natural resources
5. Others

Nearly 75% of the respondents on this question showed their concerns regarding (hazardous) waste disposal.

Efforts of Camp Crystal Lake   About half of the respondents had ever heard about CCL. Respondents of 30 years and older seemed to be more acquainted with CCL, since about 60% of this age group had heard of CCL compared to only 35% of respondents under 30 years. However, only 29% could tell more about CCL than its name. Sixty-six percent knew CCL offers summer camps and a little more than 40% mentioned the year-round camping programs. The respondents are more aware of the recreational function of CCL than of the educational role regarding environmental issues and social interaction skills (respectively mentioned by 52%, 21%, and 10%). Educational efforts of a camp like CCL are, according to most respondents, invaluable.

Environmental Education   Questions regarding environmental education were only answered by 35 respondents, whose households include school-age children. According to most parents, environmental education at school is moderate. Some parents state that they become more involved in environmental issues through their children, while others strongly disagree with this. Parents agree about the importance of environmental education at schools.

Media Use   The poll confirms the results of the qualitative media use research project of the campaign, because the information about the environment is not distributed by one particular media source. More than 50% of the respondents mentioned television and newspapers as the source for most of the information they receive about the environment.

Environmental Literature Review

Environmental Degradation

Most experts agree that the greatest sources of environmental degradation are the combustion of fossil fuels and deforestation, each producing massive amounts of carbon dioxide. Carbon dioxide is the most plentiful and effective greenhouse gas. Other greenhouse gases include methane, chlorofluorocarbons, nitrous oxide, and tropospheric ozone (Silver & DeFries, 1990).

Though the greenhouse effect is still a controversial issue, it is commonly believed that the greenhouse gases—when trapped in the atmosphere—cause a rise in the average temperature of the earth. The rise in temperature from high atmospheric concentrations of greenhouse gases are thought to lead to climatic and ecosystem changes causing dramatic worldwide effects (Ehrlich & Ehrlich, 1991).

Who contributes the most to the buildup of these gases? The earth's inhabitants don't exert equal pressure on the environment. Each person in an industrialized nation uses more natural resources and generates far more waste than a person in a developing country. The wealthy countries of the world

BOX 13.1   General Public Telephone Poll for Camp Crystal Lake

Interviewer Name:
Case Number: __ __ __
Telephone Number: (904) __ __ __ – __ __ __ __

Introduction

I.   "Hello, My name is _____, and I am a student in the department of Public Relations at the University of Florida. We are doing a telephone poll about the environment and environmental education in Alachua County. We want to ask you some questions about your involvement in environmental issues and your opinion. It will not take more than 10 minutes of your time."

II.   "Your phone number was drawn at random. Your answers will be used for statistical purposes only. They will be kept completely confidential and not connected to you in any way, by recording a number only. Can you help?"

III.   "You are free to withdraw your consent and to discontinue participation in the poll at any time. You do not have to answer any question you do not want to answer. To be clear: no immediate benefits are to be expected for you. Do you have any questions so far?"

Part 1:   Environmental Awareness and Involvement.

A)   Knowledge/Awareness
First, I would like to ask you some questions about environment-related issues, to learn about environmental awareness of residents of Alachua County.

1)   How much garbage does a Floridian on the average generate in comparison to the national average?
a   about 75% of the national average
b   about the national average
c   about 150% of the national average
d   more than 2 times the national average

2)   Can you tell me the name of any organization devoted to protecting the environment? (check all that apply)
a   Sierra Club
b   Friends of the Earth
c   Environmental Protection Agency

h   Coop America
i   1000 Friends of Florida
j   Friends of Alachua County
k   Other,   _____

          _____

B)   Behavior/Involvement
3) Do you recycle?   Y/N
4) Do you intentionally purchase products made from
     recycled products?   Y/N
5) Do you intentionally conserve water?   Y/N
6) Do you intentionally reduce your gasoline use?   Y/N
7) Do you intentionally purchase products with
     reduced packaging?   Y/N
8) Do you participate in an environmental action group?   Y/N
9) Do you ever intentionally look for information
     about environmental issues?   Y/N

C)   Importance/Opinion
10) How important do you consider these issues?
(on a 5-point scale from 1 for not important up to 5 for very important)

What about:

	n.i.				v.i.	
a) recycling:	1	2	3	4	5	6 (=don't know)
b) purchasing recycled products:	1	2	3	4	5	6 (=don't know)
c) conserving water:	1	2	3	4	5	6 (=don't know)
d) reducing gasoline use:	1	2	3	4	5	6 (=don't know)
e) purchasing products with reduced packaging:	1	2	3	4	5	6 (=don't know)
f) working with action groups:	1	2	3	4	5	6 (=don't know)
g) seeking information about the environment:	1	2	3	4	5	6 (=don't know)

(continues)

D)   Special Concerns in Alachua County
11)   What special environmental issues concern you as a resident of Alachua County?   ....

Part 2:   Efforts of Camp Crystal Lake.

12a) Have you ever heard about Camp Crystal Lake?   Y/N

12b) If no: Tell them about Camp Crystal Lake, using the 6 points of following checklist.
       If yes: Can you tell me what Camp Crystal Lake offers?

       Use Checklist (don't read it, but mark all they mention):
       1)   summer camp
       2)   year-round camping program for school groups (2nd & 5th graders)
       3)   facilities for other camp groups
       4)   environmental education
       5)   recreation
       6)   social interaction skills

13)   How important do you consider the educational efforts of a camp like Camp Crystal Lake?
       n.i.   v.i.
       1   2   3   4   5   6 (=don't know)

Part 3:   Household characteristics/ opinion about
                   environmental education.

14a) Does your household include school-age children?   Y/N

14b) How much information do your children get about environmental issues at school?
       none   very much
       1   2   3   4   5   6 (=don't know)

14c) How adequate is the information your children get at school?
       not   too
       enough   much
       1   2   3   4   5   6 (=don't know)

14d) Have you become more involved in environmental issues through your children?

not   much
at all   more
1   2   3   4   5   6 (=don't know)

15) Do you consider environmental education for children important?

n.i.   v.i.
1   2   3   4   5   6 (=don't know)

16) How do you get most of your information about the environment?
1. radio   4. newspapers
2. TV   5. friends
3. magazines   6. other, _____

17) Demographics
a) What is your age bracket? (read list if necessary, check one)
1. 16–19   5. 40–49
2. 20–25   6. 50–59
3. 26–29   7. 60–65
4. 30–39   8. over 65

b) Sex ....(observation) 1. Male   2. Female

c) Are you...... (read list, check one)
1. White
2. Black
3. Hispanic
4. Indian
5. Other – Specify _____

d) What is your occupation? _____

e) What bracket does your annual family income fall in? (read list)
1. Under $5,000   6. 20,000 to 39,999
2. 5,000 to 7,999   7. 40,000 to 59,999
3. 8,000 to 9,999   8. 60,000 or above
4. 10,000 to 14,999   9. don't know
5. 15,000 to 19,999

18) **Thank you very much for your cooperation!!!**

constitute about one-quarter of the population, but use 80 percent of the world's energy (Silver & DeFries, 1990).

In Florida, industry accounts for about one-third of all energy used. Transportation accounts for another third, but uses two-thirds of all the petroleum expended in the state. Current automobile technologies could provide a cost-effective alternative by doubling fuel efficiency through weight reduction and fuel economies that potentially double the mileage per vehicle. The last third of all energy use in Florida is in the residential sector (Capehart, 1991).

Before the Industrial Revolution the atmosphere contained about 275 parts per million (ppm) of carbon dioxide; by 1991, the concentration was about 335 ppm and rising about .4 percent annually (Ehrlich & Ehrlich, 1991).

Fossil fuels—the converted remains of plants and animals—when burned complete an age-old cycle. The energy stored in the fossil fuels (oil, natural gas, and coal) is solar, produced by photosynthesis hundreds of millions of years ago. Oxygen deprivation stopped the decomposition of these fuels. When the fuels are burned to produce energy or operate our automobiles, carbon stored over these millions of years is returned to the atmosphere. Unfortunately the return is many thousand times faster than the removal and produces a buildup of carbon dioxide in the atmosphere. About six billion tons of carbon (in the form of CO_2) is added annually to the atmosphere by fossil fuel combustion (Ehrlich & Ehrlich, 1991).

Deforestation is the second largest contributor to the greenhouse gas carbon dioxide. A study in the late 1970s by the UN Food and Agriculture Organization and the UN Environment Programme concluded that about 27 million acres of tropical forest is disappearing each year. Deforestation may account for as much as 20 percent of the buildup of carbon dioxide in the atmosphere (Silver & DeFries, 1990).

How do the forests protect the environment? Trees protect the soil from the rain and wind. Once the forest is cleared, there is a high rate of soil erosion. Normally forest ecosystems recycle rainwater back to the atmosphere through evaporation and transpiration (Silver & DeFries, 1990).

Forests also absorb energy that would reflect back into the atmosphere if the soil were bare. Plants take up carbon from the atmosphere as they grow and release carbon back when they die, decompose, or are burned. High rates of deforestation disturb the balance of plant photosynthesis and decomposition. Scientists also believe that there is a link to flooding and deforestation; once lands are cleared they act as watersheds, unable to absorb large amounts of rainfall (Silver & DeFries, 1990).

Deforestation threatens biodiversity; tropical forests contain more than half of the world's plant and animal species and because tropical soils are notoriously unproductive once cleared of their forest cover they cannot support diverse wildlife and ecosystems (Staff, 1991). It is estimated that the rate of species loss from deforestation is about 10,000 times greater than the naturally occurring extinction rate that existed prior to the appearance of human beings (Ehrlich & Ehrlich, 1991).

What can the average citizen do to reduce environmental degradation? Fossil fuel consumption can be reduced through energy conservation. By conserving and by installing more efficient air conditioners and energy-efficient lighting, the United States could eliminate the need for 85 power plants within 50 years. Raising fuel efficiency standards for cars and trucks one mile per gallon could save 300,000 barrels of oil a day (Wirth, 1990). The less energy we use, the longer our natural resources will last and the less environmental damage the earth will sustain (Capehart, 1991).

Switching to fuels like natural gas and solar power produce less carbon dioxide (Canine, 1989). Conversion of automobiles, factories, or home heating systems to natural gas and away from coal is only a temporary solution. Natural gas is found domestically, but as with the other fossil fuels, quantities are limited. Natural gas is the least polluting fossil fuel but does produce nitrous oxide, another greenhouse gas (Marinelli, 1994).

Recycling and "source reduction" (reducing waste at its source) also reduce the amount of fossil fuels used. Recycling saves energy because the manufacturing process—instead of producing the same product from natural resources—uses less energy and is less polluting. Source reduction typically involves reducing packaging materials; lighter or fewer packages also reduce air, water, and other pollutants associated with the manufacturing process (Canine, 1989; Vandervoort, 1991).

In order to reduce the overall effects of the industrial nations, we as consumers need to become better educated. Once we begin to understand the global issues and how we affect them, we can reduce our own contribution and, through legislation, the contribution of others.

Research Bibliography

Canine, C. (1989, November/December). Home Energy. *Garbage,* 20–27.

Capehart, B. (1991, October). Contemporary Issues to Energy Conservation. *Waste Management, Energy and the Environment.* Seminar conducted at the Austin Cary Forest Conference Center, Gainesville, Florida.

Ehrlich, P. R., & Ehrlich, A. H. (1991). *Healing the Planet: Strategies for Resolving the Environmental Crisis.* Addison-Wesley Publishing Company.

Shell, Paul. (1991, December). Hazardous Waste in Florida. Interview with Paul Still, assistant director, Florida Center for Solid and Hazardous Waste Management, TREEO Center, Gainesville, Florida.

Silver, C. S., & DeFries, R. S. (1990). *One Earth one Future: Our Changing Global Environment.* Washington: National Academy Press.

Staff. (1991). The Science of Saving Wildlife. *Impact,* 8(1), 16–23.

Vandervoort, S. S. (1991). Big "Green Brother" Is Watching: New Directions in Environmental Public Affairs Challenge Business. *Public Relations Review,* 47(4), 14–19 & 26.

Wirth, T. E. (1990). Conservation is the Key. *Journal of Environmental Health, Special Issue,* 25.

BOX 13.2   **Interview with Paul Still, Assistant Director**
Florida Center for Solid and Hazardous Waste Management

In Florida, the greatest proportion of hazardous waste that needs disposal comes from the citizenry. Industry produces much less hazardous waste in our state than the citizens. In Alachua County about 3 percent of the population participated in "Toxic Roundup 1990"—an annual collection of household hazardous waste—bringing about 127 tons of potentially hazardous material to the drop-off site. Materials collected included oil- and latex-based paints, flammable liquids, pesticides, used oil, aerosols, corrosives, antifreeze, lead acid and dry cell batteries, and nonregulated wastes.

Much of the flammable hazardous waste collected in Florida is mixed and burnt as a fuel source for industry within the state. Stringent mix and flow tests are run on the fluid mixture before burning and only those fuels that meet these requirements can be processed. These flammable liquids are used as fuel alternatives for producing such products as soil aggregates used as cement and asphalt bases.

To dispose of these hazardous materials through burning costs about $0.50 per gallon, which is much cheaper than trucking and disposing of these materials at a hazardous waste facility. Products that cannot be mixed as fuels must be transported to Alabama, South Carolina, or other states. Generally these materials include: batteries, photography wastes, pesticides, chlorinated solvents, metal cleaning solvents, printing solvents, dry cleaning fluids, and PCB's.

In Gainesville a "superfund site" is located near K-Mart on Main Street—the site used to house a turpentine extracting plant that produced phenol compounds as a manufacturing by-product. This hazardous by-product had originally been stored in detention ponds but was spread to the land when the site was developed. A list of other Florida or U.S. superfund sites is available from the regional Environmental Protection Agency (EPA) office in Atlanta, Georgia. In Florida, the Department of Environmental Regulation (DER) oversees hazardous waste disposal, and the EPA governs the DER.

Research Summary

1. Organizational Research—gathered information about the structure, regulations, and history of the Alachua County School Board (Ky Bradwell).
2. Population Demographics Research—assembled information about our target population. Examples include: age, sex, population size, household with children, and other variables (Ernesto Ortiz).

3. Media Research—gathered information on the best media methods to use to reach our target audience most effectively. Specifically examined Alachua County organizations that participate in environmental programs and are run by state or local government, examining what media methods worked best and why (Len Rayburn).

4. Environmental Research—compiled information on the origination of the environmental problem nationwide and specific Florida issues (Linda Tozer).

5. Public Opinion Research—using a poll, gathered data on the target population about environmental opinions, attitudes, and existing environmental knowledge (Marlies Veldhoen).

General Public Situation Analysis

Based on research findings, the general public campaign is designed to correct the following situations: low environmental awareness and involvement and limited knowledge of the specific activities provided by Camp Crystal Lake.

The program focus at CCL is teaching children about nature through a holistic approach. It is based on the concept that learning by doing in the outdoors is an effective method to develop awareness, knowledge, and skills for future effective environmental management. Planning strategies took into account the hands-on involvement that is typical of CCL. Observation, exploration, and interaction are the key to each activity.

After the situation statement was defined the group called John Christian, director at Camp Crystal Lake, to verify the statement. We asked him if he would like us to include a "twelve-month school" contingency plan. He explained that it wouldn't be necessary to include such a contingency plan, stating that if the Alachua County school board changed the length of the school year, it wouldn't take place in the near future. Throughout the planning stages, phone calls were made to him to confirm planned activities.

Our broad target audience was defined as the "general public." Specific information about this public was identified through Alachua County demographic research and by a poll conducted by our pubic relations group. Through research findings we determined the following segmented publics: parents, business/government leaders, environmental activists, media representatives, second and fifth graders, and teachers.

Lack of knowledge in the general public about the impact of technology, population growth, and development of environmentally polluting practices have all contributed to the present state of the problem.

Environmental problems indigenous to Alachua County and the state of Florida reflect and are related to the broader environmental issues, such as the greenhouse effect, ozone depletion, water quality, fossil fuel combustion, hazardous waste disposal, and destruction of vital ecosystems.

Government-sponsored organizations that were similar to CCL or participated in environmentally oriented public relations campaigns were interviewed to determine media use strategies. Some of the organizations inter-

BOX 13.3   **Total Budget—All Strategies**

Materials	Budget	Donated
Printing		
certificates	$ 190.00	
brochures, fliers		$ 300.00
booklets	$ 100.00	
info packet	$ 100.00	
Miscellaneous		
mailing	$ 200.00	
posters	$ 25.00	
prizes	$ 260.00	$ 75.00
buttons	$ 50.00	
guestbook + pens	$ 10.00	
food	$ 250.00	
collecting recyclables		$1000.00
	$1185.00	$1375.00

viewed included Alachua County Parks and Recreation, Alachua County Public Works (including water and electric divisions), and Alachua County Environmental Protection Agency.

The best appeals will be personal, specific appeals that are simple, educational, and attention getting and that call county citizens to action.

To reach the general population on a tight budget, the group used low-cost media resources and planned a fund-raising event to cover other campaign expenses.

A 10 percent increase in environmental and camp awareness and involvement in the targeted public will constitute a "successful" campaign. This goal will be measured by comparing our precampaign poll results to a postcampaign survey.

Mission Statement

The mission of Camp Crystal Lake is to promote environmental consciousness and community involvement, by providing the youth of Alachua County with outdoor learning experiences that emphasize earth conservation.

Statement of the Goal

The general public campaign seeks to position Camp Crystal Lake as the leader in youth environmental education in Alachua County by increasing recognition of the camp's activities by 10 percent* in the first campaign year.

*Will be measured with postsurvey.

Objectives

1. Involve environmental groups in at least three activities pertaining to Camp Crystal Lake.
2. Involve camp participants in demonstrating environmental concepts to 10 percent of the general public.
3. Identify teachers to promote environmental concepts to their students.
4. Involve at least 15 percent of the identified teachers in ecological school demonstrations.
5. Get funding for all costs of the Camp Crystal Lake Campaign from businesses and/or governmental agencies.
6. Get support of at least five businesses/governmental agencies for environmental education by involving them in environmental projects.
7. Establish in at least five businesses/governmental agencies an official recycling, waste reducing, and purchasing of recycled products program.
8. Establish cooperative and regular contacts with all local media to promote Camp Crystal Lake and youth environmentalists.
9. Collect a total of ten tons of recyclable materials.

Other Adaptation Elements

I. Strategies Considered and Rejected

CCL Carpool Awards program: CCL would sponsor a yearly competition between businesses and governmental agencies. The goal would be to honor businesses for taking a leadership role in stimulating carpooling, and to provide information about the importance of carpooling. Award winners would be rewarded.

CCL Christmas Cards project: This would be a fund-raising project for the CCL campaign. The alumni club would develop (on recycled paper) two series of Christmas cards, containing "simple things you can do to save the Earth" for businesses and for households. Alumni club members would also assist in selling the cards.

CCL information booths at trade shows, etc.: CCL would compile information about business recycling, waste reduction, and materials reuse programs to display at trade shows, etc.

CCL Earth Watchers Home Improvement Checklist: CCL would compile practical information about making houses more eco-friendly. This information would be distributed to Alachua County residents through newspaper and radio public service announcements (PSAs). Checklist may be distributed through local water or electric bills.

"Most Earth-Friendly House" Award: CCL would sponsor a contest where entrants would explain how earth-friendly their day-to-day life-style is. Criteria for the award would range from what types of detergents the family uses, to recycling, to how efficiently the family uses water. The award would be highly publicized and given bimonthly. The finalists' houses would be visited by a CCL representative to verify claims.

TV/Newspaper PSA ad series "The life of . . . ": CCL would create PSAs that would deliver the need for recycling efforts. The messages would be emotionally charged and have dark overtones. "The life of an aluminum can—disposable diaper—plastic bottle, etc." would follow the item's creation, use, discardment, and final fate in the landfill, with projections into the future and hints about how the problem is compounded by numbers.

"Crystal Clear—Messages for better living from CCL": Short PSAs and advertisements designed to get across a single practical informational message, such as, "Conserve water while brushing your teeth."

CCL Teachers Environmental Workshop—Provide an environmental workshop for teachers that will provide continuing education credits that all teachers need to maintain their teaching certification.

CCL Alumni Speakers Bureau—In the second year of the campaign, speech contest winners could form a speakers bureau and give presentations to fourth-grade classes about their experience at CCL.

II. Limitations Related to Calendar Time, Personnel Available and Funding

Calendar time: To take advantage of the multiplication of publicity effects when a series of events take place under an umbrella theme, the events must be implemented within a limited period of time—we suggest a year. Preparation time must be sufficient to keep volunteers interested, yet not overwhelmed.

Personnel available: CCL personnel is limited to four persons, which suggests that to implement the suggested strategies CCL must rely on volunteers. Volunteers would be taken from the alumni club the Youth Campaign is proposing.

Funds: No budget monies are specifically available for public relations activities, so costs must be avoided or events that require funding must be combined with fund-raising activities.

Implementation Strategies

Camp Crystal Lake's Earth Watchers Campaign

Team Goal The general public campaign seeks to position Camp Crystal Lake as the leader in youth environmental education for Alachua County. Targeted audiences: parents, second- and fifth-grade students, business and governmental leaders, environmental activists, media representatives, and teachers.

Team Strategy Elements All team strategies are parts of the "Earth Watchers" program theme. Each takes a different focus on delivering Camp Crystal Lake's message to specified parts of the general public while accomplishing the objectives specified in the team strategy plan.

- CCL EARTH WATCHERS BREAKFAST, CCL EARTH WATCHERS DAY
- CCL EARTH WATCHERS AWARDS
- CCL EARTH WATCHERS WORKSHOP
- CCL EARTH WATCHERS RECYCLING WEEKEND
- CCL EARTH WATCHERS 1992 EVENTS

Brief Description of Strategies, Contingencies, and Evaluation Methods
Overall evaluation of the Earth Watchers programs will be measured by a postprogram survey similar to the one used during the research part of this campaign. Increases in public awareness and involvement regarding environmental issues and CCL will be measured.

- Earth Watchers Breakfast, a fund-raising event for community leaders followed by an open house event, Earth Watchers Day, at the camp. During the breakfast, CCL will raise funds by selling Earth Watcher Contracts to business leaders and present a traveling exhibition about the meaning of the contracts. CCL alumni will help open the exhibition, with one or two business leaders already arranged to endorse the program.

Contingencies   General problems that may occur include accidents, violence, natural hazards, unruly animals, fire, illness, injuries, or death. To anticipate these problems, all staff members should have a list of emergency phone numbers and know where to find and how to use fire extinguishers and first aid equipment. Staff members may carry radio communicators for nature hikes.

- Potential problems specific to the event include absence of speaker, program changes due to weather, canceling of breakfast room reservation, and absence of project leader. To prepare for these problems in advance, an organizational guide and schedule of events for the breakfast and open house must be made, alternative leaders must be chosen and trained, and alternatives for outdoor activities must be prepared (video or indoor activity). The program director will decide when contingencies will be used.

Event Evaluation   The objectives of this strategy are:

- To involve camp participants in demonstrating environmental concepts to 10 percent of the general public.
- To get funding for all costs of the CCL campaign from businesses and governmental agencies.
- To establish in at least five businesses/governmental agencies an official recycling, waste reduction, and recycled products purchasing program.

CCL must measure:

- The number of participants in this program
- The number of sold contracts

- The amount of money received
- The number of exhibition booklets sold

In addition it would be helpful in evaluation to prepare a questionnaire for participants that measures how well they were informed, what information they understood and retained, whether they were convinced about the issues, whether they were convinced to buy the contract, and general reactions to the event.

The results have to be discussed in a staff meeting within a short period of time, so that the staff members can remember the problems involved and the positive/negative reactions received. This will help the staff to prepare for a future presentation.

Ideally, all results should be compiled and reported for use in future campaigns.

- First Annual CCL Earth Watcher Award Program: Camp Crystal Lake will sponsor an "Annual Earth Watcher Award" contest for camp alumni. Competitions for the camp alumni will include: a speech contest, poster contest, creative class project, and most-committed family contest. With the exception of the creative class project, the contest is an outside school project. Monetary awards and certificates will be provided by businesses solicited in the Earth Watchers Breakfast and Earth Watchers Day. Contest participants must have attended CCL within two years of the award submittal deadline

Contingencies The plan will include a building plan with all exits clearly marked. Back-up sites in case of emergency will be determined by the task force and told to participants. Volunteers will be used to keep things running smoothly.

- Overall, the contingency plan will include safety plans in case of fire, personal injury, an "act of God," and a plan to handle hazardous waste leaks and other potential negative effects associated with this site. Initiation of this hazardous waste plan will be decided by management.

Event Evaluation The evaluation of this event will be based on the overall survey. This analysis will be used to help plan the next annual award event.

- To measure goal achievement for this program, a follow-up questionnaire will be given to task force leaders and randomly selected participating teachers including: individuals from the general population, business and governmental leaders, environmental activists, teachers, and media representatives. This program also addresses six of the nine team strategy objectives adequately.
- The survey will include questions to determine the positive and negative event results, as well as determining changes in knowledge and support of youth education and CCL.

Survey results from teachers and task force members as well as staff observations will be used to plan the second "CCL Earth Watcher Award Program."

- CCL Earth Watchers Workshop: The "Earth Watchers Workshop" is a program designed to get parents and teachers of school-age children and young adults involved in environmental and conservation efforts by providing oral and printed information, demonstrations, and expert speakers during specified and advertised PTA meetings.
- CCL will work with local businesses and governmental agencies that work with environmental concerns (i.e., BFI, water commission) to give the program a more informed and "official" support system.

Contingencies   If any natural or man-made disaster, accident, or injury occurs, CCL will follow the policies and procedures of the host school.

CCL will have alternatives available to present the program, will insure that demonstration models and alternative visual aids are available, and will be prepared to handle any questions regarding CCL's operations and the hazardous waste situation.

Event Evaluation   In evaluating the success of the "CCL Earth Watchers Workshop," an evaluative questionnaire disguised as a "graduation test" will be given to adult participants at the PTA meetings. The questionnaire will test individual's knowledge about environmental concerns and practical home applications presented in the program. Also included will be questions regarding any parts of the program that were unclear or too complicated to remember that aren't covered in the printed information. The questionnaire will be multiple choice. Each question's results will be compiled to determine if the message covered was adequately presented.

Positive and negative results will be kept on a per question basis in a data base. Each presentation's results will be used to determine whether parts of the presentation should be changed to facilitate communication. A large percentage, to be determined by CCL, of wrong answers to a question will prompt changes to that part of the program.

The staff's performance will be evaluated with the survey.

- As the goals of this program are to communicate environmental concerns, present applicable home information, and get individuals to sign contracts to apply the information, the results of the survey and the number of contracts signed will be used to determine how well the goals have been met.
- Each presentation survey will provide valuable information for refinement of the presentation for the next campaign. The presentation will be updated after each survey.
- CCL Earth Watchers Recycling Weekend is a contest among different teams assigned to cover several neighborhoods of Alachua County. It seeks to provide residents of these neighborhoods with recycling tips and information. The teams consist of and are coordinated by children

educated in CCL. While providing information to the residents, they will be trying to achieve the goal of collecting 10 tons of recyclable material, covering 3,000 households.

Contingencies   An open line to the nearest hospital must be available. The supervisor of each group (adults or older children) must have a permanent contact with the rest of the group in order to avoid disappearances. Supervisors will count the group each 30 minutes to check for missing children. The children's parents must have signed a release form and included telephone numbers.

Event Evaluation   The objective of this event is clearly stated and perfectly measurable. We will be seeking to cover 3000 households between the preparation weekend and the actual recycling weekend and to collect 10 tons of recyclable material. A notebook accounting the reactions and attitudes of the residents reached by the students will contribute insights about the event which can be used in future events.

The evaluation of the residents' reactions is significant because of the unique situation—the education is being provided by 10 to 12 year-old children.

- CCL Earth Watchers 1992 Events: A summary of strategies to implement in "Earth Watchers 1992" theme include a "best environment" poster contest (suggested by an elementary school teacher) and a recycling drive between schools to see who can collect the most recyclable materials in a year. A school carnival will be used as a forum to disseminate information about the environment to the general public. Guest speakers from companies or environmental support groups will visit the schools at least once every two months to talk about environmental issues. The partici-learn program operates in conjunction with guidelines for fifth-grade students to learn about life cycles. On Arbor Day, students will plant trees and observe their role in the life cycle. "Earth Watchers 1992" is a series of events over the period of one year.

Contingencies   School policies will be followed in case of any problems.

Event Evaluation   A survey should be given to all fifth-grade teachers and students in Alachua County. The results from this survey should be compared to the results from the overall survey prior to these events. From this comparison, CCL should be able to determine where there was a significant increase in environmental awareness. The survey should also seek the level of involvement or any change in behavior prior to the events and whether people recognize CCL as an environmental education center.

Media coverage can be evaluated by monitoring how many news releases or stories were published about any of the events. Tabulating how much information was given out at the carnival and the effects of the guest speakers should provide valuable information on what needs to be further developed.

Weigh the amount of recyclable material collected from each elementary school participating in the drive at the end of the year. Keep records for evaluation of involvement strategy.

This program addresses five of the campaign objectives for the general public group as stated in the strategy plan. Comparison of evaluation measurement results and these objectives will determine if the goals have been met.

Each of these strategy elements addresses a number of the strategy plan objectives. All objectives are adequately addressed by the strategies. Each strategy has its own evaluation plan. How that strategy fulfills the campaign objectives it is aimed at will determine the overall success or failure of that program.

Evaluation

Overall Evaluation

Overall evaluation of the Earth Watchers programs will be measured by a postprogram survey similar to the one used in the research part of this campaign. A 10 percent increase in awareness and involvement regarding environmental issues and CCL will be measured.

Summary of Strategy Evaluations

A. CCL Earth Watchers Breakfast and CCL Earth Watchers Day

- The number of participants in this program
- The number of sold contracts
- The amount of money received
- The number of exhibition books sold

In addition it would be helpful in evaluation to prepare a questionnaire for participants that measures how well they were informed, what information they understood and retained, whether they were convinced about the issues, whether they were convinced to buy the contract, and general reactions to the event.

B. CCL Earth Watchers Awards   To measure goal achievement for this program, a follow-up questionnaire will be given to task force leaders and randomly selected participating teachers, including business and governmental leaders, environmental activists, teachers, and media representatives.

The survey will include questions to determine the positive and negative event results, as well as determining changes in knowledge and support of youth education and CCL.

C. CCL Earth Watchers Workshop   In evaluating the success of the "CCL Earth Watchers Workshop," an evaluative questionnaire disguised as a "graduation test" will be given to adult participants at the PTA meetings. The questionnaire will test individual's knowledge about environmental concerns and practical home applications presented in the program. Also included will be questions regarding any parts of the program that were unclear or too complicated to remember and aren't covered in the printed information. The questionnaire will be multiple choice. Each question's results will be compiled to determine if the message covered was adequately presented.

Positive and negative results will be kept on a per question basis in a data base. Each presentation's results should be changed to facilitate communication. A large percentage, to be determined by CCL, of wrong answers to a question will prompt changes to that part of the program.

The staff's performance will be evaluated with the survey.

D. CCL Earth Watchers Recycling Weekend   The objective of this event was clearly stated and perfectly measurable. We will need to canvass 3000 households between the preparation weekend and the actual recycling weekend and to college 10 tons of recyclable material. A file recording household reactions will contribute insight about the event that can be used in future events.

E. CCL Earth Watchers 1992 Events   A survey should be given to all fifth-grade teachers and students in Alachua County. The results from this survey should be compared to the results from the overall survey prior to these events. From this comparison, CCL should be able to determine where there was a significant increase in environmental awareness. This survey should also seek the level of involvement or any changes in behavior prior to the events, and whether people recognize CCL as an environmental education center.

Media coverage can be evaluated by monitoring how many news releases or stories were published about any of the events. Tabulating how much information was given out at the carnival and the effects of the guest speakers should provide valuable information on what needs to be further developed.

Weigh the amount of recyclable material collected from each elementary school participating in the contest between schools at the end of the year. Keep records for evaluation of involvement strategy.

➤ **CASE STUDY: A WATER UTILITY LAUNCHES CONSERVATION CAMPAIGN—1989–93**

Background

Southern States Utilities (SSU), Florida's largest investor-owned water and wastewater utility, chose to launch a water conservation campaign in spite of an industrywide corporate culture that frequently offered bonuses to managers based on total water sales and often encouraged higher customer consumption to ensure profitability. The company's executive-level decision reflected the harsh realities of a serious drought plaguing most of the Sunshine State, the demands of a rapidly growing population, and expanding residential and commercial development.

This case study was written by Kerry Anderson Crooks.

SSU corporate policy favored growth through acquisition of smaller and competing utilities. The policy prompted a hostile takeover attempt of Florida-based Deltona Utilities which, when successfully completed, would double the size of SSU. Executives of the Deltona acquisition historically opposed any conservation public information program.

To meet the company's internal and external communications requirements that were exacerbated by these developments, the company hired one public relations practitioner during the last month of 1988. The challenge of the new practitioner simultaneously dealing with the problem of building a continuing media relations and employee relations program, a hostile takeover, and a drought crisis.

Due to limited resources, SSU concentrated its efforts on the drought crisis. The new public relations administrator took his case to the new chief executive officer, and, over the objections of the Deltona executives, received a green light to start a comprehensive water conservation campaign.

Research

Historical Facts   The population of the service area perceived the state's water supply as endless. It is widely known that Florida contains the country's largest underground reservoir of fresh water. Some one quadrillion gallons of water is stored in the state's underground "aquifer" network. Since Florida contains such an extraordinary amount of this resource, many Floridians view the water supply as inexhaustible. However, the aquifer is vulnerable to salt water intrusion, especially in the coastal regions when overuse exceeds recharge from rainwater and other sources.

In 1989 the shallow well field of SSU's Venice Gardens utility began to ingest sand into its water pumps. The utility's available reserves dropped to only 1 inch of water in one of its water tanks and not much more in the other. SSU conducted an intense public information effort that included door-to-door notices, multimedia announcements, and meeting with regulators to develop a special water restriction zone. The efforts worked and SSU was able to draw a sigh of relief within two weeks.

Survey Research   To gauge whether the ongoing drought began to creep into the consciousness of its customer base, SSU included conservation questions in a survey it contracted with Cambridge Research Reports of Massachusetts. From its 100,000 total customer accounts, 600 were randomly selected yielding a chance sampling error of .04 percent. Findings revealed that 81 percent of customers felt it was important or very important that SSU "offer programs and services, such as information and advice to help customers control water use"; 86 percent felt water conservation was critical or very critical in their area. Customers were aware there was a water supply problem but were not sure what individuals could do about it.

Figure 13.1 Southern States Utilities, Florida's largest investor-owned water and wastewater utility, won awards when, in the face of drought and other threats to the water supply, it reversed an industry practice of promoting water use to launch a conservation campaign.

The Problem   These findings combined with warnings by the state's water management districts that water consumption exceeded nature's ability to replenish led the company to commit its resources to a statewide water conservation campaign. The problem would require both external steps to control demand and internal steps to enhance supplies.

Adaptation

The Goals   To reduce demand for water by initiating an inverted rate structure and a public information/education effort as well as to expand water supplies by adopting reverse osmosis technologies and water reclamation practices.

Target Publics   Customers; youth, including schools and 4-H Clubs; local and state governments, regulators, and legislators; civic associations, chambers of commerce, and libraries; Institute of Food and Agricultural Sciences (IFAS) agencies; volunteers; employees, including operations, communications, legal, and engineering personnel; the media, including newspapers, radio and television; the water supply industry; and stockholders.

Objectives

> Convince cost regulators and a majority of customers of the need for advanced treatment technologies as well as other supply technologies, and justify the cost.
>
> Incorporate into SSU's capital improvement program for employees and stockholders the need to introduce advanced treatment technologies to address water supply concerns.
>
> To create a favorable perception toward water conservation issues among the 160,000 SSU customers, as well as among youth, civic organizations, and the media within the first two years.
>
> Enhance awareness of the fragility of water supplies and elicit positive action toward conserving/protecting Florida's waters among all publics through the course of the campaign. Position SSU as a leader in the water supply industry.
>
> Convince 80 percent of customers to adopt minimum water conservation measures in the first two years.

Time Frame   A five-year campaign included start-up research and planning and implementation over the five years.

Budget   No budget was initially created for the effort; however, due to demands on funds by all departments within the corporation, the public relations budget remained fairly minimal—generally less than $30,000 was available for conservation activities. In contrast, the capital improvements costs for creating higher technology treatment systems would easily reach into the millions of dollars for one system alone. In fact the new reverse osmosis water treatment plant at Marco Island cost the company over $9 million.

Implementation Strategy

Speakers Bureau   Based on research of government and industry hydrologic and botanical sources two standard conservation speeches were created. These speeches provided information on Florida's water situation, why conservation is needed, and methods on how to conserve both indoors and out. Members of the communications department and company volunteers were trained in presenting these and in the use of supporting materials, including a 35-mm slide show, a display of water restriction devices, and conservation handouts. Business reply cards offering water conservation procedures and information were mailed on a routine basis to customers, and on a regular basis to schools and civic associations.

Customer Newsletter and Direct Mail   SSU created a customer newsletter and used it to emphasize water conservation. The newsletter, designed to be mailed on a quarterly basis, went to 160,000 customers and 233 Florida legislators, county commissioners, and administrators in each service area and 16 local area newspapers. Packets including water restriction information, Xeriscape™ brochures, and conservation kits were mailed on request. Other conservation materials the company either created or served as a conduit for free materials from Florida's water management districts.

Open Houses   SSU established a yearly goal of conducting several open house events to demonstrate the latest water/wastewater treatment technologies and water conservation techniques. On occasion, the company hosted a Chamber of Commerce function at the headquarters where water conservation displays and handouts were featured. The company held several new facility dedications to highlight both the new equipment and the company's total commitment to water conservation. During the campaign, open houses were conducted at facilities in Apopka, Venice, Marco Island, and Deltona. The open houses in Venice and Marco Island demonstrated the new reverse osmosis facilities. Reverse osmosis is a process by which potable water can be extracted from brackish (salty) groundwater. The company also held a dedication ceremony to mark the conversion of its Deltona wastewater treatment plant to an advanced water reclamation facility. This dedication was attended by members of the St. Johns Water Management District, the Florida Department of Environmental Regulation, and the media. Informal tours of SSU facilities have also been conducted for various audiences.

SSU/4-H Environmental Landscape Management (ELM) Program   SSU initiated and funded a landscape management program for youth beginning in 1991. This program helps youth members of 4-H to learn the techniques of drought-resistant landscaping and, with volunteer leaders, to develop and implement these principles in conservation landscaping projects. The program offers an opportunity for Florida youth to be hands-on researchers, planters, maintenance landscapers, evaluators, and presenters. They created a thinking gardener's landscape based on Xeriscape™ principles. The program is designed

Figure 13.2 Southern States Utilities environmental responsibility efforts included conservation of water by promoting creative low-water-use landscaping. The principle of Xeriscape® allowed 4-H youth to design landscapes and gardens that require limited use of water.

to give 4-H youths and volunteers the opportunity to experiment and examine the best methods to create drought-resistant landscapes in and for their communities. SSU promoted the new 4-H techniques during its own presentations, at various open houses, and at shareholder meetings.

Legislative Activities   SSU representatives made it a high priority to promote effective conservation legislation. The company visited various state senate and house members to voice support for water conservation and has thrown its support behind revenue-neutral conservation rate structures in its discussions with legislators, water management district officials, and the Florida Public Service Commission (FPSC).

Publications and Articles   Members of the utility staff made it their professional responsibility to publish articles regarding water resources in the commercial media. The communications department manager published several articles on international water issues and presented a paper to the National Regulators' Research Institute at the Ohio State University on water conservation efforts in Florida. The company's environmental manager coauthored an article on water resource problems on Marco Island, and the vice president for corporate development coauthored an article on water reclamation techniques. Another communications department member published a trade magazine article on water conservation and wrote several newspaper articles on the subject.

Small Change Original Theatre   Several SSU programs exist to educate youth on water conservation. In the winter of 1991–92, SSU sponsored the live production of "Captain Hydro and the Water Bandit" performed by the Small Change Original Theatre. A follow-on program, "Robin Hood and the Water Crusaders" was then planned for the 1994–95 school year.

Ongoing Research   SSU's clipping service keeps the company informed on various water issues in the media and tracks water trends affecting the state. Several staff are members of the National Association of Water Companies, where a number of employees hold board memberships. Company staff are also active in national and state activities of the American Water Works Association, and personnel in operations, communications, legal, and engineering keep current on the latest water conservation issues through direct research, continuing education, and professional associations.

Educational Videos   SSU staff wrote and produced the ADDY Award-winning 25-minute feature-length video, "Water for Florida's Future," featuring a representative each from Florida Water Management Districts, the Florida Legislature, and the Florida Public Service Commission. The video was distributed to customers, legislators, county/city commissioners and administrators, newspapers, chambers of commerce, libraries, and schools. The company also cosponsored the "Save Our Water" video, an educational musical presentation featuring fifth and sixth graders discussing the importance of water resources. Subjects highlighted include Florida's aquifer system and the state's rivers, lakes, and wetlands.

Figure 13.3 Southern States Utilities broke new ground when it designed a successful community relations campaign to educate the public in the need for water conservation and the latest techniques for responsible water use.

Evaluation

Goal Achievement   While results may be attributable to other factors including population shifts, weather conditions, and differences in rate structure, the company reported a decrease in per capita consumption between 1991 and 1993. New reclamation technologies were successfully instituted with support of employees and stockholders. In 1993 SSU was successful in its request for an increase of rates to pay for its capital improvements, an FPSC decision no doubt enhanced by the company's conservation reputation.

Communication Impact   The company reached over a million and a half water consumers through direct mail, open house events, presentations, ELM sites, theatre performances, advertisements, and periodical and newspaper stories. In 1991 alone, SSU answered over 5,000 requests for water conservation information and made over 100 presentations in response to Speakers Bureau/information request cards. In 1992 presentations increased to 130. Each year from 1991 to 1993, SSU received an increasing number of requests for its informational materials and presentations.

Activity Impact   The SSU-sponsored professional cast of the Small Change Original Theatre gave 21 performances at "Captain Hydro and the Water Bandit" at 10 schools for 6,000 elementary school students. About 10 4-H clubs have received grants and employed Environmental Landscape Management techniques around schools, libraries, and IFAS agencies. The company's total program was a topic at a regional Kiwanis Club meeting, suggesting to all members of Kiwanis Clubs that "SSU supports a good cause" and to contact the company for water conservation information.

Awards   The program has received several awards from the Florida Section of the American Water Works Association, awards from the Florida Public Relations Association, and the first education award from the National Xeriscape™ Council. Participating 4-H youth have been recognized through awards within their own state and by national organizations.

The St. Johns River Water Management District awarded the SSU program an A+ for public information and made the program a model to which other utilities must conform.

SUMMARY

Two case studies presented in the chapter offer examples of a student-planned campaign and a professional campaign that was executed. The reader may wish to reflect on the difference between a campaign plan and the report of a campaign as executed.

The evaluation plan for the Camp Crystal Lake campaign offers a full range of approaches to the evaluation challenge. The plan proposes to measure goal achievement by recording increased awareness and involvement in environmental issues. Evaluations of specific strategies and tactics include tabulation of participants, environmental "contracts" and booklets sold, amount of money raised, a follow-up survey, a "graduation test," a collection of canvass reactions, tabulation of media coverage, information distributed, school participation, recyclables collected, and a diary of the campaign execution.

The evaluation used in Southern States Utilities case lists four ways the campaign was evaluated: goal achievement, communication impact, activity impact, and awards. As a measure of goal achievement the company was able to record a decrease in per capita water consumption as well as get approval for a rate increase to pay for capital improvements—a success attributed at least in part to their conservation reputation. Evaluators measured participation in various events, published stories, requests for materials, and presentations—including an increase of requests from one year to the next. The number of theatrical performances, the number of schools, the number of children attending, 4-H Club grants, and service club spin-offs from campaign activities were also measured. Tabulation of awards resulting from the campaign provide documentation of the campaign's effectiveness from various groups.

The two case studies provide examples of the way evaluation incorporates various procedures. Not all campaign evaluations employ all the available means of evaluation; you must choose appropriate techniques.

PART SIX

Presenting and Implementing the Plan

14 Preparing and Making the Campaign Plan Presentation

- The Presentation Is Critical to the Campaign
- Adapting the Presentation to the Audience
- Putting the Presentation Together
- Presentations Using Flip Charts

- Presentations Using Slides and Script
- Guidelines for Incorporating Video in Presentations
- Making the Campaign Plan Presentation

The ultimate step in planning the public relations campaign is presenting the plan to the decision makers who will either accept or reject it. All the effort that went into the entire planning process may be lost in one brief session if the plan is not presented effectively. But how can the plan be presented in its best light? What should be said, in what order, with how much elaboration? These questions are addressed in the pages that follow.

THE PRESENTATION IS CRITICAL TO THE CAMPAIGN

Bruce Marcus, drawing on extensive experience in making presentations, reduces the process to its basic elements: "The simplest type of proposal and presentation is the face-to-face statement in which the professional says to his prospect, 'This is the problem, this is how I'm going to solve it, this is what I think will happen as a result of my efforts, and this is what it will cost'." Whether the proposal is a one-page letter of agreement or a 150-page plan book, the purpose is the same, but the format varies greatly. Marcus continues:

> . . . proposals may take advantage of graphic and visual techniques. Proposals have been done in the form of video tapes and motion picture films. A proposal may be in the form of a computer program supplied on a disk. Mixed media proposals may combine a written document with several different audio visual techniques. In fact, in requesting a prospective client's business there are no limitations, other than the imagination, to the form a proposal may take.[1]

A major part of preparing a campaign is selling it to management, whether an employer or a client. Approval usually requires the assent of several people, frequently an executive committee or a board of directors. They will usually consider the written proposal in private. Therefore, it is critical that the presentation arguments in support of the campaign be put in writing and in the most convincing manner possible. This "justification" of the plan should also be included in the plan book, because some decision makers will read it in order to decide (Box 14.1).

The presentation process differs only slightly whether the plan is being presented to corporate management or to a prospective client for a public relations counseling firm. If the presentation will be made to a management team of a corporation or other organization, there are some advantages: the presenter is most likely to know the persons who will make the decision, their biases, preferences, likes, and dislikes. That knowledge can be valuable in deciding what to say and what not to say. If the presentation is to a prospective new business client of a counseling firm, the presenter is likely to know less about the audience psychology of the decision makers. If the presentation is a competitive situation, the presenter may have to rely on nonverbal cues during the presentation when little other information is available to guide the performance.

ADAPTING THE PRESENTATION TO THE AUDIENCE

Audience adaptation is the process of matching the purpose and message of the presenter to the needs and orientations of the audience. The process involves establishing commonality with the audience in such areas as language, style, idiom, topic of common interest, examples, and references. The communication must then be adjusted to the characteristics of the audience that will make the ideas as acceptable as possible and presented in language as familiar as possible. (We use the term *client* in the following outline, but the material applies equally to employer management.)

Client *as* Audience Versus Client's Audience   The presentation is primarily concerned with the client as the audience for the presentation; the client's audience is the primary concern of the campaign.

BOX 14.1   Plan Book Guidelines

The plan book should provide the client or management with the complete detailed procedure for implementing the public relations campaign. The plan book should include the details that would not be appropriate to mention in the oral presentation of the plan. The information should be clearly organized and outlined in a table of contents for easy locating. The plan book may include such segments as the following:

1. *Title page* to identify the client, the time period covered by the campaign, name of the public relations counsel or team (optional), names of team members, course name, academic department, university, semester and date, and the course instructor (optional).

2. *Table of contents* in outline form, to identify each segment of the campaign. Headings for each major stage as well as section headings should be listed, including page numbers where they may be found within the book. (Note: Contents will be the final item you prepare, after pages have been numbered.)

3. *Team (or firm) philosophy* (optional), which explains the basic orientation of the team members to public relations and thus gives the client or management insight into why the team chose the approach it did in designing the campaign.

4. *Executive summary,* a one-page summation of the entire campaign which a busy executive may read to discover the essence of the campaign. It may be the only part of the plan book some managers read, especially those who are not directly involved in the campaign but who need to sign off on the proposal. It is not a blurb to tease the reader into reading the whole book, but should enable the client or manager to talk intelligently about the campaign without reading further. It should be written only after the plan book is complete.

5. *Situation analysis* consists of a carefully worded statement of the conditions that led to the campaign. It may include (a) a relevant history of the organization, (b) a statement of relevant competitive factors, and (c) a statement of the problem or opportunity the campaign will address.

6. *Research findings* that confirm or alter the situation as it was originally perceived. This would include findings resulting from all research projects, including history, interviews, polls, library research, comparisons with similar organizations, and the like. Research instruments should be included with percentages of response or mean scores filled in.

(continues)

7. *A mission and goals statement* that identifies the long-term purpose of the organization and fits to it the campaign goals derived from the situation analysis and the ensuing research findings.
8. *Other adaptation elements,* including especially strategies considered and rejected and limitations for implementing the campaign related to calendar time, personnel available, and funds.
9. *A strategy summary* outlining the means the campaign plan will use to achieve the goal (and thus solve the client's or organization's problem), including the overall calendar, budget, coalitions, tradeouts, and tie-ins.
10. *Evaluation plan* outlining the procedures provided in the plan book to determine how successful the campaign proves to be in achieving the goal and in producing other benefits.

Advance Analysis of Client as Audience   The client representative(s) who attends the presentation should be studied in advance of the actual presentation. The presenter should answer such questions as these:

1. Characteristics that can be measured:
   - What is the size of the audience?
   - What are the demographics, etc., of the audience?
   - What can be learned from a survey of the audience?

2. Characteristics that can be collected from other sources:
   - How does the organization compare with rivals?
   - What experiences have other firms had with the client?
   - What is the client's financial condition and reputation?

3. Characteristics that can be observed:
   - What issues or topics create excitement?
   - What does clothing, hair, personal style suggest?
   - What pressures are likely to influence responses?

4. Characteristics that can be identified by asking:
   - What does the audience want from the presentation?

Analysis of the Client's Perception of the Audience   Adjust what is presented about the client's audience according to what can be learned about the client's perceptions.

Tune in to client's perception of "its audience."
How is client perception modified by your analysis?
What clarifications should the presentation make?

Use Audience Analysis During Presentation   Interpret observations during the presentation to modify emphasis, presentation style, sound system volume, lighting, and the like.

Read attentiveness, seating patterns, body language, clothing and hair styles.

Adapt to physical setting—proximity, acoustics.

Use question-and-answer period to adjust to audience interests and concerns.

The quality of the presentation should reflect the quality of the plan. The credibility of the entire campaign plan rides on the character of the presentation. The presentation should be an accurate reflection of the campaign plan, neither more flashy nor more drab than the plan. Advertising agencies have a tradition of using "bells and whistles" in an effort to attract attention when competing with other agencies for a lucrative new account.

Agencies competing for a $14 million Microsoft advertising account used an impressive array of gimmicks to attract the prospective client's attention to features of their agency that would make them more attractive than the competition. One agency based in the same Seattle area as Microsoft headquarters rolled a rented airline boarding stairs up to the company offices. The agency had repainted the side panel to read "Redeye Airlines" and added a sign that read "Little things like this will never come between us," to make the point that company officers would not need to endure jet lag if they hired the local agency.

Another agency, in the same Microsoft competition, showed up at a presentation with all 115 employees wearing tousled, dishwater-blond wigs, horn-rimmed glasses, and baggy sweatshirts. They then asked company officials to judge a "Bill Gates look-alike contest" in honor of the owlish-looking founder and chairman of Microsoft. The agency explained, "We thought it was important to demonstrate that we are an exciting, highly motivated, entrepreneurial and turned-on group of people."[2]

During one presentation an agency pulled out a live tarantula to drive home the point that "great advertising sometimes makes advertisers uncomfortable." However, for the final presentation, the company required the final competing agencies to "design campaigns for a word processor and a computer language product, and outline an overall brand-image strategy." The winning large agency, as it turned out, had not resorted to gimmickry but had impressed the company by "using computers to analyze market data."[3]

The winning agency had succeeded by demonstrating its mastery of the technology it was being hired to promote. While such examples are only anecdotal and not necessarily representative of the entire communication field, the successful presentation demonstrated that skills relevant to the client's mission proved more effective than the flashy and spectacular. A useful principle, however, is that the presentation should reflect the character of the campaign plan being proposed.

Consider presentation audience psychology. The more the presenter can know about the decision makers who will select or approve the campaign plan proposal, the more effectively it can be adapted to those factors. Many cues can be picked up from a careful study of the decision makers involved in developing the campaign. The dynamics of personal power and the positions different people hold in the organizational structure can give clues to who might have influence on the primary decision maker who will approve the campaign plan.

In the actual presentation, an ability to read nonverbal cues can be essential in reacting to the reception of the plan. By recognizing the folded arms that cue rejection or the leaning backward that indicates disinterest, the presenter can know to go quickly to a different line of thought or topic. By knowing how to adapt to the interest indicated by a forward-inclined body or head or the open arms that suggest receptivity, the presenter can emphasize those points that seem to be well received.

Richard L. Weaver II suggests some principles of nonverbal communication that are especially useful for the business communicator. He mentions voice, appearance (especially clothes), face, eyes, eye contact, touch, and body movement as important factors in effective communication; all of these apply to the presentation situation, and they are derived from a growing body of literature on nonverbal communication. If the reader is unsure of his or her mastery of nonverbal cues, a review of Weaver's chapter or other writers in the field will be helpful.[4]

Two principles deserve further comment, the use of space and the use of time in the presentation. Both of these can have an effect on the outcome of a presentation, but both are likely to be the result of unconscious reactions. E. T. Hall has identified four zones of distance that people recognize as appropriate for different types of exchange. Hall identifies the "social distance" of 4 to 12 feet as the zone of impersonal business contact or casual conservation and the "public distance" of 12 feet or more as appropriate for public speaking or lecturing. In general, the larger the group, the farther the presenter and audiovisual materials may be removed, but for the small group likely for a presentation 4 to 12 feet is a good rule.

If there is an opportunity for social mingling before the presentation, more intimate contact may be appropriate. Blanchard and Johnson point out the potent force of touch in *The One Minute Manager.* It is a very "honest" mode of communication, which people recognize immediately and which may convey a range of feelings from the truly caring to the coldly manipulative. They suggest the rule "when you touch, don't take," which translates to the flow of power. The more powerful can "give" to the less powerful by touching; the less powerful "take" from the more powerful by touching.[5]

Time is another important variable in presentations. The unwritten rule is that the more important or powerful the person, the more permissible is lateness. This rule is peculiar to Western developed countries. In Latin American cultures everyone is late. A Latin friend of mine once announced an appointment to be at "2:00 o'clock U.S. Army time." Pressed for an explanation, he said, "In Latin cultures 2:00 o'clock means, . . . well 3:00 o'clock; 2:00 o'clock U.S. time means 2:30; but 2:00 o'clock U.S. Army time means 2:00 o'clock."

In a presentation situation the presenter should not violate the rule of time by being late, especially if the presenter is less powerful than the audience. However, it should come as no surprise if the powerful executive is late. Indeed, some artists at this craft have developed to a fine degree the use of time to put a business contact on the defensive or to unsettle the person keeping the appointment. Such gamesmanship is usually confined to relationships in which the relative status of participants has not been settled; once that "pecking order" has been conceded, appointments can be kept on time or even kept early as a sign of eagerness to please.

Other psychological factors involve trying to discern what may be going on in the heads of the decision makers. Trade publications in the business communication field have explored such pragmatic questions. Does the client know the difference between the functions of public relations and advertising, and between other related functions such as marketing, direct marketing, sales promotion, publicity, lobbying, fund-raising, and public affairs? If there are any doubts, and chances are that such education will be needed, a clear description of what public relations can do, compared to other functions, will be a useful service. Such educational points should be presented as ground rules or clarification rather than authoritative pronouncements.

A too-flashy presentation may suggest that the firm is desperate for new business because it can't keep current clients. A presentation that focuses on client problems and proposed solutions may have a psychological advantage over the glitzy, show business–type presentation. The more a presenter can put himself or herself into the shoes of the prospective client or manager, the better the presentation can be adapted to the decision-maker audience.

PUTTING THE PRESENTATION TOGETHER

There are two audiences for a presentation: the presentation audience and the campaign audience. In the campaign plan the client's concerns are addressed by a proposal to reach critical audiences with a message that will change the relationship between those audiences and the client. The entire campaign plan addresses this challenge. The audience for the presentation is the team of management decision makers who will select or reject the proposed campaign plan, and the message is the argument that the campaign proposal is the best alternative for meeting the client's challenge.

Planning the Presentation at Two Levels

Most of the material in the following pages deals with presenting the campaign plan. However, it is important to consider the significantly different audience-message situation that exists in the presentation of the plan to management. In this situation, knowing the management team audience that will attend the oral presentation is as critical as knowing the client's audience to planning an effective campaign. James G. Gray Jr. has written a book useful for those making oral presentations in business settings. He suggests, "Before beginning to write the actual presentation, write out a listener profile. List adjectives or write several paragraphs describing a typical listener or client."[6] He recommends an analysis of "listener objectives," which may be quite different from the goals or objectives of the campaign. By answering nine questions, he suggests, the presenter can identify the hidden agenda of the presentation audience:

To Determine Listener Objectives:
1. What are their reasons for attending?
2. What do they want to hear?
3. What is the listeners' likely collective attitude toward the presenter?
4. What is their opinion of my organization?
5. What is their attitude toward my topic?
6. What prior information, either true or false, do they have of me and my company?
7. What are their motives?
8. Are some motives unspoken? For example, is the manager more concerned with saving his reputation or pleasing a boss or peers than with quality?
9. Do political infighting and power struggles figure into the picture?[7]

Once the presentation audience is understood and the materials are adapted to those conditions, the campaign plan can be presented in its most persuasive form. The presentation goal should be to convince the client management audience to accept and implement the campaign plan. The campaign plan must then be adapted to both the needs of the client's audience for which the campaign is being undertaken and the biases and motivations of the management team who will make the decision about the campaign plan.

Constructing the Campaign Plan Presentation

In constructing the campaign plan presentation, seven elements must be merged: (1) the research findings that contributed to (2) the analysis of the client's audience; (3) the strategic decisions that were incorporated into (4) the campaign plan as it will be (5) structured or outlined and (6) scripted to include any audiovisual materials to be used; and (7) accommodating the pitch to the physical facilities[8] where the presentation will be made.

Research findings are often the most convincing material that can be used in a presentation. The client will be impressed at the obscure details learned about the company as background information was collected. More important, the answers to questions the client has been wondering about, which the researcher has gathered by more formal research methods, will give the client reason to trust counsel with the responsibility for solving the problem that the campaign will address.

The campaign-audience analysis resulting from research should further demonstrate an understanding of the situation and provide a credible basis for the strategy proposed. The audience analysis should identify not only the targeted segments of the public the campaign must reach but also the channels through which they may best be reached. Coalitions and tie-ins may also be mentioned here if they are not specific to elements of the strategy that will be mentioned later.

Strategic decisions arrived at as a result of the research findings will be easier to sell to the client if they are firmly based on the research findings. An important element of this research-based strategy should be discovery of the company's overall strategy and careful integration of the campaign strategy into it. Showing how the campaign will contribute to the overall company strategy as well as help solve the immediate problem will make the proposed campaign plan even more appealing.

The campaign plan must be the major part of the presentation. It should include at least the research findings, the problem statement as confirmed by research, the goal and objectives, the targeted publics, the strategy options considered, the strategy plan chosen, the theme, the communication package, calendar, contingency plans, budget, and evaluation plan. The elements of the campaign plan should be arranged and carefully structured within the outline to be incorporated in the scripted presentation.

In addition, it may be useful to mention anything that is unusual, is especially creative, reaches multiple publics, or achieves cost efficiency by cooperation with other like-minded groups. Note, for example, the Ford Tractor Operation case study, which reached its public through existing organizations (see Chapter 7).

Scripting for audiovisual materials will depend on whether the presentation requires visuals. Authorities are divided on the advisability of using them. Chester Berger, in *Experts in Action*, advises "Don't use them unless you have to."[9] This professional practitioner point of view differs from the typical textbook, which reminds the reader that "a picture is worth a thousand words."[10] Whether or not the presenter chooses to use visual aids, the material that follows assumes that the time will come when the practitioner will decide to use visuals. The material here is designed for the situation in which audiovisuals are used.

Adapting to the physical facilities demands careful coordination, because the room size, seating arrangement, conference table (if one is present), chalkboard, flip chart, and audiovisual (AV) equipment available can be quite varied. An advance run-through of the presentation at the site is highly desirable; if this is not possible, at least a visit to the room and review of the audiovisual situation is essential after rehearsal off site. If you are unfamiliar with the facility and its AV equipment, it is wise to provide your own equipment. These details must be worked out with the prospective client organization in advance.

It is wise to prepare a "justification" for the campaign plan as if your livelihood depended on it, because very likely it does. That is certainly the case with campaign plans prepared for clients of counseling firms, especially in competitive bid situations in which only one of several proposals will be accepted. For the student, realism is achieved by assuming you are preparing a proposal for a counseling firm client.

Constructing an Outline   The outline should structure the *polemic elements*, the persuasive argument most likely to lead to acceptance and approval of the campaign plan, in a logical order and with the most effective selection of supporting evidence. Each communication in general, as well as each presentation in particular, will differ from all others. Each must be carefully constructed to incorporate the outline elements, and if AV supporting materials will be used, the outline must be incorporated in a script. Whether the presentation is scripted for audiovisuals or not, it must be adapted to the physical facilities in which it will be presented.

The outline should also incorporate these *rhetorical criteria:* (1) establish the topic of the presentation, mood, and motive for listening to the presentation; (2) summarize the central idea into a single statement of no more than 18 words, shorter if possible; (3) phrase two to five points that support the central idea; (4) collect documentation to reinforce these two to five points in the form of facts, illustrations, or the like; and (5) construct a closing summary, illustration, or anecdote that motivates and provides for a behavioral response.

The **outline** of the presentation should place the elements to be presented in a logically organized sequence that will be easy to understand and will lead to client approval and acceptance. Box 14.2 shows methods of structuring and supporting the presentation argument, and an example of a presentation outline is given in Box 14.3.

BOX 14.2   Methods of Structuring and Supporting the Presentation Argument

WAYS TO ORGANIZE THE PRESENTATION STRUCTURE

Scholars in the field of rhetoric have identified at least nine methods for organizing an oral communication. These may be used either for the entire presentation or for different sections:

1. *Time order*—chronological treatment of elements that have taken place or will take place.
2. *Space order*—treatment of elements as they are situated in space, top to bottom, front to back, etc.
3. *Classification*—treatment based on an existing system, such as anatomy, engineering, ecological, atomic, planetary systems.
4. *Cause and effect*—begin with cause and then treat the possible effects.
5. *Effect to cause*—begin with an effect and think of facts, statistics, and figures of various types to make understanding of relationships easier.
6. *Case study*—real-life examples, especially if they closely relate to the point to be made, provide excellent proof.

7. *Testimony*—a high-credibility eyewitness or first-person account of an incident or experiences can be very persuasive.
8. *Evidence*—facts or figures or other logical support for the point being made.
9. *Hypothetical cases*—fictional but plausible examples help the audience to understand logical outcomes.
10. *Analogy*—a comparison or contrast, often an extended example, can help listeners to understand a case.
11. *Narrative*—a story that makes a point offers the possible dramatic and emotional appeal that can be quite forceful.
12. *Anecdote*—a short narrative often with a strong point.

SUPPORTS

Scholars have classified at least 13 ways to support an argument. Types of supporting materials that can be used to elaborate on the outlined argument, or to offer convincing proof or evidence to reinforce your points, fall into these categories:

1. *Slogan*—a well-crafted phrase that focuses attention, often by repetition.
2. *Illustration*—an actual example or word picture that helps the listener understand the point.
3. *Quotation*—a well-phrased or strongly appropriate set of words made even more effective by the credibility of the source.
4. *Logical argument*—a well-reasoned series of statements each of which leads to logical acceptance of the conclusion.
5. *Summary*—a generalization based on a larger mass of material.
6. *Citation of authority*—endorsement of a point drawn from one whose expertise or social position makes it believable.
7. *Sensory descriptive language*—appeal based on audience identification with a situation described in careful detail.
8. *Interpretation*—the meaning or significance of an incident or fact supplied by a spokesperson.
9. *Benefits*—advantages of desired action pointed out in detail.
10. *Suggestion*—an indirect indication of a desired action or outcome.
11. *Irony*—an unusual comparison that by its significance or relationship makes a strong point, often humorously.
12. *Demonstration*—contributing to understanding by showing how something works, or evidence of mass sentiment.
13. *Exhibits*—visual and often mechanical illustration of materials which pictures, demonstrates, or serves as a focus for discussion or constitutes a response to questions.

BOX 14.3   Example of Presentation Outline—Pastahhh

The following outline was used by Henry J. Kaufman & Associates, Inc., in making its initial competitive presentation to win the public relations account for the National Pasta Association (NPA). The outline served as a guide for making the in-person presentation to NPA; consequently, the outline points may not be clear to the uninitiated reader. The outline need only serve the presentation team as a reminder of the planned points to be made during the presentation.

NATIONAL PASTA ASSOCIATION PRESENTATION OUTLINE

I.   Henry J. Kaufman & Associates, Inc.
    A. 55 years old
    B. 50 employees
    C. Full-service communications
        1. KJK&A Advertising
        2. Creative Directions
        3. Marketing Research Bureau
        4. Kaufman Public Relations
    D. Clients
        1. Sears Roebuck, Thomson McKinnon Securities, Marsh-McClennan, Philips Electronics, Louis Sherry Ice Cream, U.S. Savings Bonds, Selective Service, U.S. Coast Guard, FTC, ASTA, NPCA, NABM, IMI
    E Association experience
        1. Variety of clients
        2. Working with committee/staff
        3. Understand importance of members
        4. Generic marketing programs
            a. Flowers
            b. Paint
            c. Bricks
            d. Mattresses
    F. Common elements of generic programs
        1. Products taken for granted
        2. Activities not available to individual members
        3. Must be sales-oriented

II.   Marketing Approach
    A. Advertising vs. PR discipline
    B. Developing a plan
    C. Establishing measurable results
        1. Demonstrate return on investment

D. Basics
1. Need to breakthrough clutter and malaise; therefore, a program of big ideas—quality vs. quantity
E. Review of existing program
1. Very impressive, but . . .
a. Too much like the product; taken for granted
b. Quantity—not quality
c. Not focused
d. Not sales-oriented
e. Message is not the strongest
f. Standard publicity program
F. Marketing environment
1. Secondary research
a. Simmons
b. Other
2. Primary research
a. Need more
b. Focus groups
c. In-store interviews
d. Food editor survey
G. Conclusions
1. Brand-broad use-broad appeal-better pizzazz
2. Taken for granted
3. People like pasta
4. Health/diet message is wrong for both consumer and media
5. Editors anxious for new material

III. Objectives
A. Make pasta into something people want, not need
B. Combat inroads made by imports and fresh pasta; other products—potatoes, rice
C. Broaden usage by moderate and low pasta users via segmentation to generate sales and increases in a narrowly defined audience
D. Improve environment in which members sell produce
E. Capitalize on pasta being fashionable
F. Orient program to box pasta uses
G. Use a pre/post measurement to evaluate results

IV. Strategies
A. Target audience
1. Segment
2. Target different programs to specific

(*continues*)

3. Opportunity targets
   a. Blacks
   b. Middle America
   c. Working women
   d. Singles
   e. Entertainment [in home]
B. Message
   1. Fun-Fun-Fun
   2. Sell emotion; not the product
   3. Use health and diet message secondarily to give permission to do what they really want
   4. Personalize message
   5. Develop a unified theme for campaign
C. Other strategies
   1. Big ideas—event-oriented
   2. Capitalize on favorable climate
   3. Involve editors and influentials
   4. Use both print and broadcast for each audience

V. Summary
   A. Big ideas—no more recipes
   B. Fun—health is secondary
   C. Targeted—the audiences can be defined
   D. Involving—this causes interest and sales
   E. Sales-oriented—measurable objectives and results

VI Programs
   A. *Campaign Umbrella*
      1. Theme Graphics
      2. Target pamphlets
   B. *Projects*
      1. Editor's Yearbook
      2. Yearbook Plus
      3. Cooking Seminar
      4. Feature Article Placement
      5. Newsletter
      6. Pasta Club
      7. Spokesperson
      8. Suburban Press
      9. Market Expansion
      10. Radio Features
      11. Restaurants of the Year

12. Political Pasta
13. TV news feature
14. Tie-ins
15. Meal Planning Competition

Source: From material supplied by H. J. Kaufman & Associates, Inc., Washington, D. C.

PRESENTATIONS USING FLIP CHARTS

After the outline of the presentation is complete, it must be incorporated in visuals that will help to get the points across. One way to do that is by using a flip chart to fix the main points in the mind of the presentation audience.

> In using flip charts and chalkboards, use them as carefully as you would electronic devices. Flip charts have distinctive advantages in that they supply a certain intimacy with the audience. They can be used almost anywhere and are simple and inexpensive. They can be flipped back and forth to refer to previous points more easily than can a slide. They don't require a darkened room, which means that you're always in sight of your audience and can maintain eye contact.
>
> Flip charts also have an advantage that they can be prepared beforehand or used like chalkboards to make points as you need them.[11]

The flip chart may be produced using a professional graphic artist to make the lettering, but the same procedure may be used with hand-lettered flip charts. The following procedure is suggested for classroom presentations using "quick and dirty" hand lettering. The quality of the final product depends on the time and care used in creating the flip chart. Many computer word processors allow for printing large 72- and 96-point letters that are suitable for flip charts. Ordinarily the information is typed with the appropriate words per line, then the font size is increased and the pages are printed after selecting the "landscape" option for printing. The printed pages can then be cemented to the pages of the flip chart. If outline letters are used, color can be added to make the chart more attractive. Remember that letters must be at least one-half inch high for each eight feet of viewing distance. Even with hand lettering, a little more care will result in an acceptable product for all but the most sophisticated presentations.

Techniques of the Hand-Lettered Flip Chart

Use an Art Tablet The first step is to purchase an art sketch book or tablet and several felt pens; rounded tips will hold up better. At least one pen should be black or very dark blue. Lighter blue, red, green, and orange are desirable for the other colors. For most presentations with no more than 40 people in the audience, a tablet of 14 × 17 inches is ideal; the next larger size tends to be more unstable unless a "hod" or easel is used.

Make a Grid Underlay   Next, make a guide grid using one sheet from the tablet: mark the sheet with 2-inch borders all around and 1-inch horizontal and vertical lines within the borders starting in the horizontal and vertical center; the centerline should be either a heavier line or a dotted line to make it easy to distinguish. The grid may be sketched first in pencil, but the final version should be in heavy black lines. When it is finished, the sheet should be carefully removed from the tablet with a knife; cut through the spiral binding holes so that the sheet may be easily positioned when used as an underlay beneath each page as it is lettered. The underlay serves as a guide for keeping within borders, keeping the lines straight, and centering lettering on the page as well as protection against ink going through to the next page.

Make It a Tabletop Tent   Use the first sheet in the tablet to reinforce the cover so that the tablet will stand on a table surface. You will need a knife, a pasteboard (corrugated) carton, and rubber cement. Cut the carton into flat pieces that fit the front cover of the tablet; the larger the better, but several can be pieced together to fit. Use a generous amount of rubber cement to sandwich the corrugated pieces between the front cover of the tablet and the first page. While you have the rubber cement out, apply a coat to the bottom edge of the tablet. It will soon dry and will not be noticeable, but it will give the flip chart an indispensable nonskid capability. The nonskid feature of this flip chart will allow it to stand tent-style on a tabletop with no danger of collapsing.

Flip Chart Rules   These are several rules for flip charts: *Omit needless words*, which means that only "key words" should be selected for the flip chart. Other details can be supplied orally in the presentation. *Substitute short words for long;* obviously, there will not be room on the chart for everything you may want to say, so select words that fix the idea in the mind even if a longer synonym will need to be used for clarification during the presentation. *Indent and abbreviate when necessary;* with the "magnification" effect of reducing the outline to a flip chart's dimensions, some long but indispensable words may not fit on one line. The problem can be solved by indenting and abbreviating. If the key syllables are used, even words that have letters missing in several places can be recognized; usually only one apostrophe will be necessary to cue the audience that the word has been shortened. Vowels should be the first letters to go.

Plan Each Page on a Scratch Pad   The presenter can avoid ruining art tablet sheets by using the following procedure: Print each page on a small scratch pad roughly the same dimensions as the art tablet. Count the letters, place the middle letter of each line in the center of the scratch pad sheet, and then complete the other letters, so that the line will be centered and correctly positioned on the page. This will acquaint one with the problems of later fitting the same words on the larger page. Now is the time to change the wording of the page if it becomes clear that the planned words will not fit. Letters must be at least 1 inch in size for each 16 feet of maximum viewing distance.

Draw Letters on Flip Chart Pages   Using the scratch pad, plan for each sheet. Begin by penciling the letters on the larger art tablet. Use a bit more care in placing and spacing letters than was necessary on the scratch pad. Try to keep ideas separated on the page by spacing between lines and using bullets, numbers, indentation, or other devices. After completing each page, go back over the penciled letters with a colored felt pen, being a bit more careful to shape, position, and space the letters than you were in penciling. Next, using even more care, outline each letter in black. As you do so, shape each letter to position the letter on the line and make the tops of letters a uniform height. Finally, use the color again to fill in the black-outlined letters. Other color combinations besides colors outlined in black may be more appropriate for lettering, but the outline should be in the darker of the color. As an alternative to hand lettering, pages may be prepared on a word processor. Use 65- to 72-point type to produce approximately half-inch letters, and print with the "landscape" print option. Paste pages on flip chart pages and decorate to taste.

Train Yourself in Lettering Skills   Developing skill in hand lettering is a long-time endeavor. These tips will help to improve those skills: Work on your personal lettering style. Although you may not want to try to emulate any of the hundreds of type fonts, your lettering will be more effective if you study typography. Try to develop a type style that you can use consistently; make your letters the same way each time. Keep your letters a reasonably uniform size—at least those on the same line and preferably all those on the same page. Here are some "valuable typographic hints":

- Beware of type that is set solid (lettering without spacing between lines).
- Long and heavy letters require more space between lines.
- Medium type is easier to read than either light or very bold.
- Using all capital letters retards reading speed by about 15 percent.
- Break phrases to reflect phonics.[12]

PRESENTATIONS USING SLIDES AND SCRIPT

Now that we have discussed some aspects of audience analysis and outlining for oral presentation, let's look next at structuring the presentation for use with visuals. The previously considered criteria for selecting what to include in the basic material outlined for presentation lead into some specific suggestions for a scripted presentation. Deane N. Haerer suggests 14 guidelines for planning visual presentations:

1. Research your audience. Design your presentation to meet their level of technical expertise.
2. Outline the contents of the total presentation.
3. Script your presentation.

4. Identify the graphics you will need.
5. Key all visuals to your script.
6. Give your graphics designer ample time to adequately prepare your materials.
7. Commit as much material to memory as is possible. If you must read, use key notes on 3 × 5 cards.
8. Schedule adequate rehearsal time and test run your presentation before a group of your peers.
9. If possible, use VTR [video tape recorder] for a dress rehearsal. Allow enough time to make last minute content as well as sequence changes if necessary.
10. Make sure that you are totally familiar with all data to be presented and that they are current and accurate.
11. Be totally prepared
12. Rehearse.
13. Rehearse.
14. Rehearse.[13]

There are various approaches to preparing AV presentations. Kodak's *Planning and Producing Slide Programs* suggests a two-stage process beginning with a "treatment" that "interweaves an explanation of the logical development of the presentation's content with a description of the presentation's visuals and sound." This stage is accompanied by a project proposal that incorporates objectives, theme and premise, content outline, budget, and tentative schedule.[14] If the presentation will be primarily audiovisual, the outline can be incorporated into a script for slides or video. The process of organizing a presentation using scripted slides might follow these guidelines:

Constructing the Presentation Slide Script

1. *Write out your thoughts* and ideas as they occur to you. Put them in complete sentences. Expect to struggle over the wording and phrasing of the ideas as you try to put them into complete sentence form. Include topics adapted to the audience as determined from your analysis.
2. *Compose a theme* for the presentation. It must be in summary form suitable for pickup by the media (whether or not media coverage will occur). It should also be a statement that can be repeated at transitions throughout the presentation.
3. *Build an outline* of what the presentation will say in the order in which it will be said. The outline consists ideally of two to five main points, preferably three, each in complete statement form. Used by both speechwriters and video producers, such an outline sets out the most important points to be presented and helps avoid having to redesign the script later.
4. *Leave room between major ideas* in the outline as you draft it on successive sheets of paper to allow revision, cutting, and changing material as you think it through. Don't be afraid to make major shifts of ideas or

emphasis from first to last, middle to beginning, or elsewhere. You are the final judge of when the progression of ideas seems right.

5. *Try out the ideas on other people* for their reactions. If others don't understand, redo the outline until it is understandable to a disinterested person. Many people find that the best ideas come to them as they try to explain a concept to someone else.

6. *Make a storyboard* from the outline. Use a series of 3 × 5 cards with the basic information for each visual on each card: picture idea, audio words or narration, and sound and music (if used), but don't number them until later. Some find that pictures cut from magazines can give an idea of the type of picture you will need to produce later for some of these. You can use pictures, lettering for titles or important points to make, combinations of words and pictures, charts, graphs—whatever best tells the story you want to tell.

7. *Some ideas will be easy* to illustrate; others will be hard. Start with the easy ones. They will often get you into the hard ones or suggest ways to illustrate the difficult ideas. For presentation of campaign plans, simple projection of a series of phrases or statements may be more effective than a picture.

8. *Plan transitions between main points* or between very different types of material. One good technique is to repeat the overall theme as you explain how the main points support or relate to the theme.

9. *When it all fits together* and you have had a satisfactory run-through, take a break, preferably until the next day. Then come back to it and run through it again and watch for timing. Ask yourself: Are some slides on so long that people become bored? Are some shown too briefly to read completely? Is there a rhythm that people will follow?

10. A *strong beginning and ending* will make people think they have seen a good presentation in between, so use the weakest points or imperfect pictures briefly and in the middle. It will usually work best to use your strongest material at the beginning and the second strongest at the end.

The Storyboard   A storyboard has several advantages: (1) It helps organize the presentation narrative; (2) it pinpoints the slides needed, which avoids wasted photos; and (3) it enables the producer to preview the presentation as it develops. A sample storyboard card is shown in Box 14.4.

Some Handy Hints for Slide Narration

1. Write the narration so that it flows smoothly from slide to slide.
2. Don't write for individual slides. This makes for choppy commentary. Write for groups of slides.
3. Write in paragraphs with slide changes indicated at or *two to three words* before key words. Make sure you leave adequate time for viewing slides that have heavy or complex content.

BOX 14.4   Example of Storyboard Card

Sample storyboard can be on 3 X 5 or 4 X 6 cards

	Slide No. _____
Sketch of slide	Description of slide
CONTINUITY (sound): Narration:	

By using a series of cards (each with its own visual, plus narration, music, and sound effects), the elements of the storyboard can be studied, evaluated, and, if necessary, rearranged. By spreading the cards on a tabletop the flow of the story and pictures can be visualized to identify places where new elements should be introduced, where the sequence should be shifted, or where other changes should be made.

---

4. Allow approximately three to five seconds for most slides. Depart from the three- to five-second rule only for a sound reason, such as light-content slides timed to the beat of music or heavy-content graphs or charts that take more viewing time.
5. Time your commentary first and key the music and sound effects track to it.
6. Segment the narrative into proper moods, such as action, pastoral, dramatic, or mysterious; then carefully select music and sound to establish and change moods. Use sound effects only when clearly indicated (when in doubt, don't).
7. Cue slides to the sound track (some recording systems will differ) by recording "impulse" at key words as you play both voice and sound tracks together. Impulse will, later change slides automatically.

Some Notes on Preparing Title Slides

There are many ways to create title slides suitable for use in presentations. The following are some that have proved effective.

1. **Commercial lettering** systems such as the Reynolds/Letteron™ system, which sells for under $200, will produce letters in standard fonts (Helvetica, Gothic, Clarendon) in 30 to 96 points. The letter strings can be affixed to illustrations to make slides or can be used for titles only. The system is available from Reynolds/Letteron Co., 9830 San Fernando Road, Pacoima, CA 91331.

2. **Typed titles** a less expensive way to make title slides for low-budget productions is to use a carbon ribbon typewriter on frosted-finish acrylic report covers, which are available from most bookstores or stationery shops. The steps are as follows: (a) Make a template using a scrap of 35-mm film removed from a scrap slide frame. (b) Mark squares of about $1\frac{1}{2} \times 1\frac{3}{8}$ inch on a sheet of $8\frac{1}{2} \times 11$ inch paper, and inside each square mark the dimensions of the window in a slide frame. (c) Use this template under a sheet of frosted acrylic to allow typing on the frosted side. (d) Using a carbon ribbon typewriter, types titles to fit inside the windows of successive frames, in case of mistakes go on to the next frame. (e) When finished with a series of titles, cut out the usable titles, which should be the same size as the film taken from the unusable slide, and (f) mount them in plastic slide frames, which are available from most photo stores. Colored acrylic is quite effective. These titles can also be overlaid by inserting in frame over photo slides with good effect, especially if the placement of words and images is carefully arranged.

3. **Photographed titles** with a little creativity, one can produce title slides specially adapted to the content and mood of presentations by using hand lettering on different graphic media. For example, for a travel theme, titles might be hand lettered in beach sand and then photographed with slide film. For a school theme titles might be done with chalk on a blackboard, children's books, or writing on a "steamed" or frosted window. Lipstick on a mirror, lettering made on a flour-sprinkled surface, colored cake frosting on a white surface, a child's crayon on notebook paper—the possibilities are endless.

Audiovisual Production Final Editing Checklist

The final editing process, putting slides and script into a synchronized program, requires sensitivity to overall effect, mood, timing, and the results of planned special effects. The producer's judgment is usually blurred by the pressure of last-minute production problems. Therefore, plan to complete editing three to four days before deadline, to allow time to sleep on the matter and still make changes you find necessary. Here are some things to look for during the "morning after" viewing session:

Introduction   Does the introduction establish the right mood, set the stage for the material to follow, whet the viewer's appetite for your message? Music with "establishing shots" that identify the topic with or without graphics or titles, will do the job very well. As you view it ask, "Is it too long?" That is, does it continue after the point has been made? "Is it too short?" That is, is the point obscured or not understandable? It is always helpful to have a friend who is unfamiliar with the project view it for an objective evaluation.

Main Body of Material   It usually works best to state the conclusions you want your viewers to reach as a central idea statement, which may be repeated at the beginning of each section and in a concluding summary. You will, of course, have structured your script using a three- or four-point argument stated in the way you want listeners to remember it. Check to determine whether the main points are memorable.

In moving from one section to another, make sure you provide a smooth transition, such as a repeated statement in the script, or a music bridge, and titles that indicate the next major point.

Watch for timing of slides with script. Look for slides with complex visual content that need to be on longer than usual. Avoid spending too much time on your worst shots.

Don't forget the power of pause. Silence is quite acceptable—even stronger than words, if carefully used. Plan it in your scripting. When editing, listen for a balance between music, sound effects, and voice narration. An obscure sound effect needs a "clue" word in the text to suggest what it is. The crackling of cellophane can sound like fire if you show a slide of fire or use the word just before the sound in the text.

Conclusion   Does the conclusion tie the material into a neat package and return to the mood and theme of the introduction? Is the theme repeated? Does the conclusion include or lead up to a personal request for the desired action?

Many of the techniques that have been discussed can be applied to the use of videotape for presentations. Slide presentations are probably more dramatic and have the advantage of being much more editable than video. Video does, however, have some advantages over slides.

GUIDELINES FOR INCORPORATING VIDEO IN PRESENTATIONS

Three video applications in campaign presentations include (1) presenting critical visual elements, (2) supplementing the main presentation, and (3) recording the entire presentation.

The **equipment needed** for this procedure includes one video camera with zoom lens, recorder (with or separate from camera), tripod, lavaliere microphone (optional), and lighting (daylight or three light sources for interior setting).

Recording visual elements or supplementary material to be used in the presentation requires planning these aspects as a minimum: (1) Decide what details need to be shown, in the order in which the viewer should see them, and with adequate time for each shot so that the viewer can absorb what is shown. (2) Make a "shot list" identifying the subjects to be shown so that the camera can move smoothly from the first to the last without disruption. (3) Plan related visual elements that will have to be recorded at a different site. The camera can be moved from subject to subject by *panning* the camera from side to side, by *zooming* in or out to exclude or include subjects in the frame, and by *tilting* the camera focus up or down. A camera with automatic focus will relieve the camera operator of the need to make continual focus adjustments. In all these camera movements, the tape records a continuous flow of pictures. The pause button can be used to stop the tape between segments, especially when subjects are unrelated or are located at a different site.

This application of video may be especially appropriate for showing such elements of a campaign as a headquarters building, the operation of specialized equipment, interviews that make crucial statements, or a demonstration of how something works that is critical to the campaign.

Dramatization is another application of video in presentations, but it requires much more skill to produce on videotape than the applications noted above. Dramatization can be a forceful addition to any presentation because of its power to create emotional response, but the challenge is formidable. The three most challenging aspects of producing video drama are associated with (1) finding actors who can create realistic scenarios, (2) stage blocking and camera blocking, and (3) interrupting emotional scenes to accommodate different camera placements or to allow for changing scenes. These topics are addressed in television production texts.

Recording the entire presentation involves the same blocking challenges as dramatization but not the acting problems. Blocking refers to the planned relationship of subjects to one another and to the camera. These relationships must be carefully planned to avoid such problems as appearing to go in one direction in one shot and the opposite direction in a succeeding shot, or making a disquieting shift in point of view. In blocking a presentation, avoid pitfalls by positioning two speaker stands side by side with a visual display between them, all facing a camera. This arrangement allows for a two-speaker "dialog,"[15] which breaks up the potentially boring monolog of a single speaker. It also allows each speaker to turn the flip chart or other visual aid for the other speaker. The script should be divided between the two speakers by marking two- or three-paragraph segments alternately for each in order to achieve the best dialog effect.

Recording the entire presentation should not be considered as an alternative to making the presentation in person. Even if unusual circumstances require that the presentation be recorded for subsequent viewing by decision makers, arrangements should be made to have some of the team present for a question-and-answer session. Ordinarily, the main purpose of recording a presentation is to make a record for future study, either by the team itself or by future students.

Review the Approach: Does It Sell Your Ideas?

Have you said what you needed to say? Did you cover the basic structure of the campaign plan? That is, did you reiterate the problem as confirmed by your research; did you explain why the problem can be solved by achieving the goal(s) you have set; did you explain how possible solutions were determined and why the response strategy you chose represents the best hope of achieving the goal, and thus of solving the problem; did you explain how the plan is targeted to reach precisely the public needed to achieve the goal and that the communications supporting the strategy are the best possible means of reaching the target public; did you explain why the whole strategic plan is such a financial bargain, especially considering the funds raised in the effort, the donated items, and goods and services realized in tradeout agreements?

MAKING THE CAMPAIGN PLAN PRESENTATION

When the planning is finished, you are ready to make the presentation. The more careful the preparation, the more confident the presenter usually will be. The oral presentation brings together the prospective client and the proposed campaign to solve the client's problem. In discussing how to market services to clients, Bruce Marcus describes the presentation as the "primary selling point":

> A presentation is the primary selling point at which it is explained in person why the prospect should retain the firm. It's the point at which the important element of personal chemistry is added to the marketing mix. The written proposal may supplement an oral presentation or complement it. The proposal may be sent ahead of the presentation, or left behind after the presentation has been made. Presentations offer the opportunity to deal with questions and reactions, or with new material or information.
>
> Presentations can be casual or formal; be made by one person or a team. Consideration should be made of the physical location, which should be congenial.[16]

Be prepared to interact with the actual audience. If you have made a careful analysis of the audience as outlined earlier, you should be ready to adapt your material and emphases to the individual predispositions you have determined. However, it is always possible that the people whose presence you have anticipated will be different from those actually present. The room arrangement may be different from what you expected; the lighting or AV equipment may be different or not functioning properly. The ability to demonstrate mastery of the presentation situation also offers the opportunity to demonstrate your general competence, which will inspire confidence on the part of the client.

A presentation checklist helps to keep on track and reminds the team of what to anticipate. Marcus offers the following checklist of things to remember during the presentation: Don't stray from the point you are making. Don't be overlong on any one point. Be sensitive to your listeners; watch for nonverbal cues, and be reflective of verbal questions and comments. Don't sell too hard; let the weight of research findings, the logic of your proposal, and the documentation of the firm's capability do most of the selling. Don't overemphasize personal appeal of any team member, and don't distract attention away from the central focus with irrelevant anecdotes.

Be prepared for questions; a valuable technique is to devote a session of the presentation team's rehearsal time to anticipating and answering questions. Know the competition you face for the account and be prepared to compare your proposal with those of the competition (if possible); in any case, you can offer advantageous comparisons of your firm's capability with the competition. Above all, don't forget to ask for the chance to do business, however you may phrase it: ask for the account. "We would like to have the order." "Let us know when we can start." "We're ready to begin working for you when you give the word." Or, "We can have this campaign plan producing results for you the moment you give the go-ahead."

Oral styles for presentations. The presentation may use one speaker, a series of speakers, a dialog[17] between two presenters, a panel, a combination of these, or a dialog with the client. "The presentation can be as casual as a dialogue with the prospect, or it can be formal, carefully designed and orchestrated, with several people from your firm participating, elaborate audio visual support (including slides and films), and a substantial proposal left behind or subsequently delivered."[18]

The television news team format has conditioned people generally to expect the fast-paced two-person dialog style. This format is particularly well suited to the public relations presentation. After the script is complete, the two persons who will do the dialog presentation can go through the script with highlighter pens in two colors to designate alternate blocks for delivery. This quick-moving style can give the performance a much greater aura of professionalism, overcome the tendency for any one voice to become boring, and create an impression of teamwork within the firm.

The oral style may be worked out, depending on the requirements of the individual presentation. A single speaker with a backup panel can take advantage of members of the campaign management who are present, with the account supervisor serving as the speaker and the backup people on a panel at a separate table. Thus, the artist, research staff, media people, advertising staff, and others can be represented to provide specific details on aspects of the campaign. When elaborate audiovisuals or multimedia are used, the team leader or principal speaker may need to coordinate assistants who will cue slide projector, overhead, rear screen, and video operators at critical times.

Timing and coordination depend on the elaborateness of the presentation. The single speaker need only time the outline or script to be used, with timing indications that will allow him or her to remain on schedule. If the presentation is to make use of AV materials, most of these can be timed in advance and coordinated with an overall script to ensure accurate time control. With complicated multimedia presentations, even with careful rehearsal, contingencies for equipment failure must be included in the plan.

With scripted presentations—whether slide script, video, or multimedia—most equipment is designed to allow interruption for questions or for unscripted comment or elaboration. When unscripted oral material is integrated in this way with scripted material, a careful accounting of the unscripted time is necessary to avoid exceeding a maximum time allotment. It is important to remember that the purpose of the presentation is to win the client's consent for you to provide public relations services. If the situation demands, it will be more important to deviate from the planned presentation in order to meet the client's stated desires.

Dealing with questions requires one fundamental decision: whether to have questions at designated intervals throughout or to reserve a time at the end for questions. Interrupting the presentation for questions has both pro and con sides. On the pro side, it allows the client to ask questions that are more immediate; allowing for interruptions at intervals for clarification is one example. On the con side, interruptions tend to fragment and violate the integrity of the campaign plan, as well as to encourage distracting and irrelevant discussion. Reserving time for questions only at the end keeps the questions focused on the big issues. Although clarification questions are not ruled out, the questions tend to focus on the more substantive concerns of the client. It is probably more important to be prepared to deal with the full range of questions that might be asked than to worry about where in the presentation to field the questions.

Follow-up materials. There are three classes of follow-up material: (1) the plan book (if that option is selected), (2) peripheral material that may support the presentation materials and provide additional encouragement toward a favorable decision, and, if your plan is accepted, (3) a schedule of meetings and reports to organize your relations with the client in the immediate future.

If you decide to present the campaign plan book at the conclusion of the oral presentation, as is appropriate if the client has so specified, you will need at least one copy with original artwork and graphics. You may want to provide additional copies if the management decision team consists of several people and doing so would speed a decision.

If the plan book has been presented prior to the oral presentation, and perhaps if it is presented at the same time, it may be helpful to include additional materials, such as a brochure about the firm, evidence of similar work done for other organizations, background material on the people assigned to the account, and any other information that would help the client decide in your favor.

If the client decides to award you the account on the spot, a demonstration of your businesslike practices in offering a schedule of meetings and reports will reinforce the client's belief that the right decision was made. Other indications of good personal chemistry between the account team and the client management team will also help to cement the relationship and encourage a long and mutually beneficial association. Social invitations, luncheon or dinner arrangements, and sailing, club, or golfing activities are examples of this kind of token of a new relationship.

Establish credibility by making a professional presentation. The presentation is like the cover of a book or the packaging of a product. If the first impression is not strongly positive, the content of the plan must struggle to overcome the handicap, if indeed there is such a later opportunity. How much better it is to avoid that negative possibility by making sure the presentation is the very best that it can be.

SUMMARY

The **presentation is critical to the campaign** because it is the conventional way to offer the plan to decision makers and justify it as the optimum plan.

Plan book guidelines offer an outline for preparing the plan book.

Adapting the presentation to the audience involves matching the presentation to the needs of decision makers. The quality of the presentation should reflect the quality of the plan. Consider presentation audience psychology and other psychological factors.

Putting the presentation together. Planning the presentation involves two levels. Constructing the campaign plan presentation involves ways to organize the presentation. There are some basic types of supporting evidence. An example of a presentation outline for Pastahhh reveals how the professionals do it.

Presentations using flip charts. Techniques of the hand-lettered flip chart show how to start.

Presentations using slides and script. Constructing the presentation script focuses on the storyboard. Some notes on preparing title slides help the student presenter. An AV production final editing checklist identifies flaws. Review the approach; does it sell your ideas?

Making the campaign plan presentation. Be prepared to interact with the actual audience. A presentation checklist helps to keep on track. Oral styles for presentations should consider dialog. Timing and coordination will differ with the elaborateness of the presentation. Dealing with questions requires one fundamental decision: whether to have questions throughout or at the end. Plan for follow-up materials. Establish credibility by making a professional presentation.

FOR FURTHER READING

Alten, Stanley, R. *Audio in Media.* Belmont, CA: Wadsworth, 1986. A solid production (radio and television) text.

Anderson, James A., and T. P. Meyer. *Mediated Communication.* Newbury Park, CA: Sage, 1988. A theoretic basis for communicating through the media.

Gray, James G., Jr. *Strategies and Skills of Technical Presentations.* New York: Quorum Books, 1986. A good overview of technical aspects of making presentations.

Hall, Edward T. *The Hidden Dimension*. New York: Doubleday, 1966. A basic treatment of nonverbal aspects of communication.

Marcus, Bruce W. *Competing for Clients: The Complete Guide to Marketing and Promoting Professional Services*. Chicago: Probus Publishing Co., 1986. A source for building relationships with clients.

Meeting News. This trade publication is available to people who plan meetings, sites, and arrangements on a no-cost subscription basis.

Voros, Gerald J., and Paul H. Alvarez. "Corporate Identity and Graphics." in *What Happens in Public Relations*. New York: AMACOM, 1981. A discussion of the overall visual communication aspects of public relations for organizations.

Wilcox, Dennis, and Lawrence Nolte. *Effective Publicity*. New York: HarperCollins, 1990. This textbook has a good treatment of media relations.

"Working with the Media," Chapter 10, in Newsom, Douglas A., Allen Scott, and Judy Van Slyke Turk, *This Is PR*, 5th ed. Belmont, CA: Wadsworth, 1993. This textbook chapter has a good treatment of media relations.

Wurtzel, Alan. *Television Production*. New York: McGraw-Hill, 1979.

Zettle, Herbert. *Television Production Handbook*. Belmont, CA: Wadsworth, 1976. This and the Wurtzel text are probably the most widely used television production texts.

CHAPTER

15

Implementation: Executing the Campaign Plan

- Scheduling and Coordination
- Structuring the Campaign Team
- Getting Help and Cooperation
- Performance Monitoring

- Managing Media Relations
- Training Spokespersons
- Staying Ethical and Legal Under Pressure

The campaign execution or implementation is the application of the carefully constructed plan to carry out the campaign. The implementation follows the plan as a builder would follow the architectural blueprint for a building. The outcome should be a close approximation of the plan. Of course, as with architectural blueprints, alterations of the plan may be necessary as the planned effort takes shape. The campaign plan should anticipate this need for alterations during implementation by including contingency plans or otherwise allowing for changes that may be necessary during execution.

SCHEDULING AND COORDINATION

Carrying out the plan requires somewhat different skills of coordination than does the planning process. Perhaps the most important of these are scheduling meetings, transferring information messages and materials, and making arrangements for various activities, all require careful attention to time and distance and a realistic sense of what is possible.

Activity scheduling involves task completion, meetings with other people, and the personal schedule of the campaign executive. The task completion schedule should be part of the campaign plan and will ordinarily require at most only fine-tuning at the implementation stage. Coordinating with other people for meetings, task completion, approvals, and cooperation can be less certain than working with inanimate materials. There may be a difference in what can reasonably be expected when working with salaried employees compared to working with volunteers. There are often-cited differences between working with managerial people and with creative people.

Scheduling and coordinating with other people to confer and agree on tasks require both realistic requests on their time and an appeal to their self-interest in achieving the task. The time requested and scheduled for meetings should be only what is needed to agree on tasks to be performed, and those tasks should be clearly in the self-interest of the participants. For example, in approaching an employee to perform a task, clarify what is expected and emphasize that the successful performance of the task will contribute to the purpose of the organization and will mean recognition and reward. The same is true for a task assigned to a volunteer, except that the recognition and reward will be different. Managing campaign tasks, like all effective management, depends on seeing the task from the viewpoint of the one carrying it out, in terms of the clarity of the task and reward potential.

The same principle applies to working with coalition groups. Clarifying the precise nature of the cooperative enterprise and the benefits to be derived should provide a useful framework for any discussion and planning of joint efforts in the campaign. Time is so often lost in seemingly pointless meetings that well-focused scheduling and coordination of meetings will be a welcome part of the campaign execution. Such a fundamental element of managing people in the achievement of tasks is set forth in the "One Minute Goals" and the "One Minute Praisings" that make up the popular book *The One Minute Manager* by the Ph.D. management consultant and M.D. psychologist team Blanchard and Johnson.[1]

Personal scheduling poses special challenges for the disposition of the campaign manager's personal time and may be as much of a problem as scheduling task completion and making arrangements with other people if the manager has not previously developed these skills. Indeed, some of the modern technology-based methods may benefit even the seasoned practitioner. Trip Overholt reviews several personal computer software systems that offer help for managing the busy public relations professional's schedules. He suggests:

> The program should print out daily, weekly, monthly, and yearly schedules, each in its own format, on a single piece of paper. I like to take my daily schedule home each night so I know where to be the following morning. I need my weekly schedule to schedule appointments when I'm going to be out of the office for a few days. My monthly schedule provides an overview of my monthly activities. I need it when I'm on the road, to make appointments weeks in advance, and to avoid overloading my schedule in any given week. It also helps me schedule my weekends when I'm visiting friends. . . .
>
> Besides keeping track of appointments, I expect my calendar to categorize and prioritize a substantial number of "things-to-do" lists. It should mark each item

with an entry date and tell me how many days have passed since I failed to do something. All categories and items should be modifiable, deletable, and "achievable" (stored in a file for later review). The program should merge my to-do lists with my appointment book, remind me of commitments by automatically inserting messages into my daily schedule.[2]

Another challenge to the management of the campaign director's time is the matter of backup in case of illness or conflicts. The most efficient and dependable account manager or public relations department person cannot be in two places at once. The need for someone who can take over the duties of the public relations campaign manager is critical when the campaign is carried out by a one-person firm or when responsibility falls to one person in a small department with few professionals.

E. W. Brody suggests that small or one-person public relations firms adopt the "professional association" system used widely in medical, legal, accounting, and other professional circles. The professional association "consists of a group of individual practitioners who agree to co-locate their practices in order to economically share facilities and, to a greater or lesser extent, professional support as well . . . during periods of overload, illness, or perhaps even vacations." He mentions three aspects of the arrangement that must be agreed upon:

First, billing procedures must be established. Billing usually is handled by each practitioner for his or her clients. Statements include compensation for any services provided by colleagues and appropriate remittances are made within the association.

Second, compensation scales must be established for use in the system. This usually is accomplished on an individual basis. Each associate is free to use the services of another at any time at a predetermined rate. Rates often are lower than those which individuals would charge to their own clients for two reasons. First, the individual whose services are being "contracted" has experienced no sales costs in securing the business. Second, some markup usually is allowed to the primary vendor.

Finally, agreement must be reached among two or more association members as to long-term services which might be required were one of them to become disabled through illness or mishap. Such arrangements usually involve rate structures similar to those specified above.[3]

Transfer of messages and materials is another problem faced by the person in charge of executing the public relations campaign. Exchanging the information needed to make the arrangements for decision making and for completing tasks demands that the manager be familiar with the intricacies of the telephone and mail systems. For example, in *sending messages and materials* to people you are working with on the campaign, it is critical to know how much time is required for local mail delivery and for delivery to different cities throughout the country that may be involved in the campaign. Parcel delivery using the Express Mail service of the U.S. Postal Service may be less dependable than other services such as Federal Express. Knowing the pickup or posting arrangements and times of these services is also important when deadlines approach.

Messages can be relayed most quickly by telephone or by e-mail, and printed materials can be sent most quickly by telecopier (fax). However, it is essential to know if such equipment is available to parties on both ends of the telephone line and whether staff are on hand to operate the equipment. The three-hour time difference between the Atlantic coast and the Pacific coast must be kept in mind; West Coast offices are still operating three hours after East Coast offices have closed. This means that dealing with people in different time zones can be handled after closing time if you are on the East Coast, and business can be conducted before business hours with East Coast people if you are on the West Coast. Similar adjustments can be made for at least an hour for zones in between.

Knowing how much time will be required for production of campaign materials is necessary for smooth execution of the plan. Arrangements for printing of materials must fit into the printer's schedule, and video productions must be worked into the schedule of an often overtaxed production studio. Such arrangements vary from city to city and from supplier to supplier, so each practitioner must make his or her own contacts and check with the supplier before a critical order is placed to avoid unexpected delays.

Assigning authority/responsibility and delegating. For the experienced practitioner, actually implementing the campaign plan is often easier than the research and planning phases leading up to it. The plan can be divided into parts, particularly sequential parts, that can be delegated to people in the organization, or people can be recruited to do certain tasks. It is especially important to involve employees in the campaign. By their participation they develop commitment to the project and take advantage of their past experience with the organization. Volunteers may have to be recruited and assigned to phases of the campaign. Such decisions should be based on the plan as devised in the strategy. See heading "Factors in Selecting a Strategy" in Chapter 10 and an example in the Hay Train Case Study, in Chapter 11, under the heading "Contagious Goodwill."

STRUCTURING THE CAMPAIGN TEAM

Some campaigns are relatively simple. They require only a sound working relationship between the chief executive officer or other management authority and the person responsible for carrying out the public relations aspects of the campaign. The latter would typically be the director of public relations (DPR) or the client's account executive from the outside public relations counseling firm.

More complex campaigns might involve entire divisions or subsidiaries of major corporations, large groups of employees, sales forces, external associations and organizations, inside and outside public relations professionals, printers and other suppliers, hired temporary workers in various specialties, government agencies, and other organizations cooperating in the campaign for any of a wide variety of reasons. The more complex the campaign, the more thorough and extensive must be the campaign organization. It is good practice to develop an organization chart showing all the key participants with their titles, duties, and reporting relationships and to explain the chart to all concerned.

Managing the campaign team requires determining who is responsible for specific aspects of the campaign. Delegating authority for carrying out each task is important to good management of the campaign as is a clear-cut approval process for action, especially for making midcourse corrections in the light of unanticipated events. Who is responsible for making what types of decisions must be determined and made known to all cooperating parties. In addition, almost all responsibility for decision making on routine matters should be delegated on down the line as close to the points of action or implementation as possible. This provides for an efficient organizational response to events as changes are needed. It also frees higher management and public relations executives for overall supervisory roles and the handling of major problems should they occur. It provides people at all levels with the authority needed to make key decisions within defined boundaries without having to lose time and effectiveness by seeking higher authority. Of course, everyone must know the limits of his or her own decision-making authority and how to recognize situations calling for decisions at higher levels.

Managing the creative people who are typical of public relations specialists at all levels is a special challenge to the campaign director. Linda Ray Cochran, in a review of the literature on "How to Manage Creative People," notes that "many studies identify personality characteristics which 'appear more descriptive' of creative people as a group than of the general population." The unconventional behavior of creative people can be identified even in school with the tendency to be " 'estranged' from teachers, who by and large value such norms as promptness, following directions, and self control."

> That this tendency to march to an internal drummer is carried into adulthood is documented in a widely quoted study of architects conducted by Donald W. MacKinnon. MacKinnon found that a reliable predictor of creative performance is adherence to internal rather than external standards. He also found that persons who are highly creative tend to have positive opinions of themselves and to have self-images that include inventiveness, determination, independence, individualism, enthusiasm and industry.[4]

Characteristics of managers tend to be more akin to those of teachers, so managing unconventional but creative individuals requires a "permissive" management style. Freedom for the creative person to carry out his or her tasks is the "primary environmental variable" required of managers who make the most of their creative people. A further characteristic of effective management of creative people is the independence of the creative employee "to choose assignments. The importance of this aspect is tied to the tendency of creative people to work to their own standards." A "third most often cited feature of the optimum environment for creativity: ample opportunity for interaction with colleagues within and outside the organization." A final characteristic of the working conditions the manager needs to provide is " 'maximum freedom from administrative bureaucracy'—i.e., excessive, inappropriate or inflexible regulations, arbitrary controls and routine managerial and administrative problems."[5] Managers should

> ... devote most of their attention to providing motivation through encouragement for creative performance. They should make optimum use of their staff's talents, training and interests because, [Porsche] says, "underutilizing is the surest way of dampening motivation—the most important single ingredient of (creative) productivity." ... By contrast [Hower and Orth] suggest research managers [and managers of other creative activities] should be "resource persons," facilitating rather than directing; maintaining a healthy flow of communication in all directions; knowing something about the conventional functions of management and implementing its conceptual and human relations skills.[6]

A set of guidelines for managers that was designed by Stewart Blake for managerial effectiveness in general, Cochran suggests, is also applicable to managers of creative people (Box 15.1). The campaign manager may well heed the suggestions for the job of making the campaign arrangements.

Working within the organizational structure requires that the campaign manager understand the nature of the organizational structure within which the campaign is being executed as well as the structures of other organizations with which coalitions may be formed. In putting together a task force or working team to carry out parts of the campaign, it may be necessary to draw the people from diverse units of the organization. Such task force formation is often referred to as a matrix structure or an adhocracy, in which the temporary structure is determined by the task at hand. After completion of the task, the structure will change in adapting to the new demands of the work to be performed.

Adhocracies are characterized by the need for sophisticated innovation, drawing together diverse experts from varied backgrounds, focusing their skills on a progression of projects, and requiring them to work together as ad hoc teams. There is little formalization of the work; job specialization is based on professional or technical training; project teams are market based; and liaison devices are well developed as an encouragement to mutual accommodation within and between teams.

A conscious effort is made to avoid the structures of bureaucracy in order to encourage the very qualities that are inhibited by bureaucratic hierarchies. Goodman and Goodman found that for a theatre company "role clarity" inhibited innovation: "coordination can no longer be planned but must come through interaction."[7] For the adhocracy, structure "must be flexible, self-renewing, organic, in Hedberg, et al's. (1976) terms, a 'tent' instead of a palace."[8] Toffler, who originated the term, describes adhocracies in large concerns as organizations that

> ... change their internal shape with a frequency—and sometimes a rashness—that makes the head swim. Titles change from week to week. Jobs are transformed. Responsibilities shift. Vast organizational structures are taken apart, bolted together again in new forms, then rearranged again. Departments and divisions spring up over night only to vanish in another, and yet another, reorganization.[9]

BOX 15.1   The Role of the Manager

A manager of change (which includes most, if not all, corporate managers) must be willing to accept at least the following responsibilities.

- To provide, and interpret when necessary, statements of corporate goals so as to offer direction and guidance to the innovators.
- To give up a substantial part of his decision-making prerogatives, accepting the risk involved in placing trust in the capabilities and decisions of subordinate creators and innovators.
- To commit a substantial part of his time to the process of communicating with staff members, and to do so with a considerable degree of enthusiasm. (The writer once had the acutely unpleasant experience of working under the supervision of a man who, while willing to listen, obviously was not hearing anything and was merely waiting his turn to deliver himself of his views, regardless of the comments of others.)
- To spend time and energy evaluating and controlling the activities of the inventors and the innovators by personal contact and communication with them rather than through impersonal and arbitrary written reporting procedures; and, above all, to avoid making comparisons of their work with some arbitrary standard.

Source: Blake, Stewart P. *Managing for Responsive Development* (San Francisco: W. H. Freeman, 1978), 132.

The Manned Space Flight Center of the National Aeronautics and Space Administration (NASA)—"changed its structure seventeen times in the first eight years of its existence."[10] Because of the demands of creative innovation, adhocracies often cannot even draw organizational charts "since it would change too quickly to serve any useful purpose," one such corporation executive explained.

In the adhocracy, job descriptions and tasks cannot be defined because assignments are always changing. The organization "cannot compartmentalize its activities into neat boxes" because production undergoes too many modifications; indeed, even the product itself may change as experimentation and innovation discover new substances, new processes, and new devices.

Cochran notes that most writers suggest the matrix or what some have called the adhocracy structure for public relations activities.

Blake suggests that a project/matrix approach be employed whenever possible. In this approach . . . a project leader is assigned and a team is assembled from various, project relevant functions in the organization. Blake describes it as "superimposing a cross-lines project organization on a conventional hierarchy."

Requirements for effective use of this structure are a firm understanding of the approach on the part of management and direct authority from the Chief Executive Officer to enable the project manager to communicate with and obtain action from any level of the hierarchy.

Blake stresses that there must exist a clear and complete written statement outlining the position, duties, relationships and authorities of the project leader within the organization. The leader should be given full authority over all planning, direction and control of tasks and related resources and should be assured the assistance of all the organization's elements in achieving project goals.[11]

The campaign execution team may be put together from a broad representation of a communication department, or a counseling firm may draw from the client organization for such a team. The team itself must be structured, probably using a matrix structure of subteams for larger campaign structures and assignment of tasks to individual team members for smaller efforts.

GETTING HELP AND COOPERATION

The campaign management must rely on many other people for the success of the campaign's implementation. Getting dependable help from people inside as well as outside the organization can make the difference between success and failure of the campaign.

Dealing with suppliers and service providers. Successful implementation of a campaign typically involves unusually heavy reliance on outside suppliers and service providers. Almost always there is need to rely on printers, mailers, and media distribution services. The size of the campaign and the size of the sponsoring organization have a lot to do with which services will be provided in house and which will be contracted out to suppliers. In fact, many large companies contract for services when their own service departments are overtaxed by in-house demands. The demands for printing services will depend largely on the size and complexity of the print job; if only a few hundred one-color 11 × 17 four-fold brochures are needed, most local printers could accommodate the job on relatively short notice. If the job calls for a 60-page four-color booklet with a mix of color and weight of paper stock, including a window cutout and a foil stamp, most printers would require a much longer time frame for delivery.

Mailing houses will almost always be economically sound for campaign mailings. The mailing house can affix zip code–sorted mailing labels, fold, and deliver to the post office mailings of over 500 pieces more cheaply than most organizations could by using their own staff time. Mailing lists may be developed as part of the campaign, purchased from appropriate organizations or from mailing list houses, depending on the nature of the campaign. Such a mailing list must be provided to the mailing house to keep costs to a minimum. Media distribution services provide list management, mailings, distribution of releases to selected media, monitoring, and clipping services following mailings.

Appropriate amounts of lead time must be built into the calendar in order to avoid excessive overtime costs and to allow for mistakes and rework, which happen frequently. There is much truth to the statement that "the printer is the public relations professional's best friend."

Some supplier organizations have excessive layers of bureaucracy with which the campaign manger must cope to ensure on-time delivery of needed materials. In emergencies, it is common practice to impose penalty fees on suppliers for materials delivered after deadlines. However, it is normally the best practice to deal with reliable suppliers on the basis of good faith and long-time relationships. Penalties are offensive to such good suppliers and should be avoided if at all possible.

Use of outside consultants, such as public relations counseling firms that specialize in the type of activities involved in the campaign, may be economical over the long haul for many campaigns. Even one public relations counseling firm may hire another counseling firm because of its local connections or its skills in event management or lobbying. Consultants in research, media buying, or video production may also be necessary when these skills are not regularly honed by the campaign team.

Often there is a need to coordinate the work of the outside public relations counseling firm and, perhaps, many of its far-flung offices if the campaign is national or international in scope. National and international campaigns are often best implemented by large, outside public relations counseling firms with extensive resources across the nation and around the world. Some public relations counseling firms have networks of associate offices whose services they call on when geographic or cultural requirements demand.

In cases of contracted services, monitor the work of the firm closely and make sure the overall philosophy and quality of the campaign are maintained. Public relations firms are capable of thoroughly reporting on the results of their work, and this capability is vital to the successful management of the campaign.

PERFORMANCE MONITORING

The manager of a campaign must know what the many people who carry out the campaign are doing. The manager needs a system for keeping in touch with all aspects of the campaign during implementation, and that means maintaining contact with the people who are performing the various tasks. Effective managers know that these details cannot be left to chance, nor can it be assumed that everything is going according to plan—the manager must make sure of it.

Interpersonal Communication in Campaigns

Ironically, people in the communication field often fail to communicate effectively among themselves in carrying out their broader communication duties.

The public relations professional is well advised to minimize the chances that miscommunication may jeopardize the campaign plan. That means a great deal of checking and double-checking. It involves reconciling conflicting opinions and healing bruised egos, plus some careful and sensitive "hand-holding" of the major participants in the campaign.

Perhaps the most difficult problem in a campaign is dealing with the human aspects. It is not easy to keep many people moving in one direction for a long period of time, or to motivate a task group to continue devoting themselves unselfishly to the requirements of a demanding campaign. This is why it is often said that employees, especially management itself, constitute the single most important audience for the public relations effort. If the public relations program succeeds first internally, chances for success in attaining objectives with outside audiences are greatly enhanced.

Philip Lesly has made a speciality of human relations in his public relations counseling practice. His concentration on the "human climate" in public relations has produced a set of guidelines for interpersonal communication that are quite useful for the public relations campaign manager (Box 15.2).

Monitoring Staff and Counsel

The campaign manager's primary responsibility is to see that the implementation team's activities remain on task in carrying out the plan. This is true whether the team is one person (the campaign manager), a small team of two or six, or a larger team with dozens of volunteer and temporary employees and reassigned staff from other departments. As the earlier section on managing creative people made clear, the most desirable monitoring system is personal contact between the campaign manager and team members. Such a system can be integrated with a calendar or other means of outlining the campaign plan. Calendared activities can be checked off on the master plan as a result of the "walking around" management contact with team members.

Monitoring of counsel should be incorporated in the regularly scheduled client-counsel contacts, whether the contacts are weekly telephone conferences, regular reports from counsel, personal meetings with counsel staff, or a combination of these. Renee Miller reports a list of 15 warning signs to the public relations counselor that the client-counselor relationship is faltering, which were developed by Tom Tomlin. The list might serve as a guide for a campaign manager in monitoring consultants or counsel who have been employed to help with the campaign, and perhaps some of them are suitable in monitoring staff as well (Box 15.3).

None of the items on the list should happen to the conscientious manager who keeps in touch with the business for which he or she is responsible. In addition to the problem of a failing client-counselor relationship, Miller's article describes other "big mistakes PR agencies make," which will serve well in monitoring the effectiveness of a public relations counseling firm. In other words, the campaign manager will be rated on these points in carrying out the

---

BOX 15.2   **Lesly's Rules for Effective Communication**

There are some guidelines that make effective communication possible:

- Approaching everything from the viewpoint of the audience's interest—what's on *their* minds, what's in it for *them*.
- Giving the audience a sense of involvement in the communication process and in what's going on. Get them involved and you get their interest.
- Making the subject matter part of the atmosphere the audience lives with—what they talk about, what they hear from others. That means getting the material adopted in *their* channels of communication.
- Communicating *with* people, not *at* them. Communication that approaches the audience as a target makes people put their defenses up against it.
- Localizing—getting the message conveyed as close to the individual's own milieu as possible.
- Using a number of channels of communication, not just one or two. The impact is far greater when it reaches people in a number of different forms.
- Maintaining consistency—so what's said on the subject is the same no matter which audience it's dictated to or what the context is.
- Still, tailor-making each message for the specific audience as much as possible.
- Not propagandizing but making sure that you make your point. When a communicator draws conclusions in his summation of information, it's more effective than depending on the audience to draw its own conclusions.

Source: Lesly, Philip. "The Changing Evolution of Public Relations." *Public Relations Quarterly* 27 (Winter 1982): 13.

---

campaign. In *monitoring the relationship*, the manager who employs public relations *counsel should look for:*

- Evidence of "planning, research and direction regarding client programs . . . A successful public relations campaign involves a lot more than generating clips." Counsel should submit a plan for approval and resubmit the plan with requested changes if any.
- "Failure to service the account properly. . . . Agencies don't put the same effort into keeping the account as they do to win new business using top management in the presentation. Once the account is on board, the senior 'presenters' disappear leaving the work to junior account people, and the client feels cheated."

- "Lack of sensitivity to nuances." Counsel should be able to read between the lines, read the meaning implicit in actions of the client.
- "Lack of training of junior staff people. The biggest complaint I hear from the press and clients is that junior and middle-level agency people are ill-equipped to understand the nuances of marketing and communication," said Chris Barnett, editor of *Bulldog* (an insider's report on PR and communications in the West). "Agencies don't take the time to train their junior and middle-level people well enough."
- "Failure to establish good financial controls." Billing should be prompt, accurate, and free of unexplained charges.
- Inaccurate estimates of fees. The actual time charges should not be appreciably above those estimated in winning the account. Unrealistically low estimates of costs to win new business will give the firm a bad reputation in the long run.
- "Not paying enough attention to the chemistry between the account staff and the client. The secret to a successful account is making the very best match between the account executive or staff and the client from the beginning."[12]

BOX 15.3   Warning Signs in Client-Counselor Relations

Fifteen Warning Signs in Client-Counselor Relations

1. A new employee has been working with the client a while and you are unaware of him or her.
2. Seminars and ads have been planned without your knowledge.
3. You just discovered the anniversary of the firm is two weeks away.
4. A new product or service has been introduced and you don't know about it.
5. You had no idea a new marketing thrust and direction had occurred.
6. There are top people in the company you haven't met.
7. You didn't know the client experienced a sharp decline in business.
8. The client has obtained a new client or business and you weren't aware of it.
9. You just discovered your client is planning to move in 30 days.
10. You found out about a board meeting after the fact.
11. Marketing meetings are being held and you're not invited.
12. You haven't met with the client in two weeks.
13. Collateral materials are being developed and you didn't know about them.
14. You found out about a major speech after the fact.
15. The client is not returning your telephone calls.

Source: Miller, Renee. "Big Mistakes PR Agencies Make," *Public Relations Quarterly* 29 (Winter 1984): 15–17.

MANAGING MEDIA RELATIONS

Media relations involve building mutually beneficial associations with the publicity media people and the system within which they operate.

Some Criteria for Effective Media Relations

To be effective in relations with the media, which is the first step in achieving publicity, requires, in order of importance, that you (1) know how each media system works (radio, television, newspaper, wire service), (2) know the nature of news, (3) know how to write in journalistic style, (4) know the formalities of the news release, (5) know your own organization as a news source, and (6) know eventsmanship.

Know How Each Media System Works   The more you know about how the radio system, the TV system, the newspaper system, and the wire service work, the more effective you will be in media relations. In other words, you can never know too much about the system, nor can you keep up with innovations unless you work at it. Some essentials, however, much be mastered: Know deadlines, and respect them; know the respective jobs, who reports to whom; know how to make your contact look good to his or her boss, how to submit stories and to whom; know how public service announcements are used in each broadcast station; know the pressures of coverage of various topics and industries; know how to play to TV media strengths and avoid revealing its weaknesses.

Know the Nature of News   News is what people need to know in order to cope with their lives, plus reassurances that life is predictable, as provided by feature material. Scholars identify these two categories as "need to know" and "nice to know."

Know Journalistic Style   Understand the summary-elaboration structure revealed in the inverted pyramid news story with the five W's. Use the formalities of the AP-UPI stylebook; for instance, spell out numbers one to nine, and don't start sentences with numerals. Internalize journalistic practices: the intricacies of the lead, attribution in the first two paragraphs, short sentences, brevity, active verbs, jargon-free writing style.

Know the Formalities of the News Release   Distinguish between hard news and feature material. Use letterhead paper, identify the contact person, include the release date, use a dateline in most cases, polish the lead, attribute in the first two paragraphs, use inverted pyramid form, use short paragraphs, polish a careful style, document information in the story, adapt material to readers, and submit letter-perfect copy.

Know Your Organization as a Story Source   Help journalists tell your organization's story by being an effective liaison with all news sources in the organization. Use your news judgment to help people in the organization adapt information to the media, especially when the story idea probably will not pass the editor's muster. Understand how to work with the media; you need them/ they need you. Never seek favors or offer them. Don't expect to get a clip of your story; don't even ask for one. Stand behind your story material.

Know How to Master the Event   Understand how to create news by mastering the event. Events must have a positive relation to the sponsor, be newsworthy, have a memorable name, stimulate word-of-mouth (bandwagon) effect, and take advantage of tie-ins and tradeouts.

There is much ado in the literature about the relationships between public relations professionals and the media, writers, reporters, editors, and program directors. It is probably true that there is a healthy skepticism on the media side about the newsworthiness or interest of the material being offered. It is also probably true that some public relations people have had difficulty in working with the media, especially in generating good publicity for the client or employer. By and large, most public relations people and most media people respect each other and have developed solid, long-lasting relationships and a high degree of trust and goodwill based on square dealing and truth telling over a long period of time.

The public relations person needn't be on a first-name basis with all reporters and writers in the United States, or even to have met them at all. It is vital to be knowledgeable about their requirements and their media styles and to provide them with timely and factual newsworthy or interesting material. In short, all the media want is a good story. If you give it to them or make it possible for them to have access to others who can, you will generate the desired publicity. There is much wisdom in the oft-expressed admonition of public relations pioneer Edward L. Bernays to his colleagues, "Don't make news releases; make news!"

Unfortunately, some public relations people are less than professional in this regard. They continue to bury the news media in news releases and other materials that are not news by any measure. They deserve the derogatory term *flack,* and such abuse is what gives legitimate public relations people a bad name. Before going to the media with anything, stop and ask yourself if there is any reason why it should not be given to them. If you have the slightest doubt about its newsworthiness or quality, don't send it out. Sometimes, perhaps rarely, you will have material that seems to cry out for exclusive handling by a single writer or reporter for a single medium. Exclusives should be given out only in special circumstances because this technique denies the story to the other media. This can ultimately be detrimental unless you take special care to spread such exclusives around. In general, in a campaign situation you would avoid exclusive unless the campaign is highly localized, as in a single-newspaper town.

Working with Media Gatekeepers

The term *gatekeeper* refers to the control of access to the media. Although protective secretaries and hard-to-find offices of reporters and editors are aspects of the phenomenon, the much more significant gatekeeping activity involves negative attitudes of reporters and editors. These negative attitudes are sometimes fostered by irresponsible publicists who claim they can "deliver" media coverage, as if the publicist has some control over media. The situation is illustrated by the widely reported memo sent by *Washington Post* staffer and *Newsweek* columnist Meg Greenfield to *Post* executive editor Benjamin Bradlee, in which she vows never again to deal with publicity agents. *Advertising Age* reported the incident, which reveals the gatekeeper attitudes of many in the media:

> Ms Greenfield's memo to Mr. Bradlee is replete with phrases which indicate she feels she is being used. She wrote: "Why would we be in their campaign plans as something 'deliverable' by their various agents who can 'reach' us?" She insisted: "we don't want any of that damn crowd around here, and if people want to get to us they need only to know two things: It's easy as pie, so long as they don't come in (or send their manuscripts in or make their requests) via a flack firm.[13]

The practitioner might best deal with this attitude by an unfaltering reliance on materials that meet the news test and by unfailing adherence to the Public Relations Society of America (PRSA) Code, which prohibits guaranteeing the "achievement of specified results beyond the member's direct control." The incident illustrates the practical importance of the code of ethics in preserving the credibility of practitioners. The fact that irresponsible people violate the code of ethical practice places a greater burden on ethical practitioners to preserve the fragile trust of media professionals.

The scope of the negative attitude of media gatekeepers toward public relations was revealed in a 1970s study by Aronoff that measured widely differing views of the two disciplines toward each other. Pavlik reports that "most practitioners disagreed with the following statement: PR practitioners try to deceive journalists by attaching too much importance to unimportant events. In contrast, almost all journalists agreed with this statement."[14] Although conditions may have improved since this study, the practitioner may well assume a negative attitude on the part of media gatekeepers and take pains to counter it in dealing with the media.

A 1986 study found that newspapers published releases on consumer information, coming events, research, and timely topics more frequently than releases on past events, features, or institutional "brag stories." Linda Morton summarizes the results of her research of Oklahoma newspapers as follows:

> The results indicate that Oklahoma newspaper gatekeepers are more receptive to some types of articles than to others and that their receptiveness differs according to their newspaper's frequency of publication. Daily newspapers published an average of 7.6 percent of all articles sent them, while weeklies published 9 percent and twice-weeklies published 21.6 percent. Thus the odds of getting articles published appear to be better when sent to weeklies and twice-weeklies than when sent to dailies. Newspapers in all three frequency levels published more *consumer information* articles than any other type.
>
> Three types of releases were published so infrequently that their value to public relations practitioners should be seriously questioned. These releases are *past*

events (4 percent), *features* (3 percent) and *institutional* (less than 1 percent). These results indicate that newspaper gatekeepers are not receptive to these types of articles, regardless of the newspapers' characteristics.[15]

It is probable that the principles identified in this study will apply to other media as well. Magazine, radio, and television gatekeepers are no more willing to provide their audiences with old news, features from outside, and "brag stories" than are newspaper editors.

Intermediary gatekeepers constitute another hurdle to effective media relations. These intermediary influences are organizations with which the campaign organization cooperates and which may play an important role in campaign communications that involve both organizations. Coalition members, organizations participating in tradeouts or tie-ins, will often have a stake in news releases or other communications produced as part of the campaign. Their cooperation and consent in communication are as important as their cooperation in the campaign.

When working with other organizations in a campaign, the sponsoring organization should keep control of the communication and never delegate that responsibility to intermediary gatekeepers. In a *Public Relations Quarterly* article on crisis public relations, Wayne Pines offers sound advice on working with government agencies. Having worked in public information for the U.S. Food and Drug Administration, he recommends that a company should never "lose control of your story by letting someone else announce it." Pines relates, "I was astounded at FDA to see lawyers and doctors come in to discuss a crisis situation, and, if the decision was adverse to them, let FDA announce recall or product removal or whatever the action was." There are sound reasons why the public relations campaign manager should retain control of communication involving intermediary groups, as Pines points out:

> . . . the company should, at times of crises, have professional public relations counsel, and then go ahead and handle announcement, itself. Even in a negative situation, it is infinitely better for a company to retain control of the story. There are almost too many reasons to list, but let me mention a few:
>
> - The government's announcement will sometimes generate more negative publicity for the company by making it seem the company's decision was forced by government.
> - The company's credibility will be significantly enhanced if it announces its own bad news.
> - The company will be able to time the announcement better and then control the inquiries from the media and public.
>
> In crisis situations, companies should make a major effort to pre-empt government announcements—not by circumventing the agency, but by offering to make all announcements itself.[16]

TRAINING SPOKESPERSONS

Use of the "media" carries with it the implication that such media communication is the polar opposite of the more intimate and eminently effective "person-to-person" communication. However, that assumption is no longer true with the spokesperson program. If an organization will take the time and make the effort, the trained spokesperson can command efficient use of the media to communicate person to person. If the training is not done carefully, the spokesperson runs the risk of being ineffective.

James Kilpatrick illustrated the problem quite convincingly in a column in *Nation's Business* when he told the story of an untrained spokesperson. The scene is a TV studio in which a reporter is asking an oil company executive some particularly embarrassing questions about "obscene profits," bribes to "foreign potentates," and the like. The TV cameras zoomed in on the corporate executive:

> He was a corpulent fellow in his sixties, dripping wealth and perspiration. His jowls fell in fat waterfalls over his collar, and his gut spilled over his waistband. If you had looked high and low for the worst possible image of American big business, you could not have found a better model. The gentleman could have walked out of one of the old Conde Nast cartoons depicting the robber barons.
>
> This veritable tycoon—for so he appeared—was being questioned, and questioned fairly, on what ever issue had put him before the network cameras. He had a uniform response. It began with a "well, uh" and continued evasively through a series of stammered ambiguities. Watching this wretched performance, I reflected unhappily: Here is a fellow who heads a multibillion-dollar corporation; he is paid a salary of nearly $1 million dollars a year; he must be a crackerjack executive; and he must have an encyclopedic knowledge of his industry or he wouldn't be where he is. Why doesn't somebody teach him how to handle himself when the little red light comes on?
>
> That is only one of the questions that ought to be raised. The great corporations that make the most news have whole regiments of public relations advisers. Why don't the executives take their advice?[17]

Spokespersons can be trained to be effective when the little red light comes on, or when the reporter extends the microphone toward your executive's face and asks the disarming question. A growing number of video consultants have sprung up offering short courses in executive spokesperson training. The U.S. Chamber of Commerce in Washington, D.C., offers two-day training courses for corporate executives in how to handle themselves on television. Colleges and universities also provide such services. With the advent of inexpensive video cameras and recorders, even the least sophisticated nonprofit organization can prepare its executives to meet the press (see Box 15.4).

Training spokespersons from among the organization's executives is only one possibility; a geographically broad-based organization can also train its members as effective spokespersons. James Strenski points out the benefits of an organized spokesperson program on the part of professional associations such as the American Dental Association (ADA). He details the advantages of such a program in an article in *Public Relations Quarterly*. "Building a team of trained spokespersons, geographically disseminated so that they can respond to placement opportunities, is only part of the challenge." By using direct mail circulars with reply postcards, organizational spokespersons can be scheduled for media interviews. Follow-up phone calls to arrange the actual

BOX 15.4   Chester Berger on Media Relations

Chester Berger put together a set of basic guidelines for just such a spokesperson training course in his *Harvard Business Review* article "How to Meet the Press." He offered the corporate executive spokesperson two "general criteria" that will remain valid over time: "have a sound attitude" and "always prepare carefully." The sound attitude requires the spokesperson to respect "his own competence and greater knowledge of his own subject," but realistically recognize that "the reporter or critic is skilled in the art of asking provocative questions."

Careful preparation means never "play it by ear" by improvising answers on the spur of the moment. "The best preparation consists of anticipating the most likely questions, attempting to research the facts, and structuring effective answers to be held ready for use." He advises against carrying notes into the interview, but rather having the answers "well in mind, although not literally memorized." Berger also offered ten specific guidelines to learn and remember:

1. "Talk from the viewpoint of the public's interest, not the company's." Rather than resort to the familiar corporate point of view such as, "We can't afford the increase the union is asking," phrase it: "We'd like to give our employees the increase they seek. But if our costs go up too much, our customers won't buy. That will hurt us, and in the end, it will endanger our employees' jobs."

2. "Speak in personal terms whenever possible." While corporate executives learn early on to say "we" or "our company," which reinforces the "public image of corporations as impersonal monoliths," speaking "in terms of personal experience will always make a favorable impression."

3. "If you do not want some statement quoted, do not make it." Spokespersons should avoid "off-the-record" comments. The statement the executive makes "off-the-record" may well 'turn up in the same published article, minus his name," and with a qualifying phrase added, "Meanwhile, it has been learned from other sources that. . . . "

4. "State the most important fact at the beginning." The tendency is to give background facts before the answer. But what is said first is most likely to be quoted. Such an answer to a question about a new product might be, "We are facing shortages of plastics. And their cost is rising so fast I don't think we can price the product at an attractive level. Moreover, we have a labor shortage in the plant. So I recommend we don't take any action now to develop the product." A better summary-answer first would be, "We don't plan to develop the product. We are facing materials shortages. Our costs are going up, and we also have a shortage of skilled labor."

5. "Do not argue with the reporter or lose your cool." The reporter will write the final story with any biases that might enter into the exchange. "An executive cannot win an argument with the reporter in whose power the published story lies."

6. "If a question contains offensive language or simply words you do not like, do not repeat them, even to deny them." Don't let the reporter put words in your mouth by repeating words you would not want to see in a quote attributed to you. "If you are asked a question based on a 'fact' about which you are uncertain, be wary of a trap. The so-called 'fact' may indeed be a fact, but if you are not sure, it is better to dissociate yourself from it. You might say, 'I'm not familiar with that quotation,' and then proceed to answer the question in your own positive way."

7. "If the reporter asks a direct question, he is entitled to an equally direct answer." Instead of answering with a simple yes or no, interviewees should elaborate until they have given a full reply with the context to make it a full answer. Often information the interviewee had planned to provide can be incorporated into answers to other questions.

8. "If an executive does not know the answer to a question, he should simply say, 'I don't know, but I'll find out for you'." The executive is advised "never answer 'I don't know' alone, but always to qualify the answer with a phrase like, 'I'll put you in touch with someone else who can answer that for you'." When a reporter asks a question that the executive, for legal or other reasons, cannot or wishes not to answer, it is best to respond directly, without evasion or excuses, "I'm sorry, I can't give you that information."

9. "Tell the truth, even if it hurts." Berger reminds us that "half-truths" are also "half-lies." No one likes to be in an embarrassing situation—for executives and companies as well as individuals—"telling the truth remains the best answer." Berger asks, "how much truth should a company tell? My experience answers, 'As much as the reporter wants to know'."

10. "Do not exaggerate the facts." Overly optimistic estimates or attempts to manipulate reality will lead to even more embarrassing questions in the future. The risk of loss of credibility in the ultimate disclosure of a manipulated fact is not worth it. "It's going to be that much harder for them to make themselves heard and believed next time, when they might just be right."

Source: Berger, Chester. "How to Meet the Press," *Harvard Business Review* 53 (July–August 1975): 62–70.

interviews is "the key," according to Strenski. He describes the program used by the ADA:

> The American Dental Association has long invested in professional spokesperson training for its membership. State and local Societies are offered training programs in their area. The American Dental Association has organized training "circuit riders" complete with video tape playback, role playing interview simulations, and manuals of tips and tactics. Once trained, another team swings into action in behalf of the ADA to arrange the media interviews. In 1977, more than 300 dentists were interviewed on radio and television stations alone across the country. Some 500 media exposures were recorded as a result of these interviews. Many of the shows were taped and played more than once on the same station.[18]

Whether a single executive is trained as a corporate spokesperson, representatives of the organization are trained in an organized program, or spokespersons are selected as in the Miss America contest, spokesperson remain a vital part of modern media effectiveness, especially in an organized public relations campaign.

STAYING ETHICAL AND LEGAL UNDER PRESSURE

Ethics and law are two aspects of the social force that shapes society into a coherent system by defining acceptable and unacceptable behavior. Ethics makes up the system of what coherent groups of people regard as right and wrong and have incorporated into unspoken or written rules. Law is a more formal system that identifies right and wrong by carefully defining in statute what will be regarded as wrong in specific situations.

The Basic Nature of Ethics: Conformity to Social Convention

The etymology of the word *ethics* is revealing, especially for public relations people. Ethics and ethos—credibility—are the same word in Greek, except for the first letter. Ethics (εθοs) begins with the short "e," epsilon, and ethos (ηθοs) with the long "e," or eta. The two words in Greek describe a cause-and-effect relation: ethics is conformity to social conventions of right and wrong and ethos is the result of that conformity—credibility.

The word *morals* comes from the equivalent Latin term, *mores*, but in modern usage morals generally connotes an immediate, specific, and more transitory consensus of right or wrong behavior; ethics connotes a more widely held, enduring consensus of right and wrong. Morals ordinarily involves unwritten norms of behavior, from not breaking into line ahead of people, or not taking unfair advantage, all the way to not making unwelcome sexual advances or not going back on your word.

Ethics usually involves personal or group standards of conformity to these social conventions. Individuals and groups may devise "codes" or written standards of what is right and wrong. The term *ethical* here means both the moral and the ethical senses. People earn the approval—and credibility—of their peers by their reputation for observing these social conventions. A long record of ethical conformity is necessary to achieve a good reputation and its attendant credibility; one breach of these ethical standards is often enough to destroy both reputation and credibility.

Different groups and the individuals within these groups have different standards; the standards for the "Hells Angels" would be quite different from the standards of the American Medical Association. Reputation is determined within each group by the individuals' conformity to its standards; credibility within the group follows from that conformity. Individuals earn a reputation within the group by conformity to group standards; groups earn a reputation within society at large by conforming to the prevailing standards of the whole society.

Groups earn their reputation by the behavior of their members as perceived by society. In a 1984 *Journal of Business Ethics* article, Thomas E. Shaefer argues that "business . . . is increasingly a public institution and, as such, has little choice but to answer for the effects of its activities."[19] The business community and society depend on each other to conform to the conventions regarding right and wrong behavior. Business depends on the stability of an ethical society to produce its goods, services, and profits; society depends on business for its goods and services and allows it to make profits as long as it conforms to ethical standards.

Shaefer believes that ethical business practices are based on professionalism, which he describes as putting service to society before profit: "professionalism benefits the business community in a way that, without it, commercial order must lapse into chaos. This is seen in certain undeveloped economies where there are few professionals and few who respect the restraints of law. In such a situation business cannot thrive. Incompetence and temporary gains resulting from fraud poison commerce, decreasing the wealth of the very ones who would seek profit by such means."[20]

A professional in the direct marketing field compared professionals and students in terms of how they would deal with ethical dilemmas and found that students were generally less constrained by ethical principles than professionals. Among nine other scenarios he posed this one:

The KKK Copywriter
The Problem: You are given the job of writing a piece of copy for a group—such as the Ku Klux Klan. You are in total disagreement with the group. Would you accept the assignment?

The Answers: About 35% of the students said yes—they would take the job. Among professionals, however, not a single one said they would do the job.

Conclusion: Once again, it seems as if the professionals realize that jobs are easy to get—and they can pick and choose. Also, they might understand that you can't do a good job for a product or client in which you do not believe. As we learned from history, it's easy to have ideals and principles—when you have a full stomach.[21]

Ethics and Law Are Two Limits That Society Places on Behavior

The system is a three-cornered fence. In our democratic society we place great emphasis on freedom. The ethical and legal systems are constructed to allow as much freedom of behavior as possible. Schaefer explains how they work together; if ethical standards do not succeed in producing socially acceptable behavior, the law will.

> As morality is never a matter of coercion, its practice will not be assured, either for the businessman or anyone else, through legislation. Good legislation will encourage inner compliance but it cannot touch the ethical world itself which is the realm of freedom. We know that "professional codes," even where they have the enforcement of law, could not make men ethical. These codes, in reality, will be only as good as the goodwill of those to whom they may be addressed.[22]

Ethics and law together impose effective restraints on behavior, but within these restraints our system tries to preserve as much freedom as possible (Box 15.5). Ethics, as an internalized code of conduct, represents a first line of defense against antisocial behavior and law a second line of defense. This double fence limits behavior on three sides:

1. **Personal sensitivity** to offensive behavior—or the line between what people will and will not put up with—is the basis for ethical restraint on behavior. Behind this ethical restraint lies the legal option of the injured party to seek redress in the courts. So, if someone is unwilling to bow to moral pressure and restrain himself—when he gets too close to my nose— then I, as the injured party, can bring legal charges to protect my rights.
2. **Codes and statutes** make up a second side of the fence to restrain behavior. The ethical codes make up both the unwritten and written standards stating where free behavior ends and people's rights begin. Behind the ethical codes stands the restraint of legal statute—the laws that define where freedom ends and individual rights begin. But both the ethical codes and the statutes are written *intentionally vague* to ensure that freedom of behavior is kept as broad as possible.
3. **Ethical custom and experience and legal precedents** make up the third side of the fence. When interpretation of the ethical code becomes an issue, those who disagree refer to custom and experience—whether people usually approve or disapprove of such behavior. When a case of personal injury is brought to court, a vague statute is cited as prohibiting such behavior, but the defense will claim that, when properly interpreted, the statute doesn't prohibit the behavior. Both prosecution and defense will then refer to legal precedents—previous legal interpretations of the statute—to attempt to prove their position.

We can convert this model into three questions to guide ethical decisions: (1) Who is likely to be offended or injured by the action? (2) Would the action violate any code of conduct? (3) Would experience with past ethical matters of this kind counsel restraint?

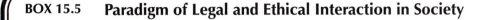

BOX 15.5   Paradigm of Legal and Ethical Interaction in Society

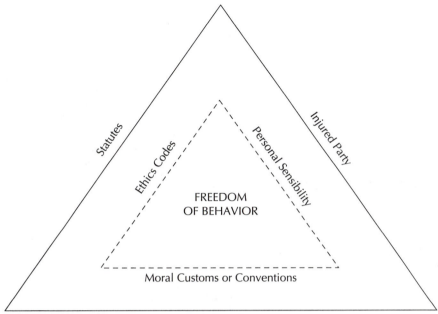

Statutes

Ethics Codes

Personal Sensibility

Injured Party

FREEDOM
OF BEHAVIOR

Moral Customs or Conventions

Legal Precedents

Both ethics and law function as restraints on behavior in a society. Of the two restraining "fences," ethics is the more breachable and law the more formally constraining. Within the double fences of ethics and law, the individual is free to act as he or she chooses. One's freedom of behavior encounters limitations when one begins to offend someone else's personal sensibility (upper right, inner fence) by threatening that person's own freedom of behavior. The limitation may also be encountered by threatening to offend the unwritten moral code (bottom inner fence) or conventions of a social group. The moral conventions may become formalized into ethical codes (upper left inner fence), which are more formal restraints on freedom of behavior, as the society develops its ethical constraints.

Beyond the constraints of a society's ethical structure lie the more formal and rigid legal barriers to freedom of behavior. Beyond the personal sensitivity of someone whose rights are threatened lies the status of the injured party who has a legal "case" (upper right outer fence) against the offending party. The "case" may be taken to court, where the complaint is compared against the formal statutes (upper left outside fence)

(*continues*)

that limit such behavior. The statutes are made intentionally vague, however, and the judge must weigh the evidence and make a decision on this particular case by consulting the

legal precedents (bottom outer fence) or decisions made on similar cases by previous courts. These precedents become a type of formal custom or convention that determines what is a just limitation on behavior in cases of similar conflict.

The American social system is constructed to provide as much freedom of behavior as possible by keeping the barriers as distant as possible. For that reason, the statutes are written "intentionally vague," with the understanding that the court system will determine individual cases. However, as society becomes more populous, interpersonal conflicts force the constraints inward, bringing more and more limitations both ethical and legal.

But ethics is more than avoiding wrong behavior; it is proactive in good behavior. Schaefer notes,

> Today's marketing manager must do more than fulfill his buyer's hopes that his product or service will perform as promised; he must also convince them that he does these things in "good faith," i.e., for their benefit as much as his or her company's. Recognizing this, marketing is striving as never before to provide service for the consumer. This centrality of service within the activity of marketing links marketing closely with professionalism.[23]

The three questions should be asked again in positive form: (1) Will society benefit from the action? (2) Is the action according to the spirit of society's code of conduct? (3) Is the action customary?

Professionalism in business as in public relations is based on a dedication to put service to society above pecuniary interests, as Edward Bernays has often pointed out. Schaefer suggests,

> By stressing dedication to service, professionalism points to a norm for business ethics: only when the interests of all who may be affected by a business decision are taken into account is a business decision truly ethical. Thus, a number of top executives have pointed out in recent years that business today must be conceived as having "many publics." It is not only the "stockholding public" or the "working public" or "the public outside the plant," but it is all of these that business must serve. Professionalism directly includes this notion that service must extend beyond the confines of special groups.[24]

For public relations people, social convention is focused in the PRSA Code. It is the first warning of what society regards as the line between right and wrong behavior. If it is ignored, legal action may follow.

The Practitioner Needs to Know the PRSA Code of Ethics

The code, as revised in 1988, can be broken down into three categories of provisions, those that protect the public, the client-employer, and the profession:

1. Six code paragraphs (1 to 8, and 11) protect the ***public;*** reduced to their essentials they are: protect the public interest, maintain honesty and integrity, deal fairly, maintain accuracy and truth, use no false or misleading information, do not corrupt the channels of public communication, be prepared to identify client/employer, and represent no undisclosed interest, nor any personal conflict of interest.

2. Five code paragraphs (5, 7, 9, 10, 12, 13) protect the ***client-;*** their essentials are: use no false or misleading information, be prepared to identify client/employer, never guarantee achievement beyond your control, represent no organization that involves professional conflict of interest, safeguard confidences, be willing to identify client-employer, accept no fees from conflicting interests.

3. Four code paragraphs (14, 15, 16, and 17) protect the ***profession;*** the essential provisions are: commit no injury to another practitioner, present ethical violations promptly, be willing to appear as witness, and sever ties with any employer who requires violation of the code.

The code includes three sets of interpretations: for *practitioners in general*, for *political practitioners*, and for *financial practitioners*. Some noteworthy interpretations include the following: Client-employer communication remains confidential even after a relationship ends. Papers produced on the job belong to the employer in the absence of a written—and signed—agreement to the contrary. It is ethical to accept gifts only of minimal value. It is unethical to offer compensation, advertising commitment, trips, loans, or investments to guarantee use of your news-ed material, but free samples and contingency fees are acceptable. Only blind solicitation for clients is acceptable, but not with adverse reference to current counsel, and "what is customary or reasonable hospitality has to be a matter of particular judgment."

Political public relations involves anything to do with candidates, holders of public office, or governments domestic or foreign and with lobbying whether official or not. The practitioner must know and adhere to the applicable laws, act the partisan in good faith as well as in accord with the public interest.

Financial public relations includes anything to do with stockholder or investor relationships. The practitioner must know and adhere to applicable laws and regulations, especially those of the Securities and Exchange Commission (SEC). Precepts which practitioners must follow include: Make full and timely disclosure of any information having a material influence on stock price. Preserve the confidentiality of corporate information, and never precondition the market during stock registration period. The code requires that practitioners satisfy themselves of the truth of information disseminated, act promptly to correct false information, clearly identify third-party sources, not use insider information for personal gain, not accept stock as compensation at below-market price, and not pay or permit to be paid to any publication any consideration in exchange for publicizing a company, except as paid advertising.

SUMMARY

This book approaches the campaign as a process that must be planned and approved before it is implemented. Not all of the campaign examples in the literature proceed in this way. Many case studies are presented with the implementation before the evaluation. While that order will apply in carrying out the campaign, this book has shown how to prepare the entire campaign plan including the evaluation plan prior to implementation.

Scheduling required for a campaign includes coordinating the activities of the team members, the scheduling of the team manager's time, backup in case of incapacity, and a system for exchange of messages.

The **campaign team** must be put together; authority and responsibility must be assigned. Some thought should be given to management of creative people during campaign implementation.

Getting help and cooperation from the broad range of suppliers, other managers, personnel, superiors, and subordinates requires careful attention to interpersonal skills. Lesly suggests ways to effective teamwork.

Performance monitoring helps ensure success by focusing on faltering performance and interpersonal relationships among team members. Techniques for monitoring outside counsel can also help internal team effectiveness.

Managing media relations should give attention to media systems, the nature of news, journalistic conventions, news release form, your organization as a news source, and how events work. The team needs to work with media gatekeepers, know what media want, and how to deal with potential problems with media.

Spokesperson training improves effectiveness of the organization in media relations. Chester Berger's guidelines for dealing with media provide the basis for media relations.

Ethics and legalities when under pressure require internalizing ethical principles. Knowing and practicing the PRSA Code of Ethics is critical for maintaining credibility for the campaign manager, the organization, and the public relations profession.

Glossary

A number of the following terms have been defined by a Terminology Committee of the Public Relations Society of America appointed by PRSA President Dwayne Summer, APR, and approved by its Spring Assembly in 1988. The committee consisted of Philip Lesly, APR chairman; John Budd, APR; Scott Cutlip, APR; Otto Lerbinger, APR; and Mary Ann Pires, APR. Italics indicate where the wording of the committee is used.

account Business relationship between a public relations counseling or consulting firm or agency and a client, whether a corporation, government agency, individual, or nonprofit organization; the term derives from the necessity of keeping records of time and other costs associated with serving the client's needs in order to have a detailed accounting to present with billing statements.

account executive (AE) Person employed by an advertising or public relations counseling or consulting concern who is responsible for serving the needs of a particular client account; the person may be assisted by other members of the agency and may hire outside specialists such as photographers, printers, or video producers to supply the needs of the client, but the AE manages the entire process and is ultimately responsible for the outcome.

account supervisor Manager within a counseling firm or agency who coordinates and supervises a number of account executives.

advance person Person who manages the publicity and arrangements for a series of public appearances or events scheduled in different geographic locations; the term arose in the circus but is now more common in political campaigns; the work involves arranging for auditorium rental, advertising, promotion, publicity, and coordinating with local organizations.

advertisement (Ad or Adv) Message created by or in behalf of an organization for paid placement in various media of mass communication, including posters and outdoor, to reach audiences attracted to those media, but may be limited to one medium.

advertising Publicity for which the media time or space is paid by the message sponsor, who also controls the appearance of the message as to time, format, placement, and recurrence; often coordinated with packaging, promotion, marketing, and public relations efforts. *Persuasive material that is presented to the public as acknowledged appeal of an identified party who pays to have it appear.* In addition to the most common form, which applies to messages about products or services, special forms include institutional advertising, public relations advertising, and corporate advertising, which place messages about the organization itself as distinct from its products or services. Advocacy advertising is characterized by its advancement of a cause or issue. Comparative advertising also is distinguished by its comparison of product or service to competitor product or service.

advertising agency   Organization that acts on behalf of clients in the preparation, production, placement, and assessment of advertising messages; the term agency refers to the organization's contracted responsibility to act for the client in the expenditure of funds to achieve anticipated outcomes.

angle   Distinctive approach to a news or feature story that sets the story off from the ordinary and thus creates reader interest.

animation   System for making filmed or computerized objects or cartoons appear to move by use of a series of pictures or acrylic overlays, each with a progressive stage in a series of movements.

annual report   Account of a corporation's yearly accomplishments of interest to stockholders; a formal version (Form 10-K) is required by the Securities and Exchange Commission (SEC) for publicly held companies (companies whose securities are offered for sale to the public and are traded on stock exchanges); the SEC also requires Forms 8-K and 10-Q for interim and quarterly reportable activities; while not a legal requirement, many other organizations, including nonprofits, issue annual reports as public relations tools.

ASCAP   American Society of Composers, Authors, and Publishers, one of three organizations that represent the royalty interests of copyright owners of musical compositions, arrangements, and performances; ASCAP and the others, Broadcast Music Inc. (BMI) and the Society of European Songwriters, Authors, and Composers (SESAC), collect royalty fees and redistribute them to copyright owners; those using music for commercial applications including public relations, advertising, and marketing must get permission from whichever organization controls the rights to the piece.

ASCII   American Standard Code for Information Interchange, a system in which the seven or eight 1's and 0's (bits) that make up a byte of computer information are uniformly translated into standard alpha (letters) or numeric (numeral) characters including some other typographic characters ($&@#). Some characters are not included in the ASCII system. Word processors that use different or nonstandard characters to indicate indentation, underlining, and other such commands produce computer files that are not compatible with other systems. Such files must be translated from one word processor system to another.

association   Group of people organized in a noncommercial organization to advance their common interest; examples, a trade association such as the National Association of Manufacturers (NAM), a professional association such as Public Relations Society of America (PRSA), and a nonprofit association such as the American Heart Association (AHA); some professionals such as physicians work cooperatively and for commercial purposes as a professional association (PA) which is a special legal designation.

attitude   Inclination, often unconscious, to behave in a given way as a result of a spectrum of information, values, beliefs, experiences, and persuasive messages.

audience   Group of people gathered to hear a speaker or other type of performance, either in one place or tuned to one or more medium of mass communication; examples are an auditorium audience, a radio or television audience, and a newspaper audience; synonymous terms include viewership for television, listenership for radio, readership for newspapers and magazines; publics may include all of these.

audience segmentation   Breakdown of an audience or audiences into demographic, psychographic, or other dimensions in order to adapt messages to audience need or interest.

audiovisuals (AVs) Range of sound, pictures, and graphics used to complement or complete the communication process; used in such public relations activities as speaking and campaign presentations; common examples include flip charts, film, sound/slide sets, video recordings, overhead projection devices, and opaque projectors. Synonymous term: visual aid.

bandwagon effect Interest stimulated by social interaction that attracts increasing numbers, such as may be seen in crowd behavior or fad-motivated activities; an attraction to a cause whose fortunes seem to be rising; the term was also used by the Institute for Propaganda Analysis (in the 1930s) to identify a propaganda device. Propaganda seeks to advance a viewpoint by use of thought-distracting appeals of an emotional nature, one-sided arguments, and half-truths—these connotations are not commonly true of the term bandwagon in current definitions.

blurb Promotional summary of a news or feature story used at the top of the first page of the published piece as an encouragement for readers to read the entire article; at times, a summary used to promote a story to media editors.

BMI Broadcast Music Incorporated is one of three organizations that represent the royalty interests of copyright owners of musical compositions, arrangements, and performances: Broadcast Music Inc. (BMI), American Society of Composers, Authors, and Publishers (ASCAP), and Society of European Songwriters, Authors, and Composers (SESAC); each collects royalty fees and redistributes them to copyright owners; those using music for commercial applications, including public relations, advertising, and marketing, must get permission from whichever organization controls the rights to the piece.

boundary spanning Term used in organizational communication to refer to the behavior of individuals or groups within units or organizations at their "boundary" or linkage with other units or organizations, usually attempting to enhance their decision-making role or power-control status; by analogy, the term is used of the public relations function in building relationships with other organizations.

brainstorming Group problem-solving or creativity process in which six to nine people think creatively, building on the ideas presented by participants to produce a collective solution to a problem, such as proposing possible campaign strategies.

briefing book Looseleaf notebook compiling the possible questions and appropriate answers prepared by public relations staff for use by a chief executive officer or other executive in a news conference or other media interaction situation.

broadside Device for communicating a simple message, usually the five W's—what, where, when, who, why—to an audience within a short time; usually printed in large letters on only one side for posting on bulletin boards and elsewhere. Synonymous terms: flier, dodger, handbill.

brochure Carefully designed message printed as a booklet with multiple pages or on both sides of a sheet, often with pictures and/or other graphics, folded for attractive display of segments and for ease of handling or mailing.

bulk mailing Category of U.S. Postal Service third-class mail that is delivered at low cost, but the pieces must be presorted and bundled by zip code.

cable Used in two senses in communication fields: the coaxial cable through which FM radio and TV signals are carried, and the medium that uses coaxial cable to transmit video programming; synonymous terms: community antenna television (CATV), and closed circuit television (CCTV).

campaign Connected series of operations designed to bring about a particular result; in public relations, advertising, marketing, political, and fund-raising contexts, the term encompasses such related activities as publicity, promotion, special events, advertising, and organizational behavior, all coordinated to sway public opinion and/or behavior.

CATV/CCTV   See **cable.**

CEO/COO   Chief executive officer (CEO) and chief operating officer (COO) are terms used in business organizations to describe the company's ultimate decision maker, whether the president, chairman of the board, executive vice president, or other job title; the term CEO is often used in other than business organizations to refer to the top decision maker.

client   In public relations, an entity, other than a regular employer, on behalf of which public relations activities are conducted; the term commonly refers to the organization contracting for the services of a counselor or consultant rather than the organization hiring a regular public relations employee.

clippings   News or feature items cut out of publications in which they were published as a result of placement efforts, or at times items clipped because they contain references to the organization or other identified terms; usually collected by clipping services, for a fee, from an agreed-upon list of publications. See also **tear sheet.**

clip sheet   Collection of news or feature items of varying length often set in type ready to be cut and pasted into a newspaper layout as filler.

communication   *(in relation to public relations) Interchange of information; also the transaction of conveying thought from one party or group to another.* A sharing of an intellectual and/or emotional experience through written, spoken, or nonverbal cues; when such cues are delivered through the mass media the result is mass communication.

community relations   Aspect of public relations having responsibility for building relationships with constituent publics such as schools, charities, clubs, and activist interests of the neighborhoods or metropolitan area(s) in which an organization operates. *Dealing and communicating with the citizens and groups within an organization's operating area.*

contingency fee   Charge for services payable on the condition that materials are successfully placed in a publication or broadcast medium; although the PRSA code of ethics prohibits the guarantee of results beyond the member's direct control, the official interpretation of this code paragraph specifies, "This paragraph should not be interpreted as prohibiting contingent fees." Synonymous term: contingent fee.

contingency plan   Procedure outlined in detail for implementation as an alternative to a portion of the primary plan to be used in a campaign or other activity; the contingency plan is a fallback option in case the primary plan encounters obstacles.

corporate culture   The pattern of behavior that distinguishes a company from other organizations even in the same line of business; the "way we do things around here" as one corporate executive described the phenomenon. Culture, whether of a company or nonprofit organization, may be described as the personality of an organization consisting of the stories, heroes, myths, anecdotes, traditions, policies, practices, and the like that characterize the organization.

counsel/counselor   Person who offers professional public relations advice and/or services either contracted or subcontracted for a fee; the term is often synonymous with public relations consultant.

coverage   Time, space, and/or prominence the media give to a story or a series of stories on an issue.

CRT/VDT   Cathode ray tube (CRT) and video display terminal (VDT) are synonymous terms describing the device in a television monitor or computer screen that displays the electronic signal involving words or pictures produced by video systems using either analog or digital signals.

customer   The purchaser, especially the "customary" purchaser, of a product or service; often used interchangeable with **consumer;** that is, one who uses or consumes a product or service, especially a nondurable product.

data   Information in coded or numeric form from a source such as survey research that may be analyzed to determine findings or the results of interviews; also, in a generic sense, undigested information.

deadline   Time after which news or other copy cannot be accepted for inclusion in media outlets because of production schedules; by analogy, the term also applies to other time limits.

defamation   General term encompassing both slanderous (verbal) and libelous (written) attack on a person's character; illegal communication that subjects a person to hatred, ridicule, or contempt or injures the person's business or is harmful to a reputation.

demonstration   Act of showing how a piece of equipment works; also, acting out of dissent from or support for an issue or petitioning for a change of practice or policy.

direct mail   Use of the U.S. Postal Service and other delivery services to communicate directly with targeted publics in the form of letters, brochures, or packets of materials, usually making use of mailing lists selected on the basis of demographic or other criteria.

distribution list   Addresses to which media news releases are sent, or targeted segments of publics used for direct mail.

dividend   Proportion of corporate earnings distributed quarterly or annually to investors based on stockholder or shareholder equity invested in an enterprise.

dodger   See **broadside.**

electronic signal   Communication encoded in an electrical current that allows for electronic transmission of messages, such as in radio, television, computer, cable, telephone, or satellite systems; the signal may be either *analog,* which includes amplitude modulation (AM) or frequency modulation (FM) of electronic waves, or *binary,* which encodes computerized bits (1's or 0's) or bytes (a series of seven or eight bits) that together make up characters such as letters, numbers, ASCII, and other computer characters.

embargo   Notation on a news release indicating a date and/or time after which the news may be published, as required of an announcement of a future event such as a resignation; conventional media practice has honored such implied requests to hold a story until after the stated time, but there is no assurance that the request will be honored.

emergency/disaster/crisis communication   Public relations activities and actions prepared in advance to deal with an emergency or disaster situation in which injury, loss of life, and/or loss of property is involved; most organizations have such plans as a responsibility of the public relations staff. Contingency plans are similar preparations for developments that will require alteration of campaign plans.

employee relations   Activities designed to build sound relationships between an organization and its employees, and a critical element in fostering positive attitudes and behavior of employees as representatives of the organization.

ethnographic   A type of research used in anthropology consisting of the detailed recording of the characteristics that make up the culture of a people. The term is made up of two Greek terms—"ethno," meaning people and "graphos," meaning to write, or writing about a people; in public relations contexts it refers to the qualitative research into the nature of a corporate or organizational culture. **Ethnography** refers to the process of compiling such a report or to such a written research report.

event   Occasion that contributes to a group's social self-understanding or identity; may include celebrations, ceremonies, recognitions, or other activities giving meaning to their membership and/or participation; variations on the term include special events, media events, and staged events.

fact sheet   Summary of facts about an organization, cause, project, or individual prepared with the five W's and correct spellings, dates, and the like for use by media reporters in writing about the subject; may also be used for other purposes such as direct mail or promotion packets. Fact sheets are usually single sheets printed on one or both sides and may include simple graphics. They are usually distinguished from fliers by more careful printing and prominent display of the words "Fact Sheet" near the top of the page.

fax or facsimile   System for nearly instantaneous transmission of pictures and/or text by telephone line to receivers who have such equipment.

feature syndicate   Distribution service organization that sells copy and rights to news feature material for use in newspapers and other media. Materials include columns, comics, weather, cartoons, and the like, which are produced by artists and writers under contract to the syndicate.

feedback   The "squawk" produced by a public address sound system when the sound is picked up by the microphone and reamplified repeatedly; by analogy, any response to communication that may be used to evaluate and improve the effort.

fillers   Short news or feature material used by newspapers and other print media to fill in the "newsholes" left after advertising and major stories are fit into the layout pages; material is usually supplied by distribution services or public relations sources.

financial public relations   Aspect of public relations responsible for building relationships with the investor public including shareholders or stockholders, potential investors, financial analysts, the financial markets such as the stock exchanges and commodities exchanges, and the Securities and Exchange Commission. The term stakeholder is sometimes used to refer to investors but includes others who have invested time, job seniority, and commitment to the organization or are otherwise dependent on an organization in a sense other than financial. *Dealing and communicating with the shareholders of an organization and the investment community.*

flack   Press agent hired to generate and distribute publicity; used in a derogatory sense by media and professional public relations people.

flier   See **broadside.**

gatekeepers   People who control the flow of information within an organization or network by restricting access or by editing news submissions, especially within media organizations such as newspapers or broadcast stations.

ghost writer   Person who writes material that will be used by and credited to another person, usually with editing changes and approval of the final draft by the one employing the service, a relationship recognized in the "works for hire" provisions of copyright law; a common service provided by public relations people for chief executives of corporations or government.

goal   End that an activity or campaign seeks to achieve; a goal is usually intended to serve the longer-range organizational "mission" and may involve the use of shorter-range "objectives." Some authorities reverse the terms goal and objective, using goal for the short-range purpose and objective for the long-range one.

gobbledygook   Confusing and meaningless use of language often involving twisted phrasing and long convoluted sentences; may result from incompetence with language or may be used to give the appearance of an effort to communicate while avoiding genuine communication.

government relations   Aspect of relationship building between an organization and government at local, state, and/or national levels especially involving flow of information to and from legislative and regulatory bodies in an effort to influence public policy decisions compatible with the organization's interests. *Dealing and communicating with legislatures and government agencies on behalf of an organization.* See **public affairs, lobbying.**

handbill   See **broadside.**

handout   Typescripted information distributed to people interested in a news issue either during a news conference or in response to individual inquiries; examples include news releases, fact sheets, lists of names, speeches, and summaries.

hard news   Information that people need to know in order to cope with developments affecting their lives; consequently, most hard news is bad news signaling unwelcome changes that will disrupt many people's lives.

hardware   Physical elements that make up a computer system, as opposed to software, which includes various forms of programmed information stored in a computer used to process other information or data.

hometowner   News release usually involving feature news or a personality profile of an individual or event of interest to people in the hometown of the news subject and sent to media in the hometown.

house publication   Newspaper, magazine, newsletter, or variations on these produced by an organization for its employees or constituents, including customers, dealers, members, supporters, and the like. Synonymous terms: house organ, house magazine, company publication, internal publication.

identity   Result of planned effort to project an impression of an organization through the concerted use of such elements as logo, trademark, coordinated signage, letterheads, packaging, uniform use of color, publication layout and design, and other visual materials; a subfunction of public relations.

image   Cumulative perception a public has of an organization based on its publicity efforts together with its behavior, including especially that behavior unintended for public consumption; the term carries a connotation of cunning manipulation at variance with reality that leads many to avoid the term, preferring instead such terms as perception, impression, or identity, which imply commitment to mutually beneficial relations.

industry relations   Public relations specialty responsible for building mutually beneficial association with other organizations competing in the same field of business in order to advance shared interests. Businesses engaged in manufacture provide an example of one means of the cooperation of competitors. They work together through a trade association called the National Association of Manufacturers. *Dealing with and communicating with firms within the industry of the organization.*

information   The mental construct of a source represented in the form of facts, news, pictures, messages, or data that justifies change in the construct of the receiver of such communicated representation. Information is often assumed to consist of "objective facts" but actually represents the point of view (theory, schema, paradigm, or construct) of the source.

in-house   Referring to activities conducted within an organization or corporation, such as in-house production of slides or computer analysis of data, as opposed to such work performed by suppliers outside the company.

institutional advancement   Public relations efforts involved in promoting the growth and development usually of nonprofit organizations such as private colleges, social service agencies, museums, symphony orchestras, or charitable organizations.

institutional advertising   Creation and placement of messages about an organization as a whole apart from its products or services; generally considered a public relations function. The term is generally interchangeable with corporate advertising and public relations advertising and is similar to advocacy advertising and issues advertising.

institutional investors   Major segment of the financial or investing public consisting of persons responsible for investing the funds of financial organizations such as banks, insurance companies, pension funds, and securities houses.

intermediating publics   Groups or publics through whom the target public may be reached, as through tradeouts or tie-ins.

issue   Controversial topic involved in public debate in the process of the formation of public opinion; issues management, a related term, refers to the tracking of issues that may affect an organization as they develop, prioritizing them by importance, planning appropriate public relations response, executing plans, and monitoring results.

issues management   Task of tracking concerns about public policies in their formative stages, identifying these issues, measuring their development, and planning and managing organizational response; often considered a specialty within the broad function of public relations and usually requiring coordination with other public relations specializations. *Systematic identification and action regarding public policy matters of concern to an organization.*

junket   Tour organized for media reporters to facilitate their coverage of news or activities of an organization in remote or widespread areas and sponsored by the organization expecting to benefit from such coverage; traditionally the travel and expenses of participants have been paid for by the sponsoring organization; while common in other parts of the world, the practice is out of favor in the United States because of ethical conflict of interest considerations.

kill   Editorial decision to withhold publication of a story in the process of preparation usually because of later developments that destroy or threaten the news value of the original story; the term may be applied in case of legal, national security, ethical, or good taste considerations. Although public relations people may be tempted to ask for kills of unfavorable stories, the practice destroys the credibility of the organization with the media and ultimately with the public.

layout   Planned arrangement of printed headlines, blocks of type, pictures, cutlines, white space, and other elements of publication design in the production of a publication.

lead   Lead sentence or paragraph of a news story (pronounced "leed") usually summarizing the entire story and ordinarily containing the five W's (who, what, where, when, why); also, the spacing between lines of type (pronounced "led") from the practice of placing strips of lead metal of varying width between lines of hand-set type and usually referred to as leading (pronounced "leding").

leaflet   See **flier, dodger, handbill.**

leak   Disclosure to media contacts, usually without attribution, of inside information that may be regarded by management as proprietary; the practice may be used with management consent to test public reaction to an issue or, when used by government staffers, may be employed to bring public pressure to bear on decision makers in cases of policy disputes.

letters to the editor   Section reserved for publishing letters from readers, usually on or opposite the newspaper's editorial page or in a special section of magazines; criteria for acceptance are usually printed in the section, but reference to items recently published is most often required. Such letters are often important aspects of campaign plans in keeping an issue in the news.

leveraged buyout   The often hostile takeover of a company in which the group organizing the takeover makes speculative purchases of securities to be used as equity in the purchase of stocks in the target company to gain a controlling interest and so to take over management of the company.

libel   See **defamation.**

lobbying   Responsibility for influencing the processes of government through the skillful dissemination of information to and from government. Individuals engaged in lobbying activities are required to register with the appropriate state or federal officer, such as the clerk of the House of Representatives. Lobbyists work in concert with other public relations functions. (See also **government relations, public affairs.**)

low profile   Concerted attempt to avoid media attention that may be adopted as a policy on certain issues or by certain organizations; the position assumes negative public reaction on the issue and creates a dangerous public relations condition that may require a response from a position of weakness if the public becomes aware of the issue.

makeup   See **layout.**

manual   Handbook of information, such as might be included in an employee policies booklet, or instructions for the operation of a product.

market   Public whose needs are addressed by a product or service, whether in a specific locality or across geographic boundaries.

marketing   Matching of product or service to the needs of consumers as discovered through research on attitudes, opinions, and behavior. "The anticipation, management, and satisfaction of demand through the exchange process"—J. R. Evans and B. Berman, *Marketing* (Macmillan, 1985).

market share   Proportion of a total market served by a specific product, brand, or service.

mass communication   Dissemination of information or impressions through written, spoken, or nonverbal cues from a source using mass media to reach a public audience, which audience is united by some shared interest but is characterized by anonymity, noncohesiveness, leaderlessness, and absence of peer influence.

media   Collective term referring to technology systems for disseminating information, which consist—in order of historical development—of print, cinema, radio, and television; more recently these technologies have blurred with the introduction of computerized distribution of print and video through cable, satellite, and other systems.

media event   See **event.**

media relations   Mutually beneficial associations between publicists and members of media organizations as a condition for reaching media audiences with messages of news or features of audience interest. Maintaining up-to-date lists of media people and knowing media audience interests are critical to the function. *Dealing with the communications media in seeking publicity or responding to their interest in the organization.*

microwaves   Radio waves of very low amplitude that can travel inside a coaxial cable or between line-of-sight points and are used to carry information by varying their frequency, which is called frequency modulation or FM.

minority relations   Mutually beneficial associations between social entities and the various minority publics in society, especially black, Hispanic, and native American groups, at the local, regional, or national level.

mission   Long-range purpose of an organization which distinguishes it from its competition and in coordination with which its shorter-range goals and objectives are determined. Public relations activities must take into account both mission and goals of an organization in establishing goals and objectives of a campaign.

model release   Agreement designed to meet legal requirements for use of a person's photograph in a commercial publication; criteria include specifying monetary considerations and the subject's signature or that of a parent or legal guardian; a monetary payment of at least a dollar gives legal weight to the agreement. Such a release is not required for news coverage in public media but is necessary for most public relations publications and for advertising.

myth   The collective self-interpretation of a group of people based on the meaning attributed to momentous shared experiences, as for example in tribes, nations, or corporations; the basis of corporate culture and much effective employee loyalty, motivation, and productivity.

news   Information that people need to know in order to cope with the challenges of their lives, which is generally termed hard news; information that people find "nice to know" in order to keep the hard news (which is often "bad news") in perspective is termed soft news or feature material. Much of what public relations people provide the media in releases is of the soft news variety, focusing on human interest or personality profiles.

news conference   Meeting of organization spokespersons with media reporters or representatives for the purpose of disclosing news that may be either too complicated to be relayed in a news release or so important that all media must be given simultaneous access to avoid playing favorites. The news conference also allows for on-the-spot clarifications and questions, as well as photo opportunities for still and video cameras.

newsletter   Publication containing news of the business organization producing it, usually for internal publics; also published commercially for subscribers on such topics as investments or distributed to supporters of advocacy organizations.

news release   News story prepared by the news-source organization for distribution to the appropriate media, usually including the words "News Release" prominently displayed, and including such criteria as letterhead information on the source organization, contact person's name and phone number, release date, dateline, the five W's in the lead, attribution in the second or third paragraph, and written in standard news reporting style.

nonprofit   Organization engaged in activities not intended to make a profit. Qualifying charitable and service organizations may file with the Internal Revenue Service (501.C.3), which exempts the organization from tax liability but prohibits certain types of political lobbying activities and requires the filing of IRS form 990 (an annual report comparable to SEC form 10-K); such organizations also generally enjoy the conventional privilege of free broadcast coverage through public service announcements (PSAs) and special bulk mailing privileges. Associations may file under IRS Code 501.C.6, which does not involve bulk mailing privileges or limit lobbying; other institutions may be nonprofit in the sense of not generating revenue beyond expenses, but these do not qualify for IRS exemptions.

op-ed piece   Category of opinion essay, commentary, and/or news feature on controversial topics; the term derives from the page opposite the editorial page where such material is usually published.

performance   The total functioning of a company or other organization in carrying out its purpose, including such typical aspects of corporate life as purchase of raw materials, manufacturing or other operations, finance, marketing, sales, service, technological and product development, and public relations.

persuasion   The intentional effort to influence a public's beliefs, attitudes, opinions or behavior—except when such compliance is forced or purchased—which shifts that public's average position, as may be measured on a negative to positive scale, when that shift is toward the position advocated by the persuader. Most authorities agree that effective persuasion is a two-way process or a symbolic interaction open to mutual adjustment. (See K.K. Reardon, *Persuasion*. Sage, 1981).

press agentry   Tradition of "stooping to anything" to get a client mentioned in the press, often involving exaggerated claims, falsehood; and/or spectacle of a propagandistic nature; such tactics are frequently associated with show business and sports, where name recognition is often more important than long-term credibility. *Creating news events of a transient nature, often of a flighty sort.*

proactive public relations   Philosophy of public relations that takes the initiative in planning the nature of the relationships desired with publics and executes programs, campaigns, or activities designed to achieve the desired ends, in contrast to reactive public relations. See **reactive public relations.**

professional association   A legal corporation of professionally employed individuals practicing in close proximity for their mutual benefit, including reciprocal support and assistance as well as for tax advantages.

promotion   Activities designed to win publicity or attention, especially the staging of special events to generate media coverage. *Special activities, such as events, designed to create and stimulate interest in a person, product, organization or cause.*

propaganda   Efforts to advance a cause using such tactics as short-term goals; half-truths; one-sided, logically flawed arguments; strong emotional and/or distorted endorsements; or unethical appeals. *Efforts to influence the opinions of a public to propagate a doctrine.*

public   A group of people concerned about an issue including the pro, the con, and the neutral or undecided. Blumer added that "they engage in discussion over the issue," and Dewey added that they are organized around the issue. Unlike crowds, their critical powers and self-awareness are heightened by discussion not necessarily face-to-face. Blumer sharpened the definition by contrasting public with **society, mass,** and **crowd. Societies** are governed by rules, norms, and social conventions. **Masses** are attracted away from social conventions by an object of interest such as an advertised product, come from all walks of life, are without organization, are unknown to one another, are puzzled and uncertain in their actions, and act as individuals—but acting collectively their influence may be enormous. **Crowds** are like masses with the added characteristics that they interact in response to rumor and spectacle, are excited by appeals to primitive impulses or traditional hatreds, mill about, "develop rapport and reach a unanimity unmarred by disagreement." Pollsters view a public as a proportionate number of people in a population who express themselves on an issue of public importance with an intensity and constancy sufficient to influence the outcome of the issue.

public affairs   The "daily link between the private sector and government" which interprets business to government and government to business within the context of a larger social responsibility to preserve the openness and integrity of the democratic process. The task involves issues management, especially issues of concern to special-interest activists in the shaping of public policy. *Working with governments and groups who help determine public policies and legislation.* See **govern-**

ment relations, lobbying, public relations. See also the Public Affairs Council Statement of Ethical Guidelines.

public information   The representation of a point of view in such collected forms as facts, news, messages, pictures, or data (see **information**); the process of disseminating such information to publics usually through the mass media; a designation describing persons charged with the task of such dissemination usually on behalf of government agencies, nonprofit organizations, colleges, or universities.

publicity   *Dissemination of purposefully planned and executed messages through selected media to further the particular interest of an organization or person without specific payment to media.* In a general sense, publicity is making information known to a public or publics by means of private or commercial media; private media include interpersonal exchange of sensory meaning by spoken, written, or nonverbal cues; mass media involve the exchange of meaning through such channels as print, radio-television, outdoor signs, and newer technology when disseminated to large audiences.

public relations   (1) Mutually beneficial associations between social entities, (2) the process of building and maintaining such relationships, and (3) the vocation devoted to that process. (4) A phenomenon of societies in which advocates of an organization manage its performance in the public interest in order to nurture mutually beneficial associations with all interdependent groups through responsible use of the instruments of one-way and two-way communication.

reactive public relations   A philosophy—or more often a lack of a philosophy—guiding the public relations of an organization, which initiates programs in response to crises and "puts out fires"; results in a defensive posture which, because it does not operate from a position of strength, weakens the character of public relations efforts. See **proactive public relations.**

release   News story, either hard news or feature material, prepared by the newssource organization for distribution to the news media. Synonymous terms: news release, press release, publicity release. See **news release.**

remote   Origination of broadcast programming, either radio or television, from a location away from the usual studio setting by use of telephone or microwave transmission of the remote signal to the station; a common practice in special events, where the station has the opportunity to reach more than its usual audience; often involves additional advertisers who sponsor the event and who receive regular mention on the air, which covers costs of the event and enables the event producer to receive extensive publicity and carry out the activity at minimum cost. Synonymous term: remote broadcast.

research   Studious inquiry designed to discover and interpret facts; see page XX for specific definitions.

research design   The plan for a research project consisting of a description of the phenomenon to be observed and the nature of the measurement to be conducted. A more detailed research design will include descriptions of: (1) The population or **body of information** one intends to measure. (2) What **specific type of information** will be collected and how, including a list of **research questions** the plan will answer, and the form the collected information will take, whether generalizations based on observation (as in interviews or library research), proportions represented (as in a poll or census), or the consensus of a sample of the population—whether random or not (as in a survey). (3) The specific **measurement technique** and specific analysis procedures to be used. (4) Any **limitations** imposed by the design, circumstances, time, money, etc. (5) As an option, a proposed **calendar** for the project.

(6) A description of the **research report** form, or how the information will be compiled, tallied, or otherwise reported.

research methodology A term frequently employed interchangeably with research design, but more frequently used after the study is completed to describe in the research report the actual procedures used in executing the research design with sufficient detail that another researcher could repeat the project to replicate the findings.

respondent In polling, a person who participates in a survey or poll by answering questions.

risk assessment In crisis public relations planning, determination of the chance of various occurrences in order to take steps to deal with such incidents in order of their probability.

sample Portion of a larger whole; in polling, a relatively small group of individuals selected to represent a population, usually by means of random probability sampling techniques, which allows for calculation of the exact probability of such representation.

satellite Device placed in stationary earth orbit that relays microwave signals to receivers across a wide geographic area and is used for distribution of television programming to commercial systems for rebroadcast or directly to home receivers.

schema The mental codification of experience that includes a particular organized way of cognitive perception and response to complex situations; similar to myth but not necessarily a collective phenomenon nor founded on the sometimes fanciful interpretation of experience.

selective attention Term used in psychology and communication to describe a phenomenon in which individuals become ready to receive information compatible with their predispositions or attitudes; selective avoidance describes a related phenomenon in which people employ various barriers to communication that is not compatible with their attitudes; a related term, selective retention, refers to the remembering only compatible information.

shareholder See **stockholder.**

shareholder relations Public relations activities designed to build continuing rapport with those who have invested money in an enterprise for which they are issued shares or stock certificates; similar to investor relations, which deals with potential investors as well as with current investors. Synonymous term: stockholder relations.

slander See **defamation.**

slant Distinctive approach to writing a story that makes it unusual or gives it an uncommon reader appeal; also an unfair bias. Synonymous term: angle.

slide Picture or graphic mounted in a frame for projection on a screen, usually in color, and often incorporated into a slide set; commonly used in presentations.

slogan Short memorable phrase conveying a desired impression of an organization, product, or campaign often using literary devices such as alliteration, rhyme, rhythm, and metaphor; from Scottish for a "war cry."

social psychology Academic discipline that studies the behavior of groups. A field important to understanding the relationships involved in public relations.

social responsibility A term applied to corporations in evaluating their humanitarian contributions to society, often applied in reference to such issues as hiring of women and minorities, fair treatment of employees, sound environmental practices, foreign trade in support of human rights, and equitable treatment of suppliers and distributors.

software Information packages that instruct computers to perform specialized operations such as word processing, statistical analysis, or spreadsheets, in contrast to hardware, which includes computer, screen, printers, modems, disks, and/or chips on which the information is stored, and other physical aspects of a computer.

speakers bureau   Organization of company employees, students, and faculty of a college or other organization constituents trained to deliver speeches on a range of topics and otherwise represent the organization before groups such as service clubs, high schools, consumer groups, or other publics as part of public relations strategy.

special event   See **event.**

spokesperson   Individual who, because of special expertise or celebrity status, is selected to represent an organization in various speaking situations, media interviews, talk shows, and the like; similar in function to speakers bureau, but usually limited to one prominent individual.

staged event   See **event.**

stakeholder   More general term than investor, stockholder, or shareholder that refers to any group or individual who has an interest in or is dependent on an organization or enterprise, including employees, customers, suppliers, dealers, government, community, and investors.

stereotype   Term derived from a printing technique that casts a metal plate from a page of set type in order to reproduce copies of the page; hence something of uncritical and unvarying conformity to a pattern, often an oversimplified notion that differs from reality.

stockholder   Investor who owns stock or shares in an enterprise in order to realize a profit, usually paid in the form of quarterly dividends but may also be realized in the increased value of the stock, which may be sold in the stock market to recover investment plus any appreciation in dollar value.

storyboard   Series of pictures or drawings of scenes or shots accompanied by scripted narration representing the planned final form of a slide show or television or film production; used in planning and preparing visual communications.

strategy   Series of planned activities designed and integrated to achieve a stated goal as incorporated into a campaign or other public relations program.

stringer   Free-lance writer, reporter, or correspondent working in a piecework arrangement for a newspaper, magazine, or broadcast station; often assigned a specific news or regional beat frequently at a distance from the publication or station and paid by the number of words or by the story.

studio   Large room equipped for photography, radio, television, or film production, usually one of several such facilities operated by a radio or television station or a film company, as opposed to outdoor shooting or production locations.

symbol   Object or activity employed for special communication functions, in which the symbol may (1) represent something, as a stop sign represents by convention the act of stopping; (2) point to something symbolized, as a wedding ring points to a marital relationship; or (3) participate in that which is symbolized, as a shared meal may symbolize participation in organizational life.

tactics   Specific methods or techniques adopted as a means for achieving strategic goals, which may vary throughout a long-term effort or strategy.

target publics   Audiences or constituencies identified as the object of communication or public relations efforts; usually segmented or subdivided by characteristics such as occupation, media use, or interest group membership to make communication more effective or efficient and help direct the impact of public relations efforts toward the specific group whose behavior is critical to the outcome. Similar term: markets.

tear sheet   Page torn or clipped from a publication, often mounted on blank pages as an illustration of originally published material to be included as part of a manuscript; by analogy, any printed piece torn from a publication. Synonymous term: clipping.

teleconference   Meeting in which participants are linked by electronic communication signals from widely dispersed locations usually through telephone (conference call) or video; in video, an electronic network links several locations so that participants may see other participants and converse, as an alternative to the greater expense and time required for traveling to a central location.

theme   A distinctive statement, phrase, or treatment—as in graphics or music—designed for repetition that characterizes the major idea in a communication or in a series of communications or messages with the intent of linking the idea, the communications, or the messages to an overall purpose and/or to enhance memorability.

third-party endorsement   Advocacy statement made to the media or public by one organization on behalf of another organization; the practice may be unethical if undisclosed considerations are involved, such as the creation and funding of an organization for the purpose of disseminating favorable information about an organization (A) without disclosing that A created and finances B; such organizations are known as "front" organizations and are violations of PRSA's code of ethics.

tie-in   Association of one campaign or communication effort with another communication effort, a well-known activity, or a calendar event, such as identifying a local charity ball with a national election by calling it a "Presidential Election Year Gala," or identifying it with a calendar holiday by calling it "New Year's Ball"; also a joint venture in which two or more organizations join forces to share in a campaign or communication effort.

timely disclosure   Term in Securities and Exchange Commission (SEC) regulatory law according to which a publicly held company is required to make "timely, full and complete disclosure" to the financial news media and to the investing community of any facts that may have a "material" effect on the price of its stock.

trade press   Publications that concentrate on coverage of news and information about, or of interest to, a particular industry, association, or profession. They may be published as commercial profit-making enterprises independent of those businesses or professions; or they may be not-for-profit publications sponsored by associations or businesses.

trade publication   A periodical identifiable as part of the trade press, they may be either profit making or nonprofit periodicals published either by the businesses, industrial associations, or professional associations themselves, or by an independent commercial enterprise.

trend analysis   Study of changes and developments that may affect an organization, generally synonymous with issue tracking but does not include the planning, execution, and measurement of results that are involved in issues management, related to the larger function of risk management which uses the outcome of risk assessment to plan and execute strategies to deal with such risks.

two-step flow   Theory of public opinion development and change in which media influence opinion leaders in the first step and opinion leaders influence their peers in the second step; generally considered to be an oversimplification of a more complex process.

video display terminal (VDT)   Cathode ray tube (CRT) used for the display of information being processed by a computer, especially the monitor connected to a personal computer (PC).

word processor   Software package of instructions used in a personal computer to write, store, change, combine, and print out written text material.

Notes

CHAPTER 1

1. *Webster's Ninth New Collegiate Dictionary* (Springfield, MA: Merriam-Webster, 1983).
2. Goldman, Jordan. *Public Relations in the Marketing Mix* (Chicago: Crain Books, 1984), xii.
3. Paisley, William J. "Public Communication Campaigns: The American Experience." In *Public Communication Campaigns*, ed. Ronald E. Rice and William J. Paisley, 1–40 (Beverly Hills: Sage, 1984), 23.
4. Paisley, 25–26.
5. Paisley, 28.
6. Paisley, 37.
7. Paisley, 40.
8. Marston, John E. *The Nature of Public Relations* (New York: McGraw-Hill, 1963), 161–289.
9. Hyman, Herbert H., and Paul B. Sheatsley. "Some Reasons Why Information Campaigns Fail," *Public Opinion Quarterly* 11 (1947): 412–23.
10. McAlister, Alfred. "Antismoking Campaigns: Progress in Developing Effective Communications." In *Public Communication Campaigns*, ed. Ronald E. Rice and William J. Paisley, 91–125 (Beverly Hills: Sage, 1984), 92.
11. O'Keefe, Garrett J. "Taking a Bite Out of Crime: The Impact of a Public Information Campaign," *Communication Research* 12 (April 1985): 147–78, p. 152.
12. O'Keefe, 172.
13. Hammall, Thomas K., and Gene Slade. "What Atlanta Is Doing to Reduce Violent Crime," *Public Relations Review* 8 (Spring 1982): 51–58.
14. Grunig, James E., and Daniel A. Ipes. "The Anatomy of a Campaign against Drunk Driving," *Public Relations Review* 9 (Summer 1983): 38 and 43.
15. Grunig, James E., and Keith R. Stamm. "Cognitive Strategies and the Resolution of Environmental Issues: A Second Study," *Journalism Quarterly* 56 (Winter 1979): 719.
16. Grunig and Ipes, 50.
17. Grunig and Ipes, 39–40.
18. Heibert, Ray E. *Courtier to the Crowd: The Life Story of Ivy Lee* (Ames, IA: Iowa State University Press, 1966), 104–106.
19. Golden, L. L. L. *Only by Public Consent* (New York: Hawthorn Books, 1968), 4.
20. Bozeman, Barry. *All Organizations Are Public* (San Francisco: Jossey-Bass, 1987). See especially the argument implicit in the title and spelled out in chapter 6 of the book.
21. Childs, Harwood. *An Introduction to Public Opinion* (New York: Wiley, 1940), 34.

22. Grunig, James E. "Symmetrical Presuppositions as a Framework for Public Relations Theory." In *Public Relations Theory*, ed. Carl H. Botan and Vincent Hazelton Jr. (Hillsdale, NJ: Lawrence Erlbaum Associates, 1989), 17–44. Compare the argument presented here with Grunig's claim that the two-way symmetric model is "a more effective as well as a more responsible approach to public relations."

23. Downey, Stephen M. "The Relationship between Corporate Culture and Corporate Identity," *Public Relations Quarterly* 31 (Winter 1986–87): 7.

24. Gray, James G., Jr. *Managing the Corporate Image* (Westport, CT: Quorum Books, 1986), 3–4.

25. Friedman, Debra. "Notes on 'Toward a Theory of Value in Social Exchange'." In *Social Exchange Theory*, ed. Karen Cook (Newbury Park, CA: Sage, 1987), 55.

26. Blau, Peter M., "Microprocess and Macrostructure," chapter 4 in *Social Exchange Theory*, ed. Karen Cook (Newbury Park, CA: Sage, 1987), 87.

27. Cupach, William R., and Sandra Metts. "Accounts of Relational Dissolution: A Comparison of Marital and Non-Marital Relationships," *Communication Monographs* 53 (December 1986): 319.

28. See especially Miller, Gerald R. *Explorations in Interpersonal Communication* (Beverly Hills: Sage, 1976) and Pilotta, Joseph J., ed. *Interpersonal Communication: Essays in Phenomenology and Hermaneutics* (Washington, DC: Center for Advanced Research in Phenomenology, and University Press of America, 1982).

29. Planalp, Sally, D. K. Rutherford, and J. M. Honycutt. "Events That Increase Uncertainty in Personal Relationships II: Replication and Extension," *Human Communication Research* 14 (Summer 1988): 516–47.

30. Compare the long-term profitability of Western Union and AT&T. When AT&T was founded, its primary competitor was Western Union under the leadership of William Vanderbilt. Vanderbilt expressed his philosophy as "the public be damned," while AT&T's Theodore Vail expressed his in inquiring of a subordinate how they could improve relations with the public. See Kendall, Robert. "Research of Organizational Culture: A Mythic History of AT&T," paper presented to the Speech Communication Association, Chicago, November, 15, 1986, and available in ERIC. See also "Controversy over NCR's Stakeholder Philosophy," *PR Week* 1 (April 11–17, 1988): 7.

31. Downey, 7.

32. Meyer, Alan D. "How Ideologies Supplant Formal Structures and Shape Responses to Environments," *Journal of Management Studies* 19 (1982): 41–62.

33. See especially Deal, Clarence E., and Allen A. Kennedy. *Corporate Cultures* (Reading, Mass.: Addison-Wesley, 1982), and Peters, Thomas J., and Robert H. Waterman Jr. *In Search of Excellence* (New York: Warner Books, 1984).

34. Tunstall, W. Brooke. "Cultural Transition at A.T.& T.," *Sloan Management Review* (Fall 1983): 18.

35. Schein, Edgar H. "Coming to a New Awareness of Organizational Culture," *Sloan Management Review* (Winter 1984): 3.

36. Deal and Kennedy, 5.

37. Ibid.

38. Deal and Kennedy; see especially chapter 3.

CHAPTER 2

1. Lerbinger, Otto. "Corporate Use of Research in Public Relations." In *Precision Public Relations*, ed. Ray Hiebert (New York: Longman, 1988), 120.
2. Lerbinger, 121.
3. Broom, Glen M., and David Dozier. *Using Research in Public Relations* (Englewood Cliffs, NJ: Prentice Hall, 1990), 141ff. See section comparing quantitative and qualitative research.
4. Greene, J. C., Joan Doughty, J. M. Marquart, M. L. Ray, and Lynn Roberts. "Qualitative Evaluation Audits in Practice," *Evaluation Review* 12 (August 1988): 352.
5. Moorhead, A. E. "Designing Ethnographic Research in Technical Communication: Case Study into Application," *Journal of Technical Writing and Communication* 17 (1987): 325–43.
6. Emmert, Philip, and Larry L. Barker, eds. *Measurement of Communication Behavior* (New York: Longman, 1989), 6.
7. Feiblemen, James K. *Scientific Method* (The Hague: Nijhoff 1972), 1–8.
8. Kerlinger, F. N. *Foundations of Behavioral Research*, 3rd ed. (New York: Holt, Rinehart & Winston, 1986).
9. Wimmer, Roger D., and J. R. Dominick. *Mass Media Research: An Introduction*, 4th ed. (Bellmont, CA: Wadsworth, 1994), 9–11.
10. Horgan, John. "Profile: Karl R. Popper—The Intellectual Warrior," *Scientific American* 267 (November 1992): 38–44, p. 38.
11. Horgan, 40.
12. Fink, Arlene, and Jacqueline Kosecoff. *How to Conduct Surveys: A Step-By-Step Guide* (Beverly Hills, CA: Sage, 1985), 73ff.
13. Suchman, Edward A. "General Considerations of Research Design." In *Handbook of Research Design and Social Measurement*, 5th ed., ed. Delbert C. Miller (New York: David McKay, 1991), 40–41.
14. Broom and Dozier, 98.
15. Suchman, 40–41.
16. For a more detailed description of research procedures, see Kibler, Robert J. "Basic Communication Research Considerations." In *Methods of Research in Communication*, ed. Philip Emmert and William D. Brooks (Boston: Houghton Mifflin, 1970), 9–49; also see specific chapters in the foregoing book as well as Philip Emmert and Larry L. Barker, eds. *Measurement of Communication Behavior* (New York: Longman, 1989).
17. Coughlin, Ellen K. "Studying Homelessness: The Difficulty of Tracking a Transient Population," *Chronicle of Higher Education* 35 (October 19, 1988): A–6, A–7, A–12.
18. Coughlin, A–6.
19. Coughlin, A–6.
20. Coughlin, A–7.
21. Coughlin, A–7.
22. Coughlin, A–12.
23. Ibid.
24. Nager, Norman R. *Strategic Public Relations Counseling: Models from the Counselors Academy* (New York: Longman, 1988), 90.
25. Grunig, James E., and Todd Hunt. *Managing Public Relations* (New York: Holt, Rinehart & Winston, 1984), 36–37.

CHAPTER 3

1. Broom, Glen M., and David M. Dozier. *Using Research in Public Relations* (Englewood Cliffs, NJ: Prentice Hall, 1990).
2. Santayana, George. *The Life of Reason,* 1906. Cited in *Bartlett's Familiar Quotations,* ed. John Bartlett (Boston: Little Brown, 1968), 867.
3. Richardson, Stephen, B. S. Dohrenwend, and D. Klein. *Interviewing: Its Form and Functions* (New York: Basic Books, 1965), 35.
4. Dexter, Lewis A. *Elite and Specialized Interviewing* (Evanston, IL: Northwestern University Press, 1970).
5. Dexter, 5.
6. Holsti, O. R. *Content Analysis for the Social Sciences and Humanities* (Reading, MA: Addison-Wesley, 1969).
7. Lindkvist, Kent. "Approaches to Textual Analysis." In *Advances in Content Analysis,* ed. Karl E. Rosengren (Beverly Hills: Sage, 1981).
8. Wells, William D. "Group Interviewing." In *Focus Group Interviewing: A Reader,* ed. Keith K. Cox and James B. Higginbotham (Chicago: American Marketing Association, 1979), 13.
9. Antilla, Susan, and Henriette Sender. "Getting Consumers in Focus," *Dun's Business Month* (May 1982): 78–79.
10. Antilla and Sender, 78.
11. Bellenger, Danny N., K. L. Bernhadt, and J. L. Goldstucker. "Qualitative Research Techniques: Focus Group Interviews." In *Focus Group Interviews: A Reader,* 14.
12. Wells, 11.
13. Santa Monica: Rand Corporation, 1962.
14. Turoff, Murray. "The Policy Delphi." In *The Delphi Method,* ed. Harold A. Linstone and Murray Turoff (Reading, MA: Addison-Wesley, 1975): 100–101.
15. Farkas, Z. Andrew, and James O. Wheeler. "Delphi Technique as Forecaster of Land Use in Appalachian Georgia," *The Geographical Review* 70 (April 1980): 218–26.
16. Morgan, David R., John P. Pelissero, and Robert E. England. "Urban Planning: Using a Delphi as a Decision-Making Aid," *Public Administration Review* (July 1979): 380–384.
17. Dalkey Norman, Daniel L. Rourke, Ralph Lewis, and David Snyder. *Studies in the Quality of Life: Delphi and Decision Making* (Lexington, MA: D. C. Heath, 1973), 20.
18. Moore, Harry W., Jr. "Delphi Analysis of Police Corruption," *The Journal of Police Science and Administration* 8 (March 1980): 107–115.
19. For detailed discussion of one approach to the Delphi techniques, see Delbecq, A. H. Van de Ven, and David A. Gustafson, in *Group Techniques for Program Planning* (Glenview, IL: Scott, Foresman, 1975).
20. *Public Opinion,* American Enterprise Institute, 1150 17th Street, N.W., Washington, D.C.
21. *The Polling Report,* 1427 21st Street, N.W., Washington, D.C. 20036.

CHAPTER 4

1. For further study of sampling methods, see Fowler, F. J. *Survey Research Methods* (Beverly Hills: Sage, 1984), and Miller, Delbert C. *Handbook of Research Design*

and *Social Measurement* (New York: McKay, 1991), 60, and Ackoff, Russell L. *The Design of Social Research* (Chicago: University of Chicago Press, 1953).

2. Kidder, L. H., and C.. M. Judd. *Research Methods in Social Relations,* 5th ed. (New York: Holt, Rinehart & Winston, 1986), 158.

3. Frey, James H. *Survey Research by Telephone* (Beverly Hills: Sage, 1983); see especially the chapter on sampling.

4. Jordan, Lawrence A., Alfred C. Marcus, and Leo G. Reeder. "Response Styles in Telephone and Household Interviewing; a Field Experiment," *Public Opinion Quarterly* 44 (Summer 1980): 210–22. Another study, by William R. Klecka and Alfred J. Tuchfarber, *POQ* 42 (Summer 1978): 105–114, found the RDD technique to be "as accurate or more accurate than personal interviews."

5. Random digit dialing sampling procedure:

   Objective: provide a random sample of chosen population in the form of systematically drawn telephone prefixes with a method of substituting random numbers for final two digits.

   Determine the sample size: Using the following formula, select a sample size that produces a chance sampling error that is within an acceptable range (.05 or better).

   $$\sigma\,\% = \sqrt{\frac{\rho \cdot q}{n}}$$

   Use the most conservative estimate for p (the homogeneity of the population, as .5) and multiply $p \times q$ (.5 $\times$ .5), which yields .25; this figure is divided by various sample sizes, for which the square root is calculated (by pressing the square root key after dividing .25 by the sample size) until an acceptable chance sampling error is determined.

   Next, the prefixes are drawn by dividing the telephone book by the size of the selected sample. These "blocks" will provide one prefix each. From the first block a random starting number is chosen by the pencil drop method on a table of random numbers. The number must be no larger than the block size and must be the same number of digits as the block size.

   With the start interval number selected, the first block is counted to identify the number corresponding to the start interval number. That number is recorded as the first in the sample. The number of the block size is then counted from the first number chosen to identify the second number, using a paper tape to measure printed lines of phone numbers. This second number is added to the sample list, and the measuring is continued through the directory to identify and record each successive phone number. Numbers are recorded on individual three-by-five inch cards, which will be distributed to interviewers.

6. See especially Converse, Jean M., and Stanley Presser. *Survey Questions: Handcrafting the Standardized Questionnaire* (Beverly Hills: Sage, 1986), and Labaw, Patricia. *Advanced Questionnaire Design* (Cambridge, MA: Abt Books, 1981).

7. See Osgood, C. E., G. J. Suci, and P. H. Tannenbaum. *The Measurement of Meaning* (Urbana, IL: The University of Illinois Press, 1971), 140. This discussion of the validation of questions suggests the need for and some techniques by which items may be validated.

8. Parten, Mildred. *Surveys, Polls and Sample; Practical Procedures* (New York: Cooper Square Publications, 1966).

9. Labaw, 9–11.

10. Labaw, 11.

11. Linden, Fabian. "The Consumer as Forecaster," *Public Opinion Quarterly* 46 (Fall 1982): 353–60.

12. Osgood, Charles, George Suci, and Percy Tannenbaum. *The Measurement of Meaning* (Champaign: University of Illinois Press, 1957).

13. Osgood, Suci, and Tannenbaum, 72–73.

14. Osgood, Suci, and Tannenbaum, 308.

15. Backstrom, Charles H., and G. D. Hursh. *Survey Research* (Evanston, IL: Northwestern University Press, 1963).

CHAPTER 6

1. For an application of this approach to analysis of corporate culture, see Kendall, Robert. "Research of Organizational Culture: A Mythic History of A.T.& T," *ERIC* (1986).

2. Mace, Myles L. "The President and Corporate Planning," *Harvard Business Review: On Management* (New York: Harper, 1975), 129–30.

3. Christopher, William F. "Is the Annual Planning Cycle Really Necessary," *Management Review* (August 1981): 40.

4. Falsey, Thomas A. *Corporate Philosophies and Mission Statements: A Survey and Guide for Corporate Communicators and Management:* (New York: Quorum Books, 1989), ix.

5. Stonich, Paul J., ed. *Implementing Strategy: Making Strategy Happen* (Cambridge, MA: Bellinger Publishing, 1982), 12.

6. Tourangeau, Kevin, W. *Strategy Management* (New York: McGraw-Hill, 1981), 46.

7. Mace, 128.

8. Nadler, David A., Richard Hackman, and Edward E. Lawler III. *Managing Organizational Behavior* (Boston: Little, Brown, 1979), 182.

9. Ibid.

10. Weisberger, Bernard. *The Dream Maker* (Boston: Little, Brown, 1979), 249.

11. Nadler et al., 181.

12. Mintzberg, Henry. *The Structuring of Organizations* (Englewood Cliffs, NJ: Prentice Hall, 1979), 10, citing Rensis Likert.

13. Mintzberg, 66.

14. Mintzberg, 67; chapters 4–11 discuss the nine "design parameters."

15. Mintzberg, 303.

16. Stonich, 24, 25.

17. Tunstall, W. Brook. "Cultural Transition at A.T. & T.," *Sloan Management Review* (Fall 1983): 20.

18. Bower, Joseph L. "Managing for Efficiency, Managing for Equity," *Harvard Business Review* 61 (July–August 1983): 83.

19. Bower, 87.

20. Godiwalla, Yezdi H. *Strategic Management* (New York: Praeger, 1983), 227.

21. Melohn, Thomas H. "How to Build Employee Trust and Productivity," *Harvard Business Review* 61 (January–February 1983): 56–61.

22. Bower, 83–84.

23. Marshall, J., and R. Stewart, "Managers' Job Perceptions. Part I: Their Overall Frameworks and Working Strategies," *Journal of Management Studies* 18 (1981): 177–89.

24. Marshall and Stewart, 183.
25. White, B. V., and B. R. Montgomery. "Corporate Codes of Conduct," *California Management Review* 23 (Winter 1980): 80–87.
26. Collins, Elizabeth G. C. "Managers and Lovers," *Harvard Business Review* 61 (September–October 1983): 152–53.
27. *Public Relations Journal* (January 1980): 10.
28. Bailey Richard N. "Issues Management: A Survey of Contemporary Practice," M.A. Thesis, University of Florida, 1983.

CHAPTER 7

1. McElreath, Mark P. "Planning Programs for Exceptional Events," *Public Relations Review* 5 (Fall 1979): 35–40. The PM approach to public relations planning is "divided into six distinct stages:" (1) *Obtaining a mandate.* This first step involves "legitimizing the planning effort by receiving specific (written) authorization from top management" to proceed with the campaign. This step is critical to get "cooperation from organizational elites and resource controllers." The mandate serves to integrate the organization and particularly to authorize the campaign management team. (2) *Identifying the problem.* This step involves all interested parties in precisely defining the "problem situation." "Both informal and formal research procedures are used to identify the problem. The initial phase of the search involves determining the overall mission; however, the focus of the entire research effort is on the causes and characteristics of the problem situation; the search procedure is not focused on solutions to the problem." (3) *Exploring for knowledge.* Following a clear and precise definition of the problem, "specialists and experts who can speak to the problem" are assembled to offer solutions and nominate a set of preferred solutions." The result should be "at least two public relations campaign options." (4) *Developing resources and reviewing the proposals.* After the expert-suggested solutions are incorporated into the process, "written proposals for feasible solutions are circulated to key decision-makers, resource controllers and people able to veto or sabotage the program." Once these people have provided input, a formal proposal is recommended for adoption. (5) *Administering the project.* When the proposal is accepted by key decision makers, "a project administrator and staff are assigned the task of implementing the project." The role of the public relations campaign manager is primarily "consensus building," with much of the detail work "delegated." (6) *Transferring technology or facilitating spin-off.* Because campaigns may "suggest major changes in organizational behavior," the effort may be pilot tested before being fully implemented. If the pilot test is successful, the campaign may be delegated to other "parts of the system."
2. Stricharchuk, Gregory. "Just Read Our Lips: No Blimps, No Tires, No Blimps, No Tires . . . ," *Wall Street Journal* (September 30, 1988): sec. 2, p. 29.
3. Ibid.
4. An influential pioneering article helped to shape the nature of segmentation: Yankelovich, Daniel. "New Criteria for Market Segmentation," *Harvard Business Review* 42 (March–April 1964): 83–90.
5. Compare: Tucker, Kerry, and Doris Derelian. *Public Relations Writing* (Englewood Cliffs, NJ: Prentice Hall, 1989); see especially pp. 35–39 and 50–51.
6. See *Chase's Annual Event Directory* (New York: Contemporary Books).
7. For a discussion of creativity in public relations planning see Holmes, Paul, ed., "Creativity: What It Is and How to Encourage It," *Inside PR* 1 (March 1991): 9–15;

also see the following readings from such collections of case studies, or more precisely "case histories," include Raymond Simon, *Public Relations Management: Cases and Simulations* (Columbus, OH: Grid 1977); and Allen Center and Pat Jackson. *Public Relations Practices: Case Studies* (Englewood Cliffs, NJ: Prentice-Hall, 1981). *PR Casebook* offered "a monthly compendium of selected case studies and programs" but is no longer in publication; *Public Relations News* is a weekly newsletter that includes two- to four-page cases; *pr reporter* is a weekly newsletter that offers helpful insights distilled from case studies and current practices.

Books from the field provide a wide range of background for campaign ideas. Edward Bernays's *Public Relations* (Norman: University of Oklahoma, 1977) is an autobiographical account of many of the public relations activities of one of the "founding fathers" of public relations, including the classic Ivory Soap carving contest. Many textbooks also include case studies. Longer case studies may be found in Craig Aronoff and Otis Baskin, *Public Relations* (St. Paul: West, 1983); Frasier H. Moore and Frank P. Kalupa, *Principles, Cases, Problems*, 9th ed. (Homewood, IL: Irwin, 1985); Doug Newsom, Alan Scott, and Judy Turk, *This Is PR*, 4th ed. (Belmont, CA: Wadsworth, 1989); and Fraser P. Sitel, *The Practice of Public Relations*, 2nd ed. (Columbus, OH: Merrill, 1984), among others.

Several handbooks are useful sources of ideas that may be adapted to specific campaign needs. These include the current editions of Philip Lesly, *Lesly's Public Relations Handbook* (Englewood Cliffs, NJ: Prentice-Hall); Howard Stephenson, *Handbook of Public Relations* (New York: McGraw-Hill); and *Dartnell Public Relations Handbook* (Chicago: Dartnell). In addition, the Public Relations Society of America (PRSA) provides, at a small fee, an annually updated bibliography that is an excellent way to keep up with new publications in the field. PRSA also provides summaries of its annual Silver Anvil Award winner case studies for a small fee; the complete cases are available for review at the information center in its New York headquarters.

8. *pr reporter*, June 24, 1985.

9. *pr reporter*, December 7, 1984.

10. A selective list of directories to stimulate creative ideas and research possibilities:

Association Meetings—Association Planner's Facilities and Services Guide Issue Lists hotels, resorts, speakers, convention services, and other suppliers for meetings. Cost: $8, from The Laux Co., Inc., 63 Great Rd., Maynard, MA 01754. Phone: 508-897-5552.

Associations Yellow Book Lists 40,000+ officers, managers, and administrators for 1,100+ trade and professional associations in the U.S. with budgets over $1 million, number of members, publications, meetings, etc., Order from: Monitor Publishing Co., 104 5th Ave., 2nd Fl., New York, NY 10011. Phone: 212-627-4140.

Awards, Honors and Prizes Includes fields of advertising, public relations, art business, government, finance, science, education, engineering, literature, technology, sports, religion, public affairs, law, radio-TV, publishing, journalism, etc. Order from: Gale Research, Inc., 835 Penobscot Bldg., Detroit, MI 48226-4094.

Bullinger's Postal and Shippers Guide for the US and Canada Provides mailing and shipping information for about 200,000 town, counties, including villages without postoffices. The book can be used not only for direct mail applications but for identifying regional place names that might be associated with historic events or tie-ins with historical anniversaries. For example it lists the towns of

George, Washington and Martha, Washington; Two Egg, Florida; a town in Indiana that has five names because it couldn't make up its mind. Order from: Alber Leland Publishing, 506 Olive St. Ste 550, St. Louis, MO 65101-1435.

Buyer's Guide to Trade Show Displays   Lists about 200 producers of portable and modular trade show exhibit systems, and custom builders including publications. Cost: $49 from Exhibitor Publications, Marquette Bank Bldg. Rm 745, Rochester, MN 55904. Phone: 507-289-6556.

Conducting International Meetings   Lists associations, corporations, embassies, chambers of commerce and other organizations of interest to meeting planners, including regulations and logistics. Contact: Greater Washington Society of Association Executives Foundation, 1426 21st St. NW Ste. 200, Washington, DC. 20036. Phone: 202-429-9370.

Convention Services & Facilities Directory   Lists about 6,472 service providers compiled from nationwide telephone yellow pages. Cost $290 from American Business Directories, Inc., 5711 S. 86th Circle, Omaha, NE 68127. Phone: 402-593-4600.

Directory of Business Information Resources (The)   Lists associations, trade shows, magazines, newsletters serving 90 business or professional specialties. Cost: $145 from Grey House Publishing, Pocket Knife Sq., P.O. Box 1866, Lakefield, CT 06039. Phone 203-435-0868.

Directory of Conventions   Lists 14,000+ meetings held throughout the US and Canada with crossindex for business, industries, professions, date, city and executive in charge, title and address; tie-in possibilities as well as exhibit and other joint ventures. Cost: $170, from Bill Communications, Inc., 355 Park Ave. S., New York, NY 10010-1789. Phone: 212-592-6200.

Directory of Research Services Provided by Members of the Marketing Research Association   Lists 950+ international market research companies and field interviewing services arranged geographically. Cost $100 from Marketing Research Association, 2189 Silas Deane Hwy, Ste 5, Rocky Hill, CT 06067. Phone: 203-257-4008.

Employee Involvement Association—Membership Directory   Lists about 1,200 companies, associations, and government organizations having employee suggestion or employee involvement programs. Available to members only, contact: Employee Involvement Association, 1735 N. Lynn St. Ste. 950, Arlington, VA 22209-2022. Phone: 703-524-3424.

EPM Entertainment Marketing Sourcebook   Lists about 2,600 media companies, sponsors, retailers and entertainment tie-ins to promote other goods or services. Cost: $250 from EPM Communications, Inc., 488 E. 18th St., Brooklyn, NY 11226. Phone: 718-469-9330.

Guinness Book of World Records   Provides categories, record holders, dates established for achievements of all sorts; an invaluable tool for planning contests and competitions or any event that may seek to set a world record whether one exists or not. Cost $1.95 from Bantum Books, 419 Park Ave. South, New York, NY 10016.

Information Industry Directory   Lists about 5,200 organizations, systems and services producing and distributing information in electronic form including database, on-line host services, CD-ROM, videotext/teletext, transactional services, etc. Cost: $495 from: Gale Research, Inc., 835 Penobscot Bldg., Detroit, MI 48226-4094. Phone: 313-961-2242.

Information Please Almanac   An annual compilation of lists of current facts, statistics, and information in many subject areas including government activities, current events, world affairs, etc. Cost $8.95 paper, from: Houghton Mifflin Co., 215 Park Ave. S., New York, NY. 10003. Phone 212-420-5879.

Journalism and Mass Communication Directory   Lists academic and related organizations in the field including purpose, objectives, number of members, headquarters, address, publications, also contacts for public relations groups, state press associations and state broadcast associations; useful as a check for enhancing coverage of meetings, conventions, also for tie-in possibilities. Cost: $20 from: AEJMC, School of Journalism, University of SC., Columbia, SC 29208-0251.

Madison Avenue Handbook   Lists advertising agencies, photographers, illustrators, art and photo suppliers, costume, prop and accessory houses, TV producers, suppliers, PR firms, fashion houses, talent agencies, artists, galleries, arranged alphabetically and geographically, for eastern metro areas. The book should prove useful for the veteran event planner as well as the beginner. For copy: Peter Glenn Publications, Ltd., 42 W 38th St., New York, NY 10018.

Meetings and Conventions—Gavel International Directory Issue   Lists 4,000+ convention halls and hotels suitable for meetings with name, address, phone, number of guest rooms, meeting rooms, etc., Cost $35, from reed Travel Group, 500 Plaza Dr., Secaucus, NJ 07094. Phone: 201-902-1700.

Meeting News Directory   Lists convention centers, hotels, resorts, visitors bureaus and suppliers serving meeting and travel industries. Cost: $10, from Miller Freeman, Inc., 1515 Broadway, Ste 3201, New York, NY 10036. Phone: 212-869-1300.

Modeling Agencies Directory   Lists organizations that provide models; valuable to the event planner for access to those involved in visual communication, may suggest tie-in possibilities. Order from: American Business Directories, Inc., 5711 S. 86th Circle, Omaha, NE 68127. Phone: 402-593-4600.

Musical America's International Directory of the Performing Arts   Lists orchestras, musicians, singers, performing arts series, dance and opera companies, festivals, contests, foundations and awards, publishers of music, artists, managers, booking agents, music magazines, and service and professional music organizations; helpful in finding music for events, conferences and the like. Copies $80, from K-III Directory Corp. 424 W. 33rd St. 11th Fl., New York, NY 10001. Phone: 212-714-3100.

National Radio Publicity Directory   Lists 7,000+ stations airing talk shows, network, syndicated and local, with time slots, area coverage, format, audience size and topics discussed; used in conjunction with segmentation by geographic or audience interest can be effective in targeting specialized publics. Cost: $99 single issue from: Morgan-Rand Media Group, 800 Masons Mill Business Park, 1800 Byberry Rd., Huntingdon Valley, PA 19006.

New York Publicity Outlets   Lists key executives and editorial people of major consumer media in New York City; useful for publicity and activities planning for New York. Cost $139.50 per year from: Public Relations Plus, Inc., P.O. Box 1197, New Millford, CT 06776. Phone: 203-354-9361.

Shopping Center Directory   Lists 32,000+ shopping centers by regional volumes including name, address, phone, owner, leasing agent, physical description, square footage, number of stores, parking availability, etc. Cost $435, from National Research Bureau, 150 N. Wacker Dr., Ste 2222, Chicago, IL 60606. Phone: 312-541-0100.

Trade Directories of the World   Lists 3,300+ publications in English, French, German, Spanish including trade and professional publications. Cost: $84.95 plus

$4.95 shipping, from: Croner Publications, Inc., 34 Jericho Tpke., Jericho, NY 11753. Phone: 516-333-9085.

Trade Show Week Data Book   Lists statistical facts on types of audience, types of exhibitors for over 4,000 trade shows with 50+ booths; useful in planning product oriented events or campaigns, targeting audiences as well as tie-in possibilities. Cost: $315 from: Tradeshow Week Inc., Reed Reference Publishing, 121 Chanlon Rd., New Providence, NJ 07974. Phone: 908-464-6800.

Trade Shows Worldwide   Lists about 6,200 trade shows and exhibitions including those in conjunction with conventions, meetings, trade and industrial events including sponsors and organizers, operators, suppliers and related information. Cost: $220 from Gale Research Inc., 835 Penobscot Bldg., Detroit, MI 48226-4094. Phone: 313-961-2242.

TV Cable Publicity Outlets   Lists 4,600+ cable and broadcast TV stations, systems, and programs that use outside scripts, film, or guests. Cost: $188 per year or $99 a single issue, from: Morgan-Rand Media Group, 800 Masons Mill Business Park, 1800 Byberry Rd., Huntingdon Valley, PA 19006. Phone: 215-938-5511.

Your Resource Guide to Environmental Organizations   Lists federal, state, and nongovernmental organizations that address environmental concerns. Cost: $15.95, from: Smiling Dolphin Press, 4 Segura, Irvine, CA 92715. Phone: 714-733-1065.

Important Note: Because prices and phone numbers change frequently the user is encouraged to consult *Directories In Print*, which lists most of the above guides, including annual updated information and many more directories that might be useful.

CHAPTER 8

1. See especially Bruce N. Carpenter and Susan M. Ruza, "Personality Characteristics of Police Applicants," *Journal of Police Science and Administration* 15 (1987): 10–17, and Edward Zamble and Phyllis Annesley, "Some Determinants of Public Attitudes Toward the Police," *Journal of Police Science and Administration* 15 (1987): 285–290.

CHAPTER 10

1. Bernays, Edward L. *Crystalizing Public Opinion* (New York: Boni and Liveright, 1923), 167.
2. Bernays, 173.
3. "Controversy over NCR's Stakeholder Philosophy," *PR Week* (April 11–17, 1988): 7.
4. Pfeffer, Jeffrey, and Gerald R. Salancik. *The External Control of Organizations* (New York: Harper & Row, 1978), 83.
5. Foster, Lawrence G., Vice President, Johnson & Johnson, remarks at PRSA Sunshine District Conference, June 8, 1989, Jacksonville, Florida.
6. Bernays, Edwrad L. *Public Relations* (Norman, OK: University of Oklahoma Press, 1952), 84.

7. Palmer, Edward. "Shaping Persuasive Messages with Formative Research." In *Public Communication Campaigns*, ed. Ronald E. Rice and William J. Paisley (Beverly Hills: Sage, 1981), 228.

8. Ibid..

9. Palmer, 231.

10. Palmer, 235.

11. Compare the "spiral of silence" described by Elizabeth Noell-Neumann in her book of the same title (Chicago: University of Chicago, 1986).

12. Midura, Edmund M. "A. J. Liebling: The Wayward Pressman as Critic," *Journalism Monographs* 33 (April 1974): 17.

13. "Schramm Says Nature of News Has Changed," *ICA Newsletter International Communication Association* 13 (Summer 1985): 8.

14. Boorstin, Daniel J. *The Image: A Guide to Pseudo Events in America* (New York: Harper & Row, 1961).

15. Adler, Ronald B., L. B. Rosenfeld, and N. Towne. *Interplay: The Process of Interpersonal Communication* (New York: Holt, Rinehart & Winston, 1980), 19–22.

16. Parker, Edwin. "Technological Change and the Mass Media." In *Handbook of Communication*, ed. Ithiel de Sola Pool et al. (Chicago: Rand McNally, 1973), 619–45.

CHAPTER 11

1. "Pastahhh" National Pasta Association, Arlington, Virginia, with Henry J. Kaufman & Associates, Washington, D.C. *1987 Silver Anvil Winners: Index and Summaries* (New York: Pubic Relations Society of America, 1987).

2. Ibid., 5.

3. Ibid., 6–7.

4. "Proposal: Public Relations Program for the National Pasta Association," Henry J. Kaufman & Associates, 2233 Wisconsin Avenue, N.W., Washington, D.C. (December 4, 1984), 70.

5. "Proposal: Public Relations Program for the National Pasta Association" (Washington, D. C.: Henry J. Kaufman & Associates, 1984), 57.

6. Ibid., 67.

7. Ibid., 56.

8. 1987 Silver Anvil Winners, 16.

9. "National Pasta Association Public Relations Plan 1987–88." (Washington, D.C.: Henry J. Kaufman & Associates, 1987), 1–2.

10. Golden, L. L. L. *Only by Public Consent* (New York: Hawthorn Books, 1968), 24.

11. Golden, 4.

12. CSX Annual Report (Jacksonville, FL, 1987).

13. Uehling, M. "Sweltering in Southland," *Newsweek* (July 28, 1986) 21.

14. Powell, S. "A Yankee Hand for a Stricken South," *U.S. News & World Report* (August 18, 1986): 16.

15. "Sweet 'Hay-Lo Specials' Swing Through the Southland," *The Locomotive Engineer* 120 (August 29, 1986): 16–17.

16. See *AP Monitor* for July 28–August 4, 1986: 21.

17. See B. Arthur, "Hay Express Winds Its Way to S.C.," *Charlotte Observer* (July 29, 1986).

18. *The Locomotive Engineer,* 1986, 16–17.
19. Peterson, R. "Trainload of Hay from Indiana on Way to Help Southeast Farmers," *Philadelphia Inquirer* (July 29, 1986).
20. *The Locomotive Engineer,* 1986, 16–17.

CHAPTER 12

1. Dozier, D. M. "Program Evaluation and the Roles of Practitioners," *Public Relations Review* 10 (Summer 1984). See also Broom and Dozier's book: *Using Research in Public Relations* (Englewood Cliffs, NJ: Prentice Hall, 1990: 13–21.
2. Pavlik, John V. *Public Relations: What Research Tells Us* (Beverly Hills: Sage, 1987), 67.
3. Ibid.
4. Ibid.
5. Bleeker, Samuel E. "Building the Public's Trust and the Bottom-Line Together," *Public Relations Quarterly* 25 (Winter 1980): 5–7.
6. Bleeker, 7.
7. Broom, Glenn M., and David M. Dozier. "An Overview: Evaluation Research in Public Relations," *Public Relations Quarterly* 28 (Fall 1983): 7.
8. Broom and Dozier, 8.
9. Grunig, James E. "Basic Research Provides Knowledge That Makes Evaluation Possible," *Public Relations Quarterly* 28 (Fall 1983): 32.
10. Pavlik, 67.
11. Krippendorff, Klaus, and Michael F. Eleey. "Monitoring a Group's Symbolic Environment," *Public Relations Review* 12 (Spring 1986): 15.
12. McClintock, Charles. "Conceptual and Action Heuristics: Tools for the Evaluator," *New Directions for Program Evaluation: Using Program Theory in Evaluation* 33 (Spring 1987): 44.
13. Levin, Henry M. "Cost-Benefit and Cost-Effectiveness Analyses," *New Directions for Program Evaluation; Evaluation Practice in Review* 34 (Summer 1987): 84.
14. Levin, 91.
15. See Levin, Henry M. *Cost Effectiveness: A Primer* (Beverly Hills: Sage, 1983), as well as the article cited here.
16. Levin, *Cost Effectiveness,* 96.
17. Faase, Thomas P., and Steve Pujdak. "Shared Understanding of Organizational Culture," *The Client Perspective on Evaluation: New Directions for Program Evaluation* 36 (Winter 1987): 76–77.
18. Ciarlo, James A., and Charles Windle. "Mental Health Program Evaluation and Needs Assessment," *Lessons from Selected Program and Policy Areas: New Directions for Program Evaluation* 37 (Spring 1988): 108–109.
19. Ciarlo and Windle, 111.
20. Lindenmann, Walter K. "Dealing with the Major Obstacles to Implementing Public Relations Research," *Public Relations Quarterly* 28 (Fall 1983): 16.
21. Scheirer, Mary Ann. "Program Theory and Implementation Theory: Implications for Evaluators," *Using Program Theory in Evaluation: New Directions for Program Evaluation* 33 (Spring 1987): 62.
22. Scheirer, 64.
23. Ibid. See also Chelimsky, E. "Comparing and Contrasting Auditing and Evaluation: Some Notes on Their Relationship," *Evaluation Review* 9 (1985): 483–503.

24. Miller, Renee. "Big Mistakes PR Agencies Make," *Public Relations Quarterly* 29 (Winter 1984): 16.

25. Patton, Michael Q. *Practical Evaluation* (Beverly Hills: Sage, 1982).

26. When considering evaluation, the costs involved may be a prime consideration. One collection of essays on the topic offers guidance: Alkin, Marvin C., and Lewis C. Solomon. *The Costs of Evaluation* (Beverly Hills: Sage, 1983).

27. See, for example, Larson, Mark A., and Karen L. Massetti-Miller. "Measuring Change after a Public Education Campaign," *Public Relations Review* 10 (Winter 1984): 23–32.

28. Patton, 196.

29. See, for example, Grant, Donald L., ed. *Monitoring Ongoing Programs,* in the *New Direction for Program Evaluation Series.* Reprint number PE3 (San Francisco: Jossey-Bass), 1978.

CHAPTER 14

1. Marcus, Bruce W. *Competing for Clients: The Complete Guide to Marketing and Promoting Professional Services* (Chicago: Probus Publishing, 1986), 283.

2. Schlender, Benton R. "Small Advertising Agencies Often Resort to Gimmicks to Grab Attention of Clients," *Wall Street Journal* (Friday, February 12, 1988), 17.

3. Ibid.

4. Weaver II, Richard L. "Nonverbal Communication." In *Understanding Business Communication* (Englewood Cliffs, NJ: Prentice-Hall, 1985), 79–95.

5. Blanchard, Kenneth, and S. Johnson, *The One Minute Manager* (New York: Berkley, 1982), 95.

6. Gray, James G., Jr. *Strategies and Skills of Technical Presentations* (New York: Quorum Books, 1986), 29–30.

7. Gray, 31–32.

8. For suggestions about evaluating facilities see, for example, Rounds, Kate. "How to Inspect Meeting Rooms for Perfectly Sound Acoustics," *Meeting News* (August 1984): 1, 50–52.

9. Feurey, Joseph. "Audio-Visual Techniques." In Bill Cantor, *Experts in Action,* ed. Chester Berger (New York: Longman, 1984), 220.

10. Weaver, 131.

11. Marcus, 290.

12. For a useful treatment of graphic design and lettering techniques appropriate for hand lettering and other public relations applications, see Berryman, Gregg. *Notes on Graphic Design and Visual Communication* (Los Altos, CA: William Kaufmann, 1979), especially p. 29.

13. Haerer, Deane N. "How to Plan Your Visual Presentations," *Public Relations Journal* (March 1978): 20–27.

14. *Planning and Producing Slide Programs,* S–30 (Rochester, NY: Eastman Kodak, 1978), 100–106.

15. While this spelling is a variant form, according to the dictionary, it is used because it conforms to the journalistic AP-UPI Stylebook, which prefers the shorter spelling in such cases.

16. Marcus, 294.

17. See note 15.

18. Marcus, 287.

CHAPTER 15

1. Blanchard, Kenneth, and Spencer Johnson. *The One Minute Manager* (New York: Berkley Books, 1983), 34–46.
2. Overholt, Trip. "How to Manage Your Time Electronically," *Public Relations Quarterly* 31 (Winter 1986–87): 17–18.
3. Brody, E. W. "The Advantages of Adopting an Association with Other Counselors," *Public Relations Quarterly* 30 (Summer 1985): 31.
4. Cochran, Linda Ray. "How to Manage Creative People: A Review of the Literature," *Public Relations Quarterly* 29 (Winter 1984): 6–12.
5. Cochran, 7–8.
6. Cochran, 9.
7. Goodman, R. A., and L. P. Goodman. "Some Management Issues in Temporary Systems: A Study of Professional Development and Manpower—the Theater Case" *Administrative Science Quarterly* 21 (September 1976): 494–95.
8. Mintzberg, Henry. *The Structuring of Organizations* (Englewood Cliffs, NJ: Prentice-Hall, 1979), 433.
9. Toffler, Alvin. *Future Shock* (New York: Bantam Books, 1981), 128.
10. Mintzberg, 433.
11. Cochran, 11.
12. Ibid.
13. *Advertising Age* (April 26, 1982), 3, 74.
14. Pavlik, John V. *Public Relations: What Research Tells Us* (Newbury Park, CA: Sage, 1987), 59.
15. Morton, Linda P. "How Newspapers Choose the Releases They Use," *Public Relations Review* 12 (Fall 1986): 26–27.
16. Pines, Wayne L. "How to Handle a PR Crisis: Five Dos and Five Don'ts," *Public Relations Quarterly* 30 (Summer 1985): 18.
17. Kilpatrick, James J. "A Short Course in Media Relations," *Nation's Business* 67 (June 1979): 17–18.
18. Strenski, James B. "Spokesperson Training Pays Off in a World of Special Interests," *Public Relations Quarterly* 24 (Spring 1979): 25–26.
19. Shaefer, Thomas E. "Professionalism: Foundation for Business Ethics," *Journal of Business Ethics* 3 (1984): 269.
20. Schaefer, 217.
21. Pierce, Milt. "Copywriting Workshops: The Morality of Direct Marketing," *Direct Marketing* 50 (October 1987): 118–22.
22. Schaefer, 273.
23. Schaefer, 272.
24. Schaefer, 273.

Index